THE **SHOCK** DOCTRINE

THE
SHOCK
DOCTRINE

THE RISE OF DISASTER CAPITALISM

. . .

NAOMI KLEIN

METROPOLITAN BOOKS   HENRY HOLT AND COMPANY   NEW YORK

m

Metropolitan Books
Henry Holt and Company, LLC
Publishers since 1866
175 Fifth Avenue
New York, New York 10010
www.henryholt.com

Metropolitan Books® and m® are registered
trademarks of Henry Holt and Company, LLC.

Library of Congress Cataloging-in-Publication Data
Klein, Naomi, 1970–
The shock doctrine : the rise of disaster capitalism / Naomi Klein. — 1st ed.
        p.   cm.
Includes bibliographical references and index.
ISBN-13: 978-0-8050-7983-8
ISBN-10: 0-8050-7983-1
1. Free enterprise.   2. Financial crises.   3. Capitalism.   I. Title.
HB95.K54 2007
330.12'2—dc22   2007018652

Henry Holt books are available for special promotions and
premiums. For details contact: Director, Special Markets.

First Edition 2007

Printed in the United States of America
9   10   8

For Avi, again

Any change is a change in the topic.
—César Aira, Argentine novelist,
Cumpleaños, 2001

CONTENTS

THE **SHOCK** DOCTRINE

BLANK IS BEAUTIFUL

THREE DECADES OF ERASING AND REMAKING THE WORLD

> Now the earth was corrupt in God's sight, and the earth was filled with violence. And God saw that the earth was corrupt; for all flesh had corrupted its ways upon the earth. And God said to Noah, "I have determined to make an end of all flesh, for the earth is filled with violence because of them; now I am going to destroy them along with the earth."
> —Genesis 6:11 (NRSV)

> Shock and Awe are actions that create fears, dangers, and destruction that are incomprehensible to the people at large, specific elements/sectors of the threat society, or the leadership. Nature in the form of tornadoes, hurricanes, earthquakes, floods, uncontrolled fires, famine, and disease can engender Shock and Awe.
> —*Shock and Awe: Achieving Rapid Dominance*, the military doctrine for the U.S. war on Iraq[1]

I met Jamar Perry in September 2005, at the big Red Cross shelter in Baton Rouge, Louisiana. Dinner was being doled out by grinning young Scientologists, and he was standing in line. I had just been busted for talking to evacuees without a media escort and was now doing my best to blend in, a white Canadian in a sea of African-American Southerners. I dodged into the food line behind Perry and asked him to talk to me as if we were old friends, which he kindly did.

Born and raised in New Orleans, he'd been out of the flooded city for a week. He looked about seventeen but told me he was twenty-three. He and his family had waited forever for the evacuation buses; when they didn't arrive, they had walked out in the baking sun. Finally they ended up here, a sprawling convention center, normally home to pharmaceutical trade shows and "Capital City Carnage: The Ultimate in Steel Cage Fighting," now jammed with two thousand cots and a mess of angry, exhausted people being patrolled by edgy National Guard soldiers just back from Iraq.

The news racing around the shelter that day was that Richard Baker, a prominent Republican congressman from this city, had told a group of lobbyists, "We finally cleaned up public housing in New Orleans. We couldn't do it, but God did."[2] Joseph Canizaro, one of New Orleans' wealthiest developers, had just expressed a similar sentiment: "I think we have a clean sheet to start again. And with that clean sheet we have some very big opportunities."[3] All that week the Louisiana State Legislature in Baton Rouge had been crawling with corporate lobbyists helping to lock in those big opportunities: lower taxes, fewer regulations, cheaper workers and a "smaller, safer city"—which in practice meant plans to level the public housing projects and replace them with condos. Hearing all the talk of "fresh starts" and "clean sheets," you could almost forget the toxic stew of rubble, chemical outflows and human remains just a few miles down the highway.

Over at the shelter, Jamar could think of nothing else. "I really don't see it as cleaning up the city. What I see is that a lot of people got killed uptown. People who shouldn't have died."

He was speaking quietly, but an older man in line in front of us overheard and whipped around. "What is wrong with these people in Baton Rouge? This isn't an opportunity. It's a goddamned tragedy. Are they blind?"

A mother with two kids chimed in. "No, they're not blind, they're evil. They see just fine."

One of those who saw opportunity in the floodwaters of New Orleans was Milton Friedman, grand guru of the movement for unfettered capitalism and the man credited with writing the rulebook for the contemporary, hypermobile global economy. Ninety-three years old and in failing health, "Uncle Miltie," as he was known to his followers, nonetheless found the strength to write an op-ed for *The Wall Street Journal* three months after the levees broke. "Most New Orleans schools are in ruins," Friedman observed, "as are the homes of the children who have attended them. The children are now scattered all over the country. This is a tragedy. It is also an opportunity to radically reform the educational system."[4]

Friedman's radical idea was that instead of spending a portion of the billions of dollars in reconstruction money on rebuilding and improving New Orleans' existing public school system, the government should provide families with vouchers, which they could spend at private institutions, many run at a profit, that would be subsidized by the state. It was crucial, Friedman wrote, that this fundamental change not be a stopgap but rather "a permanent reform."[5]

A network of right-wing think tanks seized on Friedman's proposal and descended on the city after the storm. The administration of George W. Bush backed up their plans with tens of millions of dollars to convert New Orleans schools into "charter schools," publicly funded institutions run by private entities according to their own rules. Charter schools are deeply polarizing in the United States, and nowhere more than in New Orleans, where they are seen by many African-American parents as a way of reversing the gains of the civil rights movement, which guaranteed all children the same standard of education. For Milton Friedman, however, the entire concept of a state-run school system reeked of socialism. In his view, the state's sole functions were "to protect our freedom both from the enemies outside our gates and from our fellow-citizens: to preserve law and order, to enforce private contracts, to foster competitive markets."[6] In other words, to supply the police and the soldiers—anything else, including providing free education, was an unfair interference in the market.

In sharp contrast to the glacial pace with which the levees were repaired and the electricity grid was brought back online, the auctioning off of New Orleans' school system took place with military speed and precision. Within nineteen months, with most of the city's poor residents still in exile, New Orleans' public school system had been almost completely replaced by privately run charter schools. Before Hurricane Katrina, the school board had run 123 public schools; now it ran just 4. Before that storm, there had been 7 charter schools in the city; now there were 31.[7] New Orleans teachers used to be represented by a strong union; now the union's contract had been shredded, and its forty-seven hundred members had all been fired.[8] Some of the younger teachers were rehired by the charters, at reduced salaries; most were not.

New Orleans was now, according to *The New York Times*, "the nation's preeminent laboratory for the widespread use of charter schools," while the

American Enterprise Institute, a Friedmanite think tank, enthused that "Katrina accomplished in a day . . . what Louisiana school reformers couldn't do after years of trying."[9] Public school teachers, meanwhile, watching money allocated for the victims of the flood being diverted to erase a public system and replace it with a private one, were calling Friedman's plan "an educational land grab."[10]

I call these orchestrated raids on the public sphere in the wake of catastrophic events, combined with the treatment of disasters as exciting market opportunities, "disaster capitalism."

Friedman's New Orleans op-ed ended up being his last public policy recommendation; he died less than a year later, on November 16, 2006, at age ninety-four. Privatizing the school system of a midsize American city may seem like a modest preoccupation for the man hailed as the most influential economist of the past half century, one who counted among his disciples several U.S. presidents, British prime ministers, Russian oligarchs, Polish finance ministers, Third World dictators, Chinese Communist Party secretaries, International Monetary Fund directors and the past three chiefs of the U.S. Federal Reserve. Yet his determination to exploit the crisis in New Orleans to advance a fundamentalist version of capitalism was also an oddly fitting farewell from the boundlessly energetic five-foot-two-inch professor who, in his prime, described himself as "an old-fashioned preacher delivering a Sunday sermon."[11]

For more than three decades, Friedman and his powerful followers had been perfecting this very strategy: waiting for a major crisis, then selling off pieces of the state to private players while citizens were still reeling from the shock, then quickly making the "reforms" permanent.

In one of his most influential essays, Friedman articulated contemporary capitalism's core tactical nostrum, what I have come to understand as the shock doctrine. He observed that "only a crisis—actual or perceived—produces real change. When that crisis occurs, the actions that are taken depend on the ideas that are lying around. That, I believe, is our basic function: to develop alternatives to existing policies, to keep them alive and available until the politically impossible becomes politically inevitable."[12] Some people stockpile canned goods and water in preparation for major disasters; Friedmanites stockpile free-market ideas. And once a crisis has struck, the University of Chicago professor was convinced that it was crucial to act swiftly, to impose rapid and irreversible change before the crisis-racked society slipped back into the "tyranny of the status quo." He estimated that "a new administration has some six to nine months in which to achieve major changes; if it does not seize the opportunity to act decisively during that period, it will not have another such opportunity."[13] A variation on Machiavelli's advice that injuries should be inflicted "all at once," this proved to be one of Friedman's most lasting strategic legacies.

Friedman first learned how to exploit a large-scale shock or crisis in the mid-seventies, when he acted as adviser to the Chilean dictator, General Augusto Pinochet. Not only were Chileans in a state of shock following Pinochet's violent coup, but the country was also traumatized by severe hyperinflation. Friedman advised Pinochet to impose a rapid-fire transformation of the economy—tax cuts, free trade, privatized services, cuts to social spending and deregulation. Eventually, Chileans even saw their public schools replaced with voucher-funded private ones. It was the most extreme capitalist makeover ever attempted anywhere, and it became known as a "Chicago School" revolution, since so many of Pinochet's economists had studied under Friedman at the University of Chicago. Friedman predicted that the speed, suddenness and scope of the economic shifts would provoke psychological reactions in the public that "facilitate the adjustment."[14] He coined a phrase for this painful tactic: economic "shock treatment." In the decades since, whenever governments have imposed sweeping free-market programs, the all-at-once shock treatment, or "shock therapy," has been the method of choice.

Pinochet also facilitated the adjustment with his own shock treatments; these were performed in the regime's many torture cells, inflicted on the writhing bodies of those deemed most likely to stand in the way of the capitalist transformation. Many in Latin America saw a direct connection between the economic shocks that impoverished millions and the epidemic of torture that punished hundreds of thousands of people who believed in a different kind of society. As the Uruguayan writer Eduardo Galeano asked, "How can this inequality be maintained if not through jolts of electric shock?"[15]

Exactly thirty years after these three distinct forms of shock descended on Chile, the formula reemerged, with far greater violence, in Iraq. First came the war, designed, according to the authors of the Shock and Awe military doctrine, to "control the adversary's will, perceptions, and understanding and literally make an adversary impotent to act or react."[16] Next came the radical economic shock therapy, imposed, while the country was still in flames, by the U.S. chief envoy L. Paul Bremer—mass privatization, complete free trade, a 15 percent flat tax, a dramatically downsized government. Iraq's interim trade minister, Ali Abdul-Amir Allawi, said at the time that his countrymen were "sick and tired of being the subjects of experiments. There have been enough shocks to the system, so we don't need this shock therapy in the economy."[17] When Iraqis resisted, they were rounded up and taken to jails where bodies and minds were met with more shocks, these ones distinctly less metaphorical.

I started researching the free market's dependence on the power of shock four years ago, during the early days of the occupation of Iraq. After reporting from Baghdad on Washington's failed attempts to follow Shock and Awe with shock therapy, I traveled to Sri Lanka, several months after the devastating 2004 tsunami, and witnessed another version of the same maneuver: foreign investors and international lenders had teamed up to use the atmosphere of panic to hand the entire beautiful coastline over to entrepreneurs who quickly built large resorts, blocking hundreds of thousands of fishing people from rebuilding their villages near the water. "In a cruel twist of fate, nature has presented Sri Lanka with a unique opportunity, and out of this great tragedy will come a world class tourism destination," the Sri Lankan government announced.[18] By the time Hurricane Katrina hit New Orleans, and the nexus of Republican politicians, think tanks and land developers started talking about "clean sheets" and exciting opportunities, it was clear that this was now the preferred method of advancing corporate goals: using moments of collective trauma to engage in radical social and economic engineering.

Most people who survive a devastating disaster want the opposite of a clean slate: they want to salvage whatever they can and begin repairing what was not destroyed; they want to reaffirm their relatedness to the places that formed them. "When I rebuild the city I feel like I'm rebuilding myself," said Cassandra Andrews, a resident of New Orleans' heavily damaged Lower Ninth Ward, as she cleared away debris after the storm.[19] But disaster capitalists have no interest in repairing what was. In Iraq, Sri Lanka and New Orleans, the process deceptively called "reconstruction" began with finishing the job of the original disaster by erasing what was left of the public sphere and rooted communities, then quickly moving to replace them with a kind of corporate New Jerusalem—all before the victims of war or natural disaster were able to regroup and stake their claims to what was theirs.

Mike Battles puts it best: "For us, the fear and disorder offered real promise."[20] The thirty-four-year-old ex-CIA operative was talking about how the chaos in postinvasion Iraq had helped his unknown and inexperienced private security firm, Custer Battles, to shake roughly $100 million in contracts out of the federal government.[21] His words could serve just as well as the slogan for contemporary capitalism—fear and disorder are the catalysts for each new leap forward.

When I began this research into the intersection between superprofits and megadisasters, I thought I was witnessing a fundamental change in the way the drive to "liberate" markets was advancing around the world. Having been part of the movement against ballooning corporate power that made its global debut in Seattle in 1999, I was accustomed to seeing similar business-friendly policies imposed through arm-twisting at World Trade Organization summits, or as the conditions attached to loans from the International Monetary Fund. The three trademark demands—privatization, government deregulation and deep cuts to social spending—tended to be extremely unpopular with citizens, but when the agreements were signed there was still at least the pretext of mutual consent between the governments doing the negotiating, as well as a consensus among the supposed experts. Now the same ideological program was being imposed via the most baldly coercive means possible: under foreign military occupation after an invasion, or immediately following a cataclysmic natural disaster. September 11 appeared to have provided Washington with the green light to stop asking countries if they wanted the U.S. version of "free trade and democracy" and to start imposing it with Shock and Awe military force.

As I dug deeper into the history of how this market model had swept the globe, however, I discovered that the idea of exploiting crisis and disaster has been the modus operandi of Milton Friedman's movement from the very beginning—this fundamentalist form of capitalism has always needed disasters to advance. It was certainly the case that the facilitating disasters were getting bigger and more shocking, but what was happening in Iraq and New Orleans was not a new, post-September 11 invention. Rather, these bold experiments in crisis exploitation were the culmination of three decades of strict adherence to the shock doctrine.

Seen through the lens of this doctrine, the past thirty-five years look very different. Some of the most infamous human rights violations of this era, which have tended to be viewed as sadistic acts carried out by antidemocratic regimes, were in fact either committed with the deliberate intent of terrorizing the public or actively harnessed to prepare the ground for the introduction of radical free-market "reforms." In Argentina in the seventies, the junta's "disappearance" of thirty thousand people, most of them leftist activists, was integral to the imposition of the country's Chicago School policies, just as terror had been a partner for the same kind of economic metamorphosis in Chile. In China in 1989, it was the shock of the Tiananmen Square massacre and the subsequent arrests of tens of thousands that freed the hand of the Communist Party to convert much of the country into a sprawling export zone, staffed with workers too terrified to demand their rights. In Russia in 1993, it was Boris Yeltsin's decision to send in tanks to set fire to the parliament building and lock up the opposition leaders that cleared the way for the fire-sale privatization that created the country's notorious oligarchs.

The Falklands War in 1982 served a similar purpose for Margaret Thatcher in the U.K.: the disorder and nationalist excitement resulting from the war allowed her to use tremendous force to crush the striking coal miners and to launch the first privatization frenzy in a Western democracy. The NATO attack on Belgrade in 1999 created the conditions for rapid privatizations in the former Yugoslavia—a goal that predated the war. Economics was by no means the sole motivator for these wars, but in each case a major collective shock was exploited to prepare the ground for economic shock therapy.

The traumatic episodes that have served this "softening-up" purpose have not always been overtly violent. In Latin America and Africa in the eighties, it was a debt crisis that forced countries to be "privatized or die," as one former IMF official put it.[22] Coming unraveled by hyperinflation and too indebted to say no to demands that came bundled with foreign loans, governments accepted "shock treatment" on the promise that it would save them from deeper disaster. In Asia, it was the financial crisis of 1997-98— almost as devastating as the Great Depression—that humbled the so-called Asian Tigers, cracking open their markets to what *The New York Times* described as "the world's biggest going-out-of-business sale."[23] Many of these countries were democracies, but the radical free-market transformations were not imposed democratically. Quite the opposite: as Friedman understood, the atmosphere of large-scale crisis provided the necessary pretext to overrule the expressed wishes of voters and to hand the country over to economic "technocrats."

There have, of course, been cases in which the adoption of free-market policies has taken place democratically—politicians have run on hard-line platforms and won elections, the U.S. under Ronald Reagan being the best example, France's election of Nicolas Sarkozy a more recent one. In these cases, however, free-market crusaders came up against public pressure and were invariably forced to temper and modify their radical plans, accepting piecemeal changes rather than a total conversion. The bottom line is that while Friedman's economic model is capable of being partially imposed under democracy, authoritarian conditions are required for the implementation of its true vision. For economic shock therapy to be applied without restraint—as it was in Chile in the seventies, China in the late eighties, Russia in the nineties and the U.S. after September 11, 2001—some sort of additional major collective trauma has always been required, one that either temporarily suspended democratic practices or blocked them entirely. This ideological crusade was born in the authoritarian regimes of South America, and in its largest newly conquered territories—Russia and China—it coexists most comfortably, and most profitably, with an iron-fisted leadership to this day.

Shock Therapy Comes Home

Friedman's Chicago School movement has been conquering territory around the world since the seventies, but until recently its vision had never been fully applied in its country of origin. Certainly Reagan had made headway, but the U.S. retained a welfare system, social security and public schools, where parents clung, in Friedman's words, to their "irrational attachment to a socialist system."[24]

When the Republicans gained control of Congress in 1995, David Frum, a transplanted Canadian and future speechwriter for George W. Bush, was among the so-called neoconservatives calling for a shock therapy-style economic revolution in the U.S. "Here's how I think we should do it. Instead of cutting incrementally—a little here, a little there—I would say that on a single day this summer we eliminate three hundred programs, each one costing a billion dollars or less. Maybe these cuts won't make a big deal of difference, but, boy, do they make a point. And you can do them right away."[25]

Frum didn't get his homegrown shock therapy at the time, largely because there was no domestic crisis to prepare the ground. But in 2001 that changed. When the September 11 attacks hit, the White House was packed with Friedman's disciples, including his close friend Donald Rumsfeld. The Bush team seized the moment of collective vertigo with chilling speed—not, as some have claimed, because the administration deviously plotted the crisis but because the key figures of the administration, veterans of earlier disaster capitalism experiments in Latin America and Eastern Europe, were part of a movement that prays for crisis the way drought-struck farmers pray for rain, and the way Christian-Zionist end-timers pray for the Rapture. When the long-awaited disaster strikes, they know instantly that their moment has come at last.

For three decades, Friedman and his followers had methodically exploited moments of shock in other countries—foreign equivalents of 9/11, starting with Pinochet's coup on September 11, 1973. What happened on September 11, 2001, is that an ideology hatched in American universities and fortified in Washington institutions finally had its chance to come home.

The Bush administration immediately seized upon the fear generated by the attacks not only to launch the "War on Terror" but to ensure that it is an almost completely for-profit venture, a booming new industry that has breathed new life into the faltering U.S. economy. Best understood as a "disaster capitalism complex," it has much farther-reaching tentacles than the military-industrial complex that Dwight Eisenhower warned against at the end of his presidency: this is global war fought on every level by private companies whose involvement is paid for with public money, with the unending mandate of protecting the United States homeland in perpetuity while eliminating all "evil" abroad. In only a few short years, the complex has already expanded its market reach from fighting terrorism to international peacekeeping, to municipal policing, to responding to increasingly frequent natural disasters. The ultimate goal for the corporations at the center of the complex is to bring the model of for-profit government, which advances so rapidly in extraordinary circumstances, into the ordinary and day-to-day functioning of the state—in effect, to privatize the government.

To kick-start the disaster capitalism complex, the Bush administration outsourced, with no public debate, many of the most sensitive and core functions of government—from providing health care to soldiers, to interrogating prisoners, to gathering and "data mining" information on all of us. The role of the government in this unending war is not that of an administrator managing a network of contractors but of a deep-pocketed venture capitalist, both providing its seed money for the complex's creation and becoming the biggest customer for its new services. To cite just three statistics that show the scope of the transformation, in 2003, the U.S. government handed out 3,512 contracts to companies to perform security functions; in the twenty-two-month period ending in August 2006, the Department of Homeland Security had issued more than 115,000 such contracts.[26] The global "homeland security industry"—economically insignificant before 2001—is now a $200 billion sector.[27] In 2006, U.S. government spending on homeland security averaged $545 per household.[28]

And that's just the home front of the War on Terror; the real money is in fighting wars abroad. Beyond the weapons contractors, who have seen their profits soar thanks to the war in Iraq, maintaining the U.S. military is now one of the fastest-growing service economies in the world.[29] "No two countries that both have a McDonald's have ever fought a war against each other," boldly declared the *New York Times* columnist Thomas Friedman in December 1996.[30] Not only was he proven wrong two years later, but thanks to the model of for-profit warfare, the U.S. Army goes to war with Burger King and Pizza Hut in tow, contracting them to run franchises for the soldiers on military bases from Iraq to the "mini city" at Guantánamo Bay.

Then there is humanitarian relief and reconstruction. Pioneered in Iraq, for-profit relief and reconstruction has already become the new global paradigm, regardless of whether the original destruction occurred from a preemptive war, such as Israel's 2006 attack on Lebanon, or a hurricane. With resource scarcity and climate change providing a steadily increasing flow of new disasters, responding to emergencies is simply too hot an emerging market to be left to the nonprofits—why should UNICEF rebuild schools when it can be done by Bechtel, one of the largest engineering firms in the U.S.? Why put displaced people from Mississippi in subsidized empty apartments when they can be housed on Carnival cruise ships? Why deploy UN peacekeepers to Darfur when private security companies like Blackwater are looking for new clients? And that is the post-September 11 difference: before, wars and disasters provided opportunities for a narrow sector of the economy—the makers of fighter jets, for instance, or the construction companies that rebuilt bombed-out bridges. The primary economic role of wars, however, was as a means to open new markets that had been sealed off and to generate postwar peacetime booms. Now wars and disaster responses are so fully privatized that they are themselves the new market; there is no need to wait until after the war for the boom—the medium is the message.

One distinct advantage of this postmodern approach is that in market terms, it cannot fail. As a market analyst remarked of a particularly good quarter for the earnings of the energy services company Halliburton, "Iraq was better than expected."[31] That was in October 2006, then the most violent month of the war on record, with 3,709 Iraqi civilian casualties.[32] Still, few shareholders could fail to be impressed by a war that had generated $20 billion in revenues for this one company.[33]

Amid the weapons trade, the private soldiers, for-profit reconstruction and the homeland security industry, what has emerged as a result of the Bush administration's particular brand of post-September 11 shock therapy is a fully articulated new economy. It was built in the Bush era, but it now exists quite apart from any one administration and will remain entrenched until the corporate supremacist ideology that underpins it is identified, isolated and challenged. The complex is dominated by U.S. firms, but it is global, with British companies bringing their experience in ubiquitous security cameras, Israeli firms their expertise in building high-tech fences and walls, the Canadian lumber industry selling prefab houses that are several times more expensive than those produced locally, and so on. "I don't think anybody has looked at disaster reconstruction as an actual housing market before," said Ken Baker, CEO of a Canadian forestry trade group. "It's a strategy to diversify in the long run."[34]

In scale, the disaster capitalism complex is on a par with the "emerging market" and information technology booms of the nineties. In fact, insiders say that the deals are even better than during the dot-com days and that "the security bubble" picked up the slack when those earlier bubbles popped. Combined with soaring insurance industry profits (projected to have reached a record $60 billion in 2006 in the U.S. alone) as well as super profits for the oil industry (which grow with each new crisis), the disaster economy may well have saved the world market from the full-blown recession it was facing on the eve of 9/11.[35]

In the attempt to relate the history of the ideological crusade that has culminated in the radical privatization of war and disaster, one problem recurs: the ideology is a shape-shifter, forever changing its name and switching identities. Friedman called himself a "liberal," but his U.S. followers, who associated liberals with high taxes and hippies, tended to identify as "conservatives," "classical economists," "free marketers," and, later, as believers in "Reaganomics" or "laissez-faire." In most of the world, their orthodoxy is known as "neoliberalism," but it is often called "free trade" or simply "globalization." Only since the mid-nineties has the intellectual movement, led by the right-wing think tanks with which Friedman had long associations—Heritage Foundation,

Cato Institute and the American Enterprise Institute—called itself "neocon-servative," a worldview that has harnessed the full force of the U.S. military machine in the service of a corporate agenda.

All these incarnations share a commitment to the policy trinity—the elimination of the public sphere, total liberation for corporations and skeletal social spending—but none of the various names for the ideology seem quite adequate. Friedman framed his movement as an attempt to free the market from the state, but the real-world track record of what happens when his purist vision is realized is rather different. In every country where Chicago School policies have been applied over the past three decades, what has emerged is a powerful ruling alliance between a few very large corporations and a class of mostly wealthy politicians—with hazy and ever-shifting lines between the two groups. In Russia the billionaire private players in the alliance are called "the oligarchs"; in China, "the princelings"; in Chile, "the piranhas"; in the U.S., the Bush-Cheney campaign "Pioneers." Far from freeing the market from the state, these political and corporate elites have simply merged, trading favors to secure the right to appropriate precious resources previously held in the public domain—from Russia's oil fields, to China's collective lands, to the no-bid reconstruction contracts for work in Iraq.

A more accurate term for a system that erases the boundaries between Big Government and Big Business is not liberal, conservative or capitalist but corporatist. Its main characteristics are huge transfers of public wealth to private hands, often accompanied by exploding debt, an ever-widening chasm between the dazzling rich and the disposable poor and an aggressive nationalism that justifies bottomless spending on security. For those inside the bubble of extreme wealth created by such an arrangement, there can be no more profitable way to organize a society. But because of the obvious drawbacks for the vast majority of the population left outside the bubble, other features of the corporatist state tend to include aggressive surveillance (once again, with government and large corporations trading favors and contracts), mass incarceration, shrinking civil liberties and often, though not always, torture.

Torture as Metaphor

From Chile to China to Iraq, torture has been a silent partner in the global free-market crusade. But torture is more than a tool used to enforce unwanted policies on rebellious peoples; it is also a metaphor of the shock doctrine's underlying logic.

Torture, or in CIA language "coercive interrogation," is a set of techniques designed to put prisoners into a state of deep disorientation and shock in order to force them to make concessions against their will. The guiding logic is elaborated in two CIA manuals that were declassified in the late nineties. They explain that the way to break "resistant sources" is to create violent ruptures between prisoners and their ability to make sense of the world around them.[36] First, the senses are starved of any input (with hoods, earplugs, shackles, total isolation), then the body is bombarded with overwhelming stimulation (strobe lights, blaring music, beatings, electroshock).

The goal of this "softening-up" stage is to provoke a kind of hurricane in the mind: prisoners are so regressed and afraid that they can no longer think rationally or protect their own interests. It is in that state of shock that most prisoners give their interrogators whatever they want—information, confessions, a renunciation of former beliefs. One CIA manual provides a particularly succinct explanation: "There is an interval—which may be extremely brief—of suspended animation, a kind of psychological shock or paralysis. It is caused by a traumatic or sub-traumatic experience which explodes, as it were, the world that is familiar to the subject as well as his image of himself within that world. Experienced interrogators recognize this effect when it appears and know that at this moment the source is far more open to suggestion, far likelier to comply, than he was just before he experienced the shock."[37]

The shock doctrine mimics this process precisely, attempting to achieve on a mass scale what torture does one on one in the interrogation cell. The clearest example was the shock of September 11, which, for millions of people, exploded "the world that is familiar" and opened up a period of deep disorientation and regression that the Bush administration expertly exploited. Suddenly we found ourselves living in a kind of Year Zero, in which everything we knew of the world before could now be dismissed as "pre-9/11 thinking." Never strong in our knowledge of history, North Americans had become a blank slate—"a clean sheet of paper" on which "the newest and most beautiful words can be written," as Mao said of his people.[38] A new army of experts instantly materialized to write new and beautiful words on the receptive canvas of our posttrauma consciousness: "clash of civilizations," they inscribed. "Axis of evil," "Islamo-fascism," "homeland security." With everyone preoccupied by the deadly new culture wars, the Bush administration was able to pull off what it could only have dreamed of doing before 9/11: wage privatized wars abroad and build a corporate security complex at home.

That is how the shock doctrine works: the original disaster—the coup, the terrorist attack, the market meltdown, the war, the tsunami, the hurricane— puts the entire population into a state of collective shock. The falling bombs, the bursts of terror, the pounding winds serve to soften up whole so- cieties much as the blaring music and blows in the torture cells soften up prisoners. Like the terrorized prisoner who gives up the names of comrades and renounces his faith, shocked societies often give up things they would otherwise fiercely protect. Jamar Perry and his fellow evacuees at the Baton Rouge shelter were supposed to give up their housing projects and public schools. After the tsunami, the fishing people in Sri Lanka were supposed to give up their valuable beachfront land to hoteliers. Iraqis, if all had gone ac- cording to plan, were supposed to be so shocked and awed that they would give up control of their oil reserves, their state companies and their sover- eignty to U.S. military bases and green zones.

The Big Lie

In the torrent of words written in eulogy to Milton Friedman, the role of shocks and crises to advance his worldview received barely a mention. In- stead, the economist's passing provided an occasion for a retelling of the offi- cial story of how his brand of radical capitalism became government orthodoxy in almost every corner of the globe. It is a fairy-tale version of his- tory, scrubbed clean of all the violence and coercion so intimately entwined with this crusade, and it represents the single most successful propaganda coup of the past three decades. The story goes something like this.

Friedman devoted his life to fighting a peaceful battle of ideas against those who believed that governments had a responsibility to intervene in the market to soften its sharp edges. He believed history "got off on the wrong track" when politicians began listening to John Maynard Keynes, intellec- tual architect of the New Deal and the modern welfare state.[39] The market crash of 1929 had created an overwhelming consensus that laissez-faire had failed and that governments needed to intervene in the economy to redistrib- ute wealth and regulate corporations. During those dark days for laissez-faire, when Communism conquered the East, the welfare state was embraced by the West and economic nationalism took root in the postcolonial South, Friedman and his mentor, Friedrich Hayek, patiently protected the flame of a pure version of capitalism, untarnished by Keynesian attempts to pool col- lective wealth to build more just societies.

"The major error, in my opinion," Friedman wrote in a letter to Pinochet in 1975, was "to believe that it is possible to do good with other people's money."[40] Few listened; most people kept insisting that their governments could and should do good. Friedman was dismissively described in *Time* in 1969 "as a pixie or a pest," and revered as a prophet by only a select few.[41]

Finally, after he'd spent decades in the intellectual wilderness, came the eighties and the rule of Margaret Thatcher (who called Friedman "an intellectual freedom fighter") and Ronald Reagan (who was seen carrying a copy of *Capitalism and Freedom*, Friedman's manifesto, on the presidential campaign trail).[42] At last there were political leaders who had the courage to implement unfettered free markets in the real world. According to this official story, after Reagan and Thatcher peacefully and democratically liberated their respective markets, the freedom and prosperity that followed were so obviously desirable that when dictatorships started falling, from Manila to Berlin, the masses demanded Reaganomics alongside their Big Macs.

When the Soviet Union finally collapsed, the people of the "evil empire" were also eager to join the Friedmanite revolution, as were the Communists-turned-capitalists in China. That meant that nothing was left to stand in the way of a truly global free market, one in which liberated corporations were not only free in their own countries but free to travel across borders unhindered, unleashing prosperity around the world. There was now a twin consensus about how society should be run: political leaders should be elected, and economies should be run according to Friedman's rules. It was, as Francis Fukuyama said, "the end of history" — "the end point of mankind's ideological evolution."[43] When Friedman died, *Fortune* magazine wrote that "he had the tide of history with him"; a resolution was passed in the U.S. Congress praising him as "one of the world's foremost champions of liberty, not just in economics but in all respects"; the California governor, Arnold Schwarzenegger, declared January 29, 2007, to be a statewide Milton Friedman Day, and several cities and towns did the same. A headline in *The Wall Street Journal* encapsulated this tidy narrative: "Freedom Man."[44]

This book is a challenge to the central and most cherished claim in the official story—that the triumph of deregulated capitalism has been born of freedom, that unfettered free markets go hand in hand with democracy. Instead, I will show that this fundamentalist form of capitalism has consistently been midwifed by the most brutal forms of coercion, inflicted on the collective body politic as well as on countless individual bodies. The history of the contemporary free market—better understood as the rise of corporatism—was written in shocks.

The stakes are high. The corporatist alliance is in the midst of conquering its final frontiers: the closed oil economies of the Arab world, and sectors of Western economies that have long been protected from profit making—including responding to disasters and raising armies. Since there is not even the veneer of seeking public consent to privatize such essential functions, either at home or abroad, escalating levels of violence and ever larger disasters are required in order to reach the goal. Yet because the decisive role played by shocks and crises has been so effectively purged from the official record of the rise of the free market, the extreme tactics on display in Iraq and New Orleans are often mistaken for the unique incompetence or cronyism of the Bush White House. In fact, Bush's exploits merely represent the monstrously violent and creative culmination of a fifty-year campaign for total corporate liberation.

Any attempt to hold ideologies accountable for the crimes committed by their followers must be approached with a great deal of caution. It is too easy to assert that those with whom we disagree are not just wrong but tyrannical, fascist, genocidal. But it is also true that certain ideologies are a danger to the public and need to be identified as such. These are the closed, fundamentalist doctrines that cannot coexist with other belief systems; their followers deplore diversity and demand an absolute free hand to implement their perfect system. The world as it is must be erased to make way for their purist invention. Rooted in biblical fantasies of great floods and great fires, it is a logic that leads ineluctably toward violence. The ideologies that long for that impossible clean slate, which can be reached only through some kind of cataclysm, are the dangerous ones.

Usually it is extreme religious and racially based idea systems that demand the wiping out of entire peoples and cultures in order to fulfill a purified vision of the world. But since the collapse of the Soviet Union, there has been a powerful collective reckoning with the great crimes committed in the name of Communism. The Soviet information vaults have been cracked open to researchers who have counted the dead—through forced famines, work camps and assassinations. The process has sparked heated debate around the world about how many of these atrocities stemmed from the ideology invoked, as opposed to its distortion by adherents like Stalin, Ceauşescu, Mao and Pol Pot.

"It was flesh-and-blood Communism that imposed wholesale repression, culminating in a state-sponsored reign of terror," writes Stéphane Courtois, coauthor of the contentious *Black Book of Communism*. "Is the ideology itself blameless?"[45] Of course it is not. It doesn't follow that all forms of Communism are inherently genocidal, as some have gleefully claimed, but it was certainly an interpretation of Communist theory that was doctrinaire, authoritarian, and contemptuous of pluralism that led to Stalin's purges and to Mao's reeducation camps. Authoritarian Communism is, and should be, forever tainted by those real-world laboratories.

But what of the contemporary crusade to liberate world markets? The coups, wars and slaughters to install and maintain pro-corporate regimes have never been treated as capitalist crimes but have instead been written off as the excesses of overzealous dictators, as hot fronts of the Cold War, and now of the War on Terror. If the most committed opponents of the corporatist economic model are systematically eliminated, whether in Argentina in the seventies or in Iraq today, that suppression is explained as part of the dirty fight against Communism or terrorism—almost never as the fight *for* the advancement of pure capitalism.

I am not arguing that all forms of market systems are inherently violent. It is eminently possible to have a market-based economy that requires no such brutality and demands no such ideological purity. A free market in consumer products can coexist with free public health care, with public schools, with a large segment of the economy—like a national oil company—held in state hands. It's equally possible to require corporations to pay decent wages, to respect the right of workers to form unions, and for governments to tax and redistribute wealth so that the sharp inequalities that mark the corporatist state are reduced. Markets need not be fundamentalist.

Keynes proposed exactly that kind of mixed, regulated economy after the Great Depression, a revolution in public policy that created the New Deal and transformations like it around the world. It was exactly that system of compromises, checks and balances that Friedman's counterrevolution was launched to methodically dismantle in country after country. Seen in that light, the Chicago School strain of capitalism does indeed have something in common with other dangerous ideologies: the signature desire for unattainable purity, for a clean slate on which to build a reengineered model society.

This desire for godlike powers of total creation is precisely why free-market ideologues are so drawn to crises and disasters. Nonapocalyptic reality is simply not hospitable to their ambitions. For thirty-five years, what has animated Friedman's counterrevolution is an attraction to a kind of freedom and possibility available only in times of cataclysmic change—when people, with their stubborn habits and insistent demands, are blasted out of the way—moments when democracy seems a practical impossibility.

Believers in the shock doctrine are convinced that only a great rupture—a flood, a war, a terrorist attack—can generate the kind of vast, clean canvases they crave. It is in these malleable moments, when we are psychologically unmoored and physically uprooted, that these artists of the real plunge in their hands and begin their work of remaking the world.

PART 1

TWO DOCTOR SHOCKS

RESEARCH AND DEVELOPMENT

We shall squeeze you empty, and then we shall fill you with ourselves.

—George Orwell, *Nineteen Eighty-Four*

The Industrial Revolution was merely the beginning of a revolution as extreme and radical as ever inflamed the minds of sectarians, but the problems could be resolved given an unlimited amount of material commodities.

—Karl Polanyi, *The Great Transformation*

CHAPTER 1

THE TORTURE LAB

EWEN CAMERON, THE CIA AND THE MANIACAL QUEST TO ERASE AND REMAKE THE HUMAN MIND

Their minds seem like clean slates upon which we can write.
—Dr. Cyril J. C. Kennedy and Dr. David Anchel on the benefits of electroshock therapy, 1948[1]

I went to the slaughterhouse to observe this so-called "electric slaughtering," and I saw that the hogs were clamped at the temples with big metallic tongs which were hooked up to an electric current (125 volts). As soon as the hogs were clamped by the tongs, they fell unconscious, stiffened, then after a few seconds they were shaken by convulsions in the same way as our experimental dogs. During this period of unconsciousness (epileptic coma), the butcher stabbed and bled the animals without difficulty.
—Ugo Cerletti, a psychiatrist, describing how he "invented" electroshock therapy, 1954[2]

"I don't talk to journalists anymore," says the strained voice at the other end of the phone. And then a tiny window: "What do you want?"

I figure I have about twenty seconds to make my case, and it won't be easy. How do I explain what I want from Gail Kastner, the journey that brought me to her?

The truth seems so bizarre: "I am writing a book about shock. About how countries are shocked—by wars, terror attacks, coups d'état and natural disasters. And then how they are shocked again—by corporations and politicians who exploit the fear and disorientation of this first shock to push through economic shock therapy. And then how people who dare to resist this shock politics are, if necessary, shocked for a third time—by police, soldiers and prison interrogators. I want to talk to you because you are by my estimation among the most shocked people alive, being one of the few living survivors of the CIA's covert experiments in electroshock and other 'special interrogation techniques.' And by the way, I have reason to believe that the research that was done on you in the 1950s at McGill University is now being applied to prisoners in Guantánamo Bay and Abu Ghraib."

No, I definitely can't say that. So I say this instead: "I recently traveled to Iraq, and I am trying to understand the role torture is playing there. We are told it's about getting information, but I think it's more than that—I think it may also have had to do with trying to build a model country, about erasing people and then trying to remake them from scratch."

There is a long pause, and then a different tone of voice to the reply, still strained but . . . is it relief? "You have just spelled out exactly what the CIA and Ewen Cameron did to me. They tried to erase and remake me. But it didn't work."

In less than twenty-four hours, I am knocking on the door of Gail Kastner's apartment in a grim Montreal old-age home. "It's open," comes a barely audible voice. Gail had told me she would leave the door unlocked because standing up is difficult for her. It's the tiny fractures down her spine that grow more painful as arthritis sets in. Her back pain is just one reminder of the sixty-three times that 150 to 200 volts of electricity penetrated the frontal lobes of her brain, while her body convulsed violently on the table, causing fractures, sprains, bloody lips, broken teeth.

Gail greets me from a plush blue recliner. It has twenty positions, I later learn, and she adjusts them continuously, like a photographer trying to find focus. It is in this chair that she spends her days and nights, searching for comfort, trying to avoid sleep and what she calls "my electric dreams." That's when she sees "him": Dr. Ewen Cameron, the long-dead psychiatrist who administered those shocks, as well as other torments, so many years ago. "I had two visits from the Eminent Monster last night," she announces as soon as I walk in. "I don't want to make you feel bad, but it's because of your call coming out of the blue like that, asking all those questions."

I become aware that my presence here is very possibly unfair. This feeling deepens when I scan the apartment and realize that there is no place for me. Every single surface is crowded with towers of papers and books, precariously stacked but clearly in some kind of order, the books all marked with yellowing flags. Gail motions me to the one clear surface in the room, a wooden chair that I had overlooked, but she goes into minor panic when I ask for a four-inch space for the recorder. The end table beside her chair is out of the question: it is home to about twenty empty boxes of cigarettes, Matinee Regular, stacked in a perfect pyramid. (Gail had warned me on the phone about the chain-smoking: "Sorry, but I smoke. And I'm a poor eater. I'm fat and I smoke. I hope that's okay.") It looks as if Gail has colored the insides of the boxes black, but looking closer, I realize it is actually extremely dense, minuscule handwriting: names, numbers, thousands of words.

Over the course of the day we spend talking, Gail often leans over to write something on a scrap of paper or a cigarette box—"a note to myself," she explains, "or I will never remember." The thickets of paper and cigarette boxes are, for Gail, something more than an unconventional filing system. They are her memory.

For her entire adult life, Gail's mind has failed her; facts evaporate instantly, memories, if they are there (and many aren't), are like snapshots scattered on the ground. Sometimes she will remember an incident perfectly—what she calls "a memory shard"—but when asked for a date, she will be as much as two decades off. "In 1968," she will say. "No, 1983." And so she makes lists and keeps everything, proof that her life actually happened. At first she apologizes for the clutter. But later she says, "He did this to me! This apartment is part of the torture!"

For many years, Gail was quite mystified by her lack of memory, as well as other idiosyncrasies. She did not know, for instance, why a small electrical shock from a garage door opener set off an uncontrollable panic attack. Or why her hands shook when she plugged in her hair dryer. Most of all, she could not understand why she could remember most events from her adult life but almost nothing from before she turned twenty. When she ran into someone who claimed to know her from childhood, she'd say, "'I know who you are but I can't quite place you.' I faked it."

Gail figured it was all part of her shaky mental health. In her twenties and thirties, she had struggled with depression and addiction to pills and would sometimes have such severe breakdowns that she would end up hospitalized and comatose. These episodes provoked her family to disown her, leaving her so alone and desperate that she survived by scavenging from the bins outside grocery stores.

There had also been hints that something even more traumatic had happened early on. Before her family cut ties, Gail and her identical twin sister used to have arguments about a time when Gail had been much sicker and Zella had had to take care of her. "You have no idea what I went through," Zella would say. "You would urinate on the living-room floor and suck your thumb and talk baby talk and you would demand the bottle of my baby. That's what I had to put up with!" Gail had no idea what to make of her twin's recriminations. Urinating on the floor? Demanding her nephew's bottle? She had no memory of ever doing such strange things.

In her late forties, Gail began a relationship with a man named Jacob, whom she describes as her soul mate. Jacob was a Holocaust survivor, and he was also preoccupied with questions of memory and loss. For Jacob, who died more than a decade ago, Gail's unaccountably missing years were intensely troubling. "There has to be a reason," he would say about the gaps in her life. "There has to be a reason."

In 1992, Gail and Jacob happened to pass by a newsstand with a large, sensational headline: "Brainwashing Experiments: Victims to Be Compensated." Kastner started skimming the article, and several phrases immediately leaped out: "baby talk," "memory loss," "incontinence." "I said, 'Jacob, buy this paper.'" Sitting in a nearby coffee shop, the couple read an incredible story about how, in the 1950s, the United States Central Intelligence Agency had funded a Montreal doctor to perform bizarre experiments on his psychiatric patients, keeping them asleep and in isolation for weeks, then administering huge doses of electroshock as well as experimental drug cocktails including the psychedelic LSD and the hallucinogen PCP, commonly known as angel dust. The experiments—which reduced patients to preverbal, infantile states—had been performed at McGill University's Allan Memorial Institute under the supervision of its director, Dr. Ewen Cameron. The CIA's funding of Cameron had been revealed in the late seventies through a Freedom of Information Act request, sparking hearings in the U.S. Senate. Nine of Cameron's former patients got together and sued the CIA as well as the Canadian government, which had also funded Cameron's research. Over protracted trials, the patients' lawyers argued that the experiments had violated all standards of medical ethics. They had gone to Cameron seeking relief from minor psychiatric ailments—postpartum depression, anxiety, even for help to deal with marital difficulties—and had been used, without their knowledge or permission, as human guinea pigs to satisfy the CIA's thirst for information about how to control the human mind. In 1988, the CIA settled, awarding a total of $750,000 in damages to the nine plaintiffs—at the time the largest settlement ever against the agency. Four years later, the Canadian government would agree to pay $100,000 in compensation to each patient who was part of the experiments.[3]

Not only did Cameron play a central role in developing contemporary U.S. torture techniques, but his experiments also offer a unique insight into the underlying logic of disaster capitalism. Like the free-market economists who are convinced that only a large-scale disaster—a great unmaking—can prepare the ground for their "reforms," Cameron believed that by inflicting an array of shocks to the human brain, he could unmake and erase faulty minds, then rebuild new personalities on that ever-elusive clean slate.

Gail had been dimly aware of a story involving the CIA and McGill over the years, but she hadn't paid attention—she had never had anything to do with the Allan Memorial Institute. But now, sitting with Jacob, she focused on what the ex-patients were saying about their lives—the memory loss, the regression. "I realized then that these people must have gone through the same thing I went through. I said, 'Jacob, this has got to be the reason.'"

In the Shock Shop

Kastner wrote to the Allan and requested her medical file. After first being told that they had no record of her, she finally got it, all 138 pages. The doctor who had admitted her was Ewen Cameron.

The letters, notes and charts in Gail's medical file tell a heartbreaking story, one as much about the limited choices available to an eighteen-year-old girl in the fifties as about governments and doctors abusing their power. The file begins with Dr. Cameron's assessment of Gail on her admittance: she is a McGill nursing student, excelling in her studies, whom Cameron describes as "a hitherto reasonably well balanced individual." She is, however, suffering from anxiety, caused, Cameron plainly notes, by her abusive father, an "intensely disturbing" man who made "repeated psychological assaults" on his daughter.

In their early notes, the nurses seem to like Gail; she bonds with them about nursing, and they describe her as "cheerful," "sociable" and "neat." But over the months she spent in and out of their care, Gail underwent a radical personality transformation, one that is meticulously documented in the file: after a few weeks, she "showed childish behaviour, expressed bizarre ideas, and apparently was hallucinated [*sic*] and destructive." The notes report that this intelligent young woman could now manage to count only to six; next she is "manipulative, hostile and very aggressive"; then, passive and listless, unable to recognize her family members. Her final diagnosis is "schizophrenic . . . with marked hysterical features"—far more serious than the "anxiety" she displayed when she arrived.

The metamorphosis no doubt had something to do with the treatments that are also all listed in Kastner's chart: huge doses of insulin, inducing multiple comas; strange combinations of uppers and downers; long periods when she was kept in a drug-induced sleep; and eight times as many electroshocks as was standard at the time.

Often the nurses remark on Kastner's attempts to escape from her doctors: "Trying to find way out . . . claims she is being ill treated . . . refused to have her ECT after having her injection." These complaints were invariably treated as cause for another trip to what Cameron's junior colleagues called "the shock shop."[4]

The Quest for Blankness

After reading over her medical file several times, Gail Kastner turned herself into a kind of archaeologist of her own life, collecting and studying everything that could potentially explain what happened to her at the hospital. She learned that Ewen Cameron, a Scottish-born American citizen, had reached the very pinnacle of his profession: he had been president of the American Psychiatric Association, president of the Canadian Psychiatric Association and president of the World Psychiatric Association. In 1945, he was one of only three American psychiatrists asked to testify to the sanity of Rudolf Hess at the war crimes trials in Nuremberg.[5]

By the time Gail began her investigation, Cameron was long dead, but he had left dozens of academic papers and published lectures behind. Several books had also been published about the CIA's funding of mind-control experiments, works that included plenty of detail about Cameron's relationship to the agency.* Gail read them all, marking relevant passages, making timelines and cross-referencing the dates with her own medical file. What she came to understand was that, by the early 1950s, Cameron had rejected the standard Freudian approach of using "talk therapy" to try to uncover the

*These include Anne Collins's Governor General's Award-winning *In the Sleep Room*, John Marks's *The Search for the Manchurian Candidate*, Alan Scheflin and Edward Option Jr.'s *The Mind Manipulators*, Walter Bowart's *Operation Mind Control*, Gordon Thomas's *Journey into Madness* and Harvey Weinstein's *A Father, a Son and the CIA*, written by the psychiatrist son of one of Cameron's patients.

"root causes" of his patients' mental illnesses. His ambition was not to mend or repair his patients but to re-create them using a method he invented called "psychic driving."[6]

According to his published papers from the time, he believed that the only way to teach his patients healthy new behaviors was to get inside their minds and "break up old pathological patterns."[7] The first step was "depatterning," which had a stunning goal: to return the mind to a state when it was, as Aristotle claimed, "a writing tablet on which as yet nothing actually stands written," a tabula rasa.[8] Cameron believed he could reach that state by attacking the brain with everything known to interfere with its normal functioning—all at once. It was "shock and awe" warfare on the mind.

By the late 1940s, electroshock was becoming increasingly popular among psychiatrists in Europe and North America. It caused less permanent damage than surgical lobotomy, and it seemed to help: hysterical patients frequently calmed down, and in some cases, the jolt of electricity appeared to make the person more lucid. But these were only observations, and even the doctors who developed the technique could not provide a scientific explanation for how it worked.

They were aware of its side effects, though. There was no question that ECT could result in amnesia; it was by far the most common complaint associated with the treatment. Closely related to memory loss, the other side effect widely reported was regression. In dozens of clinical studies, doctors noted that in the immediate aftermath of treatment, patients sucked their thumbs, curled up in the fetal position, needed to be spoon-fed, and cried for their mothers (often mistaking doctors and nurses for parents). These behaviors usually passed quickly, but in some cases, when large doses of shock were used, doctors reported that their patients had regressed completely, forgetting how to walk and talk. Marilyn Rice, an economist who, in the mid-seventies, spearheaded a patients' rights movement against ECT, vividly described what it was like to have her memories and much of her education erased by shock treatments. "Now I know how Eve must have felt, having been created full grown out of somebody's rib without any past history. I feel as empty as Eve."*[9]

For Rice and others, that emptiness represented an irreplaceable loss.

---

* Even today, when ECT, much refined and including procedures to ensure the safety and comfort of patients, has become a respectable and often effective treatment of psychosis, temporary short-term memory loss remains a side effect. Some patients still report that their long-term memories have also been impacted.

Cameron, on the other hand, looked into that same void and saw something else: the blank slate, cleared of bad habits, on which new patterns could be written. For him, "massive loss of all recollections" brought on by intensive ECT wasn't an unfortunate side effect; it was the essential point of the treatment, the key to bringing the patient back to an earlier stage of development "long before schizophrenic thinking and behavior made their appearance."[10] Like pro-war hawks who call for the bombing of countries "back to the stone age," Cameron saw shock therapy as a means to blast his patients back into their infancy, to regress them completely. In a 1962 paper, he described the state to which he wanted to reduce patients like Gail Kastner: "There is not only a loss of the space-time image but loss of all feeling that it should be present. During this stage the patient may show a variety of other phenomena, such as loss of a second language or all knowledge of his marital status. In more advanced forms, he may be unable to walk without support, to feed himself, and he may show double incontinence. . . . All aspects of his memorial function are severely disturbed."[11]

To "depattern" his patients, Cameron used a relatively new device called the Page-Russell, which administered up to six consecutive jolts instead of a single one. Frustrated that his patients still seemed to be clinging to remnants of their personalities, he further disoriented them with uppers, downers and hallucinogens: chlorpromazine, barbiturates, sodium amytal, nitrous oxide, desoxyn, Seconal, Nembutal, Veronal, Melicone, Thorazine, largactil and insulin. Cameron wrote in a 1956 paper that these drugs served to "disinhibit him [the patient] so that his defenses might be reduced."[12]

Once "complete depatterning" had been achieved, and the earlier personality had been satisfactorily wiped out, the psychic driving could begin. It consisted of Cameron playing his patients tape-recorded messages such as "You are a good mother and wife and people enjoy your company." As a behaviorist, he believed that if he could get his patients to absorb the messages on the tape, they would start behaving differently.*

With patients shocked and drugged into an almost vegetative state, they could do nothing but listen to the messages—for sixteen to twenty hours a day for weeks; in one case, Cameron played a message continuously for 101 days.[13]

---

* If Cameron had been slightly less powerful in his field, his "psychic driving" tapes would surely have been dismissed as a cheap joke. The entire idea came to him from an advertisement for the Cerebrophone, a bedside phonograph with pillow speakers that claimed to be "a revolutionary way to learn a foreign language while you sleep."

In the mid-fifties, several researchers at the CIA became interested in Cameron's methods. It was the start of Cold War hysteria, and the agency had just launched a covert program devoted to researching "special interrogation techniques." A declassified CIA memorandum explained that the program "examined and investigated numerous unusual techniques of interrogation including psychological harassment and such matters as 'total isolation'" as well as "the use of drugs and chemicals."[14] First code-named Project Bluebird, then Project Artichoke, it was finally renamed MKUltra in 1953. Over the next decade, MKUltra would spend $25 million on research in a quest to find new ways to break prisoners suspected of being Communists and double agents. Eighty institutions were involved in the program, including forty-four universities and twelve hospitals.[15]

The agents involved had no shortage of creative ideas for how to extract information from people who would rather not share it—the problem was finding ways to test those ideas. Activities in the first few years of Project Bluebird and Artichoke resembled those in a tragicomic spy film in which CIA agents hypnotized each other and slipped LSD into their colleagues' drinks to see what would happen (in at least one case, suicide)—not to mention torturing suspected Russian spies.[16]

The tests were more like deadly fraternity pranks than serious research, and the results didn't provide the kind of scientific certainty the agency was looking for. For this they needed large numbers of human test subjects. Several such trials were attempted, but they were risky: if word got out that the CIA was testing dangerous drugs on American soil, the entire program could be shut down.[17] Which is where the CIA's interest in Canadian researchers came in. The relationship dates back to June 1, 1951, and a trinational meeting of intelligence agencies and academics at Montreal's Ritz-Carlton Hotel. The subject of the meeting was growing concern in the Western intelligence community that the Communists had somehow discovered how to "brainwash" prisoners of war. The evidence was the fact that American GIs taken captive in Korea were going before cameras, seemingly willingly, and denouncing capitalism and imperialism. According to the declassified minutes from the Ritz meeting, those in attendance—Omond Solandt, chairman of Canada's Defense Research Board; Sir Henry Tizard, chairman of the British Defense Research Policy Committee; as well as two representatives from the CIA—were convinced that Western powers urgently needed to discover how the Communists were extracting these remarkable confessions. With that in mind, the first step was to conduct "a clinical study of actual cases" to see how brainwashing might work.[18] The stated goal of this research was not for Western powers to start using mind control on prisoners; it was to prepare Western soldiers for whatever coercive techniques they might encounter if they were taken hostage.

The CIA, of course, had other interests. Yet even in closed-door meetings like the one at the Ritz, it would have been impossible, so soon after revelations of Nazi torture had provoked worldwide revulsion, for the agency to openly admit it was interested in developing alternative interrogation methods of its own.

One of those at the Ritz meeting was Dr. Donald Hebb, director of psychology at McGill University. According to the declassified minutes, Hebb, trying to unlock the mystery of the GI confessions, speculated that the Communists might be manipulating prisoners by placing them in intensive isolation and blocking input to their senses. The intelligence chiefs were impressed, and three months later Hebb had a research grant from Canada's Department of National Defense to conduct a series of classified sensory-deprivation experiments. Hebb paid a group of sixty-three McGill students $20 a day to be isolated in a room wearing dark goggles, headphones playing white noise and cardboard tubes covering their arms and hands so as to interfere with their sense of touch. For days, the students floated in a sea of nothingness, their eyes, ears and hands unable to orient them, living inside their increasingly vivid imaginations. To see whether this deprivation made them more susceptible to "brainwashing," Hebb then began playing recordings of voices talking about the existence of ghosts or the dishonesty of science—ideas the students had said they found objectionable before the experiment began.[19]

In a confidential report on Hebb's findings, the Defense Research Board concluded that sensory deprivation clearly caused extreme confusion as well as hallucinations among the student test subjects and that "a significant temporary lowering of intellectual efficiency occurred during and immediately after the period of perceptual deprivation."[20] Furthermore, the students' hunger for stimulation made them surprisingly receptive to the ideas expressed on the tapes, and indeed several developed an interest in the occult that lasted weeks after the experiment had come to an end. It was as if the confusion from sensory deprivation partially erased their minds, and then the sensory stimuli rewrote their patterns.

A copy of Hebb's major study was sent to the CIA, as well as forty-one copies to the U.S. Navy and forty-two copies to the U.S. Army.[21] The CIA also directly monitored the findings via one of Hebb's student researchers, Maitland Baldwin, who, unbeknownst to Hebb, was reporting to the agency.[22] This keen interest was hardly surprising: at the very least, Hebb was proving that intensive isolation interfered with the ability to think clearly and made people more open to suggestion—priceless ideas for any interrogator. Hebb eventually realized that there was enormous potential for his research to be used not just to protect captured soldiers from getting "brainwashed" but also as a kind of how-to manual for psychological torture. In the last interview he gave before his death in 1985, Hebb said, "It was clear when we made our report to the Defense Research Board that we were describing formidable interrogation techniques."[23]

Hebb's report noted that four of the subjects "remarked spontaneously that being in the apparatus was a form of torture," which meant that forcing them to stay past their threshold—two or three days—would clearly violate medical ethics. Aware of the limitations this placed on the experiment, Hebb wrote that more "clearcut results" were not available because "it is not possible to force subjects to spend 30 to 60 days in conditions of perceptual isolation."[24]

Not possible for Hebb, but it was perfectly possible for his McGill colleague and academic archrival, Dr. Ewen Cameron. (In a suspension of academic niceties, Hebb would later describe Cameron as "criminally stupid.")[25] Cameron had already convinced himself that violent destruction of the minds of his patients was the necessary first step on their journey to mental health and therefore not a violation of the Hippocratic oath. As for consent, his patients were at his mercy; the standard consent form endowed Cameron with absolute power to treat, up to and including performing full frontal lobotomies.

Although he had been in contact with the agency for years, in 1957 Cameron got his first grant from the CIA, laundered through a front organization called the Society for the Investigation of Human Ecology.[26] And, as the CIA dollars poured in, the Allan Memorial Institute seemed less like a hospital and more like a macabre prison.

The first changes were the dramatically increased dosages of electroshock. The two psychiatrists who invented the controversial Page-Russell electroshock machine had recommended four treatments per patient, totaling twenty-four individual shocks.[27] Cameron started using the machine on his patients twice a day for thirty days, a terrifying 360 individual shocks to each patient—far more than his earlier patients, like Gail, had received.[28] To the already dizzying array of drugs he was giving his patients, he added more experimental, mind-altering ones that were of particular interest to the CIA: LSD and PCP.

He also added other weapons to his mind-blanking arsenal: sensory deprivation and extended sleep, a twin process he claimed would further "reduce the defensiveness of the individual," making the patient more receptive to his taped messages.[29] When the CIA dollars arrived, Cameron used the grant money to convert the old horse stables behind the hospital into isolation boxes. He also elaborately renovated the basement so that it contained a room he called the Isolation Chamber.[30] He soundproofed the room, piped in white noise, turned off the lights and put dark goggles and "rubber eardrums" on each patient, as well as cardboard tubing on the hands and arms, "preventing him from touching his body—thus interfering with his self image," as Cameron put it in a 1956 paper.[31] But, where Hebb's students fled less intense sensory deprivation after only a couple of days, Cameron kept his patients in for weeks, with one of them trapped in the isolation box for thirty-five days.[32]

Cameron further starved his patients' senses in the so-called Sleep Room, where they were kept in drug-induced reverie for twenty to twenty-two hours a day, turned by nurses every two hours to prevent bed sores and wakened only for meals and to go to the toilet.[33] Patients were kept in this state for fifteen to thirty days, though Cameron reported that "some patients have been treated up to 65 days of continuous sleep."[34] Hospital staffers were instructed not to allow patients to talk and not to give out any information about how long they would have to spend in the room. To make sure no one successfully escaped from this nightmare, Cameron gave one group of patients small doses of the drug Curare, which induces paralysis, making them literal prisoners in their own bodies.[35]

In a 1960 paper, Cameron said there are "two major factors" that allow us to "maintain a time and space image"—that allow us, in other words, to know where we are and who we are. Those two forces are "(a) our continued sensory input, and (b) our memory." With electroshock, Cameron annihilated memory; with his isolation boxes, he annihilated sensory input. He was determined to force his patients to completely lose their sense of where they were in time and space. Realizing that some patients were keeping track of time of day based on their meals, Cameron ordered the kitchen to mix it all up, changing meal times and serving soup for breakfast and porridge for dinner. "By varying these intervals and by changing the menu from the expected time we were able to break up this structuring," Cameron reported with satisfaction. Even so, he discovered that despite his best efforts, one patient had maintained a connection with the outside world by noting "the very faint rumble" of a plane that flew over the hospital every morning at nine.[36]

To anyone familiar with the testimonies of torture survivors, this detail is a harrowing one. When prisoners are asked how they survived months or years of isolation and brutality, they often speak about hearing the ring of distant church bells, or the Muslim call to prayer, or children playing in a park nearby. When life is shrunk to the four walls of the prison cell, the rhythm of these outside sounds becomes a kind of lifeline, proof that the prisoner is still human, that there is a world beyond torture. "Four times I heard the birds outside chirping with the rising sun—that's how I know it was four days," said one survivor of Uruguay's last dictatorship, recalling a particularly brutal stretch of torture.[37] The unidentified woman in the basement of the Allan Memorial Institute, straining to hear the engine of an airplane through a haze of darkness, drugs and electroshock, was not a patient in the care of a doctor; she was, for all intents and purposes, a prisoner undergoing torture.

There are several strong indications that Cameron was well aware he was simulating torture conditions and that, as a staunch anti-Communist, he relished the idea that his patients were part of a Cold War effort. In an interview with a popular magazine in 1955, he openly compared his patients to POWs facing interrogation, saying that they, "like prisoners of the Communists, tended to resist [treatment] and had to be broken down."[38] A year later, he wrote that the purpose of depatterning was "the actual 'wearing down' of defenses" and noted that "analogous to this is the breakdown of the individual under continuous interrogation."[39] By 1960, Cameron was giving lectures on his sensory deprivation research not just to other psychiatrists but also to military audiences. In a talk delivered in Texas at the Brooks Air Force Base, he made no claim that he was curing schizophrenia and in fact admitted that sensory deprivation "produces the primary symptoms of schizophrenia"—hallucinations, intense anxiety, loss of touch with reality.[40] In notes for the lecture, he mentions following sensory deprivation with "input-overload," a reference to his use of electroshock and endlessly repeated tape loops—and a foreshadowing of interrogation tactics to come.[41]

Cameron's work was funded by the CIA until 1961, and for many years it wasn't clear what, if anything, the U.S. government did with his research. In the late seventies and eighties, when proof of the CIA's funding for the experiments finally came out in Senate hearings and then in the patients'

groundbreaking class-action lawsuit against the agency, journalists and legislators tended to accept the CIA's version of events—that it was conducting
research into brainwashing techniques in order to protect captured U.S. soldiers. Most of the press attention focused on the sensational detail that the
government had been funding acid trips. In fact, a large part of the scandal,
when it finally broke, was that the CIA and Ewen Cameron had recklessly
shattered lives with their experiments for no good reason—the research appeared useless: everyone knew by then that brainwashing was a Cold War
myth. The CIA, for its part, actively encouraged this narrative, much preferring to be mocked as bumbling sci-fi buffoons than for having funded a torture laboratory at a respected university—and an effective one at that. When
John Gittinger, the CIA psychologist who first reached out to Cameron, was
forced to testify before a joint Senate hearing, he called the support for
Cameron "a foolish mistake. . . . A terrible mistake."[42] When the hearings
asked Sidney Gottlieb, former director of MKUltra, to explain why he had
ordered all the files destroyed from the $25 million program, he replied that
"the project MKUltra had not yielded any results of real positive value to the
Agency."[43] In the exposés of MKUltra from the eighties, both in investigative
accounts in the mainstream press and in books, the experiments are consistently described as "mind control" and "brainwashing." The word "torture"
is almost never used.

The Science of Fear

In 1988, *The New York Times* ran a groundbreaking investigation into U.S. involvement in torture and assassinations in Honduras. Florencio Caballero, an
interrogator with Honduras's notoriously brutal Battalion 3–16, told the *Times*
that he and twenty-four of his colleagues were taken to Texas and trained by
the CIA. "They taught us psychological methods—to study the fears and weaknesses of a prisoner. Make him stand up, don't let him sleep, keep him naked
and isolated, put rats and cockroaches in his cell, give him bad food, serve him
dead animals, throw cold water on him, change the temperature." There was
one technique he failed to mention: electroshock. Inés Murillo, a twenty-four-
year-old prisoner who was "interrogated" by Caballero and his colleagues, told
the *Times* that she was electrocuted so many times that she "screamed and fell
down from the shock. The screams just escape you," she said. "I smelled
smoke and realized I was burning from the singes of the shocks. They said they
would torture me until I went mad. I didn't believe them. But then they spread

my legs and stuck the wires on my genitals."[44] Murillo also said that there was someone else in the room: an American passing questions to her interrogators whom the others called "Mr. Mike."[45]

The revelations led to hearings of the Senate's Select Committee on Intelligence, where the CIA's deputy director, Richard Stolz, confirmed that "Caballero did indeed attend a CIA human resources exploitation or interrogation course."[46] *The Baltimore Sun* filed a Freedom of Information Act request for the course material used to train people like Caballero. For many years the CIA refused to comply; finally, under threat of a lawsuit, and nine years after the original story was published, the CIA produced a handbook called *Kubark Counterintelligence Interrogation.* The title was in code: "Kubark" is, according to *The New York Times,* "a cryptonym, KU a random diptych and BARK the agency's code word for itself at that time." More recent reports have speculated that the "ku" referred to "a country or a specific clandestine or covert activity."[47] The handbook is a 128-page secret manual on the "interrogation of resistant sources" that is heavily based on the research commissioned by MKUltra—and Ewen Cameron's and Donald Hebb's experiments have left their marks all over it. Methods range from sensory deprivation to stress positions, from hooding to pain. (The manual acknowledges early on that many of these tactics are illegal and instructs interrogators to seek "prior Headquarters approval . . . under any of the following circumstances: 1. If bodily harm is to be inflicted. 2. If medical, chemical, *or electrical* methods or materials are to be used to induce acquiescence.")[48]

The manual is dated 1963, the final year of the MKUltra program and two years after Cameron's CIA-funded experiments came to a close. The handbook claims that if the techniques are used properly, they will take a resistant source and "destroy his capacity for resistance." This, it turns out, was the true purpose of MKUltra: not to research brainwashing (that was a mere side project), but to design a scientifically based system for extracting information from "resistant sources."[49] In other words, torture.

The manual states on its first page that it is about to describe interrogation methods based on "extensive research, including scientific inquiries conducted by specialists in closely related subjects." It represents a new age of precise, refined torture—not the gory, inexact torment that had been the standard since the Spanish Inquisition. In a kind of preface, the manual states: "The intelligence service which is able to bring pertinent, modern knowledge to bear upon its problems enjoys huge advantages over a service which conducts its clandestine business in eighteenth century fashion . . . it is no longer possible to discuss interrogation significantly without reference to the psychological research conducted in the past decade."[50] What follows is a how-to guide on dismantling personalities.

The manual includes a lengthy section on sensory deprivation that refers to "a number of experiments at McGill University."[51] It describes how to build isolation chambers and notes that "the deprivation of stimuli induces regression by depriving the subject's mind of contact with an outer world and thus forcing it in upon itself. At the same time, the calculated provision of stimuli during interrogation tends to make the regressed subject view the interrogator as a father-figure."[52] The Freedom of Information Act request also produced an updated version of the manual, first published in 1983 for use in Latin America. "Window should be set high in the wall with the capability of blocking out light," it states.*[53]

It is precisely what Hebb feared: the use of his sensory deprivation methods as "formidable interrogation techniques." But it is the work of Cameron, and his recipe for disturbing "the time-space-image," that forms the core of the *Kubark* formula. The manual describes several of the techniques that were honed to depattern patients in the basement of the Allan Memorial Institute: "The principle is that sessions should be so planned as to disrupt the source's sense of chronological order. . . . Some interrogatees can be regressed by persistent manipulation of time, by retarding and advancing clocks and serving meals at odd times—ten minutes or ten hours after the last food was given. Day and night are jumbled."[54]

What most captured the imagination of *Kubark*'s authors, more than any individual technique, was Cameron's focus on regression—the idea that by depriving people of their sense of who they are and where they are in time and space, adults can be converted into dependent children whose minds are a blank slate of suggestibility. Again and again, the authors return to the theme. "All of the techniques employed to break through an interrogation roadblock, the entire spectrum from simple isolation to hypnosis and narcosis, are essentially ways of speeding up the process of regression. As the interrogatee slips back from maturity toward a more infantile state, his learned or structured personality traits fall away." That is when the prisoner goes into the state of "psychological shock" or "suspended animation" referred to earlier—that torturer's sweet spot when "the source is far more open to suggestion, far likelier to comply."[55]

---

*The 1983 version is clearly geared to classroom use, complete with pop quizzes and friendly reminders ("Always start each session with fresh batteries").

Alfred W. McCoy, a historian at the University of Wisconsin who documented the evolution of torture techniques since the Inquisition in his book *A Question of Torture: CIA Interrogation from the Cold War to the War on Terror,* describes the *Kubark* manual's shock-inducing formula of sensory deprivation followed by sensory overload as "the first real revolution in the cruel science of pain in more than three centuries."[56] And according to McCoy, it couldn't have happened without the McGill experiments in the 1950s. "Stripped of its bizarre excesses, Dr. Cameron's experiments, building upon Dr. Hebb's earlier breakthrough, laid the scientific foundation for the CIA's two-stage psychological torture method."[57]

Wherever the *Kubark* method has been taught, certain clear patterns—all designed to induce, deepen and sustain shock—have emerged: prisoners are captured in the most jarring and disorienting way possible, late at night or in early-morning raids, as the manual instructs. They are immediately hooded or blindfolded, stripped and beaten, then subjected to some form of sensory deprivation. And from Guatemala to Honduras, Vietnam to Iran, the Philippines to Chile, the use of electroshock is ubiquitous.

This was not, of course, all the influence of Cameron or MKUltra. Torture is always an improvisation, a combination of learned technique and the human instinct for brutality that is unleashed wherever impunity reigns. By the mid-fifties, electroshock was being routinely used against liberation fighters by French soldiers in Algeria, often with the help of psychiatrists.[58] In this period, French military leaders conducted seminars at a U.S. military "counterinsurgency" school in Fort Bragg, North Carolina, in which they trained students in the Algeria techniques.[59] It is also clear, however, that Cameron's particular model of using massive doses of shock not just to inflict pain but for the specific goal of erasing structured personalities made an impression on the CIA. In 1966, the CIA sent three psychiatrists to Saigon, armed with a Page-Russell, the same kind of electroshock machine favored by Cameron; it was used so aggressively that it killed several prisoners. According to McCoy, "In effect, they were testing, under field conditions, whether Ewen Cameron's McGill 'de-patterning' techniques could actually alter human behavior."[60]

For U.S. intelligence officials, that kind of hands-on approach was rare. From the seventies on, the role favored by American agents was that of mentor or trainer—not direct interrogator. Testimony from Central American torture survivors in the seventies and eighties is littered with references to mysterious English-speaking men walking in and out of cells, proposing questions or offering tips. Dianna Ortiz, an American nun who was abducted and jailed in Guatemala in 1989, has testified that the men who raped and burned her with cigarettes deferred to a man who spoke Spanish with a heavy American accent, whom they referred to as their "boss."[61] Jennifer Harbury, whose husband was tortured and killed by a Guatemalan officer on the CIA payroll, has documented many of these cases in her important book, *Truth, Torture and the American Way.*[62]

Though sanctioned by successive administrations in Washington, the U.S. role in these dirty wars had to be covert, for obvious reasons. Torture, whether physical or psychological, clearly violates the Geneva Conventions' blanket ban on "any form of torture or cruelty," as well as the U.S. Army's own Uniform Code of Military Justice barring "cruelty" and "oppression" of prisoners.[63] The *Kubark* manual warns readers on page 2 that its techniques carry "the grave risk of later lawsuits," and the 1983 version is even more blunt: "Use of force, mental torture, threats, insults, or exposure to unpleasant and inhumane treatment of any kind as an aid to interrogation is prohibited by law, both international and domestic."[64] Simply put, what they were teaching was illegal, covert by its very nature. If anyone asked, U.S. agents were tutoring their developing-world students in modern, professional policing methods—they couldn't be responsible for "excesses" that happened outside their classes.

On September 11, 2001, that longtime insistence on plausible deniability went out the window. The terrorist attack on the Twin Towers and the Pentagon was a different kind of shock from the ones imagined in the pages of the *Kubark* manual, but its effects were remarkably similar: profound disorientation, extreme fear and anxiety, and collective regression. Like the *Kubark* interrogator posing as a "father figure," the Bush administration promptly used that fear to play the role of the all-protective parent, ready to defend "the homeland" and its vulnerable people by any means necessary. The shift in U.S. policy encapsulated by Vice President Dick Cheney's infamous statement about working "the dark side" did not mark an embrace by this administration of tactics that would have repelled its more humane predecessors (as too many Democrats have claimed, invoking what the historian Garry Wills calls the particular American myth of "original sinlessness"[65]). Rather, the significant shift was that what had previously been performed by proxy, with enough distance to deny knowledge, would now be performed directly and openly defended.

Despite all the talk of outsourced torture, the Bush administration's real innovation has been its in-sourcing, with prisoners being tortured by U.S. citizens in U.S.-run prisons or directly transported, through "extraordinary rendition," to third countries on U.S. planes. That is what makes the Bush regime different: after the attacks of September 11, it dared to demand the right to torture without shame. That left the administration subject to criminal prosecution—a problem it dealt with by changing the laws. The chain of events is well known: then–secretary of defense Donald Rumsfeld, empowered by George W. Bush, decreed that prisoners captured in Afghanistan were not covered by the Geneva Conventions because they were "enemy combatants," not POWs, a view confirmed by the White House legal counsel at the time, Alberto Gonzales (subsequently U.S. attorney general).[66] Next, Rumsfeld approved a series of special interrogation practices for use in the War on Terror. These included the methods laid out in the CIA manuals: "use of isolation facility for up to 30 days," "deprivation of light and auditory stimuli," "the detainee may also have a hood placed over his head during transportation and questioning," "removal of clothing" and "using detainees' individual phobias (such as fear of dogs) to induce stress."[67] According to the White House, torture was still banned—but now to qualify as torture, the pain inflicted had to "be equivalent in intensity to the pain accompanying serious physical injury, such as organ failure."*[68] According to these new rules, the U.S. government was free to use the methods it had developed in the 1950s under layers of secrecy and deniability—only now it was out in the open, without fear of prosecution. . . . According to these new rules, the U.S. government was free to use the methods it had developed in the 1950s under layers of secrecy and deniability—only now it was out in the open, without fear of prosecution. So in February 2006, the Intelligence Sciences Board, an advisory arm of the CIA, published a report written by a veteran Defense Department interrogator. It stated openly that "a careful reading of the *Kubark* manual is essential for anyone involved in interrogation."[69]

---

* Under pressure from lawmakers in Congress and the Senate, as well as the Supreme Court, the Bush administration was forced to moderate its position somewhat when Congress approved the Military Commissions Act of 2006. But although the White House used the new bill to claim that it had renounced all use of torture, it left huge holes allowing CIA agents and contractors to continue to use *Kubark*-style sensory deprivation and overload, as well as other "creative" techniques including simulated drowning ("water-boarding"). Before signing the act, Bush attached a "signing statement" asserting his right "to interpret the meaning and application of the Geneva Conventions" as he sees fit. *The New York Times* described this as the "unilateral rewriting of more than 200 years of tradition and law."

One of the first people to come face-to-face with the new order was the U.S. citizen and former gang member José Padilla. Arrested in May 2002 at Chicago's O'Hare airport, he was accused of intending to build a "dirty bomb." Rather than being charged and taken through the court system, Padilla was classified as an enemy combatant, which stripped him of all rights. Taken to a U.S. Navy prison in Charleston, South Carolina, Padilla says he was injected with a drug that he believes was either LSD or PCP and subjected to intense sensory deprivation: he was kept in a tiny cell with the windows blacked out and forbidden to have a clock or a calendar. Whenever he left the cell he was shackled, his eyes were covered with blackout goggles and sound was blocked with heavy headphones. Padilla was kept under these conditions for 1,307 days and forbidden contact with anyone but his interrogators, who, when they questioned him, blasted his starved senses with lights and pounding sounds.[70]

Padilla was granted a court hearing in December 2006, although the dirty-bomb allegations for which he had been arrested were dropped. He was accused of having terrorist contacts, but there was little he could do to defend himself: according to expert testimony, the Cameron-style regression techniques had completely succeeded in destroying the adult he once was, which is precisely what they were designed to do. "The extended torture visited upon Mr. Padilla has left him damaged, both mentally and physically," his lawyer told the court. "The government's treatment of Mr. Padilla has robbed him of his personhood." A psychiatrist who assessed him concluded that he "lacks the capacity to assist in his own defense."[71] The Bush-appointed judge insisted that Padilla was fit to stand trial, however. The fact that he even had a public trial makes Padilla's case extraordinary. Thousands of other prisoners being held in U.S.-run prisons—who, unlike Padilla, are not U.S. citizens—have been put through a similar torture regimen, with none of the public accountability of a civilian trial.

Many languish in Guantánamo. Mamdouh Habib, an Australian who was incarcerated there, has said that "Guantánamo Bay is an experiment . . . and what they experiment in is brainwashing."[72] Indeed, in the testimonies, reports and photographs that have come out of Guantánamo, it is as if the Allan Memorial Institute of the 1950s had been transported to Cuba. When first detained, prisoners are put into intense sensory deprivation, with hoods, blackout goggles and heavy headphones to block out all sound. They are left in isolation cells for months, taken out only to have their senses bombarded with barking dogs, strobe lights and endless tape loops of babies crying, music blaring and cats meowing.

For many prisoners, the effects of these techniques have been much the same as they were at the Allan in the fifties: total regression. One released prisoner, a British citizen, told his lawyers that there is now an entire section of the prison, Delta Block, reserved for "at least fifty" detainees who are in permanently delusional states.[73] A declassified letter from the FBI to the Pentagon described one high-value prisoner who had been "subjected to intense isolation for over three months" and "was evidencing behavior consistent with extreme psychological trauma (talking to nonexistent people, reporting hearing voices, crouching in a cell covered with a sheet for hours on end)."[74] James Yee, a former U.S. Army Muslim chaplain who worked at Guantánamo, has described the prisoners on Delta Block as exhibiting the classic symptoms of extreme regression. "I'd stop to talk to them, and they would respond to me in a childlike voice, talking complete nonsense. Many of them would loudly sing childish songs, repeating the song over and over. Some would stand on top of their steel bed frames and act out childishly, reminding me of the King of the Mountain game I played with my brothers when we were young." The situation worsened markedly in January 2007, when 165 prisoners were moved into a new wing of the prison, known as Camp Six, where the steel isolation cells allowed for no human contact. Sabin Willett, a lawyer who represents several Guantánamo prisoners, warned that if the situation continued, "You're going to have an insane asylum."[75]

Human rights groups point out that Guantánamo, horrifying as it is, is actually the best of the U.S.-run offshore interrogation operations, since it is open to limited monitoring by the Red Cross and lawyers. Unknown numbers of prisoners have disappeared into the network of so-called black sites around the world or been shipped by U.S. agents to foreign-run jails through extraordinary rendition. Prisoners who have emerged from these nightmares testify to having faced the full arsenal of Cameron-style shock tactics.

The Italian cleric Hassan Mustafa Osama Nasr was kidnapped off the streets of Milan by a group of CIA agents and Italian secret police. "I didn't understand anything about what was going on," he later wrote. "They began to punch me in the stomach and all over my body. They wrapped my entire head and face with wide tape, and cut holes over my nose and face so I could breathe." They rushed him to Egypt, where he lived in a cell with no light, where "roaches and rats walked across my body" for fourteen months. Nasr remained in jail in Egypt until February 2007 but managed to smuggle out an eleven-page handwritten letter detailing his abuse.[76]

He wrote that he repeatedly faced torture by electroshock. According to the *Washington Post* account, he was "strapped to an iron rack nicknamed 'the Bride' and zapped with electric stun guns" as well as "tied to a wet mattress on the floor. While one interrogator sat on a wooden chair perched on the prisoner's shoulders, another interrogator would flip a switch, sending jolts of electricity into the mattress coils."[77] He also had electroshock applied to his testicles, according to Amnesty International.[78]

There is reason to believe that this use of electrical torture on U.S.-captured prisoners is not isolated, a fact overlooked in almost all the discussions about whether the U.S. is actually practicing torture or merely "creative interrogation." Jumah al-Dossari, a Guantánamo prisoner who has tried to commit suicide more than a dozen times, gave written testimoney to his lawyer that while he was in U.S. custody in Kandahar, "the investigator brought a small device like a mobile phone but it was an electric shock device. He started shocking my face, my back, my limbs and my genitals."[79] And Murat Kurnaz, originally from Germany, faced similar treatment in a U.S.-run prison in Kandahar. "It was the beginning, so there were absolutely no rules. They had the right to do anything. They used to beat us every time. They did use electroshocks. They dived my head in the water."[80]

The Failure to Reconstruct

Near the end of our first meeting, I asked Gail Kastner to tell me more about her "electric dreams." She told me that she often dreams of rows of patients slipping in and out of drug-induced sleep. "I hear people screaming, moaning, groaning, people saying no, no, no. I remember what it was like to wake up in that room, I was covered in sweat, nauseated, vomiting—and I had a very peculiar feeling in the head. Like I had a blob, not a head." Describing this, Gail seemed suddenly far away, slumped in her blue chair, her breath turning into a wheeze. She lowered her eyelids, and beneath them I could see her eyes fluttering rapidly. She put her hand to her right temple and said in a voice that sounded thick and drugged, "I'm having a flashback. You have to distract me. Tell me about Iraq—tell me how bad it was."

I racked my brain for a suitable war story for this strange circumstance and came up with something relatively benign about life in the Green Zone. Gail's face slowly relaxed, and her breathing deepened. Her blue eyes once again fixed on mine. "Thank you," she said. "I was having a flashback."

"I know."

"How do you know?"

"Because you told me."

She leaned over and wrote something down on a scrap of paper.

After leaving Gail that evening, I kept thinking about what I hadn't said when she'd asked me to tell her about Iraq. What I had wanted to tell her but couldn't was that she reminded me of Iraq; that I couldn't help feeling that what happened to her, a shocked person, and what happened to it, a shocked country, were somehow connected, different manifestations of the same terrifying logic.

Cameron's theories were based on the idea that shocking his patients into a chaotic regressed state would create the preconditions for him to "rebirth" healthy model citizens. It's little comfort to Gail, with her fractured spine and shattered memories, but in his own writings Cameron envisioned his acts of destruction as creation, a gift to his fortunate patients who were, under his relentless repatterning, going to be born again.

On this front Cameron was a spectacular failure. No matter how fully he regressed his patients, they never absorbed or accepted the endlessly repeated messages on his tapes. Though he was a genius at destroying people, he could not remake them. A follow-up study conducted after Cameron left the Allan Memorial Institute found that 75 percent of his former patients were worse off after treatment than before they were admitted. Of his patients who held down full-time jobs before hospitalization, more than half were no longer able to, and many, like Gail, suffered from a host of new physical and psychological ailments. "Psychic driving" did not work, not even a little, and the Allan Memorial Institute eventually banned the practice.[81]

The problem, obvious in retrospect, was the premise on which his entire theory rested: the idea that before healing can happen, everything that existed before needs to be wiped out. Cameron was sure that if he blasted away at the habits, patterns and memories of his patients, he would eventually arrive at that pristine blank slate. But no matter how doggedly he shocked, drugged and disoriented, he never got there. The opposite proved true: the more he blasted, the more shattered his patients became. Their minds weren't "clean"; rather, they were a mess, their memories fractured, their trust betrayed.

Disaster capitalists share this same inability to distinguish between destruction and creation, between hurting and healing. It's a feeling I had frequently when I was in Iraq, nervously scanning the scarred landscape for the next explosion. Fervent believers in the redemptive powers of shock, the architects of the American-British invasion imagined that their use of force would be so stunning, so overwhelming, that Iraqis would go into a kind of suspended animation, much like the one described in the *Kubark* manual. In that window of opportunity, Iraq's invaders would slip in another set of shocks — these ones economic — which would create a model free-market democracy on the blank slate that was post-invasion Iraq.

But there was no blank slate, only rubble and shattered, angry people — who, when they resisted, were blasted with more shocks, some of them based on those experiments performed on Gail Kastner all those years ago. "We're really good at going out and breaking things. But the day I get to spend more time here working on construction rather than combat, that will be a very good day," General Peter W. Chiarelli, commander of the U.S. Army's First Cavalry Division, observed a year and half after the official end of the war.[82] That day never came. Like Cameron, Iraq's shock doctors can destroy, but they can't seem to rebuild.

CHAPTER 2

THE OTHER DOCTOR SHOCK

MILTON FRIEDMAN AND THE SEARCH FOR A LAISSEZ-FAIRE LABORATORY

> Economic technocrats may be able to structure a tax reform here, a new social security law there, or a modified exchange rate regime somewhere else, but they really never have the luxury of a clean state on which to set up, in full flower as it were, their complete preferred economic policy framework.
>
> —Arnold Harberger, University of Chicago economics professor, 1998[1]

There are few academic environments as heavily mythologized as the University of Chicago's Economics Department in the 1950s, a place intensely conscious of itself not just as a school but as a School of Thought. It was not just training students; it was building and strengthening the Chicago School of economics, the brainchild of a coterie of conservative academics whose ideas represented a revolutionary bulwark against the dominant "statist" thinking of the day. To step through the doors of the Social Science Building, under the sign reading "Science Is Measurement," and into the legendary lunchroom, where students tested their intellectual mettle by daring to challenge their titanic professors, was to seek nothing so prosaic as a degree. It was to enlist in battle. As Gary Becker, the conservative economist and Nobel Prize winner, put it, "We were warriors in combat with most of the rest of the profession."[2]

Like Ewen Cameron's psychiatric department at McGill in the same period, the University of Chicago's Economics Department was in the thrall of an ambitious and charismatic man on a mission to fundamentally revolutionize his profession. That man was Milton Friedman. Though he had many mentors and colleagues who believed just as fiercely as he did in ultra laissez-faire, it was Friedman's energy that gave the school its revolutionary fervor. "People would always ask me, 'Why are you so excited? Are you going out on a date with a beautiful woman?'" recalls Becker. "I said, 'No, I'm going to a class in economics!' Being a student of Milton's was magic indeed."[3]

Friedman's mission, like Cameron's, rested on a dream of reaching back to a state of "natural" health, when all was in balance, before human interferences created distorting patterns. Where Cameron dreamed of returning the human mind to that pristine state, Friedman dreamed of depatterning societies, of returning them to a state of pure capitalism, cleansed of all interruptions—government regulations, trade barriers and entrenched interests. Also like Cameron, Friedman believed that when the economy is highly distorted, the only way to reach that prelapsarian state was to deliberately inflict painful shocks: only "bitter medicine" could clear those distortions and bad patterns out of the way. Cameron used electricity to inflict his shocks; Friedman's tool of choice was policy—the shock treatment approach he urged on bold politicians for countries in distress. Unlike Cameron, however, who was able to instantly apply his pet theories on his unwitting patients, Friedman would need two decades and several twists and turns of history before he too got the chance to put his dreams of radical erasure and creation into action in the real world.

Frank Knight, one of the founders of Chicago School economics, thought professors should "inculcate" in their students the belief that each economic theory is "a sacred feature of the system," not a debatable hypothesis.[4] The core of such sacred Chicago teachings was that the economic forces of supply, demand, inflation and unemployment were like the forces of nature, fixed and unchanging. In the truly free market imagined in Chicago classes and texts, these forces existed in perfect equilibrium, supply communicating with demand the way the moon pulls the tides. If economies suffered from high inflation, it was, according to Friedman's strict theory of monetarism, invariably because misguided policy makers had allowed too much money to enter the system, rather than letting the market find its balance. Just as ecosystems self-regulate, keeping themselves in balance, the market, left to its own devices, would create just the right number of products at precisely the right prices, produced by workers at just the right wages to buy those products—an Eden of plentiful employment, boundless creativity and zero inflation.

According to the Harvard sociologist Daniel Bell, this love of an idealized system is the defining quality of radical free-market economics. Capitalism is envisaged as "a jeweled set of movements" or a "celestial clockwork . . . a work of art, so compelling that one thinks of the celebrated pictures of Apelles who painted a cluster of grapes so realistic that the birds would come and pick at them."[5]

The challenge for Friedman and his colleagues was how to prove that a real-world market could live up to their rapturous imaginings. Friedman always prided himself on approaching economics as a science as hard and rigorous as physics or chemistry. But hard scientists could point to the behavior of the elements to prove their theories. Friedman could not point to any living economy that proved that if all "distortions" were stripped away, what would be left would be a society in perfect health and bounteous, since no country in the world met the criteria for perfect laissez-faire. Unable to test their theories in central banks and ministries of trade, Friedman and his colleagues had to settle for elaborate and ingenious mathematical equations and computer models mapped out in the basement workshops of the social sciences building.

A love of numbers and systems is what had led Friedman to economics. In his autobiography, he says his moment of epiphany came when a high-school geometry teacher wrote the Pythagorean theorem on the blackboard and then, awed by its elegance, quoted from John Keats's "Ode on a Grecian Urn": " 'Beauty is truth, truth beauty,' —that is all / Ye know on earth, and all ye need to know."[6] Friedman passed on that same ecstatic love of a beautiful all-encompassing system to generations of economics scholars—along with a search for simplicity, elegance and rigor.

Like all fundamentalist faiths, Chicago School economics is, for its true believers, a closed loop. The starting premise is that the free market is a perfect scientific system, one in which individuals, acting on their own self-interested desires, create the maximum benefits for all. It follows ineluctably that if something is wrong within a free-market economy—high inflation or soaring unemployment—it has to be because the market is not truly free. There must be some interference, some distortion in the system. The Chicago solution is always the same: a stricter and more complete application of the fundamentals.

When Friedman died in 2006, obituary writers struggled to summarize the breadth of his legacy. One settled on this statement: "Milton's mantra of free markets, free prices, consumer choice and economic liberty is responsible for the global prosperity we enjoy today."[7] This is partially true. The nature of that global prosperity—who shares in it, who doesn't, where it came from—are all highly contested, of course. What is irrefutable is the fact that Friedman's free-market rulebook, and his savvy strategies for imposing it, have made some people extremely prosperous, winning for them something approximating complete freedom—to ignore national borders, to avoid regulation and taxation and to amass new wealth.

This knack for thinking highly profitable thoughts appears to have its roots in Friedman's early childhood, when his parents, immigrants from Hungary, bought a garment factory in Rahway, New Jersey. The family apartment was in the same building as the shop floor, which, Friedman wrote, "would be termed a sweatshop today."[8] Those were volatile times for sweatshop owners, with Marxists and anarchists organizing immigrant workers into unions to demand safety regulations and weekends off—and debating the theory of worker ownership at after-shift meetings. As the boss's son, Friedman no doubt heard a very different perspective on these debates. In the end, his father's factory went under, but in lectures and television appearances, Friedman spoke of it often, invoking it as a case study for the benefits of deregulated capitalism—proof that even the worst, least-regulated jobs offer the first rung on the ladder to freedom and prosperity.

A large part of the appeal of Chicago School economics was that, at a time when radical-left ideas about workers' power were gaining ground around the world, it provided a way to defend the interests of owners that was just as radical and was infused with its own claims to idealism. To hear Friedman tell it, his ideas were not about defending the right of factory owners to pay low wages but, rather, all about a quest for the purest possible form of "participatory democracy" because in the free market, "each man can vote, as it were, for the color of tie he wants."[9] Where leftists promised freedom for workers from bosses, citizens from dictatorship, countries from colonialism, Friedman promised "individual freedom," a project that elevated atomized citizens above any collective enterprise and liberated them to express their absolute free will through their consumer choices. "What was particularly exciting were the same qualities that made Marxism so appealing to many other young people at the time," recalled the economist Don Patinkin, who studied at Chicago in the forties—"simplicity together with apparent logical completeness; idealism combined with radicalism."[10] The Marxists had their workers' utopia, and the Chicagoans had their entrepreneurs' utopia, both claiming that if they got their way, perfection and balance would follow.

The question, as always, was how to get to that wondrous place from here. The Marxists were clear: revolution—get rid of the current system, replace it with socialism. For the Chicagoans, the answer was not as straightforward. The United States was already a capitalist country, but as far as they were concerned, just barely. In the U.S., and in all supposedly capitalist economies, the Chicagoans saw interferences everywhere. To make products more affordable, politicians fixed prices; to make workers less exploited, they set minimum wages; to make sure everyone had access to education, they kept it in the hands of the state. These measures often seemed to help people, but Friedman and his colleagues were convinced—and they "proved" it with their models—that they were actually doing untold harm to the equilibrium of the market and the ability of its various signals to communicate with each other. The mission of the Chicago School was thus one of purification—stripping the market of these interruptions so that the free market could sing.

For this reason, Chicagoans did not see Marxism as their true enemy. The real source of the trouble was to be found in the ideas of the Keynesians in the United States, the social democrats in Europe and the developmentalists in what was then called the Third World. These were believers not in a utopia but in a mixed economy, to Chicago eyes an ugly hodgepodge of capitalism for the manufacture and distribution of consumer products, socialism in education, state ownership for essentials like water services, and all kinds of laws designed to temper the extremes of capitalism. Like the religious fundamentalist who has a grudging respect for fundamentalists of other faiths and for avowed atheists but disdains the casual believer, the Chicagoans declared war on these mix-and-match economists. What they wanted was not a revolution exactly but a capitalist Reformation: a return to uncontaminated capitalism.

Much of this purism came from Friedrich Hayek, Friedman's own personal guru, who also taught at the University of Chicago for a stretch in the 1950s. The austere Austrian warned that any government involvement in the economy would lead society down "the road to serfdom" and had to be expunged.[11] According to Arnold Harberger, a longtime professor at Chicago, "the Austrians," as this clique-within-a-clique was called, were so zealous that any state interference was not just wrong, but "evil. . . . It's as if there is a very pretty but highly complex picture out there, which is perfectly harmonious within itself, you see, and if there's a speck where it isn't supposed to be, well, that's just awful . . . it is a flaw that mars that beauty."[12]

In 1947, when Friedman first joined with Hayek to form the Mont Pelerin Society, a club of free-market economists named for its location in Switzerland, the idea that business should be left alone to govern the world as it wished was one barely suitable for polite company. Memories of the market crash of 1929 and the Great Depression that followed were still fresh—the life savings destroyed overnight, the suicides, the soup kitchens, the refugees. The scale of this market-created disaster had led to a surging demand for a distinctly hands-on form of government. The Depression did not signal the end of capitalism, but it was, as John Maynard Keynes forecast a few years earlier, "the end of *laissez-faire*"—the end of letting the market regulate itself.[13] The 1930s through to the early 1950s was a time of unabashed *faire:* the can-do ethos of the New Deal gave way to the war effort, with public works programs launched to create much-needed jobs, and new social programs unveiled to prevent growing numbers of people from turning hard left. It was a time when compromise between left and right was not a dirty word but part of what many saw as a noble mission to prevent a world, as Keynes wrote to President Franklin D. Roosevelt in 1933, in which "orthodoxy and revolution" are left "to fight it out."[14] John Kenneth Galbraith, heir to Keynes's mantle in the U.S., described the prime missions of politicians and economists alike as "the avoidance of depression and the prevention of unemployment."[15]

The Second World War lent new urgency to the war against poverty. Nazism had taken root in Germany at a time when the country was in a devastating depression, provoked by the punishing reparations imposed after the First World War and deepened by the 1929 crash. Keynes had warned early on that if the world took a laissez-faire approach to Germany's poverty, the blowback would be ferocious: "Vengeance, I dare predict, will not limp."[16] Those words went unheeded at the time, but when Europe was rebuilt after the Second World War, the Western powers embraced the principle that market economies needed to guarantee enough basic dignity that disillusioned citizens would not go looking once again for a more appealing ideology, whether fascism or Communism. It was this pragmatic imperative that led to the creation of almost everything that we associate today with the bygone days of "decent" capitalism—social security in the U.S., public health care in Canada, welfare in Britain, workers' protections in France and Germany.

A similar, more radical mood was on the rise in the developing world, usually going under the name developmentalism, or Third World nationalism.

Developmentalist economists argued that their countries would finally escape the cycle of poverty only if they pursued an inward-oriented industrialization strategy instead of relying on the export of natural resources, whose prices had been on a declining path, to Europe and North America. They advocated regulating or even nationalizing oil, minerals and other key industries so that a healthy share of the proceeds fed a government-led development process.

By the 1950s, the developmentalists, like the Keynesians and social democrats in rich countries, were able to boast a series of impressive success stories. The most advanced laboratory of developmentalism was the southern tip of Latin America, known as the Southern Cone: Chile, Argentina, Uruguay and parts of Brazil. The epicenter was the United Nations' Economic Commission for Latin America, based in Santiago, Chile, and headed by the economist Raúl Prebisch from 1950 to 1963. Prebisch trained teams of economists in developmentalist theory and dispatched them to act as policy advisers for governments across the continent. Nationalist politicians like Argentina's Juan Perón put their ideas into practice with a vengeance, pouring public money into infrastructure projects such as highways and steel plants, giving local businesses generous subsidies to build their new factories, churning out cars and washing machines, and keeping out foreign imports with forbiddingly high tariffs.

During this dizzying period of expansion, the Southern Cone began to look more like Europe and North America than the rest of Latin America or other parts of the Third World. The workers in the new factories formed powerful unions that negotiated middle-class salaries, and their children were sent off to study at newly built public universities. The yawning gap between the region's polo-club elite and its peasant masses began to narrow. By the 1950s, Argentina had the largest middle class on the continent, and next-door Uruguay had a literacy rate of 95 percent and offered free health care for all citizens. Developmentalism was so staggeringly successful for a time that the Southern Cone of Latin America became a potent symbol for poor countries around the world: here was proof that with smart, practical policies, aggressively implemented, the class divide between the First and Third World could actually be closed.

All this success for managed economies—in the Keynesian north and the developmentalist south—made for dark days at the University of Chicago's Economics Department. The Chicagoans' academic archrivals at Harvard, Yale and Oxford were being enlisted by presidents and prime ministers to help tame the beast of the market; almost no one was interested in Friedman's daring ideas about letting it run even more wildly than before. There were, however, a few people left who were keenly interested in Chicago School ideas—and they were a powerful few.

For the heads of U.S. multinational corporations, contending with a distinctly less hospitable developing world and with stronger, more demanding unions at home, the postwar boom years were unsettling times. The economy was growing fast, enormous wealth was being created, but owners and shareholders were forced to redistribute a great deal of that wealth through corporate taxes and workers' salaries. Everyone was doing well, but with a return to the pre–New Deal rules, a few people could have been doing a lot better.

The Keynesian revolution against laissez-faire was costing the corporate sector dearly. Clearly what was needed to regain lost ground was a counter-revolution against Keynesianism, a return to a form of capitalism even less regulated than before the Depression. This wasn't a crusade that Wall Street itself could lead—not in the current climate. If Friedman's close friend Walter Wriston, head of Citibank, had come forward and argued that the minimum wage and corporate taxes should both be abolished, he naturally would have been accused of being a robber baron. And that's where the Chicago School came in. It quickly became clear that when Friedman, a brilliant mathematician and skilled debater, made those same arguments, they took on an entirely different quality. They might be dismissed as wrong-headed but they were imbued with an aura of scientific impartiality. The enormous benefit of having corporate views funneled through academic, or quasi-academic, institutions not only kept the Chicago School flush with donations but, in short order, spawned the global network of right-wing think tanks that would churn out the counterrevolution's foot soldiers worldwide.

It all came back to Friedman's single-minded message: everything went wrong with the New Deal. That's when so many countries "including my own, got off on the wrong track."[17] To get governments back on the right track, Friedman, in his first popular book, *Capitalism and Freedom*, laid out what would become the global free-market rulebook and, in the U.S., would form the economic agenda of the neoconservative movement.

First, governments must remove all rules and regulations standing in the way of the accumulation of profits. Second, they should sell off any assets they own that corporations could be running at a profit. And third, they should dramatically cut back funding of social programs. Within the three-part formula of deregulation, privatization and cutbacks, Friedman had plenty of specifics. Taxes, when they must exist, should be low, and rich and poor should be taxed at the same flat rate. Corporations should be free to sell their products anywhere in the world, and governments should make no effort to protect local industries or local ownership. All prices, including the price of labor, should be determined by the market. There should be no minimum wage. For privatization, Friedman offered up health care, the post office, education, retirement pensions, even national parks. In short, and quite unabashedly, he was calling for the breaking of the New Deal—that uneasy truce between the state, corporations and labor that had prevented popular revolt after the Great Depression. Whatever protections workers had managed to win, whatever services the state now provided to soften the edges of the market, the Chicago School counterrevolution wanted them back.

And it wanted more than that—it wanted to expropriate what workers and governments had built during those decades of frenetic public works. The assets that Friedman urged government to sell were the end products of the years of investment of public money and know-how that had built them and made them valuable. As far as Friedman was concerned, all this shared wealth should be transferred into private hands, on principle.

Though always cloaked in the language of math and science, Friedman's vision coincided precisely with the interests of large multinationals, which by nature hunger for vast new unregulated markets. In the first stage of capitalist expansion, that kind of ravenous growth was provided by colonialism—by "discovering" new territories and grabbing land without paying for it, then extracting riches from the earth without compensating local populations. Friedman's war on the "welfare state" and "big government" held out the promise of a new font of rapid riches—only this time, rather than conquering new territory, the state itself would be the new frontier, its public services and assets auctioned off for far less than they were worth.

The War against Developmentalism

In the United States of the 1950s, access to those kinds of riches was still decades away. Even with a hard-core Republican like Dwight Eisenhower in the White House, there was no chance of a radical right turn like the one the

Chicagoans were suggesting—public services and workers' protections were far too popular, and Eisenhower was looking to the next election. Although he had little appetite for reversing Keynesianism at home, Eisenhower proved eager to take swift and radical action to defeat developmentalism abroad. It was a campaign in which the University of Chicago would eventually play a pivotal role.

When Eisenhower took office in 1953, Iran had a developmentalist leader in Mohammad Mossadegh, who had already nationalized the oil company, and Indonesia was in the hands of the increasingly ambitious Achmed Sukarno, who was talking about linking up all the nationalist governments of the Third World into a superpower on par with the West and the Soviet Bloc. Of particular concern to the State Department was the growing success of nationalist economics in the Southern Cone of Latin America. At a time when large portions of the globe were turning to Stalinism and Maoism, developmentalist proposals for "import substitution" were actually quite centrist. Still, the idea that Latin America deserved its own New Deal had powerful enemies. The continent's feudal landowners had been happy with the old status quo, which supplied them with steep profits and a limitless pool of poor peasants to work in the fields and mines. Now, they were outraged to see their profits being diverted to build up other sectors, their workers demanding land redistribution, and the government keeping the price of their crops artificially low so food could be affordable. American and European corporations doing business in Latin America began to express similar complaints to their governments: their products were being blocked at the borders, their workers were demanding higher wages and, most alarmingly, there was growing talk that everything from foreign-owned mines to banks could be nationalized to finance Latin America's dream of economic independence.

Under pressure from these corporate interests, a movement took hold in American and British foreign policy circles that attempted to pull developmentalist governments into the binary logic of the Cold War. Don't be fooled by the moderate, democratic veneer, these hawks warned: Third World nationalism was the first step on the road to totalitarian Communism and should be nipped in the bud. Two of the chief proponents of this theory were John Foster Dulles, Eisenhower's secretary of state, and his brother Allen Dulles, head of the newly created CIA. Before taking public posts, both had worked at the legendary New York law firm Sullivan & Cromwell, where they represented many of the companies that had the most to lose from developmentalism, among them J. P. Morgan & Company, the International Nickel Company, the Cuban Sugar Cane Corporation and the United Fruit Company.[18] The results of the Dulleses' ascendancy were immediate: in 1953 and 1954, the CIA staged its first two coups d'état, both against Third World governments that identified far more with Keynes than with Stalin.

The first was in 1953, when a CIA plot successfully overthrew Mossadegh in Iran, replacing him with the brutal shah. The next was the 1954 CIA-sponsored coup in Guatemala, done at the direct behest of the United Fruit Company. The corporation, which still had the ear of the Dulles brothers from their Cromwell days, was indignant that President Jacobo Arbenz Guzmán had expropriated some of its unused land (with full compensation) as part of his project to transform Guatemala, as he put it, "from a backward country with a predominantly feudal economy into a modern capitalist state"—apparently an unacceptable goal.[19] Soon enough Arbenz was out, and United Fruit was back in charge.

Eradicating developmentalism in the Southern Cone, where it had taken far deeper root, was a much greater challenge. Figuring out how to achieve that goal was the topic of discussion between two American men as they met in Santiago, Chile, in 1953. One was Albion Patterson, director of the U.S. International Cooperation Administration in Chile—the agency that would later become USAID—and the other was Theodore W. Schultz, chairman of the Department of Economics at the University of Chicago. Patterson had become increasingly concerned about the maddening influence of Raúl Prebisch and Latin America's other "pink" economists. "What we need to do is change the formation of the men, to influence the education, which is very bad," he had stressed to a colleague.[20] This objective coincided with Schultz's own belief that the U.S. government wasn't doing enough to fight the intellectual war with Marxism. "The United States must take stock of its economic programs abroad . . . we want [the poor countries] to work out their economic salvation by relating themselves to us and by using our way of achieving their economic development," he said.[21]

The two men came up with a plan that would eventually turn Santiago, a hotbed of state-centered economics, into its opposite—a laboratory for cutting-edge free-market experiments, giving Milton Friedman what he had longed for: a country in which to test his cherished theories. The original plan was simple: the U.S. government would pay to send Chilean students to study economics at what pretty much everyone recognized was the most rabidly anti-"pink" school in the world—the University of Chicago. Schultz and his colleagues at the university would also be paid to travel to Santiago to conduct research into the Chilean economy and to train students and professors in Chicago School fundamentals.

What set the plan apart from other U.S. training programs that sponsored Latin American students, of which there were many, was its unabashedly ideological character. By selecting Chicago to train Chileans—a school where the professors agitated for the near-complete dismantling of government with single-minded focus—the U.S. State Department was firing a shot across the bow in its war against developmentalism, effectively telling Chileans that the U.S. government had decided what ideas their elite students should and should not learn. This was such blatant U.S. intervention in Latin American affairs that when Albion Patterson approached the dean of the University of Chile, the country's premiere university, and offered him a grant to set up the exchange program, the dean turned him down. He said he would participate only if his faculty had input into who in the U.S. was training his students. Patterson went on to approach the dean of a lesser institution, Chile's Catholic University, a much more conservative school with no economics department. The dean at the Catholic University jumped at the offer, and what became known in Washington and Chicago as "the Chile Project" was born.

"We came here to compete, not to collaborate," said Schultz of the University of Chicago, explaining why the program would be closed to all Chilean students but the few selected.[22] This combative stance was explicit from the start: the goal of the Chile Project was to produce ideological warriors who would win the battle of ideas against Latin America's "pink" economists.

Officially launched in 1956, the project saw one hundred Chilean students pursue advanced degrees at the University of Chicago between 1957 and 1970, their tuition and expenses paid for by U.S. taxpayers and U.S. foundations. In 1965, the program was expanded to include students from across Latin America, with particularly heavy participation from Argentina, Brazil and Mexico. The expansion was funded through a grant from the Ford Foundation and led to the creation of the Center for Latin American Economic Studies at the University of Chicago. Under the program, there were forty to fifty Latin Americans studying graduate-level economics at any given time—roughly one-third of the department's total student population.

In comparable programs at Harvard or MIT, there were just four or five Latin Americans. It was a startling achievement: in just a decade, the ultra-conservative University of Chicago had become the premier destination for Latin Americans wanting to study economics abroad, a fact that would shape the course of the region's history for decades to come.

Indoctrinating the visitors in Chicago School orthodoxy became a pressing institutional priority. The head of the program, and the man in charge of making the Latin Americans feel welcome, was Arnold Harberger, a safari-suit-wearing economist who spoke fluent Spanish, had married a Chilean and described himself as "a seriously dedicated missionary."[23] When the Chilean students started arriving, Harberger created a special "Chile workshop" where University of Chicago professors presented their highly ideological diagnosis of what was wrong with the South American country—and offered their scientific prescriptions on how to fix it.

"Suddenly, Chile and its economy became a topic of daily conversation in the Department of Economics," recalled André Gunder Frank, who studied under Friedman in the 1950s and went on to become a world-renowned development economist.[24] All of Chile's policies were put under the microscope and found wanting: its strong social safety net, its protections for national industry, its trade barriers, its controls on prices. Students were taught disdain for these attempts to alleviate poverty, and many of them devoted their PhD theses to dissecting the follies of Latin American developmentalism.[25] When Harberger would return from his frequent trips to Santiago in the fifties and sixties, Gunder Frank recalled that he would lambaste Santiago, Chile's health and education systems—the best on the continent—as "absurd attempts to live beyond its underdeveloped means."[26]

Within the Ford Foundation, there were concerns about financing such an overtly ideological program. Some pointed out that the only Latin American speakers invited to address the students in Chicago were alumni of the same program. "Although the quality and impact of this endeavor cannot be denied, its ideological narrowness constituted a serious deficiency," wrote Jeffrey Puryear, a Latin American specialist with Ford, in one of the foundation's internal reviews. "The interests of developing countries are not well-served by exposure to a single point of view."[27] This assessment did not stop Ford from continuing to fund the program.

When the first group of Chileans returned home from Chicago, they were "even more Friedmanite than Friedman himself," in the words of

Mario Zañartu, an economist at Santiago's Catholic University.*[28] Many took up posts as economics professors in the Catholic University Economics Department, rapidly turning it into their own little Chicago School in the middle of Santiago—the same curriculum, the same English-language texts, the same unyielding claim to "pure" and "scientific" knowledge. By 1963, twelve of the department's thirteen full-time faculty members were graduates of the University of Chicago program, and Sergio de Castro, one of the first graduates, was appointed faculty chairman.[29] Now Chilean students didn't need to travel all the way to the U.S.—hundreds could get a Chicago School education without leaving home.

The students who went through the program, whether in Chicago or its franchise operation in Santiago, became known throughout the region as "los Chicago Boys." With more funding from USAID, Chile's Chicago Boys became enthusiastic regional ambassadors for ideas Latin Americans call "neoliberalism," traveling to Argentina and Colombia to set up more University of Chicago franchises in order to "expand this knowledge throughout Latin America, confronting the ideological positions which prevented freedom and perpetuated poverty and backwardness," according to one Chilean graduate.[30]

Juan Gabriel Valdés, Chile's foreign minister in the 1990s, described the process of training hundreds of Chilean economists in Chicago School orthodoxy as "a striking example of an organized transfer of ideology from the United States to a country within its direct sphere of influence . . . the education of these Chileans derived from a specific project designed in the 1950s to influence the development of Chilean economic thinking." He pointed out that "they introduced into Chilean society ideas that were completely new, concepts entirely absent from the 'ideas market.'"[31]

As a form of intellectual imperialism, it was certainly unabashed. There was, however, a problem: it wasn't working. According to a 1957 report from the University of Chicago to its funders at the State Department, "the central purpose of the project" was to train a generation of students "who would become the intellectual leaders in economic affairs in Chile."[32] But the Chicago Boys weren't leading their countries anywhere—in fact, they were being left behind.

In the early sixties, the main economic debate in the Southern Cone was

---

* Walter Heller, the famed Kennedy-government economist, once mocked the cultishness of Friedman's followers by dividing them into categories: "Some are Friedmanly, some Friedmanian, some Friedmanesque, some Friedmanic and some Friedmaniacs."

not about laissez-faire capitalism versus developmentalism but about how best to take developmentalism to the next stage. Marxists argued for extensive nationalization and radical land reforms; centrists argued that the key was greater economic cooperation among Latin American countries, with the goal of transforming the region into a powerful trading bloc to rival Europe and North America. At the polls and on the streets, the Southern Cone was surging to the left.

In 1962, Brazil moved decisively in this direction under the presidency of João Goulart, an economic nationalist committed to land redistribution, higher salaries and a daring plan to force foreign multinationals to reinvest a percentage of their profits back into the Brazilian economy rather than spiriting them out of the country and distributing them to shareholders in New York and London. In Argentina, a military government was trying to defeat similar demands by banning the party of Juan Perón from running in elections, but the move had only radicalized a new generation of young Peronists, many of whom were willing to use arms to retake the country.

It was in Chile—the epicenter of the Chicago experiment—that defeat in the battle of ideas was most evident. By Chile's historic 1970 elections, the country had moved so far left that all three major political parties were in favor of nationalizing the country's largest source of revenue: the copper mines then controlled by U.S. mining giants.[33] The Chile Project, in other words, was an expensive bust. As ideological warriors waging a peaceful battle of ideas with their left-wing foes, the Chicago Boys had failed in their mission. Not only was the economic debate continuing to shift leftward, but the Chicago Boys were so marginal that they did not even register on the Chilean electoral spectrum.

It might have ended there, with the Chile Project just a minor historical footnote, but something happened to rescue the Chicago Boys from obscurity: Richard Nixon was elected president of the United States. Nixon "had an imaginative, and on the whole effective, foreign policy," Friedman enthused.[34] And nowhere was it more imaginative than in Chile.

It was Nixon who would give the Chicago Boys and their professors something they had long dreamed of: a chance to prove that their capitalist utopia was more than a theory in a basement workshop—a shot at remaking a country from scratch. Democracy had been inhospitable to the Chicago Boys in Chile; dictatorship would prove an easier fit.

Salvador Allende's Popular Unity government won Chile's 1970 elections on a platform promising to put into government hands large sectors of the economy that were being run by foreign and local corporations. Allende was a new breed of Latin American revolutionary: like Che Guevara, he was a doctor, but unlike Che, he looked the part of the tweedy academic, not the romantic guerrilla. He could deliver a stump speech as fiery as any by Fidel Castro, but he was a fierce democrat who believed that socialist change in Chile needed to come through the ballot box, not the barrel of a gun. When Nixon heard that Allende had been elected president, he famously ordered the CIA director, Richard Helms, to "make the economy scream."[35] The election also reverberated throughout the University of Chicago Economics Department. When Allende won, Arnold Harberger happened to be in Chile. He wrote a letter home to his colleagues describing the event as a "tragedy" and informing them that "in rightist circles the idea of a military takeover is also sometimes broached."[36]

Although Allende pledged to negotiate fair terms to compensate companies that were losing property and investments, U.S. multinationals feared that Allende represented the beginning of a Latin America-wide trend, and many were unwilling to accept the prospect of losing what was a growing portion of their bottom line. By 1968, 20 percent of total U.S. foreign investment was tied up in Latin America, and U.S. firms had 5,436 subsidiaries in the region. The profits that these investments were able to produce were staggering. Mining companies had invested $1 billion over the previous fifty years in Chile's copper mining industry—the largest in the world—but they had sent $7.2 billion home.[37]

As soon as Allende won the vote, and before he was even inaugurated, corporate America declared war on his administration. The center of activity was the Washington-based Ad Hoc Committee on Chile, a group that included the major U.S. mining companies with holdings in Chile, as well as the de facto leader of the committee, the International Telephone and Telegraph Company (ITT), which owned 70 percent of Chile's soon-to-be-nationalized phone company. Purina, Bank of America and Pfizer Chemical also sent delegates at various stages.

The committee's single purpose was to force Allende to back off his nationalizations "by confronting him with economic collapse."[38] They had many ideas for how to make Allende feel the pain. According to declassified meeting minutes, the companies planned to block U.S. loans to Chile and "quietly have large U.S. private banks do the same. Confer with foreign banking sources with the same thing in mind. Delay buying from Chile over the next six months. Use U.S. copper stockpile instead of buying from Chile. Bring about a scarcity of U.S. dollars in Chile." And the list goes on.[39]

Allende appointed his close friend Orlando Letelier to be his ambassador to Washington; that gave him the task of negotiating the terms of expropriation with the same corporations plotting to sabotage the Allende government. Letelier, a fun-loving extrovert with a quintessential seventies moustache and a devastating singing voice, was much beloved in diplomatic circles. His son Francisco's fondest memories are of listening to his father play the guitar and belt out folk songs at gatherings of friends in their Washington home.[40] But even with all Letelier's charm and skill, the negotiations never stood a chance of success.

In March 1972, in the midst of Letelier's tense negotiation with ITT, Jack Anderson, a syndicated newspaper columnist, published an explosive series of articles based on documents that showed that the telephone company had secretly plotted with the CIA and the State Department to block Allende from being inaugurated two years earlier. In the face of these allegations, and with Allende still in power, the U.S. Senate, controlled by Democrats, launched an investigation and uncovered a far-reaching conspiracy in which ITT had offered $1 million in bribes to Chilean opposition forces and "sought to engage the CIA in a plan covertly to manipulate the outcome of the Chilean presidential election."[41]

The Senate report, released in June 1973, also found that when the plan failed and Allende took power, ITT moved to a new strategy designed to ensure that he would not "make it through the next six months." Most alarming to the Senate was the relationship between ITT executives and the U.S. government. In testimony and documents, it became clear that ITT was directly involved in shaping U.S. policy toward Chile at the highest level. At one point, a senior ITT executive wrote to National Security Adviser Henry Kissinger and suggested that "without informing President Allende, all U.S. aid funds already committed to Chile should be placed in the 'under review' status." The company also took the liberty of preparing an eighteen-point strategy for the Nixon administration that contained a clear call for a military coup: "Get to reliable sources within the Chilean military," it stated ". . . build up their planned discontent against Allende, thus, bring about necessity of his removal."[42]

When grilled by the Senate committee about his brazen attempts to harness the force of the U.S. government to subvert Chile's constitutional process in order to further ITT's own economic interests, the company's vice president, Ned Gerrity, seemed genuinely confused. "What's wrong with taking care of No. 1?" he asked. The committee offered a response in its report:

" 'No. 1' should not be allowed an undue role in determining U.S. foreign policy."[43]

Yet despite years of relentless American dirty tricks, of which ITT was only the most scrutinized example, in 1973 Allende was still in power. Eight million dollars in covert spending had failed to weaken his base. In midterm parliamentary elections that year, Allende's party actually gained support beyond the number that had first elected it in 1970. Clearly, the desire for a different economic model had taken deep root in Chile, and support for a socialist alternative was growing. For Allende's opponents, who had been plotting his overthrow since the day the 1970 election results came in, that meant their problems would not be solved by simply getting rid of him — someone else would just come along and replace him. A more radical plan was needed.

Lessons in Regime Change: Brazil and Indonesia

There were two models of "regime change" that Allende's opponents had been studying closely as possible approaches. One was in Brazil, the other in Indonesia. When Brazil's U.S.-backed junta, led by General Humberto Castello Branco, seized power in 1964, the military had a plan not merely to reverse João Goulart's pro-poor programs but to crack Brazil wide open to foreign investment. At first, the Brazilian generals tried to impose the agenda relatively peacefully — there were no obvious shows of brutality, no mass arrests, and though it was later discovered that some "subversives" had been brutally tortured during this period, their numbers were small enough (and Brazil so large) that word of their treatment barely escaped the jails. The junta also made a point of keeping some remnants of democracy in place, including limited press freedoms and freedom of assembly — a so-called gentlemen's coup.

In the late sixties, many citizens decided to use those limited freedoms to express their anger at Brazil's deepening poverty, for which they blamed the junta's pro-business economic program, much of it designed by graduates of the University of Chicago. By 1968 the streets were overrun with antijunta marches, the largest led by students, and the regime was in serious jeopardy. In a desperate bid to hold on to power, the military radically changed tactics: democracy was shut down completely, all civil liberties were crushed, torture became systematic, and, according to Brazil's later-established truth commission, "killings by the state became routine."[44]

Indonesia's 1965 coup followed a very different trajectory. Since the Second World War, the country had been led by President Sukarno, the Hugo Chávez of his day (though minus Chávez's appetite for elections). Sukarno enraged the rich countries by protecting Indonesia's economy, redistributing wealth and throwing out the International Monetary Fund and the World Bank, which he accused of being facades for the interests of Western multinationals. While Sukarno was a nationalist, not a Communist, he worked closely with the Communist Party, which had 3 million active members. The U.S. and British governments were determined to end Sukarno's rule, and declassified documents show that the CIA had received high-level directions to "liquidate President Sukarno, depending upon the situation and available opportunities."[45]

After several false starts, the opportunity came in October 1965, when General Suharto, backed by the CIA, began the process of seizing power and eradicating the left. The CIA had been quietly compiling a list of the country's leading leftists, a document that fell into Suharto's hands, while the Pentagon helped out by supplying extra weapons and field radios so Indonesian forces could communicate in the remotest parts of the archipelago. Suharto then sent out his soldiers to hunt down the four to five thousand leftists on his "shooting lists," as the CIA referred to them; the U.S. embassy received regular reports on their progress.[46] As the information came in, the CIA crossed names off their lists until they were satisfied that the Indonesian left had been annihilated. One of the people involved in the operation was Robert J. Martens, who worked for the U.S. embassy in Jakarta. "It really was a big help to the army," he told the journalist Kathy Kadane twenty-five years later. "They probably killed a lot of people, and I probably have a lot of blood on my hands, but that's not all bad. There's a time when you have to strike hard at a decisive moment."[47]

The shooting lists covered the targeted killing; the more indiscriminate massacres for which Suharto is infamous were, for the most part, delegated to religious students. They were quickly trained by the military and then sent into villages on instructions from the chief of the navy to "sweep" the countryside of Communists. "With relish," wrote one reporter, "they called out their followers, stuck their knives and pistols in their waistbands, swung their clubs over their shoulders, and embarked on the assignment for which they had long been hoping."[48] In just over a month, at least half a million and possibly as many as 1 million people were killed, "massacred by the thousands," according to *Time*.[49] In East Java, "Travelers from those areas tell of small rivers and streams that have been literally clogged with bodies; river transportation has at places been impeded."[50]

The Indonesian experience attracted close attention from the individuals and institutions plotting the overthrow of Salvador Allende in Washington and Santiago. Of interest was not only Suharto's brutality but also the extraordinary role played by a group of Indonesian economists who had been educated at the University of California at Berkeley, known as the Berkeley Mafia. Suharto was effective at getting rid of the left, but it was the Berkeley Mafia who prepared the economic blueprint for the country's future.

The parallels with the Chicago Boys were striking. The Berkeley Mafia had studied in the U.S. as part of a program that began in 1956, funded by the Ford Foundation. They had also returned home to build a faithful copy of a Western-style economics department, theirs at the University of Indonesia's Faculty of Economics. Ford sent American professors to Jakarta to establish the school, just as Chicago profs had gone to help set up the new economics department in Santiago. "Ford felt it was training the guys who would be leading the country when Sukarno got out," John Howard, then director of Ford's International Training and Research Program, bluntly explained.[51]

Ford-funded students became leaders of the campus groups that participated in overthrowing Sukarno, and the Berkeley Mafia worked closely with the military in the lead-up to the coup, developing "contingency plans" should the government suddenly fall.*[52] These young economists had enormous influence over General Suharto, who knew nothing of high finance. According to *Fortune* magazine, the Berkeley Mafia recorded economics lessons on audiotapes for Suharto to listen to at home.[53] When they met in person, "President Suharto did not merely listen, he took notes," one member of the group recalled with pride.[54] Another Berkeley grad described the relationship in this way: we "presented to the Army leadership—the crucial element in the new order—a 'cookbook' of 'recipes' for dealing with Indonesia's serious economic problems. General Suharto as the top Army commander not only accepted the cookbook, but also wanted the authors of the recipes as his economic advisers."[55] Indeed he did. Suharto packed his cabinet with

---

* Not all the U.S. professors sent under the program were comfortable with this role. "I felt that the University should not be involved in what essentially was becoming a rebellion against the government," said Len Doyle, the Berkeley professor appointed to head Ford's Indonesian economics program. That point of view got Doyle recalled to California and replaced.

members of the Berkeley Mafia, handing them all the key financial posts, including minister of trade and ambassador to Washington.[56]

This economic team, having studied at a less ideological school, were not antistate radicals like the Chicago Boys. They believed the government had a role to play in managing Indonesia's domestic economy and making sure that basics, like rice, were affordable. However, the Berkeley Mafia could not have been more hospitable to foreign investors wanting to mine Indonesia's immense mineral and oil wealth, described by Richard Nixon as "the greatest prize in the Southeast Asian area."*[57] They passed laws allowing foreign companies to own 100 percent of these resources, handed out "tax holidays," and within two years, Indonesia's natural wealth—copper, nickel, hardwood, rubber and oil—was being divided up among the largest mining and energy companies in the world.

For those plotting the overthrow of Allende just as Suharto's program was kicking in, the experiences of Brazil and Indonesia made for a useful study in contrasts. The Brazilians had made little use of the power of shock, waiting years before demonstrating their appetite for brutality. It was a near-fatal error, since it gave their opponents the chance to regroup and for some to form left-wing guerrilla armies. Although the junta managed to clear the streets, the rising opposition forced it to slow its economic plans.

Suharto, on the other hand, had shown that if massive repression was used *preemptively*, the country would go into a kind of shock and resistance could be wiped out before it even took place. His use of terror was so merciless, so far beyond even the worst expectations, that a people who only weeks earlier had been collectively striving to assert their country's independence were now sufficiently terrified that they ceded total control to Suharto and his henchmen. Ralph McGehee, a senior CIA operations manager during the years of the coup, said Indonesia was a "model operation. . . . You can trace back all major, bloody events run from Washington to the way Suharto came to power. The success of that meant that it would be repeated, again and again."[58]

The other crucial lesson from Indonesia had to do with the pre-coup partnership between Suharto and the Berkeley Mafia. Because they were ready to take up top "technocratic" positions in the new government and had already converted Suharto to their worldview, the coup did more than just get

---

* Interestingly, Arnold Harberger was hired as a consultant to Suharto's finance ministry in 1975.

rid of a nationalist threat; it transformed Indonesia into one of the most welcoming environments for foreign multinationals in the world.

As momentum began to build toward Allende's ouster, a chilling warning began appearing in red paint on the walls of Santiago. It said, "Jakarta is coming."

Shortly after Allende was elected, his opponents inside Chile began to imitate the Indonesia approach with eerie precision. The Catholic University, home of the Chicago Boys, became ground zero for the creation of what the CIA called "a coup climate."[59] Many students joined the fascist Patria y Libertad and goose-stepped through the streets in open imitation of Hitler Youth. In September 1971, a year into Allende's mandate, the top business leaders in Chile held an emergency meeting in the seaside city of Viña del Mar to develop a coherent regime-change strategy. According to Orlando Sáenz, president of the National Association of Manufacturers (generously funded by the CIA and many of the same foreign multinationals doing their own plotting in Washington), the gathering decided that "Allende's government was incompatible with freedom in Chile and with the existence of private enterprise, and that the only way to avoid the end was to overthrow the government." The businessmen formed a "war structure," one part of which would liaise with the military; another, according to Sáenz, would "prepare specific alternative programs to government programs that would systematically be passed on to the Armed Forces."[60]

Sáenz recruited several key Chicago Boys to design those alternative programs and set them up in a new office near the Presidential Palace in Santiago.[61] The group, led by the Chicago grad Sergio de Castro and by Sergio Undurraga, his colleague at the Catholic University, began holding weekly secret meetings during which they developed detailed proposals for how to radically remake their country along neoliberal lines.[62] According to the subsequent U.S. Senate investigation, "over 75 percent" of the funding for this "opposition research organization" was coming directly from the CIA.[63]

For a time, the coup planning proceeded on two distinct tracks: the military plotted the extermination of Allende and his supporters while the economists plotted the extermination of their ideas. As momentum built for a violent solution, a dialogue was opened between the two camps, with Roberto Kelly, a businessman associated with the CIA-financed newspaper *El Mercurio*, acting as the go-between. Through Kelly, the Chicago Boys sent a five-page summary of their economic program to the navy admiral in charge. The navy gave the nod, and from then on the Chicago Boys worked frantically to have their program ready by the time of the coup.

Their five-hundred-page bible—a detailed economic program that would guide the junta from its earliest days—came to be known in Chile as "The Brick." According to a later U.S. Senate Committee, "CIA collaborators were involved in preparing an initial overall economic plan which has served as the basis for the Junta's most important economic decisions."[64] Eight of the ten principal authors of "The Brick" had studied economics at the University of Chicago.[65]

Although the overthrow of Allende was universally described as a military coup, Orlando Letelier, Allende's Washington ambassador, saw it as an equal partnership between the army and the economists. "The 'Chicago boys,' as they are known in Chile," Letelier wrote, "convinced the generals that they were prepared to supplement the brutality, which the military possessed, with the intellectual assets it lacked."[66]

Chile's coup, when it finally came, would feature three distinct forms of shock, a recipe that would be duplicated in neighboring countries and would reemerge, three decades later, in Iraq. The shock of the coup itself was immediately followed by two additional forms of shock. One was Milton Friedman's capitalist "shock treatment," a technique in which hundreds of Latin American economists had by now been trained at the University of Chicago and its various franchise institutions. The other was Ewen Cameron's shock, drug and sensory deprivation research, now codified as torture techniques in the *Kubark* manual and disseminated through extensive CIA training programs for Latin American police and military.

These three forms of shock converged on the bodies of Latin Americans and the body politic of the region, creating an unstoppable hurricane of mutually reinforcing destruction and reconstruction, erasure and creation. The shock of the coup prepared the ground for economic shock therapy; the shock of the torture chamber terrorized anyone thinking of standing in the way of the economic shocks. Out of this live laboratory emerged the first Chicago School state, and the first victory in its global counterrevolution.

PART 2

THE FIRST TEST

BIRTH PANGS

The theories of Milton Friedman gave him the Nobel Prize; they gave Chile General Pinochet.

—Eduardo Galeano, *Days and Nights of Love and War*, 1983

I don't think I was ever regarded as "evil."

—Milton Friedman, quoted in *The Wall Street Journal*, July 22, 2006

CHAPTER 3

STATES OF SHOCK

THE BLOODY BIRTH OF THE COUNTERREVOLUTION

> **For injuries ought to be done all at one time, so that, being tasted less, they offend less.**
> —Niccolò Machiavelli, *The Prince*, 1513[1]

> **If this shock approach were adopted, I believe that it should be announced publicly in great detail, to take effect at a very close date. The more fully the public is informed, the more will its reactions facilitate the adjustment.**
> —Milton Friedman in a letter to General Augusto Pinochet, April 21, 1975[2]

General Augusto Pinochet and his supporters consistently referred to the events of September 11, 1973, not as a coup d'état but as "a war." Santiago certainly looked like a war zone: tanks fired as they rolled down the boulevards, and government buildings were under air assault by fighter jets. But there was something strange about this war. It had only one side.

From the start, Pinochet had complete control of the army, navy, marines and police. Meanwhile, President Salvador Allende had refused to organize his supporters into armed defense leagues, so he had no army of his own. The only resistance came from the presidential palace, La Moneda, and the rooftops around it, where Allende and his inner circle made a valiant effort to defend the seat of democracy. It was hardly a fair fight: though there were just thirty-six Allende supporters inside, the military launched twenty-four rockets into the palace.[3]

Pinochet, the operation's vain and volatile commander (built like one of the tanks he rode in on), clearly wanted the event to be as dramatic and traumatic as possible. Even if the coup was not a war, it was designed to feel like one—a Chilean precursor to Shock and Awe. It could scarcely have been more shocking. Unlike neighboring Argentina, which had been ruled by six military governments in the previous four decades, Chile had no experience with this kind of violence; it had enjoyed 160 years of peaceful democratic rule, the past 41 uninterrupted.

Now the presidential palace was in flames, the president's shrouded body was being carried out on a stretcher, and his closest colleagues were lying facedown in the street at rifle point.* A few minutes' drive from the presidential palace, Orlando Letelier, recently returned from Washington to take up a new post as Chile's defense minister, had gone to his office that morning in the ministry. As soon as he walked through the front door, he was ambushed by twelve soldiers in combat uniform, all pointing their submachine guns at him.[4]

In the years leading up to the coup, U.S. trainers, many from the CIA, had whipped the Chilean military into an anti-Communist frenzy, persuading them that socialists were de facto Russian spies, a force alien to Chilean society—a homegrown "enemy within." In fact, it was the military that had become the true domestic enemy, ready to turn its weapons on the population it was sworn to protect.

With Allende dead, his cabinet in captivity and no mass resistance in evidence, the junta's grand battle was over by mid-afternoon. Letelier and the other "VIP" prisoners were eventually taken to freezing Dawson Island in the southern Strait of Magellan, Pinochet's approximation of a Siberian work camp. Killing and locking up the government was not enough for Chile's new junta government, however. The generals knew that their hold on power depended on Chileans being truly terrified, as the people had been in Indonesia. In the days that followed, roughly 13,500 civilians were arrested, loaded onto trucks and imprisoned, according to a declassified CIA report.[5] Thousands ended up in the two main football stadiums in Santiago, the Chile Stadium and the huge National Stadium. Inside the National Stadium, death replaced football as the public spectacle. Soldiers prowled the

---

* Allende was found with his head blown apart. Debates continue over whether he was shot by one of the bullets fired into La Moneda or he shot himself rather than give Chileans the lasting image of their elected president surrendering to an insurrectionary army. The second theory is the more credible.

bleachers with hooded collaborators who pointed out "subversives"; the ones who were selected were hauled off to locker rooms and skyboxes transformed into makeshift torture chambers. Hundreds were executed. Lifeless bodies started showing up on the side of major highways or floating in murky urban canals.

To make sure that the terror extended beyond the capital city, Pinochet sent his most ruthless commander, General Sergio Arellano Stark, on a helicopter mission to the northern provinces to visit a string of prisons where "subversives" were being held. At each city and town, Stark and his roving death squad singled out the highest-profile prisoners, as many as twenty-six at a time, who were subsequently executed. The trail of blood left behind over those four days came to be known as the Caravan of Death.[6] In short order, the entire country had gotten the message: resistance is deadly.

Even though Pinochet's battle was one-sided, its effects were as real as any civil war or foreign invasion: in all, more than 3,200 people were disappeared or executed, at least 80,000 were imprisoned, and 200,000 fled the country for political reasons.[7]

The Economic Front

For the Chicago Boys, September 11 was a day of giddy anticipation and deadline adrenalin. Sergio de Castro had been working down to the wire with his contact in the navy, getting the final sections of "The Brick" approved page by page. Now, on the day of the coup, several Chicago Boys were camped out at the printing presses of the right-wing *El Mercurio* newspaper. As shots were being fired in the streets outside, they frantically tried to get the document printed in time for the junta's first day on the job. Arturo Fontaine, one of the newspaper's editors, recalled that the machines "worked non-stop to duplicate copies of this long document." And they made it—just barely. "Before midday on Wednesday, September 12, 1973, the General Officers of the Armed Forces who performed government duties had the Plan on their desks."[8]

The proposals in the final document bore a striking resemblance to those found in Milton Friedman's *Capitalism and Freedom*: privatization, deregulation and cuts to social spending—the free-market trinity. Chile's U.S.-trained economists had tried to introduce these ideas peacefully, within the confines of a democratic debate, but they had been overwhelmingly rejected. Now the Chicago Boys and their plans were back, in a climate distinctly more conducive to their radical vision. In this new era, no one besides a handful of men in uniform needed to agree with them. Their staunchest political opponents were either in jail, dead or fleeing for cover; the spectacle of fighter jets and caravans of death was keeping everyone else in line.

"To us, it was a revolution," said Cristián Larroulet, one of Pinochet's economic aides.[9] It was a fair description. September 11, 1973, was far more than the violent end of Allende's peaceful socialist revolution; it was the beginning of what *The Economist* would later describe as a "counterrevolution"—the first concrete victory in the Chicago School campaign to seize back the gains that had been won under developmentalism and Keynesianism.[10] Unlike Allende's partial revolution, tempered and compromised by the push and pull of democracy, this revolt, imposed through brute force, was free to go all the way. In the coming years, the same policies laid out in "The Brick" would be imposed in dozens of other countries under cover of a wide range of crises. But Chile was the counterrevolution's genesis—a genesis of terror.

José Piñera, an alumnus of the economics department at the Catholic University and a self-described Chicago Boy, was doing graduate work at Harvard at the time of the coup. On hearing the good news, he returned home "to help found a new country, dedicated to liberty, from the ashes of the old one." According to Piñera, who would eventually become Pinochet's minister of labor and mining, this was "the real revolution . . . a radical, comprehensive, and sustained move toward free markets."[11]

Before the coup, Augusto Pinochet had a reputation for deference that bordered on the obsequious, forever flattering and agreeing with his civilian commanders. As a dictator, Pinochet found new facets of his character. He took to power with unseemly relish, adopting the airs of a monarch and claiming that "destiny" had given him the job. In short order, he staged a coup within a coup to unseat the other three military leaders with whom he had agreed to share power and named himself Supreme Chief of the Nation as well as president. He basked in pomp and ceremony, proof of his right to rule, never missing an opportunity to put on his Prussian dress uniform, complete with cape. To get around Santiago, he chose a caravan of gold bulletproof Mercedes-Benzes.[12]

Pinochet had a knack for authoritarian rule, but, like Suharto, he knew next to nothing about economics. That was a problem because the campaign of corporate sabotage spearheaded by ITT had done an effective job of sending the economy into a tailspin, and Pinochet had a full-fledged crisis on his hands. From the start, there was a power struggle within the junta between those who simply wanted to reinstate the pre-Allende status quo and return quickly to democracy, and the Chicago Boys, who were pushing for a head-to-toe free-market makeover that would take years to impose. Pinochet, enjoying his new powers, intensely disliked the idea that his destiny was a mere cleanup operation—there to "restore order" and then get out. "We are not a vacuum cleaner that swept out Marxism to give back power to those Mr. Politicians," he would say.[13] It was the Chicago Boys' vision of a total country overhaul that appealed to his newly unleashed ambition, and, like Suharto with his Berkeley Mafia, he immediately named several Chicago grads as senior economic advisers, including Sergio de Castro, the movement's de facto leader and the main author of "The Brick." He called them the *technos*—the technicians—which appealed to the Chicago pretension that fixing an economy was a matter of science, not of subjective human choices.

Even if Pinochet understood little about inflation and interest rates, the *technos* spoke a language he did understand. Economics for them meant forces of nature that needed to be respected and obeyed because "to act against nature is counter-productive and self-deceiving," as Piñera explained.[14] Pinochet agreed: people, he once wrote, must submit to structure because "nature shows us basic order and hierarchy are necessary."[15] This mutual claim to be taking orders from higher natural laws formed the basis of the Pinochet-Chicago alliance.

For the first year and a half, Pinochet faithfully followed the Chicago rules: he privatized some, though not all, state-owned companies (including several banks); he allowed cutting-edge new forms of speculative finance; he flung open the borders to foreign imports, tearing down the barriers that had long protected Chilean manufacturers; and he cut government spending by 10 percent—except the military, which received a significant increase.[16] He also eliminated price controls—a radical move in a country that had been regulating the cost of necessities such as bread and cooking oil for decades.

The Chicago Boys had confidently assured Pinochet that if he suddenly withdrew government involvement from these areas all at once, the "natural" laws of economics would rediscover their equilibrium, and inflation—which they viewed as a kind of economic fever indicating the presence of unhealthy organisms in the market—would magically go down. They were mistaken. In 1974, inflation reached 375 percent—the highest rate in the world and almost twice the top level under Allende.[17] The cost of basics such as bread went through the roof. At the same time, Chileans were being thrown out of work because Pinochet's experiment with "free trade" was flooding the country with cheap imports. Local businesses were closing, unable to compete, unemployment hit record levels and hunger became rampant. The Chicago School's first laboratory was a debacle.

Sergio de Castro and the other Chicago Boys argued (in true Chicago fashion) that the problem didn't lie with their theory but with the fact that it wasn't being applied with sufficient strictness. The economy had failed to correct itself and return to harmonious balance because there were still "distortions" left over from nearly half a century of government interference. For the experiment to work, Pinochet had to strip these distortions away—more cuts, more privatization, more speed.

In that year and a half, many of the country's business elite had had their fill of the Chicago Boys' adventures in extreme capitalism. The only people benefiting were foreign companies and a small clique of financiers known as the "piranhas," who were making a killing on speculation. The nuts-and-bolts manufacturers who had strongly supported the coup were getting wiped out. Orlando Sáenz—the president of the National Association of Manufacturers, who had brought the Chicago Boys into the coup plot in the first place—declared the results of the experiment "one of the greatest failures of our economic history."[18] The manufacturers hadn't wanted Allende's socialism but had liked a managed economy just fine. "It is not possible to continue with the financial chaos that dominates in Chile," Sáenz said. "It is necessary to channel into productive investments the millions and millions of financial resources that are now being used in wild-cat speculative operations before the very eyes of those who don't even have a job."[19]

Their agenda now in grave danger, the Chicago Boys and the piranhas (and there was a great deal of overlap between the two) decided it was time to call in the big guns. In March 1975, Milton Friedman and Arnold Harberger flew to Santiago at the invitation of a major bank to help save the experiment.

Friedman was greeted by the junta-controlled press as something of a rock star, the guru of the new order. Each of his pronouncements made headlines, his academic lectures were broadcast on national television and he had the most important audience of all: a private meeting with General Pinochet.

Throughout his stay, Friedman hammered at a single theme: the junta was off to a good start, but it needed to embrace the free market with greater abandon. In speeches and interviews, he used a term that had never before been publicly applied to a real-world economic crisis: he called for "shock treatment." He said it was "the only medicine. Absolutely. There is no other. There is no other long-term solution."[20] When a Chilean reporter pointed out that even Richard Nixon, then president of the U.S., imposed controls to temper the free market, Friedman snapped, "I don't approve of them. I believe we should not apply them. I am against economic intervention by the government, in my own country, as well as in Chile."[21]

After his meeting with Pinochet, Friedman made some personal notes about the encounter, which he reproduced decades later in his memoirs. He observed that the general "was sympathetically attracted to the idea of a shock treatment but was clearly distressed at the possible temporary unemployment that might be caused."[22] At this point, Pinochet was already notorious the world over for ordering massacres in football stadiums; that the dictator was "distressed" by the human cost of shock therapy might have given Friedman pause. Instead, he pressed the point in a follow-up letter in which he praised the general's "extremely wise" decisions but urged Pinochet to cut government spending much further, "by 25 per cent within six months . . . across-the-board," while simultaneously adopting a package of pro-business policies moving toward "complete free trade." Friedman predicted that the hundreds of thousands of people who would be fired from the public sector would quickly get new jobs in the private sector, soon to be booming thanks to Pinochet's removal of "as many obstacles as possible that now hinder the private market."[23]

Friedman assured the general that if he followed this advice, he would be able to take credit for an "economic miracle"; he "could end inflation in months" while the unemployment problem would be equally "brief— measured in months—and that subsequent recovery would be rapid." Pinochet would need to act fast and decisively; Friedman emphasized the importance of "shock" repeatedly, using the word three times and underlining that "gradualism is not feasible."[24]

Pinochet was converted. In his letter of response, Chile's supreme chief expressed "my highest and most respectful regard for you," assuring Friedman that "the Plan is being fully applied at the present time."[25] Immediately after Friedman's visit, Pinochet fired his economic minister and handed the job to Sergio de Castro, whom he later promoted to finance minister. De Castro stacked the government with his fellow Chicago Boys, appointing one of them to head the central bank. Orlando Sáenz, who had objected to the mass layoffs and plant closures, was replaced as head of the Association of Manufacturers by someone with a more shock-friendly attitude. "If there are industrialists who complain because of this, let them 'go to hell.' I won't defend them," the new director announced.[26]

Freed of the naysayers, Pinochet and de Castro got to work stripping away the welfare state to arrive at their pure capitalist utopia. In 1975, they cut public spending by 27 percent in one blow—and they kept cutting until, by 1980, it was half of what it had been under Allende.[27] Health and education took the heaviest hits. Even *The Economist*, a free-market cheerleader, called it "an orgy of self-mutilation."[28] De Castro privatized almost five hundred state-owned companies and banks, practically giving many of them away, since the point was to get them as quickly as possible into their rightful place in the economic order.[29] He took no pity on local companies and removed even more trade barriers; the result was the loss of 177,000 industrial jobs between 1973 and 1983.[30] By the mid-eighties, manufacturing as a percentage of the economy dropped to levels last seen during the Second World War.[31]

Shock treatment was an apt description for what Friedman had prescribed. Pinochet had deliberately sent his country into a deep recession, based on the untested theory that the sudden contraction would jolt the economy into health. In its logic, it was strikingly similar to that of the psychiatrists who started mass-prescribing ECT in the 1940s and 1950s, convinced that deliberately induced grand mal seizures would magically reboot their patients' brains.

The theory of economic shock therapy relies in part on the role of expectations in feeding an inflationary process. Reining in inflation requires not only changing monetary policy but also changing the behavior of consumers, employers and workers. The role of a sudden, jarring policy shift is that it quickly alters expectations, signaling to the public that the rules of the game have changed dramatically—prices will not keep rising, nor will wages. According to this theory, the faster expectations of inflation are driven down, the shorter the painful period of recession and high unemployment will be. However, particularly in countries where the political class has lost its credibility with the public, only a major, decisive policy shock is said to have the power to "teach" the public these harsh lessons.*

---

* Some Chicago School economists claim that the first experiment in shock therapy took place in West Germany on June 20, 1948. That's when Finance Minister Ludwig Erhard eliminated

Causing a recession or a depression is a brutal idea, since it necessarily creates mass poverty, which is why no political leader had until this point been willing to test the theory. Who wants to be responsible for what *Business-Week* described as a "Dr. Strangelove world of deliberately induced depression"?[32]

Pinochet did. In the first year of Friedman-prescribed shock therapy, Chile's economy contracted by 15 percent, and unemployment—only 3 percent under Allende—reached 20 percent, a rate unheard of in Chile at the time.[33] The country was certainly convulsing under its "treatments." And contrary to Friedman's sunny predictions, the unemployment crisis lasted for years, not months.[34] The junta, which had instantly taken to Friedman's illness metaphors, was unapologetic, explaining that "this path was chosen because it is the only one that goes directly to the sickness."[35] Friedman concurred. When asked by a reporter "whether the social cost of his policies would be excessive," he responded, "Silly question."[36] To another reporter he said, "My only concern is that they push it long enough and hard enough."[37]

Interestingly, the most powerful criticism of shock therapy came from one of Friedman's own former students, André Gunder Frank. During his time at the University of Chicago in the fifties, Gunder Frank—originally from Germany—had heard so much about Chile that when he graduated with a PhD in economics, he decided to go see for himself the country his professors had portrayed as a mismanaged developmentalist dystopia. He liked what he saw and ended up teaching at the University of Chile, then serving as an economic adviser to the government of Salvador Allende, for whom he developed a great respect. As a Chicago Boy in Chile who had defected from the school's free-market orthodoxy, Gunder Frank had a unique perspective on the country's economic adventure. One year after Friedman prescribed

---

most price controls and introduced a new currency. The moves were sudden and without warning, a tremendous shock to the German economy, leading to widespread unemployment. But that is where the parallels end: Erhard's reforms were restricted to price and monetary policy, they were not accompanied by cuts to social programs or by rapid introduction of free trade, and many measures were taken to protect citizens from these shocks, including increasing wages. Even post-shock, West Germany easily met Friedman's definition of a quasi-socialist welfare state: it provided subsidized housing, government pensions, public health care and a state-run education system, while the government ran, and subsidized, everything from the phone company to aluminum plants. Crediting Erhard with inventing shock therapy makes for a palatable narrative, since his experiment took place after West Germany was liberated from tyranny. Erhard's shock, however, bears little resemblance to the sweeping transformations currently understood as economic shock therapy—that method was pioneered by Friedman and Pinochet, in a country that had just lost its liberty.

maximum shock, he wrote a rage-fueled "Open Letter to Arnold Harberger and Milton Friedman" in which he used his Chicago School education "to examine how the Chilean patient has responded to your treatment."[38]

He calculated what it meant for a Chilean family to try to survive on what Pinochet claimed was a "living wage." Roughly 74 percent of its income went simply to buying bread, forcing the family to cut out such "luxury items" as milk and bus fare to get to work. By comparison, under Allende, bread, milk and bus fare took up 17 percent of a public employee's salary.[39] Many children weren't getting milk at school either, since one of the junta's first moves had been to eliminate the school milk program. As a result of this cut compounding the desperation at home, more and more students were fainting in class, and many stopped going altogether.[40] Gunder Frank saw a direct connection between the brutal economic policies imposed by his former classmates and the violence Pinochet had unleashed on the country. Friedman's prescriptions were so wrenching, the disaffected Chicago Boy wrote, that they could not "be imposed or carried out without the twin elements that underlie them all: military force and political terror."[41]

Undeterred, Pinochet's economic team went into more experimental territory, introducing Friedman's most vanguard policies: the public school system was replaced by vouchers and charter schools, health care became pay-as-you-go, and kindergartens and cemeteries were privatized. Most radical of all, they privatized Chile's social security system. José Piñera, who brought in the program, said that he got the idea from reading *Capitalism and Freedom*.[42] George W. Bush's administration is usually credited with pioneering "the ownership society," but in fact it was Pinochet's government, thirty years earlier, that first introduced the idea of "a nation of owners."

Chile was now in bold new territory, and free-market fans the world over, accustomed to debating the merits of such policies in purely academic settings, were paying close attention. "Economics textbooks say that's the way the world should work, but where else do they practice it?" marveled the U.S. business magazine *Barron's*.[43] In an article headlined "Chile, Lab Test for a Theorist," *The New York Times* noted that "it is not often that a leading economist with strong views is given a chance to test specific prescriptions for a very sick economy. It is even more unusual when the economist's client happens to be a country other than his own."[44] Many came for an up-close look at the Chilean laboratory, including Friedrich Hayek himself, who traveled to Pinochet's Chile several times and in 1981 selected Viña del Mar (the city where the coup had been plotted) to hold the regional meeting of the Mont Pelerin Society, the brain trust of the counterrevolution.

The Myth of the Chilean Miracle

Even three decades later, Chile is still held up by free-market enthusiasts as proof that Friedmanism works. When Pinochet died in December 2006 (one month after Friedman), *The New York Times* praised him for "transforming a bankrupt economy into the most prosperous in Latin America," while a *Washington Post* editorial said he had "introduced the free-market policies that produced the Chilean economic miracle."[45] The facts behind the "Chilean miracle" remain a matter of intense debate.

Pinochet held power for seventeen years, and during that time he changed political direction several times. The country's period of steady growth that is held up as proof of its miraculous success did not begin until the mid-eighties—a full decade after the Chicago Boys implemented shock therapy and well after Pinochet was forced to make a radical course correction. That's because in 1982, despite its strict adherence to Chicago doctrine, Chile's economy crashed: its debt exploded, it faced hyperinflation once again and unemployment hit 30 percent—ten times higher than it was under Allende.[46] The main cause was that the piranhas, the Enron-style financial houses that the Chicago Boys had freed from all regulation, had bought up the country's assets on borrowed money and run up an enormous debt of $14 billion.[47]

The situation was so unstable that Pinochet was forced to do exactly what Allende had done: he nationalized many of these companies.[48] In the face of the debacle, almost all the Chicago Boys lost their influential government posts, including Sergio de Castro. Several other Chicago graduates held prominent posts with the piranhas and came under investigation for fraud, stripping away the carefully cultivated facade of scientific neutrality so central to the Chicago Boy identity.

The only thing that protected Chile from complete economic collapse in the early eighties was that Pinochet had never privatized Codelco, the state copper mine company nationalized by Allende. That one company generated 85 percent of Chile's export revenues, which meant that when the financial bubble burst, the state still had a steady source of funds.[49]

It's clear that Chile never was the laboratory of "pure" free markets that its cheerleaders claimed. Instead, it was a country where a small elite leapt from wealthy to super-rich in extremely short order—a highly profitable formula bankrolled by debt and heavily subsidized (then bailed out) with public funds. When the hype and salesmanship behind the miracle are stripped away, Chile under Pinochet and the Chicago Boys was not a capitalist state featuring a liberated market but a corporatist one. Corporatism, or "corporativism," originally referred to Mussolini's model of a police state run as an alliance of the three major power sources in society—government, businesses and trade unions—all collaborating to guarantee order in the name of nationalism. What Chile pioneered under Pinochet was an evolution of corporatism: a mutually supporting alliance between a police state and large corporations, joining forces to wage all-out war on the third power sector— the workers—thereby drastically increasing the alliance's share of the national wealth.

That war—what many Chileans understandably see as a war of the rich against the poor and middle class—is the real story of Chile's economic "miracle." By 1988, when the economy had stabilized and was growing rapidly, 45 percent of the population had fallen below the poverty line.[50] The richest 10 percent of Chileans, however, had seen their incomes increase by 83 percent.[51] Even in 2007, Chile remained one of the most unequal societies in the world—out of 123 countries in which the United Nations tracks inequality, Chile ranked 116th, making it the 8th most unequal country on the list.[52]

If that track record qualifies Chile as a miracle for Chicago school economists, perhaps shock treatment was never really about jolting the economy into health. Perhaps it was meant to do exactly what it did—hoover wealth up to the top and shock much of the middle class out of existence.

That was the way Orlando Letelier, Allende's former defense minister, saw it. After spending a year in Pinochet's prisons, Letelier managed to escape Chile, thanks to an intensive international lobbying campaign. Watching from exile the rapid impoverishment of his country, Letelier wrote in 1976 that "during the last three years several billions of dollars were taken from the pockets of wage earners and placed in those of capitalists and landowners . . . concentration of wealth is no accident, but a rule; it is not the marginal outcome of a difficult situation—as the junta would like the world to believe—but the base for a social project; it is not an economic liability but a temporary political success."[53]

What Letelier could not know at the time was that Chile under Chicago School rule was offering a glimpse of the future of the global economy, a pattern that would repeat again and again, from Russia to South Africa to Argentina: an urban bubble of frenetic speculation and dubious accounting fueling superprofits and frantic consumerism, ringed by the ghostly factories and rotting infrastructure of a development past; roughly half the population excluded from the economy altogether; out-of-control corruption and cronyism; decimation of nationally owned small and medium-sized businesses; a huge transfer of wealth from public to private hands, followed by a huge transfer of private debts into public hands. In Chile, if you were outside the wealth bubble, the miracle looked like the Great Depression, but inside its airtight cocoon the profits flowed so free and fast that the easy wealth made possible by shock therapy-style "reforms" have been the crack cocaine of financial markets ever since. And that is why the financial world did not respond to the obvious contradictions of the Chile experiment by reassessing the basic assumptions of laissez-faire. Instead, it reacted with the junkie's logic: Where is the next fix?

The Revolution Spreads, the People Vanish

For a time, the next fix came from other countries in Latin America's Southern Cone, where the Chicago School counterrevolution quickly spread. Brazil was already under the control of a U.S.-supported junta, and several of Friedman's Brazilian students held key positions. Friedman traveled to Brazil in 1973, at the height of the regime's brutality, and declared the economic experiment "a miracle."[54] In Uruguay the military had staged a coup in 1973 and the following year decided to go the Chicago route. Lacking sufficient numbers of Uruguayans who had graduated from the University of Chicago, the generals invited "Arnold Harberger and [economics professor] Larry Sjaastad from the University of Chicago and their team, which included former Chicago students from Argentina, Chile, and Brazil, to reform Uruguay's tax system and commercial policy."[55] The effects on Uruguay's previously egalitarian society were immediate: real wages dropped by 28 percent, and hordes of scavengers appeared on the streets of Montevideo for the first time.[56]

Next to join the experiment was Argentina in 1976, when a junta seized power from Isabel Perón. That meant that Argentina, Chile, Uruguay and Brazil—the countries that had been showcases of developmentalism—were now all run by U.S.-backed military governments and were living laboratories of Chicago School economics.

According to declassified Brazilian documents just released in March 2007, weeks before the Argentine generals seized power, they contacted Pinochet and the Brazilian junta and "outlined the main steps to be taken by the future regime."[57]

Despite this close collaboration, Argentina's military government did not go quite as far into neoliberal experimentation as Pinochet had; it did not privatize the country's oil reserves or social security, for instance (that would come later). However, when it came to attacking the policies and institutions that had lifted Argentina's poor into the middle class, the junta faithfully followed Pinochet, thanks in part to the abundance of Argentine economists who had gone through the Chicago program.

Argentina's newly minted Chicago Boys landed key economic posts in the junta government—as secretary of finance, president of the central bank and research director for the Treasury Department of the Finance Ministry, as well as several other lower-level economic posts.[58] But while the Argentine Chicago Boys were enthusiastic participants in the military government, the top economic job went not to one of them but to José Alfredo Martínez de Hoz. He was part of the landed gentry that belonged to the Sociedad Rural, the cattle-ranchers' association that had long controlled the country's export economy. These families, the closest thing to an aristocracy that Argentina possessed, had liked the feudal economic order just fine—a time when they didn't have to worry about their land being redistributed to peasants or the price of meat being lowered to make sure everyone could eat.

Martínez de Hoz had been president of the Sociedad Rural, as had his father and grandfather before him; he also sat on the boards of several multinational corporations, including Pan American Airways and ITT. When he took up his post in the junta government, there was no mistaking the fact that the coup represented a revolt of the elites, a counterrevolution against forty years of gains by Argentina's workers.

Martínez de Hoz's first act as minister of the economy was to ban strikes and allow employers to fire workers at will. He lifted price controls, sending the cost of food soaring. He was also determined to make Argentina once again a hospitable place for foreign multinationals. He lifted restrictions on foreign ownership and in the first few years sold off hundreds of state companies.[59] These measures earned him powerful fans in Washington. Declassified documents show William Rogers, assistant secretary of state for Latin America, telling his boss, Henry Kissinger, shortly after the coup that "Martínez de Hoz is a good man. We have been in close consultations throughout." Kissinger was so impressed that he arranged to have a high-profile meeting with Martínez de Hoz when he visited Washington "as a symbolic gesture." He also offered to make a couple of calls to help along Argentina's economic efforts: "I will call David Rockefeller," Kissinger told the junta's foreign minister, a reference to the president of Chase Manhattan Bank. "And I will call his brother, the Vice President [of the United States, Nelson Rockefeller]."[60]

To attract investment, Argentina took out a thirty-one-page advertising supplement in *BusinessWeek*, produced by the PR giant Burson-Marsteller, declaring that "few governments in history have been as encouraging to private investment. . . . We are in a true social revolution, and we seek partners. We are unburdening ourselves of statism, and believe firmly in the all-important role of the private sector."*[61]

Once again, the human impact was unmistakable: within a year, wages lost 40 percent of their value, factories closed, poverty spiraled. Before the junta took power, Argentina had fewer people living in poverty than France or the U.S.—just 9 percent—and an unemployment rate of only 4.2 percent.[62] Now the country began to display signs of the underdevelopment thought to have been left behind. Poor neighborhoods were without water, and preventable diseases ran rampant.

In Chile, Pinochet had a free hand to use economic policy to eviscerate the middle class, thanks to the shocking and terrifying way in which he had seized power. Although his fighter jets and firing squads had been enormously effective at spreading terror, they had turned out to be a public relations disaster. Press reports about Pinochet's massacres sparked a worldwide outcry, and activists in Europe and North America aggressively lobbied their governments not to trade with Chile—a distinctly unfavorable outcome for a regime whose reason for existence was to keep the country open for business.

The newly declassified documents from Brazil show that when Argentina's generals were preparing their 1976 coup, they wanted "to avoid suffering an international campaign like the one that has been unleashed against Chile."[63] To achieve that goal, less sensational repression tactics were needed—lower-profile ones capable of spreading terror but not so visible to the prying international press. In Chile, Pinochet soon settled on disappearances.

---

* The junta was so eager to auction off the country to investors that it advertised "a 10 percent discount on the price of land for ground-breaking within 60 days."

Rather than openly killing or even arresting their prey, soldiers would snatch them, take them to clandestine camps, torture and often kill them, then deny any knowledge. Bodies were thrown into mass graves. According to Chile's truth commission, established in May 1990, the secret police would dispose of some victims by dropping them into the ocean from helicopters "after first cutting their stomach open with a knife to keep the bodies from floating."[64] In addition to their lower profile, disappearances turned out to be an even more effective means of spreading terror than open massacres, so destabilizing was the idea that the apparatus of the state could be used to make people vanish into thin air.

By the mid-seventies, disappearances had become the primary enforcement tool of the Chicago School juntas throughout the Southern Cone—and none embraced the practice more zealously than the generals occupying Argentina's presidential palace. By the end of their reign, an estimated thirty thousand people had been disappeared.[65] Many of them, like their Chilean counterparts, were thrown from planes into the muddy waters of the Rio de la Plata.

The Argentine junta excelled at striking just the right balance between public and private horror, carrying out enough of its terror in the open that everyone knew what was going on, but simultaneously keeping enough secret that it could always be denied. In its first days in power, the junta made a single dramatic demonstration of its willingness to use lethal force: a man was pushed out of a Ford Falcon (a vehicle notorious for its use by the secret police), tied to Buenos Aires's most prominent monument, the 67.5-meter-high white Obelisk, and machine-gunned in plain view.

After that, the junta's killings went underground, but they were always present. Disappearances, officially denied, were very public spectacles enlisting the silent complicity of entire neighborhoods. When someone was targeted to be eliminated, a fleet of military vehicles showed up at that person's home or workplace and cordoned off the block, often with a helicopter buzzing overhead. In broad daylight and in full view of the neighbors, police or soldiers battered down the door and dragged out the victim, who often shouted his or her name before disappearing into a waiting Ford Falcon, in the hope that news of the event would reach the family. Some "covert" operations were even more brazen: police were known to board crowded city buses and drag passengers off by their hair; in the city of Santa Fe, a couple was kidnapped right at the altar on their wedding day in front of a church filled with people.[66]

The public character of terror did not stop with the initial capture. Once in custody, prisoners in Argentina were taken to one of more than three hundred torture camps across the country.[67] Many of them were located in densely populated residential areas; one of the most notorious was in a former athletic club on a busy street in Buenos Aires, another in a schoolhouse in central Bahía Blanca and yet another in a wing of a working hospital. At these torture centers, military vehicles sped in and out at odd hours, screams could be heard through the badly insulated walls and strange, body-shaped parcels were spotted being carried in and out, all silently registered by the nearby residents.

The regime in Uruguay was similarly brazen: one of its main torture centers was a navy barracks abutting Montevideo's boardwalk, an area once favored by families for ocean-side strolls and picnics. During the dictatorship, the beautiful spot was empty, as the city's residents studiously avoided hearing the screams.[68]

The Argentine junta was particularly sloppy about disposing of its victims. A country walk could end in horror because mass graves were barely concealed. Bodies would show up in public garbage bins, missing fingers and teeth (much as they do today in Iraq), or they would wash ashore on the banks of the Rio de la Plata, sometimes half a dozen at a time, after one of the junta's "death flights." On occasion, they even rained down from helicopters into farmers' fields.[69]

All Argentines were in some way enlisted as witnesses to the erasure of their fellow citizens, yet most people claimed not to know what was going on. There is a phrase Argentines use to describe the paradox of wide-eyed knowing and eyes-closed terror that was the dominant state of mind in those years: "We did not know what nobody could deny."

Since those wanted by the various juntas often took refuge in neighboring countries, the regional governments collaborated with each other in the notorious Operation Condor. Under Condor, the intelligence agencies of the Southern Cone shared information about "subversives"—aided by a state-of-the-art computer system provided by Washington—and then gave each other's agents safe passage to carry out cross-border kidnappings and torture, a system eerily resembling the CIA's "extraordinary rendition" network today.*[70]

The juntas also swapped information about the most effective means

---

* The Latin American operation was modeled on Hitler's "Night and Fog." In 1941, Hitler decreed that resistance fighters in Nazi-occupied countries would be brought to Germany to "vanish in the night and fog." Several high-profile Nazis took refuge in Chile and Argentina, and there is some speculation that they may have trained the Southern Cone intelligence agencies in these tactics.

each had found to extract information from their prisoners. Several Chileans who had been tortured at Chile Stadium in the days after the coup remarked on the unexpected detail that there were Brazilian soldiers in the room offering advice on the most scientific uses of pain.[71]

There were countless opportunities for such exchanges in this period, many of them running through the United States and involving the CIA. A 1975 U.S. Senate investigation into U.S. intervention in Chile found that the CIA had provided training to Pinochet's military in methods for "controlling subversion."[72] And U.S. training of Brazilian and Uruguayan police in interrogation techniques has been heavily documented. According to court testimony quoted in the country's truth commission report, *Brazil: Never Again*, published in 1985, military officers attended formal "torture classes" at army police units where they watched slides depicting various excruciating methods. During these sessions, prisoners were brought in for "practical demonstrations"—brutally tortured while as many as a hundred army sergeants looked on and learned. The report states that "one of the first people to introduce this practice into Brazil was Dan Mitrione, an American police officer. As a police instructor in Belo Horizonte during the early years of the Brazilian military regime, Mitrione took beggars off the streets and tortured them in classrooms so that the local police would learn the various ways of creating, in the prisoner, the supreme contradiction between the body and the mind."[73] Mitrione then moved on to conduct police training in Uruguay, where, in 1970, he was kidnapped and killed by the Tupamaro guerrillas—the group of leftist revolutionaries had planned the operation in order to to expose Mitrione's involvement in torture training.* According to one of his former students, he insisted, like the authors of the CIA manual, that effective torture was not sadism but science. "The precise pain in the precise place, in the precise amount" was his motto.[74]

The results of this training are unmistakable in all the human rights reports from the Southern Cone in this sinister period. Again and again they testify to the trademark methods codified in the *Kubark* manual: early morning arrests, hooding, intense isolation, drugging, forced nudity, electroshock. And everywhere, the terrible legacy of the McGill experiments in deliberately induced regression.

Prisoners released from Chile's National Stadium said that bright floodlights were kept on twenty-four hours a day, and the order of meals seemed

---

* The episode was the basis for Costa-Gavras's superb 1972 film, *State of Siege*.

deliberately out of sequence.[75] Soldiers forced many prisoners to wear blankets over their heads so they could neither see nor hear properly, a baffling practice since all the prisoners knew they were in the stadium. The effect of the manipulations, prisoners reported, was that they lost their sense of night and day, and the shock and panic triggered by the coup and their subsequent arrests were greatly intensified. It was almost as if the stadium had been turned into a giant laboratory, and they were the test subjects in some strange experiment in sensory manipulation.

A more faithful copy of the CIA experiments could be seen in Chile's Villa Grimaldi prison, which "was known for its 'Chile rooms'—wooden isolation compartments so small that prisoners could not kneel" or lie down.[76] Prisoners in Uruguay's Libertad prison were sent to *la isla*, the island: tiny windowless cells in which one bare bulb was illuminated at all times. High-value prisoners were kept in absolute isolation for more than a decade. "We were beginning to think we were dead, that our cells weren't cells but rather graves, that the outside world didn't exist, that the sun was a myth," one of these prisoners, Mauricio Rosencof, recalled. He saw the sun for a total of eight hours over eleven and a half years. So deprived were his senses during this time that he "forgot colors—there were no colors."*[77]

In one of Argentina's largest torture centers, the Navy School of Mechanics in Buenos Aires, the isolation chamber was called the *capucha*, the hood. Juan Miranda, who spent three months in the *capucha*, told me about that dark place. "They keep you in a blindfold and a hood with your hands and legs in chains, lying down on a foam mattress all day long, in the attic of the prison. I could not see the other prisoners—I was separated from them with plywood. When the guards would bring food, they made me face the wall, then they would pull up the hood so I could eat. It was the only time we were allowed to sit up; otherwise, we had to lie down all the time." Other Argentine prisoners had their senses starved in cells the size of coffins, called *tubos*.

The only reprieve from isolation was the worse fate of the interrogation room. The most ubiquitous technique, used in the torture chambers of all the region's military regimes, was electroshock. There were dozens of variations on how electrical currents were sent coursing through prisoners' bodies: with live wires, with army field telephones, with needles under fingernails, clamped

---

* The prison administration at Libertad worked closely with behavioral psychologists to design torture techniques tailored to each individual's psychological profile—a method now used at Guantánamo Bay.

with clothespins on gums, nipples, genitals, ears, mouths, in open wounds, attached to bodies doused in water to intensify the charge; on bodies strapped to tables or to Brazil's iron "dragon chair." Argentina's cattle-owning junta was proud of its distinctive contribution—prisoners were shocked on a metal bed, called the *parrilla* (the barbecue), where they were subject to the *picana* (cattle prod).

The exact number of people who went through the Southern Cone's torture machinery is impossible to calculate, but it is probably somewhere between 100,000 and 150,000, tens of thousands of them killed.[78]

A Witness in Difficult Times

To be a leftist in those years was to be hunted. Those who did not escape to exile were in a minute-by-minute struggle to stay one step ahead of the secret police—an existence of safe houses, phone codes and false identities. One of the people living that life in Argentina was the country's legendary investigative journalist Rodolfo Walsh. A gregarious Renaissance man, a writer of crime fiction and award-winning short stories, Walsh was also a super sleuth able to crack military codes and spy on the spies. His greatest investigative triumph took place when he was working as a journalist in Cuba, where he managed to intercept and decode a CIA telex that blew the cover of the Bay of Pigs invasion. That information is what allowed Castro to prepare for and defend against the invasion.

When Argentina's previous military junta had banned Peronism and strangled democracy, Walsh decided to join the armed Montonero movement as their intelligence expert.* That put him at the very top of the generals' Most Wanted list, with every new disappearance bringing fresh fears that information extracted by the *picana* would lead the police to the safe house he had secured with his partner, Lilia Ferreyra, in a small village outside Buenos Aires.

From his vast network of sources, Walsh had been trying to track the junta's many crimes. He compiled lists of the dead and disappeared, the locations of

---

* The Montoneros were formed as a response to the previous dictatorship. Peronism was banned, and Juan Perón, from exile, called on his young supporters to arm themselves and fight for a return to democracy. They did, and the Montoneros—though they engaged in armed attacks and kidnappings—played a significant part in forcing democratic elections with a Peronist candidate in 1973. But when Perón returned to power, he was threatened by the Montoneros' popular support and encouraged right-wing death squads to go after them, which is why the group—the subject of much controversy—was already significantly weakened by the time of the 1976 coup.

mass graves and of secret torture centers. He prided himself on his knowledge of the enemy, but in 1977 even he was stunned by the furious brutality
that the Argentine junta had unleashed on its own people. In the first year of
military rule, dozens of his close friends and colleagues had disappeared in
the death camps, and his twenty-six-year-old daughter, Vicki, was also dead,
driving Walsh mad with grief.

But with Ford Falcons circling, a life of quiet mourning was not available
to him. Knowing his time was limited, Walsh made a decision about how he
would mark the upcoming one-year anniversary of junta rule: with the official papers lavishing praise on the generals for having saved the country, he
would write his own, uncensored, version of the depravity into which his
country had descended. It would be titled "An Open Letter from a Writer to
the Military Junta," and it was composed, Walsh wrote, "without hope of being listened to, with the certainty of being persecuted, true to the commitment I took up a long time ago, to bear witness in difficult times."[79]

The letter would be the decisive condemnation of both the methods of
state terror and the economic system they served. Walsh planned to circulate
his "Open Letter" the way he had distributed previous communiqués from
the underground: by making ten copies, then posting them from different
mailboxes to select contacts who would distribute them further. "I want to
let those fuckers know that I'm still here, still alive and still writing," he told
Lilia as he sat down at his Olympia typewriter.[80]

The letter begins with an account of the generals' terror campaign, its
use of "maximum torture, unending and metaphysical," as well as the involvement of the CIA in training the Argentine police. After listing the
methods and grave sites in excruciating detail, Walsh abruptly switches
gears: "These events, which stir the conscience of the civilized world, are
not, however, the greatest suffering inflicted on the Argentinean people,
nor the worst violation for human rights which you have committed. It is
in the economic policy of this government where one discovers not only
the explanation for the crimes, but a greater atrocity which punishes
millions of human beings through planned misery. . . . You only have to
walk around greater Buenos Aires for a few hours to check the speed with
which such a policy transforms the city into a 'shantytown' of ten million
people."[81]

The system Walsh was describing was Chicago School neoliberalism, the
economic model that would sweep the world. As it took deeper root in Argentina in the decades to come, it would eventually push more than half the

population below the poverty line. Walsh saw it not as an accident but the careful execution of a plan — "planned misery."

He signed the letter on March 24, 1977, exactly one year after the coup. The next morning, Walsh and Lilia Ferreyra traveled to Buenos Aires. They split the bundle of letters between them and dropped them into mailboxes around the city. A few hours later, Walsh went to a meeting he had arranged with the family of a disappeared colleague. It was a trap: someone had talked under torture, and ten armed men were waiting outside the house in ambush, with orders to capture Walsh. "Bring that fucking bastard back alive, he's mine," Admiral Massera, one of the three junta leaders, had reportedly directed the soldiers. Walsh, whose motto was "It isn't a crime to talk; getting arrested is the crime," immediately pulled out his gun and began firing. He injured one of the soldiers and drew their fire; he was dead by the time the car arrived at the Navy School of Mechanics. Walsh's body was burned and dumped in a river.[82]

The "War on Terror" Cover Story

The juntas of the Southern Cone made no secret of their revolutionary ambitions to remake their respective societies, but they were savvy enough to publicly deny what Walsh was accusing them of: using massive violence in order to achieve those economic goals, goals that, in the absence of a system of terrorizing the public and eliminating obstacles, would have certainly provoked popular revolt.

To the extent that killings by the state were acknowledged, they were justified by the juntas on the grounds that they were fighting a war against dangerous Marxist terrorists, funded and controlled by the KGB. If the juntas used "dirty" tactics, it was because their enemy was monstrous. Using language that sounds eerily familiar today, Admiral Massera called it "a war for freedom and against tyranny . . . a war against those who favor death and by those of us who favor life. . . . We are fighting against nihilists, against agents of destruction whose only objective is destruction itself, although they disguise this with social crusades."[83]

In the run-up to Chile's coup, the CIA bankrolled a massive propaganda campaign to paint Salvador Allende as a dictator in disguise, a Machiavellian schemer who had used constitutional democracy to gain power but was on the verge of imposing a Soviet-style police state from which Chileans would never escape. In Argentina and Uruguay, the largest left-wing guerrilla groups — the Montoneros and the Tupamaros — were presented as such perilous threats to national security that the generals had no other choice but to suspend democracy, seize the state for themselves and use whatever means were necessary to crush them.

In every case, the threat was either wildly exaggerated or completely manufactured by the juntas. Among its many other revelations, the 1975 Senate investigation disclosed that the U.S. government's own intelligence reports showed that Allende posed no threat to democracy.[84] As for Argentina's Montoneros and Uruguay's Tupamaros, they were armed groups with significant popular support, able to pull off daredevil attacks on military and corporate targets. But Uruguay's Tupamaros were completely dismantled by the time the military seized absolute power, and Argentina's Montoneros were finished within the first six months of a dictatorship that stretched on for seven years (which was why Walsh was in hiding). Declassified State Department documents have proven that César Augusto Guzzetti, the Argentine junta's foreign minister, told Henry Kissinger on October 7, 1976, that "the terrorist organizations have been dismantled"—yet the junta would go on to disappear tens of thousands of citizens after that date.[85]

For many years, the U.S. State Department also presented the "dirty wars" in the Southern Cone as pitched battles between the military and dangerous guerrillas, struggles that at times got out of hand but were still deserving of economic and military aid. There is mounting evidence that in Argentina as well as in Chile, Washington knew it was supporting a very different kind of military operation.

In March 2006, the National Security Archive in Washington released the newly declassified minutes from a State Department meeting that took place just two days after the Argentine junta staged its 1976 coup. At the meeting, William Rogers, assistant secretary of state for Latin America, tells Kissinger that "we've got to expect a fair amount of repression, probably a good deal of blood, in Argentina before too long. I think they're going to have to come down very hard not only on the terrorists but on the dissidents of trade unions and their parties."[86]

Indeed they did. The vast majority of the victims of the Southern Cone's terror apparatus were not members of armed groups but non-violent activists working in factories, farms, shantytowns and universities. They were economists, artists, psychologists and left-wing party loyalists. They were killed not because of their weapons (which most did not have) but because of their beliefs. In the Southern Cone, where contemporary capitalism was born, the "War on Terror" was a war against all obstacles to the new order.

CHAPTER 4

CLEANING THE SLATE

TERROR DOES ITS WORK

> Extermination in Argentina is not spontaneous, it is not by chance,
> it is not irrational: it is the systematic destruction of a "substantial
> part" of the Argentine national group, intended to transform the
> group as such, to redefine its way of being, its social relations, its
> fate, its future.
>
> —Daniel Feierstein, an Argentine sociologist, 2004[1]

> I had just one goal—to stay alive until the next day. . . . But it
> wasn't just to survive, but to survive as me.
>
> —Mario Villani, survivor of four years in Argentina's torture camps[2]

In 1976, Orlando Letelier was back in Washington, D.C., no longer as an
ambassador but as an activist with a progressive think tank, the Institute for
Policy Studies. Haunted by thoughts of the colleagues and friends still facing
torture in junta camps, Letelier used his newly recovered freedom to expose
Pinochet's crimes and to defend Allende's record against the CIA propaganda machine.

The activism was having an effect, and Pinochet faced universal condemnation for his human rights record. What frustrated Letelier, a trained economist, was that even as the world gasped in horror at reports of summary
executions and electroshock in the jails, most were silent in the face of the
economic shock therapy; or, in the case of the international banks showering
the junta with loans, downright giddy about Pinochet's embrace of "free-
market fundamentals." Letelier rejected a frequently articulated notion that

the junta had two separate, easily compartmentalized projects—one a bold experiment in economic transformation, the other an evil system of grisly torture and terror. There was only one project, the former ambassador insisted, in which terror was the central tool of the free-market transformation.

"The violation of human rights, the system of institutionalized brutality, the drastic control and suppression of every form of meaningful dissent is discussed (and often condemned) as a phenomenon only indirectly linked, or indeed entirely unrelated, to the classical unrestrained 'free market' policies that have been enforced by the military junta," Letelier wrote in a searing essay for *The Nation*. He pointed out that "this particularly convenient concept of a social system, in which 'economic freedom' and political terror coexist without touching each other, allows these financial spokesmen to support their concept of 'freedom' while exercising their verbal muscles in defense of human rights."[3]

Letelier went so far as to write that Milton Friedman, as "the intellectual architect and unofficial adviser for the team of economists now running the Chilean economy," shared responsibility for Pinochet's crimes. He dismissed Friedman's defense that lobbying for shock treatment was merely offering "technical" advice. The "establishment of a free 'private economy' and the control of inflation a la Friedman," Letelier argued, could not be done peacefully. "The economic plan has had to be enforced, and in the Chilean context that could be done only by the killing of thousands, the establishment of concentration camps all over the country, the jailing of more than 100,000 persons in three years. . . . Regression for the majorities and 'economic freedom' for small privileged groups are in Chile two sides of the same coin." There was, he wrote, "an inner harmony" between the "free market" and unlimited terror.[4]

Letelier's controversial article was published at the end of August 1976. Less than a month later, on September 21, the forty-four-year-old economist was driving to work in downtown Washington, D.C. As he passed through the heart of the embassy district, a remote-controlled bomb planted under the driver's seat exploded, sending the car flying and blowing off both his legs. With his severed foot abandoned on the pavement, Letelier was rushed to George Washington Hospital; he was dead on arrival. The former ambassador had been driving with a twenty-five-year-old American colleague, Ronni Moffit, and she also lost her life in the attack.[5] It was Pinochet's most outrageous and defiant crime since the coup itself.

An FBI investigation revealed that the bomb had been the work of

Michael Townley, a senior member of Pinochet's secret police, later convicted in a U.S federal court for the crime. The assassins had been admitted to the country on false passports with the knowledge of the CIA.[6]

When Pinochet died in December 2006 at age ninety-one, he faced multiple attempts to put him on trial for crimes committed during his rule—from murder, kidnapping and torture to corruption and tax evasion. The family of Orlando Letelier had been trying for decades to bring Pinochet to trial for the bombing in Washington and to open the U.S. files on the incident. But the dictator got the last word in death, evading all the trials and issuing a posthumous letter in which he defended the coup and the use of "maximum rigor" in staving off a "dictatorship of the proletariat. . . . How I wish the Sep. 11, 1973, military action had not been necessary!" Pinochet wrote. "How I wish the Marxist-Leninist ideology had not entered our fatherland!"[7]

Not all the criminals of Latin America's terror years have been so fortunate. In September 2006, twenty-three years after the end of Argentina's military dictatorship, one of the main enforcers of the terror was finally sentenced to life in prison. The convicted man was Miguel Osvaldo Etchecolatz, who had been police commissioner of the province of Buenos Aires during the junta years.

During the historic trial, Jorge Julio López, a key witness, went missing—disappeared. López had been disappeared in the seventies, brutally tortured, then released—now it was happening all over again. In Argentina, López became known as the first person to be "double disappeared."[8] As of mid-2007, he was still missing, and the police were virtually certain that he had been kidnapped as a warning to other would-be witnesses—the same old tactics of the terror years.

The judge on the case, fifty-five-year-old Carlos Rozanski of Argentina's federal court, found Etchecolatz guilty of six counts of homicide, six counts of unlawful imprisonment and seven cases of torture. When he handed down his verdict, he took an extraordinary step. He said that the conviction did not do justice to the true nature of the crime and that, in the interest of "the construction of collective memory," he needed to add that these were "all crimes against humanity committed in the context of the genocide that took place in the Republic of Argentina between 1976 and 1983."[9]

With that sentence, the judge played his part in the rewriting of Argentine history: the killings of leftists in the seventies were not part of a "dirty war" in which two sides clashed and various crimes were committed, as had been the official story for decades. Nor were the disappeared merely victims of mad dictators who were drunk on sadism and their own personal power. What had happened was something more scientific, more terrifyingly rational. As the judge put it, there had been a "plan of extermination carried out by those who ruled the country."[10]

He explained that the killings were part of a system, planned far in advance, duplicated in identical fashion across the country, and committed with clear intent not of attacking individual persons but of destroying the parts of society that those people represented. Genocide is an attempt to murder a group, not a collection of individual persons; therefore, argued the judge, it was genocide.[11]

Rozanski recognized that his use of the word "genocide" was controversial, and he wrote a lengthy decision backing up the choice. He acknowledged that the UN Convention on Genocide defines the crime as an "intent to destroy, in whole or in part, a national, ethnical, religious or racial group"; the Convention does *not* include eliminating a group based on its political beliefs—as had been the case in Argentina—but Rozanski said he did not consider that exclusion to be legally legitimate.[12] Pointing to a little-known chapter in UN history, he explained that on December 11, 1946, in direct response to the Nazi Holocaust, the UN General Assembly passed a resolution by unanimous vote barring acts of genocide "when racial, religious, *political* and other groups have been destroyed, entirely or in part."[13] The reason the word "political" had been excised from the Convention two years later was that Stalin demanded it. He knew that if destroying a "political group" was genocidal, his bloody purges and mass imprisonment of political opponents would fit the bill. Stalin had enough support from other leaders who also wanted to reserve the right to wipe out their political opponents that the word was dropped.[14]

Rozanski wrote that he considered the original UN definition to be the more legitimate, since it had not been subject to this self-interested compromise.* He also made reference to a ruling by a Spanish national court that had put one of Argentina's notorious torturers on trial in 1998. That court had also ruled that Argentina's junta had committed "the crime of genocide." It defined the group the junta was trying to wipe out as "those citizens

---

* The criminal codes of many countries, including Portugal, Peru and Costa Rica, bar acts of genocide, with definitions that clearly include political groupings or "social groups." French law is even broader, defining genocide as a plan intended to destroy in whole or in part "a group determined by any arbitrary criteria."

that did not fit the model determined by the repressors to be suitable for the new order being established in the country."[15] The following year, in 1999, the Spanish judge Baltasar Garzón, famous for issuing an arrest warrant for Augusto Pinochet, also argued that Argentina had suffered genocide. He too made an attempt to define which group had been targeted for extermination. The junta's goal, he wrote, was "to establish a new order, like Hitler hoped to achieve in Germany, in which there was no room for certain types of people." The people who did not fit the new order were ones "located in those sectors that got in the way of the ideal configuration of the new Argentinean Nation."[16]

There is, of course, no comparison in scale between what happened under the Nazis, or in Rwanda in 1994, and the crimes of the corporatist dictatorships of Latin America in the seventies. If genocide means a holocaust, these crimes do not belong in that category. However, if genocide is understood as these courts define it, as an attempt to deliberately obliterate the groups who were barriers to a political project, then this process can be seen not just in Argentina but, to varying degrees of intensity, throughout the region that was turned into the Chicago School laboratory. In these countries, the people who "got in the way of the ideal" were leftists of all stripes: economists, soup kitchen workers, trade unionists, musicians, farm organizers, politicians. Members of all these groups were subjected to a clear and deliberate region-wide strategy, coordinated across borders by Operation Condor, to uproot and erase the left.

Since the fall of Communism, free markets and free people have been packaged as a single ideology that claims to be humanity's best and only defense against repeating a history filled with mass graves, killing fields and torture chambers. Yet in the Southern Cone, the first place where the contemporary religion of unfettered free markets escaped from the basement workshops of the University of Chicago and was applied in the real world, it did not bring democracy; it was predicated on the overthrow of democracy in country after country. And it did not bring peace but required the systematic murder of tens of thousands and the torture of between 100,000 and 150,000 people.

There was, as Letelier wrote, an "inner harmony" between the drive to cleanse sectors of society and the ideology at the heart of the project. The Chicago Boys and their professors, who provided advice and took up top posts in the military regimes of the Southern Cone, believed in a form of capitalism that is purist by its very nature. Theirs is a system based entirely on a belief in "balance" and "order" and the need to be free of interferences and "distortions" in order to succeed. Because of these traits, a regime committed to the faithful application of this ideal cannot accept the presence of competing or tempering worldviews. In order for the ideal to be achieved, it requires a monopoly on ideology; otherwise, according to the central theory, the economic signals become distorted and the entire system is thrown out of balance.

The Chicago Boys could scarcely have selected a part of the world less hospitable to this absolutist experiment than the Southern Cone of Latin America in the 1970s. The extraordinary rise of developmentalism meant that the area was a cacophony of precisely the policies that the Chicago School considered distortions or "uneconomic ideas." More important, it was teeming with popular and intellectual movements that had emerged in direct opposition to laissez-faire capitalism. Such views were not marginal but typical of the majority of citizens, as reflected in election after election in country after country. A Chicago School transformation was about as likely to be warmly received in the Southern Cone as a proletarian revolution in Beverly Hills.

Before the terror campaign descended on Argentina, Rodolfo Walsh had written, "Nothing can stop us, neither jail nor death. Because you can't jail or kill a whole people and because the vast majority of Argentinians . . . know that only the people will save the people."[17] Salvador Allende, as he watched the tanks roll in to lay siege to the presidential palace, had made one final radio address suffused with this same defiance: "I am certain that the seed we planted in the worthy consciousness of thousands and thousands of Chileans cannot be definitively uprooted," he said, his last public words. "They have the strength; they can subjugate us, but they cannot halt social processes by either crime or force. History is ours, and the people make it."[18]

The junta commanders of the region and their economic accomplices were well acquainted with those truths. A veteran of several Argentine military coups explained the thinking inside the military: "In 1955 we believed that the problem was [Juan] Perón, so we took him out, but by 1976 we already knew that the problem was the working class."[19] It was the same across the region: the problem was large and deep. That realization meant that if the neoliberal revolution was going to succeed, the juntas needed to do what Allende had claimed was impossible—definitively uproot the seed that was sown during Latin America's leftward surge. In its Declaration of Principles, issued after the coup, the Pinochet dictatorship described its mission as a "prolonged and profound operation to change Chilean mentality," an echo of the statement twenty years earlier by USAID's Albion Patterson, godfather of the Chile Project: "What we need to do is change the formation of the men."[20]

But how to do that? The seed that Allende referred to wasn't a single idea or even a group of political parties and trade unions. By the sixties and early seventies in Latin America, the left was the dominant mass culture—it was the poetry of Pablo Neruda, the folk music of Victor Jara and Mercedes Sosa, the liberation theology of the Third World Priests, the emancipatory theater of Augusto Boal, the radical pedagogy of Paulo Freire, the revolutionary journalism of Eduardo Galeano and Walsh himself. It was legendary heroes and martyrs of past and recent history from José Gervasio Artigas to Simón Bolívar to Che Guevara. When the juntas set out to defy Allende's prophecy and pull up socialism by its roots, it was a declaration of war against this entire culture.

The imperative was reflected in the dominant metaphors used by the military regimes in Brazil, Chile, Uruguay and Argentina: those fascist standbys of cleaning, scrubbing, uprooting and curing. In Brazil, the junta's roundups of leftists were code-named Operação Limpeza, Operation Cleanup. On the day of the coup, Pinochet referred to Allende and his cabinet as "that filth that was going to ruin the country."[21] One month later he pledged to "extirpate the root of evil from Chile," to bring about a "moral cleansing" of the nation, "purified of vices"—an echo of the Third Reich author Alfred Rosenberg's call for "a merciless cleansing with an iron broom."[22]

Cleansing Cultures

In Chile, Argentina and Uruguay, the juntas staged massive ideological cleanup operations, burning books by Freud, Marx and Neruda, closing hundreds of newspapers and magazines, occupying universities, banning strikes and political meetings.

Some of the most vicious attacks were reserved for the "pink" economists whom the Chicago Boys could not defeat before the coups. At the University of Chile, rival to the Chicago Boys' home base, the Catholic University, hundreds of professors were fired for "inobservance of moral duties" (including André Gunder Frank, the dissident Chicagoan who wrote angry letters home to his former professors).[23] During the coup, Gunder Frank reported that "six students were shot on sight in the main entrance to the School of Economics to offer an object lesson to the remainder."[24] When the junta seized power in Argentina, soldiers marched into the University of the South in Bahía Blanca and imprisoned seventeen academics on charges of "subversive instruction"; once again, most were from the economics department.[25] "It is necessary to destroy the sources which feed, form and indoctrinate the subversive delinquent," one of the generals announced at a press conference.[26] A total of eight thousand "ideologically suspect" leftist educators were purged as part of Operation Clarity.[27] In high schools, they banned group presentations—a sign of a latent collective spirit, dangerous to "individual freedom."[28]

In Santiago, the legendary left-wing folk singer Victor Jara was among those taken to the Chile Stadium. His treatment was the embodiment of the furious determination to silence a culture. First the soldiers broke both his hands so he could not play the guitar, then they shot him forty-four times, according to Chile's truth and reconciliation commission.[29] To make sure he could not inspire from beyond the grave, the regime ordered his master recordings destroyed. Mercedes Sosa, a fellow musician, was forced into exile from Argentina, the revolutionary dramatist Augusto Boal was tortured and exiled from Brazil, Eduardo Galeano was driven from Uruguay and Walsh was murdered in the streets of Buenos Aires. A culture was being deliberately exterminated.

Meanwhile, another sanitized, purified culture was replacing it. At the start of the dictatorships in Chile, Argentina and Uruguay, the only public gatherings permitted were shows of military strength and football matches. In Chile, wearing slacks was enough to get you arrested if you were a woman, long hair if you were a man. "All over the Republic a thorough cleansing is under way," declared an editorial in a junta-controlled Argentine newspaper. It called for a mass scrubbing of leftist graffiti: "Soon enough the surfaces will shine through, released from that nightmare by the action of soap and water."[30]

In Chile, Pinochet was determined to break his people's habit of taking to the streets. The tiniest gatherings were dispersed with water cannons, Pinochet's favorite crowd-control weapon. The junta had hundreds of them, small enough to drive onto sidewalks and douse cliques of schoolchildren handing out leaflets; even funeral processions, when the mourning got too rowdy, were brutally repressed. Nicknamed *guanacos*, after a llama known for its habit of spitting, the ubiquitous cannons cleared away people as if they were human garbage, leaving the streets glistening, clean and empty.

Shortly after the coup, the Chilean junta issued an edict urging citizens to "contribute to cleansing your homeland" by reporting foreign "extremists" and "fanaticized Chileans."[31]

Who Was Killed—and Why

The majority of the people swept up in the raids were not "terrorists," as the rhetoric claimed, but rather the people whom the juntas had identified as posing the most serious barriers to their economic program. Some were actual opponents, but many were simply seen as representing values contrary to the revolution's.

The systematic nature of this cleansing campaign is clearly corroborated by matching the dates and times of the disappearances documented in human rights and truth commission reports. In Brazil, the junta did not begin mass repression until the late sixties, but there was one exception: as soon as the coup was launched, soldiers rounded up the leadership of trade unions active in the factories and on the large ranches. According to *Brasil: Nunca Mais* (Never Again), they were sent to jail, where many faced torture, "for the simple reason that they were inspired by a political philosophy opposed by the authorities." This truth commission report, based on the military's own court records, notes that the General Workers Command (CGT), the main coalition of trade unions, appears in the junta's court proceedings "as an omnipresent demon to be exorcised." The report bluntly concludes that the reason "the authorities who took over in 1964 were especially careful to 'clean out' this sector" is that they "feared the spread of . . . resistance from the labor unions to their economic programs, which were based on tightening salaries and denationalizing the economy."[32]

In both Chile and Argentina, the military governments used the initial chaos of the coup to launch vicious attacks on the trade union movement. These operations were clearly planned well in advance, as the systematic raids began on the day of the coup itself. In Chile, while all eyes were on the besieged presidential palace, other battalions were dispatched to "factories in what were known as the 'industrial belts,' where troops carried out raids and arrested people. During the next few days," Chile's truth and reconciliation report notes, several more factories were raided, "leading to massive arrests of people, some of whom were later killed or disappeared."[33] In 1976, 80 percent of Chile's political prisoners were workers and peasants.[34]

Argentina's truth commission report, *Nunca Más* (Never Again), documents a parallel surgical strike against trade unions: "We notice that a large proportion of the operations [against workers] were carried out on the day of the coup itself, or immediately after."[35] Amid the list of attacks on factories, one testimony is particularly revealing about how "terrorism" was used as a smoke screen to go after non-violent worker activists. Graciela Geuna, a political prisoner in the torture camp known as La Perla, described how the soldiers guarding her became agitated by an impending strike at a power plant. The strike was to be "an important example in the resistance to the military dictatorship," and the junta did not want it to happen. So, Geuna recalled, the "soldiers in the unit decided to make it illegal or, as they said, to 'Montonerize' it" (the Montoneros being the guerrilla group the army had already effectively broken). The strikers had nothing to do with the Montoneros, but that didn't matter. The "soldiers at La Perla themselves printed leaflets they signed 'Montoneros'—leaflets calling on the power workers to strike." The leaflets then became the "proof" needed to kidnap and kill the union leadership.[36]

Corporate-Sponsored Torture

Attacks on union leaders were often carried out in close coordination with the owners of the workplaces, and court cases filed in recent years provide some of the best-documented examples of direct involvement by local subsidiaries of foreign multinationals.

In the years prior to the coup in Argentina, the rise of left-wing militancy had affected foreign companies both economically and personally; between 1972 and 1976, five executives from the auto company Fiat were assassinated.[37] The fortunes of such companies changed dramatically when the junta took power and implemented Chicago School policies; now they could flood the local market with imports, pay lower wages, lay workers off at will and send their profits home unhindered by regulations.

Several multinationals effusively expressed their gratitude. On the first new year under military rule in Argentina, Ford Motor Company took out a celebratory newspaper advertisement openly aligning itself with the regime: "1976: Once again, Argentina finds its way. 1977: New Year of faith and hope for all Argentines of good will. Ford Motor of Argentina and its people commit themselves to the struggle to bring about the great destiny of the Fatherland."[38] Foreign corporations did more than thank the juntas for their fine work; some were active participants in the terror campaigns. In Brazil, several multinationals banded together and financed their own privatized torture squads. In mid-1969, just as the junta entered its most brutal phase, an extralegal police force was launched called Operation Bandeirantes, known as OBAN. Staffed with military officers, OBAN was funded, according to *Brazil: Never Again*, "by contributions from various multinational corporations, including Ford and General Motors." Because it was outside official military and police structures, OBAN enjoyed "flexibility and impunity with regard to interrogation methods," the report states, and quickly gained a reputation for unparalleled sadism.[39]

It was in Argentina, however, that the involvement of Ford's local subsidiary with the terror apparatus was most overt. The company supplied cars to the military, and the green Ford Falcon sedan was the vehicle used for thousands of kidnappings and disappearances. The Argentine psychologist and playwright Eduardo Pavlovsky described the car as "the symbolic expression of terror. A death-mobile."[40]

While Ford supplied the junta with cars, the junta provided Ford with a service of its own—ridding the assembly lines of troublesome trade unionists. Before the coup, Ford had been forced to make significant concessions to its workers: one hour off for lunch instead of twenty minutes, and 1 percent of the sale of each car to go to social service programs. All that changed abruptly on the day of the coup, when the counterrevolution began. The Ford factory in suburban Buenos Aires was turned into an armed camp; in the weeks that followed, it was swarming with military vehicles, including tanks and helicopters buzzing overhead. Workers have testified to the presence of a battalion of one hundred soldiers permanently stationed at the factory.[41] "It looked like we were at war in Ford. And it was all directed at us, the workers," recalled Pedro Troiani, one of the union delegates.[42]

Soldiers prowled the facility, grabbing and hooding the most active union members, helpfully pointed out by the factory foreman. Troiani was among those pulled off the assembly line. He recalled that "before detaining me, they walked me around the factory, they did it right out in the open so that the people would see: Ford used this to eliminate unionism in the factory."[43] Most startling was what happened next: rather than being rushed off to a nearby prison, Troiani and others say soldiers took them to a detention facility that had been set up *inside* the factory gates. In their place of work, where they had been negotiating contracts just days before, workers were beaten, kicked and, in two cases, electroshocked.[44] They were then taken to outside prisons where the torture continued for weeks and, in some cases, months.[45] According to the workers' lawyers, at least twenty-five Ford union reps were kidnapped in this period, half of them detained on the company grounds in a facility that human rights groups in Argentina are lobbying to have placed on an official list of former clandestine detention facilities.[46]

In 2002, federal prosecutors filed a criminal complaint against Ford Argentina on behalf of Troiani and fourteen other workers, alleging that the company is legally responsible for the repression that took place on its property. "Ford [Argentina] and its executives colluded in the kidnapping of its own workers, and I think they should be held responsible for that," says Troiani.[47] Mercedes-Benz (a subsidiary of DaimlerChrysler) is facing a similar investigation stemming from allegations that the company collaborated with the military during the 1970s to purge one of its plants of union leaders, allegedly giving names and addresses of sixteen workers who were later disappeared, fourteen of them permanently.[48]

According to the Latin American historian Karen Robert, by the end of the dictatorship, "virtually all the shop-floor delegates had been disappeared from the country's biggest firms . . . such as Mercedes-Benz, Chrysler and Fiat Concord."[49] Both Ford and Mercedes-Benz deny that their executives played any role in the repression. The cases are ongoing.

It wasn't only unionists who faced preemptive attack—it was anyone who represented a vision of society built on values other than pure profit. Particularly brutal throughout the region were the attacks on farmers who had been involved in the struggle for land reform. Leaders of the Argentine Agrarian Leagues—who had been spreading incendiary ideas about the right of peasants to own land—were hunted down and tortured, often out in the fields they worked, in full view of the community. Soldiers used truck batteries to power their *picanas*, turning the ubiquitous farm implement against the farmers themselves. Meanwhile, the junta's economic policies were a windfall for the landowners and cattle ranchers. In Argentina, Martínez de Hoz had deregulated the price of meat, and the cost was up more than 700 percent, leading to record profits.[50]

In the slums, the targets of the preemptive strikes were community workers, many church-based, who organized the poorest sectors of society to demand health care, public housing and education—in other words, the "welfare state" being dismantled by the Chicago Boys. "The poor won't have any goody-goodies to look after them anymore!" Norberto Liwsky, an Argentine doctor, was told as "they applied electric shocks to my gums, nipples, genitals, abdomen and ears."[51]

An Argentine priest who collaborated with the junta explained the guiding philosophy: "The enemy was Marxism. Marxism in the church, let us say, and in the mother country—the danger of a new nation."[52] That "danger of a new nation" helps explain why so many of the juntas' victims were young. In Argentina, 81 percent of the thirty thousand people who were disappeared were between the ages of sixteen and thirty.[53] "We are working now for the next twenty years," a notorious Argentine torturer told one of his victims.[54]

Among the youngest were a group of high-school students who, in September 1976, banded together to ask for lower bus fare. For the junta, the collective action showed that the teenagers had been infected with the virus of Marxism, and it responded with genocidal fury, torturing and killing six of the high-schoolers who had dared to make this subversive request.[55] Miguel Osvaldo Etchecolatz, the police commissioner finally sentenced in 2006, was one of the key figures implicated in the attack.

The pattern of these disappearances was clear: while the shock therapists were trying to remove all relics of collectivism from the economy, the shock troops were removing the representatives of that ethos from the streets, the universities and the factory floors.

In unguarded moments, some of those on the front lines of the economic transformation have acknowledged that the achieving of their goals required mass repression. Victor Emmanuel, the Burson-Marsteller public relations executive who was in charge of selling the Argentine junta's new business-friendly regime to the outside world, told a researcher that violence was necessary to open up Argentina's "protective, statist" economy. "No one, but no one, invests in a country involved in a civil war," he said, but he admitted that it wasn't just guerrillas who died. "A lot of innocent people were probably killed," he told the author Marguerite Feitlowitz, but, "given the situation, immense force was required."[56]

Sergio de Castro, Pinochet's Chicago Boy economics minister who oversaw the implementation of shock treatment, said he could never have done it without Pinochet's iron fist backing him up. "Public opinion was very much against [us], so we needed a strong personality to maintain the policy. It was our luck that President Pinochet understood and had the character to withstand criticism." He has also observed that an "authoritarian government" is best suited to safeguarding economic freedom because of its "impersonal" use of power.[57]

As is the case with most state terror, the targeted killings served a dual purpose. First, they removed real obstacles to the project—the people most likely to fight back. Second, the fact that everyone witnessed the "troublemakers" being disappeared sent an unmistakable warning to those who might be thinking of resisting, thereby eliminating future obstacles.

And it worked. "We were confused and anguished, docile and waiting to take orders . . . people regressed; they became more dependent and fearful," recalled the Chilean psychiatrist Marco Antonio de la Parra.[58] They were, in other words, in shock. So when economic shocks sent prices soaring and wages dropping, the streets in Chile, Argentina and Uruguay remained clear and calm. There were no food riots, no general strikes. Families coped by quietly skipping meals, feeding their babies *maté,* a traditional tea that suppresses hunger, and waking up before dawn to walk for hours to work, saving on bus fare. Those who died from malnutrition or typhoid were quietly buried.

Just a decade earlier, the countries of the Southern Cone—with their exploding industrial sectors, rapidly rising middle classes and strong health and education systems—had been the hope of the developing world. Now rich and poor were hurtling into different economic worlds, with the wealthy gaining honorary citizenship in the State of Florida and the rest being pushed back into underdevelopment, a process that would deepen throughout the neoliberal "restructurings" of the postdictatorship era. No longer inspirational examples, these countries were now terrifying warnings about what happens to poor nations that think they can pull themselves out of the Third World. It was a conversion that paralleled what prisoners were going through inside the junta's torture centers: it wasn't enough to talk—they were forced to renounce their most cherished beliefs, betray their lovers and children. The ones who gave in were called *quebrados,* the broken ones. So it was in the Southern Cone: the region wasn't just beaten, it was broken, *quebrado.*

Torture as "Curing"

While the policies attempted to excise collectivism from the culture, inside the prisons torture tried to excise it from the mind and spirit. As an Argentine junta editorial noted in 1976, "minds too must be cleansed, for that is where the error was born."[59]

Many torturers adopted the posture of a doctor or surgeon. Like the Chicago economists with their painful but necessary shock treatments, these interrogators imagined that their electroshocks and other torments were therapeutic—that they were administering a kind of medicine to their prisoners, who were often referred to inside the camps as *apestosos*, the dirty or diseased ones. They would heal them of the sickness that was socialism, of the impulse toward collective action.* Their "treatments" were agonizing, certainly; they might even be lethal—but it was for the patient's own good. "If you have gangrene in an arm, you have to cut it off, right?" Pinochet demanded, in impatient response to criticisms of his human rights record.[60]

In testimony from truth commission reports across the region, prisoners tell of a system designed to force them to betray the principle most integral to their sense of self. For most Latin American leftists, that most cherished principle was what Argentina's radical historian Osvaldo Bayer called "the only transcendental theology: solidarity."[61] The torturers understood the importance of solidarity well, and they set out to shock that impulse of social interconnectedness out of their prisoners. Of course all interrogation is purportedly about gaining valuable information and therefore forcing betrayal, but many prisoners report that their torturers were far less interested in the information, which they usually already possessed, than in achieving the act of betrayal itself. The point of the exercise was getting prisoners to do irreparable damage to that part of themselves that believed in helping others above all else, that part of themselves that made them activists, replacing it with shame and humiliation.

Sometimes the betrayals were completely beyond a prisoner's control. For instance, the Argentine prisoner Mario Villani had his agenda book with him when he was kidnapped. It contained the coordinates for a meeting he had scheduled with a friend; the soldiers showed up in his place, and another activist was disappeared into the terror machinery. On the table, Villani's interrogators tortured him with the knowledge that "they got Jorge because he'd kept his date with me. They knew that my knowing this would be a far worse torment than 220 volts. The remorse is almost more than you can take."[62]

---

* This brought electroshock therapy full circle to its earliest incarnation as an exorcism technique. The first recorded use of medical electrocution was by a Swiss doctor practicing in the 1700s. Believing that mental illness was caused by the devil, he had a patient hold on to a wire that he powered with a static electricity machine; one jolt of electricity was given for each demon. The patient was then pronounced cured.

The ultimate acts of rebellion in this context were small gestures of kindness between prisoners, such as tending to each other's wounds or sharing scarce food. When such loving acts were discovered, they were met with harsh punishment. Prisoners were goaded into being as individualistic as possible, constantly offered Faustian bargains, like choosing between more unbearable torture for themselves or more torture for a fellow prisoner. In some cases, prisoners were so successfully broken that they agreed to hold the *picana* on their fellow inmates or go on television and renounce their former beliefs. These prisoners represented the ultimate triumph for their torturers: not only had the prisoners abandoned solidarity but in order to survive they had succumbed to the cutthroat ethos at the heart of laissez-faire capitalism—"looking out for No. 1," in the words of the ITT executive.*[63]

Both groups of shock "doctors" working in the Southern Cone—the generals and the economists—resorted to nearly identical metaphors for their work. Friedman likened his role in Chile to that of a physician who offered "technical medical advice to the Chilean Government to help end a medical plague"—the "plague of inflation."[64] Arnold Harberger, head of the Latin American program at the University of Chicago, went even further. In a lecture delivered to young economists in Argentina, long after the dictatorship had ended, he said that good economists are themselves the treatment—they serve "as antibodies to combat anti-economic ideas and policies."[65] The Argentine junta's foreign minister, César Augusto Guzzetti, said that "when the social body of the country has been contaminated by a disease that corrodes its entrails, it forms antibodies. These antibodies cannot be considered in the same way as the microbes. As the government controls and destroys the guerrilla, the action of the antibody will disappear, as is already happening. It is only a natural reaction to a sick body."[66]

---

* The contemporary expression of this personality-breaking process is found in the way Islam is used as a weapon against Muslim prisoners in U.S.-run jails. In the mountain of evidence that has cascaded out of Abu Ghraib and Guantánamo Bay, two forms of prisoner abuse come up again and again: nudity and the deliberate interference with Islamic practice, whether by forcing prisoners to shave their beards, kicking the Koran, wrapping prisoners in Israeli flags, forcing men into homosexual poses, even touching men with simulated menstrual blood. Moazzam Begg, a former prisoner at Guantánamo, says he was frequently forcibly shaved and a guard would say, "This is the part that really gets to you Muslims, isn't it?" Islam is desecrated not because it is hated by the guards (though it may well be) but because it is loved by the prisoners. Since the goal of torture is to unmake personalities, everything that comprises a prisoner's personality must be systematically stolen — from his clothes to his cherished beliefs. In the seventies that meant attacking social solidarity; today it means assaulting Islam.

This language is, of course, the same intellectual construct that allowed the Nazis to argue that by killing "diseased" members of society they were healing the "national body." As the Nazi doctor Fritz Klein claimed, "I want to preserve life. And out of respect for human life, I would remove a gangrenous appendix from a diseased body. The Jew is the gangrenous appendix in the body of mankind." The Khmer Rouge used the same language to justify their slaughter in Cambodia: "What is infected must be cut out."[67]

"Normal" Children

Nowhere were the parallels more chilling than in the Argentine junta's treatment of children inside its network of torture centers. The UN Convention on Genocide states that among the signature genocidal practices is "imposing measures intended to prevent births within the group" and "forcibly transferring children of the group to another group."[68]

An estimated five hundred babies were born inside Argentina's torture centers, and these infants were immediately enlisted in the plan to reengineer society and create a new breed of model citizens. After a brief nursing period, hundreds of babies were sold or given to couples, most of them directly linked to the dictatorship. The children were raised according to the values of capitalism and Christianity deemed "normal" and healthy by the junta and never told of their heritage, according to the human rights group the Grandmothers of the Plaza de Mayo that has painstakingly tracked down dozens of these children.[69] The babies' parents, considered too diseased to be salvageable, were almost always killed in the camps. The baby thefts were not individual excesses but part of an organized state operation. In one court case, an official 1977 Department of the Interior document was submitted as evidence; it was titled "Instructions on procedures to follow with underage children of political or union leaders when their parents are detained or disappeared."[70]

This chapter in Argentina's history has some striking parallels with the mass theft of indigenous children from their families in the U.S., Canada and Australia, where they were sent to residential schools, forbidden to speak their native languages, and beaten into "whiteness." In Argentina in the seventies, a similar supremacist logic was clearly at work, based not on race but on political belief, culture and class.

One of the most graphic connections between the political killings and the free-market revolution was not discovered until four years after the Argentine dictatorship had ended. In 1987, a film crew was shooting in the basement of the Galerías Pacífico, one of Buenos Aires' plushest downtown malls, and to their horror they stumbled on an abandoned torture center. It turned out that during the dictatorship, the First Army Corps hid some of its disappeared in the bowels of the mall; the dungeon walls still bore the desperate markings made by its long-dead prisoners: names, dates, pleas for help.[71]

Today, Galerías Pacífico is the crown jewel of Buenos Aires' shopping district, evidence of its arrival as a globalized consumer capital. Vaulted ceilings and lushly painted frescoes frame the vast array of brand-name stores, from Christian Dior to Ralph Lauren to Nike, unaffordable to the vast majority of the country's inhabitants but a bargain for the foreigners who flock to the city to take advantage of its depressed currency.

For Argentines who know their history, the mall stands as a chilling reminder that just as an older form of capitalist conquest was built on the mass graves of the country's indigenous peoples, the Chicago School Project in Latin America was quite literally built on the secret torture camps where thousands of people who believed in a different country disappeared.

CHAPTER 5

"ENTIRELY UNRELATED"

HOW AN IDEOLOGY WAS CLEANSED OF ITS CRIMES

> **Milton [Friedman] is the embodiment of the truth that "ideas have consequences."**
> —Donald Rumsfeld, U.S. defense secretary, May 2002[1]

> **People were in prison so that prices could be free.**
> —Eduardo Galeano, 1990[2]

For a brief period, it did seem that the crimes of the Southern Cone might actually stick to the neoliberal movement, discrediting it before it expanded beyond its first laboratory. After Milton Friedman's fateful trip to Chile in 1975, the *New York Times* columnist Anthony Lewis asked a simple but inflammatory question: "If the pure Chicago economic theory can be carried out in Chile only at the price of repression, should its authors feel some responsibility?"[3]

After the murder of Orlando Letelier, grassroots activists picked up on his call for "the intellectual architect" of Chile's economic revolution to be held responsible for the human costs of his policies. In those years, Milton Friedman couldn't give a lecture without being interrupted by someone quoting Letelier, and he was forced to enter through the kitchen at several events where he was being honored.

Students at the University of Chicago were so disturbed to learn of their professors' collaboration with the junta that they called for an academic investigation. Some academics backed them up, including the Austrian economist Gerhard Tintner, who fled European fascism and came to the U.S. in the 1930s. Tintner compared Chile under Pinochet to Germany under the Nazis and drew parallels between Friedman's support for Pinochet and the technocrats who collaborated with the Third Reich. (Friedman, in turn, accused his critics of "Nazism.")[4]

Both Friedman and Arnold Harberger gladly took credit for the economic miracles performed by their Latin American Chicago Boys. Sounding like a proud father, Friedman crowed in *Newsweek* in 1982 that the "Chicago Boys . . . combined outstanding intellectual and executive ability with the courage of their convictions and a sense of dedication to implementing them." Harberger has said, "I feel prouder about my students than of anything I have written, in fact, the *latino* group is much more mine than the contribution to the literature."[5] When it came to considering the human costs of the "miracles" their students performed, however, both men suddenly saw no relationship.

"Despite my sharp disagreement with the authoritarian political system of Chile," Friedman wrote in his *Newsweek* column, "I do not regard it as evil for an economist to render technical economic advice to the Chilean Government."[6]

In his memoir, Friedman claimed that Pinochet spent the first two years trying to run the economy on his own, and that it wasn't until "1975, when inflation still raged and a world recession triggered a depression in Chile, [that] General Pinochet turned to the 'Chicago Boys.'"[7] This was blatant revisionism—the Chicago Boys had been working with the military before the coup even took place, and the economic transformation began on the day the junta took power. At other points, Friedman even claimed that Pinochet's entire reign—seventeen years of dictatorship and tens of thousands tortured—was not a violent unmaking of democracy but its opposite. "The really important thing about the Chilean business is that free markets did work their way in bringing about a free society," Friedman said.[8]

Three weeks after Letelier was assassinated, news came that cut short the debates over how Pinochet's crimes reflected on the Chicago School movement. Milton Friedman had been awarded the 1976 Nobel Prize for Economics for his "original and weighty" work on the relationship between inflation and unemployment.[9] Friedman used his Nobel address to argue that economics was as rigorous and objective a scientific discipline as physics, chemistry and medicine, reliant on an impartial examination of the facts available. He conveniently ignored the fact that the central hypothesis for which he was receiving the prize was being graphically proven false by the breadlines, typhoid outbreaks and shuttered factories in Chile, the one regime ruthless enough to put his ideas into practice.[10]

One year later, something else happened to define the parameters of the debate about the Southern Cone: Amnesty International won the Nobel Peace Prize, largely for its courageous and crusading work exposing the human rights abuses in Chile and Argentina. The economics prize is actually independent from the peace prize, awarded by a different committee and handed out in a different city. From afar, however, it seemed as if, with the two Nobel prizes, the most prestigious jury in the world had issued its verdict: the shock of the torture chamber was to be forcefully condemned, but economic shock treatments were to be applauded—and the two forms of shock were, as Letelier had written with dripping irony, "entirely unrelated."[11]

The Blinders of "Human Rights"

This intellectual firewall went up not only because Chicago School economists refused to acknowledge any connection between their policies and the use of terror. Contributing to the problem was the particular way that these acts of terror were framed as narrow "human rights abuses" rather than as tools that served clear political and economic ends. That is partly because the Southern Cone in the seventies was not just a laboratory for a new economic model. It was also a laboratory for a relatively new activist model: the grassroots international human rights movement. That movement unquestionably played a decisive role in forcing an end to the junta's worst abuses. But by focusing purely on the crimes and not on the reasons behind them, the human rights movement also helped the Chicago School ideology to escape from its first bloody laboratory virtually unscathed.

The dilemma back to the inception of the modern-day human rights movement, with the 1948 adoption of the United Nations Universal Declaration of Human Rights. No sooner had the document been written than it became a partisan battering ram, used by both sides in the Cold War to accuse the other of being the next Hitler. In 1967, press reports revealed that the International Commission of Jurists, the preeminent human rights group focused on Soviet abuses, was not the impartial arbiter it claimed to be but was receiving secret funding from the CIA.[12]

It was in this loaded context that Amnesty International developed its doctrine of strict impartiality: its financing would come exclusively from members, and it would remain rigorously "independent of any government, political faction, ideology, economic interest or religious creed." To prove that it was not using human rights to advance a particular political agenda, each Amnesty chapter was instructed to simultaneously "adopt" three prisoners of conscience, one each "from communist, Western, and Third World countries."[13] Amnesty's position, emblematic of the human rights movement as a whole at that time, was that since human rights violations were a universal evil, wrong in and of themselves, it was not necessary to determine why abuses were taking place but to document them as meticulously and credibly as possible.

This principle is reflected in the way the terror campaign was recorded in the Southern Cone. Under constant surveillance and harassment from secret police, human rights groups sent delegations to Argentina, Uruguay and Chile to interview hundreds of victims of torture and their families; they also gained what access they could to prisons. Since independent media were banned and the juntas denied their crimes, these testimonies form the primary documentation of a history that was never supposed to be written. Important as this work was, it was also limited: the reports are legalistic lists of the most stomach-turning methods of repression, cross-referenced with the UN charters they violated.

The narrow scope is most problematic in Amnesty International's 1976 report on Argentina, a breakthrough account of the junta's atrocities and worthy of its Nobel Prize. Yet for all its thoroughness, the report sheds no light on why the abuses were occurring. It asks the question "to what extent are the violations explicable or necessary" to establish "security"—which was the junta's official rationale for the "dirty war."[14] After the evidence was examined, the report concludes that the threat posed by left-wing guerrillas was in no way commensurate with the level of repression used by the state.

But was there some other goal that made the violence "explicable or necessary"? Amnesty made no mention of it. In fact, in its ninety-two-page report, it made no mention that the junta was in the process of remaking the country along radically capitalist lines. It offered no comment on the deepening poverty or the dramatic reversal of programs to redistribute wealth, though these were the policy centerpieces of junta rule. It carefully lists all the junta laws and decrees that violated civil liberties but named none of the economic decrees that lowered wages and increased prices, thereby violating the right to food and shelter—also enshrined in the UN charter. If the junta's revolutionary economic project had been even superficially examined, it would have been clear why such extraordinary repression was necessary, just as it would have explained why so many of Amnesty's prisoners of conscience were peaceful trade unionists and social workers.

In another major omission, Amnesty presented the conflict as one restricted to the local military and the left-wing extremists. No other players are mentioned—not the U.S. government or the CIA; not local landowners; not multinational corporations. Without an examination of the larger plan to impose "pure" capitalism on Latin America, and the powerful interests behind that project, the acts of sadism documented in the report made no sense at all—they were just random, free-floating bad events, drifting in the political ether, to be condemned by all people of conscience but impossible to understand.

Every facet of the human rights movement was functioning under highly restricted circumstances, though for different reasons. Inside the affected countries, the first people to call attention to the terror were friends and relatives of the victims, but there were severe limits on what they could say. They didn't talk about the political or economic agendas behind the disappearances because to do so was to risk being disappeared themselves. The most famous human rights activists to emerge under these dangerous circumstances were the Mothers of the Plaza de Mayo, known in Argentina as the Madres. At their weekly demonstrations outside the house of government in Buenos Aires, the Madres did not dare hold up protest signs—instead they clasped photographs of their missing children with the caption ¿Dónde están? Where are they? In the place of chants, they circled silently, wearing white headscarves embroidered with their children's names. Many of the Madres had strong political beliefs, but they were careful to present themselves as nothing more threatening to the regime than grieving mothers, desperate to know where their innocent children had been taken.*

In Chile, the largest of the human rights groups was the Peace Committee, formed by opposition politicians, lawyers and Church leaders. These were lifelong political activists who knew that the attempt to stop torture and to free political prisoners was only one front in a much broader battle over who would have control of Chile's wealth. But in order to avoid becoming the regime's next victims, they dropped their usual old-left denunciations of the bourgeoisie and learned the new language of "universal human rights."

---

* After the end of dictatorship, the Madres became some of the fiercest critics of the new economic order in Argentina, as they still are today.

Scrubbed clean of references to the rich and the poor, the weak and strong, the North and the South, this way of explaining the world, so popular in North America and Europe, simply asserted that everyone has the right to a fair trial and to be free from cruel, inhuman and degrading treatment. It didn't ask why, it just asserted *that*. In the mixture of legalese and human interest that characterizes the human rights lexicon, they learned that their imprisoned *compañeros* were actually prisoners of conscience whose right to freedom of thought and speech, protected under articles 18 and 19 of the Universal Declaration of Human Rights, had been violated.

For those living under dictatorship, the new language was essentially a code; just as musicians hid the political messages in their lyrics in sly metaphors, they were disguising their leftism in legalese—a way of engaging in politics without mentioning politics.*

When Latin America's terror campaign was picked up by the fast-expanding international human rights movement, those activists had their own, very different, reasons for avoiding talk of politics.

Ford on Ford

The refusal to connect the apparatus of state terror to the ideological project it served is characteristic of almost all the human rights literature from this period. Although Amnesty's reticence can be understood as an attempt to remain impartial amid Cold War tensions, there was, for many other groups, another factor at play: money. By far the most significant source of funding for this work was the Ford Foundation, then the largest philanthropic organization in the world. In the sixties, the organization spent only a small portion of its budget on human rights, but in the seventies and eighties, the foundation spent a staggering $30 million on work devoted to human rights in Latin America. With these funds, the foundation backed Latin American groups like Chile's Peace Committee as well as new U.S.-based groups, including Americas Watch.[15]

Prior to the military coups, the Ford Foundation's primary role in the Southern Cone had been to fund the training of academics, mostly in economics

---

* Even with these precautions, human rights activists were not safe from the terror. Chile's jails were filled with human rights lawyers, and in Argentina the junta sent one of its top torturers to infiltrate the Madres, posing as a grieving relative. In December 1977, the group was raided; twelve mothers were permanently disappeared, including the leader of the Madres, Azucena de Vicenti, along with two French nuns.

and agricultural science, working closely with the U.S. State Department.[16] Frank Sutton, the deputy vice president of Ford's international division, explained the organization's philosophy: "You can't have a modernizing country without a modernizing elite."[17] Although squarely within the Cold War logic of attempting to foster an alternative to revolutionary Marxism, most of Ford's academic grants did not betray a strong right-wing bias—Latin American students were sent to a wide range of U.S. universities, and funding for graduate departments was provided to diverse Latin American universities, including large public ones with left-leaning reputations.

But there were several significant exceptions. As discussed earlier, the Ford Foundation was the primary funder of the University of Chicago's Program of Latin American Economic Research and Training, which churned out hundreds of Latino Chicago Boys. Ford also financed a parallel program at the Catholic University in Santiago, designed to attract undergraduate economics students from neighboring countries to study under Chile's Chicago Boys. That made the Ford Foundation, intentionally or not, the leading source of funding for the dissemination of the Chicago School ideology throughout Latin America, more significant even than the U.S. government.[18]

When the Chicago Boys came to power in a hail of gunfire alongside Pinochet, it did not reflect particularly well on the Ford Foundation. The Chicago Boys had been funded as part of the foundation's mission to "improve economic institutions for the better realization of democratic goals."[19] Now the economic institutions that Ford had helped build in both Chicago and Santiago were playing a central role in the overthrow of Chile's democracy, and its former students were in the process of applying their U.S. education in a context of shocking brutality. Making matters more complicated for the foundation, this was the second time in just a few years that its protégés had chosen a violent route to power, the first case being the Berkeley Mafia's meteoric rise to power in Indonesia after Suharto's bloody coup.

Ford had built the economics department at the University of Indonesia from the ground up, but when Suharto came to power, "nearly all the economists that the program produced were recruited into the government," a Ford document notes. There was practically no one left to teach the students.[20] In 1974, nationalist riots broke out in Indonesia against "foreign subversion" of the economy; the Ford Foundation became a target of popular rage—it was the foundation, many pointed out, that had trained Suharto's economists to sell Indonesia's oil and mineral wealth to Western multinationals.

Between the Chicago Boys in Chile and the Berkeley Mafia in Indonesia, Ford was gaining an unfortunate reputation: graduates from two of its flagship programs were now dominating the most notoriously brutal right-wing dictatorships in the world. Although Ford could not have known that the ideas in which its grads were trained would be enforced with such barbarism, uncomfortable questions were nonetheless raised about why a foundation dedicated to peace and democracy was neck-deep in authoritarianism and violence.

Whether as a result of panic, social conscience or some combination of both, the Ford Foundation dealt with its dictatorship problem the way any good business would: proactively. In the mid-seventies, Ford transformed itself from a producer of "technical expertise" for the so-called Third World to its leading funder of human rights activism. That about-face was particularly jarring in both Chile and Indonesia. After the left in those countries had been obliterated by regimes that Ford had helped shape, it was none other than Ford that funded a new generation of crusading lawyers dedicated to freeing the hundreds of thousands of political prisoners being held by those same regimes.

Given its own highly compromised history, it is hardly surprising that when Ford dived into human rights, it defined the field as narrowly as possible. The foundation strongly favored groups that framed their work as legalistic struggles for the "rule of law," "transparency" and "good governance." As one Ford Foundation officer put it, the organization's attitude in Chile was, "How can we do this and not get involved in politics?"[21] It wasn't just that Ford was an inherently conservative institution, accustomed to working hand in hand, and not at cross purposes, with official U.S. foreign policy.* It was also that any serious investigation of the goals served by the repression in Chile would inevitably have led directly back to the Ford Foundation and the central role it played in indoctrinating the country's current rulers in a fundamentalist sect of economics.

There was also the question of the foundation's inescapable association with the Ford Motor Company, a complicated relationship, especially for activists on the ground. Today, the Ford Foundation is wholly independent

---

* In the 1950s, the Ford Foundation often served as a front organization for the CIA, allowing the agency to channel funds to anti-Marxist academics and artists who did not know where the money was coming from, a process extensively documented in *The Cultural Cold War* by Frances Stonor Saunders. Amnesty was not funded by the Ford Foundation; nor were the most radical of Latin America's human rights defenders, the Mothers of the Plaza de Mayo.

of the car company and its heirs, but that was not the case in the fifties and sixties when it was funding education projects in Asia and Latin America. The foundation was started in 1936 with donations of stock from three Ford Motor executives, including Henry and Edsel Ford. As the foundation's wealth expanded, it began to operate independently, but its divestment of Ford Motor stock was not completed until 1974, the year after the coup in Chile and several years after the coup in Indonesia, and it had Ford family members on its board until 1976.[22]

In the Southern Cone, the contradictions were surreal: the philanthropic legacy of the very company most intimately associated with the terror apparatus—accused of having a secret torture facility on its property and of helping to disappear its own workers—was the best, and often the only, chance of putting an end to the worst of the abuses. Through its funding of human rights campaigners, the Ford Foundation saved many lives in those years. And it deserves at least part of the credit for persuading the U.S. Congress to cut military support to Argentina and Chile, gradually forcing the juntas of the Southern Cone to scale back the most brutal of their repressive tactics. But when Ford rode to the rescue, its assistance came at a price, and that price was—consciously or not—the intellectual honesty of the human rights movement. The foundation's decision to get involved in human rights but "not get involved in politics" created a context in which it was all but impossible to ask the question underlying the violence it was documenting: Why was it happening, in whose interests?

That omission has played a disfiguring role in the way the history of the free-market revolution has been told, largely absent any taint of the extraordinarily violent circumstances of its birth. Just as the Chicago economists had nothing to say about the torture (it had nothing to do with their areas of expertise), the human rights groups had little to say about the radical transformations taking place in the economic sphere (it was beyond their narrow legal purview).

The idea that the repression and the economics were in fact a single unified project is reflected in only one major human rights report from this period: *Brasil: Nunca Mais*. Significantly, it is the only truth commission report published independently of both the state and foreign foundations. It is based on the military's court records, secretly photocopied over years by tremendously brave lawyers and Church activists while the country was still under dictatorship. After detailing some of the most horrific crimes, the authors pose that central question so studiously avoided by others: Why? They answer matter-of-factly: "Since the economic policy was extremely unpopular among the most numerous sectors of the population, it had to be implemented by force."[23]

The radical economic model that took such deep root during dictatorship would prove hardier than the generals who implemented it. Long after the soldiers returned to their barracks, and Latin Americans were permitted to elect their governments once again, the Chicago School logic remained firmly entrenched.

Claudia Acuña, an Argentine journalist and educator, told me how difficult it had been in the seventies and eighties to fully grasp that violence was not the goal of the junta but only the means. "Their human rights violations were so outrageous, so incredible, that stopping them of course became the priority. But while we were able to destroy the secret torture centers, what we couldn't destroy was the economic program that the military started and continues to this day."

In the end, as Rodolfo Walsh predicted, many more lives would be stolen by "planned misery" than by bullets. In a way, what happened in the Southern Cone of Latin America in the seventies is that it was treated as a murder scene when it was, in fact, the site of an extraordinarily violent armed robbery. "It was as if that blood, the blood of the disappeared, covered up the cost of the economic program," Acuña told me.

The debate about whether "human rights" can ever truly be separated from politics and economics is not unique to Latin America; these are questions that surface whenever states use torture as a weapon of policy. Despite the mystique that surrounds it, and the understandable impulse to treat it as aberrant behavior beyond politics, torture is not particularly complicated or mysterious. A tool of the crudest kind of coercion, it crops up with great predictability whenever a local despot or a foreign occupier lacks the consent needed to rule: Marcos in the Philippines, the shah in Iran, Saddam in Iraq, the French in Algeria, the Israelis in the occupied territories, the U.S. in Iraq and Afghanistan. The list could stretch on and on. The widespread abuse of prisoners is a virtually foolproof indication that politicians are trying to impose a system—whether political, religious or economic—that is rejected by large numbers of the people they are ruling. Just as ecologists define ecosystems by the presence of certain "indicator species" of plants and birds, torture is an indicator species of a regime that is engaged in a deeply anti-democratic project, even if that regime happens to have come to power through elections.

As a means of extracting information during interrogations, torture is notoriously unreliable, but as a means of terrorizing and controlling populations, nothing is quite as effective. It was for this reason that, in the fifties and sixties, many Algerians grew impatient with French liberals who expressed their moral outrage over news that their soldiers were electrocuting and water-boarding liberation fighters—and yet did nothing to end the occupation that was the reason for these abuses.

In 1962, Gisèle Halimi, a French lawyer for several Algerians who had been brutally raped and tortured in prison, wrote in exasperation, "The words were the same stale clichés: ever since torture had been used in Algeria there had always been the same words, the same expression of indignation, the same signatures to public protests, the same promises. This automatic routine had not abolished one set of electrodes or water-hoses; nor had it in any remotely effective way curbed the power of those who used them." Simone de Beauvoir, writing on the same subject, concurred: "To protest in the name of morality against 'excesses' or 'abuses' is an error which hints at active complicity. There are no 'abuses' or 'excesses' here, simply an all-pervasive *system*."[24]

Her point was that the occupation could not be done humanely; there is no humane way to rule people against their will. There are two choices, Beauvoir wrote: accept occupation and all the methods required for its enforcement, "or else you reject, not merely certain specific practices, but the greater aim which sanctions them, and for which they are essential." The same stark choice is available in Iraq and Israel/Palestine today, and it was the only option in the Southern Cone in the seventies. Just as there is no kind, gentle way to occupy people against their determined will, there is no peaceful way to take away from millions of citizens what they need to live with dignity—which is what the Chicago Boys were determined to do. Robbery, whether of land or a way of life, requires force or at least its credible threat; it's why thieves carry guns, and often use them. Torture is sickening, but it is often a highly rational way to achieve a specific goal; indeed, it may be the only way to achieve those goals. Which raises the deeper question, one that so many were incapable of asking at the time in Latin America. Is neoliberalism an inherently violent ideology, and is there something about its goals that demands this cycle of brutal political cleansing, followed by human rights cleanup operations?

One of the most moving testimonies on this question comes from Sergio

Tomasella, a tobacco farmer and secretary-general of Argentina's Agrarian Leagues, who was tortured and imprisoned for five years, as were his wife and many friends and family members.* In May 1990, Tomasella took the overnight bus to Buenos Aires from the rural province of Corrientes in order to add his voice to the Argentine Tribunal against Impunity, which was hearing testimony on human rights abuses during the dictatorship. Tomasella's testimony was different from the others. He stood before the urban audience in his farming clothes and work boots and explained that he was the casualty of a long war, one between poor peasants who wanted pieces of land to form cooperatives and the all-powerful ranchers who owned half the land in his province. "The line is continuous—those who took the land from the Indians continue to oppress us with their feudal structures."[25]

He insisted that the abuse he and his fellow members of the Agrarian Leagues suffered could not be isolated from the huge economic interests served by the breaking of their bodies and destruction of their activist networks. So instead of naming the soldiers who abused him, he chose to name the corporations, both foreign and national, that profit from Argentina's continued economic dependence. "Foreign monopolies impose crops on us, they impose chemicals that pollute our earth, impose technology and ideology. All this through the oligarchy which owns the land and controls the politics. But we must remember—the oligarchy is also controlled, by the very same monopolies, the very same Ford Motors, Monsanto, Philip Morris. It's the *structure* we have to change. This is what I have come to denounce. That's all."

The auditorium erupted in applause. Tomasella concluded his testimony with these words: "I believe that truth and justice will eventually triumph. It will take generations. If I am to die in this fight, then so be it. But one day we will triumph. In the meantime, I know who the enemy is, and the enemy knows who I am, too."[26]

The Chicago Boys' first adventure in the seventies should have served as a warning to humanity: theirs are dangerous ideas. By failing to hold the ideology accountable for the crimes committed in its first laboratory, this subculture of unrepentant ideologues was given immunity, freed to scour the world for its

---

* For this account I am indebted to Marguerite Feitlowitz's inspiring book, *A Lexicon of Terror*.

next conquest. These days, we are once again living in an era of corporatist massacres, with countries suffering tremendous military violence alongside organized attempts to remake them into model "free market" economies; disappearances and torture are back with a vengeance. And once again the goals of building free markets, and the need for such brutality, are treated as entirely unrelated.

PART 3

SURVIVING DEMOCRACY

BOMBS MADE OF LAWS

An armed conflict between nations horrifies us. But the economic war is no better than an armed conflict. This is like a surgical operation. An economic war is prolonged torture. And its ravages are no less terrible than those depicted in the literature on war properly so called. We think nothing of the other because we are used to its deadly effects. . . . The movement against war is sound. I pray for its success. But I cannot help the gnawing fear that the movement will fail if it does not touch the root of all evil—human greed.

—M. K. Gandhi, "Non-Violence—The Greatest Force," 1926

CHAPTER 6

SAVED BY A WAR

THATCHERISM AND ITS USEFUL ENEMIES

Sovereign is he who decides the state of emergency.

—Carl Schmitt, Nazi lawyer[1]

When Friedrich Hayek, patron saint of the Chicago School, returned from a visit to Chile in 1981, he was so impressed by Augusto Pinochet and the Chicago Boys that he sat down and wrote a letter to his friend Margaret Thatcher, prime minister of Britain. He urged her to use the South American country as a model for transforming Britain's Keynesian economy. Thatcher and Pinochet would later become firm friends, with Thatcher famously visiting the aging general under house arrest in England as he faced charges of genocide, torture and terrorism.

The British prime minister was well acquainted with what she called "the remarkable success of the Chilean economy," describing it as "a striking example of economic reform from which we can learn many lessons." Yet despite her admiration for Pinochet, when Hayek first suggested that she emulate his shock therapy policies, Thatcher was far from convinced. In February 1982, the prime minister bluntly explained the problem in a private letter to her intellectual guru: "I am sure you will agree that, in Britain with our democratic institutions and the need for a high degree of consent, some of the measures adopted in Chile are quite unacceptable. Our reform must be in line with our traditions and our Constitution. At times the process may seem painfully slow."[2]

The bottom line was that Chicago-style shock therapy just wasn't possible in a democracy like the U.K. Thatcher was three years into her first term, sinking in the polls and not about to guarantee a loss in the next election by doing anything as radical or unpopular as Hayek was suggesting.

For Hayek and the movement he represented, it was a disappointing assessment. The Southern Cone's experiment had generated such spectacular profits, albeit for a small number of players, that there was tremendous appetite from increasingly global multinationals for new frontiers—and not just in developing countries but in rich ones in the West too, where states controlled even more lucrative assets that could be run as for-profit interests: phones, airlines, television airwaves, power companies. If anyone could have championed this agenda in the wealthy world, it would surely have been either Thatcher in England or the American president at the time, Ronald Reagan.

In 1981, *Fortune* magazine ran an article extolling the virtues of "Chile's Brave New World of Reaganomics." Praising Santiago's "glittering, luxury filled shops" and "shiny new Japanese cars," the article was oblivious to the pervasive repression and the explosion of shantytowns. "What can we learn from Chile's experiment in economic orthodoxy?" it asked, and quickly provided the correct answer: "If a small undeveloped country can live by the theory of competitive advantage, then surely our infinitely more resourceful economy can."[3]

However, as Thatcher's letter to Hayek made clear, it wasn't quite as simple as that. Elected leaders have to worry about what voters think of their job performance, which comes up for regular review. And in the early eighties, even with Reagan and Thatcher in power and Hayek and Friedman serving as influential advisers, it was not at all clear that the kind of radical economic agenda that had been imposed with such ferocious violence in the Southern Cone would ever be possible in Britain and the United States.

A decade earlier, Friedman and his movement had faced a great disappointment in the U.S. at the hands of none other than Richard Nixon, one that seemed to confirm this point. Even though Nixon had helped put the Chicago Boys in power in Chile, he had taken a very different route at home—an inconsistency Friedman would never forgive. When Nixon took office in 1969, Friedman thought his time had finally come to lead his domestic counterrevolution against the legacy of the New Deal. "Few presidents have come closer to expressing a philosophy compatible with my own," Friedman wrote of Nixon.[4] The two men met regularly in the Oval Office, and Nixon named several of Friedman's like-minded friends and colleagues to key economics posts. One was the University of Chicago professor

George Shultz, whom Friedman helped recruit to work for Nixon; another was Donald Rumsfeld, then thirty-seven. In the sixties, Rumsfeld used to attend seminars at the University of Chicago, gatherings he later described in reverential terms. Rumsfeld called Friedman and his colleagues "a cluster of geniuses," while he and other self-described "young pups" would "come in and learn at their feet. . . . I was so privileged."[5] With true disciples making policy and a strong personal rapport with the president, Friedman had every reason to believe that his ideas were about to be put into practice in the most powerful economy in the world.

But in 1971, the U.S. economy was in a slump; unemployment was high and inflation was pushing prices way up. Nixon knew that if he followed Friedman's laissez-faire advice, millions of angry citizens would vote him out of a job. He decided to put caps on the prices of necessities such as rent and oil. Friedman was outraged: of all possible government "distortions," price controls were the absolute worst. He called them "a cancer that can destroy an economic system's capacity to function."[6]

Even more disgraceful, it was his own disciples who were the Keynesian enforcers: Rumsfeld was in charge of the wage-and-price-control program, and he answered to Shultz, who at the time was director of the Office of Management and Budget. At one point, Friedman called Rumsfeld at the White House and berated his former "young pup." According to Rumsfeld, Friedman instructed him, "You have got to stop doing what you are doing." The novice bureaucrat replied that it seemed to be working—inflation was going down, the economy was growing. Friedman fired back that that was the greatest crime of all: "People are going to think that you're doing it . . . they're going to learn the wrong lesson."[7] They did indeed, and they re-elected Nixon with 60 percent of the popular vote the following year. In his second term, the president proceeded to shred even more of Friedman's orthodoxies, passing a slew of new laws imposing higher environmental and safety standards on industry. "We are all Keynesians now," Nixon famously proclaimed—the cruelest cut of all.[8] So deep was this betrayal that Friedman would later describe Nixon as "the most socialist of the presidents of the United States in the 20th century."[9]

Nixon's tenure was a stark lesson for Friedman. The University of Chicago professor had built a movement on the equation of capitalism and freedom, yet free people just didn't seem to vote for politicians who followed his advice. Worse, dictatorships—where freedom was markedly absent—were the only governments who were ready to put pure free-market doctrine into practice. So while they griped about being betrayed at home, Chicago School luminaries junta-hopped their way through the seventies. Almost everywhere that right-wing military dictatorships were in power, the University of Chicago's presence could be felt. Harberger worked as a consultant to Bolivia's military regime in 1976 and accepted an honorary degree from Argentina's University of Tucuman in 1979, a time when universities were under the control of the junta.[10] And farther afield, he advised Suharto and the Berkeley Mafia in Indonesia. Friedman wrote an economic liberalization program for the repressive Chinese Communist Party when it decided to convert to a market economy.[11]

Stephen Haggard, a staunch neoliberal political scientist at the University of California, conceded the "sad fact" that "some of the widest-ranging reform efforts in the developing world were undertaken following military coups"—in addition to the Southern Cone and Indonesia, he listed Turkey, South Korea and Ghana. Other success stories took place not after military coups but in one-party states like Mexico, Singapore, Hong Kong and Taiwan. In direct contradiction of Friedman's central claim, Haggard concluded that "good things—such as democracy and market-oriented economic policy—do not always go together."[12] Indeed, in the early eighties, *there was not a single case* of a multiparty democracy going full-tilt free market.

Leftists in the developing world have long argued that genuine democracy, with fair rules preventing corporations from buying elections, would necessarily result in governments committed to the redistribution of wealth. The logic is simple enough: in these countries, there are far more poor people than rich ones. Policies that directly redistribute land and raise wages, not trickle-down economics, are in the clear self-interest of a poor majority. Give all citizens the vote and a reasonably fair process, and they will elect the politicians who appear most likely to deliver jobs and land, not more free-market promises.

For all these reasons, Friedman had spent a fair bit of time staring down an intellectual paradox: as the heir to Adam Smith's mantle, he believed passionately that humans are governed by self-interest and that society works best when self-interest is allowed to govern almost all activities—except when it comes to a little activity called voting. Since most people in the world are either poor or live below the average income in their countries (including in the U.S.), it is in their short-term self-interest to vote for politicians promising to redistribute wealth from the top of the economy down to them.[13] Friedman's longtime friend Allan Meltzer, a fellow monetarist economist, put the conundrum this way: "Votes are more equally distributed than income. . . . Voters with incomes at the median or below gain by transferring income to themselves." Meltzer described this reaction as "part of the cost of democratic government and political freedom" but said that "the Friedmans [Milton and his wife, Rose] swam against this strong current. They could not stop or reverse it, but they influenced far more than most the ways in which people and politicians think and act."[14]

Across the Atlantic, Thatcher was attempting an English version of Friedmanism by championing what has become known as "the ownership society." The effort centered on Britain's public housing, or council estates, which Thatcher opposed on philosophical grounds, believing that the state had no role to play in the housing market. The council estates were filled with the type of people who wouldn't vote Tory because it wasn't in their economic self-interest; Thatcher was convinced that if they could be brought into the market, they would start to identify with the interests of the wealthier people who opposed redistribution. With that in mind, she offered strong incentives to the residents of public housing to buy their flats at reduced rates. Those who could became homeowners, while those who couldn't faced rents that were almost twice as high as before. It was a divide-and-conquer strategy, and it worked: the renters continued to oppose Thatcher, the streets of Britain's large cities saw a visible increase in homelessness, but polls showed that more than half of the new owners did switch their party affiliation to the Tories.[15]

Although the estate sales offered a glimmer of hope for the possibility of hard-right economics in a democracy, Thatcher still looked poised to lose her job after just one term. In 1979, she had run on the slogan "Labor isn't working," but by 1982, the number of unemployed had doubled under her watch, as had the inflation rate.[16] She had tried to take on one of the most powerful unions in the country, the coal miners, and had failed. After three years in office, Thatcher saw her personal approval rating drop to only 25 percent—lower than George W. Bush at his lowest point and lower than any British prime minister in the history of opinion polls. Approval for her government as a whole had sunk to 18 percent.[17] With a general election looming, Thatcherism was about to come to an early and inglorious close, well before the Tories had achieved their most ambitious goals of mass privatization and breaking the blue-collar unions. It was in those trying circumstances that Thatcher wrote to Hayek, politely informing him that a Chilean-style transformation was "quite unacceptable" in the U.K.

Thatcher's catastrophic first term seemed to further confirm the lessons of the Nixon years: that the radical and highly profitable policies of the Chicago School couldn't survive in a democratic system. It seemed clear that the successful imposition of economic shock therapy required some other sort of shock—whether of a coup, or of the torture chamber delivered by a repressive regime.

That was an especially disturbing prospect on Wall Street because, in the early eighties, authoritarian regimes were starting to collapse around the world—Iran, Nicaragua, Ecuador, Peru, Bolivia—and many more would follow in what the conservative political scientist Samuel Huntington would term the "third wave" of democracy.[18] These were worrying developments— what would prevent the emergence of another Allende, winning votes and support with populist policies?

Washington had watched as that very scenario played out in both Iran and Nicaragua in 1979. In Iran, the U.S.-backed shah was overthrown by a coalition of leftists and Islamists. While the stories of hostages and ayatollahs made the news, the economic side of the program was also raising alarms in Washington. The Islamic regime, which had not yet transitioned to full-blown authoritarianism, nationalized the banking sector and then brought in a land redistribution program. It also imposed controls on imports and exports, a reversal of the shah's free-trade policies.[19] Five months later in Nicaragua, the U.S.-backed dictatorship of Anastasio Somoza Dabayle fell to a popular revolt that installed the left-wing Sandinista government. It controlled imports and, like the Iranians, nationalized the banking industry.

It added up to a grim prognosis for the dream of a global free market. By the early eighties, Friedmanites were facing the prospect that their revolution, less than a decade old, could not survive a new populist wave.

War to the Rescue

Six weeks after Thatcher wrote that letter to Hayek, something happened that changed her mind and altered the destiny of the corporatist crusade: on April 2, 1982, Argentina invaded the Falkland Islands, a relic of British colonial rule. The Falklands War, or the Malvinas War if you are Argentine, went down in history as a vicious but fairly minor battle. At the time, the Falklands appeared to have no strategic importance. The cluster of islands off the Argentine coast was thousands of miles from Britain and costly to guard and maintain. Argentina, too, had little use for them, though having a British outpost in its waters was regarded as an affront to national pride. The legendary Argentine writer Jorge Luis Borges scathingly described the land dispute as "a fight between two bald men over a comb."[20]

From a military standpoint, the eleven-week battle appears to have almost no historic significance. Overlooked, however, was the war's impact on the free-market project, which was enormous: it was the Falklands War that gave Thatcher the political cover she needed to bring a program of radical capitalist transformation to a Western liberal democracy for the first time.

Both sides in the conflict had good reasons to want a war. In 1982, Argentina's economy was collapsing under the weight of its debt and corruption, and human rights campaigns were gaining momentum. A new junta government, led by General Leopoldo Galtieri, calculated that the only thing more powerful than the anger at its continued suppression of democracy was anti-imperialist sentiment, which Galtieri expertly unleashed on the British for their refusal to give up the islands. Soon enough, the junta had Argentina's blue-and-white flag planted on that rocky outpost, and the country cheered on cue.

When news arrived that Argentina had laid claim to the Falklands, Thatcher recognized it as a last-ditch hope to turn around her political fortunes and immediately went into Churchillian battle mode. Until this point, she had shown only disdain for the financial burden that the Falklands placed on government coffers. She had cut grants to the islands and announced major cutbacks to the navy, including the armed ships that guarded the Falklands—moves read by the Argentine generals as clear indications that Britain was ready to cede the territory. (One of Thatcher's biographers characterized her Falklands policy as "practically an invitation to Argentina to invade.")[21] In the lead-up to the war, critics across the political spectrum accused Thatcher of using the military for her own political goals. The Labour MP Tony Benn said, "It looks more and more as if what is at stake is Mrs. Thatcher's reputation, not the Falkland Islands at all," while the conservative *Financial Times* noted, "What is deplorable is that the issue is rapidly becoming mixed up with political differences within Britain itself which have nothing to do with the matter in hand. Not only the pride of the Argentine Government is involved. So is the standing, perhaps even the survival, of the Tory Government in Britain."[22]

Yet even with all of this healthy cynicism in the run-up, as soon as troops were deployed, the country was swept up in what a draft Labour Party resolution described as a "jingoistic, militaristic frame of mind," embracing the

Falkland Islands as a last blast of glory for Britain's faded empire.[23] Thatcher praised the "Falklands spirit" gripping the nation, which in practice meant that shouts of "Ditch the bitch!" subsided while "Up Your Junta!" T-shirts sold briskly.[24] Neither London nor Buenos Aires made any serious attempt to avoid a showdown. Thatcher brushed aside the United Nations much as Bush and Blair did in the run-up to the war in Iraq, uninterested in sanctions or negotiations. Glorious victory was the only outcome that either side had any interest in.

Thatcher was fighting for her political future—and she succeeded spectacularly. After the Falklands victory, which took the lives of 255 British soldiers and 655 Argentines, the prime minister was heralded as a war hero, her moniker "Iron Lady" transformed from insult to high praise.[25] Her poll numbers were similarly transformed. Thatcher's personal approval rating more than doubled over the course of the battle, from 25 percent at the start to 59 percent at the end, paving the way for a decisive victory in the following year's election.[26]

The British military's counterinvasion of the Falklands was code-named Operation Corporate, and though it was an odd name for a military campaign, it proved prescient. Thatcher used the enormous popularity afforded her by the victory to launch the very corporatist revolution she had told Hayek was impossible before the war. When the coal miners went on strike in 1984, Thatcher cast the standoff as a continuation of the war with Argentina, calling for similarly brutal resolve. She famously declared, "We had to fight the enemy without in the Falklands and now we have to fight the enemy within, which is much more difficult but just as dangerous to liberty."[27] With British workers now categorized as "the enemy within," Thatcher unleashed the full force of the state on the strikers, including, in a single confrontation, eight thousand truncheon-wielding riot police, many on horseback, to storm a plant picket line, leading to roughly seven hundred injuries. Over the course of the long strike, the number of injuries reached into the thousands. As the *Guardian* reporter Seumas Milne documents in his definitive account of the strike, *The Enemy Within: Thatcher's Secret War against the Miners*, the prime minister pressed the security services to intensify surveillance of the union and, in particular, its militant president, Arthur Scargill. What ensued was "the most ambitious counter-surveillance operation ever mounted in Britain." The union was infiltrated by multiple agents and informers, and all its phones were bugged, as were the homes and even the fish-and-chips shop frequented by its leadership.

The chief executive of the union was alleged, on the floor of the House of Commons, to have been an MI5 agent sent in to "destabilize and sabotage the union," though he denied the charge.[28]

Nigel Lawson, U.K. chancellor of the exchequer during the strike, explained that the Thatcher government considered the union to be its enemy. "It was just like arming to face the threat of Hitler in the late 1930s," Lawson said a decade later. "One had to prepare."[29] As in the Falklands, there was little interest in bargaining, just a focused determination to break the union, regardless of the cost (and with three thousand extra police a day, the cost was enormous). Colin Naylor, an acting police sergeant who was on the front lines of the conflict, described it as "a civil war."[30]

By 1985, Thatcher had won this war too: workers were going hungry and couldn't hold out; in the end 966 people were fired.[31] It was a devastating setback for Britain's most powerful union, and it sent a clear message to the others: if Thatcher was willing to go to the wall to break the coal miners, on whom the country depended for its lights and warmth, it would be suicide for weaker unions producing less crucial products and services to take on her new economic order. Better just to accept whatever was on offer. It was a message very similar to the one Ronald Reagan had sent a few months after he took office with his response to a strike by the air-traffic controllers. By not showing up to work, they had "forfeited their jobs and will be terminated," Reagan said. Then he fired 11,400 of the country's most essential workers in a single blow—a shock from which the U.S. labor movement has yet to fully recover.[32]

In Britain, Thatcher parlayed her victory in the Falklands and over the miners into a major leap forward for her radical economic agenda. Between 1984 and 1988, the government privatized, among others, British Telecom, British Gas, British Airways, British Airport Authority and British Steel, while it sold its shares in British Petroleum.

Much as the terrorist attacks of September 11, 2001, would take an unpopular president and hand him an opportunity to launch a massive privatization initiative (in Bush's case, the privatization of security, warfare and reconstruction), Thatcher used her war to launch the first mass privatization auction in a Western democracy. This was the real Operation Corporate, one with historic implications. Thatcher's successful harnessing of the Falklands War was the first definitive evidence that a Chicago School economic program did not need military dictatorships and torture chambers in order to advance. She had proved that with a large enough political crisis to rally around, a limited version of shock therapy could be imposed in a democracy.

Still, Thatcher had needed an enemy to unite the country, a set of extraordinary circumstances that justified her use of emergency measures and repression—a crisis that made her look tough and decisive rather than cruel and regressive. The war had served her purpose perfectly, but the Falklands War was an anomaly in the early eighties, a throwback to earlier colonial conflicts. If the eighties were really going to be the dawn of a new age of peace and democracy, as many claimed, then Falklands-type clashes would be far too infrequent to form the basis of a global political project.

It was in 1982 that Milton Friedman wrote the highly influential passage that best summarizes the shock doctrine: "Only a crisis—actual or perceived—produces real change. When that crisis occurs, the actions that are taken depend on the ideas that are lying around. That, I believe, is our basic function: to develop alternatives to existing policies, to keep them alive and available until the politically impossible becomes politically inevitable."[33] It was to become a kind of mantra for his movement in the new democratic era. Allan Meltzer elaborated on the philosophy: "Ideas are alternatives waiting on a crisis to serve as the catalyst of change. Friedman's model of influence was to legitimize ideas, to make them bearable, and worth trying when the opportunity comes."[34]

The kind of crisis Friedman had in mind was not military but economic. What he understood was that in normal circumstances, economic decisions are made based on the push and pull of competing interests—workers want jobs and raises, owners want low taxes and relaxed regulation, and politicians have to strike a balance between these competing forces. However, if an economic crisis hits and is severe enough—a currency meltdown, a market crash, a major recession—it blows everything else out of the water, and leaders are liberated to do whatever is necessary (or said to be necessary) in the name of responding to a national emergency. Crises are, in a way, democracy-free zones—gaps in politics as usual when the need for consent and consensus do not seem to apply.

The idea that market crashes can act as catalysts for revolutionary change has a long history on the far left, most notably in the Bolshevik theory that hyperinflation, by destroying the value of money, takes the masses one step closer to the destruction of capitalism itself.[35] This theory explains why a certain breed of sectarian leftist is forever calculating the exact conditions under which capitalism will reach "the crisis," much as evangelical Christians calibrate signs of the coming Rapture. In the mid-eighties, this Communist idea began to experience a powerful revival, picked up by Chicago School economists who argued that just as market crashes could precipitate left-wing revolutions, so too could they be used to spark right-wing counterrevolutions, a theory that became known as "the crisis hypothesis."[36]

Friedman's interest in crisis was also a clear attempt to learn from the victories of the left after the Great Depression: when the market crashed, Keynes and his disciples, previously voices in the wilderness, had been ready and waiting with their ideas, their New Deal solutions. In the seventies and early eighties, Friedman and his corporate underwriters had attempted to mimic this process with their unique brand of intellectual disaster preparedness. They painstakingly built up a new network of right-wing think tanks, including Heritage and Cato, and produced the most significant vehicle to disseminate Friedman's views, the ten-part PBS miniseries *Free to Choose*—underwritten by some of the largest corporations in the world, including Getty Oil, Firestone Tire & Rubber Co., PepsiCo, General Motors, Bechtel and General Mills.[37] When the next crisis hit, Friedman was determined that it would be his Chicago Boys who would be the ones ready with their ideas and their solutions.

At the time he first articulated the crisis theory in the early eighties, the U.S. was in a recession—a double whammy of high inflation and unemployment. And Chicago School policies, now known as Reaganomics, certainly held sway in Washington. But even Reagan didn't dare implement the kind of sweeping shock therapy that Friedman dreamed of, the kind he had prescribed in Chile.

Once again, it would be a Latin American country that would be the testing ground for Friedman's crisis theory—and this time, it wouldn't be a Chicago Boy who would lead the way, but a new breed of shock doctor, one more suited to the new democratic age.

CHAPTER 7

THE NEW DOCTOR SHOCK

ECONOMIC WARFARE REPLACES DICTATORSHIP

> Bolivia's situation could well be compared with the case of a person who has cancer. He knows he faces that most dangerous and painful operation which monetary stabilization and a number of other measures will undoubtedly be. Yet he has no alternative.
> —Cornelius Zondag, U.S. economic adviser to Bolivia, 1956.[1]

> The use of cancer in political discourse encourages fatalism and justifies "severe" measures—as well as strongly reinforcing the widespread notion that the disease is necessarily fatal. The concept of disease is never innocent. But it could be argued that the cancer metaphors are in themselves implicitly genocidal.
> —Susan Sontag, *Illness as Metaphor*, 1977[2]

In 1985, Bolivia was part of the democratic wave sweeping the developing world. For eighteen of the previous twenty-one years, Bolivians had been living under some form of dictatorship. Now they were getting the chance to choose their president in national elections.

Winning control over Bolivia's economy at this particular juncture looked less like a prize than a punishment, however: its debt was so high that the amount Bolivia owed in interest surpassed its entire national budget. A year earlier, in 1984, Ronald Reagan's administration pushed the country over the edge by funding an unprecedented attack on its coca farmers, who grow the green leaf that can be refined into cocaine. The siege, which turned a large section of Bolivia into a military zone, didn't just choke the coca trade, but cut off the source of roughly half of the country's export revenues, triggering an economic meltdown. As *The New York Times* reported, "When the army marched into the Chapare in August, closing the narcodollar pipeline part way, the shock wave immediately hit the thriving black market in dollars . . . less than a week after the Chapare occupation, the Government was forced to drop the peso's official value by more than half." A few months later, inflation had increased tenfold, and thousands were leaving the country in search of jobs in Argentina, Brazil, Spain and the United States.[3]

It was in those volatile circumstances, with inflation up to 14,000 percent, that Bolivia entered its historic 1985 national elections. The election was a race between two familiar figures for Bolivians—their former dictator, Hugo Banzer, and their former elected president, Víctor Paz Estenssoro. The vote was very close, and the final decision would be left to Bolivia's Congress, but Banzer's team was sure it had won. Before the results were announced, the party enlisted the help of a little-known thirty-year-old economist named Jeffrey Sachs to help develop an anti-inflation economic plan. Sachs was the rising star of Harvard's economics department, raking in academic awards and becoming one of the university's youngest tenured professors. A few months earlier, a delegation of Bolivian politicians had visited Harvard and seen Sachs in action; they had been impressed by his bravado—he had told them that he could turn around their inflationary crisis in a day. Sachs had no experience in development economics, but, by his own admission, "I thought that I knew just about everything that needed to be known" about inflation.[4]

Sachs had been heavily influenced by Keynes's writings on the connection between hyperinflation and the spread of fascism in Germany after the First World War. The peace agreement imposed on Germany had sent it into severe economic crisis—including a hyperinflation rate of 3.25 million percent in 1923—which was then compounded by the Great Depression a few years later. With an unemployment rate of 30 percent and generalized rage at what seemed a global conspiracy, the country was fertile ground for Nazism.

Sachs liked to quote Keynes's warning that "there is no subtler, no surer means of overturning the existing basis of society than to debauch the currency. The process engages all the hidden forces of economic law on the side of destruction."[5] He shared Keynes's view that it was the sacred duty of economists to suppress those forces of destruction at all costs. "The thing I got from Keynes," Sachs says, "was this deep sadness and sense of risk that things can go completely awry. And how incredibly stupid it was of us to leave Germany in a state of disrepair."[6] Sachs also told journalists that he regarded Keynes's lifestyle as a politically engaged, globe-trotting economist as a model for his own career.

Although Sachs shared Keynes's belief in the power of economics to fight poverty, he was also a product of Reagan's America, which was, in 1985, in the midst of a Friedman-inspired backlash against all that Keynes represented. Chicago School precepts about the supremacy of the free market had rapidly become the unquestioned orthodoxy in Ivy League economics departments, including Harvard's, and Sachs was definitely not immune. He admired Friedman's "faith in markets, his constant insistence on proper monetary management," calling it "far more accurate than fuzzy structuralist or pseudo-Keynesian arguments one hears a lot in the developing world."[7]

Those "fuzzy" arguments were the same ones that in Latin America had been suppressed by violence a decade earlier—the conviction that in order to escape poverty, the continent needed to break the colonial ownership structures with such interventionist policies as land reform, trade protections and subsidies, nationalization of natural resources, and cooperatively run workplaces. Sachs had little time for such structural changes. So although he knew next to nothing about Bolivia and its long history of colonial exploitation, the suppression of its indigenous inhabitants and the hard-won gains of its 1952 revolution, he was convinced that in addition to hyperinflation, Bolivia suffered from "socialist romanticism"—the same delusion of developmentalism that an earlier generation of U.S.-trained economists had tried to stamp out in the Southern Cone.[8]

Where Sachs parted ways with Chicago School orthodoxy was that he believed free-market policies needed to be supported by debt relief and generous aid—for the young Harvard economist, the invisible hand was not enough. This discrepancy eventually led Sachs to part ways from his more laissez-faire colleagues and devote his efforts exclusively to aid. But that split was years away. In Bolivia, Sachs's hybrid ideology merely made for some strange contradictions. For instance, when he got off the plane in La Paz, breathing the thin Andean air for the first time, he imagined himself as a latter-day Keynes arriving to save the Bolivian people from the "chaos and disorder" of hyperinflation.* Although the core tenet of Keynesianism is that

---

* Beating hyperinflation had not saved Germany from depression and then fascism, a contradiction Sachs has never addressed in his persistent use of this analogy.

countries in severe economic recession should spend money to stimulate the economy, Sachs took the opposite approach, advocating government austerity and price increases in the midst of the crisis—the same recipe for contraction that *BusinessWeek* had described in Chile as a "Dr. Strangelove world of deliberately induced depression."[9]

Sachs's advice to Banzer was straightforward: only sudden shock therapy would cure Bolivia's hyperinflation crisis. He proposed raising the price of oil tenfold and a range of other price deregulations and budget cuts. In a speech to the Bolivian-American Chamber of Commerce, Sachs again predicted that hyperinflation could be ended in a day, reporting that "the crowd was startled, and delighted, at the prospect."[10] Like Friedman, Sachs was a firm believer that, with a sudden policy jolt, "an economy can be reoriented from a dead end, a dead end of socialism or a dead end of mass corruption or a dead end of central planning, to a normal market economy."[11]

At the time Sachs made these bold promises, the results of Bolivia's elections were still up in the air. The former dictator Hugo Banzer was acting as if he had won, but his rival in the race, Victor Paz Estenssoro, hadn't yet given up. During the campaign, Paz Estenssoro had provided few concrete details about how he planned to deal with inflation. But he had served three times before as Bolivia's elected president, most recently in 1964, before he was overthrown in a coup. It was Paz who had been the face of Bolivia's developmentalist transformation, nationalizing the large tin mines, beginning to distribute land to indigenous peasants, defending the right of all Bolivians to vote. Like Argentina's Juan Perón, Paz was a complicated, omnipresent fixture on the political landscape, often switching allegiances abruptly in order to hold on to power or make a comeback. During the 1985 campaign, an aging Paz pledged allegiance to his "nationalist revolutionary" past and made vague statements about fiscal responsibility. He was not a socialist, but he was no Chicago School neoliberal—or so Bolivians believed.[12]

Since the final decision about who would be named president was up to Congress, this was a period of high-stakes backroom negotiations and horse-trading between the parties, the Congress and the Senate. One newly elected senator ended up playing a pivotal role: Gonzalo Sánchez de Lozada (known in Bolivia as Goni). He had lived in the United States for so long that he spoke Spanish with a heavy American accent and had returned to Bolivia to become one of the country's wealthiest businessmen. He owned Comsur, the second-largest private mine in the country, soon to be the largest. As a young man, Goni had studied at the University of Chicago, and though he was not an economist, he was strongly influenced by Friedman's ideas and recognized that they held tremendously profitable implications in the mining sector, which in Bolivia was still largely controlled by the state. When Sachs laid out his shock plans to Banzer's team, Goni was impressed.

The details of the backroom negotiations have never been disclosed, but the results are clear enough. On August 6, 1985, it was Paz who was sworn in as president of Bolivia. Only four days later, Paz appointed Goni to head up a top-secret bipartisan emergency economic team charged with radically re-structuring the economy. The group's starting point was Sachs's shock ther-apy, but it would go much further than anything he had suggested. In fact, it would propose dismantling the entire state-centered economic model that Paz himself had constructed decades earlier. At this point Sachs was back at Harvard, but he says he "was happy to hear that the ADN [Banzer's party] had shared a copy of our stabilization plan with the new president and his team."[13]

Paz's party had no idea that their leader had struck this backroom deal. With the exception of the minister of finance and the minister of planning, who were part of the secret group, Paz did not even tell his newly elected cabinet about the existence of the emergency economic team.[14]

For seventeen days straight, the emergency team met in the living room of Goni's palatial home. "We holed ourselves up there in a cautious and almost clandestine way," recalled the planning minister, Guillermo Bedregal, in an interview given in 2005, revealing these details for the first time.*[15] What they were contemplating was a radical overhaul of a national economy so sweeping that nothing like it had ever been attempted in a democracy. Pres-ident Paz was convinced that his only hope was to move as fast and suddenly as possible. That way, Bolivia's notoriously militant trade unions and peasant groups would be caught off guard and wouldn't have a chance to organize a response, or so he hoped. As Goni recalled, Paz "kept saying, 'If you are go-ing to do it, do it now. I can't operate twice.'"[16] The reason for Paz's post-election about-face remains something of a mystery. He died in 2001 and never did explain whether he had agreed to adopt Banzer's shock therapy program in exchange for being awarded the presidency, or whether he had

---

* For two decades, Bolivians did not know how their shock therapy program had been de-vised. In August 2005, twenty years after the drafting of the original decree, the Bolivian journalist Susan Velasco Portillo interviewed the original members of the emergency eco-nomic team, and several of them shared information about the clandestine operation. This account is primarily based on those memories.

undergone a heartfelt ideological conversion. Some insight was provided to me by Edwin Corr, the U.S. ambassador to Bolivia at the time. He recalled that he had met with all the political parties and made it clear that U.S. aid would flow if they went the shock route.

After seventeen days, Bedregal, the planning minister, had the draft of a textbook shock therapy program. It called for the elimination of food subsidies, the canceling of almost all price controls and a 300 percent hike in the price of oil.[17] Despite the fact that life was about to get a lot more expensive in an already desperately poor country, the plan froze government wages at their already low levels for a year. It also called for deep cuts to government spending, flung open Bolivia's borders to unrestricted imports and called for a downsizing of state companies, the precursor to privatization. Bolivia had missed the neoliberal revolution imposed on the rest of the Southern Cone in the seventies; now it was going to make up for lost time.

When the members of the emergency team had finished drafting the new laws, they still weren't ready to share them with Bolivia's elected representatives, let alone its voters, who had never cast their ballots for such a plan. They had one more task to complete. As a group, they drove over to the office of the International Monetary Fund's representative in Bolivia and told him what they were planning to do. His response was at once encouraging and harrowing: "This is what every official at the IMF has dreamed about. But if it doesn't work, luckily I have diplomatic immunity and I can catch a plane and flee."[18]

The Bolivians proposing the plan had no such escape hatch, and several were terrified of how the public was going to react. "They are going to kill us," predicted Fernando Prado, the youngest member of the group. Bedregal, the plan's main author, attempted to stiffen spines by comparing the team to fighter pilots attacking an enemy. "We have to be like the pilot of Hiroshima. When he dropped the atomic bomb he didn't know what he was doing, but when he saw the smoke he said: 'Oops, sorry!' And that's exactly what we have to do, launch the measures and then: Oops, sorry!"[19]

The idea that policy change should be like launching a surprise military attack is a recurring theme for economic shock therapists. In *Shock and Awe: Achieving Rapid Dominance*, the U.S. military doctrine published in 1996 that eventually formed the basis of the 2003 invasion of Iraq, the authors state that the invading force should "seize control of the environment and paralyze or so overload an adversary's perceptions and understanding of events so that the enemy would be incapable of resistance."[20] Economic shock works according to a similar theory: the premise is that people can develop responses to gradual change—a slashed health program here, a trade deal there—but if dozens of changes come from all directions at once, a feeling of futility sets in, and populations go limp.

Hoping to induce that sense of hopelessness, the Bolivian planners required all of their radical measures to be adopted at the same time, and all within the first hundred days of the new government. Rather than presenting each section of the plan as its own individual law (the new tax code, the new pricing law and so on), Paz's team insisted on bundling the entire revolution into a single executive decree, D.S. 21060. It contained 220 separate laws and covered every aspect of economic life in the country, making it the equivalent, in scope and ambition, to "The Brick," the hefty blueprint written by the Chicago Boys in preparation for Pinochet's coup. According to its authors, the entire program had to be accepted or rejected; it couldn't be amended. It was the economic equivalent of Shock and Awe.

When the document was complete, the team made five copies: one for Paz, one for Goni and one for the treasury minister. The destination of the other two copies revealed how certain Paz and his team were that many Bolivians would regard the plan as an act of war: one was for the head of the army and the other was for the chief of police. Paz's cabinet, however, was still in the dark. They continued to be under the mistaken impression that they were working for the same man who had nationalized the mines and redistributed land all those years ago.

Three weeks after being sworn in as president, Paz finally called his cabinet together to let them in on the surprise he had in store. He ordered the doors closed to the governing chambers and "instructed the secretaries to hold all of the ministers' telephone calls." Bedregal read the full sixty pages to the stunned audience. He was so nervous, he confessed, that he "even got a nosebleed only minutes later." Paz informed his cabinet members that the decree was not up for debate; in yet another backroom deal, he had already secured support from Banzer's right-wing opposition party. If they disagreed, he said, they could resign.

"I don't agree," announced the minister of industry.

"Please leave," Paz replied. The minister stayed. With inflation still soaring and strong hints that a shock therapy approach would be rewarded with significant financial aid from Washington, no one dared leave. Two days later, in a televised presidential address titled "Bolivia Is Dying," Paz dropped Bolivia's "Brick" on a completely unsuspecting public.

Sachs was correct in predicting that price increases would end hyperinflation. Within two years, inflation was down to 10 percent, impressive by any standard.[21] The broader legacy of Bolivia's neoliberal revolution is far more contentious. All economists agree that rapid inflation is enormously damaging, unsustainable and must be controlled—a process that imposes significant pain during the adjustment. The debate is over how a credible program can be achieved, as well as who, in any given society, is forced to bear the brunt of that pain. Ricardo Grinspun, a professor of economics specializing in Latin America at York University, explains that an approach in the Keynesian or developmentalist tradition seeks to mobilize support and share the burden through "a negotiated process involving key stakeholders—government, employers, farmers, unions and so on. In this way, the parties come to agreements over income policies, like wages and prices, at the same time that stabilization measures are implemented." In sharp contrast, says Grinspun, "the orthodox approach is to shift all the social cost onto the poor through shock therapy." That, he told me, is precisely what happened in Bolivia.

Just as Friedman had promised in Chile, freer trade was supposed to create jobs for the newly jobless. It didn't, and the unemployment rate increased from 20 percent at the time of the elections to between 25 and 30 percent two years later.[22] The state mining corporation alone—the same one that Paz had nationalized in the 1950s—was downsized from twenty-eight thousand employees to just six thousand.[23]

The minimum wage never recovered its value, and two years into the program, real wages were down 40 percent; at one point they would drop 70 percent.[24] In 1985, the year of shock therapy, the per capita average income in Bolivia was $845; two years later it had fallen to $789. This is the measure used by Sachs and the government, and despite the lack of progress it conveys, it does not begin to capture the degradation of daily life for many Bolivians. Average income is derived by adding up the country's total income and dividing by the number of people in the country; it glosses over the fact that shock therapy in Bolivia had the same effects that it had in the rest of the region: a small elite grew far wealthier while large portions of what had been the working class were discarded from the economy altogether and turned into surplus people. In 1987, Bolivian peasants, known as campesinos, were earning, on average, just $140 a year, less than one-fifth of the "average income."[25] That is the problem with measuring only the "average": it effectively erases these sharp divisions.

A leader of the peasants' union explained that "the government's statistics don't reflect the growing number of families forced to live in tents; the thousands of malnourished kids who get only a piece of bread and a cup of tea a day; the hundreds of campesinos who have come to the capital in search of work and end up begging on the streets."[26] That was the hidden story of Bolivia's shock therapy: hundreds of thousands of full-time jobs with pensions were eliminated, replaced with precarious ones with no protections at all. Between 1983 and 1988, the number of Bolivians eligible for social security dropped by 61 percent.[27]

Sachs, who returned to Bolivia as an adviser in the midst of the transition, opposed raising salaries to keep up with the price of food and gasoline and instead favored an emergency fund to help the hardest hit—a Band-Aid on what had become a gaping wound. Sachs returned to Bolivia at Paz Estenssoro's request and was working directly for the president. He is remembered as an unyielding presence. According to Goni (who would later become president of Bolivia), Sachs helped to stiffen the resolve of policy makers when public pressure was building against the human cost of shock therapy. "In his visits [Sachs] said, 'Look, all this gradualist stuff, it just doesn't work. When it really gets out of control you've got to stop it, like a medicine. You've got to take some radical steps; otherwise your patient is going to die."[28]

One immediate result of this resolve was that many of Bolivia's desperately poor were pushed to become coca growers, because it paid roughly ten times as much as other crops (somewhat of an irony since the original economic crisis was set off by the U.S.-funded siege on the coca farmers.)[29] By 1989, an estimated one in ten workers was turning to work in some aspect of the coca or cocaine industries.[30] These workers would include the family of Evo Morales, future president of Bolivia and a former leader of the militant coca growers' union.

The coca industry played a significant role in resuscitating Bolivia's economy and beating inflation (a fact now recognized by historians but never mentioned by Sachs in explanations of how his reforms triumphed over inflation).[31] Just two years after the "atomic bomb," illegal drug exports were generating more income for Bolivia than all its legal exports combined, and an estimated 350,000 people were earning a living in some facet of the drug trade. "For now," a foreign banker observed, "the Bolivian economy is hooked on cocaine."[32]

In the immediate aftermath of shock therapy, few outside Bolivia were talking about such complex repercussions. They were telling a far simpler story:

about a bold, boyish professor from Harvard who had, virtually single-handedly, "salvaged the inflation-wracked economy of Bolivia," according to *Boston Magazine*.[33] The victory over inflation that Sachs had helped engineer was enough to qualify Bolivia as a stunning free-market success story, "the most remarkable of modern times," as *The Economist* described it.[34] "Bolivia's Miracle" gave Sachs immediate star status in powerful financial circles and launched his career as the leading expert on crisis-struck economies, sending him on to Argentina, Peru, Brazil, Ecuador and Venezuela in the coming years.

The praise heaped on Sachs was not just about beating inflation in a poor country. It was that he had achieved what so many had claimed was impossible: he had helped stage a radical neoliberal transformation within the confines of a democracy and without a war, a change far more sweeping than those attempted by either Thatcher or Reagan. Sachs was fully aware of the historical significance of what he had accomplished. "Bolivia was really the first, in my view, combination of democratic reform combined with economic institutional change," he said years later. "And Bolivia much more than Chile showed that you could combine political liberalization and democracy with economic liberalization. That's an extremely important lesson, to have both of those working in parallel and each one reinforcing the other."[35]

The comparison with Chile was not incidental. Thanks to Sachs—"evangelist for democratic capitalism," as *The New York Times* described him—shock therapy had finally shaken off the stench of dictatorships and death camps that had been clinging to it ever since Friedman made his fateful trip to Santiago a decade earlier.[36] Sachs had proven, contrary to what the critics claimed, that the free-market crusade could not only survive but ride the democratic wave now sweeping the world. And Sachs, with his praise for Keynes and his unabashedly idealistic commitment to improving the lot of the developing world, was the perfect man to steer the crusade into this kinder, more peaceful era.

The Bolivian left had taken to calling Paz's decree *pinochetismo económico*—economic Pinochetism.[37] As far as the business community was concerned, both inside and outside Bolivia, that was the whole point: Bolivia had brought in Pinochet-style shock therapy, without a Pinochet—and under a center-left government, no less. As one Bolivian banker put it with admiration, "The things Pinochet did with a bayonet, Paz has done within a democratic system."[38]

The story of the Bolivian miracle has been told and retold, in newspaper and magazine articles, in profiles of Sachs, in Sachs's own best-selling book, and in documentary productions such as PBS's three-part series *Commanding Heights: The Battle for the World Economy*. There is one major problem: it isn't true. Bolivia did show that shock therapy could be imposed in a country that had just had elections, but it did not show that it could be imposed democratically or without repression—in fact, it proved, once again, that the opposite was still the case.

First, there was the obvious problem that President Paz had no mandate from Bolivian voters to remake the entire economic architecture of the country. He had run on a nationalist platform, which he abruptly abandoned in a backroom deal. Some years later, the influential free-market economist John Williamson coined a term for what Paz did: he called it "voodoo politics"; most people simply call it lying.[39] That was by no means the only problem with the democracy narrative.

Predictably, many of the voters who elected Paz were furious at his betrayal, and as soon as the decree was handed down, tens of thousands took to the streets to try to block a plan that would mean layoffs and deepening hunger. The major opposition came from the country's main labor federation, which called a general strike that brought industry to a halt. Paz's response made Thatcher's treatment of the miners seem tame. He immediately declared a "state of siege," and army tanks rolled through the streets of the capital, which was placed under a strict curfew. To travel through their own country, Bolivian citizens now needed special passes. Riot police raided union halls, a university and a radio station, as well as several factories. Political assemblies and marches were forbidden, and state permission was required to hold meetings.[40] Oppositional politics was effectively banned—just as it had been during the Banzer dictatorship.

To clear the streets, police arrested fifteen hundred demonstrators, dispersed crowds with tear gas and fired on strikers who they said had attacked their officers.[41] Paz also took further measures to make sure that the protests stopped for good. With the leaders of the labor federation on a hunger strike, Paz directed the police and military to round up the country's top two hundred union leaders, load them on planes and fly them to remote jails in the Amazon.[42] According to Reuters, the detainees included "the leadership of the Bolivian Labor Federation and other senior trade union officials," and they were taken "to isolated villages in the Amazon basin in northern Bolivia, where their movements [were] restricted."[43] It was a mass kidnapping, complete with a ransom demand: the prisoners would be released only if the unions called off their protests, which they eventually agreed to do. Filemon Escobar was a miner and labor activist on the streets in those years. In a recent telephone interview from Bolivia, he recalled that "they plucked the labor leaders from the streets and took them to the jungle to be eaten alive by the bugs. When they were released, the new economic plan was in place." According to Escobar, "The government didn't take people to the jungle to be tortured or killed, but so that they could go ahead with their economic plan."

This extraordinary state of siege stayed in place for three months, and since the plan was pushed through in one hundred days, that meant the country was under lockdown during the decisive shock therapy period. One year later, when the Paz government moved ahead with mass layoffs in the tin mines, the unions once again took to the streets, and the same series of dramatic events unfolded: a state of siege was declared, and two Bolivian Air Force planes carried one hundred of the country's top labor leaders to internment camps in Bolivia's tropical flatlands. This time, the kidnapped leaders included two former labor ministers and a former senator—recalling Pinochet's "VIP prison" in Southern Chile where Orlando Letelier had been taken. The leaders were held in the camps for two and half weeks until, once again, the unions agreed to call off their protests and hunger strike.[44]

It was a kind of junta lite. In order for the regime to impose economic shock therapy, certain people needed to disappear—if only temporarily. Though certainly less brutal, these disappearances served the same purpose as they had in the seventies. Interning Bolivia's trade unionists so that they could not resist the reforms cleared the path for the economic erasure of whole sectors of workers; their jobs were soon lost, and they ended up warehoused in the shantytowns and slums surrounding La Paz.

Sachs had gone to Bolivia quoting Keynes's warning about economic collapse breeding fascism, but he had proceeded to prescribe measures so painful that quasi-fascist measures were required for their enforcement.

The Paz government's crackdown was covered in the international press at the time, but only as a one- or two-day news story about generic riots in Latin America. When it came time to tell the tale of the triumph of "free-market reforms" in Bolivia, however, the events did not make it into the narrative (much as the symbiosis of Pinochet's violence and Chile's "economic miracle" is so often omitted). Jeffrey Sachs, of course, is not the one who called in the riot police or declared the state of siege, but he does devote a chapter of his book *The End of Poverty* to Bolivia's victory over inflation, and while he seems happy to take a share of the credit, he makes no mention of the repression required to carry out the plan. The closest he comes is an oblique reference to "tense moments in the early months of the stabilization program."[45]

In other accounts, even that admission is erased. Goni went so far as to claim that "stabilization had been achieved in a democracy without going against people's human liberties, letting people express themselves."[46] A less idealized assessment came from a minister in the Paz government, who said that they "behaved like authoritarian pigs."[47]

That dissonance may be the most lasting legacy of Bolivia's shock therapy experiment. Bolivia had shown that wrenching shock therapy still needed to be accompanied by shocking attacks on inconvenient social groups and on democratic institutions. It also showed that the corporatist crusade could advance by these baldly authoritarian means and still be applauded as democratic because elections had taken place, regardless of how completely civil liberties were suppressed in the aftermath or how fully democratic wishes were ignored. (It was a lesson that would prove particularly handy for Russia's Boris Yeltsin, among other leaders, in the years to come.) In this way, Bolivia provided a blueprint for a new, more palatable kind of authoritarianism, a civilian coup d'état, one carried out by politicians and economists in business suits rather than soldiers in military uniforms—all unfolding within the official shell of a democratic regime.

CHAPTER 8

CRISIS WORKS

THE PACKAGING OF SHOCK THERAPY

> Well, what is the sense of ruining my head and erasing my memory, which is my capital, and putting me out of business? It was a brilliant cure but we lost the patient.
>
> —Ernest Hemingway on his electroshock therapy, shortly before committing suicide, 1961[1]

For Jeffrey Sachs, the lesson of his first international adventure was that hyperinflation could indeed be stopped in its tracks, with the right tough and drastic measures. He had gone to Bolivia to slay inflation and he had done it. Case closed.

John Williamson, one of the most influential right-wing economists in Washington and a key adviser to the IMF and the World Bank, was watching Sachs's experiment closely, and he saw something of far greater significance in Bolivia. He described the shock therapy program as "the big bang" moment—a breakthrough in the campaign to bring the Chicago School doctrine to the entire globe.[2] The reason had little to do with economics and everything to do with tactics.

It may not have been his intention, but in quite spectacular fashion Sachs had proven that Friedman's theory about crisis was absolutely correct. Bolivia's hyperinflation meltdown was the excuse that was needed to push through a program that would have been politically impossible under normal circumstances. Here was a country with a strong, militant labor movement and a powerful left tradition, site of Che Guevara's last stand. Yet it had been forced to accept draconian shock therapy in the name of stabilizing its out-of-control currency.

By the mid-eighties, several economists had observed that a true hyperinflation crisis simulates the effects of a military war—spreading fear and confusion, creating refugees and causing large loss of life.[3] It was strikingly clear that in Bolivia, hyperinflation had played the same role as had Pinochet's "war" in Chile and the Falklands War for Margaret Thatcher—it had created the context for emergency measures, a state of exception during which the rules of democracy could be suspended and economic control could be temporarily handed over to the team of experts in Goni's living room. For hard-core Chicago School ideologues like Williamson, that meant that hyperinflation was not a problem to be solved, as Sachs believed, but a golden opportunity to be seized.

There was no shortage of such opportunities in the eighties. In fact, much of the developing world, but particularly Latin America, was at that very moment spiraling into hyperinflation. The crisis was the result of two main factors, both with roots in Washington financial institutions. The first was their insistence on passing on illegitimate debts accumulated under dictatorships to new democracies. The second was the Friedman-inspired decision at the U.S. Federal Reserve to allow interest rates to soar, which massively increased the size of those debts overnight.

Passing on Odious Debts

Argentina was a textbook case. In 1983, when the junta collapsed after the Falklands War, Argentines elected Raúl Alfonsín as their new president. The newly liberated country was rigged to detonate, thanks to the planting of a so-called debt bomb. As part of what the outgoing junta had termed a "dignified transition" to democracy, Washington insisted that the new government agree to pay off the debts amassed by the generals. During junta rule, Argentina's external debt had ballooned from $7.9 billion the year before the coup to $45 billion at the time of the handover—debts owed to the International Monetary Fund, the World Bank, the U.S. Export-Import Bank and private banks based in the U.S. It was much the same across the region. In Uruguay, the junta took a debt of half a billion dollars when it seized power and expanded it to $5 billion, a huge load in a country of only 3 million people. In Brazil, the most dramatic case, the generals, who came to power in 1964 promising financial order, managed to take the debt from $3 billion to $103 billion in 1985.[4]

At the time of the transitions to democracy, powerful arguments were made, both moral and legal, that these debts were "odious" and that newly liberated people should not be forced to pay the bills of their oppressors and tormentors. The case was especially strong in the Southern Cone because so much of the foreign credit had gone straight to the military and police during the dictatorship years—to pay for guns, water cannons and state-of-the-art torture camps. In Chile, for instance, the loans bankrolled a tripling in military spending, enlarging Chile's army from forty-seven thousand in 1973 to eighty-five thousand in 1980. In Argentina, the World Bank estimates that roughly $10 billion of the money borrowed by the generals went to military purchases.[5]

Much of what wasn't spent on weapons simply vanished. A culture of corruption permeated junta rule—a glimpse of the debauched future to come when the same free-wheeling economic policies spread to Russia, China and the "free fraud zone" of occupied Iraq (to borrow a phrase from a disaffected U.S. adviser).[6] According to a 2005 U.S. Senate report, Pinochet maintained a byzantine web of at least 125 secret foreign bank accounts listed under the names of various family members and combinations of his own name. The accounts, the most notorious of which were at the Washington, D.C.–based Riggs Bank, hid an estimated $27 million.[7]

In Argentina, the junta has been accused of being even more acquisitive. In 1984, José Martínez de Hoz, architect of the economic program, was arrested on fraud charges relating to a massive state subsidy to one of the companies he used to head (the case was later dismissed).[8] The World Bank, meanwhile, later tracked what happened to $35 billion in foreign loans borrowed by the junta and found that $19 billion—46 percent of the total—was moved offshore. Swiss officials have confirmed that much of it ended up in numbered accounts.[9] The U.S. Federal Reserve observed that in 1980 alone, Argentina's debt expanded by $9 billion; in that same year, the amount of money deposited abroad by Argentine citizens increased by $6.7 billion.[10] Larry Sjaastad, a famed University of Chicago professor who personally trained many of Argentina's Chicago Boys, has described these missing billions (stolen under the noses of his students) as "the greatest fraud of the twentieth century."*[11]

The junta embezzlers even enlisted their victims in these crimes. At the

---

* It may well have been at the time, but the century was not over—Russia's Chicago School experiment was to come.

ESMA torture center in Buenos Aires, prisoners with strong language skills or university educations were regularly pulled out of their cells to perform clerical tasks for their captors. One survivor, Graciela Daleo, was instructed to type a document advising officers on offshore tax havens for the money they were embezzling.[12]

The remainder of the national debt was mostly spent on interest payments, as well as shady bailouts for private firms. In 1982, just before Argentina's dictatorship collapsed, the junta did one last favor for the corporate sector. Domingo Cavallo, president of Argentina's central bank, announced that the state would absorb the debts of large multinational and domestic firms that had, like Chile's piranhas, borrowed themselves to the verge of bankruptcy. The tidy arrangement meant that these companies continued to own their assests and profits, but the public had to pay off between $15 and $20 billion of their debts; among the companies to receive this generous treatment were Ford Motor Argentina, Chase Manhattan, Citibank, IBM and Mercedes-Benz.[13]

Those who favored defaulting on these illegitimately accumulated debts argued that the lenders knew, or ought to have known, that the money was being spent on repression and corruption. This case was bolstered recently when the State Department declassified the transcript of a meeting held on October 7, 1976, between Henry Kissinger, then secretary of state, and Argentina's foreign minister under the military dictatorship, the admiral César Augusto Guzzetti. After discussing the international human rights outcry following the coup, Kissinger said, "Look, our basic attitude is that we would like you to succeed. I have an old-fashioned view that friends ought to be supported. . . . The quicker you succeed, the better." Kissinger then moved on to the topic of loans, encouraging Guzzetti to apply for as much foreign assistance as possible and fast, before Argentina's "human rights problem" tied the hands of the U.S. administration. "There are two loans in the bank," Kissinger said, referring to the Inter-American Development Bank. "We have no intention of voting against them." He also instructed the minister, "Proceed with your Export-Import Bank requests. We would like your economic program to succeed and we will do our best to help you."[14]

The transcript proves that the U.S. government approved loans to the junta knowing they were being used in the midst of a campaign of terror. In the early eighties, it was these odious debts that Washington insisted Argentina's new democratic government had to repay.

The Debt Shock

On their own, the debts would have been an enormous burden on the new democracies, but that burden was about to get much heavier. A new kind of shock was in the news: the Volcker Shock. Economists used this term to describe the impact of the decision made by Federal Reserve chairman Paul Volcker when he dramatically increased interest rates in the United States, letting them rise as high as 21 percent, reaching a peak in 1981 and lasting through the mid-eighties.[15] In the U.S., rising interest rates led to a wave of bankruptcies, and in 1983 the number of people who defaulted on their mortgages tripled.[16]

The deepest pain, however, was felt outside the U.S. In developing countries carrying heavy debt loads, the Volcker Shock—also known as the "debt shock" or the "debt crisis"—was like a giant Taser gun fired from Washington, sending the developing world into convulsions. Soaring interest rates meant higher interest payments on foreign debts, and often the higher payments could only be met by taking on more loans. The debt spiral was born. In Argentina, the already huge debt of $45 billion passed on by the junta grew rapidly until it reached $65 billion in 1989, a situation reproduced in poor countries around the world.[17] It was after the Volcker Shock that Brazil's debt exploded, doubling from $50 billion to $100 billion in six years. Many African countries, having borrowed heavily in the seventies, found themselves in similar straits: Nigeria's debt in the same short time period went from $9 billion to $29 billion.[18]

These were not the only economic shocks zapping the developing world in the eighties. A "price shock" occurs every time the price of an export commodity like coffee or tin drops by 10 percent or more. According to the IMF, developing countries experienced 25 such shocks between 1981 and 1983; between 1984 and 1987, the height of the debt crisis, they experienced 140 such shocks, pushing them deeper into debt.[19] One hit Bolivia in 1986, the year after it had swallowed Jeffrey Sachs's bitter medicine and submitted to a capitalist makeover. The price of tin, Bolivia's major export other than coca, dropped by 55 percent, devastating the country's economy through no fault of its own. (This was precisely the kind of dependence on raw resource exports that developmentalist economics had been trying to transcend in the fifties and sixties—an idea dismissed as "fuzzy" by the Northern economic establishment.)

This is where Friedman's crisis theory became self-reinforcing. The more the global economy followed his prescriptions, with floating interest rates, deregulated prices and export-oriented economies, the more crisis-prone the system became, producing more and more of precisely the type of meltdowns he had identified as the only circumstances under which governments would take more of his radical advice.

In this way, crisis is built into the Chicago School model. When limitless sums of money are free to travel the globe at great speed, and speculators are able to bet on the value of everything from cocoa to currencies, the result is enormous volatility. And, since free-trade policies encourage poor countries to continue to rely on the export of raw resources such as coffee, copper, oil or wheat, they are particularly vulnerable to getting trapped in a vicious circle of continuing crisis. A sudden drop in the price of coffee sends entire economies into depression, which is then deepened by currency traders who, seeing a country's financial downturn, respond by betting against its currency, causing its value to plummet. When soaring interest rates are added, and national debts balloon overnight, you have a recipe for potential economic mayhem.

Chicago School believers tend to portray the mid-eighties onward as a smooth and triumphant victory march for their ideology: at the same time that countries were joining the democratic wave, they had the collective epiphany that free people and unfettered free markets go hand in hand. That epiphany was always fictional. What actually happened is that just as citizens were finally winning their long-denied freedoms, escaping the shock of the torture chambers under the likes of the Philippines' Ferdinand Marcos and Uruguay's Juan María Bordaberry, they were hit with a perfect storm of financial shocks—debt shocks, price shocks and currency shocks—created by the increasingly volatile, deregulated global economy.

Argentina's experience of how the debt crisis was compounded by these other shocks was, unfortunately, typical. Raúl Alfonsín took office in 1983, in the midst of the Volcker Shock, which placed the new government in crisis mode from day one. In 1985, inflation was so bad that Alfonsín was forced to unveil a brand-new currency, the austral, gambling that a fresh start would allow him to regain control. Within four years, prices had soared so high that massive food riots broke out, and Argentine restaurants were using the currency as wallpaper because it was cheaper than paper. In June 1989, with inflation up 203 percent that month alone, and five months before his term was set to expire, Alfonsín gave up: he resigned and called early elections.[20]

Other options were available to politicians in Alfonsín's position. He could have defaulted on Argentina's huge debts. He could have joined with neighboring governments in the same crisis and formed a debtors' cartel. These governments could have created a common market based on developmentalist principles, a process that had begun when the region was torn apart by sadistic military regimes. But part of the challenge at the time had to do with the legacy of state terror faced by new democracies. In the eighties and nineties, much of the developing world was in the grip of a kind of terror hangover, free on paper but still cautious and wary. Having finally escaped the darkness of dictatorship, few elected politicians were willing to risk inviting another round of U.S.-supported coups d'état by pushing the very policies that had provoked the coups of the seventies—especially when the military officials who had staged them were, for the most part, not in prison but, having negotiated immunity, in their barracks, watching.

Understandably unwilling to go to war with the Washington institutions that owned their debts, crisis-struck new democracies had little choice but to play by Washington's rules. And then, in the early eighties, Washington's rules got a great deal stricter. That's because the debt shock coincided precisely, and not coincidentally, with a new era in North-South relations, one that would make military dictatorships largely unnecessary. It was the dawn of the era of "structural adjustment"—otherwise known as the dictatorship of debt.

Philosophically, Milton Friedman did not believe in the IMF or the World Bank: they were classic examples of big government interfering with the delicate signals of the free market. So it was ironic that there was a virtual conveyor belt delivering Chicago Boys to the two institutions' hulking headquarters on Nineteenth Street in Washington, D.C., where they took up many of the top positions.

Arnold Harberger, who headed the University of Chicago's Latin America program, often brags about how many of his graduates landed powerful jobs at the World Bank and the IMF. "There was one moment in time when four regional chief economists at the World Bank had been my students in Chicago. One of them, Marcelo Selowsky, went off to be the chief economist for the newly minted ex-Soviet empire area, which is the biggest such job in the whole Bank. And guess what? He was replaced by yet another former student, Sebastian Edwards. So it's very nice to see these people moving up, and I'm proud to have played a part in their development as economists."[21]

Another star was Claudio Loser, an Argentine who graduated from the University of Chicago in 1971 and went on to become director of the Western Hemisphere Department of the IMF, the most senior post dealing with Latin America.* Chicagoans occupied many other senior IMF posts as well, including the second-highest position, first deputy managing director, as well as chief economist, director of research and senior economist of the African Department.[22]

Friedman may have opposed the institutions on philosophical grounds, but practically, there were no institutions better positioned to implement his crisis theory. When countries were sent spiraling into crisis in the eighties, they had nowhere else to turn but the World Bank and the IMF. When they did, they hit a wall of orthodox Chicago Boys, trained to see their economic catastrophes not as problems to solve but as precious opportunities to leverage in order to secure a new free-market frontier. Crisis opportunism was now the guiding logic of the world's most powerful financial institutions. It was also a fundamental betrayal of their founding principles.

Like the UN, the World Bank and the IMF were created in direct response to the horror of the Second World War. With the goal of never again repeating the mistakes that had allowed fascism to rise in the heart of Europe, the world powers came together in 1944 in Bretton Woods, New Hampshire, to create a new economic architecture. The World Bank and the IMF, financed through contributions by their initial forty-three member countries, were given the explicit mandate to prevent future economic shocks and crashes like the ones that had so destabilized Weimar Germany. The World Bank would make long-term investments in development to pull countries out of poverty, while the IMF would act as a kind of global shock absorber, promoting economic policies that reduced financial speculation and market volatility. When a country looked as though it was falling into crisis, the IMF would leap in with stabilizing grants and loans, thereby preventing crises before they occurred.[23] The two institutions, located across the street from each other in Washington, would coordinate their responses.

John Maynard Keynes, who headed the U.K. delegation, was convinced that the world had finally recognized the political perils of leaving the mar-

---

* Loser was fired after Argentina's 2001 collapse. The consensus was that the IMF under his watch was so enamored of free-market policies that, as long as countries kept cutting spending and privatizing their economies, it continued to lavish loans on them, overlooking glaring weaknesses in their economies, such as mass unemployment and rampant corruption—not to mention unsustainable debt to the IMF.

ket to regulate itself. "Few believed it possible," Keynes said at the conference's end. But if the institutions stayed true to their founding principles, "the brotherhood of man will have become more than a phrase."[24]

The IMF and the World Bank did not live up to that universal vision; from the start they allocated power not on the basis of "one country, one vote," like the UN General Assembly, but rather on the size of each country's economy—an arrangement that gives the United States an effective veto over all major decisions, with Europe and Japan controlling most of the rest. That meant that when Reagan and Thatcher came to power in the eighties, their highly ideological administrations were essentially able to harness the two institutions for their own ends, rapidly increasing their power and turning them into the primary vehicles for the advancement of the corporatist crusade.

The colonization of the World Bank and the IMF by the Chicago School was a largely unspoken process, but it became official in 1989 when John Williamson unveiled what he called "the Washington Consensus." It was a list of economic policies that he said both institutions now considered the bare minimum for economic health—"the common core of wisdom embraced by all serious economists."[25] These policies, masquerading as technical and uncontentious, included such bald ideological claims as all "state enterprises should be privatized" and "barriers impeding the entry of foreign firms should be abolished."[26] When the list was complete, it made up nothing less than Friedman's neoliberal triumvirate of privatization, deregulation/free trade and drastic cuts to government spending. These were the policies, Williamson said, "that were being urged on Latin America by the powers-that-be in Washington."[27] Joseph Stiglitz, former chief economist of the World Bank and one of the last holdouts against the new orthodoxy, wrote that "Keynes would be rolling over in his grave were he to see what has happened to his child."[28]

Officials with the World Bank and the IMF had always made policy recommendations when they handed out loans, but in the early eighties, emboldened by the desperation of developing countries, those recommendations morphed into radical free-market demands. When crisis-struck countries came to the IMF seeking debt relief and emergency loans, the fund responded with sweeping shock therapy programs, equivalent in scope to "The Brick" drafted by the Chicago Boys for Pinochet and the 220-law decree cooked up in Goni's living room in Bolivia.

The IMF issued its first full-fledged "structural adjustment" program in

1983. For the next two decades, every country that came to the fund for a major loan was informed that it needed to revamp its economy from top to bottom. Davison Budhoo, an IMF senior economist who designed structural adjustment programs in Latin America and Africa throughout the eighties, admitted later that "everything we did from 1983 onward was based on our new sense of mission to have the south 'privatised' or die; towards this end we ignominiously created economic bedlam in Latin America and Africa in 1983–88."[29]

Despite this radical (and highly profitable) new mission, the IMF and the bank always claimed that everything they did was in the interest of stabilization. The fund's official mandate was still crisis prevention—not social engineering or ideological transformation—so stabilization needed to be the official rationale. The reality was that in country after country, the international debt crisis was being methodically leveraged to advance the Chicago School agenda, based on a ruthless application of Friedman's shock doctrine.

Economists at the World Bank and the IMF admitted this at the time, although the admissions were generally made in coded economic language and restricted to specialized forums and publications for fellow "technocrats." Dani Rodrik, a renowned Harvard economist who worked extensively with the World Bank, described the entire construct of "structural adjustment" as an ingenious marketing strategy. "The World Bank must be given credit," Rodrik wrote in 1994, "for having invented and successfully marketed the concept of 'structural adjustment,' a concept that *packaged together* microeconomic and macroeconomic reforms. *Structural adjustment was sold as the process that countries needed to undergo in order to save their economies from the crisis.* For governments that bought into the package, the distinction between sound macroeconomic policies that maintain external balance and stable prices, on the one hand, and policies that determine openness [like free trade], on the other, *was obfuscated.*"[30]

The principle was simple: countries in crisis desperately need emergency aid to stabilize their currencies. When privatization and free-trade policies are packaged together with a financial bailout, countries have little choice but to accept the whole package. The really clever part was that the economists themselves knew that free trade had nothing to do with ending a crisis, but that information was expertly "obfuscated." Rodrik meant his comment as a compliment. Not only did this bundling work in getting poor countries to accept the policies selected for them by Washington, but it was the only thing that worked—and Rodrik had the numbers to back up his claim. He had studied all the countries that adopted radical free-trade policies in the eighties and found that "no significant case of trade reform in a developing country in the 1980s took place outside the context of a serious economic crisis."[31]

It was a staggering admission. At this point in history, the bank and the fund were publicly insisting that governments the world over had seen the light and realized that the Washington Consensus policies were the only recipe for stability, and therefore democracy. Yet here was an acknowledgment, made inside the Washington establishment, that developing countries were submitting to them only through a combination of false pretenses and bald extortion: Want to save your country? Sell it off. Rodrik even conceded that privatization and free trade—two central pieces of the structural adjustment package—had no direct link with creating stability. To argue otherwise, according to Rodrik, was "bad economics."[32]

Argentina—the "model student" of the IMF in this period—once again offers a clear window into the mechanics of the new order. After the hyperinflation crisis forced President Alfonsín to resign, he was replaced by Carlos Menem, a Peronist governor from a small province who wore leather jackets, had muttonchop sideburns and seemed tough enough to stand up to both the still-ominous military and the creditors. After all the violent attempts that had been made to erase the Peronist party and the trade union movement, Argentina now had a president who had run a pro-union campaign promising to revive Juan Perón's nationalist economic policies. It was a moment with many of the same emotional echoes as Paz's inauguration in Bolivia.

Too many, as it turned out. After a year in office, and under intense pressure from the IMF, Menem embarked on a defiant course of "voodoo politics." Elected as the symbol of the party that had opposed the dictatorship, Menem appointed Domingo Cavallo as his economy minister, bringing back to power the junta-era official responsible for bailing out the debts of the corporate sector—the dictatorship's parting gift.[33] His appointment was what economists call "a signal"—an unmistakable indication, in this case, that the new government would pick up and continue the corporatist experiment started by the junta. The Buenos Aires stock market responded with the equivalent of a standing ovation: a 30 percent spike in trading on the day Cavallo's name was announced.[34]

Cavallo immediately called for ideological reinforcements, stacking the government with former students of Milton Friedman and Arnold Harberger.

Virtually all the country's top economic posts were filled by Chicago Boys: president of the central bank was Roque Fernández, who had worked at both the IMF and the World Bank; vice president of the central bank was Pedro Pou, a Chicago Boy who had worked for the dictatorship; the chief central bank adviser was the Pablo Guidotti, who came directly from his job working at the IMF under another former University of Chicago professor, Michael Mussa.

Argentina was not unique in this regard. By 1999, the Chicago School international alumni included more than twenty-five government ministers and more than a dozen central bank presidents from Israel to Costa Rica, an extraordinary level of influence for one university department.[35] In Argentina, as in so many other countries, the Chicago Boys formed a kind of ideological pincer around the elected government, one group squeezing from within, another exerting its pressure from Washington. For instance, the IMF delegations to Buenos Aires were often led by Claudio Loser, the Argentine Chicago Boy, which meant that when he met with the finance ministry and the central bank, the meetings were not adversarial negotiations but collegial discussions among friends, former classmates at the University of Chicago and recent coworkers on Nineteenth Street. A book published in Argentina about the effect of this global economic fraternity is aptly titled *Buenos Muchachos,* a reference to Martin Scorsese's mafia classic, *Goodfellas.*[36]

The members of this fraternity were in enthusiastic agreement about what needed to be done with Argentina's economy—and how to pull it off. The Cavallo Plan, as it came to be called, was based on the clever packaging trick that both the World Bank and the IMF had perfected: harnessing the chaos and desperation of a hyperinflation crisis to pass privatization off as an integral part of the rescue mission. So, to stabilize the money system, Cavallo quickly made massive cuts to public spending and launched another new currency, the Argentine peso, pegged to the U.S. dollar. Within a year, inflation was down to 17.5 percent and was virtually eliminated a few years later.[37] This dealt with the runaway currency but "obfuscated" the other half of the program.

Argentina's dictatorship, for all its commitment to pleasing foreign investors, had left large and desirable pieces of the economy in state hands, from the national airline to Patagonia's impressive oil reserves. As far as Cavallo and his Chicago Boys were concerned, the revolution was only half finished, and they were determined to use the economic crisis to complete their work.

In the early nineties, the Argentine state sold off the riches of the country so rapidly and so completely that the project far surpassed what had taken place in Chile a decade earlier. By 1994, 90 percent of all state enterprises had been sold to private companies, including Citibank, Bank Boston, France's Suez and Vivendi, Spain's Repsol and Telefónica. Before making the sales, Menem and Cavallo had generously performed a valuable service for the new owners: they had fired roughly 700,000 of their workers, according to Cavallo's own estimates; some put the number much higher. The oil company alone lost 27,000 workers during the Menem years. An admirer of Jeffrey Sachs, Cavallo called this process "shock therapy." Menem had an even more brutal phrase for it: in a country still traumatized by mass torture, he called it "major surgery without anesthetic."*[38]

In the midst of the transformation, *Time* magazine put Menem on its cover, his face grinning out of the middle of a sunflower, under the headline "Menem's Miracle."[39] And it was a miracle—Menem and Cavallo had pulled off a radical and painful privatization program without sparking a national revolt. How had they done it?

Years later, Cavallo explained. "At the time of hyperinflation it's terrible for the people, particularly for low-income people and small savers, because they see that in a few hours or in a few days they are being told their salaries got destroyed by the price increases, which take place at an incredible speed. That is why the people ask the government, 'Please do something.' And if the government comes with a good stabilization plan, that is the opportunity to also accompany that plan with other reforms . . . the most important reforms were related to the opening up of the economy and to the deregulation and the privatization process. But the only way to implement all those reforms was, at that time, to take advantage of the situation created by hyperinflation, because the population was ready to accept drastic changes in order to eliminate hyperinflation and to go back to normality."[40]

---

* In January 2006, long after Cavallo and Menem were out of office, Argentines received some surprising news. It turned out that the Cavallo Plan wasn't Cavallo's at all, nor was it the IMF's: Argentina's entire early-nineties shock therapy program was written in secret by JP Morgan and Citibank, two of Argentina's largest private creditors. In the course of a lawsuit against the Argentine government, the noted historian Alejandro Olmos Gaona uncovered a jaw-dropping 1,400-page document written by the two U.S. banks for Cavallo in which "the policies carried out by the government from '92 on are drawn up . . . the privatization of utilities, the labour law reform, the privatization of the pension system. It is all laid out with great attention to detail. . . . Everyone believes that the economic plan pursued since 1992 was Domingo Cavallo's creation, but that's not the way it is."

In the long term, Cavallo's program in its entirety would prove disastrous for Argentina. His method of stabilizing the currency—pegging the peso to the U.S. dollar—made it so expensive to produce goods inside the country that local factories could not compete with the cheap imports flooding the country. So many jobs were lost that well over half the country would eventually be pushed below the poverty line. In the short term, however, the plan worked brilliantly: Cavallo and Menem had smuggled privatization in while the country was in shock from hyperinflation. Crisis had done its job.

What Argentina's leaders pulled off in this period was a psychological more than an economic technique. As Cavallo, a junta veteran, well understood, in moments of crisis, people are willing to hand over a great deal of power to anyone who claims to have a magic cure—whether the crisis is a financial meltdown or, as the Bush administration would later show, a terrorist attack.

And that is how the crusade that Friedman began managed to survive the dreaded transition to democracy—not by its proponents persuading electorates of the wisdom of their worldview, but by moving deftly from crisis to crisis, expertly exploiting the desperation of economic emergencies to push through policies that would tie the hands of fragile new democracies. Once the tactic was perfected, opportunities just seemed to multiply. The Volcker Shock would be followed by the Mexican Tequila Crisis in 1994, the Asian Contagion in 1997 and the Russian Collapse in 1998, which was followed shortly afterward by one in Brazil. When these shocks and crises started to lose their power, even more cataclysmic ones would appear: tsunamis, hurricanes, wars and terrorist attacks. Disaster capitalism was taking shape.

PART 4

LOST IN TRANSITION

WHILE WE WEPT, WHILE WE TREMBLED, WHILE WE DANCED

These worst of times give rise to the best of opportunities for those who understand the need for fundamental economic reform.

—Stephan Haggard and John Williamson, *The Political Economy of Policy Reform*, 1994

CHAPTER 9

SLAMMING THE DOOR ON HISTORY

A CRISIS IN POLAND, A MASSACRE IN CHINA

I live in a Poland that is now free, and I consider Milton Friedman to be one of the main intellectual architects of my country's liberty.
—Leszek Balcerowicz, former finance minister of Poland, November 2006[1]

There's a certain chemical that gets released in your stomach when you make ten times your money. And it's addictive.
—William Browder, a U.S. money manager, on investing in Poland in the early days of capitalism[2]

We certainly must not stop eating for fear of choking.
—*People's Daily*, the official state newspaper, on the need to continue free-market reforms after the Tiananmen Square massacre[3]

Before the Berlin Wall fell, becoming the defining symbol of the collapse of Communism, there was another image that held out the promise of Soviet barriers coming down. It was Lech Walesa, a laid-off electrician with a handlebar moustache and disheveled hair, climbing over a steel fence festooned with flowers and flags in Gdańsk, Poland. The fence protected the Lenin shipyards and the thousands of workers who had barricaded themselves inside to protest a Communist Party decision to raise the price of meat.

The workers' strike was an unprecedented show of defiance against the Moscow-controlled government, which had ruled Poland for thirty-five years. No one knew what would happen: Would Moscow send tanks? Would they fire on the strikers and force them to work? As the strike wore on, the shipyard became a pocket of popular democracy within an authoritarian country, and the workers expanded their demands. They no longer wanted their work lives controlled by party apparatchiks claiming to speak for the working class. They wanted their own independent trade union, and they wanted the right to negotiate, bargain and strike. Not waiting for permission, they voted to form that union and called it Solidarność, Solidarity.[4] That was 1980, the year the world fell in love with Solidarity and with its leader, Lech Walesa.

Walesa, then thirty-six, was so in tune with the aspirations of Poland's workers that they seemed in spiritual communion. "We eat the same bread!" he bellowed into the microphone in the Gdańsk shipyard. It was a reference not only to Walesa's own unassailable blue-collar credentials but also to the powerful role that Catholicism played in this trail-blazing new movement. With religion frowned upon by party officials, the workers wore their faith as a badge of courage, lining up to take Communion behind the barricades. Walesa, a bracing mix of bawdy and pious, opened the Solidarity office with a wooden crucifix in one hand and a bouquet of flowers in the other. When it came time to sign the first landmark labor agreement between Solidarity and the government, Walesa marked his name with "a giant souvenir pen bearing the likeness of John Paul II." The admiration was mutual; the Polish pope told Walesa that his prayers were with Solidarity.[5]

Solidarity spread through the country's mines, shipyards and factories with ferocious speed. Within a year, it had 10 million members—almost half of Poland's working-age population. Having won the right to bargain, Solidarity started making concrete headway: a five-day work week instead of six, and more say in the running of factories. Tired of living in a country that worshipped an idealized working class but abused actual workers, Solidarity members denounced the corruption and brutality of the party functionaries who answered not to the people of Poland but to remote and isolated bureaucrats in Moscow. All the desire for democracy and self-determination suppressed by one-party rule was being poured into local Solidarity unions, sparking a mass exodus of members from the Communist Party.

Moscow recognized the movement as the most serious threat yet to its Eastern empire. Inside the Soviet Union, opposition was still coming largely from human rights activists, many of whom were on the political right. But Solidarity's members couldn't easily be dismissed as stooges of capitalism—they were workers with hammers in their hands and coal dust in their pores, the people who should, according to Marxist rhetoric, have been the party's base.* Even more threatening, Solidarity's vision was everything the party was not: democratic where it was authoritarian; dispersed where it was centralized; participatory where it was bureaucratic. And its 10 million members had the power to bring Poland's economy to a standstill. As Walesa taunted, they might lose their political battles, "but we will not be compelled to work. Because if people want us to build tanks, we will build streetcars. And trucks will go backward if we build them that way. We know how to beat the system. We are pupils of that system."

Solidarity's commitment to democracy inspired even party insiders to rebel. "Once I was so naive as to think that a few evil men were responsible for the errors of the party," Marian Arendt, a member of the Central Committee, told a Polish newspaper. "Now I no longer have such illusions. There is something wrong in our whole apparatus, in our entire structure."[6]

In September 1981, Solidarity's members were ready to take their movement to the next stage. Nine hundred Polish workers gathered once again in Gdańsk for the union's first national congress. There, Solidarity turned into a revolutionary movement with aspirations to take over the state, with its own alternative economic and political program for Poland. The Solidarity plan stated, "We demand a self-governing and democratic reform at every management level and a new socioeconomic system combining the plan, self-government and the market." The centrepiece was a radical vision for the huge state-run companies, which employed millions of Solidarity members, to break away from governmental control and become democratic workers' cooperatives. "The socialized enterprise," the program stated, "should be the basic organizational unit in the economy. It should be controlled by the workers council representing the collective and should be operatively run by the director, appointed through competition and recalled by the council."[7] Walesa opposed this demand, fearing it was such a challenge to party control that it would provoke a crackdown. Others argued that the movement needed a goal, a positive hope for the future, not just an enemy. Walesa lost the debate, and the economic program became official Solidarity policy.

Walesa's fears of a crackdown turned out to be well founded. Solidarity's

---

* One of the popular Solidarity slogans in 1980 was "Socialism—YES, Its distortions—NO" (which no doubt works better in Polish).

mounting ambition frightened and infuriated Moscow. Under intense pressure, Poland's leader, General Wojciech Jaruzelski, declared martial law in December 1981. Tanks rolled through the snow to surround factories and mines, Solidarity's members were rounded up in the thousands, and its leaders, including Walesa, were arrested and imprisoned. As *Time* reported, "Soldiers and police used force to clear out resisting workers, leaving at least seven dead and hundreds injured when miners in Katowice fought back with axes and crowbars."[8]

Solidarity was forced underground, but during the eight years of police-state rule, the movement's legend only grew. In 1983, Walesa was awarded the Nobel Peace Prize, although his activities were still restricted and he could not accept the prize in person. "The Peace Prize laureate's seat is empty," the representative from the Nobel Committee said at the ceremony. "Let us therefore try even harder to listen to the silent speech from his empty place."

The empty space was a fitting metaphor because, by that time, everyone seemed to see what they wanted in Solidarity: the Nobel Committee saw a man who "espoused no other weapon than the peaceful strike weapon."[9] The left saw redemption, a version of socialism that was not tainted by the crimes of Stalin or Mao. The right saw evidence that Communist states would meet even moderate expressions of dissent with brutal force. The human rights movement saw prisoners jailed for their beliefs. The Catholic Church saw an ally against Communist atheism. And Margaret Thatcher and Ronald Reagan saw an opening, a crack in the Soviet armor, even though Solidarity was fighting for the very rights that both leaders were doing their best to stamp out at home. The longer the ban lasted, the more powerful the Solidarity mythology became.

By 1988, the terror of the initial crackdown had eased, and Polish workers were once again staging huge strikes. This time, with the economy in free fall, and the new, moderate regime of Mikhail Gorbachev in power in Moscow, the Communists gave in. They legalized Solidarity and agreed to hold snap elections. Solidarity split in two: there was now the union and a new wing, Citizens' Committee Solidarity, that would participate in the elections. The two bodies were inextricably linked; Solidarity leaders were the candidates, and because the electoral platform was vague, the only specifics of what a Solidarity future might look like were provided by the union's economic program. Walesa himself didn't run, choosing to maintain his role as head of the union wing, but he was the face of the campaign, which ran under the slogan "With us, you're safer."[10] The results were humiliating for the

Communists and glorious for Solidarity: of the 261 seats in which Solidarity ran candidates, it won 260 of them.* Walesa, maneuvering behind the scenes, had the post of prime minister filled by Tadeusz Mazowiecki. He had little of Walesa's charisma, but as the editor of the Solidarity weekly newspaper, he was considered one of the movement's leading intellectuals.

The Shock of Power

As Latin Americans had just learned, authoritarian regimes have a habit of embracing democracy at the precise moment when their economic projects are about to implode. Poland was no exception. The Communists had been mismanaging the economy for decades, making one disastrous, expensive mistake after another, and it was at the point of collapse. "To our misfortune, we have won!" Walesa famously (and prophetically) declared. When Solidarity took office, debt was $40 billion, inflation was at 600 percent, there were severe food shortages and a thriving black market. Many factories were making products that, with no buyers in sight, were destined to rot in warehouses.[11] For Poles, the situation made for a cruel entry into democracy. Freedom had finally come, but few had the time or the inclination to celebrate because their paychecks were worthless. They spent their days lining up for flour and butter if there happened to be any in the stores that week.

All summer following its triumph at the polls, the Solidarity government was paralyzed by indecision. The speed of the collapse of the old order and the sudden election sweep had been shocks in themselves: in a matter of months, Solidarity activists went from hiding from the secret police to being responsible for paying the salaries of those same agents. And now they had the added shock of discovering that they barely had enough money to make the payroll. Rather than building the post-Communist economy they had dreamed of, the movement had the far more pressing task of avoiding a complete meltdown and potential mass starvation.

Solidarity's leaders knew they wanted to put an end to the state's viselike grip on the economy, but they weren't at all clear about what could replace it. For the movement's militant rank and file, this was the chance to test their economic program: if the state-run factories were converted to workers'

---

* The elections, while a breakthrough, were still rigged: from the outset, the Communist Party was guaranteed 65 percent of the seats in parliament's lower house, and Solidarity was allowed to contest only the remaining ones. Nevertheless, the win was so sweeping that Solidarity gained effective control of the government.

cooperatives, there was a chance they could become economically viable again—worker management could be more efficient, especially without the added expense of party bureaucrats. Others argued for the same gradual approach to transition that Gorbachev was advocating at the time in Moscow—slow expansion of the areas in which supply-and-demand monetary rules apply (more legal shops and markets), combined with a strong public sector modeled on Scandinavian social democracy.

But as had been the case in Latin America, before anything else could happen, Poland needed debt relief and some aid to get out of its immediate crisis. In theory, that's the central mandate of the IMF: providing stabilizing funds to prevent economic catastrophes. If any government deserved that kind of lifeline it was the one headed by Solidarity, which had just pulled off the Eastern Bloc's first democratic ouster of a Communist regime in four decades. Surely, after all the Cold War railing against totalitarianism behind the Iron Curtain, Poland's new rulers could have expected a little help.

No such aid was on offer. Now in the grips of Chicago School economists, the IMF and the U.S. Treasury saw Poland's problems through the prism of the shock doctrine. An economic meltdown and a heavy debt load, compounded by the disorientation of rapid regime change, meant that Poland was in the perfect weakened position to accept a radical shock therapy program. And the financial stakes were even higher than in Latin America: Eastern Europe was untouched by Western capitalism, with no consumer market to speak of. All of its most precious assets were still owned by the state—prime candidates for privatization. The potential for rapid profits for those who got in first was tremendous.

Confident in the knowledge that the worse things got, the more likely the new government would be to accept a total conversion to unfettered capitalism, the IMF let the country fall deeper and deeper into debt and inflation. The White House, under George H. W. Bush, congratulated Solidarity on its triumph against Communism but made it clear that the U.S. administration expected Solidarity to pay the debts accumulated by the regime that had banned and jailed its members—and it offered only $119 million in aid, a pittance in a country facing economic collapse and in need of fundamental restructuring.

It was in this context that Jeffrey Sachs, then thirty-four, started working as an adviser to Solidarity. Since his Bolivian exploits, the hype surrounding Sachs had reached feverish levels. Marveling at how he could serve as economic shock doctor to half a dozen countries and still hold down his teaching job, the *Los Angeles Times* pronounced Sachs—who still looked like a member of the Harvard debate team— the "Indiana Jones of Economics."[12]

Sachs's work in Poland had begun before Solidarity's election victory, at the request of the Communist government. It started with a one-day trip, during which he met with the Communist government and with Solidarity. It was George Soros, the billionaire financier and currency trader, who had enlisted Sachs to play a more hands-on role. Soros and Sachs traveled to Warsaw together, and as Sachs recalls, "I told the Solidarity group and the Polish government that I would be willing to become more involved to help address the deepening economic crisis."[13] Soros agreed to cover the costs for Sachs and his colleague David Lipton, a staunch free-market economist then working at the IMF, to set up an ongoing Poland mission. When Solidarity swept the elections, Sachs began working closely with the movement.

Though he was a free agent, not on the payroll of either the IMF or the U.S. government, Sachs, in the eyes of many of Solidarity's top officials, possessed almost messianic powers. With his high-level contacts in Washington and legendary reputation, he seemed to hold the key to unlocking the aid and debt relief that was the new government's only chance. Sachs said at the time that Solidarity should simply refuse to pay the inherited debts, and he expressed confidence that he could mobilize $3 billion in support—a fortune compared with what Bush had offered.[14] He had helped Bolivia land loans with the IMF and renegotiated its debts; there seemed no reason to doubt him.

That help, however, came at a price: for Solidarity to get access to Sachs's connections and powers of persuasion, the government first needed to adopt what became known in the Polish press as "the Sachs Plan" or "shock therapy."

It was an even more radical course than the one imposed on Bolivia: in addition to eliminating price controls overnight and slashing subsidies, the Sachs Plan advocated selling off the state mines, shipyards and factories to the private sector. It was a direct clash with Solidarity's economic program of worker ownership, and though the movement's national leaders had stopped talking about the controversial ideas in that plan, they remained articles of faith for many Solidarity members. Sachs and Lipton wrote the plan for Poland's shock therapy transition in one night. It was fifteen pages long and, Sachs claimed, was "the first time, I believe, that anyone had written down a comprehensive plan for the transformation of a socialist economy to a market economy."[15]

Sachs was convinced that Poland had to take this "leap across the institutional chasm" right away because, in addition to all its other problems, it was on the verge of entering hyperinflation. Once that happened, he said, it would be "fundamental breakdown . . . just pure, unmitigated disaster."[16]

He gave several one-on-one seminars explaining the plan to key Solidarity officials, some lasting up to four hours, and he also addressed Poland's elected officials as a group. Many of Solidarity's leaders didn't like Sachs's ideas—the movement had formed in a revolt against drastic price increases imposed by the Communists—and now Sachs was telling them to do the same on a far more sweeping scale. He argued that they could get away with it precisely because "Solidarity had a reservoir of trust of the public, which was absolutely phenomenal and critical."[17]

Solidarity's leaders hadn't planned to expend that trust on policies that would cause extreme pain to their rank and file, but the years spent in the underground, in jail and in exile had also alienated them from their base. As the Polish editor Przemyslaw Wielgosz explains, the top tier of the movement "became effectively cut off . . . their support came not from the factories and industrial plants, but the church."[18] The leaders were also desperate for a quick fix, even if it was painful, and that was what Sachs was offering. "Will this work? That's what I want to know. Will this work?" demanded Adam Michnik, one of Solidarity's most celebrated intellectuals. Sachs did not waver: "This is good. This will work."*[19]

Sachs often held up Bolivia as the model that Poland should emulate, so often that the Poles grew tired of hearing about the place. "I would love to see Bolivia," one Solidarity leader told a reporter at the time. "I'm sure it's very lovely, very exotic. I just don't want to see Bolivia *here*." Lech Walesa developed a particularly acute antipathy to Bolivia, as he admitted to Gonzalo Sánchez de Lozada (Goni) when the two men met years later at a summit, when they were both presidents. "He came up to me," Goni recalled, "and said, 'I've always wanted to meet a Bolivian, especially a Bolivian president, because they're always making us take this very bitter medicine, saying you have to do it because this is what the Bolivians did. Now I know you, you're not that bad a guy, but I sure used to hate you.' "[20]

In Sachs's talk of Bolivia, he failed to mention that in order to push through the shock therapy program, the government had imposed a state of

---

* Michnik later observed bitterly that "the worst thing about Communism is what comes after."

emergency and, on two separate occasions, kidnapped and interned the union leadership—much as the Communist Party secret police had snatched and imprisoned Solidarity's leaders under a state of emergency not so long before.

What was most persuasive, many now recall, was Sachs's promise that if they followed his harsh advice, Poland would cease being exceptional and become "normal"—as in "a normal European country." If Sachs was right, and they really could fast-forward to becoming a country like France or Germany simply by hacking off the structures of the old state, wasn't the pain worth it? Why take an incremental route to change that could well fail—or pioneer a new third way—when this insta-Europe version was right there, calling out? Sachs predicted that shock therapy would cause "momentary dislocations" as prices spiked. "But then they'll stabilize—people will know where they stand."[21]

He formed an alliance with Poland's newly appointed finance minister, Leszek Balcerowicz, an economist at the Main School of Planning and Statistics in Warsaw. Little was known of Balcerowicz's political leanings when he was appointed (all economists were officially socialist), but it would soon become clear that he saw himself as an honorary Chicago Boy, having pored over an illegal Polish edition of Friedman's *Free to Choose*. It helped "to inspire me, and many others, to dream of a future of freedom during the darkest years of communist rule," Balcerowicz later explained.[22]

Friedman's fundamentalist version of capitalism was a long way from what Walesa had been promising the country that summer. He was still insisting that Poland was going to find that more generous third way, which he described in an interview with Barbara Walters as "a mixture. . . . It won't be capitalism. It will be a system that is better than capitalism, that will reject everything that is evil in capitalism."[23]

Many did argue that the sudden fix that Sachs and Balcerowicz were selling was a myth, that, rather than jolting Poland into health and normalcy, shock therapy would create an even bigger mess of poverty and deindustrialization than before. "This is a poor, weak country. We simply cannot take the shock," a leading doctor and health care advocate told the *New Yorker* journalist Lawrence Weschler.[24]

For three months after their historic victory at the polls and their abrupt transition from outlaws to lawmakers, the Solidarity inner circle debated, paced, yelled and chain-smoked, unable to decide what to do. Every day, the country fell deeper into economic crisis.

A Very Hesitant Embrace

On September 12, 1989, the Polish prime minister, Tadeusz Mazowiecki, rose before the first elected parliament. The Solidarity caucus had at last decided what it was going to do about the economy, but only a handful of people knew the final decision—was it the Sachs Plan, the Gorbachev gradualist route or Solidarity's platform of workers' cooperatives?

Mazowiecki was on the verge of announcing the verdict, but in the middle of his momentous speech, before he could confront the country's most burning question, something went terribly wrong. He started to sway, clasped the lectern and, according to one witness, "grew pale, gasped for breath and was heard to mutter under his breath, 'I'm not feeling too well.' "[25] His aides whisked him out of the chamber, leaving the 415 deputies to trade rumors. Was it a heart attack? Had he been poisoned? By the Communists? By the Americans?

One floor below, a team of doctors examined Mazowiecki and administered an electrocardiogram. It wasn't a heart attack or poison. The prime minister was simply suffering from "acute fatigue," from too little sleep and too much stress. After almost an hour of tense uncertainty, he reentered the parliamentary chamber, where he was greeted with thunderous applause. "Excuse me," said the bookish Mazowiecki. "The state of my health is the same as the state of the Polish economy."[26]

At long last, the verdict: the Polish economy would be treated for its own acute fatigue with shock therapy, a particularly radical course of it that would include "privatization of state industry, the creation of a stock exchange and capital markets, a convertible currency, and a shift from heavy industry to consumer goods production" as well as "budget cuts"—as fast as possible and all at once.[27]

If the dream of Solidarity began with Walesa's energetic vault over the steel fence in Gdańsk, then Mazowiecki's exhaustedly succumbing to shock therapy represented the end of that dream. Finally, the decision came down to money. Solidarity's members did not decide that their vision for a cooperatively run economy was wrongheaded, but their leaders became convinced that all that mattered was winning relief from the Communist debts and immediately stabilizing the currency. As Henryk Wujec, one of Poland's leading advocates of cooperatives, put it at the time, "If we had enough time, we might even be able to pull it off. But we don't have time."[28] Sachs, meanwhile, could deliver the money. He helped Poland negotiate an agreement with the IMF and secured some debt relief and $1 billion to stabilize the currency— but all of it, particularly the IMF funds, was strictly conditional on Solidarity's submitting to shock therapy.

Poland became a textbook example of Friedman's crisis theory: the disorientation of rapid political change combined with the collective fear generated by an economic meltdown to make the promise of a quick and magical cure—however illusory—too seductive to turn down. Halina Bortnowska, a human rights activist, described the velocity of change in this period as "the difference between dog years and human years, the way we're living these days . . . you start witnessing these semi-psychotic reactions. You can no longer expect people to act in their own best interests when they're so disoriented they don't know—or no longer care—what those interests are."[29]

Balcerowicz, the finance minister, has since admitted that capitalizing on the emergency environment was a deliberate strategy—a way, like all shock tactics, to clear away the opposition. He explained that he was able to push through policies that were antithetical to the Solidarity vision in both content and form because Poland was in what he dubbed a period of "extraordinary politics." He described that condition as a short-lived window in which the rules of "normal politics" (consultation, discussion, debate) do not apply— in other words, a democracy-free pocket within a democracy.[30]

"Extraordinary politics," he said, "by definition is a period of very clear discontinuity in a country's history. It could be a period of very deep economic crisis, of a breakdown of the previous institutional system, or of a liberation from external domination (or end of war). In Poland, all three phenomena converged in 1989."[31] Because of those extraordinary circumstances, he was able to shunt aside due process and force "a radical acceleration of the legislative process" to pass the shock therapy package.[32]

In the early nineties, Balcerowicz's theory about periods of "extraordinary politics" attracted considerable interest among Washington economists. And no wonder: only two months after Poland announced that it would accept shock therapy, something happened that would change the course of history and invest Poland's experiment with global significance. In November 1989, the Berlin Wall was joyously dismantled, the city was turned into a festival of possibility and the MTV flag was planted in the rubble, as if East Berlin were the face of the moon. Suddenly it seemed that the whole world was living the same kind of fast-forward existence as the Poles: the Soviet Union was on the verge of breaking apart, apartheid in South Africa seemed on its last legs, authoritarian regimes continued to crumble in Latin America, Eastern Europe and Asia, and long wars were coming to an end from Namibia to Lebanon. Everywhere, old regimes were collapsing, and the new ones rising in their place had yet to take shape.

Within a few years it seemed as if half the world was in a period of "extraordinary politics," or "in transition," as liberated countries came to be called in the nineties—suspended in an existential in-betweenness of past and future. According to Thomas Carothers, a leader in the U.S. government's so-called democracy-promotion apparatus, "in the first half of the 1990s . . . the set of 'transitional countries' swelled dramatically, and nearly 100 countries (approximately 20 in Latin America, 25 in Eastern Europe and the former Soviet Union, 30 in sub-Saharan Africa, 10 in Asia, and 5 in the Middle East) were in some kind of dramatic transition from one model to another."[33]

Many were claiming that all of this flux, and the fall of real and metaphorical walls, would lead to an end of ideological orthodoxy. Freed from the polarizing effects of dueling superpowers, countries would finally be able to choose the best of both worlds—some hybrid of political freedom and economic security. As Gorbachev put it, "Many decades of being mesmerized by dogma, by a rule-book approach, have had their effect. Today we want to introduce a genuinely creative spirit."[34]

In Chicago School circles, such talk of mix-and-match ideologies was met with open contempt. Poland had clearly shown that this kind of chaotic transition opened up a window for decisive men, acting swiftly, to push through rapid change. Now was the moment to convert former Communist countries to pure Friedmanism, not some mongrel Keynesian compromise. The trick, as Friedman had said, was for Chicago School believers to be ready with their solutions when everyone else was still asking questions and regaining their bearings.

A sort of revival meeting for those who embraced this worldview was held in that eventful winter of 1989; the location, fittingly, was the University of Chicago. The occasion was a speech by Francis Fukuyama titled "Are We Approaching the End of History?"* For Fukuyama, then a senior policy maker at the U.S. State Department, the strategy for advocates of unfettered

---

* The lecture formed the foundation for Fukuyama's book *The End of History and the Last Man*, published three years later.

capitalism was clear: don't debate with the third-way crowd; instead, pre-emptively declare victory. Fukuyama was convinced that there should be no abandonment of extremes, no best of both worlds, no splitting the difference. The collapse of Communism, he told his audience, was leading "not to an 'end of ideology' or a convergence between capitalism and socialism . . . but to an unabashed victory of economic and political liberalism." It was not ide-ology that had ended but "history as such."[35]

The talk was sponsored by John M. Olin, longtime funder of Milton Friedman's ideological crusade and bankroller of the boom in right-wing think tanks.[36] The synergy was fitting since Fukuyama was essentially restat-ing Friedman's claim that free markets and free people are part of an insep-arable project. Fukuyama took that thesis into bold new terrain, arguing that deregulated markets in the economic sphere, combined with liberal democ-racy in the political sphere, represented "the end point of mankind's ideo-logical evolution and . . . final form of human government."[37] Democracy and radical capitalism were fused not only with each other but also with modernity, progress and reform. Those who objected to the merger were not just wrong but "still in history," as Fukuyama put it, the equivalent of being left behind after the Rapture, since everyone else had already transcended to a celestial "posthistorical" plane.[38]

The argument was a magnificent example of the democracy avoidance honed by the Chicago School. Much as the IMF had sneaked privatization and "free trade" into Latin America and Africa under cover of emergency "stabilization" programs, Fukuyama was now trying to smuggle this same highly contested agenda into the pro-democracy wave rising up from War-saw to Manila. It was true, as Fukuyama noted, that there was an emerging and irrepressible consensus that all people have the right to govern them-selves democratically, but only in the State Department's most vivid fan-tasies was that desire for democracy accompanied by citizens' clamoring for an economic system that would strip away job protections and cause mass layoffs.

If there was a genuine consensus about anything, it was that for people es-caping both left-wing and right-wing dictatorships, democracy meant finally having a say in all major decisions rather than having somebody else's ideol-ogy imposed unilaterally and with force. In other words, the universal princi-ple that Fukuyama identified as "the sovereignty of the people" *included* the sovereignty of the people to choose how the wealth of their countries would be distributed, from the fate of state-owned companies to the level of funding for schools and hospitals. Around the world, citizens were ready to exercise their hard-won democratic powers to become the authors of their national destinies, at last.

In 1989, history was taking an exhilarating turn, entering a period of genuine openness and possibility. So it was no coincidence that Fukuyama, from his perch at the State Department, chose precisely that moment to attempt to slam the history book shut. Nor was it a coincidence that the World Bank and the IMF chose that same volatile year to unveil the Washington Consensus—a clear effort to halt all discussion and debate about any economic ideas outside the free-market lockbox. These were democracy-containment strategies, designed to undercut the kind of unscripted self-determination that was, and always had been, the greatest single threat to the Chicago School crusade.

The Shock of Tiananmen Square

One place where Fukuyama's bold pronouncement came in for early discrediting was China. Fukuyama's speech took place in February 1989; two months later, a pro-democracy movement exploded in Beijing, with mass protests and sit-ins in Tiananmen Square. Fukuyama had claimed that democratic and "free market reforms" were a twin process, impossible to pry apart. Yet in China, the government had done precisely that: it was pushing hard to deregulate wages and prices and expand the reach of the market—but it was fiercely determined to resist calls for elections and civil liberties. The demonstrators, on the other hand, demanded democracy, but many opposed the government's moves toward unregulated capitalism, a fact largely left out of the coverage of the movement in the Western press. In China, democracy and Chicago School economics were not proceeding hand in hand; they were on opposite sides of the barricades surrounding Tiananmen Square.

In the early 1980s, the Chinese government, then led by Deng Xiaoping, was obsessed with avoiding a repeat of what had just happened in Poland, where workers had been allowed to form an independent movement that challenged the party's monopoly hold on power. It was not that China's leaders were committed to protecting the state-owned factories and farm communes that formed the foundation of the Communist state. In fact, Deng was enthusiastically committed to converting to a corporate-based economy—so committed that, in 1980, his government invited Milton Friedman to come to China and tutor hundreds of top-level civil servants, professors and party economists in the fundamentals of free-market theory. "All were invited guests, who had to show a ticket of invitation to attend," Friedman recalled of his audiences in Beijing and Shanghai. His central message was "how much better ordinary people lived in capitalist than in communist countries."[39] The example he held up was Hong Kong, a zone of pure capitalism that Friedman had long admired for its "dynamic, innovative character that has been produced by personal liberty, free trade, low taxes, and minimal government intervention." He claimed that Hong Kong, despite having no democracy, was freer than the United States, since its government participated less in the economy.[40]

Friedman's definition of freedom, in which political freedoms were incidental, even unnecessary, compared with the freedom of unrestricted commerce, conformed nicely with the vision taking shape in the Chinese Politburo. The party wanted to open the economy to private ownership and consumerism while maintaining its own grip on power—a plan that ensured that once the assets of the state were auctioned off, party officials and their relatives would snap up the best deals and be first in line for the biggest profits. According to this version of "transition," the same people who controlled the state under Communism would control it under capitalism, while enjoying a substantial upgrade in lifestyle. The model the Chinese government intended to emulate was not the United States but something much closer to Chile under Pinochet: free markets combined with authoritarian political control, enforced by iron-fisted repression.

From the start, Deng clearly understood that repression would be crucial. Under Mao, the Chinese state had exerted brutal control over the people, dispensing with opponents and sending dissidents for reeducation. But Mao's repression took place in the name of the workers and against the bourgeoisie; now the party was going to launch its own counterrevolution and ask workers to give up many of their benefits and security so that a minority could collect huge profits. It was not going to be an easy task. So, in 1983, as Deng opened up the country to foreign investment and reduced protections for workers, he also ordered the creation of the 400,000-strong People's Armed Police, a new, roving riot squad charged with quashing all signs of "economic crimes" (i.e., strikes and protests). According to the China historian Maurice Meisner, "The People's Armed Police kept American helicopters and electric cattle prods in its arsenal." And "several units were sent to Poland for anti-riot training"—where they studied the tactics that had been used against Solidarity during Poland's period of martial law.[41]

Many of Deng's reforms were successful and popular—farmers had more control over their lives, and commerce returned to the cities. But in the late eighties, Deng began introducing measures that were distinctly unpopular, particularly among workers in the cities—price controls were lifted, sending prices soaring; job security was eliminated, creating waves of unemployment; and deep inequalities were opening up between the winners and losers in the new China. By 1988, the party was confronting a powerful backlash and was forced to reverse some of its price deregulation. Outrage was also mounting in the face of the party's defiant corruption and nepotism. Many Chinese citizens wanted more freedom in the market, but "reform" increasingly looked like code for party officials turning into business tycoons, as many illegally took posession of the assets they had previously managed as bureaucrats.

With the free-market experiment in peril, Milton Friedman was once again invited to pay a visit to China—much as the Chicago Boys and the piranhas had enlisted his help in 1975, when their program had sparked an internal revolt in Chile.[42] A high-profile visit from the world-famous guru of capitalism was just the boost China's "reformers" needed.

When Friedman and his wife, Rose, arrived in Shanghai in September 1988, they were dazzled by how quickly mainland China was beginning to look and feel like Hong Kong. Despite the rage simmering at the grass roots, everything they saw served to confirm "our faith in the power of free markets." Friedman described this moment as "the most hopeful period of the Chinese experiment."

In the presence of official state media, Friedman met for two hours with Zhao Ziyang, general secretary of the Communist Party, as well as with Jiang Zemin, then party secretary of the Shanghai Committee and the future Chinese president. Friedman's message to Jiang echoed the advice he had given to Pinochet when the Chilean project was on the skids: don't bow to the pressure and don't blink. "I emphasized the importance of privatization and free markets, and of liberalizing at one fell stroke," Friedman recalled. In a memo to the general secretary of the Communist Party, Friedman stressed that more, not less, shock therapy was needed. "China's initial steps of reform have been dramatically successful. China can make further dramatic progress by placing still further reliance on *free private markets*."[43]

Shortly after his return to the U.S., Friedman, remembering the heat he had taken for advising Pinochet, wrote "out of sheer devilry" a letter to the editor of a student newspaper, denouncing his critics for their double standards. He explained that he had just spent twelve days in China, where "I was mostly the guest of governmental entities," and had met with Communist Party officials at the highest level. Yet these meetings had provoked no human rights outcry on American university campuses, Friedman pointed out. "Incidentally, I gave precisely the same advice to both Chile and China." He concluded by asking sarcastically, "Should I prepare myself for an avalanche of protests for having been willing to give advice to so evil a government?"[44]

A few months later, that devilish letter took on sinister overtones, as the Chinese government began to emulate many of Pinochet's most infamous tactics.

Friedman's trip did not have the desired results. The pictures in the official papers of the professor offering his blessing to party bureaucrats did not succeed in bringing the public onside. In subsequent months, protests grew more determined and radical. The most visible symbols of the opposition were the demonstrations by student strikers in Tiananmen Square. These historic protests were almost universally portrayed in the international media as a clash between modern, idealistic students who wanted Western-style democratic freedoms and old-guard authoritarians who wanted to protect the Communist state. Recently, another analysis of the meaning of Tiananmen has emerged, one that challenges the mainstream version while putting Friedmanism at the heart of the story. This alternative narrative is being advanced by, among others, Wang Hui, one of the organizers of the 1989 protests, and now a leading Chinese intellectual of what is known as China's "New Left." In his 2003 book, *China's New Order*, Wang explains that the protesters spanned a huge range of Chinese society—not just elite university students but also factory workers, small entrepreneurs and teachers. What ignited the protests, he recalls, was popular discontent in the face of Deng's "revolutionary" economic changes, which were lowering wages, raising prices and causing "a crisis of layoffs and unemployment."[45] According to Wang, "These changes were the catalyst for the 1989 social mobilization."[46]

The demonstrations were not against economic reform per se; they were against the specific Friedmanite nature of the reforms—their speed, ruthlessness and the fact that the process was highly antidemocratic. Wang says that the protesters' call for elections and free speech were intimately connected to this economic dissent. What drove the demand for democracy was the fact that the party was pushing through changes that were revolutionary in scope, entirely without popular consent. There was, he writes, "a general request for democratic means to supervise the fairness of the reform process and the reorganization of social benefits."[47]

These demands forced the Politburo to make a definite choice. The choice was not, as was so often claimed, between democracy and Communism, or "reform" versus the "old guard." It was a more complex calculation: Should the party bulldoze ahead with its free-market agenda, which it could do only by rolling over the bodies of the protesters? Or should it bow to the protesters' demands for democracy, cede its monopoly on power and risk a major setback to the economic project?

Some of the free-market reformers within the party, most notably General Secretary Zhao Ziyang, appeared willing to gamble on democracy, convinced that economic and political reform could still be compatible. More powerful elements in the party were not willing to take the risk. The verdict came down: the state would protect its economic "reform" program by crushing the demonstrators.

That was the clear message when, on May 20, 1989, the government of the People's Republic of China declared martial law. On June 3, the tanks of the People's Liberation Army rolled into the protests, shooting indiscriminately into the crowds. Soldiers stormed onto buses where student demonstrators were taking cover and beat them with sticks; more troops broke through the barricades protecting Tiananmen Square, where students had erected a Goddess of Democracy statue, and rounded up the organizers. Similar crackdowns took place simultaneously across the country.

There will never be reliable estimates for how many people were killed and injured in those days. The party admits to hundreds, and eyewitness reports at the time put the number of dead at between two thousand and seven thousand and the number of injured as high as thirty thousand. The protests were followed by a national witch hunt against all regime critics and opponents. Some forty thousand were arrested, thousands were jailed and many—possibly hundreds—were executed. As in Latin America, the government reserved its harshest repression for the factory workers, who represented the most direct threat to deregulated capitalism. "Most of those arrested, and virtually all who were executed, were workers. With the obvious aim of terrorizing the population, it became a well-publicized policy to systematically subject arrested individuals to beatings and torture," writes Maurice Meisner.[48]

For the most part, the massacre was covered in the Western press as another example of Communist brutality: just as Mao had wiped out his opponents during the Cultural Revolution, now Deng, "the Butcher of Beijing," crushed his critics under the watchful eye of Mao's giant portrait. A *Wall Street Journal* headline claimed that "China's Harsh Actions Threaten to Set Back [the] 10-Year Reform Drive"—as if Deng was an enemy of those reforms and not their most committed defender, determined to take them into bold new territory.[49]

Five days after the bloody crackdown, Deng addressed the nation and made it perfectly clear that it wasn't Communism he was protecting with his crackdown, but capitalism. After dismissing the protesters as "a large quantity of the dregs of society," China's president reaffirmed the party's commitment to economic shock therapy. "In a word, this was a test, and we passed," Deng said, adding, "Perhaps this bad thing will enable us to go ahead with reform and the open-door policy at a more steady, better, even a faster pace. . . . We haven't been wrong. There's nothing wrong with the four cardinal principles [of economic reform]. If there is anything amiss, it's that these principles haven't been thoroughly implemented."*[50]

Orville Schell, a China scholar and journalist, summarized Deng Xiaoping's choice: "After the massacre of 1989, he in effect said we will not stop economic reform; we will in effect halt political reform."[51]

For Deng and the rest of the Politburo, the free-market possibilities were now limitless. Just as Pinochet's terror had cleared the streets for revolutionary change, so Tiananmen paved the way for a radical transformation free from fear of rebellion. If life grew harder for peasants and workers, they would either have to accept it quietly or face the wrath of the army and the secret police. And so, with the public in a state of raw terror, Deng rammed through his most sweeping reforms yet.

Before Tiananmen, he had been forced to ease off some of the more painful measures; three months after the massacre, he brought them back, and he implemented several of Friedman's other recommendations, including price deregulation. For Wang Hui, there is an obvious reason why "market

---

* Deng had some notable defenders. After the massacre, Henry Kissinger wrote an op-ed arguing that the party had no choice. "No government in the world would have tolerated having the main square of its capital occupied for eight weeks by tens of thousands of demonstrators. . . . A crackdown was therefore inevitable."

reforms that had failed to be implemented in the late 1980s just happened to have been completed in the post-1989 environment"; the reason, he writes, "is that the violence of 1989 served to check the social upheaval brought about by this process, and the new pricing system finally took shape."[52] The shock of the massacre, in other words, made shock therapy possible.

In the three years immediately following the bloodbath, China was cracked open to foreign investment, with special export zones constructed throughout the country. As he announced these new initiatives, Deng reminded the country that "if necessary, every possible means will be adopted to eliminate any turmoil in the future as soon as it has appeared. Martial law, or even more severe methods, may be introduced."*[53]

It was this wave of reforms that turned China into the sweatshop of the world, the preferred location for contract factories for virtually every multinational on the planet. No country offered more lucrative conditions than China: low taxes and tariffs, corruptible officials and, most of all, a plentiful low-wage workforce that, for many years, would be unwilling to risk demanding decent salaries or the most basic workplace protections for fear of the most violent reprisals.

For foreign investors and the party, it has been a win-win arrangement. According to a 2006 study, 90 percent of China's billionaires (calculated in Chinese yuan) are the children of Communist Party officials. Roughly twenty-nine hundred of these party scions—known as "the princelings"—control $260 billion.[54] It is a mirror of the corporatist state first pioneered in Chile under Pinochet: a revolving door between corporate and political elites who combine their power to eliminate workers as an organized political force. Today, this collaborative arrangement can be seen in the way that foreign multinational media and technology companies help the Chinese state to spy on its citizens, and to make sure that when students do Web searches on phrases like "Tiananmen Square Massacre," or even "democracy," no documents turn up. "The creation of today's market society was not the result of a sequence of spontaneous events," writes Wang Hui, "but rather of state interference and violence."[55]

One of the truths revealed by Tiananmen was the stark similarity between the tactics of authoritarian Communism and Chicago School capitalism—a

---

* As the New York University anthropologist David Harvey notes, it was only after Tiananmen, when Deng went on his famous "southern tour" of China, "that the full force of the central government was put behind the opening to foreign trade and foreign direct investment."

shared willingness to disappear opponents, to blank the slate of all resistance and begin anew.

Despite the fact that the massacre happened just months after he had encouraged Chinese officials to push forward with painful and unpopular free-market policies, Friedman never did face "an avalanche of protests for having been willing to give advice to so evil a government." And as usual, he saw no connection between the advice he had given and the violence required to enforce it. While condemning China's use of repression, Friedman continued to hold it up as an example of "the efficacy of free-market arrangements in promoting both prosperity and freedom."[56]

In a strange coincidence, the Tiananmen Square massacre took place on the same day as Solidarity's historic election sweep in Poland—June 4, 1989. They were, in a way, two very different studies in the shock doctrine. Both countries had needed to exploit shock and fear to push through a free-market transformation. In China, where the state used the gloves-off methods of terror, torture and assassination, the result was, from a market perspective, an unqualified success. In Poland, where only the shock of economic crisis and rapid change were harnessed—and there was no overt violence—the effects of the shock eventually wore off, and the results were far more ambiguous.

In Poland, shock therapy may have been imposed after elections, but it made a mockery of the democratic process since it directly conflicted with the wishes of the overwhelming majority of voters who had cast their ballots for Solidarity. As late as 1992, 60 percent of Poles still opposed privatization for heavy industry. Defending his unpopular actions, Sachs claimed he had no choice, likening his role to that of a surgeon in an emergency room. "When a guy comes into the emergency room and his heart's stopped, you just rip open the sternum and you don't worry about the scars that you leave," he said. "The idea is to get the guy's heart beating again. And you make a bloody mess. But you don't have any choice."[57]

But once Poles recovered from the initial surgery, they had questions about both the doctor and the treatment. Shock therapy in Poland did not cause "momentary dislocations," as Sachs had predicted. It caused a full-blown depression: a 30 percent reduction in industrial production in the two years after the first round of reforms. With government cutbacks and cheap imports flooding in, unemployment skyrocketed, and in 1993 it reached 25 percent in some areas—a wrenching change in a country that, under Communism, for all its many abuses and hardships, had no open joblessness. Even when the economy began growing again, high unemployment remained chronic. According to the World Bank's most recent figures, Poland has an unemployment rate of 20 percent—the highest in the European Union. For those under twenty-four, the situation is far worse: 40 percent of young workers were unemployed in 2006, twice the EU average. Most dramatic are the number of people in poverty: in 1989, 15 percent of Poland's population was living below the poverty line; in 2003, 59 percent of Poles had fallen below the line.[58] Shock therapy, which eroded job protection and made daily life far more expensive, was not the route to Poland's becoming one of Europe's "normal" countries (with their strong labor laws and generous social benefits) but to the same gaping disparities that have accompanied the counterrevolution everywhere it has triumphed, from Chile to China.

The fact that it was Solidarity, the party built by Poland's blue-collar workers, that oversaw the creation of this permanent underclass represented a bitter betrayal, one that bred a deep cynicism and anger in the country that has never fully lifted. Solidarity's leaders often play down the party's socialist roots, with Walesa now claiming that as far back as 1980 he knew they would "have to build capitalism." Karol Modzelewski, a Solidarity militant and intellectual who spent eight and a half years in Communist jails, retorts angrily, "I wouldn't have spent a week nor a month, let alone eight and a half years in jail for capitalism!"[59]

For the first year and a half of Solidarity rule, workers believed their heroes when they were assured that the pain was temporary, a necessary stop on the way to bringing Poland into modern Europe. Even in the face of soaring unemployment, they staged only a smattering of strikes and waited patiently for the therapeutic part of their shock therapy to take effect. When the promised recovery didn't arrive, at least not in the form of jobs, Solidarity's members were simply confused: How could their own movement have delivered a standard of living worse than that under Communism? "[Solidarity] defended me in 1980 when I set up a union committee," one forty-one-year-old construction worker said. "But when I went to them for help this time, they told me that I have to suffer for the sake of reform."[60]

About eighteen months into Poland's period of "extraordinary politics," Solidarity's base had had enough and demanded an end to the experiment. The extreme dissatisfaction was reflected in a marked increase in the number of strikes: in 1990, when workers were still giving Solidarity a free pass, there were only 250 strikes; by 1992 there were more than 6,000 such protests.[61] Faced with this pressure from below, the government was forced to slow down its more ambitious privatization plans. By the end of 1993—a year that saw almost 7,500 strikes—62 percent of Poland's total industry was still public.[62]

The fact that Polish workers managed to stop the wholesale privatization of their country means that as painful as the reforms were, they could have been far worse. The wave of strikes unquestionably saved hundreds of thousands of jobs that would otherwise have been lost if these supposedly inefficient firms had been allowed to close or be radically downsized and sold off. Interestingly, Poland's economy began growing quickly in this same period, proving, according to the prominent Polish economist and former Solidarity member Tadeusz Kowalik, that those who were ready to write off the state firms as inefficient and archaic were "obviously wrong."

Besides going on strike, Polish workers found another way to express their anger with their onetime allies in Solidarity: they used the democracy they had fought for to punish the party decisively at the polls, including their once-beloved leader Lech Walesa. The most dramatic trouncing came on September 19, 1993, when a coalition of left parties, including the former ruling Communists (rebranded Democratic Left Alliance), won 66 percent of the seats in parliament. Solidarity had, by this time, splintered into warring factions. The trade union faction won less than 5 percent, losing official party status in the parliament, and a new party led by Mazowiecki, the prime minister, won just 10.6 percent—a resounding rejection of shock therapy.

Yet somehow, in the years to come, as dozens of countries struggled with how to reform their economies, the inconvenient details—the strikes, the election defeats, the policy reversals—would be lost. Instead, Poland would be held up as a model, proof that radical free-market makeovers can take place democratically and peacefully.

Like so many stories about countries in transition, this one was mostly a myth. But it was better than the truth: in Poland, democracy was used as a weapon against "free markets" on the streets and at the polls. Meanwhile in China, where the drive for free-wheeling capitalism rolled over democracy in Tiananmen Square, shock and terror unleashed one of the most lucrative and sustained investor booms in modern history. Another miracle born of a massacre.

CHAPTER 10

DEMOCRACY BORN IN CHAINS

SOUTH AFRICA'S CONSTRICTED FREEDOM

> Reconciliation means that those who have been on the underside of history must see that there is a qualitative difference between repression and freedom. And for them, freedom translates into having a supply of clean water, having electricity on tap; being able to live in a decent home and have a good job; to be able to send your children to school and to have accessible health care. I mean, what's the point of having made this transition if the quality of life of these people is not enhanced and improved? If not, the vote is useless.
>
> —Archbishop Desmond Tutu, chair of South Africa's Truth and Reconciliation Commission, 2001[1]

> Before transferring power, the Nationalist Party wants to emasculate it. It is trying to negotiate a kind of swap where it will give up the right to run the country its way in exchange for the right to stop blacks from running it their own way.
>
> —Allister Sparks, South African journalist[2]

In January 1990, Nelson Mandela, age seventy-one, sat down in his prison compound to write a note to his supporters outside. It was meant to settle a debate over whether twenty-seven years behind bars, most of it spent on Robben Island off the coast of Cape Town, had weakened the leader's commitment to the economic transformation of South Africa's apartheid state. The note was only two sentences long, and it decisively put the matter to rest: "The nationalisation of the mines, banks and monopoly industries is the policy of the ANC, and the change or modification of our views in this regard is inconceivable. Black economic empowerment is a goal we fully support and encourage, but in our situation state control of certain sectors of the economy is unavoidable."[3]

History, it turned out, was not over just yet, as Fukuyama had claimed. In South Africa, the largest economy on the African continent, it seemed that some people still believed that freedom included the right to reclaim and redistribute their oppressors' ill-gotten gains.

That belief had formed the basis of the policy of the African National Congress for thirty-five years, ever since it was spelled out in its statement of core principles, the Freedom Charter. The story of the charter's drafting is the stuff of folklore in South Africa, and for good reason. The process began in 1955, when the party dispatched fifty thousand volunteers into the townships and countryside. The task of the volunteers was to collect "freedom demands" from the people—their vision of a postapartheid world in which all South Africans had equal rights. The demands were handwritten on scraps of paper: "Land to be given to all landless people," "Living wages and shorter hours of work," "Free and compulsory education, irrespective of color, race or nationality," "The right to reside and move about freely" and many more.[4] When the demands came back, leaders of the African National Congress synthesized them into a final document, which was officially adopted on June 26, 1955, at the Congress of the People, held in Kliptown, a "buffer zone" township built to protect the white residents of Johannesburg from the teeming masses of Soweto. Roughly three thousand delegates—black, Indian, "colored" and a few white—sat together in an empty field to vote on the contents of the document. According to Nelson Mandela's account of the historic Kliptown gathering, "the charter was read aloud, section by section, to the people in English, Sesotho and Xhosa. After each section, the crowd shouted its approval with cries of 'Afrika!' and 'Mayibuye!'"[5] The first defiant demand of the Freedom Charter reads, "The People Shall Govern!"

In the mid-fifties, that dream was decades away from fulfillment. On the Congress's second day, the gathering was violently broken up by police, who claimed the delegates were plotting treason.

For three decades, South Africa's government, dominated by white Afrikaners and British, banned the ANC and the other political parties that were intent on ending apartheid. Throughout this period of intense repression, the Freedom Charter continued to circulate, passed from hand to hand in the revolutionary underground, its power to inspire hope and resistance undiminished. In the 1980s, it was picked up by a new generation of young militants who emerged in the townships. Fed up with patience and good behavior and braced to do whatever it took to topple white domination, the young radicals stunned their parents with their fearlessness. They took to the streets without illusion, chanting, "Neither bullets nor tear gas will stop us." They faced massacre after massacre, buried friends, kept singing and kept coming. When the militants were asked what they were fighting against, they answered, "Apartheid" or "Racism"; asked what they were fighting for, many replied "Freedom" and, often, "The Freedom Charter."

The charter enshrines the right to work, to decent housing, to freedom of thought, and, most radically, to a share in the wealth of the richest country in Africa, containing, among other treasures, the largest goldfield in the world. "The national wealth of our country, the heritage of South Africans, shall be restored to the people; the mineral wealth beneath the soil, the Banks and monopoly industry shall be transferred to the ownership of the people as a whole; all other industry and trade shall be controlled to assist the well-being of the people," the charter states.[6]

At the time of its drafting, the charter was viewed by some in the liberation movement as positively centrist, by others as unforgivably weak. The Pan-Africanists castigated the ANC for conceding too much to white colonizers (why did South Africa belong to "everyone, black *and* white?" they asked; the manifesto should have demanded, as the Jamaican black nationalist Marcus Garvey had, "Africa for the Africans.") The staunch Marxists dismissed the demands as "petty bourgeois": it wasn't revolutionary to divide the ownership of the land among all people; Lenin said that private property itself must be abolished.

What was taken as a given by all factions of the liberation struggle was that apartheid was not only a political system regulating who was allowed to vote and move freely. It was also an *economic* system that used racism to enforce a highly lucrative arrangement: a small white elite had been able to amass enormous profits from South Africa's mines, farms and factories because a large black majority was prevented from owning land and forced to provide its labor for far less than it was worth—and was beaten and imprisoned when it dared to rebel. In the mines, whites were paid up to ten times more than blacks, and, as in Latin America, the large industrialists worked closely with the military to have unruly workers disappeared. [7]

What the Freedom Charter asserted was the baseline consensus in the liberation movement that freedom would not come merely when blacks took control of the state but when the wealth of the land that had been illegitimately confiscated was reclaimed and redistributed to the society as a whole. South Africa could no longer be a country with Californian living standards for whites and Congolese living standards for blacks, as the country was described during the apartheid years; freedom meant that it would have to find something in the middle.

That was what Mandela was confirming with his two-sentence note from prison: he still believed in the bottom line that there would be no freedom without redistribution. With so many other countries now also "in transition," it was a statement with enormous implications. If Mandela led the ANC to power and nationalized the banks and the mines, the precedent would make it far more difficult for Chicago School economists to dismiss such proposals in other countries as relics of the past and insist that only unfettered free markets and free trade had the ability to redress deep inequalities.

On February 11, 1990, two weeks after writing that note, Mandela walked out of prison a free man, as close to a living saint as existed anywhere in the world. South Africa's townships exploded in celebration and renewed conviction that nothing could stop the struggle for liberation. Unlike the movement in Eastern Europe, South Africa's was not beaten down but a movement on a roll. Mandela, for his part, was suffering from such an epic case of culture shock that he mistook a camera microphone for "some newfangled weapon developed while I was in prison."[8]

It was definitely a different world from the one he had left twenty-seven years earlier. When Mandela was arrested in 1962, a wave of Third World nationalism was sweeping the African continent; now it was torn apart by war. While he was in prison, socialist revolutions had been ignited and extinguished: Che Guevara had been killed in Bolivia in 1967; Salvador Allende had died in the coup of 1973; Mozambique's liberation hero and president, Samora Machel, had perished in a mysterious plane crash in 1986. The late eighties and early nineties saw the fall of the Berlin Wall, the repression in Tiananmen Square and the collapse of Communism. Amid all this change there was little time for catching up: immediately on his release, Mandela had a people to lead to freedom while preventing a civil war and an economic collapse—both of which looked like distinct possibilities.

If there was a third path between Communism and capitalism—a way of democratizing the country and redistributing wealth at the same time—South Africa under the ANC looked uniquely positioned to turn that persistent dream into reality. It wasn't only the global outpouring of admiration and support for Mandela but also the particular way in which the anti-apartheid struggle had taken shape in the preceding years. In the eighties, it had become a truly global mass movement, and outside South Africa, the weapon that activists wielded most effectively was the corporate boycott—both of South African–made products and of international firms that did business with the apartheid state. The goal of the boycott strategy was to put enough of a squeeze on the corporate sector that it would lobby the intransigent South African government to end apartheid. But there was also a moral component to the campaign: many consumers firmly believed that companies that were profiting from white supremacist laws deserved to take a financial hit.

It was this attitude that gave the ANC a unique opportunity to reject the free-market orthodoxy of the day. Since there was already widespread agreement that corporations shared responsibility for the crimes of apartheid, the stage was set for Mandela to explain why key sectors of South Africa's economy needed to be nationalized just as the Freedom Charter demanded. He could have used the same argument to explain why the debt accumulated under apartheid was an illegitimate burden to place on any new, popularly elected government. There would have been plenty of outrage from the IMF, the U.S. Treasury and the European Union in the face of such undisciplined behavior, but Mandela was also a living saint—there would have been enormous popular support for it as well.

We will never know which of these forces would have proved more powerful. In the years that passed between Mandela's writing his note from prison and the ANC's 1994 election sweep in which he was elected president, something happened to convince the party hierarchy that it could not use its grass-roots prestige to reclaim and redistribute the country's stolen wealth. So, rather than meeting in the middle between California and the Congo, the ANC adopted policies that exploded both inequality and crime to such a degree that South Africa's divide is now closer to Beverly Hills and Baghdad. Today, the country stands as a living testament to what happens when economic reform is severed from political transformation. Politically, its people have the right to vote, civil liberties and majority rule. Yet economically, South Africa has surpassed Brazil as the most unequal society in the world.

I went to South Africa in 2005 to try to understand what had happened in the transition, in those key years between 1990 and 1994, to make Mandela take a route that he had described so unequivocally as "inconceivable."

The ANC went into negotiations with the ruling National Party determined to avoid the kind of nightmare that neighboring Mozambique had experienced when the independence movement forced an end to Portuguese colonial rule in 1975. On their way out the door, the Portuguese threw a vindictive temper tantrum, pouring cement down elevator shafts, smashing tractors and stripping the country of all they could carry. To its enormous credit, the ANC did negotiate a relatively peaceful handover. However, it did not manage to prevent South Africa's apartheid-era rulers from wreaking havoc on their way out the door. Unlike their counterparts in Mozambique, the National Party didn't pour concrete—their sabotage, equally crippling, was far subtler, and was all in the fine print of those historic negotiations.

The talks that hashed out the terms of apartheid's end took place on two parallel tracks that often intersected: one was political, the other economic. Most of the attention, naturally, focused on the high-profile political summits between Nelson Mandela and F. W. de Klerk, leader of the National Party.

De Klerk's strategy in these negotiations was to preserve as much power as possible. He tried everything—breaking the country into a federation, guaranteeing veto power for minority parties, reserving a certain percentage of the seats in government structures for each ethnic group—anything to prevent simple majority rule, which he was sure would lead to mass land expropriations and the nationalizing of corporations. As Mandela later put it, "What the National Party was trying to do was to maintain white supremacy with our consent." De Klerk had guns and money behind him, but his opponent had a movement of millions. Mandela and his chief negotiator, Cyril Ramaphosa, won on almost every count.[9]

Running alongside these often explosive summits were the much lower profile economic negotiations, primarily managed on the ANC side by Thabo Mbeki, then a rising star in the party, now South Africa's president. As the political talks progressed, and it became clear to the National Party that Parliament would soon be firmly in the hands of the ANC, the party of South Africa's elites began pouring its energy and creativity into the economic negotiations. South Africa's whites had failed to keep blacks from taking over the government, but when it came to safeguarding the wealth they had amassed under apartheid, they would not give up so easily.

In these talks, the de Klerk government had a twofold strategy. First, drawing on the ascendant Washington Consensus that there was now only one way to run an economy, it portrayed key sectors of economic decision making—such as trade policy and the central bank—as "technical" or "administrative." Then it used a wide range of new policy tools—international trade agreements, innovations in constitutional law and structural adjustment programs—to hand control of those power centers to supposedly impartial experts, economists and officials from the IMF, the World Bank, the General Agreement on Tariffs and Trade (GATT) and the National Party—anyone except the liberation fighters from the ANC. It was a strategy of balkanization, not of the country's geography (as de Klerk had originally attempted) but of its economy.

This plan was successfully executed under the noses of ANC leaders, who were naturally preoccupied with winning the battle to control Parliament. In the process, the ANC failed to protect itself against a far more insidious strategy—in essence, an elaborate insurance plan against the economic clauses in the Freedom Charter ever becoming law in South Africa. "The people shall govern!" would soon become a reality, but the sphere over which they would govern was shrinking fast.

While these tense negotiations between adversaries were unfolding, the ANC was also busily preparing within its own ranks for the day when it would take office. Teams of ANC economists and lawyers formed working groups charged with figuring out exactly how to turn the general promises of the Freedom Charter—for housing amentites and health care—into practical policies. The most ambitious of these plans was Make Democracy Work, an economic blueprint for South Africa's postapartheid future, written while the high-level negotiations were taking place. What the party loyalists didn't know at the time was that while they were hatching their ambitious plans, the negotiating team was accepting concessions at the bargaining table that would make their implementation a practical impossibility. "It was dead before it was even launched," the economist Vishnu Padayachee told me of Make Democracy Work. By the time the draft was complete, "there was a new ball game."

As one of the few classically trained economists active in the ANC, Padayachee was enlisted to play a leading role in Make Democracy Work ("doing the number-crunching," as he puts it). Most of the people he worked alongside in those long policy meetings went on to top posts in the ANC government, but Padayachee did not. He has turned down all the offers of government jobs, preferring academic life in Durban, where he teaches, writes and owns the much-loved Ike's Bookshop, named after Ike Mayet, the first non-white South African bookseller. It was there, surrounded by carefully preserved out-of-print volumes on African history, that we met to discuss the transition.

Padayachee entered the liberation struggle in the seventies, as an adviser to South Africa's trade union movement. "We all had the Freedom Charter stuck on the back of our doors in those days," he recalled. I asked him when he knew its economic promises were not going to be realized. He first suspected it, he said, in late 1993, when he and a colleague from the Make Democracy Work group got a call from the negotiating team who were in the final stages of haggling with the National Party. The call was a request for them to write a position paper on the pros and cons of making South Africa's central bank an independent entity, run with total autonomy from the elected government—oh, and the negotiators needed it by morning.

"We were caught completely off guard," recalled Padayachee, now in his early fifties. He had done his graduate studies at Johns Hopkins University in Baltimore. He knew that at the time, even among free-market economists in the U.S., central bank independence was considered a fringe idea, a pet policy of a handful of Chicago School ideologues who believed that central banks should be run as sovereign republics within states, out of reach of the meddling hands of elected lawmakers.*[10] For Padayachee and his colleagues, who strongly believed that monetary policy needed to serve the new government's "big goals of growth, employment and redistribution," the ANC's position was a no-brainer: "There was not going to be an independent central bank in South Africa."

Padayachee and a colleague stayed up all night writing a paper that gave the negotiating team the arguments it needed to resist this curveball from the National Party. If the central bank (in South Africa called the Reserve Bank) was run separately from the rest of the government, it could restrict the ANC's ability to keep the promises in the Freedom Charter. Besides, if the central bank was not accountable to the ANC government, to whom, exactly, would it be accountable? The IMF? The Johannesburg Stock Exchange?

---

* Milton Friedman often joked that if he had his way, central banks would be based so purely on "economic science" that they would be run by giant computers—no humans required.

Obviously, the National Party was trying to find a backdoor way to hold on to power even after it lost the elections—a strategy that needed to be resisted at all costs. "They were locking in as much as possible," Padayachee recalled. "That was a clear part of the agenda."

Padayachee faxed the paper in the morning and didn't hear back for weeks. "Then, when we asked what happened, we were told, 'Well, we gave that one up.'" Not only would the central bank be run as an autonomous entity within the South African state, with its independence enshrined in the new constitution, but it would be headed by the same man who ran it under apartheid, Chris Stals. It wasn't just the central bank that the ANC had given up: in another major concession, Derek Keyes, the white finance minister under apartheid, would also remain in his post—much as the finance ministers and central bank heads from Argentina's dictatorship somehow managed to get their jobs back under democracy. *The New York Times* praised Keyes as "the country's ranking apostle of low-spending business-friendly government."[11]

Until that point, Padayachee said, "we were still buoyant, because, my God, this was a revolutionary struggle; at least there'd be *something* to come out of it." When he learned that the central bank and the treasury would be run by their old apartheid bosses, it meant "everything would be lost in terms of economic transformation." When I asked him whether he thought the negotiators realized how much they had lost, after some hesitation, he replied, "Frankly, no." It was simple horse-trading: "In the negotiations, something had to be given, and our side gave those things—I'll give you this, you give me that."

From Padayachee's point of view, none of this happened because of some grand betrayal on the part of ANC leaders but simply because they were outmaneuvered on a series of issues that seemed less than crucial at the time—but turned out to hold South Africa's lasting liberation in the balance.

What happened in those negotiations is that the ANC found itself caught in a new kind of web, one made of arcane rules and regulations, all designed to confine and constrain the power of elected leaders. As the web descended on the country, only a few people even noticed it was there, but when the new government came to power and tried to move freely, to give its voters the tangible benefits of liberation they expected and thought they had voted for, the strands of the web tightened and the administration discovered that its powers were tightly bound. Patrick Bond, who worked as an economic adviser in Mandela's office during the first years of ANC rule, recalls that the in-house quip was "Hey, we've got the state, where's the power?" As the new government attempted to make tangible the dreams of the Freedom Charter, it discovered that the power was elsewhere.

Want to redistribute land? Impossible—at the last minute, the negotiators agreed to add a clause to the new constitution that protects all private property, making land reform virtually impossible. Want to create jobs for millions of unemployed workers? Can't—hundreds of factories were actually about to close because the ANC had signed on to the GATT, the precursor to the World Trade Organization, which made it illegal to subsidize the auto plants and textile factories. Want to get free AIDS drugs to the townships, where the disease is spreading with terrifying speed? That violates an intellectual property rights commitment under the WTO, which the ANC joined with no public debate as a continuation of the GATT. Need money to build more and larger houses for the poor and to bring free electricity to the townships? Sorry—the budget is being eaten up servicing the massive debt, passed on quietly by the apartheid government. Print more money? Tell that to the apartheid-era head of the central bank. Free water for all? Not likely. The World Bank, with its large in-country contingent of economists, researchers and trainers (a self-proclaimed "Knowledge Bank"), is making private-sector partnerships the service norm. Want to impose currency controls to guard against wild speculation? That would violate the $850 million IMF deal, signed, conveniently enough, right before the elections. Raise the minimum wage to close the apartheid income gap? Nope. The IMF deal promises "wage restraint."[12] And don't even think about ignoring these commitments—any change will be regarded as evidence of dangerous national untrustworthiness, a lack of commitment to "reform," an absence of a "rules-based system." All of which will lead to currency crashes, aid cuts and capital flight. The bottom line was that South Africa was free but simultaneously captured; each one of these arcane acronyms represented a different thread in the web that pinned down the limbs of the new government.

A longtime antiapartheid activist, Rassool Snyman, described the trap to me in stark terms. "They never freed us. They only took the chain from around our neck and put it on our ankles." Yasmin Sooka, a prominent South African human rights activist, told me that the transition "was business saying, 'We'll keep everything and you [the ANC] will rule in name. . . . You can have political power, you can have the façade of governing, but the real governance will take place somewhere else.'"*[13] It was a process of infantilization that is common to so-called transitional countries—new governments are, in effect, given the keys to the house but not the combination to the safe.

Part of what I wanted to understand was how, after such an epic struggle for freedom, any of this could have been allowed to happen. Not just how the leaders of the liberation movement gave up the economic front, but how the ANC's base—people who had already sacrificed so much—let their leaders give it up. Why didn't the grassroots movement *demand* that the ANC keep the promises of the Freedom Charter and rebel against the concessions as they were being made?

I put the question to William Gumede, a third-generation ANC activist who, as a leader of the student movement during the transition, was on the streets in those tumultuous years. "Everyone was watching the political negotiations," he recalled, referring to the de Klerk–Mandela summits. "And if people felt it wasn't going well there would be mass protests. But when the economic negotiators would report back, people thought it was technical; no one was interested." This perception, he said, was encouraged by Mbeki, who portrayed the talks as "administrative" and of no popular concern (much like the Chileans with their "technified democracy"). As a result, he told me, with great exasperation, "We missed it! We missed the real story."

Gumede, who today is one of South Africa's most respected investigative journalists, says he came to understand that it was in those "technical" meetings that the true future of his country was being decided—though few understood it at the time. Like many people I spoke with, Gumede reminded me that South Africa was very much on the brink of civil war throughout the transition period—townships were being terrorized by gangs who had been

---

* It was the Chicago Boys in Chile, fittingly, who pioneered this process of democracy-proofing capitalism, or building what they called "new democracy." In Chile, before handing over power to an elected government after seventeen years of junta rule, the Chicago Boys rigged the constitution and the courts so it was legally next to impossible to reverse their revolutionary laws. They had many names for this process: building a "technified democracy," a "protected democracy," or, as Pinochet's young minister José Piñera put it, ensuring "insulation from politics." Alvaro Bardón, Pinochet's undersecretary of the economy, explained the classic Chicago School reasoning: "If we acknowledge economics as a science, this immediately implies less power for government or the political structure, since both lose responsibility for making such decisions."

armed by the National Party, police massacres were still taking place, leaders were still being assassinated and there was constant talk of the country descending into a bloodbath. "I was focusing on the politics—mass action, going to Bisho [site of a definitive showdown between demonstrators and police], shouting, 'Those guys must go!'" Gumede recalled. "But that was not the real struggle—the real struggle was over economics. And I *am* disappointed in myself for being so naive. I thought I was politically mature enough to understand the issues. How did I miss this?"

Since then, Gumede has been making up for lost time. When we met, he was in the middle of a national firestorm sparked by his new book, *Thabo Mbeki and the Battle for the Soul of the* ANC. It is an exhaustive exposé of precisely how the ANC negotiated away the country's economic sovereignty in those meetings he was too busy to pay attention to at the time. "I wrote the book out of anger," Gumede told me. "Anger at myself and at the party."

It's hard to see how the outcome could have been different. If Padayachee is right and the ANC's own negotiators failed to grasp the enormity of what they were bargaining away, what chance was there for the movement's street fighters?

During those key years when the deals were being signed, South Africans were in a constant state of crisis, ricocheting between the intense exuberance of watching Mandela walk free and the rage of learning that Chris Hani, the younger militant many hoped would succeed Mandela as leader, had been shot dead by a racist assassin. Other than a handful of economists, nobody wanted to talk about the independence of the central bank, a topic that works as a powerful soporific even under normal circumstances. Gumede points out that most people simply assumed that no matter what compromises had to be made to get into power, they could be unmade once the ANC was firmly in charge. "We were going to be the government—we could fix it later," he said.

What ANC activists didn't understand at the time was that it was the nature of democracy itself that was being altered in those negotiations, changed so that—once the web of constraints had descended on their country—there would effectively be no *later*.

In the first two years of ANC rule, the party still tried to use the limited resources it had to make good on the promise of redistribution. There was a flurry of public investment—more than a hundred thousand homes were built for the poor, and millions were hooked up to water, electricity and phone lines.[14] But, in a familiar story, weighed down by debt and under international pressure to privatize these services, the government soon began raising prices. After a decade of ANC rule, millions of people had been cut off from newly connected water and electricity because they couldn't pay the bills.* At least 40 percent of the new phones lines were no longer in service by 2003.[15] As for the "banks, mines and monopoly industry" that Mandela had pledged to nationalize, they remained firmly in the hands of the same four white-owned megaconglomerates that also control 80 percent of the Johannesburg Stock Exchange.[16] In 2005, only 4 percent of the companies listed on the exchange were owned or controlled by blacks.[17] Seventy percent of South Africa's land, in 2006, was still monopolized by whites, who are just 10 percent of the population.[18] Most distressingly, the ANC government has spent far more time denying the severity of the AIDS crisis than getting lifesaving drugs to the approximately 5 million people infected with HIV, though there were, by early 2007, some positive signs of progress.[19] Perhaps the most striking statistic is this one: since 1990, the year Mandela left prison, the average life expectancy for South Africans has dropped by thirteen years.[20]

Underlying all these facts and figures is a fateful choice made by the ANC after the leadership realized it had been outmaneuvered in the economic negotiations. At that point, the party could have attempted to launch a second liberation movement and break free of the asphyxiating web that had been spun during the transition. Or it could simply accept its restricted power and embrace the new economic order. The ANC's leadership chose the second option. Rather than making the centerpiece of its policy the redistribution of wealth that was already in the country—the core of the Freedom Charter on which it had been elected—the ANC, once it became the government, accepted the dominant logic that its only hope was to pursue new foreign investors who would create new wealth, the benefits of which would trickle down to the poor. But for the trickle-down model to have a hope of working, the ANC government had to radically alter its behavior to make itself appealing to investors.

This was not an easy task, as Mandela had learned when he walked out of prison. As soon as he was released, the South African stock market collapsed

---

* The question of whether more people have been cut off from new services than connected to them is highly contested in South Africa. At least one credible study has found that the cutoffs outnumber the connections: the government says it has connected nine million people to water; the study calculated ten million disconnections.

in panic; South Africa's currency, the rand, dropped by 10 percent.[21] A few weeks later, De Beers, the diamond corporation, moved its headquarters from South Africa to Switzerland.[22] This kind of instant punishment from the markets would have been unimaginable three decades earlier, when Mandela was first imprisoned. In the sixties, it was unheard of for multinationals to switch nationalities on a whim and, back then, the world money system was still firmly linked to the gold standard. Now South Africa's currency had been stripped of controls, trade barriers were down and most trading was short-term speculation.

Not only did the volatile market not like the idea of a liberated Mandela, but just a few misplaced words from him or his fellow ANC leaders could lead to an earth-shaking stampede by what the *New York Times* columnist Thomas Friedman has aptly termed "the electronic herd."[23] The stampede that greeted Mandela's release was just the start of what became a call-and-response between the ANC leadership and the financial markets—a shock dialogue that trained the party in the new rules of the game. Every time a top party official said something that hinted that the ominous Freedom Charter might still become policy, the market responded with a shock, sending the rand into free fall. The rules were simple and crude, the electronic equivalent of monosyllabic grunts: justice—expensive, sell; status quo—good, buy. When, shortly after his release, Mandela once again spoke out in favor of nationalization at a private lunch with leading businessmen, "the All-Gold Index plunged by 5 per cent."[24]

Even moves that seemed to have nothing to do with the financial world but betrayed some latent radicalism seemed to provoke a market jolt. When Trevor Manuel, an ANC minister, called rugby in South Africa a "white minority game" because its team was an all-white one, the rand took another hit.[25]

Of all the constraints on the new government, it was the market that proved most confining—and this, in a way, is the genius of unfettered capitalism: it's self-enforcing. Once countries have opened themselves up to the global market's temperamental moods, any departure from Chicago School orthodoxy is instantly punished by traders in New York and London who bet against the offending country's currency, causing a deeper crisis and the need for more loans, with more conditions attached. Mandela acknowledged the trap in 1997, telling the ANC's national conference, "The very mobility of capital and the globalisation of the capital and other markets, make it impossible for countries, for instance, to decide national economic policy without regard to the likely response of these markets."[26]

The person inside the ANC who seemed to understand how to make the shocks stop was Thabo Mbeki, Mandela's right hand during his presidency and soon to be his successor. Mbeki had spent many of his years of exile in England, studying at the University of Sussex, then moving to London. In the eighties, while the townships of his country were flooded with tear gas, he was breathing in the fumes of Thatcherism. Of all the ANC leaders, Mbeki was the one who mingled most easily with business leaders, and before Mandela's release, he organized several secret meetings with corporate executives who were afraid of the prospect of black majority rule. In 1985, after a night of drinking Scotch with Mbeki and a group of South African businesspeople at a Zambian game lodge, Hugh Murray, the editor of a prestigious business magazine, commented, "The ANC supremo has a remarkable ability to instill confidence, even in the most fraught circumstances."[27]

Mbeki was convinced that the key to getting the market to calm down was for the ANC to instill that kind of clubby confidence on a much larger scale. According to Gumede, Mbeki took on the role of free-market tutor within the party. The beast of the market had been unleashed, Mbeki would explain; there was no taming it, just feeding it what it craved: growth and more growth.

So, rather than calling for the nationalization of the mines, Mandela and Mbeki began meeting regularly with Harry Oppenheimer, former chairman of the mining giants Anglo-American and De Beers, the economic symbols of apartheid rule. Shortly after the 1994 election, they even submitted the ANC's economic program to Oppenheimer for approval and made several key revisions to address his concerns, as well as those of other top industrialists.[28] Hoping to avoid getting another shock from the market, Mandela, in his first postelection interview as president, carefully distanced himself from his previous statements favoring nationalization. "In our economic policies . . . there is not a single reference to things like nationalization, and this is not accidental," he said. "There is not a single slogan that will connect us with any Marxist ideology."*[29] The financial press offered steady encouragement for this conversion: "Though the ANC still has a powerful leftist wing," *The Wall Street Journal* observed, "Mr. Mandela has in recent days sounded more like Margaret Thatcher than the socialist revolutionary he was once thought to be."[30]

* In fact, the ANC's official economic platform, on which it had been elected, called for "increasing the public sector in strategic areas through, for example, nationalisation." Then there was the Freedom Charter, which continued to be the party's manifesto.

The memory of its radical past still clung to the ANC, and despite the new government's best efforts to appear unthreatening, the market kept inflicting its painful shocks: in a single month in 1996, the rand dropped 20 percent, and the country continued to hemorrhage capital as South Africa's jittery rich moved their money offshore.[31]

Mbeki convinced Mandela that what was needed was a definitive break with the past. The ANC needed a completely new economic plan—something bold, something shocking, something that would communicate, in the broad, dramatic strokes the market understood, that the ANC was ready to embrace the Washington Consensus.

As in Bolivia, where the shock therapy program was prepared with all the secrecy of a covert military operation, in South Africa only a handful of Mbeki's closest colleagues even knew that a new economic program was in the works, one very different from the promises they had all made during the 1994 elections. Of the people on the team, Gumede writes, "all were sworn to secrecy and the entire process was shrouded in deepest confidentiality lest the left wing get wind of Mbeki's plan."[32] The economist Stephen Gelb, who took part in drafting the new program, admitted that "this was 'reform from above' with a vengeance, taking to an extreme the arguments in favour of insulation and autonomy of policymakers from popular pressures."[33] (This emphasis on secrecy and insulation was particularly ironic given that, under the tyranny of apartheid, the ANC had pulled off a remarkably open and participatory process to come up with the Freedom Charter. Now, under a new order of democracy, the party was opting to hide its economic plans from its own caucus.)

In June 1996, Mbeki unveiled the results: it was a neoliberal shock therapy program for South Africa, calling for more privatization, cutbacks to government spending, labor "flexibility," freer trade and even looser controls on money flows. According to Gelb, its overriding aim "was to signal to potential investors the government's (and specifically the ANC's) commitment to the prevailing orthodoxy."[34] To make sure the message was loud and clear to traders in New York and London, at the public launch of the plan, Mbeki quipped, "Just call me a Thatcherite."[35]

Shock therapy is always a market performance—that is part of its underlying theory. The stock market loves overhyped, highly managed moments that send stock prices soaring, usually provided by an initial public stock offering, the announcement of a huge merger or the hiring of a celebrity CEO. When economists urge countries to announce a sweeping shock therapy package, the advice is partially based on an attempt to imitate this kind of high-drama market event and trigger a stampede—but rather than selling an individual stock, they are selling a country. The hoped-for response is "Buy Argentine stocks!" "Buy Bolivian bonds!" A slower, more careful approach, on the other hand, may be less brutal, but it deprives the market of these hype-bubbles, during which the real money gets made. Shock therapy is always a significant gamble, and in South Africa it didn't work: Mbeki's grand gesture failed to attract long-term investment; it resulted only in speculative betting that ended up devaluing the currency even further.

The Shock of the Base

"The new convert is always more zealous at these things. They want to please even more," remarked the Durban-based writer Ashwin Desai when we met to discuss his memories of the transition. Desai spent time in jail during the liberation struggle, and he sees parallels between the psychology in prisons and the ANC's behavior in government. In prison, he said, "if you please the warden more, you get a better status. And that logic obviously transposed itself into some of the things that South African society did. They did want to somehow prove that they were much better prisoners. Much more disciplined prisoners than other countries, even."

The ANC base, however, proved distinctly more unruly—which created a need for yet more discipline. According to Yasmin Sooka, one of the jurors on South Africa's Truth and Reconciliation Commission, the discipline mentality reached into every aspect of the transition—including the quest for justice. After hearing years of testimony about torture, killings and disappearances, the truth commission turned to the question of what kind of gestures could begin to heal the injustices. Truth and forgiveness were important, but so was compensation for the victims and their families. It made little sense to ask the new government to make compensation payouts, as these were not its crimes, and anything spent on reparations for apartheid abuses was money not spent building homes and schools for the poor in the newly liberated nation.

Some commissioners felt that multinational corporations that had benefited from apartheid should be forced to pay reparations. In the end the Truth and Reconciliation Commission made the modest recommendation of a onetime 1 percent corporate tax to raise money for the victims, what it called "a solidarity tax." Sooka expected support for this mild recommendation from the ANC; instead, the government, then headed by Mbeki, rejected any suggestion of corporate reparations or a solidarity tax, fearing that it would send an antibusiness message to the market. "The president decided not to hold business accountable," Sooka told me. "It was that simple." In the end, the government put forward a fraction of what had been requested, taking the money out of its own budget, as the commissioners had feared.

South Africa's Truth and Reconciliation Commission is frequently held up as a model of successful "peace building," exported to other conflict zones from Sri Lanka to Afghanistan. But many of those who were directly involved in the process are deeply ambivalent. When he unveiled the final report in March 2003, the commission's chairman, Archbishop Desmond Tutu, confronted journalists with freedom's unfinished business. "Can you explain how a black person wakes up in a squalid ghetto today, almost 10 years after freedom? Then he goes to work in town, which is still largely white, in palatial homes. And at the end of the day, he goes back home to squalor? I don't know why those people don't just say, 'To hell with peace. To hell with Tutu and the truth commission.'"[36]

Sooka, who now heads South Africa's Foundation for Human Rights, says that she feels that although the hearings dealt with what she described as "outward manifestations of apartheid such as torture, severe ill treatment and disappearances," it left the economic system served by those abuses "completely untouched"—an echo of the concerns about the blindness of "human rights" expressed by Orlando Letelier three decades earlier. If she had the process to do over again, Sooka said, "I would do it completely differently. I would look at the *systems* of apartheid—I would look at the question of land, I would certainly look at the role of multinationals, I would look at the role of the mining industry very, very closely because I think that's the real sickness of South Africa. . . . I would look at the systematic effects of the policies of apartheid, and I would devote only *one* hearing to torture because I think when you focus on torture and you don't look at what it was serving, that's when you start to do a revision of the real history."

Reparations in Reverse

The fact that the ANC dismissed the Commission's call for corporate reparations is particularly unfair, Sooka pointed out, because the government continues to pay the apartheid debt. In the first years after the handover, it cost the new government 30 billion rand annually (about $4.5 billion) in servicing—a sum that provides a stark contrast with the paltry total of $85 million that the government ultimately paid out to more than nineteen thousand victims of apartheid killings and torture and their families. Nelson Mandela has cited the debt burden as the single greatest obstacle to keeping the promises of the Freedom Charter. "That is 30 billion [rand] we did not have to build houses as we planned, before we came into government, to make sure that our children go to the best schools, that unemployment is properly addressed and that everybody has the dignity of having a job, a decent income, of being able to provide shelter to his beloved, to feed them. . . . We are limited by the debt that we inherited."[37]

Despite Mandela's acknowledgment that paying the apartheid bills has become a disfiguring burden, the party has opposed all suggestions that it default. The fear is that even though there is a strong legal case that the debts are "odious," any move to default would make South Africa look dangerously radical in the eyes of investors, thus provoking another market shock. Dennis Brutus, a longtime ANC member and a former prisoner on Robben Island, ran directly into that wall of fear. In 1998, seeing the financial stress the new government was under, he and a group of South African activists decided that the best way they could support the ongoing struggle was to start a "debt jubilee" movement. "I must say, I was so naive," Brutus, now in his seventies, told me. "I expected that the government would express appreciation to us, that the grass roots are taking up the issue of debt, you know, that it would reinforce the government taking up debt." To his astonishment, "the government repudiated us and said, 'No, we don't accept your support.'"

What makes the ANC's decision to keep paying the debt so infuriating to activists like Brutus is the tangible sacrifice made to meet each payment. For instance, between 1997 and 2004, the South African government sold eighteen state-owned firms, raising $4 billion, but almost half the money went to servicing the debt.[38] In other words, not only did the ANC renege on Mandela's original pledge of "the nationalisation of the mines, banks and monopoly industry" but because of the debt, it was doing the opposite—selling off national assets to make good on the debts of its oppressors.

Then there is the matter of where, precisely, the money is going. During the transition negotiations, F. W. de Klerk's team demanded that all civil servants be guaranteed their jobs even after the handover; those who wanted to leave, they argued, should receive hefty lifelong pensions. This was an extraordinary demand in a country with no social safety net to speak of, yet it was one of several "technical" issues on which the ANC ceded ground.[39] The concession meant that the new ANC government carried the cost of two governments—its own, and a shadow white government that was out of power. Forty percent of the government's annual debt payments go to the country's massive pension fund. The vast majority of the beneficiaries are former apartheid employees.*[40]

In the end, South Africa has wound up with a twisted case of reparations in reverse, with the white businesses that reaped enormous profits from black labor during the apartheid years paying not a cent in reparations, but the victims of apartheid continuing to send large paychecks to their former victimizers. And how do they raise the money for this generosity? By stripping the state of its assets through privatization—a modern form of the very looting that the ANC had been so intent on avoiding when it agreed to negotiations, hoping to prevent a repeat of Mozambique. Unlike what happened in Mozambique, however, where civil servants broke machinery, stuffed their pockets and then fled, in South Africa the dismantling of the state and the pillaging of its coffers continue to this day.

When I arrived in South Africa, the fiftieth anniversary of the signing of the Freedom Charter was approaching, and the ANC had decided to mark the event with a media spectacle. The plan was for Parliament to relocate for the day from its usual commanding home in Cape Town to the far more humble surroundings of Kliptown, where the charter was first ratified. The South African president, Thabo Mbeki, was going to take the occasion to rename Kliptown's main intersection the Walter Sisulu Square of Dedication, after one of the ANC's most revered leaders. Mbeki would also inaugurate a new Freedom Charter Monument, a brick tower in which the words of the Charter had been engraved on stone tablets, and light an eternal "flame of

---

* In fact, this one apartheid-era burden is simultaneously driving the growth of the country's overall debt and putting billions of rand of public money out of reach every year. A "technical" accounting change in 1989 switched the state pension fund from a "pay as you go" system, in which benefits are paid from contributions made in any given year, to a "fully funded" system, in which the fund has to have on hand enough capital to pay out 70 to 80 percent of its total liabilities at any given time—not a scenario it will ever face. As a result, the fund ballooned from 30 billion rand in 1989 to more than 300 billion rand in 2004—certainly qualifying as a debt shock. What this means for South Africans is that the huge pool of capital administered independently by the pension fund has been cordoned off and placed out of reach for spending on housing, health care or basic services. The pension agreement was actually negotiated on the ANC side by Joe Slovo, the legendary leader of the South African Communist Party, a fact that continues to be a source of great resentment in the country today.

freedom." Adjacent to this building, work was progressing on another monument, this one called the Freedom Towers, a pavilion of black and white concrete pillars designed to symbolize the charter's famous clause that says, "South Africa belongs to all those who live in it, black and white."[41]

The overall message of the event was hard to miss: fifty years ago, the party had promised to bring freedom to South Africa and now it had delivered—it was the ANC's own "mission accomplished" moment.

Yet there was something strange about the event. Kliptown—an impoverished township with dilapidated shacks, raw sewage in the streets and an unemployment rate of 72 percent, far higher than under apartheid—seems more like a symbol of the Freedom Charter's broken promises than an appropriate backdrop for such a slickly produced celebration.[42] As it turned out, the anniversary events were staged and art-directed not by the ANC but by an odd entity called Blue IQ. Though officially an arm of the provincial government, Blue IQ "operates in a carefully constructed environment which makes it look and feel more like a private sector company than a government department," according to its very glossy, and very blue, brochure. Its goal is to drum up new foreign investment in South Africa—part of the ANC program of "re-distribution through growth."

Blue IQ had identified tourism as a major growth area for investment, and its market research showed that for tourists visiting South Africa, a large part of the attraction is the ANC's global reputation for having triumphed over oppression. Hoping to build on this powerful draw, Blue IQ determined that there was no better symbol of the South African triumph-over-adversity narrative than the Freedom Charter. With that in mind, it launched a project to transform Kliptown into a Freedom Charter theme park, "a world-class tourist destination and heritage site offering local and international visitors a unique experience"—complete with museum, a freedom-themed shopping mall and a glass-and-steel Freedom Hotel. What is now a slum is set to be remade "into a desirous and prosperous" Johannesburg suburb, while many of its current residents will be relocated to slums in less historic locales.[43]

With its plans to rebrand Kliptown, Blue IQ is following the free-market playbook—providing incentives for business to invest, in the hope that it will create jobs down the road. What sets this particular project apart is that, in Kliptown, the foundation on which the entire trickle-down apparatus rests is a fifty-year-old piece of paper that called for a distinctly more direct road to poverty elimination. Redistribute the land so millions can sustain themselves from it, demanded the framers of the Freedom Charter, and take back the mines so the bounty can be used to build houses and infrastructure and create jobs in the process. In other words, cut out the middleman. Those ideas may sound like utopian populism to many ears, but after so many failed experiments in Chicago School orthodoxy, the real dreamers may be those who still believe that a scheme like the Freedom Charter theme park, which provided handouts to corporations while further dispossessing the neediest people, will solve the pressing health and economic problems for the 22 million South Africans still living in poverty.[44]

After more than a decade since South Africa made its decisive turn toward Thatcherism, the results of its experiment in trickle-down justice are scandalous:

- Since 1994, the year the ANC took power, the number of people living on less than $1 a day has doubled, from 2 million to 4 million in 2006.[45]
- Between 1991 and 2002, the unemployment rate for black South Africans more than doubled, from 23 percent to 48 percent.[46]
- Of South Africa's 35 million black citizens, only five thousand earn more than $60,000 a year. The number of whites in that income bracket is twenty times higher, and many earn far more than that amount.[47]
- The ANC government has built 1.8 million homes, but in the meantime 2 million people have lost their homes.[48]
- Close to 1 million people have been evicted from farms in the first decade of democracy.[49]
- Such evictions have meant that the number of shack dwellers has grown by 50 percent. In 2006, more than one in four South Africans lived in shacks located in informal shantytowns, many without running water or electricity.[50]

Perhaps the best measure of the betrayed promises of freedom is the way the Freedom Charter is now regarded in different parts of South African society. Not so long ago, the document represented the ultimate threat to white privilege in the country; today it is embraced in business lounges and gated communities as a statement of good intentions, at once flattering and totally unthreatening, on a par with a flowery corporate code of conduct. But in the townships where the document adopted in a field in Kliptown was once electric with possibility, its promises are almost too painful to contemplate. Many South Africans boycotted the government-sponsored anniversary celebrations completely. "What is in the Freedom Charter is very good," S'bu Zikode, a leader of Durban's burgeoning shack dwellers' movement, told me. "But all I see is the betrayal."

In the end, the most persuasive argument for abandoning the redistribution promises of the Freedom Charter was the least imaginative one: everyone is doing it. Vishnu Padayachee summed up for me the message that the ANC leadership was getting from the start from "Western governments, the IMF and the World Bank. They would say, 'The world has changed; none of that left stuff means anything anymore; this is the only game in town.'" As Gumede writes, "It was an onslaught for which the ANC was wholly unprepared. Key economic leaders were regularly ferried to the head offices of international organizations such as the World Bank and IMF, and during 1992 and 1993 several ANC staffers, some of whom had no economic qualifications at all, took part in abbreviated executive training programs at foreign business schools, investment banks, economic policy think tanks and the World Bank, where they were 'fed a steady diet of neo-liberal ideas.' It was a dizzying experience. Never before had a government-in-waiting been so seduced by the international community."[51]

Mandela received a particularly intense dose of this elite form of schoolyard peer pressure when he met with European leaders at the 1992 World Economic Forum in Davos. When he pointed out that South Africa wanted to do nothing more radical than what Western Europe had done under the Marshall Plan after the Second World War, the Dutch minister of finance dismissed the parallel. "That was what we understood then. But the economies of the world are interdependent. The process of globalization is taking root. No economy can develop separately from the economies of other countries."[52]

As leaders like Mandela traveled the globalization circuit, it was pounded into them that even the most left-wing governments were embracing the Washington Consensus: the Communists in Vietnam and China were doing it, and so were the trade unionists in Poland and the social democrats in Chile, finally free from Pinochet. Even Russians had seen the neoliberal light—at the time the ANC was in its heaviest negotiations, Moscow was in the midst of a corporatist feeding frenzy, selling off its state assets to apparatchiks-turned-entrepreneurs as fast as it could. If Moscow had given in, how could a raggedy band of freedom fighters in South Africa resist such a forceful global tide?

That, at least, was the message being peddled by the lawyers, economists and social workers who made up the rapidly expanding "transition" industry—the teams of experts who hop from war-torn country to crisis-racked city, regaling overwhelmed new politicians with the latest best practice from Buenos Aires, the most inspiring success story from Warsaw, the most fearsome roar from the Asian Tigers. "Transitionologists" (as the NYU political scientist Stephen Cohen has called them) have a built-in advantage over the politicians they advise: they are a hypermobile class, while the leaders of liberation movements are inherently inward-looking.[53] By their very nature, people spearheading intense national transformations are narrowly focused on their own narratives and power struggles, often unable to pay close attention to the world beyond their borders. That's unfortunate, because if the ANC leadership had been able to cut through the transitionology spin and find out for itself what was really going on in Moscow, Warsaw, Buenos Aires and Seoul, it would have seen a very different picture.

CHAPTER 11

BONFIRE OF A YOUNG DEMOCRACY

RUSSIA CHOOSES "THE PINOCHET OPTION"

> Pieces of a living city cannot be auctioned off without taking into consideration that there are indigenous traditions, even if they seem odd to foreigners. . . . But these are our traditions and our city. For a long time we lived under the dictatorship of the Communists, but now we have found out that life under the dictatorship of business people is no better. They couldn't care less about what country they are in.
> —Grigory Gorin, Russian writer, 1993[1]

> Spread the truth—the laws of economics are like the laws of engineering. One set of laws works everywhere.
> —Lawrence Summers, chief economist of the World Bank, 1991[2]

When Soviet president Mikhail Gorbachev flew to London to attend his first G7 Summit in July 1991, he had every reason to expect a hero's welcome. For the previous three years, he had seemed not so much to stride across the international stage as to float, charming the media, signing disarmament treaties and picking up peace prizes, including the Nobel in 1990.

He had even managed to do the previously unthinkable: win over the American public. The Russian leader so thoroughly challenged Evil Empire caricatures that the U.S. press had taken to calling him by a cuddly nickname, "Gorby," and in 1987, *Time* magazine took the risky decision of making the Soviet president their Man of the Year. The editors explained that unlike his predecessors ("gargoyles in fur hats"), Gorbachev was Russia's own Ronald Reagan — "a Kremlin version of the Great Communicator." The Nobel Prize committee declared that thanks to his work, "It is our hope that we are now celebrating the end of the Cold War."[3]

By the beginning of the nineties, with his twin policies of *glasnost* (openness) and *perestroika* (restructuring), Gorbachev had led the Soviet Union through a remarkable process of democratization: the press had been freed, Russia's parliament, local councils, president and vice president had been elected, and the constitutional court was independent. As for the economy, Gorbachev was moving toward a mixture of a free market and a strong safety net, with key industries under public control — a process he predicted would take ten to fifteen years to be completed. His end goal was to build social democracy on the Scandinavian model, "a socialist beacon for all mankind."[4]

At first it seemed that the West also wanted Gorbachev to succeed in loosening up the Soviet economy and transforming it into something close to Sweden's. The Nobel Committee explicitly described the prize as a way of offering support to the transition — "a helping hand in an hour of need." And on a visit to Prague, Gorbachev made it clear that he couldn't do it all alone: "Like mountain climbers on one rope, the world's nations can either climb together to the summit or fall together into the abyss," he said.[5]

So what happened at the G7 meeting in 1991 was totally unexpected. The nearly unanimous message that Gorbachev received from his fellow heads of state was that, if he did not embrace radical economic shock therapy immediately, they would sever the rope and let him fall. "Their suggestions as to the tempo and methods of transition were astonishing," Gorbachev wrote of the event.[6]

Poland had just completed its first round of shock therapy under the IMF's and Jeffrey Sachs's tutelage, and the consensus among British prime minister John Major, U.S. president George H. W. Bush, Canadian prime minister Brian Mulroney and Japanese prime minister Toshiki Kaifu was that the Soviet Union had to follow Poland's lead on an even faster timetable. After the meeting, Gorbachev got the same marching orders from the IMF, the World Bank and every other major lending institution. Later that year, when Russia asked for debt forgiveness to weather a catastrophic economic crisis, the stern answer was that the debts had to be honored.[7] Since the time when Sachs had marshaled aid and debt relief for Poland, the political mood had changed — it was meaner.

What happened next — the dissolution of the Soviet Union, Gorbachev's eclipse by Yeltsin, and the tumultuous course of economic shock therapy in Russia—is a well-documented chapter of contemporary history. It is, however, a story too often told in the bland language of "reform," a narrative so generic that it has hidden one of the greatest crimes committed against a democracy in modern history. Russia, like China, was forced to choose between a Chicago School economic program and an authentic democratic revolution. Faced with that choice, China's leaders had attacked their own people in order to prevent democracy from disturbing their free-market plans. Russia was different: the democratic revolution was already well under way—in order to push through a Chicago School economic program, that peaceful and hopeful process that Gorbachev began had to be violently interrupted, then radically reversed.

Gorbachev knew that the only way to impose the kind of shock therapy being advocated by the G7 and the IMF was with force—as did many in the West pushing for these policies. *The Economist* magazine, in an influential 1990 piece, urged Gorbachev to adopt "strong-man rule . . . to smash the resistance that has blocked serious economic reform."[8] Only two weeks after the Nobel Committee had declared an end to the Cold War, *The Economist* was urging Gorbachev to model himself after one of the Cold War's most notorious killers. Under the heading "Mikhail Sergeevich Pinochet?" the article concluded that even though following its advice could cause "possible blood-letting . . . it might, just might, be the Soviet Union's turn for what could be called the Pinochet approach to liberal economics." *The Washington Post* was willing to go further. In August 1991, the paper ran a commentary under the headline "Pinochet's Chile a Pragmatic Model for Soviet Economy." The article supported the idea of a coup for getting rid of the slow-going Gorbachev, but the author, Michael Schrage, worried that the Soviet president's opponents "had neither the savvy nor the support to seize the Pinochet option." They should model themselves, Schrage wrote, after "a despot who really knew how to run a coup: retired Chilean general Augusto Pinochet."[9]

Gorbachev soon found himself facing an adversary who was more than willing to play the role of a Russian Pinochet. Boris Yeltsin, though holding the post of Russian president, had a much lower profile than Gorbachev, who headed all the Soviet Union. That was to change dramatically on August 19, 1991, one month after the G7 Summit. A group from the Communist old guard drove tanks up to the White House, as the Russian parliament building is called. In a bid to halt the democratization process, they threatened to attack the country's first elected parliament. Amid a crowd of Russians determined to defend their new democracy, Yeltsin stood on one of the tanks and denounced the aggression as "a cynical, right-wing coup attempt."[10] The tanks retreated, and Yeltsin emerged as a courageous defender of democracy. One demonstrator who stood in the streets that day described it as "the first time I felt that I could really affect the situation in my country. Our souls soared. It was such a feeling of unity. We felt invincible."[11]

And so did Yeltsin. As a leader, he had always been a kind of anti-Gorbachev. Where Gorbachev had projected propriety and sobriety (one of his most controversial measures was an aggressive anti-vodka-drinking campaign), Yeltsin was a notorious glutton and a heavy drinker. Prior to the coup, many Russians harbored reservations about Yeltsin, but he had helped save democracy from a Communist coup, and that made him, at least for the time being, a people's hero.

Yeltsin immediately parlayed his triumphant showdown into increased political power. As long as the Soviet Union remained intact, he would always have less control than Gorbachev, but in December 1991, four months after the aborted coup, Yeltsin pulled off a political masterstroke. He formed an alliance with two other Soviet republics, a move that had the effect of abruptly dissolving the Soviet Union, thereby forcing Gorbachev's resignation. The abolition of the Soviet Union, "the only country most Russians had ever known," was a powerful shock to the Russian psyche—and as the political scientist Stephen Cohen put it, it was the first of "three traumatic shocks" that Russians would endure over the next three years.[12]

Jeffrey Sachs was in the room at the Kremlin on the day Yeltsin announced that the Soviet Union was no more. Sachs recalled the Russian president saying, "'Gentlemen, I just want to announce that the Soviet Union has ended. . . .' And I said, 'Gee, you know, this is once in a century. This is the most incredible thing you can imagine; this is a true liberation; let's help these people.'"[13] Yeltsin had invited Sachs to come to Russia to serve as an adviser, and Sachs was more than game: "If Poland can do it, so can Russia," he declared.[14]

But Yeltsin didn't just want advice, he wanted the kind of gold-plated fund-raising that Sachs had pulled off for Poland. "The only hope," Yeltsin said, "was the promises of the Group of Seven quickly to grant us large sums of financial aid."[15] Sachs told Yeltsin he was confident that if Moscow was willing to go with the "big bang" approach to establishing a capitalist economy, he could raise something in the area of $15 billion.[16] They would need to be ambitious, and they would need to move fast. What Yeltsin did not know was that Sachs's luck was about to run out.

Russia's conversion to capitalism had much in common with the corrupt approach that had sparked the Tiananmen Square protests in China two years earlier. Moscow's mayor, Gavriil Popov, has claimed that there were really only two options for how to break up the centrally controlled economy: "Property can be divided among all members of society, or the best pieces can be given to the leaders. . . . In a word, there's the democratic approach, and there's the nomenklatura, apparatchik approach."[17] Yeltsin took the latter approach—and he was in a hurry. In late 1991, he went to the parliament and made an unorthodox proposal: if they gave him one year of special powers, under which he could issue laws by decree rather than bring them to parliament for a vote, he would solve the economic crisis and give them back a thriving, healthy system. What Yeltsin was asking for was the kind of executive power enjoyed by dictators, not democrats, but the parliament was still grateful to the president for his role during the attempted coup, and the country was desperate for foreign aid. The answer was yes: Yeltsin could have one year of absolute power to remake Russia's economy.

He immediately assembled a team of economists, many of whom, in the final years of Communism, had formed a kind of free-market book club, reading the basic texts of the Chicago School thinkers and discussing how the theories could be applied in Russia. Though they had never studied in the U.S., they were such devoted fans of Milton Friedman that the Russian press took to calling Yeltsin's team "the Chicago Boys," a knock-off of the original title, and fitting in the context of Russia's thriving black market economy. In the West they were dubbed "the young reformers." The group's figurehead was Yegor Gaidar, whom Yeltsin named as one of his two deputy prime ministers. Pyotr Aven, a Yeltsin minister in 1991–92 who was part of this inner circle, said of his former clique, "Their identification of themselves with God, which flowed naturally from their belief in their all-round superiority, was, unfortunately, typical of our reformers."[18]

Surveying the group that had suddenly ascended to power in Moscow, the Russian newspaper *Nezavisimaya Gazeta* observed the rather astonishing development that "for the first time Russia will get in its government a team of liberals who consider themselves followers of Friedrich von Hayek and the 'Chicago school' of Milton Friedman." Their policies were "quite clear—'strict financial stabilization' according to 'shock therapy' recipes." At the same time as Yeltsin made these appointments, the newspaper noted, he had also put the notorious strongman Yury Skokov "in charge of the defense and repressive departments: the Army, the Ministry of Internal Affairs and the State Security Committee." The decisions were clearly connected: "Probably the 'strong' Skokov can 'ensure' strict stabilization in politics while the 'strong' economists guarantee it in the economy." The article ended with a prediction: "It will come as no surprise if they attempt to construct something like a homegrown Pinochet system, in which the role of the 'Chicago boys' will be played by Gaidar's team."[19]

To provide ideological and technical backup for Yeltsin's Chicago Boys, the U.S. government funded its own transition experts whose jobs ranged from writing privatization decrees, to launching a New York–style stock exchange, to designing a Russian mutual fund market. In the fall of 1992, US-AID awarded a $2.1 million contract to the Harvard Institute for International Development, which sent teams of young lawyers and economists to shadow the Gaidar team. In May 1995, Harvard named Sachs director of the Harvard Institute for International Development, which meant that he played two roles in Russia's reform period: he began as a freelance adviser to Yeltsin, then moved on to overseeing Harvard's large Russia outpost, funded by the U.S. government.

Once again a group of self-described revolutionaries huddled in secret to write a radical economic program. As Dimitry Vasiliev, one of the key reformers, recalled, "At the start, we didn't have a single employee, not even a secretary. We didn't have any equipment, not even a fax machine. And in those conditions, in just a month and a half, we had to write a comprehensive privatization program, we had to write twenty normative laws. . . . It was a really romantic period."[20]

On October 28, 1991, Yeltsin announced the lifting of price controls, predicting that "the liberalization of prices will put everything in its right place."[21] The "reformers" waited only one week after Gorbachev resigned to launch their economic shock therapy program—the second of the three traumatic shocks. The shock therapy program also included free-trade policies and the first phase of the rapid-fire privatization of the country's approximately 225,000 state-owned companies.[22]

"The country was taken by surprise by the 'Chicago School' program," one of Yeltsin's original economic advisers recalled.[23] That surprise was deliberate, part of Gaidar's strategy of unleashing change so suddenly and quickly that resistance would be impossible. The problem his team was up against was the usual one: the threat of democracy obstructing their plans. Russians did not want their economy organized by a Communist central committee, but most still believed firmly in wealth redistribution and in an activist role for government. Like the Polish supporters of Solidarity, 67 percent of Russians told pollsters in 1992 they believed workers' cooperatives were the most equitable way to privatize the assets of the Communist state, and 79 percent said they considered maintaining full employment to be a core function of government.[24] That meant that if Yeltsin's team had submitted their plans to democratic debate, rather than launching a stealth attack on an already deeply disoriented public, the Chicago School revolution would not have stood a chance.

Vladimir Mau, an adviser to Boris Yeltsin in this period, explained that "the most favorable condition for reform" is a "weary public, exhausted by the previous political struggle. . . . That is why the government was confident, on the eve of price liberalization, that a drastic social clash was impossible, that the government would not be overthrown by a popular revolt." The vast majority of Russians—70 percent—were opposed to lifting price controls, he explained, but "we could see that the people, then and now, were concentrating on the yields of their private [garden] plots and in general on their individual economic circumstances."[25]

Joseph Stiglitz, who at the time was serving as chief economist at the World Bank, summarized the mentality that guided the shock therapists. His metaphors should by now be familiar: "Only a blitzkrieg approach during the 'window of opportunity' provided by the 'fog of transition' would get the changes made before the population had a chance to organize to protect its previous vested interests."[26] In other words, the shock doctrine.

Stiglitz called Russia's reformers "market Bolsheviks" for their fondness for cataclysmic revolution.[27] However, where the original Bolsheviks fully intended to build their centrally planned state in the ashes of the old, the market Bolsheviks believed in a kind of magic: if the optimal conditions for profit making were created, the country would rebuild itself, no planning required. (It was a faith that would reemerge, a decade later, in Iraq.)

Yeltsin made wild promises that "for approximately six months, things will be worse," but then the recovery would begin, and soon enough Russia would be an economic titan, one of the top four economies in the world.[28] This logic of so-called creative destruction resulted in scarce creation and spiraling destruction. After only one year, shock therapy had taken a devastating toll: millions of middle-class Russians had lost their life savings when money lost its value, and abrupt cuts to subsidies meant millions of workers had not been paid in months.[29] The average Russian consumed 40 percent less in 1992 than in 1991, and a third of the population fell below the poverty line.[30] The middle class was forced to sell personal belongings from card tables on the streets—desperate acts that the Chicago School economists praised as "entrepreneurial," proof that a capitalist renaissance was indeed under way, one family heirloom and second-hand blazer at a time.[31]

As in Poland, Russians did, eventually, regain their bearings and began to demand an end to the sadistic economic adventure ("no more experiments" was a popular piece of graffiti in Moscow at the time). Under pressure from voters, the country's elected parliament—the same body that had supported Yeltsin's rise to power—decided it was time to rein in the president and his ersatz Chicago Boys. In December 1992, they voted to unseat Yegor Gaidar, and three months later, in March 1993, the parliamentarians voted to repeal the special powers they had given to Yeltsin to impose his economic laws by decree. The grace period had expired, and the results were abysmal; from now on, laws had to go through parliament, a standard measure in any liberal democracy and following the procedures set out in Russia's constitution.

The deputies were acting within their rights, but Yeltsin had grown accustomed to his augmented powers and had come to think of himself less as a president and more as a monarch (he had taken to calling himself Boris I). He retaliated against the parliament's "mutiny" by going on television and declaring a state of emergency, which conveniently restored his imperial powers. Three days later, Russia's independent Constitutional Court (the creation of which was one of Gorbachev's most significant democratic breakthroughs) ruled 9–3 that Yeltsin's power grab violated, on eight different counts, the constitution he had sworn to uphold.

Until this point, it had still been possible to present "economic reform" and democratic reform as part of the same project in Russia. But once Yeltsin declared a state of emergency, the two projects were on a collision course, with Yeltsin and his shock therapists in direct opposition to the elected parliament and the constitution.

Nevertheless, the West threw its weight behind Yeltsin, who was still cast in the role of a progressive "genuinely committed to freedom and democracy, genuinely committed to reform," in the words of then U.S. president Bill Clinton.[32] The majority of the Western press also sided with Yeltsin against the entire parliament, whose members were dismissed as "communist hardliners" trying to roll back democratic reforms.[33] They suffered, according to the *New York Times* Moscow bureau chief, from "a Soviet mentality—suspicious of reform, ignorant of democracy, disdainful of intellectuals or 'democrats.'"[34]

In fact, these were the same politicians, for all their flaws (and with 1,041 deputies there were plenty), who had stood with Yeltsin and Gorbachev against the coup by the hardliners in 1991, who had voted to dissolve the Soviet Union and who had, until recently, thrown their support behind Yeltsin. Yet *The Washington Post* opted to cast Russia's parliamentarians as "antigovernment"—as if they were interlopers and not themselves part of the government.[35]

In the spring of 1993, the collision drew closer when parliament brought forward a budget bill that did not follow IMF demands for strict austerity. Yeltsin responded by trying to eliminate the parliament. He hastily threw together a referendum, supported in Orwellian fashion by the press, which asked voters if they agreed to dissolve parliament and hold snap elections. Not enough voters turned out to give Yeltsin the mandate he needed. He still claimed victory, however, maintaining that the exercise proved the country was behind him, because he had slipped in an entirely non-binding question about whether voters supported his reforms. A slim majority said yes.[36]

In Russia, the referendum was widely seen as a propaganda exercise, and a failed one at that. The reality was that Yeltsin and Washington were still stuck with a parliament that had the constitutional right to do what it was doing: slowing down the shock therapy transformation. An intense pressure campaign began. Lawrence Summers, then U.S. Treasury undersecretary, warned that "the momentum for Russian reform must be reinvigorated and intensified to ensure sustained multilateral support."[37] The IMF got the message, and an unnamed official leaked to the press that a promised $1.5 billion loan was being rescinded because the IMF was "unhappy with Russia's backtracking on reforms."[38] Pyotr Aven, the former Yeltsin minister, said, "The maniacal obsession of the IMF with budgetary and monetary policy, and its absolutely superficial and formal attitude to everything else . . . played not a small role in what happened."[39]

What happened was that the day after the IMF leak, Yeltsin, confident that he had the West's support, took his first irreversible step toward what was now being openly referred to as the "Pinochet option": he issued decree 1400, announcing that the constitution was abolished and parliament dissolved. Two days later, a special session of parliament voted 636–2 to impeach

Yeltsin for this outrageous act (the equivalent of the U.S. president unilaterally dissolving Congress). Vice President Aleksandr Rutskoi announced that Russia had already "paid a dear price for the political adventurism" of Yeltsin and the reformers.[40]

Some kind of armed conflict between Yeltsin and the parliament was now inevitable. Despite the fact that Russia's Constitutional Court once again ruled Yeltsin's behavior unconstitutional, Clinton continued to back him, and Congress voted to give Yeltsin $2.5 billion in aid. Emboldened, Yeltsin sent in troops to surround the parliament and got the city to cut off power, heat and phone lines to the White House parliament building. Boris Kagarlitsky, director of the Institute of Globalization Studies in Moscow, told me that supporters of Russian democracy "were coming in by the thousands trying to break the blockade. There were two weeks of peaceful demonstrations confronting the troops and police forces, which led to partial unblocking of the parliament building, with people able to bring food and water inside. Peaceful resistance was growing more popular and gaining broader support every day."

With each side becoming more entrenched, the only compromise that could have resolved the standoff would have been for both sides to agree to early elections, putting everybody's job up for public review. Many were urging this outcome, but just as Yeltsin was weighing his options, and reportedly leaning toward elections, news came from Poland that voters had rained down their decisive punishment on Solidarity, the party that had betrayed them with shock therapy.

After they witnessed Solidarity get pounded at the polls, it was obvious to Yeltsin and his Western advisers that early elections were far too risky. In Russia, too much wealth hung in the balance: huge oil fields, about 30 percent of the world's natural gas reserves, 20 percent of its nickel, not to mention weapons factories and the state media apparatus with which the Communist Party had controlled the vast population.

Yeltsin abandoned negotiations and moved into war posture. Having just doubled military salaries, he had most of the army on his side, and he "surrounded the parliament with thousands of Interior Ministry troops, barbed wire and water cannons and refused to let anyone pass," according to *The Washington Post*.[41] Vice President Rutskoi, Yeltsin's main rival in parliament, had by this point armed his guards and welcomed proto-fascist nationalists into his camp. He urged his supporters to "not give a moment of peace" to Yeltsin's "dictatorship."[42] Kagarlitsky, who participated in the protests and wrote a book about the episode, told me that on October 3, crowds of supporters of the parliament "marched to the Ostankino TV center to demand that news be announced. Some people in the crowd were armed, but most were not. There were children in the crowd. It was met by Yeltsin's troops and machine-gunned." About one hundred demonstrators, and one member of the military, were killed. Yeltsin's next move was to dissolve all city and regional councils in the country. Russia's young democracy was being destroyed piece by piece.

There is no doubt that some parliamentarians showed antipathy for a peaceful settlement by egging on the crowds, but as even the former U.S. State Department official Leslie Gelb wrote, the parliament was "not dominated by a bunch of right-wing crazies."[43] It was Yeltsin's illegal dissolution of parliament and his defiance of the country's highest court that precipitated the crisis—moves that were bound to be met by desperate measures in a country that had little desire to give up the democracy it had just won.*

A clear signal from Washington or the EU could have forced Yeltsin to engage in serious negotiations with the parliamentarians, but he received only encouragement. Finally, on the morning of October 4, 1993, Yeltsin fulfilled his long-prescribed destiny and became Russia's very own Pinochet, unleashing a series of violent events with unmistakable echoes of the coup in Chile exactly twenty years earlier. In what was the third traumatic shock inflicted by Yeltsin on the Russian people, he ordered a reluctant army to storm the Russian White House, setting it on fire and leaving charred the very building he had built his reputation defending just two years earlier. Communism may have collapsed without the firing of a single shot, but Chicago-style capitalism, it turned out, required a great deal of gunfire to defend itself: Yeltsin called in five thousand soldiers, dozens of tanks and armored personnel carriers, helicopters and elite shock troops armed with automatic machine guns—all to defend Russia's new capitalist economy from the grave threat of democracy.

This is how *The Boston Globe* reported on Yeltsin's parliamentary siege:

---

* In one of the most remarkable bits of sensational reporting, *The Washington Post* noted, "About 200 demonstrators then surged to Russia's Defense Ministry, where the nation's nuclear controls are located and its top generals were meeting"—raising the absurd prospect that the crowd of Russians attempting to defend their democracy might start a nuclear war. "The ministry locked its doors and kept the crowd out without incident," reported *The Post*.

"For 10 hours yesterday, about 30 Russian army tanks and armored personnel carriers encircled the parliament building in downtown Moscow, known as the White House, and pelted it with explosive rounds, while infantry troops sprayed machine-gun fire. At 4:15 p.m., about 300 guards, congressional deputies and staff workers marched single-file out of the building with their hands up."[44]

By the end of the day, the all-out military assault had taken the lives of approximately five hundred people and wounded almost a thousand, the most violence Moscow had seen since 1917.[45] Peter Reddaway and Dmitri Glinski, who wrote the definitive account of the Yeltsin years (*The Tragedy of Russia's Reforms: Market Bolshevism against Democracy*), point out that "during the mopping-up operation in and around the White House, 1,700 persons had been arrested, and 11 weapons seized. Some of the arrested were interned in a sports stadium, recalling the procedures used by Pinochet after the 1973 coup in Chile."[46] Many were taken to police stations, where they were severely beaten. Kagarlitsky recalls that while he was being struck on the head, an officer shouted, "You wanted democracy, you sons of bitches? We'll show you democracy!"[47]

But Russia wasn't a repeat of Chile—it was Chile in reverse order: Pinochet staged a coup, dissolved the institutions of democracy and then imposed shock therapy; Yeltsin imposed shock therapy in a democracy, then could defend it only by dissolving democracy and staging a coup. Both scenarios earned enthusiastic support from the West.

"Yeltsin Receives Widespread Backing for Assault," read a headline in *The Washington Post* the day after the coup, "Victory Seen for Democracy." *The Boston Globe* went with "Russia Escapes a Return to the Dungeon of Its Past." The U.S. secretary of state, Warren Christopher, traveled to Moscow to stand with Yeltsin and Gaidar and declared, "The United States does not easily support the suspension of parliaments. But these are extraordinary times."[48]

The events looked different in Russia. Yeltsin, the man who had risen to power by defending the parliament, had now literally set it on fire, leaving it so badly charred that it was nicknamed the black house. A middle-age Muscovite told a foreign camera crew in horror, "People supported [Yeltsin] because he promised us democracy, but he shot up that democracy. Not only did he violate it, but he shot it up."[49] Vitaly Neiman, who had stood guard at the entrance of the White House during the 1991 coup, put the betrayal this way: "What we got was entirely the opposite of what we dreamed of. We went to the barricades for them, laid our lives on the line, but they didn't keep their promises."[50]

Jeffrey Sachs, lauded for proving that radical free-market reforms could be compatible with democracy, continued to publicly support Yeltsin after his assault on the parliament, dismissing his opponents as "a group of former communists intoxicated by power."[51] In his book *The End of Poverty*, in which he gives his definitive account of his involvement in Russia, Sachs completely glosses over this dramatic episode, not mentioning it once, just as he left out the state of siege and attacks on labor leaders that accompanied his shock program in Bolivia.[52]

Following the coup, Russia was under unchecked dictatorial rule: its elected bodies were dissolved, the Constitutional Court was suspended, as was the constitution; tanks patrolled the streets, a curfew was in effect, and the press faced pervasive censorship, though civil liberties were soon restored.

So what did the Chicago Boys and their Western advisers do at this critical moment? The same thing they did when Santiago smoldered, and the same thing they would do when Baghdad burned: liberated from the meddling of democracy, they went on a law-making binge. Three days after the coup, Sachs observed that up to this point "there was no shock therapy" because the plan was "only incoherently and fitfully put into practice. Now there is a chance to do something," he said.[53]

And do something they did. "These days, Yeltsin's liberal economic team is on a roll," reported *Newsweek*. "The day after the Russian president dissolved Parliament, the word came down to the market reformers: start writing decrees." The magazine quoted a "jubilant Western economist working closely with the government" who made it absolutely clear that in Russia, democracy was always a hindrance to the market plan: "With Parliament out of the way, this is a great time for reform. . . . The economists around here were pretty depressed. Now we're working day and night." Indeed, there seems to be nothing quite as cheering as a coup, as Charles Blitzer, the World Bank's chief economist for Russia, told *The Wall Street Journal*. "I've never had so much fun in my life."[54]

The fun was just beginning. With the country reeling from the attack, Yeltsin's own Chicago Boys rammed through the most contentious measures in their program: huge budget cuts, the removal of price controls on basic food items, including bread, and even more and faster privatizations—the standard policies that cause so much instant misery that they seem to require a police state to stave off rebellion.

After Yeltsin's coup, Stanley Fischer, first deputy managing director of the IMF (and a 1970s Chicago Boy), advocated "moving as fast as possible on all fronts."[55] So did Lawrence Summers, who was helping to shape Russia policy in the Clinton administration. The "three '-ations,'" as he called them— "privatization, stabilization and liberalization—must all be completed as soon as possible."[56]

Change was so rapid that it was impossible for Russians to keep up. Workers often did not even know that their factories and mines had been sold—let alone how they had been sold or to whom (a profound confusion I would witness a decade later in the state-owned factories of Iraq). In theory, all this wheeling and dealing was supposed to create the economic boom that would lift Russia out of desperation; in practice, the Communist state was simply replaced with a corporatist one: the beneficiaries of the boom were confined to a small club of Russians, many of them former Communist Party apparatchiks, and a handful of Western mutual fund managers who made dizzying returns investing in newly privatized Russian companies. A clique of nouveaux billionaires, many of whom were to become part of the group universally known as "the oligarchs" for their imperial levels of wealth and power, teamed up with Yeltsin's Chicago Boys and stripped the country of nearly everything of value, moving the enormous profits offshore at a rate of $2 billion a month. Before shock therapy, Russia had no millionaires; by 2003, the number of Russian billionaires had risen to seventeen, according to the *Forbes* list.[57]

That is partly because, in a rare departure from Chicago School orthodoxy, Yeltsin and his team did not allow foreign multinationals to buy up Russia's assets directly; they kept the prizes for Russians, then opened up the newly privatized companies, owned by so-called oligarchs, to foreign shareholders. The returns were still astronomical. "Looking for an investment that could gain 2,000 per cent in three years?" *The Wall Street Journal* asked. "Only one stock market offers that hope . . . Russia."[58] Many investment banks, including Credit Suisse First Boston, as well as a few deep-pocketed financiers, quickly set up dedicated Russian mutual funds.

For the country's oligarchs and foreign investors, only one cloud loomed on the horizon: Yeltsin's plummeting popularity. The effects of the economic program were so brutal for the average Russian, and the process was so self-evidently corrupt, that his approval ratings fell to the single digits. If Yeltsin was pushed from office, whoever replaced him would likely put a halt to Russia's adventure in extreme capitalism. Even more worrying for the oligarchs and the "reformers," there would be a strong case for renationalizing many of the assets that had been handed out under such unconstitutional political circumstances.

In December 1994, Yeltsin did what so many desperate leaders have done throughout history to hold on to power: he started a war. His national security chief, Oleg Lobov, had confided to a legislator, "We need a small, victorious war to raise the president's ratings," and the defense minister predicted that his army could defeat the forces in the breakaway republic of Chechnya in a matter of hours—a cakewalk.[59]

For a while at least, the plan seemed to work. In its first phase, the Chechen independence movement was partially suppressed, and Russian troops took over the already abandoned presidential palace in Grozny, allowing Yeltsin to declare glorious victory. It would prove to be a short-term triumph, both in Chechnya and in Moscow. When Yeltsin faced reelection in 1996, he was still so unpopular and his defeat looked so certain that his advisers toyed with canceling the vote altogether; a letter signed by a group of Russian bankers published in all the Russian national newspapers strongly hinted at this possibility.[60] Yeltsin's privatization minister, Anatoly Chubais (whom Sachs once described as "a freedom fighter"), became one of the most outspoken proponents of the Pinochet option.[61] "In order to have a democracy in society there must be a dictatorship in power," he pronounced.[62] It was a direct echo of both the excuses made for Pinochet by Chile's Chicago Boys and Deng Xiaoping's philosophy of Friedmanism without the freedom.

In the end, the election went ahead and Yeltsin won, thanks to an estimated $100 million in financing from oligarchs (thirty-three times the legal amount) as well as eight hundred times more coverage on oligarch-controlled TV stations than his rivals.[63] With the threat of a sudden change in government removed, the knockoff Chicago Boys were able to move to the most contentious, and most lucrative, part of their program: selling off what Lenin had once called "the commanding heights."

Forty percent of an oil company comparable in size to France's Total was sold for $88 million (Total's sales in 2006 were $193 billion). Norilsk Nickel, which produced a fifth of the world's nickel, was sold for $170 million—even though its profits alone soon reached $1.5 billion annually. The massive oil company Yukos, which controls more oil than Kuwait, was sold for $309 million; it now earns more than $3 billion in revenue a year. Fifty-one percent of the oil giant Sidanko went for $130 million; just two years later that stake would be valued on the international market at $2.8 billion. A huge weapons factory sold for $3 million, the price of a vacation home in Aspen.[64]

The scandal wasn't just that Russia's public riches were auctioned off for a fraction of their worth—it was also that, in true corporatist style, they were purchased with public money. As the *Moscow Times* journalists Matt Bivens and Jonas Bernstein put it, "a few hand-picked men took over Russia's state-developed oil fields for free, as part of a giant shell game in which one arm of government paid another arm." In a bold act of cooperation between the politicians selling the public companies and the businessmen buying them, several of Yeltsin's ministers transferred large sums of public money, which should have gone into the national bank or treasury, into private banks that had been hastily incorporated by oligarchs.* The state then contracted with the same banks to run the privatization auctions for the oil fields and mines. The banks ran the auctions, but they also bid in them—and sure enough, the oligarch-owned banks decided to make themselves the proud new owners of the previously public assets. The money that they put up to buy the shares in these public companies was likely the same public money that Yeltsin's ministers had deposited with them earlier.[65] In other words, the Russian people fronted the money for the looting of their own country.

As one of Russia's "young reformers" put it, when Russia's Communists decided to break up the Soviet Union, they made an "exchange [of] power for property."[66] Just like his mentor Pinochet's, Yeltsin's own family grew exceedingly rich, his children and several of their spouses appointed to top posts at large privatized firms.

With oligarchs firmly in control of the key assets of the Russian state, they opened up their new companies to blue-chip multinationals, who snapped up large portions. In 1997, Royal Dutch/Shell and BP entered into partnerships with two key Russian oil giants, Gazprom and Sidanko.[67] These were highly profitable investments, but the principal share of the wealth in Russia was in the hands of Russian players, not their foreign partners. It is an oversight that the IMF and the U.S. Treasury would successfully rectify in future

---

* The two major oligarch-connected banks were Mikhail Khodorkovsky's Bank Menatep and Vladimir Potanin's Uneximbank.

privatization auctions in Bolivia and Argentina. And in Iraq after the invasion, the U.S. would go even further, attempting to cut the local elite out of
lucrative privatization deals entirely.

Wayne Merry, the chief political analyst at the U.S. embassy in Moscow
during the key years of 1990 to 1994, has admitted that the choice between
democracy and market interests in Russia was a stark one. "The U.S. government chose the economic over the political. We chose the freeing of prices,
privatization of industry, and the creation of a really unfettered, unregulated
capitalism, and essentially hoped that rule of law, civil society, and representative democracy would develop somehow automatically as a result of
that. . . . Unfortunately, the choice was to ignore popular will and to press on
with the policy."[68]

So much wealth was being made in Russia in this period that some of the
"reformers" couldn't resist getting in on the action. Indeed, more than anywhere else up to this point, the situation in Russia exposed the myth of the
technocrat, the egghead free-market economist supposedly imposing textbook models out of pure conviction. As in Chile and China, where rampant
corruption and economic shock therapy went hand in hand, several of
Yeltsin's Chicago School ministers and deputy ministers ended up losing
their posts in high-profile corruption scandals.[69]

Then there were the whiz kids from Harvard's Russia Project, tasked with
organizing the country's privatizations and the mutual fund market. The two
academics who headed the project—Harvard economics professor Andrei
Shleifer and his deputy Jonathan Hay—were discovered to have been directly profiting from the market they were busily creating. While Shleifer
was the lead adviser to the Gaidar team on privatization policy, his wife was
investing heavily in privatized Russian assets. Hay, a thirty-year-old graduate
of Harvard Law School, also made personal investments in privatized Russian oil stocks, allegedly in direct violation of Harvard's USAID contract.
And while Hay was helping the Russian government to set up a new mutual
fund market, his girlfriend, later wife, was awarded the first license to open a
mutual fund company in Russia, which, when it started, was managed out of
the U.S. government–funded Harvard office. (Technically, as head of the
Harvard Institute for International Development, which housed the Russia
Project, Sachs was Shleifer's and Hay's boss for part of this time. However,
Sachs was no longer working on the ground in Russia and has never been
implicated in any of the questionable actions.)[70]

When these tangles came to light, the U.S. Department of Justice sued Harvard, alleging that the business dealings of Shleifer and Hay violated contracts they had signed agreeing not to profit personally from their high-level work. After a seven-year investigation and legal battle, the U.S. District Court in Boston found that Harvard had breached its contract, that the two academics "conspired to defraud the United States," that "Shleifer engaged in apparent self-dealing," that "Hay attempted to launder $400,000 through his father and girlfriend."[71] Harvard paid a settlement of $26.5 million, the largest in the institution's history. Shleifer agreed to pay $2 million, and Hay agreed to pay between $1 and $2 million, depending on his earnings, though neither admitted any liability.*[72]

Perhaps this kind of "self-dealing" was inevitable, given the nature of the Russian experiment. Anders Åslund, one of the most influential Western economists working in Russia at the time, claimed that shock therapy would work because "the miraculous incentives or temptations of capitalism conquer more or less anything."[73] So if greed was to be the engine for rebuilding Russia, then surely the Harvard men and their wives and girlfriends, as well as Yeltsin's staff and family, by taking part in the frenzy themselves, were simply leading by example.

This points to a nagging and important question about free-market ideologues: Are they "true believers," driven by ideology and faith that free markets will cure underdevelopment, as is often asserted, or do the ideas and theories frequently serve as an elaborate rationale to allow people to act on unfettered greed while still invoking an altruistic motive? All ideologies are corruptible, of course (as Russia's apparatchiks made abundantly clear when, during the Communist era, they collected their abundant privileges), and there are certainly honest neoliberals. But Chicago School economics does seem particularly conducive to corruption. Once you accept that profit and greed as practiced on a mass scale create the greatest possible benefits for any society, pretty much any act of personal enrichment can be justified as a contribution to the great creative cauldron of capitalism, generating wealth and spurring economic growth—even if it's only for yourself and your colleagues.

George Soros's philanthropic work in Eastern Europe—including his funding of Sachs's travels through the region—has not been immune to controversy.

---

* Unfortunately, the money didn't go to the Russian people, the true victims of the corrupt privatization process, but back to the U.S. government—the same way that the "whistle-blower" lawsuits against U.S. contractors in Iraq divvy up the settlement between the U.S. government and the American whistle-blower.

There is no doubt that Soros was committed to the cause of democratization in the Eastern Bloc, but he also had clear economic interests in the kind of economic reform accompanying that democratization. As the world's most powerful currency trader, he stood to benefit greatly when countries implemented convertible currencies and lifted capital controls, and when state companies were put on the auction block, he was one of the potential buyers.

It would have been perfectly legal for Soros to profit directly from the markets he—as a philanthropist—was helping to open up, but it would not have looked particularly good. For a time, he dealt with the appearance of conflict of interest by barring his companies from investing in countries where his foundations were active. But by the time Russia went up for sale, Soros could no longer resist. In 1994, he explained that his policy "has been modified due to the fact that markets are really developing in the region and I have no rhyme or reason or right to deny my funds, or my shareholders, the possibility of investing there, or to deny those countries the chance to get hold of some of these funds." Soros had already purchased shares in Russia's privatized phone system in 1994, for example (a very bad investment, as it turned out), and acquired a piece of a large food company in Poland.[74] In the early days of the fall of Communism, Soros, through Sachs's work, had been one of the prime movers behind the push for the shock approach to economic transformation. By the late nineties, however, he had an apparent change of heart, becoming one of the leading critics of shock therapy and directing his foundations to fund NGOs that focus on putting anticorruption measures in place before privatizations occur.

That epiphany came much too late to save Russia from casino capitalism. Shock therapy had cracked it open to flows of hot money—short-term speculative investment and currency trading, which are highly profitable. Such intense speculation meant that in 1998, when the Asian financial crisis (the subject of chapter 13) started spreading, Russia was left wholly unprotected. Its already precarious economy crashed definitively. The public blamed Yeltsin, and his approval rating dropped to an utterly untenable 6 percent.[75] With the futures of many of the oligarchs in jeopardy once again, it was going to take yet another major shock to save the economic project and stave off the threat of genuine democracy coming to Russia.

In September 1999, the country was hit with a series of exceedingly cruel terrorist attacks: seemingly out of the blue, four apartment buildings were blown up in the middle of the night, killing close to three hundred people.

In a narrative all too familiar to Americans after September 11, 2001, every other issue was blasted off the political map by the only force on earth capable of doing the job. "It was this sort of very simple fear," explains the Russian journalist Yevgenia Albats. "All of a sudden, it appeared that all these discussions about democracy, oligarchs—nothing compared to this fear to die inside your own apartment."[76]

The man put in charge of hunting down the "animals" was Russia's prime minister, the steely and vaguely sinister Vladimir Putin.*[77] Immediately after the apartment bombings, in late September 1999, Putin launched air strikes on Chechnya, attacking civilian areas. In the new light of terror, the fact that Putin was a seventeen-year veteran of the KGB—the most feared symbol of the Communist era—suddenly seemed reassuring to many Russians. With Yeltsin's alcoholism making him increasingly dysfunctional, Putin the protector was perfectly positioned to succeed him as president. On December 31, 1999, with the war in Chechnya foreclosing serious debate, several oligarchs engineered a quiet handover from Yeltsin to Putin, no elections necessary. Before he left power, Yeltsin took one last page out of the Pinochet playbook and demanded legal immunity for himself. Putin's first act as president was signing a law protecting Yeltsin from any criminal prosecution, whether for corruption or for the military's killing of pro-democracy demonstrators that took place on his watch.

Yeltsin is regarded by history more as a corrupt buffoon than a menacing strongman. Yet his economic policies, and the wars he waged in order to protect them, contributed significantly to the Chicago School crusade death toll, which has been mounting steadily since Chile in the seventies. In addition to the casualties of Yeltsin's October coup, the wars in Chechnya have killed an estimated 100,000 civilians.[78] The larger massacres he precipitated have taken place in slow motion, but their numbers are much higher—the "collateral damage" of economic shock therapy.

In the absence of major famine, plague or battle, never have so many lost so much in so short a time. By 1998, more than 80 percent of Russian farms had gone bankrupt, and roughly seventy thousand state factories had closed, creating an epidemic of unemployment. In 1989, before shock therapy, 2

---

* Not surprisingly, given the defiant criminality of Russia's ruling class, conspiracy theories swirl around these events. Many Russians believe that Chechens had nothing to do with the apartment bombings and that they were a covert operation designed to turn Putin into Yeltsin's heir apparent.

million people in the Russian Federation were living in poverty, on less than $4 a day. By the time the shock therapists had administered their "bitter medicine" in the mid-nineties, 74 million Russians were living below the poverty line, according to the World Bank. That means that Russia's "economic reforms" can claim credit for the impoverishment of 72 *million people in only eight years.* By 1996, 25 percent of Russians—almost 37 million people—lived in poverty described as "desperate."[79]

Although millions of Russians have been pulled out of poverty in recent years, thanks largely to soaring oil and gas prices, Russia's underclass of extreme poor has remained permanent—with all the sicknesses associated with that discarded status. As miserable as life under Communism was, with crowded, cold apartments, Russians at least were housed; in 2006 the government admitted that there were 715,000 homeless kids in Russia, and UNICEF has put the number as high as 3.5 million children.[80]

During the Cold War, widespread alcoholism was always seen in the West as evidence that life under Communism was so dismal that Russians needed large quantities of vodka to get through the day. Under capitalism, however, Russians drink more than twice as much alcohol as they used to—and they are reaching for harder painkillers as well. Russia's drug czar, Aleksandr Mikhailov, says that the number of users went up 900 percent from 1994 to 2004, to more than 4 million people, many of them heroin addicts. The drug epidemic has contributed to another silent killer: in 1995, fifty thousand Russians were HIV positive, and in only two years that number doubled; ten years later, according to UNAIDS, nearly a million Russians were HIV positive.[81]

These are the slow deaths, but there are fast ones as well. As soon as shock therapy was introduced in 1992, Russia's already high suicide rate began to rise; 1994, the peak of Yeltsin's "reforms," saw the suicide rate climb to almost double what it had been eight years earlier. Russians also killed each other with much greater frequency: by 1994, violent crime had increased more than fourfold.[82]

"What have our motherland and her people gotten out of the last 15 criminal years?" Vladimir Gusev, a Moscow academic, asked at a 2006 democracy demonstration. "The years of criminal capitalism have killed off 10 percent of our population." Russia's population is indeed in dramatic decline—the country is losing roughly 700,000 people a year. Between 1992, the first full year of shock therapy, and 2006, Russia's population shrank by 6.6 million.[83] Three decades ago, André Gunder Frank, the dissident

Chicago economist, wrote a letter to Milton Friedman accusing him of "economic genocide." Many Russians describe the slow disappearance of their fellow citizens in similar terms today.

This planned misery is made all the more grotesque because the wealth accumulated by the elite is flaunted in Moscow as nowhere else outside of a handful of oil emirates. In Russia today, wealth is so stratified that the rich and the poor seem to be living not only in different countries but in different centuries. One time zone is downtown Moscow, transformed in fast-forward into a futuristic twenty-first-century sin city, where oligarchs race around in black Mercedes convoys, guarded by top-of-the-line mercenary soldiers, and where Western money managers are seduced by the open investment rules by day and by on-the-house prostitutes by night. In the other time zone, a seventeen-year-old provincial girl, asked about her hopes for the future, replied, "It's difficult to talk about the twenty-first century when you're sitting here reading by candlelight. The twenty-first century does not matter. It's the nineteenth century here."[84]

This pillage of a country with as much wealth as Russia required extreme acts of terror—from the torching of the parliament to the invasion of Chechnya. "Policy that breeds poverty and crime," writes Georgi Arbatov, one of Yeltsin's original (and ignored) economic advisers, ". . . can survive only if democracy is suppressed."[85] Just as it had been in the Southern Cone, in Bolivia under the state of siege, in China during Tiananmen. Just as it would be in Iraq.

When in Doubt, Blame Corruption

Rereading Western news reports on Russia's shock therapy period, it is striking how closely discussions at that time paralleled debates about Iraq that would unfold more than a decade later. For both the Clinton and Bush Sr. administrations, not to mention the European Union, the G7 and the IMF, the clear goal in Russia was to erase the preexisting state and create the conditions for a capitalist feeding frenzy, which in turn would kick-start a booming free-market democracy—managed by overconfident Americans barely out of school. In other words, it was Iraq without the explosives.

When the zeal for shock therapy in Russia was at its peak, its cheerleaders were absolutely convinced that only total destruction of every single institution would create the conditions for a national rebirth—the dream of the blank slate that would recur in Baghdad. It is "desirable," wrote the Harvard historian Richard Pipes, "for Russia to keep on disintegrating until nothing remains of its institutional structures."[86] And the Columbia University economist Richard Ericson wrote in 1995, "Any reform must be disruptive on a historically unprecedented scale. An entire world must be discarded, including all of its economic and most of its social and political institutions, and concluding with the physical structure of production, capital, and technology."[87]

Another Iraq parallel: no matter how baldly Yeltsin defied anything resembling democracy, his rule was still characterized in the West as part of "a transition to democracy," a narrative that would change only when Putin began cracking down on the illegal activities of several of the oligarchs. Similarly, the Bush administration has always portrayed Iraq as on the road to freedom, even in the face of overwhelming evidence of rampant torture, out-of-control death squads and pervasive press censorship. Russia's economic program was always described as "reform," just as Iraq is perennially under "reconstruction," even after the U.S. contractors have mostly all fled, leaving the infrastructure in a shambles, as the destruction roars on. In Russia in the mid-nineties, anyone who dared question the wisdom of "the reformers" was dismissed as nostalgic for Stalin, just as critics of Iraq's occupation were, for years, met with accusations that they thought life was better under Saddam Hussein.

When it was no longer possible to hide the failures of Russia's shock therapy program, the spin turned to Russia's "culture of corruption," as well as speculation that Russians "aren't ready" for genuine democracy because of their long history of authoritarianism. Washington's think-tank economists hastily disavowed the Frankenstein economy they helped create in Russia, deriding it as "mafia capitalism"—supposedly a phenomenon peculiar to the Russian character. "Nothing good will ever come of Russia," *The Atlantic Monthly* reported in 2001, quoting a Russian office worker. In the *Los Angeles Times*, the journalist and novelist Richard Lourie pronounced that "the Russians are such a calamitous nation that even when they undertake something sane and banal, like voting and making money, they make a total hash of it."[88] The economist Anders Åslund had claimed that the "temptations of capitalism" alone would transform Russia, that the sheer power of greed would provide the momentum to rebuild the country. Asked a few years later what went wrong, he replied, "Corruption, corruption and corruption," as if corruption was something other than the unrestrained expression of the "temptations of capitalism" that he had so enthusiastically praised.[89]

The entire charade would be replayed a decade later to explain away the billions of missing reconstruction dollars in Iraq, with the disfiguring legacy of Saddam and the pathologies of "radical Islam" standing in for the legacy of Communism and czarism. In Iraq, U.S. rage at the apparent inability of Iraqis to accept their gift of gunpoint "freedom" would also turn abusive — except that in Iraq the rage would not be found only in nasty editorials about "ungrateful" Iraqis but would also be pounded out on the bodies of Iraqi civilians by U.S. and British soldiers.

The real problem with the blame-Russia narrative is that it pre-empts any serious examination of what the whole episode has to teach about the true face of the crusade for unfettered free markets, the most powerful political trend of the past three decades. The corruption of many of the oligarchs is still spoken of as an alien force that infected otherwise worthy free-market plans. But corruption wasn't an intruder to Russia's free-market reforms: quick and dirty deals were actively encouraged by Western powers at every stage as the fastest way to kick-start the economy. National salvation through the harnessing of greed was the closest thing Russia's Chicago Boys and their advisers had to a plan for what they were going to do after they finished destroying Russia's institutions.

Nor were these catastrophic results unique to Russia; the entire thirty-year history of the Chicago School experiment has been one of mass corruption and corporatist collusion between security states and large corporations, from Chile's piranhas, to Argentina's crony privatizations, to Russia's oligarchs, to Enron's energy shell game, to Iraq's "free fraud zone." The point of shock therapy is to open up a window for enormous profits to be made very quickly — not despite the lawlessness but precisely because of it. "Russia Has Become a Klondike for International Fund Speculators," ran a headline in a Russian newspaper in 1997, while *Forbes* described Russia and Central Europe as "the new frontier."[90] The colonial-era terms were entirely appropriate.

The movement that Milton Friedman launched in the 1950s is best understood as an attempt by multinational capital to recapture the highly profitable, lawless frontier that Adam Smith, the intellectual forefather of today's neoliberals, so admired — but with a twist. Rather than journeying through Smith's "savage and barbarous nations" where there was no Western law (no longer a practical option), this movement set out to systematically dismantle existing laws and regulations to re-create that earlier lawlessness. And where

Smith's colonists earned their record profits by seizing what he described as "waste lands" for "but a trifle," today's multinationals see government programs, public assets and everything that is not for sale as terrain to be conquered and seized—the post office, national parks, schools, social security, disaster relief and anything else that is publicly administered.[91]

Under Chicago School economics, the state acts as the colonial frontier, which corporate conquistadors pillage with the same ruthless determination and energy as their predecessors showed when they hauled home the gold and silver of the Andes. Where Smith saw fertile green fields turned into profitable farmlands on the pampas and the prairies, Wall Street saw "green field opportunities" in Chile's phone system, Argentina's airline, Russia's oil fields, Bolivia's water system, the United States' public airwaves, Poland's factories—all built with public wealth, then sold for a trifle.[92] Then there are the treasures created by enlisting the state to put a patent and a price tag on life-forms and natural resources never dreamed of as commodities—seeds, genes, carbon in the earth's atmosphere. By relentlessly searching for new profit frontiers in the public domain, Chicago School economists are like the mapmakers of the colonial era, identifying new waterways through the Amazon, marking off the location of a hidden cache of gold inside an Inca temple.

Corruption has been as much a fixture on these contemporary frontiers as it was during the colonial gold rushes. Since the most significant privatization deals are always signed amid the tumult of an economic or political crisis, clear laws and effective regulators are never in place—the atmosphere is chaotic, the prices are flexible and so are the politicians. What we have been living for three decades is frontier capitalism, with the frontier constantly shifting location from crisis to crisis, moving on as soon as the law catches up.

And so, far from acting as a cautionary tale, the rise of Russia's billionaire oligarchs proved precisely how profitable the strip mining of an industrialized state could be—and Wall Street wanted more. Immediately following the Soviet collapse, the U.S. Treasury and the IMF became much tougher in their demands for instant privatizations from other crisis-racked countries. The most dramatic case to date came in 1994, the year after Yeltsin's coup, when Mexico's economy suffered a major meltdown known as the Tequila Crisis: the terms of the U.S. bailout demanded rapid-fire privatizations, and *Forbes* announced that the process had minted twenty-three new billionaires. "The lesson here is fairly obvious: to predict whence the next bursts of billionaires will issue, look for countries where markets are opening." It also cracked Mexico open to unprecedented foreign ownership: in 1990, only one of Mexico's banks was foreign owned, but "by 2000 twenty-four out of thirty were in foreign hands."[93] Clearly the only lesson learned from Russia is that the faster and more lawless the transfer of wealth, the more profitable it will be.

One person who understood that was Gonzalo Sánchez de Lozada (Goni), the businessman in whose living room the Bolivian shock therapy plan had been drafted in 1985. As president of the country in the mid-nineties, he sold off Bolivia's national oil company, as well as the national airline, railway, electricity and phone companies. Unlike what transpired in Russia, where the biggest prizes were awarded to locals, the winners of Bolivia's fire sale included Enron, Royal Dutch/Shell, Amoco Corp. and Citicorp—and the sales were direct; there was no need to partner with local firms.[94] *The Wall Street Journal* described the Wild West scene in La Paz in 1995: "The Radisson Plaza Hotel is crammed with executives from major U.S. companies like AMR Corp.'s American Airlines, MCI Communications Corp., Exxon Corp. and Salomon Brothers Inc. They have been invited by the Bolivians to rewrite laws governing the sectors to be privatized and to bid on the companies on the block"—a tidy arrangement. "The important thing is to make these changes irreversible and to get them done before the anti-bodies kick in," said President Sánchez de Lozada, explaining his shock therapy approach. To make absolutely sure those "antibodies" didn't kick in, Bolivia's government did something it had done before under similar circumstances: it imposed yet another prolonged "state of siege" that banned political gatherings and authorized the arrest of all opponents of the process.[95]

These were also the years of Argentina's notoriously corrupt privatization circus, hailed as "A Bravo New World" in an investment report by Goldman Sachs. Carlos Menem, the Peronist president who came to power promising to be the voice of the working man, was in charge during those years, downsizing and then selling the oil fields, the phone system, the airline, the trains, the airport, the highways, the water system, the banks, the Buenos Aires zoo and, eventually, the post office and the national pension plan. As the country's wealth moved offshore, the lifestyles of Argentina's politicians grew increasingly lavish. Menem, once known for his leather jackets and working-class sideburns, began wearing Italian suits and reportedly making trips to the plastic surgeon ("a bee sting" is how he explained his swollen features). María Julia Alsogaray, Menem's minister in charge of privatization, posed for the cover of a popular magazine wearing nothing but an artfully draped fur coat, while Menem began driving a bright red Ferrari Testarossa— a "gift" from a grateful businessman.[96]

The countries that emulated Russia's privatizations also experienced milder versions of Yeltsin's coups-in-reverse—governments that came to power peacefully and, through elections, found themselves resorting to increasing levels of brutality to hold on to power and defend their reforms. In Argentina, the rule of unfettered neoliberalism ended on December 19, 2001, when President Fernando de la Rúa and his finance minister, Domingo Cavallo, tried to impose further IMF-prescribed austerity measures. The population revolted, and de la Rúa sent in federal police on orders to disperse the crowds by whatever means were required. De la Rúa was forced to flee in a helicopter, but not before twenty-one protesters were killed by police and 1,350 people were injured.[97] Goni's last months and days in office were even bloodier. His privatizations sparked a series of "wars" in Bolivia: first the water war, against Bechtel's water contract that sent prices soaring 300 percent; then a "tax war" against an IMF-prescribed plan to make up a budget shortfall by taxing the working poor; then the "gas wars" against his plans to export gas to the U.S. In the end, Goni was also forced to flee the presidential palace to live in exile in the U.S., but, as in de la Rúa's case, not before many lives were lost. After Goni ordered the military to put down street demonstrations, soldiers killed close to seventy people—many of them bystanders—and injured four hundred others. As of early 2007, Goni was wanted by Bolivia's Supreme Court on charges relating to the massacre.[98]

The regimes that imposed mass privatization on Argentina and Bolivia were both held up in Washington as examples of how shock therapy could be imposed peacefully and democratically, without coups or repression. Although it's true that they did not begin in a hail of gunfire, it is surely significant that both ended in one.

In much of the Southern Hemisphere, neoliberalism is frequently spoken of as "the second colonial pillage": in the first pillage, the riches were seized from the land, and in the second they were stripped from the state. After every one of these profit frenzies come the promises: next time, there will be firm laws in place before a country's assets are sold off, and the entire process will be watched over by eagle-eyed regulators and investigators with unimpeachable ethics. Next time there will be "institution building" before privatizations (to use the post-Russia parlance). But calling for law and order after the profits have all been moved offshore is really just a way of legalizing the theft ex post facto, much as the European colonizers locked in their land grabs with treaties. Lawlessness on the frontier, as Adam Smith understood, is not the problem but the point, as much a part of the game as the contrite hand-wringing and the pledges to do better next time.

CHAPTER 12

THE CAPITALIST ID

RUSSIA AND THE NEW ERA OF THE BOOR MARKET

> **You have made yourself the trustee for those in every country who seek to mend the evils of our condition by reasoned experiment within the framework of the existing social system. If you fail, rational change will be gravely prejudiced throughout the world, leaving orthodoxy and revolution to fight it out.**
>
> —John Maynard Keynes in a letter to
> President Franklin D. Roosevelt, 1933[1]

On the day I went to visit Jeffrey Sachs in October 2006, New York City was under a damp blanket of gray drizzle punctuated, every five paces or so, by a vibrant burst of red. It was the week of the grand launch of Bono's (Product) Red brand, and the city was getting the full blitz. Red iPods and Armani sunglasses loomed from billboards overhead, every bus shelter featured Steven Spielberg or Penélope Cruz in a different red garment, every Gap outlet in the city had given itself over to the launch, and the Apple store on Fifth Avenue was emitting a rosy glow. "Can a tank top change the world?" asked one ad. Yes it can, we were assured, because a portion of the profits was going to the Global Fund to Fight AIDS, TB and malaria. "Shop till it stops!" Bono had pronounced, in the midst of a televised shopping spree with Oprah a couple of days earlier.[2]

I had a hunch that most of the journalists wanting to talk to Sachs that week would be looking for the superstar economist's view on this fashionable new way to raise aid money. After all, Bono refers to Sachs as "my professor," and a photo of the two men greeted me as I entered Sachs's office at Columbia

University (he left Harvard in 2002). In the midst of all this glamorous charity, I felt like a bit of a spoiler, because I wanted to talk about the professor's least favorite topic of all, one that has prompted him to threaten to hang up on reporters mid-interview. I wanted to talk about Russia and what went wrong there.

It was in Russia, after the first year of shock therapy, that Sachs began his own transition, from global shock doctor to one of the world's most outspoken campaigners for increasing aid to impoverished countries. It is a transition that, in the years since, has put him in conflict with many former colleagues and collaborators in orthodox economic circles. As far as Sachs is concerned, he isn't the one who changed—he was always committed to helping countries develop market-based economies bolstered by generous aid and debt forgiveness. For years he had found it possible to achieve these goals by working in partnership with the IMF and the U.S. Treasury. But by the time he was on the ground in Russia, the tenor of discussion had changed and he came up against a level of official indifference that shocked him and pushed him into a more confrontational stance with Washington's economic establishment.

Seen with hindsight, there is no doubt that Russia marked the beginning of a new chapter in the evolution of the Chicago School crusade. In earlier shock therapy laboratories of the seventies and eighties, there had been some desire at the U.S. Treasury and the IMF to make the experiments at least superficially successful—precisely because they were experiments, meant to serve as models for other countries to follow. The Latin American dictatorships of the seventies were rewarded for their attacks on trade unions and their open borders with steady loans, which were granted despite such departures from Chicago School orthodoxy as Chile's continued state control over the world's largest copper mines and the Argentine junta's slow action on privatizations. Bolivia, as the first democracy to adopt shock therapy in the eighties, was granted aid and had a portion of its debt erased—well before Goni moved ahead with privatization in the nineties. In Poland, the first Eastern Bloc country to impose shock therapy, Sachs had no trouble securing substantial loans, and, once again, major privatizations were slowed and staggered when the original plan encountered strong opposition.

Russia was different. "Too much shock, not enough therapy" was the widespread verdict. Western powers were totally unyielding in their demand for the most painful "reforms," at the same time as they were assiduously stingy in the amount of aid they would offer in return. Even Pinochet had cushioned the pain of shock therapy with food programs for the poorest children; Washington lenders saw no reason to help Yeltsin do the same, pushing the country instead into its Hobbesian nightmare.

Having a substantive discussion about Russia with Sachs isn't easy. I was hoping to take the conversation beyond his initial defensiveness ("I was right and they were completely wrong," he told me. Then, "Ask Larry Summers, don't ask me; ask Bob Rubin, ask Clinton, ask Cheney how happy they were with the way Russia went"). I also wanted to get beyond the genuine despondency ("I was trying to do something at the time, which proved to be completely useless"). What I was aiming to understand better was why he was so unsuccessful in Russia, why Jeffrey Sachs's famous luck ran out at that particular juncture.

Sachs now says that he knew something was different as soon as he arrived in Moscow. "I had a sense of foreboding from the first moment . . . I was furious from the first moment." Russia was facing "a first-class macroeconomic crisis, one of the most intense and unstable I had ever seen in my life," he said. And as far as he was concerned, the way out was clear: the shock therapy measures he had prescribed for Poland "to get basic market forces working quickly—plus a heck of a lot of aid. I was thinking of $30 billion a year, roughly divided, $15 billion for Russia and $15 billion for the republics, in order to be able to pull off a peaceful and democratic transition."

Sachs, it must be said, has a notoriously selective memory when it comes to the draconian policies he pushed in both Poland and Russia. In our interview, he repeatedly glossed over his own calls for swift privatization and large cutbacks (in short, shock therapy, a phrase he now disavows, claiming he was referring only to narrow pricing policies, not wholesale country makeovers). The way he remembers his role, shock therapy played a minor part, and he was almost exclusively focused on fund-raising; his plan for Poland, he says, was a "stabilization fund, debt cancellation, short-term financial help, integration with the Western European economy. . . . When I was asked by Yeltsin's team to help them, I proposed basically the same thing."*

There is no debate about the key fact in Sachs's account: securing a major aid infusion was a central pillar of his plan for Russia—that was Yeltsin's

* As John Cassidy noted in a 2005 *New Yorker* profile, "The fact is that in both Poland and Russia Sachs favored large-scale social engineering over gradual change and institution-building. The disastrous privatization policy is one example. Although most of the privatization took place after Sachs left Russia, at the end of 1994, the original policy framework was put in place in 1992 and 1993, when he was still there."

incentive for submitting to the entire program. Sachs based this vision, he says, on the Marshall Plan, the $12.6 billion ($130 billion in today's dollars) that the U.S. allotted for Europe to reconstruct its infrastructure and industry after the Second World War—a scheme widely regarded as Washington's most successful diplomatic initiative.[3] Sachs says the Marshall Plan showed that "when a country is in disarray, you can't just expect it to get back up on its feet in a coherent way by itself. So, for me the interesting thing about the Marshall Plan . . . is how a modest amount of monetary infusion created a base for [Europe's] economic recovery to take hold." At the start, he had been convinced that there was a similar political will in Washington to transform Russia into a successful capitalist economy, just as there had been a genuine commitment to West Germany and Japan after the Second World War.

Sachs was confident that he could shake a new Marshall Plan out of the U.S. Treasury and the IMF, and not without reason. "Probably the most important economist in the world" is how *The New York Times* described him in this period.[4] When he was an adviser to Poland's government, he recalled that he "raised $1 billion in one day in the White House." But, Sachs told me, "when I suggested the same thing for Russia, there was absolutely no interest at all. None. And the IMF just stared me down like I was crazy."

Although Yeltsin and his Chicago Boys had plenty of admirers in Washington, no one was willing to come up with the kind of aid they were talking about. That meant Sachs had urged wrenching policies on Russia, and he couldn't keep up his end of the bargain. It was in this period that he came close to self-criticism: "My greatest personal mistake," Sachs said in the midst of the Russia debacle, "was to say to President Boris Yeltsin, 'Don't worry; help is on the way.' I believed deeply that the assistance was too important, and too crucial to the West, for it to be messed up as significantly and fundamentally as it has been."[5] But the problem wasn't only that the IMF and the Treasury hadn't listened to Sachs, it was that Sachs had pushed hard for shock therapy before he had any guarantee that they would—a gamble for which millions paid dearly.

When I revisited the question with Sachs, he reiterated that his real failing was in misreading Washington's political mood. He recalled a discussion with Lawrence Eagleburger, U.S. secretary of state under George H. W. Bush. Sachs made his case: if Russia was allowed to descend further into economic chaos, it could unleash forces no one could control—mass famine, resurgent nationalism, even fascism, surely unwise in a country where virtually the only product held in surplus was nuclear arms. "Your analysis may be just right, but it's not going to happen," Eagleburger replied. Then he asked Sachs, "Do you know what year this is?"

It was 1992, the year of the U.S. election in which Bill Clinton was about to defeat Bush Sr. The core of Clinton's campaign was that Bush had neglected economic hardship at home to pursue glory abroad ("It's the economy, stupid"). Sachs believes that Russia was a casualty of that domestic battle. And, he says, he now sees that there was something else at work: many of Washington's power brokers were still fighting the Cold War. They saw Russia's economic collapse as a geopolitical victory, the decisive one that ensured U.S. supremacy. "I had none of that mind-set," Sachs told me, sounding, as he often does, like a Boy Scout who has stumbled into an episode of *The Sopranos*. "For me it was just, 'Great, this is the final end of this abominable regime. Now, let's really help [the Russians]. Let's throw everything into it. . . .' I'm sure that in retrospect, in the minds of the policy planners, that was viewed as crazy."

Despite his failure, Sachs does not feel that the policy toward Russia in this period was driven by free-market ideology. It was mostly, he said, characterized by "sheer laziness." He would have welcomed a heated debate about whether to offer aid to Russia or leave it all to the market. Instead, there was a collective shrug. He said he was amazed by the absence of serious research and debate informing momentous decisions. "To me, it was just the lack of effort that was the dominant thing. Let's at least spend two days and debate this—well, we never even did that! I never saw the hard work of 'Roll up your sleeves, let's get down and solve these problems, let's figure out what's really going on.' "

When Sachs talks passionately about "hard work," he is harking back to the days of the New Deal, the Great Society and the Marshall Plan, when young men from Ivy League schools sat around commanding tables in their shirt sleeves, surrounded by empty coffee cups and piles of policy papers, having heated debates about the interest rate and the price of wheat. That is how policy makers behaved in the heyday of Keynesianism, and that is the kind of "seriousness" that Russia's catastrophe clearly deserved.

But attributing the abandonment of Russia to a bout of collective laziness in Washington offers little by way of explanation. Perhaps a better way to understand the episode is through the lens favored by free-market economists: competition in the market. When the Cold War was in full swing and the Soviet Union was intact, the people of the world could choose (at least theoretically) which ideology they wanted to consume; there were the two poles, and there was much in between. That meant capitalism had to win customers; it

needed to offer incentives; it needed a good product. Keynesianism was always an expression of that need for capitalism to compete. President Roosevelt brought in the New Deal not only to address the desperation of the Great
Depression but to undercut a powerful movement of U.S. citizens who, having been dealt a savage blow by the unregulated free market, were demanding
a different economic model. Some wanted a radically different one: in the
1932 presidential elections, one million Americans voted for Socialist or
Communist candidates. Growing numbers of Americans were also paying
close attention to Huey Long, the populist senator from Louisiana who believed that all Americans should receive a guaranteed annual income of
$2,500. Explaining why he had added more social welfare benefits to the
New Deal in 1935, FDR said he wanted to "steal Long's thunder."[6]

It was in this context that American industrialists grudgingly accepted
FDR's New Deal. The edges of the market needed to be softened with public sector jobs and by making sure no one went hungry—the very future of
capitalism was at stake. During the Cold War, no country in the free world
was immune to this pressure. In fact, the achievements of mid-century capitalism, or what Sachs calls "normal" capitalism—workers' protections, pensions, public health care and state support for the poorest citizens in North
America—all grew out of the same pragmatic need to make major concessions in the face of a powerful left.

The Marshall Plan was the ultimate weapon deployed on this economic
front. After the war, the German economy was in crisis, threatening to bring
down the rest of Western Europe. Meanwhile, so many Germans were
drawn to socialism that the U.S. government opted to split Germany into two
parts rather than risk losing it all, either to collapse or to the left. In West Germany, the U.S. government used the Marshall Plan to build a capitalist system that was not meant to create fast and easy new markets for Ford and
Sears but, rather, to be so successful on its own terms that Europe's market
economy would thrive and socialism would be drained of its appeal.

By 1949, that meant tolerating from the West German government all
kinds of policies that were positively uncapitalist: direct job creation by the
state, huge investment in the public sector, subsidies for German firms and
strong labour unions. In a move that would have been unthinkable in Russia
in the 1990s or Iraq under U.S. occupation, the U.S. government infuriated
its own corporate sector by imposing a moratorium on foreign investment
so that war-battered German companies would not be forced to compete
before they had recovered. "The feeling was that letting foreign companies

come in at that point would have been like piracy," I was told by Carolyn Eisenberg, author of an acclaimed history of the Marshall Plan.[7] "The main difference between now and then is that the U.S. government did not see Germany as a cash cow. They didn't want to antagonize people. The belief was that if you come in and start pillaging the place, you interfere with the recovery of Europe as a whole."

This approach, Eisenberg points out, was not born of altruism. "The Soviet Union was like a loaded gun. The economy was in crisis, there was a substantial German left, and they [the West] had to win the allegiance of the German people fast. They really saw themselves battling for the soul of Germany."

Eisenberg's account of the battle of ideologies that created the Marshall Plan points to a persistent blind spot in Sachs's work, including his recent laudable efforts to dramatically increase aid spending for Africa. Rarely are mass popular movements even mentioned. For Sachs, the making of history is a purely elite affair, a matter of getting the right technocrats settled on the right policies. Just as shock therapy programs are drafted in secret bunkers in La Paz and Moscow, so, apparently, should a $30 billion aid program for the Soviet republics have materialized based solely on the commonsense arguments he was making in Washington. As Eisenberg notes, however, the original Marshall Plan came about not out of benevolence, or even reasoned argument, but fear of popular revolt.

Sachs admires Keynes, but he seems uninterested in what made Keynesianism finally possible in his own country: the messy, militant demands of trade unionists and socialists whose growing strength turned a more radical solution into a credible threat, which in turn made the New Deal look like an acceptable compromise. This unwillingness to recognize the role of mass movements in pressuring reluctant governments to embrace the very ideas he advocates has had serious ramifications. For one, it meant that Sachs could not see the most glaring political reality confronting him in Russia: there was never going to be a Marshall Plan for Russia because there was only ever a Marshall Plan *because of* Russia. When Yeltsin abolished the Soviet Union, the "loaded gun" that had forced the development of the original plan was disarmed. Without it, capitalism was suddenly free to lapse into its most savage form, not just in Russia but around the world. With the Soviet collapse, the free market now had a global monopoly, which meant all the "distortions" that had been interfering with its perfect equilibrium were no longer required.

This was the real tragedy of the promise made to the Poles and Russians—that if they followed shock therapy they would suddenly wake up in a "normal

European country." Those normal European countries (with their strong social safety nets, workers' protections, powerful trade unions and socialized
health care) emerged as a compromise between Communism and capitalism. Now that there was no need for compromise, all those moderating social policies were under siege in Western Europe, just as they were under
siege in Canada, Australia and the U.S. Such policies were not about to be
introduced in Russia, certainly not subsidized with Western funds.

This liberation from all constraints is, in essence, Chicago School economics (otherwise known as neoliberalism or, in the U.S., neoconservatism): not
some new invention but capitalism stripped of its Keynesian appendages, capitalism in its monopoly phase, a system that has let itself go—that no longer
has to work to keep us as customers, that can be as antisocial, antidemocratic
and boorish as it wants. As long as Communism was a threat, the gentlemen's
agreement that was Keynesianism would live on; once that system lost ground,
all traces of compromise could finally be eradicated, thereby fulfilling the
purist goal Friedman had set out for his movement a half century earlier.

That was the real point of Fukuyama's dramatic "end of history" announcement at the University of Chicago lecture in 1989: he wasn't actually
claiming that there were no other ideas in the world, but merely that, with
Communism collapsing, there were no other ideas sufficiently powerful to
constitute a head-to-head competitor.

So while Sachs saw the collapse of the Soviet Union as a liberation from authoritarian rule and was ready to roll up his sleeves and start helping, his
Chicago School colleagues saw it as a freedom of a different sort—as the final
liberation from Keynesianism and the do-gooder ideas of men like Jeffrey
Sachs. Seen in that light, the do-nothing attitude that so infuriated Sachs when
it came to Russia was not "sheer laziness" but laissez-faire in action: let it go,
do nothing. By not lifting a finger to help, all the men charged with Russian
policy—from Dick Cheney, as Bush Sr.'s defense secretary, to Lawrence Summers, Treasury undersecretary, to Stanley Fischer at the IMF—were indeed
doing something: they were practicing pure Chicago School ideology, letting
the market do its worst. Russia, even more than Chile, was what this ideology
looked like in practice, a foreshadowing of the get-rich-or-die-trying dystopia
that many of these same players would create a decade later in Iraq.

The new rules of the game were on display in Washington, D.C., on January
13, 1993. The occasion was a small but important conference, by invitation
only, on the tenth floor of the Carnegie Conference Center on Dupont

Circle, a seven-minute drive from the White House and a stone's throw from the headquarters of the IMF and the World Bank. John Williamson, the powerful economist known for shaping the missions of both the bank and the fund, had convened the event as a historic gathering of the neoliberal tribe. In attendance was an impressive array of the star "technopols" who were at the forefront of the campaign to spread the Chicago doctrine throughout the world. There were present and former finance ministers from Spain, Brazil and Poland, central bank heads from Turkey and Peru, the chief of staff for the president of Mexico and a former president of Panama. There was Sachs's old friend and hero, Leszek Balcerowicz, architect of Poland's shock therapy, as well as his Harvard colleague Dani Rodrik, the economist who had proven that every country that had accepted neoliberal restructuring had been in deep crisis. Anne Krueger, future first deputy managing director of the IMF, was there, and although José Piñera, Pinochet's most evangelical minister, couldn't make it because he was trailing in Chile's presidential election, he sent a detailed paper in his place. Sachs, who was still advising Yeltsin at the time, was to deliver the keynote address.

All day long, the conference participants had been indulging in that favorite economists' pastime of strategizing how to get reluctant politicians to embrace policies that are unpopular with voters. How soon after elections should shock therapy be launched? Are center-left parties more effective than right-wing ones because the attack is unexpected? Is it better to warn the public or take people by surprise with "voodoo politics"? Though the conference was called "The Political Economy of Policy Reform"—so willfully bland a title that it seemed designed to deflect media interest—one participant remarked slyly that what it was really about was "Machiavellian economics."[8]

Sachs listened to all this talk for several hours, and after dinner he went to the podium to give his address, titled, in true Sachsian fashion, "Life in the Economic Emergency Room."[9] He was visibly agitated. The crowd was ready to hear a speech from one of their idols, the man who had carried the torch of shock therapy into the democratic era. Sachs was in no mood for self-congratulation. Instead, he was determined to use the speech, he later explained to me, to try to get this powerful crowd to grasp the gravity of what was unfolding in Russia.

He reminded his audience of the infusions of aid that had gone to Europe and Japan after the Second World War, "vital for Japan's later magnificent success." He told a story about getting a letter from an analyst at the Heritage Foundation—ground zero of Friedmanism—who "believed strongly in Russia's reforms but not in foreign aid for Russia. This is a common view of free-market ideologues—of which I am one," Sachs said. "It is plausible but it is mistaken. The market cannot do it all by itself; international help is crucial." The laissez-faire obsession was taking Russia into catastrophe, where, he said, "no matter how valiant, brilliant, and lucky are Russia's reformers, they won't make it without large-scale external assistance . . . we are close to missing a historic opportunity."

Sachs got a round of applause, of course, but the response was tepid. Why was he praising such lavish social spending? This crowd was on a global crusade to dismantle the New Deal, not to forge a new one. In the conference sessions that followed, not a single participant supported Sachs's challenge, and several spoke out against it.

What he was trying to do with the speech, Sachs told me, was "explain what a real crisis was like . . . to convey a sense of urgency." People who make policy from Washington, he said, often "don't understand what economic chaos is. They don't understand the disarray that comes." He wanted to confront them with the reality that "there's also a dynamic that things get farther and farther out of control, until you have other disasters, until Hitler comes back in power, until you have civil war, or mass famine or whatever it is. . . . You need to do emergency things to help, because an unstable situation definitely has a path of increasing instability, not just a path to normal equilibrium."

I couldn't help thinking that Sachs wasn't giving his audience enough credit. The people in that room were well versed in Milton Friedman's crisis theory, and many had applied it in their own countries. Most understood perfectly how wrenching and volatile an economic meltdown could be, but they were taking a different lession from Russia: that a painful and disorienting political situation was forcing Yeltsin to rapidly auction off the riches of the state, a distinctly favorable outcome.

It was left to John Williamson, the host of the conference, to steer the discussion back to those pragmatic priorities. Sachs was the one with the star power at the event, but it was Williamson who was the crowd's real guru. Balding and untelegenic but thrillingly politically incorrect, Williamson was the one who coined the phrase "the Washington Consensus"—perhaps the most quoted and contentious three words in modern economics. He is famous for his tightly structured closed-door conferences and seminars, each designed to test one of his bold hypotheses. At the conference in January, he had a pressing agenda: he wanted to test what he called the "crisis hypothesis" once and for all.[10]

In his lecture, Williamson offered no warnings of the imperative to save any country from crisis; in fact, he spoke rhapsodically of cataclysmic events. He reminded his audience of the indisputable evidence that only when countries are truly suffering do they agree to swallow their bitter market medicine; only when they are in shock do they lie down for shock therapy. "These worst of times give rise to the best of opportunities for those who understand the need for fundamental economic reform," he declared.[11]

With his unparalleled knack for verbalizing the subconscious of the financial world, Williamson casually pointed out that this raised some intriguing questions:

> One will have to ask whether it could conceivably make sense to think of deliberately provoking a crisis so as to remove the political logjam to reform. For example, it has sometimes been suggested in Brazil that it would be worthwhile stoking up a hyperinflation so as to scare everyone into accepting those changes. . . . Presumably no one with historical foresight would have advocated in the mid-1930s that Germany or Japan go to war in order to get the benefits of the supergrowth that followed their defeat. But could a lesser crisis have served the same function? Is it possible to conceive of a pseudo-crisis that could serve the same positive function without the cost of a real crisis?[12]

Williamson's remarks represented a major leap forward for the shock doctrine. In a room filled with enough finance ministers and central bank chiefs to hold a major trade summit, the idea of actively creating a serious crisis so that shock therapy could be pushed through was now being openly discussed.

At least one conference participant felt obliged to distance himself in his own speech from these risqué ideas. "Williamson's suggestion that it might be a good move to provoke an artificial crisis in order to trigger reform should best be read as an idea designed to provoke and tease," said John Toye, a British economist from the University of Sussex.[13] There was no evidence that Williamson was teasing. In fact, there was plenty of evidence that his ideas were already being acted on at the highest levels of financial decision making in Washington and beyond.

The month after Williamson's conference in Washington, we caught a glimpse of the new enthusiasm for "pseudo crisis" in my country, although few understood it as part of a global strategy at the time. In February 1993, Canada was in the midst of financial catastrophe, or so one would have concluded by reading the newspapers and watching TV. "Debt Crisis Looms," screamed a banner front-page headline in the national newspaper, the *Globe and Mail*. A major national television special reported that "economists are predicting that sometime in the next year, maybe two years, the deputy minister of finance is going to walk into cabinet and announce that Canada's credit has run out. . . . Our lives will change dramatically."[14]

The phrase "debt wall" suddenly entered the vocabulary. What it meant was that, although life seemed comfortable and peaceful now, Canada was spending so far beyond its means that, very soon, powerful Wall Street firms like Moody's and Standard and Poor's would downgrade our national credit rating from its perfect Triple A status to something much lower. When that happened, hypermobile investors, liberated by the new rules of globalization and free trade, would simply pull their money from Canada and take it somewhere safer. The only solution, we were told, was to radically cut spending on such programs as unemployment insurance and health care. Sure enough, the governing Liberal Party did just that, despite having just been elected on a platform of job creation (Canada's version of "voodoo politics").

Two years after the deficit hysteria peaked, the investigative journalist Linda McQuaig definitively exposed that a sense of crisis had been carefully stoked and manipulated by a handful of think tanks funded by the largest banks and corporations in Canada, particularly the C. D. Howe Institute and the Fraser Institute (which Milton Friedman had always actively and strongly supported).[15] Canada did have a deficit problem, but it wasn't caused by spending on unemployment insurance and other social programs. According to Statistics Canada, it was caused by high interest rates, which exploded the worth of the debt much as the Volcker Shock had ballooned the developing world's debt in the eighties. McQuaig went to Moody's Wall Street head office and spoke with Vincent Truglia, the senior analyst in charge of issuing Canada's credit rating. He told her something remarkable: that he had come under constant pressure from Canadian corporate executives and bankers to issue damning reports about the country's finances, something he refused to do because he considered Canada an excellent, stable investment. "It's the only country that I handle where, usually, nationals from that country want the country downgraded even more—on a regular basis. They think it's rated too highly." He said he was used to getting calls from country representatives telling him he had issued too low a rating. "But Canadians usually, if anything, disparage their country far more than foreigners do."

That's because, for the Canadian financial community, the "deficit crisis" was a critical weapon in a pitched political battle. At the time Truglia was getting those strange calls, a major campaign was afoot to push the government to lower taxes by cutting spending on social programs such as health and education. Since these programs are supported by an overwhelming majority of Canadians, the only way the cuts could be justified was if the alternative was national economic collapse—a full-blown crisis. The fact that Moody's kept giving Canada the highest possible bond rating—the equivalent of an A++— was making it extremely difficult to maintain the apocalyptic mood.

Investors, meanwhile, were getting confused by the mixed messages: Moody's was upbeat about Canada, but the Canadian press contantly presented the national finances as catastrophic. Truglia got so fed up with the politicized statistics coming out of Canada, which he felt were calling his own research into question, that he took the extraordinary step of issuing a "special commentary" clarifying that Canada's spending was "not out of control," and he even aimed some veiled shots at the dodgy math practiced by right-wing think tanks. "Several recently published reports have grossly exaggerated Canada's fiscal debt position. Some of them have double counted numbers, while others have made inappropriate international comparisons. . . . These inaccurate measurements may have played a role in exaggerated evaluations of the severity of Canada's debt problems." With Moody's special report, word was out that there was no looming "debt wall"—and Canada's business community was not pleased. Truglia says that when he put out the commentary, "one Canadian . . . from a very large financial institution in Canada called me up on the telephone screaming at me, literally screaming at me. That was unique."*[16]

By the time Canadians learned that the "deficit crisis" had been grossly manipulated by the corporate-funded think tanks, it hardly mattered—the budget cuts had already been made and locked in. As a direct result, social programs for the country's unemployed were radically eroded and have never recovered, despite many subsequent surplus budgets. The crisis strategy was

* It must be said that Truglia is a rarity on Wall Street—bond and credit ratings are often influenced by political pressure, and are used to increase the pressure to enact "market reforms."

used again and again in this period. In September 1995, a video was leaked to the Canadian press of John Snobelen, Ontario's minister of education, telling a closed-door meeting of civil servants that before cuts to education and other unpopular reforms could be announced, a climate of panic needed to be created by leaking information that painted a more dire picture than he "would be inclined to talk about." He called it "creating a useful crisis."[17]

"Statistical Malpractice" in Washington

By 1995, political discourse in most Western democracies was saturated with talk of debt walls and imminent economic collapse, demanding ever-deeper cuts and more ambitious privatizations, with the Friedmanite think tanks always out front crying crisis. At Washington's most powerful financial institutions, however, there was a willingness not only to create an appearance of crisis through the media but also to take concrete measures to generate crises that were all too real. Two years after Williamson made his observations about "stoking up" crisis, Michael Bruno, chief economist of development economics at the World Bank, publicly echoed the same line, once again without attracting media scrutiny. In a lecture to the International Economic Association in Tunis in 1995, later published as a paper by the World Bank, Bruno informed five hundred assembled economists from sixty-eight countries that there was a growing consensus about "the idea that a large enough crisis may shock otherwise reluctant policymakers into instituting productivity-enhancing reforms."*[18] Bruno pointed to Latin America as "a prime example of seemingly beneficial deep crises" and to Argentina in particular, where, he said, President Carlos Menem and his finance minister, Domingo Cavallo, were doing a fine job of "taking advantage of the emergency atmosphere" to push through deep privatization. Just in case the audience missed the point, Bruno said, "I have emphasized one major theme: the political economy of deep crises tends to yield radical reforms with positive outcomes."

In light of this fact, he argued that international agencies needed to do more than just take advantage of existing economic crises to push through the Washington Consensus—they needed to preemptively cut off aid to make those crises worse. "An adverse shock (such as a drop in government

---

* Though Bruno did not attend the University of Chicago, he studied under and was mentored by the prominent Chicagoan Don Patinkin, quoted earlier comparing Chicago economics to Marxism for its "logical completeness."

revenue or in external transfers) may actually *increase* welfare because it shortens the delay [before reforms are adopted]. The notion that 'things have to get worse before they can get better' emerges naturally. . . . In fact, a high-inflation crisis may leave a country better off than if it had muddled along through less severe crises."

Bruno conceded that deepening or creating a serious economic melt-down was frightening—government salaries would go unpaid, public infra-structure would rot—but, Chicago disciple that he was, he urged his audience to embrace this destruction as the first stage of creation. "Indeed, as the crisis deepens the *government may gradually wither away*," Bruno said. "This development has a positive outcome; namely, at the time of re-form the power of entrenched groups may have been weakened—and a leader who opts for the long-run solution over short-term expediency may win support for reform."[19]

The Chicago School crisis addicts were certainly on a speedy intellectual trajectory. Only a few years earlier, they had speculated that a hyperinflation crisis could create the shocking conditions required for shock policies. Now a chief economist at the World Bank, an institution funded, by this time, with tax dollars from 178 countries and whose mandate was to rebuild and strengthen struggling economies, was advocating the creation of failed states because of the opportunities they provided to start over in the rubble.[20]

For years, there had been rumors that the international financial institutions had been dabbling in the art of "pseudo-crisis," as Williamson put it, in order to bend countries to their will, but it was difficult to prove. The most exten-sive testimony came from Davison Budhoo, an IMF staffer turned whistle-blower, who accused the organization of cooking the books in order to doom the economy of a poor but strong-willed country.

Budhoo was a Grenadian-born, London School of Economics-trained economist who stood out in Washington thanks to an unconventional ap-proach to personal style: he let his hair stand straight on end, à la Albert Ein-stein, and preferred the windbreaker to the pinstripe suit. He had worked at the IMF for twelve years, where his job was designing structural adjustment programs for Africa, Latin America and his native Caribbean. After the orga-nization took its sharp right turn during the Reagan/Thatcher era, the inde-pendent-minded Budhoo felt increasingly ill at ease in his place of work. The fund was packed with zealous Chicago Boys under the leadership of its man-aging director, the staunch neoliberal Michel Camdessus. When Budhoo quit in 1988, he decided to devote himself to exposing the secrets of his former workplace. It began when he wrote a remarkable open letter to Camdessus, adopting the *j'accuse* tone of André Gunder Frank's letters to Friedman a decade earlier.

Showing an enthusiasm for language rare for senior fund economists, the letter began: "Today I resigned from the staff of the International Monetary Fund after over twelve years, and after 1000 days of official Fund work in the field, hawking your medicine and your bag of tricks to governments and to peoples in Latin America and the Caribbean and Africa. To me resignation is a priceless liberation, for with it I have taken the first big step to that place where I may hope to wash my hands of what in my mind's eye is the blood of millions of poor and starving peoples. . . . The blood is so much, you know, it runs in rivers. It dries up, too; it cakes all over me; sometimes I feel that there is not enough soap in the whole world to cleanse me from the things that I did do in your name."[21]

He then went on to build his case. Budhoo accused the fund of using statistics as "lethal" weapons. He exhaustively documented how, as a fund employee in the mid-eighties, he was involved in elaborate "statistical malpractices" to exaggerate the numbers in IMF reports on oil-rich Trinidad and Tobago in order to make the country look far less stable than it actually was. Budhoo contended that the IMF had more than doubled a crucial statistic measuring the labor costs in the country, making it appear highly unproductive—even though, as he said, the fund had the correct information on hand. In another instance, he claimed that the fund "invented, literally out of the blue," huge unpaid government debts.[22]

Those "gross irregularities," which Budhoo claims were deliberate and not mere "sloppy calculations," were taken as fact by the financial markets, which promptly classified Trinidad as a bad risk and cut off its financing. The country's economic problems—triggered by a drop in the price of oil, its primary export—quickly became calamitous, and it was forced to beg the IMF for a bailout. The fund then demanded that it accept what Budhoo described as the IMF's "deadliest medicine": layoffs, wage cuts and the "whole gamut" of structural adjustment policies. He described the process as the "deliberate blocking of an economic lifeline to the country through subterfuge" in order to see "Trinidad and Tobago destroyed economically first, and converted thereafter."

In his letter, Budhoo, who died in 2001, made it clear that his dispute was over more than the treatment of one country by a handful of officials. He characterized the IMF's entire program of structural adjustment as a form of mass torture in which "'screaming-in-pain' governments and peoples [are] forced to bend on their knees before us, broken and terrified and disintegrating, and begging for a sliver of reasonableness and decency on our part. But we laugh cruelly in their face, and the torture goes on unabated."

After the letter was published, the government of Trinidad commissioned two independent studies to investigate the allegations and found that they were correct: the IMF had inflated and fabricated numbers, with tremendously damaging results for the country.[23]

Even with this substantiation, however, Budhoo's explosive allegations disappeared virtually without a trace; Trinidad and Tobago is a collection of tiny islands off the coast of Venezuela, and unless its people storm the headquarters of the IMF on Nineteenth Street, its complaints are unlikely to capture world attention. The letter was, however, turned into a play in 1996 called *Mr. Budhoo's Letter of Resignation from the I.M.F. (50 Years Is Enough)*, put on in a small theater in New York's East Village. The production received a surprisingly positive review in *The New York Times*, which praised its "uncommon creativity" and "inventive props."[24] The short theater review was the only time Budhoo's name was ever mentioned in *The New York Times*.

CHAPTER 13

LET IT BURN

THE LOOTING OF ASIA AND "THE FALL OF A SECOND BERLIN WALL"

> **Money flows to where opportunity is, and, right now, Asia appears to be cheap.**
> —Gerard Smith, a financial institutions banker at UBS Securities in New York, on the Asian economic crisis of 1997–98[1]

> **Good times make bad policy.**
> —Mohammad Sadli, economic adviser to Indonesia's General Suharto[2]

They seemed like simple questions. What can your salary buy? Is it enough for room and board? Is there any left over to send money back to your parents? How about transportation costs to and from the factory? But no matter how I phrased them, the answers I kept getting were "It depends." Or "I don't know."

"A few months ago," a seventeen-year-old worker who sewed Gap clothing near Manila explained, "I used to have enough money to send a little bit home to my family every month, but now I don't even make enough to buy food for myself."

"Are they lowering your wages?" I asked.

"No, I don't think so," she said, a little confused. "It just doesn't buy as much. The prices keep rising."

It was the summer of 1997, and I was in Asia researching the working conditions inside the region's booming export factories. I found workers facing a problem bigger than forced overtime or abusive supervisors: their countries were rapidly falling into what would soon become a full-fledged depression. In Indonesia, where the crisis was even deeper, the atmosphere felt dangerously volatile. The Indonesian currency dropped between morning and nightfall over and over and again. One day factory workers could buy fish and rice, and the next day they were subsisting on rice alone. In casual conversations at restaurants and in taxis, everyone seemed to have the same theory about who was to blame: "the Chinese," I was told. It was ethnic Chinese people, as Indonesia's merchant class, who seemed to be profiting most directly from the rising prices, and so they were bearing the brunt of the anger. This is what Keynes had meant when he warned of the dangers of economic chaos—you never know what combination of rage, racism and revolution will be unleashed.

Southeast Asian countries were particularly vulnerable to conspiracy theories and ethnic scapegoating because, on the face of it, the financial crisis had no rational cause. On television and in newspapers, analysis kept referring to the region as if it had contracted some mysterious but highly contagious disease—"the Asian Flu," as the market crash was immediately labeled, later upgraded to "the Asian Contagion" when it spread to Latin America and Russia.

Just weeks before it all went wrong, these countries were being held up as paragons of economic fitness and vitality—the so-called Asian Tigers, globalization's most robust success stories. One minute, stockbrokers were telling their clients that there was no surer route to wealth than sinking your savings in Asian "emerging market" mutual funds; the next they were cashing out in droves, while traders "attacked" the currencies—the baht, the ringgit, the rupiah—creating what *The Economist* called "a destruction of savings on a scale more usually associated with a full-scale war."[3] And yet, within Asia's Tiger economies, nothing observable had changed—for the most part, they were still run by the same crony elite; they had not been hit by a natural disaster or war; they were not running large deficits—some had none at all. Many large conglomerates were carrying heavy debts, but they were still producing everything from sneakers to cars, and their sales were as strong as ever. So how was it possible that, in 1996, investors had seen fit to pour $100 billion into South Korea and then, the very next year, the country had a negative investment of $20 billion—a discrepancy of $120 billion?[4] What could explain this kind of monetary whiplash?

It turned out that the countries were victims of pure panic, made lethal by the speed and volatility of globalized markets. What began as a rumor—that

Thailand did not have enough dollars to back up its currency—triggered a stampede by the electronic herd. Banks called in their loans, and the real estate market, which had been growing so quickly that it had become a bubble, promptly popped. Construction ground to a halt on half-built malls, skyscrapers and resorts; motionless construction cranes loomed over Bangkok's crowded skyline. In a slower era of capitalism, the crisis might have stopped there, but because mutual fund brokers had marketed the Asian Tigers as part of a single investment package, when one Tiger went down, they all did: after Thailand, panic spread and money fled from Indonesia, Malaysia, the Philippines and even South Korea, the eleventh-largest economy in the world and a star in the globalization firmament.

Asian governments were forced to drain their reserve banks in an effort to prop up their currencies, turning the original fear into a reality: now these countries really were going broke. The market responded with more panic. In one year, $600 billion had disappeared from the stock markets of Asia—wealth that had taken decades to build.[5]

The crisis provoked desperate measures. In Indonesia, impoverished citizens stormed urban stores and took what they could carry. In one particularly horrific incident, a Jakarta shopping mall caught fire while it was being looted, and hundreds of people were burned alive.[6]

In South Korea, television stations ran a massive campaign calling on citizens to donate their gold jewelry so that it could be melted down and used to pay off the country's debts. In just a few weeks, 3 million people had handed over necklaces, earrings, sports medals and trophies. At least one woman donated her wedding ring, and a cardinal donated his golden cross. The television stations ran kitschy give-away-your-gold game shows, but even with two hundred tons of gold collected, enough to drive down the world price, Korea's currency continued to plummet.[7]

As had happened during the Great Depression, the crisis led to a wave of suicides as families saw their life savings disappear and tens of thousands of small businesses shut their doors. In South Korea, the suicide rate went up by 50 percent in 1998. The spike was steepest among people over sixty, with older parents attempting to lessen the economic burden on their struggling children. The Korean press also reported an alarming increase in family suicide pacts in which fathers led their debt-ridden households in group hangings. Authorities pointed out that since "only the [family] leader's death is classified as suicide while the rest are listed as murders, the actual number of suicides is far higher than the statistics released."[8]

Asia's crisis was caused by a classic fear cycle, and the only move that might have arrested it was the same one that had rescued Mexico's currency during the so-called Tequila Crisis of 1994: a quick, decisive loan—proof to the market that the U.S. Treasury would simply not let Mexico fail.[9] No such timely move was forthcoming for Asia. In fact, as soon as the crisis hit, a surprising array of heavy hitters from the financial establishment stepped forward with a unified message: Don't help Asia.

Milton Friedman himself, now in his mid-eighties, made a rare appearance on CNN to tell the news anchor Lou Dobbs that he opposed any kind of bailout and that the market should be left to correct itself. "Well, Professor, I can't tell you what it means to have your support in this semantic discussion," said an embarassingly starstruck Dobbs. The let-them-sink position was echoed by Friedman's old friend Walter Wriston, former head of Citibank, and George Shultz, now working alongside Friedman at the right-wing Hoover Institution and a board member at the brokerage house Charles Schwab.[10]

The view was openly shared by one of Wall Street's premier investment banks, Morgan Stanley. Jay Pelosky, the firm's hotshot emerging-market strategist, told a conference in Los Angeles hosted by the Milken Institute (of junk bonds fame) that it was imperative that the IMF and the U.S. Treasury do nothing to lessen the pain of a crisis of 1930s proportions. "What we need now in Asia is more bad news. Bad news is needed to keep stimulating the adjustment process," Pelosky said.[11]

The Clinton administration took its cue from Wall Street. When the Asia Pacific Economic Cooperation Summit was held in November 1997 in Vancouver, four months into the crash, Bill Clinton enraged his Asian counterparts by dismissing what they viewed as an economic apocalypse as "a few little glitches in the road."[12] The message was clear: the U.S. Treasury was in no rush to stop the pain. As for the IMF, the world body created to prevent crashes like this one, it took the do-nothing approach that had become its trademark since Russia. It did, eventually, respond—but not with the sort of fast, emergency stabilization loan that a purely financial crisis demanded. Instead, it came up with a long list of demands, pumped up by the Chicago School certainty that Asia's catastrophe was an opportunity in disguise.

Back in the early nineties, whenever advocates of free trade wanted a persuasive success story to invoke in debates, they invariably pointed to the Asian Tigers. These were the miracle economies that were growing by leaps and bounds, supposedly because they had flung open their borders to unrestricted globalization. It was a useful story—the Tigers were certainly developing with whirlwind speed—but to suggest that their expansion was based on free trade was fiction. Malaysia, South Korea and Thailand still had highly protectionist policies that barred foreigners from owning land and from buying out national firms. They had also maintained a significant role for the state, keeping sectors like energy and transportation in public hands. The Tigers had also blocked many foreign imports from Japan, Europe and North America, as they built up their own domestic markets. They were economic success stories unquestionably, but ones that proved that mixed, managed economies grew faster and more equitably than those following the Wild West Washington Consensus.

The situation did not please Western and Japanese investment banks and multinational firms; watching Asia's consumer market explode, they understandably longed for unfettered access to the region to sell their products. They also wanted the right to buy up the best of the Tigers' corporations— particularly Korea's impressive conglomerates like Daewoo, Hyundai, Samsung and LG. In the mid-nineties, under pressure from the IMF and the newly created World Trade Organization, Asian governments agreed to split the difference: they would maintain the laws that protected national firms from foreign ownership and resist pressure to privatize their key state companies, but they would lift barriers to their financial sectors, allowing a surge of paper investing and currency trading.

In 1997, when the flood of hot money suddenly reversed current in Asia, it was a direct result of this kind of speculative investment, which was legalized only because of Western pressure. Wall Street, of course, didn't see it that way. Top investment analysts instantly recognized the crisis as the chance to level the remaining barriers protecting Asia's markets once and for all. Pelosky, the Morgan Stanley strategist, was particularly forthright about the logic: if the crisis was left to worsen, all foreign currency would be drained from the region and Asian-owned companies would have either to close down or to sell themselves to Western firms—both beneficial outcomes for Morgan Stanley. "I'd like to see closure of companies and asset sales. . . . Asset sales are very difficult; typically owners don't want to sell unless they're forced to. Therefore, we need more bad news to continue to put the pressure on these corporates to sell their companies."[13]

Some saw the breaking of Asia in even grander terms. José Piñera, Pinochet's star minister who was now working at the Cato Institute in Washington, D.C., greeted the crisis with undisguised glee, pronouncing that "the

day of reckoning has arrived." In Piñera's eyes, the crisis was the latest chapter in the war that he and his fellow Chicago Boys had started in Chile in the
seventies. The fall of the Tigers, he said, represented nothing less than "the
fall of a second Berlin Wall," the collapse of "the notion that there is a 'Third
Way' between free-market democratic capitalism and socialist statism."[14]

Piñera's was not a fringe perspective. It was openly shared by Alan
Greenspan, chairman of the U.S. Federal Reserve and probably the single
most powerful economic policy maker in the world. Greenspan described
the crisis as "a very dramatic event towards a consensus of the type of market
system which we have in this country." He also observed that "the current
crisis is likely to accelerate the dismantling in many Asian countries of the
remnants of a system with large elements of government-directed investment."[15] In other words, the destruction of Asia's managed economy was actually a process of creating a new American-style economy—birth pangs for
a new Asia, to borrow a phrase that would be used in an even more violent
context a few years later.

Michel Camdessus, who as head of the IMF was arguably the world's second most powerful monetary policy maker, expressed a similar view. In a
rare interview, he spoke of the crisis as an opportunity for Asia to shed its old
skin and be born anew. "Economic models are not eternal," he said. "There
are times when they are useful and other times . . . where they become out-
dated and must be abandoned."[16] The crisis sparked by a rumor that turned
fiction into fact apparently provided such a time.

Eager not to let this opportunity slip by, the IMF—after months of doing
nothing while the emergency worsened—finally entered into negotiations
with the ailing governments of Asia. The only country to resist the fund in
this period was Malaysia, thanks to its relatively small debt. Malaysia's controversial prime minister, Mahathir Mohamad, said that he did not think he
should have to "destroy the economy in order that it should become better,"
which was enough to brand him as a raving radical at the time.[17] The rest of
Asia's crisis-struck economies were too desperate for foreign currency to refuse the possibility of tens of billions in IMF loans: Thailand, the Philippines, Indonesia and South Korea all came to the table. "You can't force a
country to ask you for help. It has to ask. But when it's out of money, it hasn't
got many places to turn," said Stanley Fischer, who was in charge of the talks
for the IMF.[18]

Fischer had been one of the most vocal advocates of shock therapy in
Russia, and despite the harrowing human costs there, his attitude was just as

unyielding in Asia. Several governments suggested that since the crisis was caused by the ease with which money could gush in and out of their countries with nothing to slow down the flow, perhaps it made sense to put some barriers back up—the dreaded "capital controls." China had kept its controls up (ignoring Friedman's advice in this regard), and it was the only country in the region that was not being ravaged by the crisis. And Malaysia had put controls back up, and they seemed to be working.

Fischer and the rest of the IMF team dismissed the idea out of hand.[19] The IMF displayed no interest in what had actually caused the crisis. Instead, like a prison interrogator looking for a weakness, the fund was exclusively focused on how the crisis could be used as leverage. The meltdown had forced a group of strong-willed countries to beg for mercy; to fail to take advantage of that window of opportunity was, for the Chicago School economists running the IMF, tantamount to professional negligence.

With their treasuries empty, the Tigers were, as far as the IMF was concerned, broken; now they were primed to be remade. The first stage of this process was to strip the countries of all the "trade and investment protectionism and activist state intervention that were the key ingredients of the 'Asian miracle,'" as the political scientist Walden Bello put it.[20] The IMF also demanded that the governments make deep budget cuts, leading to mass layoffs of public sector workers in countries where people were already taking their own lives in record numbers. Fischer admitted after the fact that the IMF had concluded that in Korea and Indonesia, the crisis was unrelated to government overspending. Nonetheless, he used the extraordinary leverage granted by the crisis to extract these painful austerity measures. As one *New York Times* reporter wrote, the IMF's actions were "like a heart surgeon who, in the middle of an operation, decides to do some work on the lungs and kidneys, too."[*21]

After the IMF had stripped the Tigers of their old habits and ways, they were now ready to be reborn, Chicago-style: privatized basic services, independent central banks, "flexible" workforces, low social spending and, of

---

* The IMF is often portrayed as a puppet of the U.S. Treasury, but rarely have the strings been as clearly visible as during these negotiations. To make sure the interests of U.S. firms were reflected in the final agreements, David Lipton, U.S. Treasury undersecretary for international affairs (and Sachs's former partner for Poland's shock therapy program), flew to South Korea and checked into the Seoul Hilton—the hotel where the negotiations between the IMF and the Korean government were taking place. Lipton's presence was, according to *The Washington Post*'s Paul Blustein, "a visible manifestation of the influence the United States wields over IMF policy."

course, total free trade. According to the new agreements, Thailand would allow foreigners to own large stakes in its banks, Indonesia would cut food subsidies, and Korea would lift its law protecting workers against mass layoffs.[22] The IMF even set strict layoff targets in Korea: in order to get the loan, the country's banking sector needed to shed 50 percent of its workforce (later lowered to 30 percent).[23] This kind of demand was crucial for many Western multinationals who wanted assurances that they could radically downsize the Asian firms they were about to buy. Piñera's "Berlin Wall" was falling down.

Such measures would have been unthinkable a year before the crisis hit, when South Korea's trade unions had been at their peak of militancy. They had greeted a proposed new labor law that would have reduced job security with the largest and most radical series of strikes in South Korea's history. But, thanks to the crisis, the rules of the game had changed. The economic meltdown was so dire that it gave governments the license (as similar crises had from Bolivia to Russia) to declare temporary authoritarian rule; it didn't last long—just long enough to impose the IMF decrees.

Thailand's shock therapy package, for instance, was pushed through the National Assembly not in a normal process of debate but as a result of four emergency decrees. "We have lost our autonomy, our ability to determine our macroeconomic policy. This is unfortunate," conceded Thailand's deputy premier, Supachai Panitchpakdi (later rewarded for this kind of cooperative attitude by being named head of the WTO).[24] In South Korea, the IMF subversion of democracy was even more overt. There, the end of the IMF negotiations coincided with scheduled presidential elections in which two of the candidates were running on anti-IMF platforms. In an extraordinary act of interference with a sovereign nation's political process, the IMF refused to release the money until it had commitments from all four main candidates that they would stick to the new rules if they won. With the country effectively held at ransom, the IMF was triumphant: each candidate pledged his support in writing.[25] Never before had the central Chicago School mission to protect economic matters from the reach of democracy been more explicit: you can vote, South Koreans were told, but your vote can have no bearing on the managing and organization of the economy. (The day the deal was signed was instantly dubbed Korea's "National Humiliation Day.")[26]

In one of the worst-hit countries, such acts of democracy containment were not required. Indonesia, first in the region to fling open its doors to deregulated foreign investment, was still under the control of General Suharto, after more than thirty years. Suharto, however, had become less compliant with the West in his old age (as dictators often do). After decades of selling off Indonesia's oil and mineral wealth to foreign corporations, he had grown bored with enriching others and had spent the previous decade or so taking care of himself, his children and his golfing buddies. For instance, the general had given heavy subsidies to a car company—owned by his son Tommy—much to the consternation of Ford and Toyota, who saw no reason why they should have to compete with what analysts called "Tommy's toys."[27]

For a few months, Suharto tried to resist the IMF, issuing a budget that did not contain the massive cuts it was demanding. The fund fought back by increasing the pain levels. Officially, IMF representatives are not allowed to talk to the press during a negotiation since the slightest indication of how talks are going can dramatically influence the market. That didn't stop an unnamed "senior IMF official" from telling *The Washington Post* that "the markets are asking themselves the question of just how much the senior Indonesian leadership is committed to this program, and particularly to the major reform measures." The article went on to predict that the IMF would punish Indonesia by withholding billions in promised loans. As soon as it appeared, Indonesia's currency fell through the floor, losing 25 percent of its value in a single day.[28]

With that massive blow, Suharto gave in. "Can someone find me an economist who knows what's going on?" Indonesia's foreign minister reportedly pleaded.[29] Suharto found such an economist; in fact, he found several. Guaranteeing that the final IMF negotiations would go smoothly, he brought back the Berkeley Mafia who, after playing such a central role in the early days of his regime, had lost their influence with the aging general. After years in the political wilderness, they were once again in charge, with Widjojo Nitisastro, now seventy years old and known in Indonesia as "the dean of the Berkeley Mafia," heading up the negotiations. "When times are good, Widjojo and the economists are put in an obscure corner and President Suharto speaks to the cronies," explained Mohammad Sadli, a former Suharto minister. "The technocrat group is at its best in times of crisis. Suharto listens to them more for the time being and he orders the other ministers to shut up."[30] Talks with the IMF now took a distinctly more collegial tone, more "like intellectual discussions. No pressure from one side on the other," explained a member of Widjojo's team. Naturally, the IMF got almost everything it wanted—140 "adjustments" in all.[31]

The Reveal

As far as the IMF was concerned, the crisis was going extremely well. In less than a year, it had negotiated the economic equivalent of extreme makeovers for Thailand, Indonesia, South Korea and the Philippines.[32] It was finally ready for the defining moment in every makeover drama: the Reveal, the moment when the nipped-and-tucked, coached-and-buffed subject is unveiled to the awestruck public — in this case, the global stock and currency markets. If all had gone smoothly, when the IMF pulled back the curtain on its newest creations, the hot money that had fled Asia the previous year would have come rushing back in to buy up the Tigers' now irresistible stocks, bonds and currencies. Something else happened; the market panicked. The reasoning went like this: if the fund thought that the Tigers were such hopeless cases that they needed to be remade from scratch, then Asia was obviously in much worse shape than anyone had previously feared.

So rather than rushing back, traders responded to the IMF's big Reveal by promptly yanking out even more money and further attacking Asia's currencies. Korea was losing $1 billion a day and its debt was downgraded to junk bond status. The IMF's "help" had turned crisis into catastrophe. Or, as Jeffrey Sachs, now in open warfare with the international financial institutions, put it, "Instead of dousing the fire, the IMF in effect screamed fire in the theatre."[33]

The human costs of the IMF's opportunism were nearly as devastating in Asia as in Russia. The International Labor Organization estimates that a staggering 24 million people lost their jobs in this period and that Indonesia's unemployment rate increased from 4 to 12 percent. Thailand was losing 2,000 jobs a day at the height of the "reforms" — 60,000 a month. In South Korea, 300,000 workers were fired every month — largely the result of the IMF's totally unnecessary demands to slash government budgets and hike interest rates. By 1999, South Korea's and Indonesia's unemployment rates had nearly tripled in only two years. As in Latin America in the seventies, what disappeared in these parts of Asia was what was so remarkable about the region's "miracle" in the first place: its large and growing middle class. In 1996, 63.7 percent of South Koreans identified as middle class; by 1999 that number was down to 38.4 percent. According to the World Bank, 20 million Asians were thrown into poverty in this period of what Rodolfo Walsh would have called "planned misery."[34]

Behind every statistic was a story of wrenching sacrifice and degraded decisions. As is always the case, women and children suffered the worst of the crisis. Many rural families in the Philippines and South Korea sold their daughters to human traffickers who took them to work in the sex trade in Australia, Europe and North America. In Thailand, public health officials reported a 20 percent increase in child prostitution in just one year—the year after the IMF reforms. The Philippines tracked the same trend. "It was the rich who benefited from the boom, but we the poor pay the price of the crisis," said Khun Bunjan, a community leader in northeast Thailand who was forced to send her children to work as scavengers after her husband lost his factory job. "Even our limited access to schools and health [care] is now beginning to disappear."[35]

It was in this context that the U.S. secretary of state, Madeleine Albright, visited Thailand in March 1999 and saw fit to scold the Thai public for turning to prostitution and the "dead end of drugs." It is "essential that girls not be exploited and abused and exposed to AIDS. It's very important to fight back," Albright said, filled with moral resolve. She apparently saw no connection between the fact that so many Thai girls were being forced into the sex trade and the austerity policies for which she expressed her "strong support" on the same trip. It was the Asian financial crisis's equivalent of Milton Friedman expressing his displeasure with Pinochet's or Deng Xiaoping's human rights violations while praising their bold embrace of economic shock therapy.[36]

Feeding Off the Ruins

The story of Asia's crisis usually ends there—the IMF tried to help; it didn't work. Even the IMF's own internal audit came to that conclusion. The fund's Independent Evaluation Office concluded that the structural adjustment demands were "ill-advised" and "broader than seemed necessary" as well as "not critical to resolving the crisis." It also warned that "crisis should not be used as an opportunity to seek a long agenda of reforms just because leverage is high, irrespective of how justifiable they may be on merits."* A particularly forceful section of the internal report accused the fund of being so blinded by free-market ideology that even considering capital controls was institutionally unimaginable. "If it was heresy to suggest that financial markets were not distributing world capital in a rational and stable way, then it was a mortal sin to contemplate" capital controls.[37]

---

* For some reason, that highly critical report did not come out until 2003, five years after the crisis. By then, it was a little late to be issuing warnings against crisis opportunism; the IMF was already structurally adjusting Afghanistan and drawing up plans for Iraq.

What few were willing to admit at the time is that, while the IMF certainly failed the people of Asia, it did not fail Wall Street—far from it. The hot money may have been spooked by the IMF's drastic measures, but the large investment houses and multinational firms were emboldened. "Of course these markets are highly volatile," said Jerome Booth, head of research at London's Ashmore Investment Management. "That's what makes them fun."[38] These fun-seeking firms understood that as a result of the IMF's "adjustments," pretty much everything in Asia was now up for sale—and the more the market panicked, the more desperate Asian companies would be to sell, pushing their prices through the floor. Morgan Stanley's Jay Pelosky had said that what Asia needed was "more bad news to continue to put pressure on these corporates to sell their companies"—and that's exactly what happened, thanks to the IMF.

Whether the IMF planned the deepening of Asia's crisis or was merely recklessly indifferent remains a subject of debate. Perhaps the most charitable interpretation is that the fund knew it could not lose: if its adjustments inflated another bubble in emerging-market stocks, that would be a boon; if they sparked more capital flight, it would be a bonanza for vulture capitalists. Either way, the IMF was comfortable enough with the possibility of total meltdown to be willing to roll the dice. It's now clear who won the gamble.

Two months after the IMF came to its final agreement with South Korea, *The Wall Street Journal* ran an article headlined "Wall Street Scavenging in Asia-Pacific." It reported that Pelosky's firm, as well as several other prominent houses, had "dispatched armies of bankers to the Asia-Pacific region to scout for brokerage firms, asset management firms and even banks that they can snap up at bargain prices. The hunt for Asian acquisitions is urgent because many U.S. securities firms, led by Merrill Lynch & Co. and Morgan Stanley, have made overseas expansion their priority."[39] In short order, several major sales went through: Merrill Lynch bought Japan's Yamaichi Securities as well as Thailand's largest securities firm, while AIG bought Bangkok Investment for a fraction of its worth. JP Morgan bought a stake in Kia Motors, while Travelers Group and Salomon Smith Barney bought one of Korea's largest textile companies as well as several other companies. Interestingly, the chair of Salomon Smith Barney's International Advisory Board, which was providing advice to the company on mergers and acquisitions in this period, was Donald Rumsfeld (appointed in May 1999). Dick Cheney was also on the board. Another winner was the Carlyle Group, the secretive

Washington-based firm known for being the preferred soft landing for ex-presidents and ministers, from former secretary of state James Baker, to former U.K. prime minister John Major, to Bush Sr., who served as a consultant. Carlyle used its top-level connections to snap up Daewoo's telecom division, Ssangyong Information and Communication (one of Korea's largest high-tech firms), and it became a major shareholder in one of Korea's largest banks.[40]

Jeffrey Garten, former U.S. undersecretary of commerce, had predicted that when the IMF was finished, "there is going to be a significantly different Asia, and it will be an Asia in which American firms have achieved much deeper penetration, much greater access."[41] He wasn't kidding. Within two years, the face of much of Asia was utterly transformed, with hundreds of local brands replaced by multinational giants. It was dubbed "the world's biggest going-out-of-business sale," by *The New York Times*, and a "business-buying bazaar" by *BusinessWeek*.[42] In fact, it was a preview of the kind of disaster capitalism that would become the market norm after September 11: a terrible tragedy was exploited to allow foreign firms to storm Asia. They were there not to build their own businesses and compete but to snap up the entire apparatus, workforce, customer base and brand value built over decades by Korean companies, often to break them apart, downsize them or shut them completely in order to eliminate competition for their imports.

The Korean titan Samsung, for instance, was broken up and sold for parts: Volvo got its heavy industry division, SC Johnson & Son its pharmaceutical arm, General Electric its lighting division. A few years later, Daewoo's once-mighty car division, which the company had valued at $6 billion, was sold off to GM for just $400 million—a steal worthy of Russia's shock therapy. But this time, unlike what happened in Russia, local firms were getting wiped out by the multinationals.[43]

Other big players who got a piece of the Asian distress sale included Seagram's, Hewlett-Packard, Nestlé, Interbrew and Novartis, Carrefour, Tesco and Ericsson. Coca-Cola bought a Korean bottling company for half a billion dollars; Procter and Gamble bought a Korean packaging company; Nissan bought one of Indonesia's largest car companies. General Electric acquired a controlling stake in Korea's refrigerator manufacturer LG; and Britain's Powergen nabbed LG Energy, a large Korean electricity-and-gas company. According to *BusinessWeek*, the Saudi prince Alwaleed bin Talal was "jetting across Asia in his cream-colored Boeing 727, collecting bargains"—including a stake in Daewoo.[44]

Fittingly, Morgan Stanley, which had been the loudest in calling for a deepening of the crisis, inserted itself into many of these deals, collecting huge commissions. It acted as Daewoo's adviser on the sale of its automotive division and on brokering the privatization of several South Korean banks.[45]

It wasn't only private Asian firms that were being sold to foreigners. Like earlier crises in Latin America and Eastern Europe, this one also forced governments to sell public services to raise badly needed capital. The U.S. government eagerly anticipated this effect early on. In arguing why Congress should authorize billions to the IMF for the Asia makeover, the U.S. trade representative Charlene Barshefsky offered assurances that the agreements would "create new business opportunities for US firms": Asia would be forced to "accelerate privatization of certain key sectors—including energy, transportation, utilities and communications."[46]

Sure enough, the crisis set off a wave of privatizations, and foreign multi-nationals cleaned up. Bechtel got the contract to privatize the water and sewage systems in eastern Manila, as well as one to build an oil refinery in Sulawesi, Indonesia. Motorola got full control over Korea's Appeal Telecom. The New York–based energy giant Sithe got a large stake in Thailand's public gas company, the Cogeneration. Indonesia's water systems were split between Britain's Thames Water and France's Lyonnaise des Eaux. Canada's Westcoast Energy snapped up a huge Indonesian power plant project. British Telecom purchased a large stake in both Malaysia's and Korea's postal services. Bell Canada got a piece of Korea's telecom Hansol.[47]

All told, there were 186 major mergers and acquisitions of firms in Indonesia, Thailand, South Korea, Malaysia and the Philippines by foreign multinationals in a span of only twenty months. Watching this sale unfold, Robert Wade, an LSE economist, and Frank Veneroso, an economic consultant, predicted that the IMF program "may even precipitate the biggest peacetime transfer of assets from domestic to foreign owners in the past fifty years anywhere in the world."[48]

The IMF, while admitting some errors in its early responses to the crisis, claims that it quickly corrected them and that the "stabilization" programs were successful. It's true that Asia's markets eventually calmed down, but at a tremendous and ongoing cost. Milton Friedman, at the height of the crisis, had cautioned against panic, insisting that "it will be over. . . . As they get this financial mess settled, you can see a return to growth in Asia, but whether it will be one year, two years, three years, nobody can tell you."[49]

The truth is that Asia's crisis is still not over, a decade later. When 24 million people lose their jobs in a span of two years, a new desperation takes root that no culture can easily absorb. It expresses itself in different forms across the region, from a significant rise in religious extremism in Indonesia and Thailand to the explosive growth in the child sex trade.

Employment rates have still not reached pre-1997 levels in Indonesia, Malaysia and South Korea. And it's not just that workers who lost their jobs during the crisis never got them back. The layoffs have continued, with new foreign owners demanding ever-higher profits for their investments. The suicides have also continued: in South Korea, suicide is now the fourth most common cause of death, more than double the pre-crisis rate, with thirty-eight people taking their own lives every day.[50]

That is the untold story of the policies that the IMF calls "stabilization programs," as if countries were ships being tossed around on the market's high seas. They do, eventually, stabilize, but that new equilibrium is achieved by throwing millions of people overboard: public sector workers, small-business owners, subsistence farmers, trade unionists. The ugly secret of "stabilization" is that the vast majority never climb back aboard. They end up in slums, now home to 1 billion people; they end up in brothels or in cargo ship containers. They are the disinherited, those described by the German poet Rainer Maria Rilke as "ones to whom neither the past nor the future belongs."[51]

These people weren't the only victims of the IMF's demand for perfect orthodoxy in Asia. In Indonesia, the anti-Chinese sentiment I witnessed in the summer of 1997 continued to build, stoked by a political class happy to deflect attention away from itself. It got much worse after Suharto raised the price of basic survival items. Riots broke out across the country, and many of them targeted the Chinese minority; approximately twelve hundred people were killed, and dozens of Chinese women were gang-raped.[52] They too should be counted among the victims of Chicago School ideology.

Anger in Indonesia did, finally, direct itself at Suharto and the presidential palace. For three decades, Indonesians had been kept more or less in line by the memory of the bloodbath that brought Suharto to power, a memory that was refreshed by periodic massacres in the provinces and in East Timor. Anti-Suharto rage had burned under the surface all this time, but it took the IMF to pour the gasoline—which it did, ironically, by demanding that he raise the price of gasoline. After that, Indonesians rose up and pushed Suharto from power.

Like a prison interrogator, the IMF used the extreme pain of the crisis to break the Asian Tigers' will, to reduce the countries to total compliance. But the CIA's interrogation manuals warn that this process can go too far—apply too much direct pain and, instead of regression and compliance, the interrogators face confidence and defiance. In Indonesia that line was crossed, a reminder that it is possible to take shock therapy too far, provoking a kind of blowback that was about to become very familiar, from Bolivia to Iraq.

Free-market crusaders are, however, slow learners when it comes to the unintended consequences of their policies. The only lesson learned from the enormously lucrative Asian sell-off appears to have been yet more confirmation for the shock doctrine, more evidence (as if any more was needed) that there is nothing like a true disaster, a genuine churning of society, to open up a new frontier. A few years after the peak of the crisis, several prominent commentators were even willing to go so far as to say that what happened in Asia, despite all the devastation, was a blessing in disguise. *The Economist* noted that "it took a national crisis for South Korea to turn from an inward-looking nation to one that embraced foreign capital, change and competition." And Thomas Friedman, in his best-selling book *The Lexus and the Olive Tree*, declared that what happened in Asia wasn't a crisis at all. "I believe globalization did us all a favor by melting down the economies of Thailand, Korea, Malaysia, Indonesia, Mexico, Russia, and Brazil in the 1990s, because it laid bare a lot of rotten practices and institutions," he wrote, adding that "exposing the crony capitalism in Korea was no crisis in my book."[53] In his *New York Times* columns supporting the invasion of Iraq, a similar logic would be on display, except that the melting down would be done with cruise missiles, not currency trades.

The Asian crisis certainly showed how well disaster exploitation worked. At the same time, the destructiveness of the market crash and the cynicism of the West's response sparked powerful countermovements.

The forces of multinational capital got their way in Asia, but they provoked new levels of public rage, with the rage eventually directed squarely at the institutions advancing the ideology of unfettered capitalism. As an unusually balanced *Financial Times* editorial put it, Asia was a "warning signal that public unease with capitalism and the forces of globalization is reaching a worrying level. The Asian crisis showed the world how even the most successful countries could be brought to their knees by a sudden outflow of capital. People were outraged at how the whims of secretive hedge funds could apparently cause mass poverty on the other side of the world."[54]

Unlike in the former Soviet Union, where the planned misery of shock therapy could be passed off as part of the "painful transition" from Communism to market democracy, Asia's crisis was plainly a creation of the global markets. Yet when the high priests of globalization sent missions to the disaster zone, all they wanted to do was deepen the pain.

The result was that these missions lost the comfortable anonymity they had enjoyed previously. The IMF's Stanley Fischer recalled the "circus atmosphere" around the Seoul Hilton when he visited South Korea at the start of the negotiations. "I got imprisoned in my hotel room—couldn't move out because [if] I opened the door, there were 10,000 photographers." According to another account, in order to reach the banquet room where the negotiations were taking place, IMF representatives were forced "to take a circuitous route to a back entrance that involved going up and down flights of stairs and through the Hilton's vast kitchen."[55] At the time, IMF officials were unaccustomed to such attention. The experience of being prisoners in five-star hotels and conference centers would become familiar for emissaries of the Washington Consensus in the years to come, as mass protests started to greet their gatherings around the world.

After 1998, it became increasingly difficult to impose the shock therapy-style makeovers by peaceful means—through the usual IMF bullying or arm-twisting at trade summits. The defiant new mood coming from the South made its global debut when the World Trade Organization talks collapsed in Seattle in 1999. Though the college-age protesters received the bulk of the media coverage, the real rebellion took place inside the conference center, when developing countries formed a voting bloc and rejected demands for deeper trade concessions as long as Europe and the U.S. continued to subsidize and protect their domestic industries.

At the time, it was still possible to dismiss the Seattle breakdown as a minor pause in the steady advance of corporatism. Within a few years, however, the depth of the shift would be undeniable: the U.S. government's ambitious dream of creating a unified free-trade zone encompassing all of Asia-Pacific was abandoned, as were a global investors' treaty and plans for a Free Trade Area of the Americas, stretching from Alaska to Chile.

Perhaps the greatest impact of the so-called antiglobalization movement was that it forced the Chicago School ideology into the dead center of the international debate. For a brief moment at the turn of the millennium, there was no pressing crisis to deflect attention—the debt shocks had faded, the "transitions" were complete, and a new global war had not yet arrived. What was left was the real world track record of the free-market crusade: the dismal reality of inequality, corruption and environmental degradation left behind when government after government embraced Friedman's advice, given to Pinochet all those years ago, that it was a mistake to try "to do good with other people's money."

In retrospect, it is striking that capitalism's monopoly period, when it no longer had to deal with competing ideas or counterpowers, was extremely brief—only eight years, from the collapse of the Soviet Union in 1991 to the collapse of the WTO talks in 1999. But rising opposition would not slow the determination to advance this extraordinarily profitable agenda; its advocates would simply ride the waves of fear and disorientation created by bigger shocks than ever before.

PART 5

SHOCKING TIMES

THE RISE OF THE DISASTER CAPITALISM COMPLEX

Creative destruction is our middle name, both within our own society and abroad. We tear down the old order every day, from business to science, literature, art, architecture, and cinema to politics and the law. . . . They must attack us in order to survive, just as we must destroy them to advance our historic mission.

—Michael Ledeen, *The War against the Terror Masters,* 2002

George's answer to any problem at the ranch is to cut it down with a chain saw—which I think is why he and Cheney and Rumsfeld get along so well.

—Laura Bush, White House Correspondents' Association Dinner, April 30, 2005

CHAPTER 14

SHOCK THERAPY IN THE U.S.A.

THE HOMELAND SECURITY BUBBLE

He's a ruthless little bastard. You can be sure of that.
—Richard Nixon, U.S. president, referring to Donald Rumsfeld, 1971[1]

Today I fear that we are in fact waking up to a surveillance society that is already all around us.
—Richard Thomas, U.K. information commissioner, November 2006[2]

Homeland security may have just reached the stage that Internet investing hit in 1997. Back then, all you needed to do was put an "e" in front of your company name and your IPO would rocket. Now you can do the same with "fortress."
—Daniel Gross, *Slate*, June 2005[3]

It was a muggy Monday in Washington, and Donald Rumsfeld was about to do something he hated: talk to his staff. Since taking office as defense secretary, he had solidified his reputation among the Joint Chiefs of Staff as high-handed, secretive and—a word that kept coming up—arrogant. Their animosity was understandable. Since setting foot in the Pentagon, Rumsfeld had brushed aside the prescribed role of leader and motivator and acted instead like a blood-less hatchet man—a CEO secretary on a downsizing mission.

When Rumsfeld accepted the post, many wondered why he would even want it. He was sixty-eight years old, had five grandchildren and a personal fortune estimated at as much as $250 million—and he had already held the same post in the Gerald Ford administration.[4] Rumsfeld, however, had no desire to be a traditional defense secretary, defined by the wars waged on his watch; he had greater ambitions than that.

The incoming defense secretary had spent the past twenty-odd years heading up multinational corporations and sitting on their boards, often leading companies through dramatic mergers and acquisitions, as well as painful restructurings. In the nineties, he had come to see himself as a man of the New Economy, directing a company specializing in digital TV, sitting on the board of another promising "e-business solutions," and serving as board chairman of the very sci-fi biotech firm that held the exclusive patent on a treatment for avian flu as well as on several important AIDS medications.[5] When Rumsfeld joined the cabinet of George W. Bush in 2001, it was with a personal mission to reinvent warfare for the twenty-first century—turning it into something more psychological than physical, more spectacle than struggle, and far more profitable than it had ever been before.

Much has been written about Rumsfeld's controversial "transformation" project, which prompted eight retired generals to call for his resignation and eventually forced him to step down after the 2006 midterm elections. When Bush announced the resignation he described the "sweeping transformation" project—and not the war in Iraq or the broader "War on Terror"—as Rumsfeld's most profound contribution: "Don's work in these areas did not often make the headlines. But the reforms that set in motion—that he has set in motion—are historic."[6] They are indeed, but it has not always been clear what those reforms consist of.

Senior military officials derided "transformation" as "empty buzz words," and Rumsfeld often seemed determined (almost comically) to prove the critics right: "The Army is going through what is a major modernization," Rumsfeld said in April 2006. "It's moving from a division-oriented force to a modular brigade combat team force . . . from service-centric war-fighting to deconfliction war-fighting to interoperability and now toward interdependence. That's a hard thing to do."[7] But the project was never quite as complicated as Rumsfeld made it sound. Beneath the jargon, it was simply an attempt to bring the revolution in outsourcing and branding that he had been part of in the corporate world into the heart of the U.S. military.

During the 1990s, many companies that had traditionally manufactured their own products and maintained large, stable workforces embraced what became known as the Nike model: don't own any factories, produce your products through an intricate web of contractors and subcontractors, and pour your resources into design and marketing. Other companies opted for the alternative, Microsoft model: maintain a tight control center of shareholder/employees who perform the company's "core competency" and outsource everything else to temps, from running the mailroom to writing code. Some called the companies that underwent these radical restructurings "hollow corporations" because they were mostly form, with little tangible content left over.

Rumsfeld was convinced that the U.S. Department of Defense needed an equivalent makeover; as *Fortune* said when he arrived at the Pentagon, "Mr. CEO" was "about to oversee the same sort of restructuring that he orchestrated so well in the corporate world."[8] There were, of course, some necessary differences. Where corporations unburdened themselves of geography-bound factories and full-time workers, Rumsfeld saw the army shedding large numbers of full-time troops in favor of a small core of staffers propped up by cheaper temporary soldiers from the Reserve and National Guard. Meanwhile, contractors from companies such as Blackwater and Halliburton would perform duties ranging from high-risk chauffeuring to prisoner interrogation to catering to health care. And where corporations poured their savings on labor into design and marketing, Rumsfeld would spend his savings from fewer troops and tanks on the latest satellite and nanotechnology from the private sector. "In the twenty-first century," Rumsfeld said of the modern military, "we're going to have to stop thinking about things, numbers of things, and mass, and think also and maybe even first about speed and agility and precision." He sounded very much like the hyperactive management consultant Tom Peters, who declared in the late nineties that companies had to decide if they were "pure 'players' in brainware" or "lumpy-object purveyors."[9]

Not surprisingly, the generals who were used to holding sway in the Pentagon were pretty sure that "things" and "mass" still mattered when it came to fighting wars. They soon became deeply hostile to Rumsfeld's vision of a hollow military. After a little more than seven months in office, the secretary had already stepped on so many powerful toes that it was rumored his days were numbered.

It was at this moment that Rumsfeld called a rare "town hall meeting" for Pentagon staff. The speculation began immediately: Was he going to announce his resignation? Was he going to try his hand at a pep talk? Was he belatedly trying to sell the old guard on transformation? As hundreds of Pentagon senior staff filed into the auditorium that Monday morning, "the mood was definitely one of curiosity," one staffer told me. "The feeling was, How are you going to convince us? Because there was already a huge amount of animosity toward him."

When Rumsfeld made his entrance, "we politely stood up and sat down." It rapidly became clear that this was not a resignation, and it most certainly was not a pep talk. It may have been the most extraordinary speech ever given by a U.S. secretary of defense. It began like this:

> The topic today is an adversary that poses a threat, a serious threat, to the security of the United States of America. This adversary is one of the world's last bastions of central planning. It governs by dictating five-year plans. From a single capital, it attempts to impose its demands across time zones, continents, oceans and beyond. With brutal consistency, it stifles free thought and crushes new ideas. It disrupts the defense of the United States and places the lives of men and women in uniform at risk.
>
> Perhaps this adversary sounds like the former Soviet Union, but that enemy is gone: our foes are more subtle and implacable today. . . . The adversary's closer to home. It's the Pentagon bureaucracy.[10]

As Rumsfeld's rhetorical gimmick revealed itself, the faces in the audience went stony. Most of the people listening had devoted their careers to fighting the Soviet Union and didn't appreciate being compared to Commies at this stage in the game. Rumsfeld wasn't finished. "We know the adversary. We know the threat. And with the same firmness of purpose that any effort against a determined adversary demands, we must get at it and stay at it . . . today we declare war on bureaucracy."

He'd done it: the defense secretary had not only described the Pentagon as a grave threat to America but declared war against the institution where he worked. The audience was stunned. "He was saying we were the enemy, that the enemy was us. And here we were thinking we were doing the nation's business," the staffer told me.

It wasn't that Rumsfeld wanted to save taxpayer dollars—he had just asked Congress for an 11 percent budget increase. But following the corporatist principles of the counterrevolution, in which Big Government joins forces with Big Business to redistribute funds upward, he wanted less spent on staff and far more public money transferred directly into the coffers of private companies. And with that, Rumsfeld launched his "war." Every department needed to slash its staff by 15 percent, including "every base headquarters building in the world. It's not just the law, it's a good idea, and we're going to get it done."[11]

He had already directed his senior staff to "scour the Department [of Defense] for functions that could be performed better and more cheaply through commercial outsourcing." He wanted to know, "Why is DoD one of the last organizations around that still cuts its own checks? When an entire industry exists to run warehouses efficiently, why do we own and operate so many of our own? At bases around the world, why do we pick up our own garbage and mop our own floors, rather than contracting services out, as many businesses do? And surely we can outsource more computer systems support."

He even went after the sacred cow of the military establishment: health care for soldiers. Why were there so many doctors? Rumsfeld wanted to know. "Some of those needs, especially where they may involve general practice or specialties unrelated to combat, might be more efficiently delivered by the private sector." And how about the houses for soldiers and their families—surely these could be done through "public-private partnerships."

The Defense Department should focus on its core competency: "warfighting . . . But in all other cases, we should seek suppliers who can provide these non-core activities efficiently and effectively."

After the speech, plenty of Pentagon staffers griped that the only thing standing in the way of Rumsfeld's bold vision of outsourcing the army was the small matter of the U.S. Constitution, which clearly defined national security as the duty of government, not private companies. "I thought the speech was going to cost Rumsfeld his job," my source told me.

It didn't, and the coverage of his declaration of war on the Pentagon was sparse. That's because the date of his contentious address was September 10, 2001.

It is a strange historical footnote that CNN *Evening News* on September 10 carried a short story under the headline "Defense Secretary Declares War on the Pentagon's Bureaucracy" and that, the next morning, the network would report on an attack on that institution of a distinctly less metaphorical kind, one that killed 125 Pentagon employees and seriously wounded another 110 of the people whom Rumsfeld had portrayed as enemies of the state less than twenty-four hours earlier.[12]

Cheney and Rumsfeld: Proto-Disaster Capitalists

The idea at the heart of Rumsfeld's forgotten speech is nothing less than the central tenet of the Bush regime: that the job of government is not to govern but to subcontract the task to the more efficient and generally superior private sector. As Rumsfeld made clear, this task was about nothing as prosaic as trimming the budget, but was, for its advocates, a world-changing crusade on a par with defeating Communism.

By the time the Bush team took office, the privatization mania of the eighties and nineties (fully embraced by the Clinton administration, as well as state and local governments) had successfully sold off or outsourced the large, publicly owned companies in several sectors, from water and electricity to highway management and garbage collection. After these limbs of the state had been lopped off, what was left was "the core"—those functions so intrinsic to the concept of governing that the idea of handing them to private corporations challenged what it meant to be a nation-state: the military, police, fire departments, prisons, border control, covert intelligence, disease control, the public school system and the administering of government bureaucracies. The earlier stages of the privatization wave had been so profitable, however, that many of the companies that had devoured the appendages of the state were greedily eyeing these essential functions as the next source of instant riches.

By the late nineties, a powerful move was afoot to break the taboos protecting "the core" from privatization. It was, in many ways, merely a logical extension of the status quo. Just as Russia's oil fields, Latin America's telecoms, and Asia's industry had supplied the stock market with superprofits in the nineties, now it would be the U.S. government itself that would play that central economic role—all the more crucial because the backlash against privatization and free trade was spreading rapidly through the developing world, closing off other avenues for growth.

It was a move that brought the shock doctrine to a new, self-referential phase: until that point, disasters and crises had been harnessed to push through radical privatization plans after the fact, but the institutions that had the power both to create and respond to cataclysmic events—the military, the CIA, the Red Cross, the UN, emergency "first responders"—had been some of the last bastions of public control. Now, with the core set to be devoured, the crisis-exploiting methods that had been honed over the previous three decades would be used to leverage the privatization of the infrastructure of disaster creation and disaster response. Friedman's crisis theory was going postmodern.

At the vanguard of the push to create what can only be described as a privatized police state were the most powerful figures in the future Bush administration: Dick Cheney, Donald Rumsfeld and George W. Bush himself.

For Rumsfeld, the idea of applying "market logic" to the U.S. military was a project that dated back four decades. It began in the early sixties, when he used to attend seminars at the University of Chicago's Economics Department. He had developed a particularly close connection with Milton Friedman, who, after Rumsfeld was elected to Congress at the age of thirty, took the precocious Republican under his wing, helping him to develop a bold free-market policy platform and tutoring him in economic theory. The two men remained close over the years, with Rumsfeld attending an annual birthday celebration for Friedman, organized every year by the Heritage Foundation's president, Ed Feulner. "There is something about Milton that when I am around him, and talking to him, I feel smarter," Rumsfeld said of his mentor when Friedman turned ninety.[13]

The admiration was mutual. Friedman was so impressed with Rumsfeld's commitment to deregulated markets that he aggressively lobbied Reagan to name Rumsfeld as his running mate in the 1980 election instead of George H. W. Bush—and he never did quite forgive Reagan for disregarding his advice. "I believe that Reagan made a mistake when he chose Bush as his vice-presidential candidate," Friedman wrote in his memoirs; "indeed, I regard it as the worst decision not only of his campaign but of his presidency. My favorite candidate was Donald Rumsfeld. Had he been chosen, I believe he would have succeeded Reagan as president, and the sorry Bush-Clinton period would never have occurred."[14]

Rumsfeld survived being passed over as Reagan's running mate by throwing himself into his burgeoning business career. As CEO of the international drug and chemical company Searle Pharmaceuticals, he used his political connections to secure the controversial and extraordinarily lucrative Food and Drug Administration (FDA) approval for aspartame (marketed as NutraSweet); and when Rumsfeld brokered the deal to sell Searle to Monsanto, he personally earned an estimated $12 million.[15]

The high-stakes sale established Rumsfeld as a corporate power player, landing him seats on the boards of such blue-chip firms as Sears and Kellogg's. His status as a former defense secretary, meanwhile, made him a score for any company that was part of what Eisenhower had called the "military-industrial complex." Rumsfeld sat on the board of the aircraft manufacturer Gulfstream and was also paid $190,000 a year as a board member of ASEA Brown Boveri (ABB), the Swiss engineering giant that gained unwanted attention when it was revealed to have sold nuclear technology to North Korea, including the capacity to produce plutonium. The nuclear reactor sale went through in 2000, and at the time Rumsfeld was the only North American on the ABB board. He claims to have no memory of the reactor sale coming before the board, though the company insists that "board members were informed about the project."[16]

It was in 1997, when Rumsfeld was named chairman of the board of the biotech firm Gilead Sciences, that he would firmly establish himself as a proto disaster capitalist. The company had registered the patent for Tamiflu, a treatment for many kinds of influenza and the preferred drug for avian flu.* If there was ever an outbreak of the highly contagious virus (or the threat of one), governments would be forced to buy billions of dollars' worth of the treatment from Gilead Sciences.

The patenting of drugs and vaccines to treat public health emergencies remains a controversial subject. The U.S. has been epidemic-free for several decades, but when the polio outbreak was at its peak in the mid-fifties, the ethics of disease profiteering were hotly debated. With close to sixty thousand known cases of polio, and parents terrified that their children were going to contract the crippling, often fatal, disease, the search for a cure was frantic. When Jonas Salk, a scientist at the University of Pittsburgh, found it and developed the first polio vaccine in 1952, he did not patent the lifesaving treatment. "There is no patent," Salk told the broadcaster Edward R. Murrow: "Could you patent the sun?"[17]

It's safe to say that if you could patent the sun, Donald Rumsfeld would have long since put in an application with the U.S. Patent and Trademark Office. His former company Gilead Sciences, which also owns the patents on four AIDS treatments, spends a great deal of energy trying to block the distribution of cheaper generic versions of its lifesaving drugs in the developing

---

* Tamiflu has become highly controversial. In a growing number of reported cases, young people who took the drug became confused, paranoid, delusional and suicidal. Between November 2005 and November 2006, twenty-five deaths around the world were linked to Tamiflu, and in the United States the drug is now issued with a health warning alerting patients to an "increased risk of self-injury and confusion" and urging them to "be closely monitored for signs of unusual behavior."

world. It has been targeted for these activities by public health activists in the U.S., who point out that some of Gilead's key medicines were developed on grants funded by taxpayers.[18] Gilead, for its part, sees epidemics as a growth market, and it has an aggressive marketing campaign to encourage businesses and individuals to stockpile Tamiflu, just in case. Before he reentered government, Rumsfeld was so convinced that he was on to a hot new industry that he helped found several private investment funds specializing in biotechnology and pharmaceuticals.[19] These companies are banking on an apocalyptic future of rampant disease, one in which governments are forced to buy, at top dollar, whatever lifesaving products the private sector has under patent.

Dick Cheney, a protégé of Rumsfeld's in the Ford administration, has also built a fortune based on the profitable prospect of a grim future, though where Rumsfeld saw a boom market in plagues, Cheney was banking on a future of war. As secretary of defense under Bush Sr., Cheney scaled down the number of active troops and dramatically increased reliance on private contractors. He contracted Brown & Root, the engineering division of the Houston-based multinational Halliburton, to identify tasks being performed by U.S. troops that could be taken over by the private sector for a profit. Not surprisingly, Halliburton identified all kinds of jobs that the private sector could perform, and those findings led to a bold new Pentagon contract: the Logistics Civil Augmentation Program, or LOGCAP. The Pentagon was notorious for its multi-billion-dollar contracts with weapons manufacturers, but this was something new: not supplying the military with gear but serving as manager for its operations.[20]

A select group of companies was invited to apply to provide unlimited "logistical support" for U.S. military missions, an extremely vague work description. Furthermore, no dollar value was attached to the contract: the winning company was simply assured that whatever it did for the military, it would have its costs covered by the Pentagon, plus a guaranteed profit— what is known as a "cost plus" contract. These were the final days of the Bush Sr. administration, and the company that won the contract in 1992 was none other than Halliburton. As the *Los Angeles Times*'s T. Christian Miller noted, Halliburton "beat out thirty-six other bidders to win a five-year contract—not surprising perhaps, given that it was the company that drew up the plans."

In 1995, with Clinton in the White House, Halliburton recruited Cheney as its new boss. While the Halliburton division Brown & Root had a long history as a U.S. military contractor, under Cheney's leadership Halliburton's role was to expand so dramatically that it would transform the nature of modern war. Thanks to the loosely worded contract that Halliburton and Cheney had crafted when he was at the Pentagon, the company was able to stretch and expand the meaning of the term "logistical support" until Halliburton was responsible for creating the entire infrastructure of a U.S. military operation overseas. All that was required of the army was to provide the soldiers and the weapons—they were, in a way, content providers, while Halliburton ran the show.

The result, first on display in the Balkans, was a kind of McMilitary experience in which deploying abroad resembled a heavily armed and perilous package vacation. "The first person to greet our soldiers as they arrive in the Balkans and the last one to wave goodbye is one of our employees," a Halliburton spokesperson explained, making the company's staff sound more like cruise directors than army logistics coordinators.[21] That was the Halliburton difference: Cheney saw no reason why war shouldn't be a thriving part of America's highly profitable service economy—invasion with a smile.

In the Balkans, where Clinton deployed nineteen thousand soldiers, U.S. bases sprang up as mini Halliburton cities: neat, gated suburbs, built and run entirely by the company. And Halliburton was committed to providing the troops with all the comforts of home, including fast-food outlets, supermarkets, movie theaters and high-tech gyms.[22] Some senior officers wondered what the strip-malling of the military would do to troop discipline—but they too were enjoying the perks. "Everything with Halliburton was gold-plated," one told me. "So we weren't complaining." As far as Halliburton was concerned, keeping the customer satisfied was good business—it guaranteed more contracts, and because profits were calculated as a percentage of costs, the higher the costs, the higher the profits. "Don't worry, it's cost plus," was a saying made famous in Baghdad's Green Zone, but the deluxe war spending was pioneered during the Clinton era. In just five years at Halliburton, Cheney almost doubled the amount of money the company extracted from the U.S. Treasury, from $1.2 billion to $2.3 billion, while the amount it received in federal loans and loan guarantees increased fifteenfold.[23] And he was well rewarded for his efforts. Before taking office as vice president, Cheney "valued his net worth at between $18 million and $81.9 million, including between $6 million and $30 million worth of stock in Halliburton Co. . . . Overall, Cheney was given some 1,260,000 Halliburton options, with 100,000 already used, 760,000 eligible to be redeemed and 166,667 to become valid this December [2000]."[24]

The push to expand the service economy into the heart of government was, for Cheney, a family affair. In the late nineties, while he was turning military bases into Halliburton suburbs, his wife, Lynne, was earning stock options in addition to her salary as a board member at Lockheed Martin, the world's largest defense contractor. Lynne's time on the board, from 1995 to 2001, coincided with a key period of transition for companies like Lockheed.[25] The Cold War was over, defense spending was dropping, and with nearly their entire budgets coming from government weapons contracts, these firms needed a new business model. At Lockheed and its fellow arms manufacturers, a strategy emerged to aggressively pursue a new line of work: running the government for a fee.

In the mid-nineties, Lockheed began taking over information technology divisions of the U.S. government, running its computer systems and a great deal of its data management. Largely under the public radar, the company went so far in this direction that, in 2004, *The New York Times* reported, "Lockheed Martin doesn't run the United States. But it does help run a breathtakingly big part of it. . . . It sorts your mail and totals your taxes. It cuts Social Security checks and counts the United States census. It runs space flights and monitors air traffic. To make all that happen, Lockheed writes more computer code than Microsoft.*[26]

It made for a powerful husband-and-wife team. While Dick was steering Halliburton to take over the infrastructure of warfare abroad, Lynne was helping Lockheed to take over the day-to-day running of government at home. At times husband and wife found themselves in direct competition. In 1996, when the state of Texas announced that corporations could bid to run its welfare program—a contract worth up to $2 billion over five years— both Lockheed and the IT giant Electronic Data Systems, which boasted Dick Cheney as a board member, bid on the contract. In the end, the Clinton administration intervened and halted the auction. Though it was generally an enthusiastic supporter of outsourcing, deciding who was eligible to receive welfare was determined to be an essential role of government, not suitable for privatization. Both Lockheed and EDS cried foul, as did the

---

* All the large weapons makers got into the business of running government in this period. Computer Sciences, which provides information technologies to the military, including biometric IDs, won a $644 million contract from the county of San Diego to run all its information technology—one of the largest contracts of its kind ever awarded. The county became dissatisfied with Computer Sciences' performance and did not renew the contract, only to give it to yet another weapons giant, Northrop Grumman, maker of the B-2 stealth bomber.

governor of Texas, George W. Bush, who thought privatizing the welfare system was a terrific idea.[27]

George W. Bush didn't distinguish himself as governor in too many
ways, but there was one area in which he excelled: parceling out to private
interests the various functions of the government he was elected to run—
especially security-related functions, a preview of the privatized War on
Terror he would soon unleash. Under his watch, the number of private
prisons in Texas grew from twenty-six to forty-two, prompting *The American Prospect* magazine to call Bush's Texas "the world capital of the
private-prison industry." In 1997, the FBI launched an investigation into a
jail in Brazoria County, forty miles outside Houston, after a local television
station aired a videotape of guards kicking unresisting inmates in the
groin, shooting them with stun guns and attacking them with dogs. At least
one of the violent guards in the video was wearing the uniform of Capital
Correctional Resources, a private company contracted to supply guards for
the prison.[28]

Bush's enthusiasm for privatization was in no way dampened by the Brazoria incident. A few weeks later, he had what appears to have been an
epiphany when he met José Piñera, the Chilean minister who had privatized
social security during the Pinochet dictatorship. This is Piñera's description
of the meeting: "By his concentrated focus, his body language [and] his relevant questions, I knew immediately that Mr. Bush had fully understood the
essence of my idea: that Social Security reform could be used both to provide a decent retirement and to create a world of worker-capitalists, an ownership society. . . . He was so enthusiastic that at the end he whispered in my
ear with a smile, 'Go and tell all this to my little brother in Florida. He will
also love it.' "[29]

The future president's commitment to auctioning off the state, combined
with Cheney's leadership in outsourcing the military and Rumsfeld's patenting of drugs that might prevent epidemics, provided a preview of the kind of
state the three men would construct together—it was a vision of a perfectly
hollow government. Though this radical program did not form the centerpiece of Bush's campaign for the presidency in 2000, there were hints of
what was in store: "There are hundreds of thousands of full-time federal employees that are performing tasks that could be done by companies in the
private sector," Bush said in one campaign speech. "I will put as many of
these tasks as possible up for competitive bidding. If the private sector can do
a better job, the private sector should get the contract."[30]

September 11 and the Civil Service Comeback

As Bush and his cabinet took their posts in January 2001, the need for new sources of growth for U.S. corporations took on even greater urgency. With the tech bubble now officially popped and the Dow Jones tumbling 824 points in their first two and half months in office, they found themselves staring in the face of a serious economic downturn. Keynes had argued that governments should spend their way out of recessions, providing economic stimulus with public works. Bush's solution was for the government to deconstruct itself—hacking off great chunks of the public wealth and feeding them to corporate America, in the form of tax cuts on the one hand and lucrative contracts on the other. Bush's budget director, the think-tank ideologue Mitch Daniels, pronounced, "The general idea—that the business of government is not to provide services, but to make sure that they are provided—seems self-evident to me."[31] That assessment included disaster response. Joseph Allbaugh, the Republican Party operative whom Bush put in charge of the Federal Emergency Management Agency (FEMA)—the body responsible for responding to disasters, including terrorist attacks—described his new place of work as "an oversized entitlement program."[32]

Then came 9/11, and all of a sudden having a government whose central mission was self-immolation did not seem like a very good idea. With a frightened population wanting protection from a strong, solid government, the attacks could well have put an end to Bush's project of hollowing out government just as it was beginning.

For a while, that even seemed to be the case. "September 11 has changed everything," said Ed Feulner, Milton Friedman's old friend and president of the Heritage Foundation, ten days after the attack, making him one of the first to utter the fateful phrase. Many naturally assumed that part of that change would be a reevaluation of the radical antistate agenda that Feulner and his ideological allies had been pushing for three decades, at home and around the world. After all, the nature of the September 11 security failures exposed the results of more than twenty years of chipping away at the public sector and outsourcing government functions to profit-driven corporations. Much as the flooding of New Orleans exposed the rotting condition of public infrastructure, the attacks pulled back the curtain on a state that had been allowed to grow dangerously weak: radio communications for the New York City police and firefighters broke down in the middle of the rescue operation, air traffic controllers didn't notice the off-course planes in time, and the attackers had passed through airport security checkpoints staffed by contract workers, some of whom earned less than their counterparts at the food court.[33]

The first major victory of the Friedmanite counterrevolution in the United States had been Ronald Reagan's attack on the air traffic controllers' union and his deregulation of the airlines. Twenty years later, the entire air transit system had been privatized, deregulated and downsized, with the vast majority of airport security work performed by underpaid, poorly trained, nonunion contractors. After the attacks, the inspector general of the Department of Transportation testified that the airlines, which were responsible for security on their flights, had skimped significantly to keep costs down. The "counterpressures in turn manifested themselves as significant weaknesses in security," he told the Bush-convened 9/11 Commission. A longtime Federal Aviation Authority security official testifed before the commission that the airlines' approach to security was "decry, deny and delay."[34]

On September 10, as long as flights were cheap and plentiful, none of that seemed to matter. But on September 12, putting $6-an-hour contract workers in charge of airport security seemed reckless. Then, in October, envelopes with white powder were sent to lawmakers and journalists, spreading panic about the possibility of a major anthrax outbreak. Once again, nineties privatization looked very different in this new light: Why did a private lab have the exclusive right to produce the anthrax vaccine? Had the federal government signed away its responsibility to protect the public from a major public health emergency? It didn't help that Bioport, the privatized lab in question, had failed a series of inspections and that the FDA wasn't even authorizing it to distribute its vaccines at the time.[35] Furthermore, if it was true, as media reports kept claiming, that anthrax, smallpox and other deadly agents could be spread through the mail, the food supply or the water systems, was it really such a good idea to be pushing ahead with Bush's plans to privatize the postal service? And what about all those laid-off food and water inspectors—could somebody bring them back?

The backlash against the pro-corporate consensus only deepened in the face of new scandals like that of Enron. Three months after the 9/11 attacks, Enron declared bankruptcy, leading thousands of employees to lose their retirement savings while executives acting on insider knowledge cashed out. The crisis contributed to a general plummeting of faith in private industry to perform essential services, especially when it came out that it was Enron's manipulation of energy prices that had led to the massive blackouts in California a few months earlier. Milton Friedman, aged ninety, was so concerned that the tides were shifting back toward Keynesianism that he complained that "businessmen are being presented in the public as second-class citizens."[36]

While CEOs were falling from their pedestals, unionized public sector workers—the villains of Friedman's counterrevolution—were rapidly ascending in the public's estimation. Within two months of the attacks, trust in government was higher than it had been since 1968—and that, remarked Bush to a crowd of federal employees, is "because of how you've performed your jobs."[37] The uncontested heroes of September 11 were the blue-collar first responders—the New York firefighters, police and rescue workers, 403 of whom lost their lives as they tried to evacuate the towers and aid the victims. Suddenly, America was in love with its men and women in all kinds of uniforms, and its politicians—slapping on NYPD and FDNY baseball caps with unseemly speed—were struggling to keep up with the new mood.

When Bush stood with the firefighters and rescue workers at Ground Zero on September 14—what his advisers call "the bullhorn moment"—he was embracing some of the very unionized civil servants that the modern conservative movement had devoted itself to destroying. Of course he had to do it (even Dick Cheney put on a hard hat in those days), but he didn't have to do it so convincingly. Through some combination of genuine feeling on Bush's part, and the public's projected desire for a leader worthy of the moment, these were the most moving speeches of Bush's political career.

For weeks after the attacks, the president went on a grand tour of the public sector—public schools, firehouses and memorials, the Centers for Disease Control and Prevention—embracing and thanking civil servants for their contributions and humble patriotism. "We have gained new heroes," Bush said in a speech, praising not only emergency services personnel but teachers, postal employees and health care workers.[38] At these events, he treated work done in the public interest with a level of respect and dignity that had not been seen in the United States in four decades. Cost-cutting was suddenly off the agenda, and in every speech the president gave, he announced some ambitious new public program.

"The twin demands of a sagging economy and an urgent new war on terrorism have transformed the philosophical heart of President Bush's agenda," confidently declared John Harris and Dana Milbank in *The Washington Post* eleven days after the attacks. "A man who came to power offering himself as an ideological descendant of Ronald Reagan has emerged nine months later as something closer to an heir of Franklin D. Roosevelt." They further observed that "Bush is working on a large economic stimulus package to stave off recession. He said a weak economy needs its pump primed by government with a big infusion of money—a basic precept of Keynesian economics that was at the heart of FDR's New Deal."[39]

A Corporate New Deal

Public pronouncements and photo ops aside, Bush and his inner circle had no intention of converting to Keynesianism. Far from shaking their determination to weaken the public sphere, the security failures of 9/11 reaffirmed their deepest ideological (and self-interested) beliefs—that only private firms possessed the intelligence and innovation to meet the new security challenge. Although it was true that the White House was on the verge of spending huge amounts of taxpayer money to stimulate the economy, it most certainly was not going to be on the model of FDR. Rather, Bush's New Deal would be exclusively with corporate America, a straight-up transfer of hundreds of billions of public dollars a year into private hands. It would take the form of contracts, many offered secretively, with no competition and scarcely any oversight, to a sprawling network of industries: technology, media, communications, incarceration, engineering, education, health care.*

What happened in the period of mass disorientation after the attacks was, in retrospect, a domestic form of economic shock therapy. The Bush team, Friedmanite to the core, quickly moved to exploit the shock that gripped the nation to push through its radical vision of a hollow government in which everything from war fighting to disaster response was a for-profit venture.

It was a bold evolution of shock therapy. Rather than the nineties approach of selling off existing public companies, the Bush team created a whole new framework for its actions—the War on Terror—built to be private from the start. This feat required two stages. First, the White House used the omnipresent sense of peril in the aftermath of 9/11 to dramatically increase the policing, surveillance, detention and war-waging powers of the executive branch—a power grab that the military historian Andrew Bacevich has termed "a rolling coup."[40] Then those newly enhanced and richly funded functions

* The lack of competition in awarding contracts has been one of the distinguishing features of the Bush years. A *New York Times* analysis in February 2007 found that "fewer than half of all 'contract actions'—new contracts and payments against existing contracts—are now subject to full and open competition. Just 48 percent were competitive in 2005, down from 79 percent in 2001."

of security, invasion, occupation and reconstruction were immediately out-sourced, handed over to the private sector to perform at a profit.

Although the stated goal was fighting terrorism, the effect was the creation of the disaster capitalism complex—a full-fledged new economy in home-land security, privatized war and disaster reconstruction tasked with nothing less than building and running a privatized security state, both at home and abroad. The economic stimulus of this sweeping initiative proved enough to pick up the slack where globalization and the dot-com booms had left off. Just as the Internet had launched the dot-com bubble, 9/11 launched the di-saster capitalism bubble. "When the IT industry shut down, post-bubble, guess who had all the money? The government," said Roger Novak of Novak Biddle Venture Partners, a venture capitalism firm that invests in homeland security companies. Now, he says, "every fund is seeing how big the trough is and asking, How do I get a piece of that action?"[41]

It was the pinnacle of the counterrevolution launched by Friedman. For decades, the market had been feeding off the appendages of the state; now it would devour the core.

Bizarrely, the most effective ideological tool in this process was the claim that economic ideology was no longer a primary motivator of U.S. foreign or domestic policy. The mantra "September 11 changed everything" neatly dis-guised the fact that for free-market ideologues and the corporations whose interests they serve, the only thing that changed was the ease with which they could pursue their ambitious agenda. Now, rather than subjecting new poli-cies to fractious public debate in Congress or bitter conflict with public sec-tor unions, the Bush White House could use the patriotic alignment behind the president and the free pass handed out by the press to stop talking and start doing. As *The New York Times* observed in February 2007, "Without a public debate or formal policy decision, contractors have become a virtual fourth branch of government."[42]

Rather than meet the security challenge posed by September 11 with a com-prehensive plan to plug the holes in the public infrastructure, the Bush team devised a new role for government, one in which the job of the state was not to provide security but to purchase it at market prices. And so, in November 2001, just two months after the attacks, the Department of Defense brought together what it described as "a small group of venture capitalist consultants" with experience in the dot-com sector. The mission was to identify "emerg-ing technology solutions that directly assist in the U.S. efforts in the Global

War on Terrorism." By early 2006, this informal exchange had become an official arm of the Pentagon: the Defense Venture Catalyst Initiative (De-VenCI), a "fully operational office" that continually feeds security information to politically connected venture capitalists, who, in turn, scour the private sector for start-ups that can produce new surveillance and related products. "We're a search engine," explains Bob Pohanka, director of De-VenCI.[43] According to the Bush vision, the role of government is merely to raise the money necessary to launch the new war market, then buy the best products that emerge out of that creative cauldron, encouraging industry to even greater innovation. In other words, the politicians create the demand, and the private sector supplies all manner of solutions—a booming economy in homeland security and twenty-first-century warfare entirely underwritten by taxpayer dollars.

The Department of Homeland Security, as a brand-new arm of the state created by the Bush regime, is the clearest expression of this wholly outsourced mode of government. As Jane Alexander, deputy director of the research wing of the Department of Homeland Security, explained, "We don't make things. If it doesn't come from industry, we are not going to be able to get it."[44]

Another is Counterintelligence Field Activity (CIFA), a new intelligence agency created under Rumsfeld that is independent of the CIA. This parallel spy agency outsources 70 percent of its budget to private contractors; like the Department of Homeland Security, it was built as a hollow shell. As Ken Minihan, former director of the National Security Agency, explained, "Homeland security is too important to be left to the government." Minihan, like hundreds of other Bush administration staffers, has already left his government post to work in the bourgeoning homeland security industry, which, as a top spy, he helped create.[45]

Every aspect of the way the Bush administration has defined the parameters of the War on Terror has served to maximize its profitability and sustainability as a market—from the definition of the enemy to the rules of engagement to the ever-expanding scale of the battle. The document that launched the Department of Homeland Security declares, "Today's terrorists can strike at any place, at any time, and with virtually any weapon"—which conveniently means that the security services required must protect against every imaginable risk in every conceivable place at every possible time. And it's not necessary to prove that a threat is real for it to merit a full-scale response—not with Cheney's famous "1 percent doctrine," which justified the invasion of Iraq on the grounds that if there is a 1 percent chance that something is a threat, it requires that the U.S. respond as if the threat is a 100 percent certainty. This logic has been a particular boon for the makers of various high-tech detection devices: for instance, because we can conceive of a smallpox attack, the Department of Homeland Security has handed out half a billion dollars to private companies to develop and install detection equipment to guard against this unproven threat.[46]

Through all its various name changes—the War on Terror, the war on radical Islam, the war against Islamofascism, the Third World War, the long war, the generational war—the basic shape of the conflict has remained unchanged. It is limited by neither time nor space nor target. From a military perspective, these sprawling and amorphous traits make the War on Terror an unwinnable proposition. But from an economic perspective, they make it an unbeatable one: not a flash-in-the-pan war that could potentially be won but a new and permanent fixture in the global economic architecture.

That was the business prospectus that the Bush administration put before corporate America after September 11. The revenue stream was a seemingly bottomless supply of tax dollars to be funneled from the Pentagon ($270 billion a year to private contractors, a $137 billion increase since Bush took office); U.S. intelligence agencies ($42 billion a year to contractors for outsourced intelligence, more than double 1995 levels); and the newest arrival, the Department of Homeland Security. Between September 11, 2001, and 2006, the Department of Homeland Security handed out $130 billion to private contractors—money that was not in the economy before and that is more than the GDP of Chile or the Czech Republic. In 2003, the Bush administration spent $327 billion on contracts to private companies—nearly 40 cents of every discretionary dollar.[47]

In a remarkably short time, the suburbs ringing Washington, D.C., became dotted with gray buildings housing security "start-ups" and "incubator" companies, hastily thrown together operations where, as in late-nineties Silicon Valley, the money came in faster than the furniture could be assembled. The Bush administration, meanwhile, played the part of the free-spending venture capitalist of that same heady era. Whereas in the nineties the goal was to develop the killer application, the "next new new thing," and sell it to Microsoft or Oracle, now it was to come up with a new "search and nail" terrorist-catching technology and sell it to the Department of Homeland Security or the Pentagon. That is why, in addition to the start-ups and investment funds, the disaster industry also gave birth to an army of new lobby firms promising to hook up new companies with the right people on Capitol Hill—in 2001, there were two such security-oriented lobby firms, but by mid-2006 there were 543. "I've been in private equity since the early '90s," Michael Steed, managing director of the homeland security firm Paladin told *Wired*, "and I've never seen a sustained deal flow like this."[48]

A Market for Terrorism

Like the dot-com bubble, the disaster bubble is inflating in an ad hoc and chaotic fashion. One of the first booms for the homeland security industry was surveillance cameras, 4.2 million of which have been installed in Britain, one for every fourteen people, and 30 million in the U.S., shooting about 4 billion hours of footage a year. That created a problem: Who's going to watch 4 billion hours of footage? So a new market emerged for "analytic software" that scans the tapes and creates matches with images already on file (networking various security systems has been the source of some of the most lucrative contracts, such as $9 billion from the air force to a consortium of companies including Booz Allen Hamilton, one of the oldest strategy consulting firms, and some of the largest defense contractors).[49]

This development created another problem, because facial recognition software can really make positive IDs only if people present themselves front and center to the cameras, which they rarely do while rushing to and from work. So another market was created for digital image enhancement. Salient Stills, a company that sells software to isolate and enhance video images, started by pitching its technology to media companies, but it turned out that there was more potential revenue from the FBI and other law-enforcement agencies.[50] And with all the snooping going on—phone logs, wiretapping, financial records, mail, surveillance cameras, Web surfing—the government is drowning in data, which has opened up yet another massive market in information management and data mining, as well as software that claims to be able to "connect the dots" in this ocean of words and numbers and pinpoint suspicious activity.

In the nineties, tech companies endlessly trumpeted the wonders of the borderless world and the power of information technology to topple authoritarian regimes and bring down walls. Today, inside the disaster capitalism complex, the tools of the information revolution have been flipped to serve the opposite purpose. In the process, cell phones and Web surfing have been turned into powerful tools of mass state surveillance by increasingly authoritarian regimes, with the full cooperation of privatized phone companies and search engines, whether it's Yahoo collaborating with the Chinese government to pinpoint the location of dissidents or AT&T helping the U.S. National Security Agency to wiretap its customers without a warrant (a practice the Bush administration claims it has discontinued). The dismantling of borders, the great symbol and promise of globalization, has been replaced with the exploding industry of border surveillance, from optical scanning and biometric IDs to the planned high-tech fence on the border between Mexico and the U.S., worth up to $2.5 billion for Boeing and a consortium of other companies.[51]

As high-tech firms have jumped from one bubble to another, the result has been a bizarre merger of security and shopping cultures. Many technologies in use today as part of the War on Terror—biometric identification, video surveillance, Web tracking, data mining, sold by companies like Verint Systems and Seisint, Accenture and ChoicePoint—had been developed by the private sector before September 11 as a way to build detailed customer profiles, opening up new vistas for micromarketing. They also promised to reduce the number of retail workers at supermarkets and shopping malls, because biometric IDs, combined with cash cards, would eliminate the need for tellers. When widespread discomfort about big-brother technologies stalled many of these initiatives, it caused dismay to both marketers and retailers. September 11 loosened this logjam in the market: suddenly the fear of terror was greater than the fear of living in a surveillance society. So now, the same information collected from cash cards or "loyalty" cards can be sold not only to a travel agency or the Gap as marketing data but also to the FBI as security data, flagging a "suspicious" interest in pay-as-you-go cell phones and Middle Eastern travel.[52]

As an exuberant article in the business magazine *Red Herring* explained, one such program "tracks terrorists by figuring out if a name spelled a hundred different ways matches a name in a homeland security database. Take the name Mohammad. The software contains hundreds of possible spellings for the name, and it can search terabytes of data in a second."[53] Impressive, unless they nail the wrong Mohammad, which they have a bad habit of doing, from Iraq to Afghanistan to the suburbs of Toronto.

This potential for error is where the incompetence and greed that have been the hallmark of the Bush years, from Iraq to New Orleans, becomes harrowing. One false ID coming out of any of these electronic fishing expeditions is enough for an apolitical family man, who sort of looks like someone whose name sort of sounds like his (at least to someone with no knowledge of Arabic or Muslim culture), to be flagged as a potential terrorist. And the process of putting names and organizations on watch lists is also now handled by private companies, as are the programs to cross-check the names of travelers with the names in the data bank. As of June 2007, there were half a million names on a list of suspected terrorists kept by the National Counterterrorism Center. Another program, the Automated Targeting System (ATS), made public in November 2006, has already assigned a "risk assessment" rating to tens of millions of travelers passing through the U.S. The rating, never disclosed to passengers, is based on suspicious patterns revealed through commercial data mining—for instance, information provided by airlines about "the passenger's history of one-way ticket purchase, seat preferences, frequent flyer records, number of bags, how they pay for tickets and even what meals they order."[54] Incidents of supposedly suspicious behaviour are tallied up to generate each passenger's risk rating.

Anyone can be blocked from flying, denied an entry visa to the U.S. or even arrested and named as an "enemy combatant" based on evidence from these dubious technologies—a blurry image identified through facial recognition software, a misspelled name, a misunderstood snippet of a conversation. If "enemy combatants" are not U.S. citizens, they will probably never even know what it was that convicted them, because the Bush administration has stripped them of habeas corpus, the right to see the evidence in court, as well as the right to a fair trial and a vigorous defense.

If the suspect is taken, as a result, to Guantánamo, he may well end up in the new two-hundred-person maximum-security prison constructed by Halliburton. If he is a victim of the CIA's "extraordinary rendition" program, kidnapped off the streets of Milan or while changing planes at a U.S. airport, then whisked to a so-called black site somewhere in the CIA's archipelago of secret prisons, the hooded prisoner will likely fly in a Boeing 737, designed as a deluxe executive jet, retrofitted for this purpose. According to *The New Yorker*, Boeing has been acting as the "CIA's travel agent"—blocking out flight plans for as many as 1,245 rendition voyages, arranging ground crews and even booking hotels. A Spanish police report explains that the work was done by Jeppesen International Trip Planning, a Boeing subsidiary in San Jose. In May 2007, the American Civil Liberties Union launched a lawsuit against the Boeing subsidiary; the company has refused to confirm or deny the allegations.[55]

Once the prisoners arrive at the destination, they face interrogators, some of whom will not be employed by the CIA or the military but by private

contractors. According to Bill Golden, who runs the job Web site www
.IntelligenceCareers.com, "Over half of the qualified counter-intelligence
experts in the field work for contractors."[56] If these freelance interrogators are
to keep landing lucrative contracts, they must extract from prisoners the kind
of "actionable intelligence" their employers in Washington are looking for.
It's a dynamic ripe for abuse: just as prisoners under torture will usually say
anything to make the pain stop, contractors have a powerful economic incentive to use whatever techniques are necessary to produce the sought-after
information, regardless of its reliability. (Part of the reason the Bush administration has relied so heavily on private intelligence contractors working in
new structures like Rumsfeld's secretive Office of Special Plans is that they
have proven far more willing than their counterparts in governments to mas-
sage and manipulate information to meet the political goals of the administration—after all, their next contract depends on it.)

Then there is the low-tech version of this application of market "solutions" to the War on Terror—the willingness to pay top dollar to pretty much
anyone for information about alleged terrorists. During the invasion of
Afghanistan, U.S. intelligence agents let it be known that they would pay
anywhere from $3,000 to $25,000 for al Qaeda or Taliban fighters handed
over to them. "Get wealth and power beyond your dreams," stated a typical
flyer handed out by the U.S. in Afghanistan, introduced as evidence in a
2002 U.S. federal court filing on behalf of several Guantánamo prisoners.
"You can receive millions of dollars helping the anti-Taleban forces. . . . This
is enough money to take care of your family, your village, your tribe for the
rest of your life."[57]

Soon enough, the cells of Bagram and Guantánamo were overflowing
with goatherds, cabdrivers, cooks and shopkeepers—all lethally dangerous
according to the men who turned them over and collected the rewards.

"Do you have any theories about why the government and the Pakistani
intel folks would sell you out and turn you over to the Americans?" a member of a military tribunal asked an Egyptian prisoner held in the Guantánamo prison.

In the declassified transcript, the prisoner appears incredulous. "Come
on, man," he replied, "you know what happened. In Pakistan you can buy
people for $10. So what about $5,000?"

"So they sold you?" the tribunal member asked, as if the thought had
never before occurred to him.

"Yes."

According to the Pentagon's own figures, 86 percent of the prisoners at Guantánamo were handed over by Afghan and Pakistani fighters or agents after the bounties were announced. As of December 2006, the Pentagon had released 360 prisoners from Guantánamo. The Associated Press was able to track down 245 of them; 205 had been freed or cleared of all charges when they returned to their home countries.[58] It is a track record that is a grave indictment of the quality of intelligence produced by the administration's market-based approach to terrorist identification.

In just a few years, the homeland security industry, which barely existed before 9/11, has exploded to a size that is now significantly larger than either Hollywood or the music business.[59] Yet what is most striking is how little the security boom is analyzed and discussed *as an economy*, as an unprecedented convergence of unchecked police powers and unchecked capitalism, a merger of the shopping mall and the secret prison. When information about who is or is not a security threat is a product to be sold as readily as information about who buys Harry Potter books on Amazon or who has taken a Caribbean cruise and might enjoy one in Alaska, it changes the values of a culture. Not only does it create an incentive to spy, torture and generate false information but it creates a powerful impetus to perpetuate the fear and sense of peril that created the industry in the first place.

When new economies emerged in the past, from the Fordist revolution to the IT boom, they sparked a flood of analysis and debate about how such seismic shifts in the production of wealth were also altering the way we as a culture worked, the way we traveled, even the way our brains process information. The new disaster economy has been subject to none of this kind of far-reaching discussion. There have been and are debates, of course—about the constitutionality of the Patriot Act, about indefinite detention, about torture and extraordinary rendition—but discussion of what it means to have these functions performed as commercial transactions has been almost completely avoided. What passes for debate is restricted to individual cases of war profiteering and corruption scandals, as well as the usual hand-wringing about the failure of government to adequately oversee private contractors—rarely about the much broader and deeper phenomenon of what it means to be engaged in a fully privatized war built to have no end.

Part of the problem is that the disaster economy sneaked up on us. In the eighties and nineties, new economies announced themselves with great pride and fanfare. The tech bubble in particular set a precedent for a new ownership class inspiring deafening levels of hype—endless media lifestyle profiles of dashing young CEOs beside their private jets, their remote-controlled yachts, their idyllic Seattle mountain homes.

That kind of wealth is being generated by the disaster complex today, though we rarely hear about it. According to a 2006 study, "Since the 'War on Terror' began, the CEOs of the top 34 defense contractors have enjoyed average pay levels that are double the amounts they received during the four years leading up to 9/11." While these CEOs saw their compensation go up an average of 108 percent between 2001 and 2005, chief executives at other large American companies averaged only 6 percent over the same period.[60]

The disaster industry may be approaching dot-com levels of profit, but it generally has CIA levels of discretion. Disaster capitalists dodge the press, play down their wealth and know better than to brag. "We are not celebrating that there is this huge industry blossoming around protecting ourselves from terrorism," said John Elstner of the Chesapeake Innovation Center, a homeland security incubator. "But there is big business going on, and CIC is in the middle of it."[61]

Peter Swire, who served as the U.S. government's privacy counselor during the Clinton administration, describes the convergence of forces behind the War on Terror bubble like this: "You have government on a holy mission to ramp up information gathering and you have an information technology industry desperate for new markets."[62] In other words, you have corporatism: big business and big government combining their formidable powers to regulate and control the citizenry.

CHAPTER 15

A CORPORATIST STATE

REMOVING THE REVOLVING DOOR, PUTTING IN AN ARCHWAY

> I think that's weird and it's nuts. To suggest that everything we do is because we're hungry for money, I think that's crazy. I think you need to go back to school.
> —George H. W. Bush in response to an accusation that his son invaded Iraq to open up new markets for U.S. companies[1]

> There's something civil servants have that the private sector doesn't. And that is the duty of loyalty to the greater good—the duty of loyalty to the collective best interest of all rather than the interest of a few. Companies have duties of loyalty to their shareholders, not to the country.
> —David M. Walker, comptroller general of the United States, February 2007[2]

> He doesn't see the difference between public and private interests.
> —Sam Gardiner, retired U.S. Air Force colonel, on Dick Cheney, February 2004[3]

In the heat of the midterm elections in 2006, three weeks before announcing Donald Rumsfeld's resignation, George W. Bush signed the Defense Authorization Act in a private Oval Office ceremony. Tucked into its fourteen hundred pages is a rider that went almost completely unnoticed at the time. It gave the president the power to declare martial law and "employ the armed forces, including the National Guard," overriding the wishes of state governors, in the event of a "public emergency" in order to "restore public order" and "suppress" the disorder. That emergency could be a hurricane, a mass protest or a "public health emergency," in which case the army could be used to impose quarantines and to safeguard vaccine supplies.[4] Before this act, the president had these martial law powers only in the face of an insurrection.

With his colleagues on the campaign trail, Democratic Senator Patrick Leahy was a lone voice of alarm, entering into the public record that "using the military for law enforcement goes against one of the founding tenets of our democracy" and pointing out that "the implications of changing the act are enormous, but this change was just slipped in the defense bill as a rider with little study. Other congressional committees with jurisdiction over these matters had no chance to comment, let alone hold hearings on, these proposals."[5]

In addition to the executive branch, which gained the extraordinary new powers, there was at least one other clear winner: the pharmaceutical industry. In the case of any kind of disease outbreak, the military can now be called in to safeguard their labs and drug supplies and impose quarantines — a long-standing policy goal of the Bush administration. That was good news for Rumsfeld's former company Gilead Sciences, which owns the patent on Tamiflu, used to treat avian flu. The new law, as well as continued avian flu scares, may even have contributed to Tamiflu's stellar performance after Rumsfeld left office; in just five months, its stock price went up 24 percent.[6]

What role did industry interests play in shaping the specifics of the law? Perhaps none, but the question is worth asking. Similarly, and on a much wider scale, what role did the benefits to contractors such as Halliburton and Bechtel and oil companies such as ExxonMobil play in the Bush team's enthusiasm for invading and occupying Iraq? These questions of motivation are impossible to answer with any precision, because the people involved are notorious for conflating corporate interests with the national interest, to the extent that they themselves are seemingly incapable of drawing distinctions.

In his 2006 book *Overthrow,* the former *New York Times* correspondent Stephen Kinzer tries to get to the bottom of what has motivated the U.S. politicians who have ordered and orchestrated foreign coups d'état over the past century. Studying U.S. involvement in regime change operations from Hawaii in 1893 to Iraq in 2003, he observes that there is often a clear three-stage process that takes place. First, a U.S.-based multinational corporation faces some kind of threat to its bottom line by the actions of a foreign government demanding that the company "pay taxes or that it observe labor laws or environmental laws. Sometimes that company is nationalized or is somehow required to sell some of its land or its assets," Kinzer says. Second, U.S. politicians hear of this corporate setback and reinterpret it as an attack on the United States: "They transform the motivation from an economic one into a political or geo-strategic one. They make the assumption that any regime that would bother an American company or harass an American company must be anti-American, repressive, dictatorial, and probably the tool of some foreign power or interest that wants to undermine the United States." The third stage happens when the politicians have to sell the need for intervention to the public, at which point it becomes a broadly drawn struggle of good versus evil, "a chance to free a poor oppressed nation from the brutality of a regime that we assume is a dictatorship, because what other kind of a regime would be bothering an American company?"[7] Much of U.S. foreign policy, in other words, is an exercise in mass projection, in which a tiny self-interested elite conflates its needs and desires with those of the entire world.

Kinzer points out that this tendency has been especially pronounced in politicians who move directly from the corporate world into public office. For instance, Eisenhower's secretary of state, John Foster Dulles, worked as a high-powered international corporate lawyer for most of his life, representing some of the richest firms in the world in their conflicts with foreign governments. Dulles's various biographers have concluded, like Kinzer, that the secretary of state was simply incapable of distinguishing between the interests of corporations and the interests of his country. "Dulles had two lifelong obsessions: fighting Communism and protecting the rights of multinational corporations," writes Kinzer. "In his mind they were . . . 'interrelated and mutually reinforcing.'"[8] That meant he didn't need to choose between his obsessions: if the Guatemalan government took an action that hurt the interests of the United Fruit Company, for instance, that was a de facto attack on America and worthy of a military response.

As it pursues its twin obsessions of fighting terrorism and protecting the interests of multinational corporations, the Bush administration, packed with CEOs fresh from the boardroom, is subject to the same confusions and conflations. But there is a significant difference. The companies with which Dulles identified were multinationals with large international investments in foreign countries—in mining, agriculture, banking and oil. These companies generally shared a straightforward objective: they wanted stable, profitable environments in which to do business—loose investment laws, pliant workers and no nasty expropriation surprises. Coups and military interventions were a means to that end, not the goal itself.

As proto-disaster capitalists, the architects of the War on Terror are part of a different breed of corporate-politicians from their predecessors, one for whom wars and other disasters are indeed ends in themselves. When Dick Cheney and Donald Rumsfeld conflate what is good for Lockheed, Halliburton, Carlyle and Gilead with what is good for the United States and indeed the world, it is a form of projection with uniquely dangerous consequences. That's because what is unquestionably good for the bottom line of these companies is cataclysm—wars, epidemics, natural disasters and resource shortages—which is why all their fortunes have improved dramatically since Bush took office. What makes their acts of projection even more perilous is the fact that, to an unprecedented degree, key Bush officials have maintained their interests in the disaster capitalism complex even as they have ushered in a new era of privatized war and disaster response, allowing them to simultaneously profit from the disasters they help unleash.

For instance, when Rumsfeld resigned his post after the Republican defeat in the 2006 midterm elections, the press reported that he was returning to the private sector. The truth was that he never actually left. When he accepted Bush's nomination as defense secretary, Rumsfeld, like all public officials, was required to divest himself of any holdings that stood to lose or gain from decisions he might make while in office. Simple enough—that meant selling everything related to national security or defense. But Rumsfeld had a great deal of trouble. He was so weighed down with holdings in various disaster-related industries that he claimed it was impossible to disentangle himself in time to meet the deadlines, and he tied the ethics rules in knots trying to hold on to everything he could.

He sold off his directly owned stocks in Lockheed, Boeing and other defense companies and put up to $50 million worth of stocks in a blind trust. But he still was part or complete owner of private investment firms that were devoted to defense and biotechnology stocks. Rumsfeld was unwilling to take losses to sell those companies quickly and instead asked for two three-month extensions to the time limit—extremely rare at that level of government. That meant he was still looking for what he considered suitable buyers for his companies and assets a full six months into his term as defense secretary, possibly even longer.[9]

When it came to Gilead Sciences, the company Rumsfeld used to chair and that held the patent on Tamiflu, the secretary of defense put his foot down. Asked to choose between his business interests and his public calling, he simply refused. Epidemics are national security issues and therefore squarely within the portfolio of the defense secretary. Yet despite this glaring conflict of interest, Rumsfeld failed to sell off his Gilead stocks for his entire term in office, holding on to somewhere between $8 million and $39 million worth of Gilead holdings.[10]

As the Senate Ethics Committee tried to bring him into compliance with standard conflict rules, Rumsfeld was openly belligerent. At one point, he wrote a letter to the Office of Government Ethics complaining that he had to spend $60,000 on accountants' fees to help him with "excessively complex and confusing" disclosure forms. For a man bent on holding on to $95 million in shares while in office, $60,000 in finessing fees hardly seemed out of proportion.[11]

Rumsfeld's adamant refusal to stop making money from disaster while in the top security post in the country affected his job performance in several concrete ways. For much of his first year in office, while he looked to off-load his holdings, Rumsfeld had to recuse himself from an alarming range of crucial policy decisions: according to the Associated Press, "he has avoided Pentagon meetings in which AIDS is discussed." And when the federal government had to decide whether to intervene in several high-profile mergers and sales involving top defense contractors, including General Electric, Honeywell, Northrop Grumman and Silicon Valley Graphics, Rumsfeld recused himself from those top-level talks as well. It turned out, according to his official spokesperson, that he had financial ties to several of the companies listed above. "I have tended to stay away from them thus far," Rumsfeld told a reporter who asked about one of the sales.[12]

For the six years that he held office, Rumsfeld had to leave the room whenever talk turned to the possibility of avian flu treatment and the purchase of drugs for it. According to the letter outlining the arrangement that allowed him to hold on to his stocks, he had to stay out of decisions that "may directly and predictably affect Gilead."[13] His colleagues, however, took good care of his interests. In July 2005, the Pentagon purchased $58 million worth of Tamiflu, and the Department of Health and Human Services announced that it would order up to $1 billion worth of the drug a few months later.[14]

Rumsfeld's defiance definitely paid off. If he had sold his Gilead stocks at inauguration, in January 2001, he would have received a mere $7.45 each. By keeping them through all the avian flu scares, all the bioterror hysteria and through his own administration's decisions to invest heavily in the company, Rumsfeld ended up with stocks worth $67.60 each when he left office—an 807 percent increase. (By April 2007 the price had reached $84 each.)[15] That meant that when Rumsfeld left his post as defense secretary, he did so a significantly wealthier man than when he arrived—a rare occurrence for a multimillionaire in public office.

If Rumsfeld never really left Gilead behind, Cheney was equally reluctant to fully sever his ties to Halliburton—an arrangement that, unlike Rumsfeld's with Gilead, has been the subject of a great deal of media attention. Before stepping down as CEO to be George Bush's running mate, Cheney negotiated a retirement package that left him loaded with Halliburton stocks and options. After some uncomfortable press questions, he agreed to sell some of his Halliburton shares, making an impressive $18.5 million profit in the process. But he didn't cash out entirely. According to *The Wall Street Journal,* Cheney hung on to 189,000 Halliburton shares and 500,000 unvested options even as he entered the vice presidency.[16]

The fact that Cheney still maintains such a quantity of Halliburton shares means that throughout his term as vice president, he has collected millions every year in dividends from his stocks and has also been paid an annual deferred income by Halliburton of $211,000—roughly equivalent to his government salary. When he leaves office in 2009 and is able to cash in his Halliburton holdings, Cheney will have the opportunity to profit extravagantly from the stunning improvement in Halliburton's fortunes. The company's stock price rose from $10 before the war in Iraq to $41 three years later—a 300 percent jump, thanks to a combination of soaring energy prices and Iraq contracts, both of which flow directly from Cheney's steering the country into war with Iraq.[17] Iraq seems to fit Kinzer's formula perfectly. Saddam did not pose a threat to U.S. security, but he did pose a threat to U.S. energy companies, since he had recently signed contracts with a Russian oil giant and was in negotiations with France's Total, leaving U.S. and British oil firms with nothing; the third-largest proven oil reserves in the world were slipping out of the Anglo-American grasp.[18] Saddam's removal from power has opened vistas of opportunities for the oil giants, including ExxonMobil, Chevron, Shell and BP, all of whom have been laying the groundwork for new deals in Iraq, as well as for Halliburton, which, with its move to Dubai, is perfectly positioned to sell its energy services to all these companies.[19] Already the war itself has been the single most profitable event in Halliburton's history.

Both Rumsfeld and Cheney could have taken simple measures to divest themselves completely of their disaster-related holdings, thereby eliminating any doubt about what role profit has played in their enthusiasm for disaster-producing situations. But then they would have missed the boom years in their own industries. Asked to choose between private profit and public life, again and again they chose profit, forcing the government ethics committees to adapt to their defiant stance.

During the Second World War, President Franklin D. Roosevelt spoke out strongly against war profiteers, saying, "I don't want to see a single war millionaire created in the United States as a result of this world disaster." One wonders what he would have made of Cheney, whose millions in war profits accumulated while he was a sitting vice president. Or Rumsfeld, who, in 2004, couldn't resist cashing in a few Gilead stocks, making an easy $5 million, according to his annual disclosure report, while he was defense secretary—a small taste of the profits that awaited him when he left office.[20] In the Bush administration, the war profiteers aren't just clamoring to get access to government, they are the government; there is no distinction between the two.

The Bush years have, of course, been characterized by some of the seediest and most blatant corruption scandals in recent memory: Jack Abramoff and his golfing vacations offered to members of Congress; Randy "Duke" Cunningham, now serving eight years for accepting bribes and donating his yacht the *Duke-Stir* as part of a "bribe menu" listed on official congressional letterhead to a defense contractor; and the parties at the Watergate hotel with courtesy prostitutes—all sounding very much like Moscow and Buenos Aires in the mid-nineties.[21]

Then there is the whirling revolving door between government and industry. It has always been there, but for the most part political figures used to wait until their administration was out of office before cashing in on government connections. Under Bush, the nonstop homeland security market bonanza has proved too tempting for many administration officials to resist. So, rather than wait until the end of their terms, hundreds, from a wide range of government agencies, have already charged for the door. According to Eric Lipton, who has tracked this phenomenon in the Department of Homeland Security for *The New York Times*, "veteran Washington lobbyists and watchdog groups say the exodus of such a sizable share of an agency's senior management before the end of an administration has few modern parallels." Lipton identified ninety-four examples of civil servants who had been working on domestic security and who are now working in some aspect of the home-land security industry.[22]

There are far too many such cases to detail here, but a few stand out, since they involve the key architects of the War on Terror. John Ashcroft, for-mer attorney general and prime mover behind the Patriot Act, now heads up the Ashcroft Group, specializing in helping homeland security firms pro-cure federal contracts. Tom Ridge, the first head of the Department of Homeland Security, is now at Ridge Global and an adviser to the communi-cation technology company Lucent, which is active in the security sector. Rudy Giuliani, the former New York mayor and hero of the September 11 re-sponse, started Giuliani Partners four months later to sell his services as a cri-sis consultant. Richard Clarke, counterterrorism czar under Clinton and Bush and an outspoken critic of the administration, is now chairman of Good Harbor Consulting, specializing in homeland security and counterter-rorism. James Woolsey, head of the CIA until 1995, is now at Paladin Capi-tal Group, a private equity firm that invests in homeland security companies, and a vice president at Booz Allen, one of the leaders in the homeland secu-rity industry. Joe Allbaugh, head of FEMA on September 11, cashed out just eighteen months later to start New Bridge Strategies, promising to be the "bridge" between business and the lucrative world of government contracts and investment opportunities in Iraq. He was replaced by Michael Brown, who bolted after only two years to start Michael D. Brown LLC, specializing in disaster preparedness.[23]

"Can I quit now?" Brown wrote in an infamous e-mail to a fellow FEMA staffer in the middle of the Hurricane Katrina disaster.[24] That is pretty much the philosophy: stay in government just long enough to get an impressive ti-tle in a department handing out big contracts and to collect inside informa-tion on what will sell, then quit and sell access to your former colleagues. Public service is reduced to little more than a reconnaissance mission for fu-ture work in the disaster capitalism complex.

In some ways, however, the stories about corruption and revolving doors leave a false impression. They imply that there is still a clear line between the state and the complex, when in fact that line disappeared long ago. The innovation of the Bush years lies not in how quickly politicians move from one world to the other but in how many feel entitled to occupy both worlds simultaneously. People like Richard Perle and James Baker make policy, of-fer top-level advice and speak in the press as disinterested experts and states-men when they are at the same time utterly embedded in the business of privatized war and reconstruction. They embody the ultimate fulfillment of the corporatist mission: a total merger of political and corporate elites in the name of security, with the state playing the role of chair of the business guild—as well as the largest source of business opportunities, thanks to the contract economy.

Wherever it has emerged over the past thirty-five years, from Santiago to Moscow to Beijing to Bush's Washington, the alliance between a small corporate elite and a right-wing government has been written off as some sort of aberration—mafia capitalism, oligarchy capitalism and now, under Bush, "crony capitalism." But it's not an aberration; it is where the entire Chicago School crusade—with its triple obsessions—privatization, deregulation and union-busting—has been leading.

Rumsfeld's and Cheney's dogged refusals to choose between their disaster-connected holdings and their public duties were the first sign that a genuine corporatist state had arrived. There are many others.

The Power of the Formers

One of the distinguishing features of the Bush administration has been its reliance on outside advisers and freelance envoys to perform key functions: James Baker, Paul Bremer, Henry Kissinger, George Shultz, Richard Perle, as well as the members of the Defense Policy Board and the Committee for the Liberation of Iraq, to name just a few. While Congress played a rubber-stamp role during the pivotal decision-making years, and Supreme Court rulings are treated as little more than gentle suggestions, these mostly volunteer advisers have wielded enormous influence.

Their power stems from the fact that these advisers used to perform key roles in government—they are former secretaries of state, former ambassadors and former undersecretaries of defense. All have been out of government for years and, in the meantime, have set up lucrative careers in the disaster capitalism complex. Because they are classified as contractors, not staff, most are not subject to the same conflict-of-interest rules as elected or appointed politicians—if they are subject to any restrictions at all. The effect has been to eliminate the so-called revolving door between government and industry and put in "an archway" (as the disaster management specialist Irwin Redlener put it to me). It has allowed the disaster industries to set up shop inside the government, using the reputations of such illustrious ex-politicians as cover.

When in March 2006 James Baker was named cochair of the Iraq Study Group, the advisory panel charged with recommending a new way forward in Iraq, there was palpable bipartisan relief: here was a politician of the old school, one who had steered the country in more stable times, a grown-up. Certainly Baker is a veteran of a less reckless era of U.S. foreign policy than the current one. But that was fifteen years ago. Who is James Baker now?

Like Cheney, when he left office at the end of Bush Sr.'s term, James Baker III made a fortune from his government contacts. Particularly lucrative were the friends he made in Saudi Arabia and Kuwait during the first Gulf War.[25] His Houston-based law firm, Baker Botts, represents the Saudi royal family as well as Halliburton and Gazprom, Russia's largest oil company, and is one of the leading oil and gas law firms in the world. He also became an equity partner in the Carlyle Group, earning an estimated $180 million stake in the highly secretive company.[26]

Carlyle has benefited enormously from the war, thanks to sales of robotics systems, defense communications systems, and a major Iraq contract to train police awarded to its holding, USIS. The $56 billion company has a defense-oriented equity firm that specializes in collecting defense contractors and taking them public, a very profitable enterprise in recent years. "It's the best 18 months we ever had," said Carlyle's chief investment officer, Bill Conway, referring to the first eighteen months of the war in Iraq. "We made money and we made it fast." The war in Iraq, already clearly a disaster, translated into a record-breaking $6.6 billion payout to Carlyle's select investors.[27]

When Bush Jr. pulled Baker back into public life by naming him his special envoy on Iraq's debt, Baker did not have to cash out of the Carlyle Group or Baker Botts, despite their direct interests in the war. At first, several commentators pointed out these serious potential conflicts. *The New York Times* published an editorial calling on Baker to resign his posts at the Carlyle Group and Baker Botts to preserve the integrity of the debt envoy position. "Mr. Baker is far too tangled in a matrix of lucrative private business relationships that leave him looking like a potentially interested party in any debt-restructuring formula," stated the editorial. It concluded that it wasn't enough for Baker to "forgo earnings from clients with obvious connections to Iraqi debts. . . . To perform honorably in his new public job, Mr. Baker must give up these two private ones."[28]

In keeping with the example set at the top of the administration, Baker simply refused, and Bush backed his decision, leaving Baker in charge of the effort of persuading governments around the world to forgive Iraq's crushing foreign debt. After he had been in the role for nearly a year, I obtained a copy of a confidential document that proved that he was in a far more serious and direct conflict of interest than previously understood. The document was a sixty-five-page business plan submitted by a consortium of companies, including the Carlyle Group, to the government of Kuwait, one of Iraq's main creditors. The consortium offered to use its high-level political connections to collect from Iraq $27 billion in unpaid debts to Kuwait stemming from Saddam's invasion of Kuwait—in other words, to do exactly the opposite of what Baker was supposed to be doing as envoy, which was to convince governments that Saddam-era debts should be canceled.[29]

The document, titled "Proposal to Assist the Government of Kuwait in Protecting and Realizing Claims against Iraq," was submitted almost two months *after* Baker's appointment. It named James Baker personally eleven times, making it clear that Kuwait would benefit from working with a company that employed the man in charge of erasing Iraq's debts. But there was a price. In exchange for these services, the documents said, the government of Kuwait would have to invest $1 billion with the Carlyle Group. It was straight-up influence peddling: pay Baker's company to get protection from Baker. I showed the document to Kathleen Clark, a law professor at Washington University and a leading expert on government ethics and regulations, and she said Baker was in a "classic conflict of interest. Baker is on two sides of this transaction: he is supposed to be representing the interests of the United States, but he is also a senior counselor at Carlyle, and Carlyle wants to get paid to help Kuwait recover its debts from Iraq." After examining the documents, Clark determined that "Carlyle and the other companies are exploiting Baker's current position to try to land a deal with Kuwait that would undermine the interests of the U.S. government."

The day after my story about Baker was published in *The Nation*, Carlyle backed out of the consortium, forfeiting its hope of landing the $1 billion; several months later, Baker cashed out of the Carlyle Group and resigned as general counsel. But the real damage had been done: Baker had performed miserably as envoy, failing to secure the kind of debt forgiveness that Bush had pledged and Iraq required. In 2005 and 2006, Iraq made $2.59 billion in reparation payments for Saddam's war, most to Kuwait—resources that were desperately needed to meet Iraq's humanitarian crisis and to rebuild the country, especially after U.S. firms pulled out with the aid money squandered and the job left undone. Baker's mandate was to erase 90 to 95 percent of Iraq's debt. Instead, the debt was merely rescheduled and is still equivalent to 99 percent of the country's GDP.[30]

Other key aspects of Iraq policy were also handed to freelance envoys whose companies earned record profits from the war. Former secretary of state George Shultz headed up the Committee for the Liberation of Iraq, a pressure group formed in 2002 at the request of the Bush White House to help it build the case for war in the public mind. Shultz certainly obliged. Since his role was at arm's length from the administration, he was able to whip up hysteria about the imminent danger posed by Saddam, entirely free from any burden of proof or fact. "If there is a rattlesnake in the yard, you don't wait for it to strike before you take action in self-defense," he wrote in *The Washington Post* in September 2002 under the headline "Act Now: The danger is immediate. Saddam Hussein must be removed." Shultz did not disclose to his readers that he was, at the time, a member of the board of directors of Bechtel, where he had served many years earlier as CEO. The company would collect $2.3 billion to reconstruct the country that Shultz was so eager to see destroyed.[31] So, in retrospect, it seems worth asking, when Shultz called on the world to Act Now, was he speaking as a concerned elder statesman or as a representative of Bechtel—or perhaps Lockheed Martin?

According to Danielle Brian, executive director of the Project on Government Oversight, a nonprofit watchdog group, "It's impossible to tell where the government ends and Lockheed begins." It's even harder to tell where Lockheed ends and the Committee for the Liberation of Iraq begins. The group Shultz headed and used as a pro-war platform was convened by Bruce Jackson, who, just three months earlier, held the job of vice president for strategy and planning at Lockheed Martin. Jackson says that he was asked to form the group by "people in the White House," but he stacked it with old colleagues from Lockheed. Besides Jackson, Lockheed's representatives included Charles Kupperman, Lockheed Martin's vice president for space and strategic missiles, and Douglas Graham, Lockheed's director of defense systems. Even though the committee was formed at the explicit request of the White House to be the propaganda arm of the war, no one had to step down from Lockheed or sell his shares. Which was certainly good for committee members, since Lockheed's share price jumped 145 percent thanks to the war they helped engineer—from $41 in March 2003 to $102 in February 2007.[32]

And then there is Henry Kissinger, the man who kicked off the counter-revolution with his support for Pinochet's coup. In his 2006 book *State of*

Denial, Bob Woodward revealed that Dick Cheney holds monthly meetings with Kissinger, while Bush meets with Kissinger about half as frequently, "making him the most regular and frequent outside adviser to Bush on foreign affairs." Cheney told Woodward, "I probably talk to Henry Kissinger more than I talk to anybody else."[33]

But who was Kissinger representing in all those top-level meetings? Like Baker and Shultz, he used to be a secretary of state, but hasn't held that post for three decades. Since 1982, when he started his privately held and secretive company, Kissinger Associates, his job has been to represent a roster of clients that is said to have included everyone from Coca-Cola to Union Carbide to Hunt Oil to the engineering giant Fluor (one of the biggest reconstruction contract winners in Iraq)—and even his old partner in the Chilean covert action, ITT.[34] So when he met with Cheney, was he acting as elder statesman, or as high-priced lobbyist for his oil and engineering clients?

Kissinger gave a strong indication of where his loyalties lay in November 2002, when Bush named him to chair the 9/11 Commission, perhaps the most crucial role any patriot could be called out of retirement to perform. Yet when the families of the victims asked Kissinger to produce a list of his corporate clients, pointing to potential conflicts of interest with the investigation, he refused to cooperate with this basic gesture of public accountability and transparency. Rather than disclose the names of his clients, he stepped down as chair of the commission.[35]

Richard Perle, a friend and business associate of Kissinger's, would make that precise choice a year later. Perle, a defense official under Reagan, was asked by Rumsfeld to chair the Defense Policy Board. Before Perle took over, the board was a quiet advisory panel, a way to pass on the knowledge of former administrations to the one in office. Perle turned it into a platform for himself, using the impressive title to argue forcefully in the press for a preemptive attack on Iraq. He also used it in other ways. According to a Seymour Hersh investigation in *The New Yorker,* he touted the title to solicit investment for his new company. Perle, it turned out, was one of the first post-9/11 disaster capitalists—just two months after the attacks, he launched his venture capital firm Trireme Partners, which would invest in firms developing products and services relevant to homeland security and defense. In letters soliciting business, Trireme boasted of its political connections: "Three of Trireme's Management Group members currently advise the U.S. Secretary of Defense by serving on the U.S. Defense Policy Board." Those three were Perle, his friend Gerald Hillman and Henry Kissinger.[36]

One of Perle's early investors was Boeing—the Pentagon's second-largest contractor—which kicked in $20 million to get Trireme going. Perle became an outspoken Boeing fan, writing an op-ed supporting Boeing's controversial $17 billion tanker contract with the Pentagon.*[37]

Although Perle told his investors all about his pull at the Pentagon, several of his colleagues on the Defense Policy Board say he failed to tell them about Trireme. On hearing about the company, one described it as "at the edge of or off the ethical charts." In the end, all the knots of conflict caught up with Perle and he, like Kissinger, had to choose: make defense policy or profit from the War on Terror. In March 2003, just as the war in Iraq was starting and the contractor bonanza was about to begin, Perle stepped down as chairman of the Defense Policy Board.[38]

There is nothing that enrages Richard Perle more than the suggestion that his advocacy of unlimited war to end all evil is in any way influenced by the enormous profitability of that proposition for him personally. On CNN, Wolf Blitzer confronted Perle with Hersh's observation that "he has set up a company that may gain from a war." It would seem self-evidently true, yet Perle blew up, calling Hersh, a Pulitzer Prize winner, "the closest thing American journalism has to a terrorist, frankly." He told Blitzer, "I don't believe that a company would gain from a war. . . . The suggestion that my views are somehow related for the potential for investments in homeland defense is complete nonsense."[39]

It was a strange claim. If a venture capital firm that was set up to invest in security and defense companies managed not to gain from a war, it would surely be failing its investors. The episode raised larger questions about the role played by figures such as Perle, who exist in a gray zone between disaster capitalist, public intellectual and policy maker. If a Lockheed or Boeing executive went on Fox News to make the case for regime change in Iran (as Perle has done), their obvious self-interest would negate any intellectual arguments they

---

* The tanker deal became the biggest scandal in recent Pentagon history, ultimately landing a senior Department of Defense official and a Boeing executive in jail. The official had been negotiating for a job at Boeing while the deal was going down. In a subsequent investigation, Rumsfeld was questioned about why he didn't catch the rotten deal under his watch. He replied that he could not recall the details of his role in a contract that would consume between $17 billion and $30 billion of taxpayer money. "I don't remember approving it. But I certainly don't remember not approving it, if you will." Rumsfeld was slammed for poor management, but his forgetfulness may also have been a casualty of how frequently the secretary of defense recused himself from purchasing discussions in order to avoid the appearance of conflicts with his many defense-related holdings.

offered. Yet Perle continues to be introduced as an "analyst" or as a Pentagon adviser, perhaps as "a neocon," but certainly there is never any suggestion that he might just be an arms dealer with an impressive vocabulary.

Whenever members of this Washington clique are confronted with their economic interests in the wars they support, they invariably respond the way Perle did: the entire suggestion is preposterous, simple-minded, vaguely terrorist. The neocons—a group that includes Cheney, Rumsfeld, Shultz, Jackson and, I would argue, Kissinger—take great pains to project themselves as egghead intellectuals or hawkish realists, driven by ideology and big ideas, not anything so worldly as profit. Bruce Jackson, for instance, says Lockheed did not approve of his extracurricular foreign policy work. Perle says that his association with the Pentagon has hurt him in business since "it means there are . . . things you can't say and do." Perle's partner Gerald Hillman insists that Perle "is not a financial creature. He doesn't have any desire for financial gain." Douglas Feith, when he was undersecretary of defense for policy, claimed that "the vice president's former connection [with Halliburton] made people in the government reluctant to award the contract, not eager to do it, even though awarding it to KBR [Kellogg, Brown and Root, the former Halliburton subsidiary] was the right thing to do."[40]

Even their most committed critics tend to portray the neocons as true believers, motivated exclusively by a commitment to the supremacy of American and Israeli power that is so all-consuming they are prepared to sacrifice economic interests in favor of "security." This distinction is both artificial and amnesiac. The right to limitless profit-seeking has always been at the center of neocon ideology. Before 9/11, demands for radical privatization and attacks on social spending fuelled the neocon movement—Friedmanite to its core—at think tanks such as the American Enterprise Institute, Heritage and Cato.

With the War on Terror, the neocons didn't abandon their corporatist economic goals; they found a new, even more effective way to achieve them. Of course these Washington hawks are committed to an imperial role for the United States in the world and for Israel in the Middle East. It is impossible, however, to separate that military project—endless war abroad, and a security state at home—from the interests of the disaster capitalism complex, which has built a multibillion-dollar industry based on these very assumptions. Nowhere has the merger of these political and profit-making goals been clearer than on the battlefields of Iraq.

PART 6

IRAQ, FULL CIRCLE

OVERSHOCK

One of the risks in shock-based operations has to do with the likelihood of "unintended consequences," or in precipitating reactions that have not been anticipated. For example, extensive attacks against a nation's infrastructure, electrical grid, or economic system can create such extreme hardship that the resulting backlash bolsters rather than weakens our opponent's national will to fight.

—Lieutenant Colonel John N. T. Shanahan, "Shock-Based Operations," *Air & Space Power*, October 15, 2001

Direct physical brutality creates only resentment, hostility, and further defiance. . . . Interrogatees who have withstood pain are more difficult to handle by other methods. The effect has been not to repress the subject but to restore his confidence and maturity.

—*Kubark Counterintelligence Interrogation*,
CIA manual, 1963

CHAPTER 16

ERASING IRAQ

IN SEARCH OF A "MODEL"
FOR THE MIDDLE EAST

> The introverted schizophrenic or melancholic may be likened to a
> walled city which has closed its gates and refuses to trade with
> the rest of the world. . . . A breach is blown in the wall, and rela-
> tions with the world are re-established. Unfortunately we cannot
> control the amount of damage done in the bombardment.
> —Andrew M. Wyllie, a British psychiatrist, on electroshock therapy,
> 1940[1]

> In a post-Sept. 11 world, I thought the prudent use of violence
> could be therapeutic.
> —Richard Cohen, a *Washington Post* columnist, on his support for
> the invasion of Iraq[2]

It was March 2004. I had been in Baghdad for less than three hours, and it
wasn't going well. First, our car hadn't shown up at the airport checkpoint,
and my photographer, Andrew Stern, and I had to hitch a ride on what was
already being called "the most dangerous road in the world." When we
made it to the hotel in the busy Karada district, we were greeted by Michael
Birmingham, an Irish peace activist who had moved to Baghdad before the
invasion. I had asked if he could introduce me to a few Iraqis concerned
about the plans to privatize their economy. "No one here cares about privatization," Michael told us. "What they care about is surviving."

A tense debate followed about the ethics of bringing a political agenda to
a war zone. Michael wasn't saying that Iraqis supported the privatization

plans—only that most people had more urgent concerns. They were worried about bombs going off in their mosques or finding a cousin who has disappeared into the U.S.-run Abu Ghraib prison. They were thinking about how to get drinking and bathing water for tomorrow, not whether a foreign company wanted to privatize their water system and sell it back to them in a year. The job of an outsider, he argued, is to try to document the reality of war and occupation, not to decide what Iraqi priorities ought to be.

I defended myself as best as I could, pointing out that selling this country off to Bechtel and ExxonMobil wasn't an idea I had dreamed up—it was already in its early stages, spearheaded by the White House's top envoy to Iraq, L. Paul Bremer III. For months I had been reporting on the auctioning off of Iraq's state assets from trade shows in hotel ballrooms, surreal events where body-armor salesmen terrified businessmen with stories of severed limbs while U.S. trade officials assured everyone that it really wasn't as bad as it seemed on TV. "The best time to invest is when there is still blood on the ground," I was told earnestly by a delegate at the "Rebuilding Iraq 2" conference in Washington, D.C.

The fact that it was hard to find people in Baghdad who were interested in talking about economics was not surprising. The architects of this invasion were firm believers in the shock doctrine—they knew that while Iraqis were consumed with daily emergencies, the country could be auctioned off discreetly and the results announced as a done deal. As for journalists and activists, we seemed to be exhausting our attention on the spectacular physical attacks, forgetting that the parties with the most to gain never show up on the battlefield. And in Iraq there was plenty to gain: not just the world's third-largest proven oil reserves but territory that was one of the last remaining holdouts from the drive to build a global market based on Friedman's vision of unfettered capitalism. After the crusade had conquered Latin America, Africa, Eastern Europe and Asia, the Arab world called out as its final frontier.

While Michael and I debated back and forth, Andrew went to have a cigarette on the balcony. As he opened the glass door, all the air seem to be sucked out of the room. Outside the window was a ball of lavalike fire, deep red flecked with black. We grabbed our shoes and ran in our socks down five flights of stairs. The lobby was covered in shattered glass. Around the corner, the Mount Lebanon Hotel lay in rubble, along with a neighboring house, destroyed by a thousand-pound bomb, making it, at that point, the largest attack of its kind since the end of the war.

Andrew ran with his camera to the wreckage; I tried not to, but ended up following. After only three hours in Baghdad, I was already breaking my one rule: no bomb chasing. Back at the hotel, all the indie reporters and NGO types were drinking arak and trying to get their adrenalin under control. Everybody kept grinning at me and saying, "Welcome to Baghdad!" I glanced at Michael, and we both silently acknowledged that, yes, he had won the argument. The last word came from the war itself: "Bombs, not journalists, set the agenda here." And they certainly do. They don't just suck oxygen into their vortex, they demand everything: our attention, our compassion, our outrage.

That night I thought about Claudia Acuña, the extraordinary journalist I had met in Buenos Aires two years earlier who had given me a copy of Rodolfo Walsh's "Open Letter from a Writer to the Military Junta." She had warned me that extreme violence has a way of preventing us from seeing the interests it serves. In a way, it had happened already to the antiwar movement. Our explanations for why the war was waged rarely went beyond one-word answers: oil, Israel, Halliburton. Most of us chose to oppose the war as an act of folly by a president who mistook himself for a king, and his British sidekick who wanted to be on the winning side of history. There was little interest in the idea that war was a rational policy choice, that the architects of the invasion had unleashed ferocious violence because they could not crack open the closed economies of the Middle East by peaceful means, that the level of terror was proportional to what was at stake.

The invasion of Iraq was sold to the public on the basis of fear of weapons of mass destruction because, as Paul Wolfowitz explained, WMDs were "the one issue that everyone could agree on"—it was, in other words, the lowest-common-denominator excuse.[3] The more rarefied reason, favored by the most intellectual proponents of the war, was the "model" theory. According to the pundits who advanced this theory, many of them identified as neocons, terrorism was coming from multiple locations in the Arab and Muslim world: the September 11 hijackers were from Saudi Arabia, Egypt, the United Arab Emirates and Lebanon; Iran was funding Hezbollah; Syria was housing Hamas's leadership; Iraq was sending money to the families of Palestinian suicide bombers. For these war advocates, who conflated attacks on Israel with attacks on the U.S., as if there were no differences between the two, that was enough to qualify the entire region as a potential terrorist breeding ground.

So what was it about this part of the world, they asked, that produced terrorism? Ideologically blinded from seeing either U.S. or Israeli policies as contributing factors, let alone provocations, they identified the true cause as something else—the region's deficit in free-market democracy.*[4]

Since the entire Arab world could not be conquered all at once, a single country needed to serve as the catalyst. The U.S. would invade that country and turn it into, as Thomas Friedman, chief media proselytizer of the theory, put it, "a different model in the heart of the Arab-Muslim world," one that in turn would set off a series of democratic/neoliberal waves throughout the region. Joshua Muravchik, an American Enterprise Institute pundit, forecast a "tsunami across the Islamic world" in "Tehran and Baghdad," while the archconservative Michael Ledeen, an adviser to the Bush administration, described the goal as "a war to remake the world."[†5]

Within the internal logic of this theory, fighting terrorism, spreading frontier capitalism and holding elections were bundled into a single unified project. The Middle East would be "cleaned out" of terrorists and a giant free-trade zone would be created; then it would all be locked in with after-the-fact elections—a sort of three-for-one special. George W. Bush later simplified this agenda to a single phrase: "spreading freedom in a troubled region," and many mistook the sentiment as a starry-eyed commitment to democracy.[6] But it was always that other kind of freedom, the one offered to Chile in the seventies and to Russia in nineties—the freedom for Western

---

* The free-market wave had bypassed this region for several reasons. The richest countries—Kuwait, Saudi Arabia, the emirates—were so flush with oil cash that they managed to keep out of debt and thus out of the grip of the IMF (84 percent of Saudi Arabia's economy, for instance, is state controlled). Iraq had a heavy debt, accumulated during the war with Iran, but just as the era of globalization was beginning, the first Gulf War ended and Iraq was locked away under strict sanctions: not only would there be no "free trade," there would be virtually no legal trade at all.

† The idea that a failure to join the Washington Consensus could be enough to provoke a foreign invasion may seem far-fetched, but there was a precedent. When NATO bombed Belgrade in 1999, the official reason was Slobodan Milošević's egregious human rights violations that had horrified the world. But in a little-reported revelation years after the Kosovo war, Strobe Talbott, deputy secretary of state under President Clinton and the lead U.S. negotiator during the war, provided a distinctly less idealistic explanation. "As nations throughout the region sought to reform their economies, mitigate ethnic tensions, and broaden civil society, Belgrade seemed to delight in continually moving in the opposite direction. It is small wonder NATO and Yugoslavia ended up on a collision course. It was Yugoslavia's resistance to the broader trends of political and economic reform—not the plight of the Kosovar Albanians—that best explains NATO's war." The revelation came out in a 2005 book, *Collision Course: NATO, Russia, and Kosovo* by Talbott's former communications director, John Norris.

multinationals to feed off freshly privatized states—that was at the center of the model theory. The president made that perfectly clear only eight days after declaring an end to major combat in Iraq when he announced plans for the "establishment of a U.S.-Middle East free trade area within a decade."[7] Dick Cheney's daughter Liz, a veteran of the Soviet shock therapy adventure, was put in charge of the project.

When the idea of invading an Arab country and turning it into a model state first gained currency after September 11, the names of several possible countries were floated—Iraq, Syria, Egypt and, Michael Ledeen's preference, Iran. Iraq had a great deal to recommend it, however. In addition to its vast oil reserves, it also made a good central location for military bases now that Saudi Arabia looked less dependable, and Saddam's use of chemical weapons on his own people made him easy to hate. Another factor, often overlooked, was that Iraq had the advantage of familiarity.

The 1991 Gulf War had been the U.S.'s last major ground offensive involving hundreds of thousands of troops, and in the twelve years since, the Pentagon had been using the battle as a template in workshops, training and elaborate war games. One example of this postgame theory was a paper that had captured the imagination of Donald Rumsfeld called *Shock and Awe: Achieving Rapid Dominance*. Written by a group of maverick strategists at the National Defense University in 1996, the paper positions itself as an all-purpose military doctrine, but it is really about refighting the Gulf War. Its lead author, the retired navy commander Harlan Ullman, explained that the project began when General Chuck Horner, the commander of the air war in the 1991 invasion, was asked about his greatest frustration in fighting Saddam Hussein. He replied that he did not know where to "stick the needle" to make the Iraqi army collapse. "Shock and Awe," writes Ullman (who coined the phrase) "was intended to address this question: If Desert Storm could be refought, how could we win in half the time or less and with far fewer forces? . . . The key to its success is finding the entry points for Horner's needles—the spots that, when targeted, get an enemy to collapse immediately."[8] The authors were convinced that if the U.S. military ever got the chance to fight Saddam again, it would now be in a far better position to find those "entry points," thanks to new satellite technologies and breakthroughs in precision weaponry that would allow it to insert the "needles" with unprecedented accuracy.

Iraq had another advantage. While the U.S. military was busy fantasizing about refighting Desert Storm with a technological upgrade equivalent to "the difference between Atari and PlayStation," as one commentator put it, Iraq's military capacity had been hurtling backward, eroded by sanctions and virtually disassembled by the United Nations–administered weapons inspection program.[9] That meant that, compared with Iran or Syria, Iraq seemed the site for the most winnable war.

Thomas Friedman was forthright about what it meant for Iraq to be selected as the model. "We are not doing nation-building in Iraq. We are doing nation-creating," he wrote—as if shopping around for a large, oil-rich Arab nation to create from scratch was a natural, even "noble" thing to do in the twenty-first century.[10] Friedman is among many of the onetime war advocates who has since claimed that he did not foresee the carnage that would follow from the invasion. It's hard to see how he could have missed that detail. Iraq was not an empty space on a map; it was and remains a culture as old as civilization, with fierce anti-imperialist pride, strong Arab nationalism, deeply held faiths and a majority of the adult male population with military training. If "nation creating" was going to happen in Iraq, what exactly was supposed to become of the nation that was already there? The unspoken assumption from the beginning was that much of it would have to disappear, to clear the ground for the grand experiment—an idea that contained, at its core, the certainty of extraordinary colonialist violence.

Thirty years earlier, when the Chicago School counterrevolution took its first leap from the textbook to the real world, it also sought to erase nations and create new ones in their place. Like Iraq in 2003, Chile in 1973 was meant to serve as a model for the entire rebellious continent, and for many years it did. The brutal regimes that implemented Chicago School ideas in the seventies understood that, for their idealized new nations to be born in Chile, Argentina, Uruguay and Brazil, whole categories of people and their cultures would need to be pulled up "from the root."

In the countries that suffered the political cleansings, there have been collective efforts to come to terms with this violent history—truth commissions, excavations of unmarked graves and the beginnings of war crimes trials for the perpetrators. But the Latin American juntas did not act alone: they were propped up before and after their coups by Washington, as has been amply documented. For instance, in 1976, the year of Argentina's coup, when thousands of young activists were snatched from their homes, the junta had full financial support from Washington. ("If there are things that have to be done, you should do them quickly," Kissinger had said.)[11] That year, Gerald Ford was president, Dick Cheney was his chief of staff, Donald Rumsfeld was his secretary of defense, and Kissinger's executive assistant was an ambitious young man named Paul Bremer. These men faced no truth-and-justice process for their roles in supporting the juntas and went on to enjoy long and prosperous careers. So long, in fact, that they would be around three decades later to implement a strikingly similar—if far more violent—experiment in Iraq.

In his 2005 inaugural address, George W. Bush described the era between the end of the Cold War and the start of the War on Terror as "years of repose, years of sabbatical—and then there came a day of fire."[12] The Iraq invasion marked the ferocious return to the early techniques of the free-market crusade—the use of ultimate shock to forcibly wipe out and erase all obstacles to the construction of model corporatist states free from all interference.

Ewen Cameron, the CIA-funded psychiatrist who had tried to "depattern" his patients by regressing them to infantile states, had believed that if a little shock was good for this purpose, more was better. He blasted brains with everything he could think of—electricity, hallucinogens, sensory deprivation, sensory overload—anything that would wipe out what was and give him a blank slate on which to imprint new thoughts, new patterns. With a far larger canvas, that was the invasion and occupation strategy for Iraq. The architects of the war surveyed the global arsenal of shock tactics and decided to go with all of them—blitzkrieg military bombardment supplemented with elaborate psychological operations, followed up with the fastest and most sweeping political and economic shock therapy program attempted anywhere, backed up, if there was any resistance, by rounding up those who resisted and subjecting them to "gloves-off" abuse.

Often, in the analyses of the war in Iraq, the conclusion is that the invasion was a "success" but the occupation was a failure. What this assessment overlooks is that the invasion and occupation were two parts of a unified stategy—the initial bombardment was designed to erase the canvas on which the model nation could be built.

War as Mass Torture

For the strategists of the 2003 invasion of Iraq, the answer to the question of "where to stick the needles" appears to have been: everywhere. During the 1991 Gulf War, roughly three hundred Tomahawk cruise missiles were fired over the course of five weeks. In 2003, more than three hundred and eighty were launched in a single day. Between March 20 and May 2, the weeks of "major combat," the U.S military dropped more than thirty thousand bombs on Iraq, as well as twenty thousand precision-guided cruise missiles—67 percent of the total number ever made.[13]

"I am so scared," Yasmine Musa, a Baghdad mother of three said during the bombings. "Not a single minute passes by without hearing and feeling a drop of a bomb somewhere. I don't think that a single meter in the whole of Iraq is safe."[14] That meant Shock and Awe was doing its job. In open defiance of the laws of war barring collective punishment, Shock and Awe is a military doctrine that prides itself on not merely targeting the enemy's military forces but, as its authors stress, the "society writ large"—mass fear is a key part of the strategy.

Another element that distinguishes Shock and Awe is its acute consciousness of war as a cable news spectacle, one playing to several audiences at once: the enemy, Americans at home and anyone else thinking of making trouble. "When the video results of these attacks are broadcast in real time worldwide on CNN, the positive impact on coalition support and negative impact on potential threat support can be decisive," the Shock and Awe manual states.* From the start, the invasion was conceived as a message from Washington to the world, one spoken in the language of fireballs, deafening explosions and city-shattering quakes. In *The One Percent Doctrine*, Ron Suskind explains that for Rumsfeld and Cheney, "the primary impetus for invading Iraq" was the desire "to create a demonstration model to guide the behavior of anyone with the temerity to acquire destructive weapons or, in any way, flout the authority of the United States." Less than a war strategy, it was a "global experiment in behaviorism."[15]

Warfare is always partly a performance, always a form of mass communication, but Rumsfeld's marshaling of his tech and media know-how from the business world put the marketing of fear at the center of U.S. military doctrine. During the Cold War, the fear of a nuclear attack was the core of the deterrence strategy, but the idea was for the nuclear missiles to stay in their silos. This attack was different: Rumsfeld's war would use everything short of a nuclear bomb to put on a show designed to bombard the senses, pull and play on emotion, and convey lasting messages, with targets carefully chosen for their symbolic value and their made-for-TV impact. In this way, Rumsfeld's theory of war, part of his project of "transformation," had far less in common with the "force-on-force" battlefield strategies of the generals, who

---

*The 1991 Gulf War was the first CNN battle, but since the idea of twenty-four-hour live coverage was still young, the military had not by then fully incorporated it into its war planning.

were always slowing him down, and far more in common with the terrorists against whom Rumsfeld had declared permanent war. Terrorists don't try to win through direct confrontation; they attempt to break public morale with spectacular, televisual displays that at once expose their enemy's vulnerability and their own capacity for cruelty. That was the theory behind the 9/11 attacks, just as it was the theory behind the invasion of Iraq.

Shock and Awe is often presented as merely a strategy of overwhelming firepower, but the authors of the doctrine see it as much more than that: it is, they claim, a sophisticated psychological blueprint aimed "directly at the public will of the adversary to resist." The tools are ones familiar from another arm of the U.S. military complex: sensory deprivation and sensory overload, designed to induce disorientation and regression. With clear echoes of the CIA's interrogation manuals, "Shock and Awe" states, "In crude terms, Rapid Dominance would seize control of the environment and paralyze or so overload an adversary's perceptions and understanding of events." The goal is "rendering the adversary completely impotent." This includes such strategies as "real-time manipulation of senses and inputs . . . literally 'turning on and off' the 'lights' that enable any potential aggressor to see or appreciate the conditions and events concerning his forces and ultimately, his society" as well as "depriving the enemy, in specific areas, of the ability to communicate, observe."[16] The country of Iraq was subjected to this experiment in mass torture for months, with the process beginning well before the bombs started falling.

Fear Up

When the Canadian citizen Maher Arar was grabbed by U.S. agents at JFK airport in 2002 and taken to Syria, a victim of extraordinary rendition, his interrogators engaged in a tried-and-tested torture technique. "They put me on a chair, and one of the men started asking me questions. . . . If I did not answer quickly enough, he would point to a metal chair in the corner and ask, 'Do you want me to use this?' . . . I was terrified, and I did not want to be tortured. I would say anything to avoid torture."[17] The technique Arar was being subjected to is known as "the showing of the instruments," or, in U.S. military lingo, "fear up." Torturers know that one of their most potent weapons is the prisoner's own imagination—often just showing fearsome instruments is more effective than using them.

As the day of the invasion of Iraq drew closer, U.S. news media outlets were conscripted by the Pentagon to "fear up" Iraq. "They're calling it 'A-Day,'" began a report on *CBS News* that aired two months before the war began. "'A' as in airstrikes so devastating they would leave Saddam's soldiers unable or unwilling to fight." Viewers were introduced to Harlan Ullman, a *Shock and Awe* author, who explained that "you have this simultaneous effect, rather like the nuclear weapons at Hiroshima, not taking days or weeks but in minutes." The anchor, Dan Rather, ended the telecast with a disclaimer: "We assure you this report contains no information that the Defense Department thinks could help the Iraqi military."[18] He could have gone further: the report, like so many others in this period, was an integral part of the Department of Defense's strategy—fear up.

Iraqis, who picked up the terrifying reports on contraband satellites or in phone calls from relatives abroad spent months imagining the horrors of Shock and Awe. The phrase itself became a potent psychological weapon. Would it be worse than 1991? If the Americans really thought Saddam had WMDs, would they launch a nuclear attack?

One answer was provided a week before the invasion. The Pentagon invited Washington's military press corps on a special field trip to Eglin Air Force Base in Florida to witness the testing of the MOAB, which officially stands for Massive Ordnance Air Blast but which everyone in the military calls the "Mother of All Bombs." At twenty-one thousand pounds, it is the largest nonnuclear explosive ever built, able to create, in the words of CNN's Jamie McIntyre, "a ten-thousand-foot-high mushroom-like cloud that looks and feels like a nuclear weapon."[19]

In his report, McIntyre said that even if it was never used, the bomb's very existence "could still pack a psychological wallop"—a tacit acknowledgment of the role he himself was playing in delivering that wallop. Like prisoners in interrogation cells, Iraqis were being shown the instruments. "The goal is to have the capabilities of the coalition so clear and so obvious that there's an enormous disincentive for the Iraqi military to fight," Rumsfeld explained on the same program.[20]

When the war began, the residents of Baghdad were subjected to sensory deprivation on a mass scale. One by one, the city's sensory inputs were cut off; the ears were the first to go.

On the night of March 28, 2003, as U.S. troops drew closer to Baghdad, the ministry of communication was bombed and set ablaze, as were four Baghdad telephone exchanges, with massive bunker-busters, cutting off millions of phones across the city. The targeting of the phone exchanges continued—twelve in total—until, by April 2, there was barely a phone working in all of Baghdad.*[21] During the same assault, television and radio transmitters were also hit, making it impossible for families in Baghdad, huddling in their homes, to pick up even a weak signal carrying news of what was going on outside their doors.

Many Iraqis say that the shredding of their phone system was the most psychologically wrenching part of the air attack. The combination of hearing and feeling bombs going off everywhere while being unable to call a few blocks away to find out if loved ones were alive, or to reassure terrified relatives living abroad, was pure torment. Journalists based in Baghdad were swarmed by desperate local residents begging for a few moments with their satellite phones or pressing numbers into the reporters' hands along with pleas to call a brother or an uncle in London or Baltimore. "Tell him everything is okay. Tell him his mother and father are fine. Tell him hello. Tell him not to worry."[22] By then, most drugstores in Baghdad had sold out of sleeping aids and antidepressants, and the city was completely cleaned out of Valium.

Next to go were the eyes. "There was no audible explosion, no discernible change in the early evening bombardments, but in an instant, an entire city of 5 million people was plunged into an awful, endless night," *The Guardian* reported on April 4. Darkness was "relieved only by the headlights of passing cars."[23] Trapped in their homes, Baghdad's residents could not speak to each other, hear each other or see outside. Like a prisoner destined for a CIA black site, the entire city was shackled and hooded. Next it was stripped.

Comfort Items

In hostile interrogations, the first stage of breaking down prisoners is stripping them of their own clothes and any items that have the power to evoke their sense of self—so-called comfort items. Often objects that are of particular value to a prisoner, like the Koran or a cherished photograph, are treated

---

* The official reason for the wholesale annihilation of Baghdad's phone system was to sever Saddam's ability to communicate with his elite commandos. But after the war, U.S. interrogators conducted extensive "interviews" with top Iraqi prisoners and discovered that for years Saddam had been convinced that spies were tracking him through his phone calls and therefore had used a phone only twice in the previous thirteen years. As usual, reliable intelligence wasn't necessary; there would be plenty of ready money for Bechtel to build a new system.

with open disrespect. The message is "You are no one, you are who we want you to be," the essence of dehumanization. Iraqis went through this unmaking process collectively, as they watched their most important institutions desecrated, their history loaded onto trucks and disappeared. The bombing badly injured Iraq, but it was the looting, unchecked by occupying troops, that did the most to erase the heart of the country that was.

"The hundreds of looters who smashed ancient ceramics, stripped display cases and pocketed gold and other antiquities from the National Museum of Iraq pillaged nothing less than records of the first human society," reported the *Los Angeles Times.* "Gone are 80 per cent of the museum's 170,000 priceless objects."[24] The national library, which contained copies of every book and doctoral thesis ever published in Iraq, was a blackened ruin. Thousand-year-old illuminated Korans had disappeared from the Ministry of Religious Affairs, which was left a burned-out shell. "Our national heritage is lost," pronounced a Baghdad high-school teacher.[25] A local merchant said of the museum, "It was the soul of Iraq. If the museum doesn't recover the looted treasures, I will feel like a part of my own soul has been stolen." McGuire Gibson, an archaeologist at the University of Chicago, called it "a lot like a lobotomy. The deep memory of an entire culture, a culture that has continued for thousands of years, has been removed."[26]

Thanks mostly to the efforts of clerics who organized salvage missions in the midst of the looting, a portion of the artifacts has been recovered. But many Iraqis were, and still are, convinced that the memory lobotomy was intentional—part of Washington's plans to excise the strong, rooted nation that was and replace it with their own model. "Baghdad is the mother of Arab culture," seventy-year-old Ahmed Abdullah told *The Washington Post*, "and they want to wipe out our culture."[27]

As the war planners were quick to point out, the looting was done by Iraqis, not foreign troops. And it's true that Rumsfeld did not plan for Iraq to be sacked—but he did not take measures to prevent it from happening either, or to stop it once it had begun. These were failures that cannot be dismissed as mere oversights.

During the 1991 Gulf War, thirteen Iraqi museums were attacked by looters, so there was every reason to believe that poverty, anger at the old regime and the general atmosphere of chaos would prompt some Iraqis to respond in the same way (especially given that Saddam had emptied the prisons several months earlier). The Pentagon had been warned by leading archaeologists that it needed to have an airtight strategy to protect museums and libraries before any attack, and a March 26 Pentagon memo to coalition command listed "in order of importance, 16 sites that were crucial to protect in Baghdad." Second on the list was the museum. Other warnings had urged Rumsfeld to send an international police contingent in with the troops to maintain public order—another suggestion that was ignored.[28]

Even without the police, however, there were enough U.S. soldiers in Baghdad for a few to be dispatched to the key cultural sites, but they weren't sent. There are numerous reports of U.S. soldiers hanging out by their armored vehicles and watching as trucks loaded with loot drove by—a reflection of the "stuff happens" indifference coming straight from Rumsfeld. Some units took it upon themselves to stop the looting, but in other instances, soldiers joined in. The Baghdad International Airport was completely trashed by soldiers who, according to *Time*, smashed furniture and then moved on to the commercial jets on the runway: "U.S. soldiers looking for comfortable seats and souvenirs ripped out many of the planes' fittings, slashed seats, damaged cockpit equipment and popped out every windshield." The result was an estimated $100 million worth of damage to Iraq's national airline—which was one of the first assets to be put on the auction block in an early and contentious partial privatization.[29]

Some insight into why there was so little official interest in stopping the looting has since been provided by two men who played pivotal roles in the occupation—Peter McPherson, the senior economic adviser to Paul Bremer, and John Agresto, director of higher education reconstruction for the occupation. McPherson said that when he saw Iraqis taking state property—cars, buses, ministry equipment—it didn't bother him. His job, as Iraq's top economic shock therapist, was to radically downsize the state and privatize its assets, which meant that the looters were really just giving him a jump-start. "I thought the privatization that occurs sort of naturally when somebody took over their state vehicle, or began to drive a truck that the state used to own, was just fine," he said. A veteran bureaucrat of the Reagan administration and a firm believer in Chicago School economics, McPherson termed the pillage a form of public sector "shrinkage."*[30]

* It's a spin that puts Halliburton's overcharging of U.S. taxpayers and the Pentagon's willingness to let it slide in a new light—perhaps the Department of Defense saw the missing millions not as theft but as shrinkage, all part of the campaign to scale back government and beef up business.

His colleague John Agresto also saw a silver lining as he watched the looting of Baghdad on TV. He envisioned his job—"a never to be repeated adventure"—as the remaking of Iraq's system of higher education from scratch. In that context, the stripping of the universities and the education ministry was, he explained, "the opportunity for a clean start," a chance to give Iraq's schools "the best modern equipment." If the mission was "nation creating," as so many clearly believed it to be, then everything that remained of the old country was only going to get in the way. Agresto was the former president of St. John's College in New Mexico, which specializes in a Great Books curriculum. He explained that although he knew nothing of Iraq, he had refrained from reading books about the country before making the trip so that he would arrive "with as open a mind as I could have."[31] Like Iraq's colleges, Agresto would be a blank slate.

If Agresto had read a book or two, he might have thought twice about the need to erase everything and start over. He could have learned, for instance, that before the sanctions strangled the country, Iraq had the best education system in the region, with the highest literacy rates in the Arab world—in 1985, 89 percent of Iraqis were literate. By contrast, in Agresto's home state of New Mexico, 46 percent of the population is functionally illiterate, and 20 percent are unable do "basic math to determine the total on a sales receipt."*[32] Yet Agresto was so convinced of the superiority of American systems that he seemed unable to entertain the possibility that Iraqis might want to salvage and protect their own culture and that they might feel its destruction as a wrenching loss.

This neocolonialist blindness is a running theme in the War on Terror. At the U.S.-run prison at Guantánamo Bay, there is a room known as "the love shack." Detainees are taken there after their captors have decided they are not enemy combatants and will soon be released. Inside the love shack, prisoners are allowed to watch Hollywood movies and are plied with American junk food. Asif Iqbal, one of three British detainees known as the "Tipton Three," was permitted several visits there before he and his two friends were finally sent home. "We would get to watch DVDs, eat McDonald's, eat Pizza Hut and basically chill out. We were not shackled in this area. . . . We had no idea why they were being like that to us. The rest of the week we were

---

* When Agresto failed miserably at his job of rebuilding Iraq's university system, leaving the country with the job undone, he revised his early enthusiasm for looting, describing himself as "a neoconservative who's been mugged by reality." This and other details come from Rajiv Chandrasekaran's vivid account of the Green Zone, *Imperial Life in the Emerald City*.

back in the cages as usual. . . . On one occasion Lesley [an FBI official] brought Pringles, ice cream and chocolates, this was the final Sunday before we came back to England." His friend Rhuhel Ahmed speculated that the special treatment "was because they knew they had messed us about and tortured us for two and half years and they hoped we would forget it."[33]

Ahmed and Iqbal had been grabbed by the Northern Alliance while visiting Afghanistan on their way to a wedding. They had been violently beaten, injected with unidentified drugs, put in stress positions for hours, sleep deprived, forcibly shaven and denied all legal rights for twenty-nine months.[34] And yet they were supposed to "forget it" in the face of the overwhelming allure of Pringles. That was actually the plan.

It's hard to believe—but then again, that was pretty much Washington's game plan for Iraq: shock and terrorize the entire country, deliberately ruin its infrastructure, do nothing while its culture and history are ransacked, then make it all okay with an unlimited supply of cheap household appliances and imported junk food. In Iraq, this cycle of culture erasing and culture replacing was not theoretical; it all unfolded in a matter of weeks.

Paul Bremer, appointed by Bush to serve as director of the occupation authority in Iraq, admits that when he first arrived in Baghdad, the looting was still going strong and order was far from restored. "Baghdad was on fire, literally, as I drove in from the airport. . . . There was no traffic on the streets; there was no electricity anywhere; no oil production; no economic activity; there wasn't a single policeman on duty anywhere." And yet his solution to this crisis was to immediately fling open the country's borders to absolutely unrestricted imports: no tariffs, no duties, no inspections, no taxes. Iraq, Bremer declared two weeks after he arrived, was "open for business."[35] Overnight, Iraq went from being one of the most isolated countries in the world, sealed off from the most basic trade by strict UN sanctions, to becoming the widest-open market anywhere.

While the pickup trucks stuffed with loot were still being driven to buyers in Jordan, Syria and Iran, passing them in the opposite direction were convoys of flatbeds piled high with Chinese TVs, Hollywood DVDs and Jordanian satellite dishes, ready to be unloaded on the sidewalks of Baghdad's Karada district. Just as one culture was being burned and stripped for parts, another was pouring in, prepackaged, to replace it.

One of the U.S. businesses ready and waiting to be the gateway to this experiment in frontier capitalism was New Bridge Strategies, started by Joe Allbaugh, Bush's ex-head of FEMA. It promised to use its top-level political connections to help U.S. multinationals land a piece of the action in Iraq. "Getting the rights to distribute Procter & Gamble products would be a gold mine," one of the company's partners enthused. "One well-stocked 7-Eleven could knock out 30 Iraqi stores; a Wal-Mart could take over the country."[36]

Like the prisoners in Guantánamo's love shack, all of Iraq was going to be bought off with Pringles and pop culture—that, at least, was the Bush administration's idea of a postwar plan.

CHAPTER 17

IDEOLOGICAL BLOWBACK

A VERY CAPITALIST DISASTER

> **The world is a messy place, and someone has to clean it up.**
> —Condoleezza Rice, September 2002, on the need to invade Iraq[1]

> **Bush's capacity to imagine a different Middle East may actually be related to his relative ignorance of the region. Had he traveled to the Middle East and seen its many dysfunctions, he might have been disheartened. Freed from looking at the day-to-day realities, Bush maintained a vision of what the region could look like.**
> —Fareed Zakaria, *Newsweek* columnist[2]

> **And the one who was seated on the throne said, "See, I am making all things new." Also he said, "Write this, for these words are trustworthy and true."**
> —Revelation 21:5 (NRSV)

The war in Iraq has been in damage control mode for so long that it's easy to forget the original vision for the way it was supposed to work out. But there was a vision, one neatly encapsulated at a conference held by the U.S. State Department in Baghdad in the early months of the occupation. The gathering featured fourteen high-level politicians and bureaucrats from Russia and Eastern Europe—an assortment of finance ministers, central bank chiefs and former deputy prime ministers. They were flown to the Baghdad International Airport in September 2003, kitted out in combat helmets and body armor, then raced to the Green Zone, the walled city within a city that housed the U.S.-run government of Iraq, the Coalition Provisional Authority (CPA), and now houses the U.S. embassy. Inside Saddam's former conference center, the VIP guests gave a small group of influential Iraqis lessons in capitalist transformation.

One of the main speakers was Marek Belka, Poland's former right-wing finance minister who worked under Bremer in Iraq for several months. According to an official State Department report on the gathering, Belka pounded the Iraqis with the message that they had to seize this moment of chaos to be "forceful" in pushing through policies that "would throw many people out of work." The first lesson from Poland, Belka said, was that "unproductive state-owned enterprises should be sold off immediately without efforts to salvage them with public funds." (He failed to mention that popular pressure had forced Solidarity to abandon its plans for rapid privatization, saving Poland from a Russian-style meltdown.) His second lesson was even bolder. It was five months after the fall of Baghdad, and Iraq was in the midst of a humanitarian emergency. Unemployment was at 67 percent, malnutrition was rampant and the only thing holding off mass starvation was the fact that Iraqi households still received government-subsidized food and other essentials, just as they had under the UN-administered oil-for-food program during the sanctions period. They were also able to fill their gas tanks for pennies, when gas was available. Belka told the Iraqis that these market-distorting giveaways had to be scrapped immediately. "Develop the private sector, starting with the elimination of subsidies." He stressed that these measures were "much more important and divisive than privatization."[3]

Next up was none other than Yegor Gaidar, Yeltsin's former deputy prime minister, regarded as the architect of Russia's shock therapy program. In inviting Gaidar to come to Baghdad, the State Department seems to have assumed that the Iraqis would not know that he was regarded as a pariah back in Moscow, tainted by his close association with the oligarchs and by policies that had impoverished tens of millions of Russians.* While it was true that under Saddam the Iraqis had only limited access to outside news, the people at the Green Zone conference were mostly recently returned exiles; in the

---

* Many of the key players in Iraq's invasion and occupation were veterans of the original team in Washington that had demanded shock therapy in Russia: Dick Cheney was defense secretary when George Bush Sr. crafted his post-Soviet Russia policy, and Paul Wolfowitz was Cheney's deputy, while Condoleezza Rice served as Bush Sr.'s chief adviser on Russia's transition. For all these top players, and dozens of lesser ones, Russia's experience in the nineties, despite its abysmal results for ordinary people, was often invoked, without irony, as the model for Iraq to emulate in its transition.

nineties, while Russia was imploding, they were reading *The International Herald Tribune.*

It was Mohamad Tofiq, Iraq's interim industry minister, who told me about this strange conference, which wasn't covered in the press at the time. Months later, when we met in his temporary office in Baghdad (the old ministry was a charred shell), Tofiq was still laughing about it. He said the Iraqis had blasted the flak-jacket-wearing visitors, informing them that Paul Bremer's decision to fling open the borders to unrestricted imports had already dramatically worsened the lives of a war-ravaged people—if it was pushed further by cutting gas subsidies and eliminating food aid, the occupation would have a revolution on its hands. As for the star speaker, Tofiq said, "I told some of the people who organized the conference that if I was to encourage privatization in Iraq, I'd bring Gaidar to tell them, 'Do exactly the opposite of what we did.'"

When Bremer started issuing legal decrees in Baghdad, Joseph Stiglitz, the former World Bank chief economist, warned that Iraq was getting "an even more radical form of shock therapy than pursued in the former Soviet world." That was quite true. In the original Washington plan, Iraq was going to become a frontier just as Russia had been in the early nineties, but this time it would be U.S. firms—not local ones or European, Russian or Chinese competitors—that would be first in line for the easy billions. And nothing would deter even the most painful economic changes because, in contrast to the former Soviet Union, or Latin America and Africa, the transformation would not involve a mannered dance between IMF officials and quixotic local politicians while the U.S. Treasury called the shots from the suite down the hall. In Iraq, Washington cut out the middlemen: the IMF and the World Bank were relegated to supporting roles, and the U.S. was front and center. Paul Bremer was the government; as a top U.S. military official told the Associated Press, there was no point in negotiating with the local government because "at this point, we'd be negotiating with ourselves."[4]

This dynamic was what set the economic transformation of Iraq apart from earlier laboratories. All the careful efforts during the nineties to present "free trade" as something other than an imperial project were abandoned. Elsewhere, there would still be free trade lite, with its hothouse negotiations, but now there would also be free trade heavy, without proxies or puppets, seizing new markets directly for Western multinationals on the battlefields of preemptive wars.

The proponents of the "model theory" now claim that this was where their war went horribly wrong—as Richard Perle said in late 2006, "the seminal mistake" was "bringing Bremer in." David Frum concurred, saying they should have had "any kind of an Iraqi face" on the remaking of Iraq right away.[5] Instead they had Paul Bremer, ensconced in Saddam's turquoise-domed Republican Palace, receiving trade and investment laws by e-mail from the Department of Defense, printing them out, signing them and imposing them by fiat on the Iraqi people. Bremer was no quiet American, maneuvering and manipulating behind the scenes. With his movie-of-the-week looks and his fondness for news crews, he seemed intent on flaunting his absolute power over Iraqis, crisscrossing the country in a flashy Blackhawk helicopter flanked by GI Joe private security guards from Blackwater and always in his trademark uniform: immaculately pressed Brooks Brothers suits and beige Timberland boots. The boots were a going-to-Baghdad present from his son; "Go kick some butt, Dad," the card had said.[6]

By his own admission, Bremer knew little of Iraq ("I had lived in Afghanistan," he told one interviewer). That ignorance hardly mattered, however, because if there was one thing Bremer knew a great deal about, it was the central mission in Iraq: disaster capitalism.[7]

On September 11, 2001, he had been working as managing director and "senior political adviser" at the insurance giant Marsh & McLennan. The company had its offices in the North Tower of the World Trade Center and was devastated by the attacks. In the first few days, 700 of its workers were unaccounted for; in the end, 295 were confirmed dead. Exactly one month later, on October 11, 2001, Paul Bremer launched Crisis Consulting Practice, a new division of Marsh specializing in helping multinational corporations prepare for possible terrorist attacks and other crises. Advertising his experience as ambassador-at-large for counterterrorism under the Reagan administration, Bremer and his company offered clients comprehensive counterterrorism services, from political risk insurance to public relations and even advice on what to stockpile.[8]

Bremer's vanguard participation in the homeland security industry was ideal preparation for Iraq. That's because the Bush administration used the same formula to rebuild Iraq that it had pioneered to respond to 9/11: it treated postwar Iraq as if it was an exciting IPO, brimming with free-wheeling, quick-profit potential. So while Bremer may have stepped on plenty of toes, his mission never was to win Iraqi hearts and minds. Rather, it was to get the country ready for the launch of Iraq Inc. Seen in that light, his early, much-maligned decisions have an unmistakable logical coherence.

After replacing the cautious general Jay Garner as the top U.S. envoy, Bremer spent his first four months in Iraq almost exclusively focused on economic transformation, passing a series of laws that together make up a classic Chicago School shock therapy program. Before the invasion, Iraq's economy had been anchored by its national oil company and by two hundred state-owned companies, which produced the staples of the Iraqi diet and the raw materials of its industry, everything from cement to paper and cooking oil. The month after he arrived in his new job, Bremer announced that the two hundred firms were going to be privatized immediately. "Getting inefficient state enterprises into private hands," Bremer said, "is essential for Iraq's economic recovery."[9]

Next came the new economic laws. To entice foreign investors to take part in the privatization auction and to build new factories and retail outlets in Iraq, Bremer enacted a radical set of laws described by The Economist in glowing terms as the "wish-list that foreign investors and donor agencies dream of for developing markets."[10] One law lowered Iraq's corporate tax rate from roughly 45 percent to a flat 15 percent (straight out of the Milton Friedman playbook). Another allowed foreign companies to own 100 percent of Iraqi assets—preventing a repeat of Russia, where the prizes went to the local oligarchs. Even better, investors could take 100 percent of the profits they made in Iraq out of the country; they would not be required to reinvest, and they would not be taxed. The decree also stipulated that investors could sign leases and contracts that would last for forty years and then be eligible for renewal, which meant that future elected governments would be saddled with deals signed by their occupiers. The one area on which Washington held back was oil: its Iraqi advisers warned that any move to privatize the state oil company or to lay claim to untapped reserves before an Iraqi government was in place would be seen as an act of war. But the occupation authority did take possession of $20 billion worth of revenues from Iraq's national oil company, to spend as it wished.*[11]

The White House was so focused on unveiling a shiny new Iraqi economy that it decided, in the early days of the occupation, to launch a brand-new

---

* Some $8.8 billion of this money is often referred to as "Iraq's missing billions" because it disappeared into U.S.-controlled Iraqi ministries in 2004, virtually without a trace. Bremer defended this lax oversight to a U.S. congressional committee in February 2007, saying: "Our top priority was to get the economy moving again. The first step was to get money into the hands of the Iraqi people as quickly as possible." When Bremer's financial adviser, the retired admiral David Oliver, was asked by the committee about the missing billions, he replied, "Yeah, I understand. I'm saying what difference does it make?"

currency, a massive logistical undertaking. The U.K. firm De La Rue did the printing, and bills were delivered in fleets of planes and distributed in armored vehicles and trucks that ran at least a thousand missions throughout the country—at a time when 50 percent of the people still lacked drinking water, the traffic lights weren't working and crime was rampant.[12]

Although it was Bremer who implemented these plans, the priorities were coming straight from the top. Testifying before a Senate committee, Rumsfeld described Bremer's "sweeping reforms" as creating "some of the most enlightened—and inviting—tax and investment laws in the free world." At first, investors seemed to appreciate the effort. Within a few months, there was talk of a McDonald's opening in downtown Baghdad—the ultimate symbol of Iraq joining the global economy—funding was almost in place for a Starwood luxury hotel, and General Motors was planning to build an auto plant. On the financial side, HSBC, the international bank headquartered in London, was awarded a contract to open branches all over Iraq, while Citigroup announced plans to offer substantial loans guaranteed against future sales of Iraqi oil. The oil majors—Shell, BP, ExxonMobil, Chevron and Russia's Lukoil—made tentative approaches, signing agreements to train Iraqi civil servants in the latest extraction technologies and management models, confident that their time would soon arrive.[13]

Bremer's laws, designed to create the conditions for an investor frenzy, were not exactly original—they were merely an accelerated version of what had been implemented in previous shock therapy experiments. But Bush's disaster capitalism cabinet was not content to wait for the laws to take effect. Where the Iraq experiment entered bold new terrain was that it transformed the invasion, occupation and reconstruction into an exciting, fully privatized new market. This market was created, just as the homeland security complex was, with a huge pot of public money. For reconstruction alone, the boom was kicked off with $38 billion from the U.S. Congress, $15 billion from other countries and $20 billion of Iraq's own oil money.[14]

When the initial billions were announced, there were, inevitably, laudatory comparisons with the Marshall Plan. Bush invited the parallels, declaring the reconstruction "the greatest financial commitment of its kind since the Marshall Plan," and stating in a televised address in the early months of the occupation that "America has done this kind of work before. Following World War II, we lifted up the defeated nations of Japan and Germany, and stood with them as they built representative governments."[15]

What happened to the billions earmarked for Iraq's reconstruction, however, bore no relationship to the history Bush invoked. Under the original Marshall Plan, American firms benefited by sending equipment and food to Europe, but the explicit goal was to help war-torn economies recover as self-sufficient markets, creating local jobs and developing tax bases capable of funding domestic social services—the results of which are in evidence in Germany's and Japan's mixed economies today.

The Bush cabinet had in fact launched an anti-Marshall Plan, its mirror opposite in nearly every conceivable way. It was a plan guaranteed from the start to further undermine Iraq's badly weakened industrial sector and to send Iraqi unemployment soaring. Where the post-Second World War plan had barred foreign firms from investing, to avoid the perception that they were taking advantage of countries in a weakened state, this scheme did everything possible to entice corporate America (with a few bones tossed to corporations based in countries that joined the "Coalition of the Willing"). It was this theft of Iraq's reconstruction funds from Iraqis, justified by unquestioned, racist assumptions about U.S. superiority and Iraqi inferiority—and not merely the generic demons of "corruption" and "inefficiency"—that doomed the project from the start.

None of the money went to Iraqi factories so they could reopen and form the foundation of a sustainable economy, create local jobs and fund a social safety net. Iraqis had virtually no role in this plan at all. Instead, the U.S. federal government contracts, most of them issued by USAID, commissioned a kind of country-in-a-box, designed in Virginia and Texas, to be assembled in Iraq. It was, as the occupation authorities repeatedly said, "a gift from the people of the United States to the people of Iraq"—all Iraqis needed to do was unwrap it.[16] Even Iraqis' low-wage labor wasn't required for the assembly process because the major U.S. contractors such as Halliburton, Bechtel and the California-based engineering giant Parsons preferred to import foreign workers whom they felt confident they could control. Once again Iraqis were cast in the role of awed spectators—first awed by U.S. military technology and then by its engineering and management prowess.

As in the homeland security industry, the role for government employees—even U.S. government employees—was cut to the bone. Bremer's staff was a mere fifteen hundred people to govern a sprawling country of 25 million. By contrast, Halliburton had fifty thousand workers in the region, many of them lifelong public servants lured into the private sector by offers of better salaries.[17]

The weak public presence and the robust corporate one reflected the fact that the Bush cabinet was using Iraq's reconstruction (over which it had complete control, in contrast to the federal bureaucracy back home) to implement its vision of a fully outsourced, hollow government. In Iraq, there was not a single governmental function that was considered so "core" that it could not be handed to a contractor, preferably one who provided the Republican Party with financial contributions or Christian foot soldiers during election campaigns. The usual Bush motto governed all aspects of the foreign forces' involvement in Iraq: if a task could be performed by a private entity, it must be.

So while Bremer may have signed the laws, it was private accountants who designed and managed the economy. (BearingPoint, an offshoot of the major international accounting and consulting firm KPMG, was paid $240 million to build a "market-driven system" in Iraq—the 107-page contract mentions the word "privatization" fifty-one times; much of the original contract was written by BearingPoint.) Think tanks were paid to think (Britain's Adam Smith Institute was contracted to help privatize Iraq's companies). Private security firms and defense contractors trained Iraq's new army and police (Dyn-Corp, Vinnell and the Carlyle Group's USIS, among others). And education companies drafted the post-Saddam curriculum and printed the new textbooks. (Creative Associates, a management-and-education-consulting firm based in Washington, D.C., was given contracts worth more than $100 million for these tasks.)*[18]

Meanwhile, the model pioneered by Cheney for Halliburton in the Balkans, where bases were transformed into mini Halliburton towns, was adopted on a vastly larger scale. In addition to Halliburton's construction and management of military bases across the country, the Green Zone was, from the start, a Halliburton-run city-state, with the company in charge of everything from road maintenance to pest control to movie and disco nights.

The CPA was far too understaffed to monitor all the contractors, and besides, the Bush administration saw oversight as a noncore function to be outsourced. The Colorado-based engineering and construction company CH2M Hill was paid $28.5 million in a joint venture with Parsons to oversee four other major contractors. Even the job of building "local democracy" was privatized, given to the North Carolina–based Research Triangle Institute in a contract worth up to $466 million, though it's not at all clear what qualified

---

* Ahmed al-Rahim, an Iraqi American who worked with Creative Associates, explained, "The initial idea was that we would write a curriculum and bring it into Iraq." As it turned out, Iraqis complained that "something packaged in America was not acceptable, and it was scrapped."

RTI to bring democracy to a Muslim country. The leadership of the company's Iraq operation was dominated by high-level Mormons—people like James Mayfield, who told his mission back in Houston that he thought Muslims could be persuaded to embrace the Book of Mormon as compatible with the teachings of the prophet Muhammad. In an e-mail home, he imagined that Iraqis would erect a statue to him as their "founder of democracy."*[19]

As these foreign corporations descended on the country, the machinery in Iraq's two hundred state firms stood still, frozen by chronic power blackouts. Iraq once had one of the most sophisticated industrial economies in the region; now its largest firms couldn't even get a subsubsubcontract in their own country's reconstruction. To participate in the gold rush at all, Iraqi firms would have needed emergency generators and some basic repairs—which should not have been insurmountable, given Halliburton's speed in building military bases that look like Midwestern suburbs.

Mohamad Tofiq at the Industry Ministry told me he had made repeated requests for generators, pointing out that Iraq's seventeen state-owned cement factories were perfectly positioned both to supply the reconstruction effort with building materials and to put tens of thousands of Iraqis to work. The factories received nothing—no contracts, no generators, no help. American companies preferred to import their cement, like their workforce, from abroad, at up to ten times the price. One of Bremer's economic edicts specifically prohibited Iraq's central bank from offering financing to state-owned enterprises (a fact not reported until years later).[20] The reason for this effective boycott of Iraqi industry was not practical, Tofiq told me, but ideological. Among those making the decisions, he said, "no one believes in the public sector."

While private Iraqi firms closed in droves, unable to compete with imports streaming across the open borders, Bremer's staff had few comforting words to offer. Addressing a gathering of Iraqi businessmen, Michael Fleischer, one of Bremer's deputies, confirmed that many of their businesses would indeed fail in the face of foreign competition, but that was the beauty of the free market. "Will you be overwhelmed by foreign businesses?" he asked rhetorically. "The answer depends on you. Only the best of you will survive." He sounded like Yegor Gaidar, who reportedly said of small Russian businesses going under as a result of shock therapy, "So what? One who is dying deserves to die."[21]

---

* In fact, RTI was driven out of the country after it helped block local Islamic parties from democratically taking power in several cities and towns.

—

As is now well known, nothing about Bush's anti–Marshall Plan went as intended. Iraqis did not see the corporate reconstruction as "a gift"; most saw it as a modernized form of pillage, and U.S. corporations didn't wow anyone with their speed and efficiency; instead they have managed to turn the word "reconstruction" into, as one Iraqi engineer put it, "a joke that nobody laughs at."[22] Each miscalculation provoked escalating levels of resistance, answered with counterrepression by foreign troops, ultimately sending the country spiraling into an inferno of violence. As of July 2006, according to the most credible study, the war in Iraq had taken the lives of 655,000 Iraqis who would not have died had there been no invasion or occupation.[23]

In November 2006, Ralph Peters, a retired U.S. Army officer, wrote in *USA Today* that "we did give the Iraqis a unique chance to build a rule-of-law democracy," but Iraqis "preferred to indulge in old hatreds, confessional violence, ethnic bigotry and a culture of corruption. It appears that the cynics were right: Arab societies can't support democracy as we know it. And people get the government they deserve. . . . The violence staining Baghdad's streets with gore isn't only a symptom of the Iraqi government's incompetence, but of the comprehensive inability of the Arab world to progress in any sphere of organized human endeavor. We are witnessing the collapse of a civilization."[24] Though Peters was particularly blunt, many Western observers have arrived at the same verdict: blame the Iraqis.

But the sectarian divisions and religious extremism engulfing Iraq cannot be neatly detached from the invasion and the occupation. Although these forces were certainly present in advance of the war, they were far weaker before Iraq was turned into a U.S. shock lab. It's worth remembering that in February 2004, eleven months after the invasion, an Oxford Research International poll found that a majority of Iraqis wanted a secular government: only 21 percent of respondents said their favored political system was "an Islamic state," and only 14 percent ranked "religious politicians" as their preferred political actors. Six months later, with the occupation in a new and more violent phase, another poll found that 70 percent of Iraqis wanted Islamic law as the basis of the state.[25] As for sectarian violence, it was virtually unknown for the first year of the occupation. The first major incident, the bombing of Shia mosques during the holiday of Ashoura, was in March 2004, a full year after the invasion. There can be no doubt that the occupation deepened and ignited these hatreds.

In fact, all the forces tearing Iraq apart today—rampant corruption, ferocious sectarianism, the surge in religious fundamentalism and the tyranny of
death squads—escalated in lockstep with the implementation of Bush's anti—
Marshall Plan. After the toppling of Saddam Hussein, Iraq badly needed and
deserved to be repaired and reunited, a process that could only have been
led by Iraqis. Instead, at precisely that precarious moment, the country was
transformed into a cutthroat capitalist laboratory—a system that pitted individuals and communities against each other, that eliminated hundreds of
thousands of jobs and livelihoods and that replaced the quest for justice with
rampant impunity for foreign occupiers.

Iraq's current state of disaster cannot be reduced either to the incompetence
and cronyism of the Bush White House or to the sectarianism or tribalism of
Iraqis. It is a very capitalist disaster, a nightmare of unfettered greed unleashed
in the wake of war. The "fiasco" of Iraq is one created by a careful and faithful
application of unrestrained Chicago School ideology. What follows is an initial (and not exhaustive) account of the links between the "civil war" and the
corporatist project at the heart of the invasion. It is a process of ideology
boomeranging on the people who unleashed it—ideological blowback.

The most widely recognized case of blowback was provoked by Bremer's first
major act, the firing of approximately 500,000 state workers, most of them
soldiers, but also doctors, nurses, teachers and engineers. "De-Baathification,"
as it was called, was supposedly driven by a desire to clean out the government of Saddam loyalists. No doubt that was part of the motivation, but it
does not explain the scale of the layoffs or how deeply they savaged the public sector as a whole, punishing workers who were not high-level officials.

The purge resembled similar attacks on the public sector that have accompanied shock therapy programs ever since Milton Friedman advised
Pinochet to slash government spending by 25 percent. Bremer made no secret of his antipathy for Iraq's "Stalinist economy," as he described the country's state-run companies and large ministries, and he had no appreciation
for the specialized skills and the years of accumulated knowledge possessed
by Iraq's engineers, doctors, electricians and road builders.[26] Bremer knew
people would be upset about losing their jobs, but as his memoir makes
clear, he did not consider how the sudden amputation of Iraq's professional
class would make it impossible for the Iraqi state to function and therefore
hinder his own work. That blindness had little to do with anti-Saddamism

and everything to do with free-market fervor. Only someone deeply inclined to see government purely as a burden and public sector workers as dead wood could have made the choices Bremer did.

That ideological blindness had three concrete effects: it damaged the possibility of reconstruction by removing skilled people from their posts, it weakened the voice of secular Iraqis, and it fed the resistance with angry people. Dozens of senior U.S. military and intelligence officers have acknowledged that many of the 400,000 soldiers Bremer laid off went straight to the emerging resistance. As Marine Colonel Thomas Hammes put it, "Now you have a couple hundred thousand people who are armed—because they took their weapons home with them—who know how to use the weapons, who have no future, who have a reason to be angry at you."[27]

At the same time, Bremer's classic Chicago School decision to fling open the borders to unrestricted imports while allowing foreign companies to own 100 percent of Iraqi assets infuriated Iraq's business class. Many responded by funding the resistance with what little revenue they had left. After covering the first year of the Iraqi resistance in the Sunni Triangle, the investigative reporter Patrick Graham wrote in *Harper's* that Iraqi businessmen "are outraged by the new foreign-investment laws, which allow foreign companies to buy up factories for very little. Their revenues have collapsed, because the country has been flooded with foreign goods. . . . The violence, these businessmen realize, is their only competitive edge. It is simple business logic: the more problems there are in Iraq, the harder it is for outsiders to get involved."[28]

More ideological blowback came from the White House's determination to prevent future Iraqi governments from changing Bremer's economic laws—the same drive to "lock in" changes made in the wake of a crisis has been in effect since the first IMF-issued "structural adjustment" program. From Washington's perspective, there was no point in having the most enlightened investment rules in the world if a sovereign Iraqi government could take power in a few months and rewrite them. Because most of Bremer's decrees were in a legal gray zone, the Bush administration solution was to draft a new constitution for Iraq, a goal it pursued with bloody-minded determination—first with an interim constitution that locked in Bremer's laws, and then with a permanent constitution that attempted (but failed) to do the same.

Many legal experts were baffled by Washington's constitutional obsession. On the surface, there was no pressing need to write a new document from scratch—Iraq's 1970 constitution, ignored by Saddam, was perfectly serviceable, and the country had far more urgent needs. More important, the process of writing a constitution is among the most wrenching any nation can go through, even a nation at peace. It brings every tension, rivalry, prejudice and latent grievance to the surface. To foist that process—twice—on a country as divided and shattered as Iraq after Saddam greatly exacerbated the possibility of civil strife. The social cleavages cracked open by the negotiations have in no way healed, and may yet result in the partition of the country.

Like the lifting of all trade restrictions, Bremer's plan to privatize Iraq's two hundred state companies was regarded by many Iraqis as yet another U.S. act of war. Workers learned that in order to make the companies attractive to foreign investors, as many as two-thirds of them would have to lose their jobs. At one of Iraq's large state firms—a compound of seven factories that produced cooking oil, soap, dishwashing liquid and other basics—I heard a story that brought into sharp relief how many new enemies had been created by the privatization announcement.

On a tour of the factory complex in a Baghdad suburb, I met Mahmud, a confident twenty-five-year-old with a neat beard. He said that when he and his fellow workers heard about the plans to sell their workplace, six months into the U.S. occupation, they "were shocked. If the private sector buys our company, the first thing they would do is reduce the staff to make more money. And we will be forced into a very hard destiny, because the factory is our only way of living." Frightened by this prospect, a group of seventeen workers, including Mahmud, went to confront one of the managers in his office. A fight broke out: one worker struck a manager and the manager's bodyguard fired at the workers, who then turned on him. He spent a month in the hospital. A couple of months later, there was even more violence. The manager and his son were shot and badly injured on their way to work. At the end of our meeting, I asked Mahmud what would happen if the plant was sold despite their objections. "There are two choices," he said, smiling kindly. "Either we will set the factory on fire and let the flames devour it to the ground, or we will blow ourselves up inside it. But it will not be privatized." It was an early warning—one of many—that the Bush team had definitely overestimated its ability to shock Iraqis into submission.

There was another obstacle to Washington's privatization dreams: the free-market fundamentalism that shaped the structure of the occupation itself. Thanks to their rejections of all things "statist," the occupation authority running out of the Green Zone was far too understaffed and underresourced to pull off its own ambitious plans—especially in the face of the kind of hard-core resistance expressed by workers like Mahmud. As *The Washington Post's* Rajiv Chandrasekaran revealed, the CPA was such a skeletal organization that it had just three people assigned to the enormous task of privatizing Iraq's state-owned factories. "Don't bother starting," the three lonely staffers were counseled by a delegation from East Germany—which, when it sold off its state assets, had assigned eight thousand people to the project.[29] In short, the CPA was itself too privatized to privatize Iraq.

The problem wasn't just that the CPA was understaffed, it was also that it was staffed by people who lacked the baseline belief in the public sphere that is required for the complex task of reconstructing a state from the ground up. As the political scientist Michael Wolfe puts it, "Conservatives cannot govern well for the same reason that vegetarians cannot prepare a world-class boeuf bourguignon: If you believe that what you are called upon to do is wrong, you are unlikely to do it very well." He adds, "As a way of governing, conservatism is another name for disaster."[30]

It certainly was in Iraq. Much has been made of the youth and inexperience of the U.S. political appointees in the CPA—the fact that a handful of twentysomething Republicans were given key roles overseeing Iraq's $13 billion budget.[31] While there is no question that the members of the so-called brat pack were alarmingly young, that was not their greatest liability. These were not just any political cronies; they were frontline warriors from America's counterrevolution against all relics of Keynesianism, many of them linked to the Heritage Foundation, ground zero of Friedmanism since it was launched in 1973. So whether they were twenty-two-year-old Dick Cheney interns or sixtysomething university presidents, they shared a cultural antipathy to government and governing that, while invaluable for the dismantling of social security and the public education system back home, had little use when the job was actually to build up public institutions that had been destroyed.

In fact, many seemed to believe that the process was unnecessary. James Haveman, in charge of rebuilding Iraq's health care system, was so ideologically opposed to free, public health care that, in a country where 70 percent of child deaths are caused by treatable illnesses such as diarrhea, and incubators are held together with duct tape, he decided that an overarching priority was to privatize the drug distribution system.[32]

The paucity of experienced civil servants in the Green Zone was not an oversight—it was an expression of the fact that the occupation of Iraq was, from the start, a radical experiment in hollow governance. By the time the think-tank lifers arrived in Baghdad, the crucial roles in the reconstruction had already all been outsourced to Halliburton and KPMG. Their job as the public servants was simply to administer the petty cash, which in Iraq took the form of handing shrink-wrapped bricks of hundred-dollar bills to contractors. It was a graphic glimpse into the acceptable role of government in a corporatist state—to act as conveyor belt for getting public money into private hands, a job for which ideological commitment is far more relevant than elaborate field experience.

That nonstop conveyor belt was part of what was so enraging to Iraqis about the U.S. insistence that they adapt to a strict free market, without state subsidies or trade protections. In one of his many lectures to Iraqi businesspeople, Michael Fleischer explained that "protected businesses never, never become competitive."[33] He appeared to be impervious to the irony that Halliburton, Bechtel, Parsons, KPMG, RTI, Blackwater and all the other U.S. corporations that were in Iraq to take advantage of the reconstruction were part of a vast protectionist racket whereby the U.S. government had created their markets with war, barred their competitors from even entering the race, then paid them to do the work, while guaranteeing them a profit to boot—all at taxpayer expense. The Chicago School crusade, which emerged with the core purpose of dismantling the welfare statism of the New Deal, had finally reached its zenith in this corporate New Deal. It was a simpler, more stripped-down form of privatization—the transfer of bulky assets wasn't even necessary: just straight-up corporate gorging on state coffers. No investment, no accountability, astronomical profits.

The double standards were explosive, as was the systematic exclusion of Iraqis from the plan. Having suffered through the sanctions and the invasion, most Iraqis naturally assumed that they had the right to benefit from the reconstruction of their country—not just from the final product but from the jobs created along the way. When tens of thousands of foreign workers poured across Iraq's borders to take up jobs with foreign contractors, it was seen as an extension of the invasion. Rather than reconstruction, this was destruction in a different guise—the wholesale wiping out of the country's industry, which had been a powerful source of national pride, one that cut across sectarian lines. Only fifteen thousand Iraqis were hired to work for the U.S.-funded reconstruction during Bremer's tenure, a staggeringly low figure.[34] "When the Iraqi people see all these contracts going to foreigners and these people bring in their own security guards and all their own engineers, and we're just supposed to watch them, what do you expect?" Nouri Sitto, an

Iraqi American, told me when we met in the Green Zone. Sitto had moved back to Baghdad to assist the CPA with the reconstruction, but he was tired of being diplomatic. "The economy is the number-one reason for the terrorism and the lack of security."

Much of the violence took direct aim at the foreign-run occupation, its projects and its workers. Some of the attacks clearly came from elements in Iraq, like al Qaeda, that are guided by a strategy of spreading chaos. However, if the reconstruction had been seen as part of a national project from the start, the general Iraqi population might have defended it as an extension of their communities, making the work of provocateurs far more difficult.

The Bush administration could easily have stipulated that any company receiving U.S. tax dollars had to staff its projects with Iraqis. It could also have contracted for many jobs directly with Iraqi firms. Such simple, common-sense measures did not happen for years because they conflicted with the underlying strategy of turning Iraq into an emerging market economic bubble—and everyone knows that bubbles are not inflated with rules and regulations but by their absence. So, in the name of speed and efficiency, contractors could hire whomever they wished, import from wherever they liked and subcontract to whatever company they wanted.

If within six months of the invasion, Iraqis had found themselves drinking clean water from Bechtel pipes, their homes illuminated by GE lights, their infirm treated in sanitary Parsons-built hospitals, their streets patrolled by competent DynCorp-trained police, many citizens (though not all) would probably have overcome their anger at being excluded from the reconstruction process. But none of this happened, and well before Iraqi resistance forces began systematically targeting reconstruction sites it was clear that applying laissez-faire principles to such a huge government task had been a disaster.

Freed of all regulations, largely protected from criminal prosecution and on contracts that guaranteed their costs would be covered, plus a profit, many foreign corporations did something entirely predictable: they scammed wildly. Known in Iraq as "the primes," the big contractors engaged in elaborate subcontracting schemes. They set up offices in the Green Zone, or even Kuwait City and Amman, then subcontracted to Kuwaiti companies, who subcontracted to Saudis, who, when the security situation got too rough, finally subcontracted to Iraqi firms, often from Kurdistan, for a fraction of what the contracts were worth. The Democratic senator Byron Dorgan described this web, using an air-conditioning contract in Baghdad as an example: "The contract goes to a subcontractor, which goes to another subcontractor, and a fourth-level subcontractor. And the payment for air-conditioning turns out to be payments to four contractors, the fourth of which puts a fan in a room. Yes, the American taxpayer paid for an air-conditioner and, after the money goes through four hands like ice cubes travel around the room, there is a fan put in a room in Iraq."[35] More to the point, all this time Iraqis watched their aid money stolen as their country boiled.

When Bechtel packed up and left Iraq in November 2006, it blamed "the overlay of violence" for its inability to fulfill its projects. But the contractor failure began well before the armed resistance in Iraq built up steam. The first schools that Bechtel reconstructed drew complaints immediately.[36] In early April 2004, before Iraq had spiraled into violence, I visited the Baghdad Central Children's Hospital. It had supposedly been rebuilt by a different U.S. contractor, but there was raw sewage in the hallways, none of the toilets worked and the men trying to fix the mess were so poor that they didn't have shoes—they were subsubsubcontractors, like the women who sew piecework at their kitchen tables for a Wal-Mart contractor's contractor's contractor.

The mismanagement continued for three and a half years until all the major U.S. reconstruction contractors pulled out of Iraq, their billions spent, the bulk of the work still undone. Parsons was handed $186 million to build 142 health clinics. Only 6 were ever completed. Even the projects held up as reconstruction success stories have been called into question. In April 2007, U.S. inspectors in Iraq looked into eight projects completed by U.S. contractors—including a maternity hospital and a water purification system—and found that "seven were no longer operating as designed," according to *The New York Times*. The paper also reported that Iraq's power grid was producing significantly less electricity in 2007 than it did in 2006.[37] As of December 2006, when all the main reconstruction contracts were ending, the Inspector General's Office was investigating eighty-seven cases of possible fraud relating to U.S. contractors in Iraq.[38] Corruption during the occupation was not the result of poor management but of a policy decision: if Iraq was to be the next frontier for Wild West capitalism, it needed to be liberated from laws."

Bremer's CPA would not try to stop the various scams, side deals and shell games because the CPA was itself a shell game. Though it was billed as the U.S. occupation authority, it's unclear that it held that distinction in any-thing other than name. This point was forcefully made by a judge in the in-famous Custer Battles corruption case.

Two former employees of the security firm launched a whistle-blower lawsuit against the company, accusing it of cheating on reconstruction-related contracts with the CPA and defrauding the U.S. government of millions of dol-lars, mostly for work done at the Baghdad International Airport. The case was based on documents produced by the company that clearly showed it was keep-ing two sets of numbers—one for itself, one for invoicing the CPA. Retired Brigadier General Hugh Tant testified that the company's performance was "probably the worst I've ever seen in my 30 years in the army." (Among Custer Battles' many alleged violations, it is said to have appropriated Iraqi-owned fork-lifts from the airport, repainted them and billed the CPA for the cost of leasing the machines.)[39]

In March 2006, a federal jury in Virginia ruled against the company, find-ing it guilty of fraud, and forced it to pay $10 million in damages. The com-pany then asked the judge to overturn the verdict, with a revealing defense. It claimed that the CPA was not part of the U.S. government, and therefore not subject to its laws, including the False Claims Act. The implications of this defense were enormous: the Bush administration had indemnified U.S. cor-porations working in Iraq from any liability under Iraqi laws; if the CPA wasn't subject to U.S. law either, it meant that the contractors weren't subject to any law at all—U.S. or Iraqi. This time, the judge ruled in the company's favor: he said there was plenty of evidence that Custer Battles had submitted to the CPA "false and fraudulently inflated invoices," but he ruled that the plaintiffs had "failed to prove that the claims were presented to the United States."[40] In other words, the U.S. government presence in Iraq during the first year of its economic experiment had been a mirage—there had been no government, just a funnel to get U.S. taxpayer and Iraqi oil dollars to foreign corporations, completely outside the law. In this way, Iraq represented the most extreme expression of the anti-state counterrevolution—a hollow state, where, as the courts finally established, there was no there, there.

After handing out its billions to contractors, the CPA melted away. Its for-mer staffers returned to the private sector and, when the scandals hit, there was no one left to defend the Green Zone's dismal record. But in Iraq, the missing billions were keenly felt. "The situation now is much worse and it seems not to be improving despite the huge contracts signed with American companies," remarked an engineer with the Ministry of Electricity the week after Bechtel announced its departure from Iraq. "It is strange how billions of dollars spent on electricity brought no improvement whatsoever, but in fact worsened the situation." A taxi driver in Mosul asked, "What reconstruction? Today we are drinking untreated water from a plant built decades ago that was never maintained. The electricity only visits us two hours a day. And now we are going backward. We cook on the firewood we gather from the forests because of the gas shortage."[41]

The catastrophic failure to reconstruct also shared direct responsibility for the most lethal form of blowback—the dangerous rise of religious fundamentalism and sectarian conflict. When the occupation proved unable to provide the most basic services, including security, the mosques and local militias filled the vacuum. The young Shia cleric Moqtada al-Sadr proved particularly adept at exposing the failures of Bremer's privatized reconstruction by running his own shadow reconstruction in Shia slums from Baghdad to Basra, earning himself a devoted following. Funded through donations to mosques, and perhaps later with help from Iran, the centers dispatched electricians to fix power and phone lines, organized local garbage collection, set up emergency generators, ran blood drives and directed traffic. "I found a vacuum, and no one filled the vacuum," al-Sadr said in the early days of the occupation, adding, "What I can do, I do."[42] He also took the young men who saw no jobs and no hope in Bremer's Iraq, dressed them in black and armed them with rusty Kalashnikovs. The result was the Mahdi Army, now one of the most brutal forces in Iraqi's sectarian battles. These militias are corporatism's legacy too: if the reconstruction had provided jobs, security and services to Iraqis, al-Sadr would have been deprived of both his mission and many of his newfound followers. As it was, corporate America's failures laid the groundwork for al-Sadr's successes.

Iraq under Bremer was the logical conclusion of Chicago School theory: a public sector reduced to a minimal number of employees, mostly contract workers, living in a Halliburton city state, tasked with signing corporate-friendly laws drafted by KPMG and handing out duffle bags of cash to Western contractors protected by mercenary soldiers, themselves shielded by full legal immunity. All around them were furious people, increasingly turning to religious fundamentalism because it's the only source of power in a hollowed-out state. Like Russia's gangsterism and Bush's cronyism, contemporary Iraq is a creation of the fifty-year crusade to privatize the world. Rather than being disowned by its creators, it deserves to be seen as the purest incarnation yet of the ideology that gave it birth.

CHAPTER 18

FULL CIRCLE

FROM BLANK SLATE TO SCORCHED EARTH

Would it not be easier
In that case for the government
To dissolve the people
And elect another?
—Bertolt Brecht, "The Solution," 1953[1]

Iraq is the last great frontier in the Middle East. . . . In Iraq, 80 per
cent of the oil wells ever drilled have been discoveries.
—David Horgan, chief executive of the Irish oil company Petrel, January 2007[2]

Is it possible that the Bush administration was unaware that its economic program had the potential to spark a violent backlash in Iraq? One person likely to have been aware of possible negative consequences was the man who implemented the policies, Paul Bremer. In November 2001, shortly after he had launched his new counter-terrorism company, Crisis Consulting Practice, Bremer wrote a policy paper for his clients explaining why multinational corporations faced increased risks of terrorist attacks at home and abroad. In the paper, titled "New Risks in International Business," he told his elite clients that they faced increased dangers because of the economic model that had made them so wealthy. Free trade, he wrote, has led to "the creation of unprecedented wealth," but it has "immediate negative consequences for many." It "requires laying off workers. And opening markets to foreign trade puts enormous pressure on traditional retailers and trade monopolies." All these changes lead to "growing income gaps and social tensions," which in turn can lead to a range of attacks on U.S. firms, including terrorist attacks.[3]

That certainly is what happened in Iraq. If the war's architects convinced themselves that there would be no political blowback from their economic program, it was probably not because they believed Iraqis would actively consent to such policies of systematic dispossession. Rather, the war planners were banking on something else—the disorientation of Iraqis, their collective regression, their inability to keep up with the pace of transformation. They were banking, in other words, on the power of shock. The guiding assumption of Iraq's military and economic shock therapists, best articulated by the former deputy secretary of state Richard Armitage, was that Iraqis would be so stunned by U.S. firepower, and so relieved to be rid of Saddam, "that they could be easily marshaled from point A to point B."[4] Then, after a few months, they would emerge from their postwar daze, pleasantly surprised to be living in an Arabic Singapore, a "Tiger on the Tigris," as some market analysts were excitedly calling it.

Instead, a great many Iraqis immediately demanded a say in the transformation of their country. And it was the Bush administration's response to this unexpected turn of events that generated the most blowback of all.

Dismantling Democracy

In the summer after Iraq's invasion, there was so much pent-up hunger for political participation that Baghdad, for all its daily hardships, displayed an almost carnival-like atmosphere. There was anger at Bremer's layoffs, and frustration with the blackouts and the foreign contractors, but for months that anger was primarily expressed through outbursts of unregulated, exuberant free speech. All summer there were daily protests outside the gates of the Green Zone, many by workers demanding their old jobs back. Hundreds of new newspapers flew off printing presses, filled with articles critical of Bremer and his economic program. Clerics preached politics during the Friday sermons, a freedom impossible under Saddam.

Most exciting of all, there were spontaneous elections breaking out in cities, towns and provinces across the country. Finally free of Saddam's iron grip, neighbors were convening town hall meetings and electing leaders to represent them in this new era. In cities like Samarra, Hilla and Mosul, religious leaders, secular professionals and tribespeople worked together to set local priorities for reconstruction, defying the worst predictions about sectarianism and fundamentalism. Meetings were heated, but by many accounts they were also joyous: the challenges were enormous but freedom was becoming a reality. In many cases, U.S. forces, believing their president when he said the army had been sent to Iraq to spread democracy, played a facilitating role, helping to organize the elections, even building ballot boxes.

The democratic enthusiasm, combined with the clear rejection of Bremer's economic program, put the Bush administration in an extremely difficult position. It had made bold promises to hand over power to an elected Iraqi government in a matter of months and to include Iraqis in decision making right away. But that first summer left no doubt that any relinquishing of power would mean abandoning the dream of turning Iraq into a model privatized economy dotted with sprawling U.S. military bases; economic nationalism was far too deeply ingrained in the populace, particularly when it came to the national oil reserves, the greatest prize of all. So Washington abandoned its democratic promises and instead ordered increases in the shock levels in the hope that a higher dosage would finally do the trick. It was a decision that brought the crusade for a pure free market back full circle to its roots in the Southern Cone of Latin America, when economic shock therapy was enforced by brutally suppressing democracy and by disappearing and torturing anyone who stood in the way.

When Paul Bremer first arrived, the U.S. plan was to convene a large constituent assembly, representing all sectors of Iraqi society, where delegates would vote for the members of an interim executive council. After spending two weeks in Baghdad, Bremer scrapped the idea. Instead, he decided to handpick the members of an Iraqi Governing Council. In a message to President Bush, Bremer described his process for selecting the Iraqi members of the council as "a cross between blind man's bluff and three-dimensional tic-tac-toe."[5]

Bremer had said that the council would have governing power, but once again he changed his mind. "My experience with the Governing Council at this point suggested this would not be a great idea," the former envoy later said, explaining that the council members were too slow and deliberative—traits unsuitable for his shock therapy plans. "They couldn't organize a two-car parade," Bremer said. "They were simply not able to make decisions in a timely fashion, or any decisions. Moreover, I still felt very strongly about the importance of getting a constitution in place before we handed sovereignty to anybody."[6]

Bremer's next problem was the elections breaking out in towns and cities across the country. At the end of June, only his second month in Iraq, Bremer sent word that all local elections must stop immediately. The new plan was for Iraq's local leaders to be appointed by the occupation, just as the Governing Council had been. A defining showdown took place in Najaf, the holiest city for Iraq's Shia, the largest religious denomination in the country. Najaf was in the process of organizing citywide elections with the help of U.S. troops when, only one day before registration, the lieutenant colonel in charge got a call from Marine Major General Jim Mattis. "The election had to be canceled. Bremer was concerned that an unfriendly Islamic candidate would prevail. . . . Bremer would not allow the wrong guy to win the election. The Marines were advised to select a group of Iraqis they thought were safe and have them pick a mayor. That was how the United States would control the process," wrote Michael Gordon and General Bernard Trainor, the authors of *Cobra II*, regarded as the definitive military history of the invasion. In the end, the U.S. military appointed a Saddam-era army colonel as Najaf's mayor, as they did in cities and towns across the country.*[7]

In some cases, Bremer's ban came after Iraqis had already voted in elections for local representatives. Undaunted, Bremer ordered the creation of new councils. In the province of Taji, RTI, the Mormon-dominated contractor tasked with building local government, dismantled the council that local people had elected months before it arrived and insisted on starting from scratch. "We feel we are going backwards," one man complained. Bremer insisted that there was "no blanket prohibition" against democracy. "I'm not opposed to it, but I want to do it a way that takes care of our concerns. . . . Elections that are held too early can be destructive. It's got to be done very carefully."[8]

At that point, Iraqis were still expecting Washington to make good on its promise to organize national elections and hand over power directly to a government elected by the majority of citizens. But in November 2003, after he canceled local elections, Bremer flew back to Washington for huddled meetings at the White House. When he returned to Baghdad, he announced

---

* This was one of the reasons why "de-Baathification" inspired such rage: while low-level soldiers had all lost their jobs, along with teachers and doctors who had been required to join the party in order to advance professionally, top-level Baathist military officials, well known for their human rights abuses, were being enlisted to bring order to the cities and towns.

that general elections were off the table. Iraq's first "sovereign" government would be appointed, not elected.

The about-turn may well have had something to do with a poll, conducted in this period by the Washington-based International Republican Institute. It asked Iraqis what kind of politicians they would vote for if they had the chance. The results were a wake-up call for the Green Zone corporatists: 49 percent of Iraqi respondents said they would vote for a party promising to create "more government jobs." Asked if they would vote for a party promising to create "more private sector jobs," only 4.6 percent said yes. Asked if they would vote for a party promising to "keep coalition forces until security is good," only 4.2 percent said they would.[9] Put simply, if Iraqis were allowed to freely elect the next government, and if that government had real power, Washington would have to give up on two of the war's main goals: access to Iraq for U.S. military bases and full access to Iraq for U.S. multinationals.

Some critics of the neocon wing of the Bush regime fault its Iraq plan for relying too heavily on democracy, for displaying a wide-eyed faith in self-determination. Airbrushed from this narrative is the actual track record of the entire first year of occupation, when Bremer cut down democracy wherever it reared its hydra head. Within his first six months in the job, he had canceled a constituent assembly, nixed the idea of electing the drafters of the constitution, annulled and called off dozens of local and provincial elections and then vanquished the beast of national elections—hardly the actions of an idealistic democrat. And not one of the high-profile neocons who now blame the problems in Iraq on the absence of "an Iraqi face" supported the calls for direct elections coming from the streets of Baghdad and Basra.

Many who were posted in Iraq in the early months draw a direct link between the various decisions to delay and defang democracy and the ferocious rise of the armed resistance. Salim Lone, a UN diplomat who was in Iraq after the invasion, saw the pivotal moment as Bremer's first antidemocratic decision. "The first devastating attacks on the foreign presence in Iraq, for example, came soon after the United States selected in July 2003 the first Iraqi leadership body, the Iraqi Governing Council: The Jordanian mission and then, soon after, the UN's Baghdad headquarters were blown up, killing scores of innocents . . . the anger over the composition of this council, and for UN support for it, was palpable in Iraq." Lone lost many friends and colleagues in the attack.[10]

Bremer's canceling of national elections was a bitter betrayal for Iraq's Shia. As the largest ethnic group, they were certain to dominate an elected government after decades of subjugation. At first, Shia resistance took the form of massive peaceful demonstrations: 100,000 protesters in Baghdad, 30,000 in Basra. Their unified chant was "Yes, yes, elections. No, no selections." "Our main demand in this process is to establish all the constitutional institutions through elections and not appointments," wrote Ali Abdel Hakim al-Safi, the second most senior Shia cleric in Iraq, in a letter to George Bush and Tony Blair. He declared Bremer's new plan "nothing other than replacing one dictatorship with another" and warned that if they went ahead with it, they would find themselves fighting a losing battle.[11] Bush and Blair were unmoved—they praised the demonstrations as evidence of freedom's flowering but bulldozed ahead with the plan to appoint Iraq's first post-Saddam government.

It was at this juncture that Moqtada al-Sadr became a political force to be reckoned with. When the other main Shia parties decided to participate in the appointed government and to abide by an interim constitution that was written inside the Green Zone, al-Sadr broke ranks, denouncing the process and the constitution as illegitimate and openly comparing Bremer to Saddam Hussein. He also started building up the Mahdi Army in earnest. After peaceful protests had no effect, many Shia became convinced that if majority-rule democracy was ever to become a reality, they would have to fight for it.

Had the Bush administration kept its promise to hand over power quickly to an elected Iraqi government, there is every chance that the resistance would have remained small and containable, rather than becoming a countrywide rebellion. But keeping that promise would have meant sacrificing the economic agenda behind the war, something that was never going to happen—and that is why the violent repercussions of America's denial of democracy in Iraq must also be counted as a form of ideological blowback.

Body Shocks

As resistance mounted, the occupation forces fought back with escalating shock tactics. These came late at night or very early in the morning, with soldiers bursting through doors, shining flashlights into darkened homes, shouting in English (a few words are understood: "motherfucker," "Ali Baba," "Osama bin Laden"). Women reached frantically for scarves to cover their heads in front of intruding strangers; men's heads were forcibly bagged before they were thrown into army trucks and sped to prisons and holding camps. In the first three and half years of occupation, an estimated 61,500 Iraqis were captured and imprisoned by U.S. forces, usually with methods designed to "maximize capture shock." Roughly 19,000 remained in custody in the spring of 2007.[12] Inside the prisons, more shocks followed: buckets of freezing water; snarling, teeth-baring German shepherds; punching and kicking; and sometimes the shock of electrical currents running from live wires.

Three decades earlier, the neoliberal crusade had begun with tactics like these—with so-called subversives and alleged terrorists grabbed from their homes, blindfolded and hooded, taken to dark cells where they faced beatings and worse. Now, to defend the hope of a model free market in Iraq, the project had come full circle.

One factor that made the surge in torture tactics all but inevitable was Donald Rumsfeld's determination to run the military like a modern, outsourced corporation. He had planned the troop deployment less like a defense secretary and more like a Wal-Mart vice president looking to shave a few more hours from the payroll. Having whittled the generals down from their early requests for 500,000 troops to fewer than 200,000, he still saw fat to trim: at the last minute, satisfying his inner CEO, he cut tens of thousands more troops from the battle plans.[13]

Although his just-in-time forces were capable of toppling Saddam, they had no hope of handling what Bremer's edicts created in Iraq—a population in open rebellion and a gaping hole where Iraq's army and police used to be. Lacking the numbers to bring control to the streets, the occupation forces did the next best thing: they scooped the people off the streets and put them in the jails. The thousands of prisoners rounded up in the raids were brought to CIA agents, U.S. soldiers and private contractors—many of them untrained—who conducted aggressive interrogations to find out whatever they could about the resistance.

In the early days of the occupation, the Green Zone had played host to economic shock therapists from Poland and Russia; now it became a magnet for a different breed of shock experts, those specializing in the darker arts of suppressing resistance movements. The private security companies padded their ranks with veterans of the dirty wars in Colombia, South Africa and Nepal. According to journalist Jeremy Scahill, Blackwater and other private security firms hired more than seven hundred Chilean troops—many of them special forces operators—for Iraq deployment, some of whom had trained and served under Pinochet.[14]

One of the highest-ranking shock specialists was the U.S. commander James Steele, who arrived in Iraq in May 2003. Steele had been a key figure in Central America's right-wing crusades, where he had served as chief U.S. adviser to several Salvadoran army battalions accused of being death squads. More recently, he had been a vice president at Enron and had originally gone to Iraq as an energy consultant, but when the resistance rose up, he switched back to his old persona, becoming Bremer's chief security adviser. Steele was eventually directed to bring to Iraq what unnamed sources at the Pentagon were chillingly calling "the Salvador option."[15]

John Sifton, senior researcher at Human Rights Watch, told me that the abuse of prisoners in Iraq did not fit the usual pattern. Usually in conflict zones, abuses take place early on, in the so-called fog of war, when the battlefield is chaotic and no one knows the rules. That's what happened in Afghanistan, Sifton said, "but Iraq was different—things started off professional and then they got worse, not better." He dates the shift to late August 2003—four months after Baghdad fell. It was at that point, he says, that the reports of abuse began streaming in.

According to this timeline, the shock of the torture chamber emerged immediately following Bremer's most controversial economic shocks. Late August was the end of Bremer's long summer of lawmaking and election canceling. As those moves sent ever more recruits to the resistance, U.S. soldiers were sent to break down doors and try to shake the defiance out of Iraq, one military-age man at a time.

The timing of this shift can be clearly tracked through a series of declassified documents that came to light in the wake of the Abu Ghraib scandal. The paper trail begins on August 14, 2003, when Captain William Ponce, an intelligence officer at the top U.S. military headquarters in Iraq, sent an e-mail to his fellow officers stationed around the country. It contained the now notorious statement: "The gloves are coming off gentlemen regarding these detainees . . . [a colonel] has made it clear that we want these individuals broken. Casualties are mounting and we need to start gathering info to help protect our fellow soldiers from any further attacks." Ponce solicited ideas for the techniques that interrogators would like to use on prisoners— what he called a "wish list." Suggestions came shooting back into his inbox, including "low-voltage electrocution."[16]

Two weeks later, on August 31, Major General Geoffrey Miller, warden of the Guantánamo Bay prison, was brought to Iraq on his mission to "Gitmoize" the Abu Ghraib prison.[17] Two weeks after that, on September 14,

Lieutenant General Ricardo Sanchez, top commander in Iraq, authorized a wide range of new interrogation procedures based on the Guantánamo model, including deliberate humiliation (called "pride and ego down"), "exploit[ing] Arab fear of dogs," sensory deprivation (called "light control"), sensory overload (yelling, loud music) and "stress positions." It was shortly after the Sanchez memo was sent out, in early October, that the incidents documented in the infamous Abu Ghraib photographs took place.[18]

The Bush team had failed to shock Iraqis into obedience either with Shock and Awe or with economic shock therapy. Now the shock tactics became more personal, using the *Kubark* interrogation manual's unmistakable formula for inducing regression.

Many of the most important prisoners were taken to a secured area near the Baghdad International Airport, run by a military task force and the CIA. Accessible only by special ID and kept hidden from the Red Cross, the facility was so clandestine that even high-level military officials were denied entry. To maintain its cover it repeatedly changed names—from Task Force 20 to 121 to 6-26 to Task Force 145.[19]

Prisoners were held in a small generic building, designed to create the textbook *Kubark* conditions, including complete sensory deprivation. The building was divided into five areas: a medical exam room, a "soft room" that looked like a living room (for co-operative prisoners), a red room, a blue room and the much-feared black room—a small cell with every surface painted black and speakers in all four corners.

The existence of the secret facility became public only when a sergeant who worked there, using the pseudonym Jeff Perry, approached Human Rights Watch to describe this strange place. Compared with the bedlam of Abu Ghraib, with its untrained guards mostly making it up as they went along, the CIA's airport facility was spookily ordered and clinical. According to Perry, when interrogators wanted to use "harsh tactics" against prisoners in the black room, they went to a computer terminal and printed out a form that was a kind of torture menu. "It was all already typed out for you," Perry recalled, "environmental controls, hot and cold, you know, strobe lights, music, so forth. Working dogs . . . you would just check what you want to use off." When they completed the forms, the interrogators took them to a superior officer for authorization. "I never saw a sheet that wasn't signed," Perry said.

He and other interrogators became concerned that the techniques violated the Geneva Conventions' prohibition against "humiliating and degrading treatment." Worried that they could face prosecution if their work ever became public, Perry and three others confronted their colonel and "told him we were uneasy about this type of abuse." The secret prison was so efficient that within two hours, a team of military lawyers descended on the facility with a PowerPoint presentation on why the detainees were not protected by the Geneva Conventions, and why sensory deprivation—despite the CIA's own research to the contrary—was not torture. "Oh, it was very fast," Perry said of the response time. "It was like they were ready. I mean they had this two hour slide show all prepared."

There were other facilities dotted around Iraq where prisoners were subjected to the same *Kubark*-style sensory deprivation tactics, some even more reminiscent of the McGill experiments all those years ago. Another sergeant told of a prison on a military base called Tiger, near al Qaim, close to the Syrian border, which held twenty to forty prisoners. They were blindfolded, shackled and put in sweltering hot metal shipping containers for twenty-four hours—"no sleep, no food, no water," the sergeant reported. After they had been softened up by the sensory deprivation box, prisoners were blasted with strobe lights and heavy-metal music.[20]

Similar methods were used at a Special Operations base near Tikrit—except that prisoners there were put in boxes even smaller: four feet by four feet and twenty inches deep, too small for an adult to stand or lie down, strongly reminiscent of many of the cells described in Latin America's Southern Cone. They were kept in that extreme sensory isolation for up to a week. At least one of the prisoners also reported being electrocuted by U.S. soldiers, though the soldiers denied it.[21] There is, however, a significant and little discussed body of evidence suggesting that U.S. soldiers have indeed used electrocution as a torture technique in Iraq. On May 14, 2004, in a case that received almost no publicity, two Marines were sentenced to prison for electrocuting an Iraqi prisoner one month earlier. According to government documents obtained by the American Civil Liberties Union, one soldier "shock[ed] an Iraqi detainee with an electric transformer . . . held the wires against the shoulder area of the detainee" until "the detainee 'danced' as he was shocked."[22]

When the infamous Abu Ghraib photographs were published, including the one of a hooded prisoner standing on a box with electrical wires dangling from his arms, the military had a strange problem: "We have had several detainees claim they were the person depicted in the photograph in question," explained the spokesperson for the Army's Criminal Investigation Command, the agency charged with investigating prisoner abuse. One of those detainees was Haj Ali, a former district mayor. Ali said that he too had been hooded, made to stand on a box and had electrical wires attached to his body parts. But, contradicting the accounts of the guards at Abu Ghraib who claimed the wires were not live, Ali told PBS, "When they shocked me with electricity, it felt like my eyeballs were coming out of their sockets."[23]

Like thousands of his fellow prisoners, Ali was released from Abu Ghraib without charge, pushed off a truck after being told "You were arrested by mistake." The Red Cross has said that U.S. military officials have admitted that somewhere between 70 and 90 percent of the detentions in Iraq were "mistakes." According to Ali, many of those human errors emerged from U.S.-run jails looking for revenge. "Abu Ghraib is a breeding ground for insurgents. . . . All the insults and torture make them ready to do just about anything. Who can blame them?"[24]

Many U.S. soldiers understand and fear this response. "If he's a good guy, you know, now he's a bad guy because of the way we treated him," said a sergeant with the 82nd Airborne, who had been stationed at a particularly brutal makeshift prison on a U.S. army base outside Fallujah, home to a battalion proudly known as the "Murderous Maniacs."[25]

The situation is far worse in jails run by Iraqis. Saddam had always relied heavily on torture to hold on to power. If torture was to recede in post-Saddam Iraq, it would have required a focused effort to repudiate such tactics on the part of a new government. Instead, the U.S. embraced torture for its own purposes, setting a degraded standard at the very time it was training and supervising the new Iraqi police force.

In January 2005, Human Rights Watch found that torture within Iraqi-run (and U.S.-supervised) jails and detention facilities was "systematic," including the use of electroshock. An internal report from the 1st Cavalry Division states that "electrical shock and choking" are "consistently used to achieve confessions" by Iraqi police and soldiers. Iraqi jailers were also using the ubiquitous symbol of Latin American torture, the *picana*, the electric cattle prod. In December 2006, *The New York Times* reported on the case of Faraj Mahmoud, who "was stripped and hanged from the ceiling. An electric prod applied to his genitals made his body bounce off the walls, he said."[26]

In March 2005, *The New York Times Magazine* reporter Peter Maass was embedded with a Special Police Commando unit that had been trained by James Steele. Maass visited a public library in Samarra that had been converted into a macabre prison. Inside, he saw blindfolded and shackled prisoners, some beaten bloody, as well as a desk with "bloodstains running down its side." He heard vomiting and screams that he described as "chilling, like the screams of a madman, or of someone being driven mad." He also clearly heard the sound of two gunshots "from within or behind the detention center."[27]

In El Salvador, death squads were notorious for using murder not just to get rid of political opponents but to send messages of terror to the broader public. Mutilated bodies that appeared on roadsides told the wider community that if individuals stepped out of line, they could be the next corpse. Often the tortured bodies were left with a sign bearing the signature of the death squad: Mano Blanco or Maximiliano Hernandez Brigade. By 2005, these sorts of messages had become a regular sight on roadsides in Iraq: prisoners, last seen in the custody of Iraqi commandos who were usually linked to the Ministry of Interior, found with a single bullet hole in the head, hands still cuffed behind their backs, or with holes in the skull made by electric drills. In November 2005, the *Los Angeles Times* reported that at the Baghdad morgue, "dozens of bodies arrive at the same time on a weekly basis, including scores of corpses with wrists bound by police handcuffs." Often the morgues kept the metal cuffs and returned them to the police.[28]

In Iraq, there are also more high-tech ways of conveying messages of terror. *Terrorism in the Grip of Justice* is a widely watched TV show on the U.S.-funded Al Iraqiya network. The series is produced in conjunction with the Salvadorized Iraqi commandos. Several released prisoners have explained how the show's content is produced: detainees, often grabbed at random in neighborhood sweeps, are beaten and tortured, and threats are made against their families until they are ready to confess to any crime—even crimes that lawyers have proved never took place. Then the video cameras come out to record the prisoners "confessing" to being insurgents, as well as thieves, homosexuals and liars. Every night, Iraqis watch these confessions, coming from the bruised and swollen faces of the unmistakably tortured. "The show has a good effect on civilians," Adnan Thabit, leader of the Salvadorized commandos, told Maass.[29]

Ten months after "the Salvador option" was first mentioned in the press, its full terrifying implications became clear. The Iraqi commandos, originally trained by Steele, were officially working under Iraq's Ministry of the Interior, which had insisted, when Maass questioned them about what he had seen in the library, that it "does not allow any human rights abuses of prisoners that are in the hands of Ministry of Interior Security Forces." But in

November 2005, 173 Iraqis were discovered in an Interior Ministry dungeon, some tortured so badly that their skin was falling off, others with drill marks in their skulls and teeth and toenails removed. The released prisoners said that not everyone made it out alive. They compiled a list of 18 people who had been tortured to death inside the ministry dungeon—Iraq's disappeared.[30]

When I was researching Ewen Cameron's electroshock experiments in the 1950s, I came across an observation made by one of his colleagues, a psychiatrist named Fred Lowy. "The Freudians had developed all these subtle methods of peeling the onion to get at the heart of the problem," he said. "Cameron wanted to drill right through and to hell with the layers. But, as we later discovered, the layers are all there is."[31] Cameron thought he could blast away all his patients' layers and start again; he dreamed of creating brand-new personalities. But his patients weren't reborn: they were confused, injured, broken.

Iraq's shock therapists blasted away at the layers too, seeking that elusive blank slate on which to create their new model country. They found only the piles of rubble that they themselves had created, and millions of psychologically and physically shattered people—shattered by Saddam, shattered by war, shattered by one another. Bush's in-house disaster capitalists didn't wipe Iraq clean, they just stirred it up. Rather than a tabula rasa, purified of history, they found ancient feuds, brought to the surface to merge with fresh vendettas from each new attack—on a mosque in Karbala, in Samarra, on a market, a ministry, a hospital. Countries, like people, don't reboot to zero with a good shock; they just break and keep on breaking.

Which of course requires more blasting—upping the dosage, holding down the button longer, more pain, more bombs, more torture. Former deputy secretary of state Richard Armitage, who had predicted that Iraqis would be easily marshaled from A to B, has since concluded that the real problem was that the U.S. was too soft. "The humane way in which the coalition fought the war," he said, "actually has led to a situation where it is more difficult to get people to come together, not less. In Germany and Japan [after the Second World War], the population was exhausted and deeply shocked by what had happened, but in Iraq it's been the opposite. A very rapid victory over enemy forces has meant we've not had the cowed population we had in Japan and Germany. . . . The US is dealing with an Iraqi population that is un-shocked and un-awed."[32] By January 2007, Bush and his advisers were still convinced that they could gain control of Iraq with one good "surge," one that wiped out Moqtada al-Sadr—"a cancer that undermines" the Iraq government. The report on which the surge strategy was based aimed for "the successful clearing of central Baghdad" and, when al-Sadr's forces moved to Sadr City, to "clear that Shiite stronghold by force" as well.[33]

In the seventies, when the corporatist crusade began, it used tactics that courts ruled were overtly genocidal: the deliberate erasure of a segment of the population. In Iraq, something even more monstrous has happened— the erasure not of a segment of the population but of an entire country; Iraq is disappearing, disintegrating. It began, as it often does, with the disappearance of women behind veils and doors, then the children disappeared from the schools—as of 2006, two-thirds of them stayed home. Next came the professionals: doctors, professors, entrepreneurs, scientists, pharmacists, judges, lawyers. An estimated three hundred Iraqi academics have been assassinated by death squads since the U.S. invasion, including several deans of departments; thousands more have fled. Doctors have fared even worse: by February 2007, an estimated two thousand had been killed and twelve thousand had fled. In November 2006, the UN High Commission for Refugees estimated that three thousand Iraqis were fleeing the country every day. By April 2007, the organization reported that four million people had been forced to leave their homes—roughly one in seven Iraqis. Only a few hundred of those refugees had been welcomed into the United States.[34]

With Iraqi industry all but collapsed, one of the only local businesses booming is kidnapping. Over just three and a half months in early 2006, nearly twenty thousand people were kidnapped in Iraq. The only time the international media pays attention is when a Westerner is taken, but the vast majority of abductions are Iraqi professionals, grabbed as they travel to and from work. Their families either come up with tens of thousands in U.S. dollars for the ransom money or identify their bodies at the morgue. Torture has also emerged as a thriving industry. Human rights groups have documented numerous cases of Iraqi police demanding thousands of dollars from the families of prisoners in exchange for a halt to torture.[35] It's Iraq's own domestic version of disaster capitalism.

This was not what the Bush administration intended for Iraq when it was selected as the model nation for the rest of the Arab world. The occupation had begun with cheerful talk of clean slates and fresh starts. It didn't take long, however, for the quest for cleanliness to slip into talk of "pulling Islamism up

from the root" in Sadr City or Najaf and removing "the cancer of radical Islam" from Fallujah and Ramadi—what was not clean would be scrubbed
out by force.

That is what happens with projects to build model societies in other people's countries. The cleansing campaigns are rarely premeditated. It is only
when the people who live on the land refuse to abandon their past that the
dream of the clean slate morphs into its doppelgänger, the scorched earth—
only then that the dream of total creation morphs into a campaign of total
destruction.

The unanticipated violence that now engulfs Iraq is the creation of the
lethally optimistic architects of the war—it was preordained in that original
seemingly innocuous, even idealistic phrase: "a model for a new Middle
East." The disintegration of Iraq has its roots in the ideology that demanded
a tabula rasa on which to write its new story. And when no such pristine
tableau presented itself, the supporters of that ideology proceeded to blast
and surge and blast again in the hope of reaching that promised land.

Failure: The New Face of Success

On my flight leaving Baghdad, every seat was filled by a foreign contractor
fleeing the violence. It was April 2004, and both Fallujah and Najaf were under siege; fifteen hundred contractors pulled out of Iraq that week alone.
Many more would follow. At the time, I was convinced that we were seeing
the first full-blown defeat of the corporatist crusade. Iraq had been blasted
with every shock weapon short of a nuclear bomb, and yet nothing could
subdue this country. The experiment, clearly, had failed.

Now I'm not sure. On one level, there is no question that parts of the project were a disaster. Bremer was sent to Iraq to build a corporate utopia; instead, Iraq became a ghoulish dystopia where going to a simple business
meeting could get you lynched, burned alive or beheaded. By May 2007,
more than 900 contractors had been reported killed and "more than 12,000
wounded in battle or injured on the job," according to a *New York Times*
analysis. The investors Bremer had done so much to attract had never shown
up—not HSBC, or Procter & Gamble, which put its joint venture on hold,
as did General Motors. New Bridge Strategies, the company that had gushed
about how "a Wal-Mart could take over the country," conceded that "Mc-
Donald's is not opening any time soon."[36] Bechtel's reconstruction contracts
did not roll easily into long-term contracts to run the water and electricity

systems. And by late 2006, the privatized reconstruction efforts that were at the center of the anti–Marshall Plan had almost all been abandoned on the ground—and some rather dramatic policy reversals were in evidence.

Stuart Bowen, U.S. special inspector general for Iraq reconstruction, reported that in the few cases where contracts were awarded directly to Iraqi firms, "it was more efficient and cheaper. And it has energized the economy because it puts the Iraqis to work." It turns out that funding Iraqis to rebuild their own country is more efficient than hiring lumbering multinationals who don't know the country or the language, surround themselves with $900-a-day mercenaries and spend as much as 55 percent of their contract budgets on overhead.[37] Jon C. Bowersox, who worked as the health adviser at the U.S. embassy in Baghdad, offered this radical observation: the problem with Iraq's reconstruction, he said, was its desire to build everything from scratch. "We could have gone in and done low-cost rehabs, and not tried to transform their health-care system in two years."[38]

An even more dramatic about-face came from the Pentagon. In December 2006, it announced a new project to get Iraq's state-owned factories up and running—the same ones that Bremer had refused to supply with emergency generators because they were Stalinist throwbacks. Now the Pentagon realized that instead of buying cement and machine parts from Jordan and Kuwait, it could be purchasing them from languishing Iraqi factories, putting tens of thousands to work and sending revenue to surrounding communities. Paul Brinkley, U.S. deputy undersecretary of defense for business transformation in Iraq, said, "We've looked at some of these factories more closely and found they aren't quite the rundown Soviet-era enterprises we thought they were"—though he did admit that some of his colleagues had begun calling him a Stalinist.[39]

Army Lieutenant General Peter W. Chiarelli, the top U.S. field commander in Iraq, explained that "we need to put the angry young men to work. . . . A relatively small decrease in unemployment would have a very serious effect on the level of sectarian killing going on." He couldn't help adding, "I find it unbelievable after four years that we haven't come to that realization. . . . To me, it's huge. It's as important as just about any other part of the campaign plan."[40]

Do these about-faces signal the death of disaster capitalism? Hardly. By the time U.S. officials came to the realization that they didn't need to rebuild a shiny new country from scratch, that it was more important to provide Iraqis with jobs and for their industry to share in the billions raised for reconstruction, the money that would have financed such an undertaking had already been spent.

Meanwhile, in the midst of the wave of neo-Keynesian epiphanies, Iraq was hit with the boldest attempt at crisis exploitation yet. In December 2006, the bipartisan Iraq Study Group fronted by James Baker issued its long-awaited report. It called for the U.S. to "assist Iraqi leaders to reorganize the national oil industry as a commercial enterprise" and to "encourage invest-ment in Iraq's oil sector by the international community and by international energy companies."[41]

Most of the Iraq Study Group's recommendations were ignored by the White House, but not this one: the Bush administration immediately pushed ahead by helping to draft a radical new oil law for Iraq, which would allow companies like Shell and BP to sign thirty-year contracts in which they could keep a large share of Iraq's oil profits, amounting to tens or even hun-dreds of billions of dollars—unheard of in countries with as much easily ac-cessible oil as Iraq, and a sentence to perpetual poverty in a country where 95 percent of government revenues come from oil.[42] This was a proposal so wildly unpopular that even Paul Bremer had not dared make it in the first year of occupation. Yet it was coming up now, thanks to deepening chaos. Explaining why it was justified for such a large percentage of the profits to leave Iraq, the oil companies cited the security risks. In other words, it was the disaster that made the radical proposed law possible.

Washington's timing was extremely revealing. At the point when the law was pushed forward, Iraq was facing its most profound crisis to date: the country was being torn apart by sectarian conflict with an average of one thousand Iraqis killed every week. Saddam Hussein had just been put to death in a depraved and provocative episode. Simultaneously, Bush was un-leashing his "surge" of troops in Iraq, operating with "less restricted" rules of engagement. Iraq in this period was far too volatile for the oil giants to make major investments, so there was no pressing need for a new law—except to use the chaos to bypass a public debate on the most contentious issue facing the country. Many elected Iraqi legislators said they had no idea that a new law was even being drafted, and had certainly not been included in shaping its outcome. Greg Muttitt, a researcher with the oil-watch group Platform, reported. "I was recently at a meeting of Iraqi MPs and asked them how many of them had seen the law. Out of 20, only one MP had seen it." Ac-cording to Muttitt, if the law was passed, Iraqis "would lose out massively be-cause they don't have the capacity at the moment to strike a good deal."[43]

Iraq's main labor unions declared that "the privatization of oil is a red line that may not be crossed" and, in a joint statement, condemned the law as an attempt to seize Iraq's "energy resources at a time when the Iraqi people are seeking to determine their own future while still under conditions of occupation."[44] The law that was finally adopted by Iraq's cabinet in February 2007 was even worse than anticipated: it placed no limits on the amount of profits that foreign companies can take from the country and made no specific requirements about how much or how little foreign investors would partner with Iraqi companies or hire Iraqis to work in the oil fields. Most brazenly, it excluded Iraq's elected parliamentarians from having any say in the terms for future oil contracts. Instead, it created a new body, the Federal Oil and Gas Council, which, according to *The New York Times*, would be advised by "a panel of oil experts from inside and outside Iraq." This unelected body, advised by unspecified foreigners, would have ultimate decision-making power on all oil matters, with the full authority to decide which contracts Iraq did and did not sign. In effect, the law called for Iraq's publicly owned oil reserves, the country's main source of revenues, to be exempted from democratic control and run instead by a powerful, wealthy oil dictatorship, which would exist alongside Iraq's broken and ineffective government.[45]

It's hard to overstate the disgrace of this attempted resource grab. Iraq's oil profits are the country's only hope of financing its own reconstruction when some semblance of peace returns. To lay claim to that future wealth in a moment of national disintegration was disaster capitalism at its most shameless.

There was another, little discussed, consequence of the chaos in Iraq: the longer it wore on, the more privatized the foreign presence became, ultimately forging a new paradigm for the way wars are fought and how human catastrophes are responded to.

This is where the ideology of radical privatization at the heart of the anti–Marshall Plan paid off handsomely. The Bush administration's steadfast refusal to staff the war in Iraq—whether with troops or with civilian administrators under its control—had some very clear benefits for its other war, the one to outsource the U.S. government. This crusade, while it ceased to be the subject of the administration's public rhetoric, has remained a driving obsession behind the scenes, and it has been far more successful than all the administration's more public battles combined.

Because Rumsfeld designed the war as a just-in-time invasion, with soldiers there to provide only core combat functions, and because he eliminated fifty-five thousand jobs in the Department of Defense and the Department of Veterans Affairs in the first year of the Iraq deployment, the private sector was left to fill in the gaps at every level.[46] In practice, what this configuration meant was that, as Iraq spiraled into turmoil, an ever more elaborate privatized war industry took shape to prop up the bare-bones army—whether on the ground in Iraq or back home treating soldiers at the Walter Reed Medical Center.

Since Rumsfeld steadfastly rejected all solutions that required increasing the size of the army, the military had to find ways to get more soldiers into combat roles. Private security companies flooded into Iraq to perform functions that had previously been done by soldiers—providing security for top officials, guarding bases, escorting other contractors. Once they were there, their roles expanded further in response to the chaos. Blackwater's original contract in Iraq was to provide private security for Bremer, but a year into the occupation, it was engaging in all-out street combat. During the April 2004 uprising of Moqtada al-Sadr's movement in Najaf, Blackwater actually assumed command over active-duty U.S. marines in a daylong battle with the Mahdi Army, during which dozens of Iraqis were killed.[47]

At the start of the occupation, there were an estimated ten thousand private soldiers in Iraq, already far more than during the first Gulf War. Three years later, a report by the U.S. Government Accountability Office found that there were forty-eight thousand private soldiers, from around the world, deployed in Iraq. Mercenaries represented the largest contingent of soldiers after the U.S. military—more than all the other members of the "Coalition of the Willing" combined. The "Baghdad boom," as it was called in the financial press, took what was a frowned-upon, shadowy sector and fully incorporated it into the U.S. and U.K. war-fighting machines. Blackwater hired aggressive Washington lobbyists to erase the word "mercenary" from the public vocabulary and turn its company into an all-American brand. According to its CEO, Erik Prince, "This goes back to our corporate mantra: We're trying to do for the national security apparatus what FedEx did for the postal service."[48]

When the war moved inside the jails, the military was so short on trained interrogators and Arabic translators that it couldn't get information out of its new prisoners. Desperate for more interrogators and translators, it turned to the defense contractor CACI International Inc. In its original contract, CACI's role in Iraq was to provide information technology services to the military, but the wording of the work order was vague enough that "information technology" could be stretched to mean interrogation.[49] The flexibility was intentional: CACI is part of a new breed of contractor that acts as a temp agency for the federal government—it has ongoing, loosely worded contracts and keeps large numbers of potential workers on call, ready to fill whatever positions come up. Calling CACI, whose workers did not need to meet the rigorous training and security clearances required of government employees, was as easy as ordering new office supplies; dozens of new interrogators arrived in a flash.*

The corporation that gained most from the chaos was Halliburton. Before the invasion, it had been awarded a contract to put out oil fires set by Saddam's retreating armies. When those fires did not materialize, Halliburton's contract was stretched to include a new function: providing fuel for the entire nation, a job so big that "it bought up every available tanker truck in Kuwait, and imported hundreds more."[50] In the name of freeing up soldiers for the battlefield, Halliburton took on dozens more of the army's traditional functions, including maintaining army vehicles and radios.

Even recruiting, long since seen as the job of soldiers, rapidly became a for-profit business as the war wore on. By 2006, new soldiers were being recruited by private head-hunting firms such as Serco or a division of the weapons giant L-3 Communications. The private recruiters, many of whom had never served in the military, were paid bonuses every time they signed up a soldier, so, one company spokesperson bragged, "If you want to eat steak, you have to put people in the army."[51] Rumsfeld's reign also fueled a boom in outsourced training: companies such as Cubic Defense Applications and Blackwater ran soldiers through live combat training and war games, bringing them to privately owned training facilities, where they practiced house-to-house combat in simulated villages.

And thanks to Rumsfeld's privatization obsession, as he first suggested in his speech on September 10, 2001, when soldiers came home sick or suffering from posttraumatic stress, they were treated by private health care companies

* The catch is that the contractors were operating with little supervision. As the U.S. military's own investigation into the Abu Ghraib scandal concluded, the government officials in charge of overseeing the interrogators' performance were not even in Iraq, let alone in Abu Ghraib, making it "very difficult, if not impossible, to effectively administer a contract." Army General George Fay, author of the report, concluded that the government's "interrogators, analysts, and leaders were unprepared for the arrival of contract interrogators and had no training to fall back on in the management, control, and discipline of these personnel. . . . It is apparent that there was no credible exercise of appropriate oversight of contract performance at Abu Ghraib."

for whom the trauma-heavy war in Iraq generated windfall profits. One of these companies, Health Net, became the seventh-strongest performer in the Fortune 500 in 2005, owing largely to the number of traumatized soldiers returning from Iraq. Another was IAP Worldwide Services Inc., which won the contract to take over many of the services at the military hospital Walter Reed. The move to privatize the running of the medical center allegedly contributed to a shocking deterioration in maintenance and care, as more than a hundred skilled federal employees left the facility.[52]

The greatly expanded role of private companies was never openly debated as a question of policy (much in the way Iraq's proposed oil law suddenly materialized). Rumsfeld did not have to engage in pitched battles with federal employees' unions or high-ranking generals. Instead, it all just happened on the fly in the field, in what the military describes as mission creep. The longer the war wore on, the more it became a privatized war, and soon enough, this was simply the new way of war. Crisis was the enabler of the boom, just as it had been for so many before.

The numbers tell the dramatic story of corporate mission creep. During the first Gulf War in 1991, there was one contractor for every hundred soldiers. At the start of the 2003 Iraq invasion, the ratio had jumped to one contractor for every ten soldiers. Three years into the U.S. occupation, the ratio had reached one to three. Less than a year later, with the occupation approaching its fourth year, there was one contractor for every 1.4 U.S. soldiers. But that figure includes only contractors working directly for the U.S. government, not for other coalition partners or the Iraqi government, and it doesn't account for the contractors based in Kuwait and Jordan who had farmed out their jobs to subcontractors.[53]

British soldiers in Iraq are already far outnumbered by their countrymen working for private security firms at a ratio of three to one. When Tony Blair announced in February 2007 that he was pulling sixteen hundred soldiers out of Iraq, the press reported instantly that "civil servants hope 'mercenaries' can help fill the gap left behind," with the companies paid directly by the British government. At the same time, the Associated Press put the number of contractors in Iraq at 120,000, almost equivalent to the number of U.S. troops.[54] In scale, this kind of privatized warfare has already overshadowed the United Nations. The UN's budget for peacekeeping in 2006–2007 was $5.25 billion—that's less than a quarter of the $20 billion Halliburton got in Iraq contracts, and the latest estimates are that the mercenary industry alone is worth $4 billion.[55]

So while the reconstruction of Iraq was certainly a failure for Iraqis and for U.S. taxpayers, it has been anything but for the disaster capitalism complex. Made possible by the September 11 attacks, the war in Iraq represented nothing less than the violent birth of a new economy. This was the genius of Rumsfeld's "transformation" plan: since every possible aspect of both destruction and reconstruction has been outsourced and privatized, there's an economic boom when the bombs start falling, when they stop and when they start up again—a closed profit-loop of destruction and reconstruction, of tearing down and building up. For companies that are clever and farsighted, like Halliburton and the Carlyle Group, the destroyers and rebuilders are different divisions of the same corporations.*[56]

The Bush administration has taken several important and little-examined measures to institutionalize the privatized warfare model forged in Iraq, making it a permanent fixture of foreign policy. In July 2006, Bowen, the inspector general for Iraq reconstruction, issued a report on "lessons learned" from the various contractor debacles. It concluded that the problems stemmed from insufficient planning and called for the creation of "a deployable reserve corps of contracting personnel who are trained to execute rapid relief and reconstruction contracting during contingency operations" and to "pre-qualify a diverse pool of contractors with expertise in specialized reconstruction areas"—in other words, a standing contractor army. In his 2007 State of the Union address, Bush championed the idea, announcing the creation of a brand-new civilian reserve corps. "Such a corps would function much like our military reserve. It would ease the burden on the Armed Forces by allowing us to hire civilians with critical skills to serve on missions abroad when America needs them," he said. "It would give people across America who do not wear the uniform a chance to serve in the defining struggle of our time."[57]

A year and half into the Iraq occupation, the U.S. State Department launched a new branch: the Office of Reconstruction and Stabilization. On any given day, it is paying private contractors to draw up detailed plans to reconstruct twenty-five different countries that may, for one reason or another,

---

* Lockheed Martin has gone furthest in this direction. In early 2007, it began "buying companies in the $1,000bn-a-year healthcare market," according to *The Financial Times*, and it also snapped up the engineering giant Pacific Architects and Engineers. The wave of acquisitions signified a new era of morbid vertical integration in the disaster capitalism complex: in future conflicts, Lockheed is poised to profit not only from making the weapons and fighter jets but from rebuilding what they destroy, and even from the treating the people injured by its own weapons.

find themselves the target of U.S.-sponsored destruction, from Venezuela to Iran. Corporations and consultants are lined up on "presigned contracts" so that they are ready to leap into action as soon as disaster strikes.[58] For the Bush administration, it was a natural evolution: after claiming it had a right to cause unlimited preemptive destruction, it then pioneered preemptive reconstruction—rebuilding places that have not yet been destroyed.

So in the end, the war in Iraq did create a model economy—it was just not the Tiger on the Tigris that the neocons had advertised. Instead, it was a model for privatized war and reconstruction—a model that quickly became export-ready. Until Iraq, the frontiers of the Chicago crusade had been bound by geography: Russia, Argentina, South Korea. Now a new frontier can open up wherever the next disaster strikes.

PART 7

THE MOVABLE GREEN ZONE

BUFFER ZONES AND BLAST WALLS

Because you are able to start new, you can start fundamentally at the leading edge, which is a very good thing. It is a privilege for you to have that opportunity, because there are other places that haven't had such systems or are burdened with systems that are a hundred or two hundred years old. In a way, this is an advantage for Afghanistan to start anew with the best ideas and the best technical knowledge.

—Paul O'Neill, U.S. Treasury secretary, November 2002, in postinvasion Kabul

CHAPTER 19

BLANKING THE BEACH

"THE SECOND TSUNAMI"

> The tsunami that cleared the shoreline like a giant bulldozer has presented developers with an undreamed-of opportunity, and they have moved quickly to seize it.
>
> —Seth Mydans, *International Herald Tribune*, March 10, 2005[1]

I went to the beach at sunrise, hoping to meet some fishing people before they went out on the turquoise waters for the day. It was July 2005 and the beach was almost deserted, but there was a small cluster of hand-painted wooden catamarans, and beside one of them a small family was getting ready to go to sea. Roger, forty years old and sitting shirtless in his sarong on the sand, was repairing a tangled red net with his twenty-year-old son, Ivan. Jenita, Roger's wife, was circling the boat, waving a small tin of smoldering incense. "Asking for luck," she explained of the ritual, "and safety."

Not so long ago, this beach and dozens like it up and down Sri Lanka's coast had been the site of a frantic rescue mission after the most devastating natural disaster in recent memory—the December 26, 2004, tsunami, which took the lives of 250,000 people and left 2.5 million people homeless throughout the region.[2] I had come to Sri Lanka, one of the hardest-hit countries, six months later to see how the reconstruction efforts here compared with those in Iraq.

My travel companion, Kumari, an activist from Colombo, had been a part of the rescue and rehabilitation effort and had agreed to act as guide and translator through the tsunami-struck region. Our trip began in Arugam Bay, a fishing and faded resort village on the east coast of the island, which was being held up by the government's reconstruction team as the showcase for its plans to "build back better."

That's where we met Roger, who gave us, after only a few minutes, a very different version. He called it "a plan to drive the fishing people from the beach." He claimed that this mass eviction plan long predated the giant wave, but the tsunami, like so many other disasters, was being harnessed to push through a deeply unpopular agenda. For fifteen years, Roger told us, his family had spent fishing season in a thatched hut on the beach in Arugam Bay, near where we were sitting. Along with dozens of other fishing families, they had kept their boats beside their huts and dried their catch on banana leaves in the fine white sand. They mingled easily with tourists, most of whom were Australian and European surfers staying in hostels along the beach, the kind of place with ratty hammocks out front and London club music playing on speakers lodged in palm trees. The restaurants bought fish straight off the boats, and the fishing people, with their colorful traditional lifestyles, provided just the splash of authenticity most rugged travelers were looking for.

For a long time, there was no particular conflict between the hotels and the fishing people in Arugum Bay, in part because the ongoing civil war in Sri Lanka ensured that neither industry could grow beyond a small scale. The east coast of Sri Lanka saw some of the worst of the fighting as it was claimed by both sides—the Liberation Tigers of Tamil Eelam (known as the Tamil Tigers) in the North, and the Sinhalese central government in Colombo—but was never fully controlled by either. Reaching Arugam Bay required navigating a maze of checkpoints and running the risk of getting caught in a shootout or a suicide bombing (the Tamil Tigers are credited with having invented the exploding suicide belt). All the guidebooks contained stern warnings about steering clear of Sri Lanka's volatile east coast; the wave breaks were notoriously good, but only worth the trouble for the seriously hard core.

The breakthrough came in February 2002, when Colombo and the Tigers signed a cease-fire agreement. It wasn't exactly peace but more like a taut pause in the action, one punctured by the occasional bombing or assassination. Despite this precarious state, as soon as the roads were opened, the guidebooks began pumping up the east coast as the next Phuket: great surfing, beautiful beaches, funky hotels, spicy food, full-moon raves . . . "a hot party spot," according to *Lonely Planet*.[3] And Arugam Bay was the center of the action. At the same time, the opening of checkpoints meant that fishing people from around the country could return in large numbers to some of the most plentiful waters along the eastern coast, including Arugam Bay.

The beach was getting crowded. Arugam Bay was zoned as a fishing port, but local hotel owners began complaining that the huts blocked their views, that the fragrance of drying fish turned off their customers (one hotelier, a Dutch expat, told me that "there is such a thing as smell pollution"). Some of the hoteliers started lobbying the local government to relocate the boats and fishing huts to a different bay, one less popular with foreigners. The villagers pushed back, pointing out that they had been living on these lands for generations, and that Arugam Bay was more than a boat launch — it was fresh water and electricity, schools for their children and buyers for their catch.

These tensions threatened to explode six months before the tsunami hit, when there was a mysterious fire on the beach in the middle of the night. Twenty-four fishing huts were reduced to ash. Roger and his family, he told me, "lost everything, our belongings, our nets and ropes." Kumari and I spoke with many fishing people in Arugam Bay, and all insisted that the fire was arson. They blamed the hotel owners, who obviously wanted the beach to themselves.

But if the fire really was a bid to scare off the fishing people, it didn't work; the villagers became more determined than ever to stay, and the people who lost their huts quickly rebuilt.

When the tsunami came, it did what the fire couldn't: it cleared the beach completely. Every single fragile structure was washed away — every boat, every fishing hut, as well as every tourist cabana and bungalow. In a community of only 4,000, about 350 were killed, most of them people like Roger, Ivan and Jenita, who make their living from the sea.[4] And yet, underneath the rubble and the carnage was what the tourism industry had been angling for all along — a pristine beach, scrubbed clean of all the messy signs of people working, a vacation Eden. It was the same up and down the coast: once the rubble was cleared away, what was left was . . . paradise.

When the emergency subsided and fishing families returned to the spots where their homes once stood, they were greeted by police who forbade them to rebuild. "New rules," they were told — no homes on the beach, and everything had to be at least two hundred meters back from the high-water mark. Most would have accepted building farther from the water, but there was no available land there, leaving the fishing people with nowhere to go. And the new "buffer zone" was being imposed not only in Arugam Bay but along the entire east coast. The beaches were off-limits.

The tsunami killed approximately thirty-five thousand Sri Lankans and displaced nearly a million. Small-boat fishing people like Roger made up 80 percent of the victims; in some areas the number was closer to 98 percent. In order to receive food rations and small relief allowances, hundreds of thousands of people moved away from the beach and into temporary camps inland, many of them long, grim barracks made of tin sheet that trapped the heat so unbearably that many abandoned them to sleep outside. As time dragged on, the camps became dirty and disease ridden and were patrolled by menacing, machine-gun-wielding soldiers.

Officially, the government said the buffer zone was a safety measure, meant to prevent a repeat of the devastation should another tsunami strike. On the surface it made sense, but there was a glaring problem with that rationale—it was not being applied to the tourism industry. On the contrary, hotels were being encouraged to expand onto the valuable oceanfront where fishing people had lived and worked. Resorts were completely exempted from the buffer-zone rule—as long as they classified their construction, no matter how elaborate or close to the water, as "repair," they were free and clear. So all along the beach in Arugam Bay, construction workers hammered and drilled. "Don't tourists have to fear a tsunami?" Roger wanted to know.

To him and his colleagues, the buffer zone looked like little more than an excuse for the government to do what it had wanted to do before the wave: clear the beach of fishing people. The catch they used to pull from the waters had been enough to sustain their families, but it did not contribute to economic growth as measured by institutions like the World Bank, and the land where their huts once stood could clearly be put to more profitable use. Shortly before I arrived, a document called the "Arugam Bay Resource Development Plan" was leaked to the press, and it confirmed the fishing community's worst fears. The federal government had commissioned a team of international consultants to develop a reconstruction blueprint for Arugam Bay, and this plan was the result. Even though it had been only the beachfront properties that were damaged by the tsunami, with most of the town still standing, it called for Arugam Bay to be leveled and rebuilt, transformed from a hippie-charming seaside town into a high-end "boutique tourism destination"—five-star resorts, luxury $300-a-night ecotourism chalets, a floatplane pier and a helipad. The report enthused that Arugam Bay was to serve as a model for up to thirty new nearby "tourism zones," turning the previously war-torn east coast of Sri Lanka into a South Asian Riviera.[5]

Missing from all the artists' impressions and blueprints were the victims of the tsunami—the hundreds of fishing families who used to live and work on the beach. The report explained that villagers would be moved to more suitable locations, some several kilometers away and far from the ocean. Making matters worse, the $80 million redevelopment project was to be financed with aid money raised in the name of the victims of the tsunami.

It was the weeping faces of these fishing families and others like them in Thailand and Indonesia that had triggered the historic outpouring of international generosity after the tsunami—it had been their relatives piled up in mosques, their wailing mothers trying to identify a drowned baby, their children swept to sea. Yet for communities like Arugam Bay, the "reconstruction" meant nothing less than the deliberate destruction of their culture and way of life and the theft of their land. As Kumari said, the entire reconstruction process would result in "victimizing the victims, exploiting the exploited."

When the plan got out, it sparked outrage across the country, and nowhere more than in Arugam Bay. As soon as we arrived in town, Kumari and I stumbled into a crowd of several hundred demonstrators dressed in a kaleidoscopic mix of saris, sarongs, hijabs and flip-flops. They were gathered on the beach and were just beginning a march that would pass in front of the hotels, then on to the neighboring town of Pottuvil, home of the local government.

As they marched past the hotels, a young man in a white T-shirt with a red megaphone led the demonstrators in a call-and-response. "We don't want, we don't want . . ." he called out, and the crowd shouted back, "Tourist hotels!" Then he shouted, "Whites . . ." and they cried, "Get out!" (Kumari translated from Tamil with apologies.) Another young man, skin toughened by the sun and the ocean, took over megaphone duties and yelled, "We *do* want, we *do* want . . ." and the answers came flying: "Our land back!" "Our homes back!" "A fishing port!" "Our aid money!" "Famine, famine!" he shouted, and the crowd replied, "Fisher people are facing famine!"

Outside the gates of the district government, leaders of the march accused their elected representatives of abandonment, of corruption, of spending aid money meant for the fishing people "on dowries for their daughters and jewelry for their wives." They spoke of special favors handed out to the Sinhalese, of discrimination against Muslims, of the "foreigners profiting from our misery."

It seemed unlikely that their chants would have much effect. In Colombo I spoke with the director general of the Sri Lankan Tourist Board, Seenivasagam Kalaiselvam, a middle-aged bureaucrat with a bad habit of quoting from his country's multimillion-dollar "brand personality profile." I asked him what would become of the fishing people in places like Arugam Bay. He leaned back in a rattan chair and explained. "In the past, in the coastal belt, there were a lot of unauthorized establishments . . . not constructed according to the tourism plan. With the tsunami, the good thing that happened to tourism is that most of these unauthorized establishments [have been] affected by the tsunami, and the buildings are no longer there." If fishing people come back and rebuild, he explained, "We again will be forced to demolish. . . . The beach will be clean."

It hadn't started this way. When Kumari first came to the east coast in the days after the tsunami, none of the official aid had arrived yet. That meant everyone was a relief worker, a medic, a gravedigger. The ethnic barriers that had divided this region suddenly melted away. "The Muslim side was running to the Tamil side to bury the dead," she recalled, "and Tamil people were running to the Muslim side to eat and drink. People from the interior of the country were sending two lunch parcels each day from each house, which was a lot because they are very poor. It was not to get anything back; it was just the feeling 'I have to support my neighbor; we have to support the sisters, the brothers, the daughters, the mothers.' Just that."

Similar cross-cultural aid was breaking out across the country. Tamil teenagers drove their tractors from the farms to help find bodies. Christian children donated their school uniforms to be turned into white Muslim funeral shrouds, while Hindu women gave their white saris. It was as if this invasion of salt water and rubble was so humblingly powerful that, in addition to grinding up homes and buckling highways, it also scrubbed away intractable hatreds, blood feuds and the tally of who last killed whom. For Kumari, who had done years of frustrating work with peace groups trying to bridge the divides, it was overwhelming to see such tragedy met with such decency. Instead of endlessly talking about peace, Sri Lankans, in their moment of greatest stress, were actually living it.

It also seemed that the country could count on international support for its recovery efforts. At first, the help wasn't coming from governments, which were slow to respond, but from individuals who saw the disaster on TV: schoolchildren in Europe held bake sales and bottle drives, musicians organized star-studded concerts, religious groups collected clothes, blankets and money. Citizens then demanded that their governments match their generosity with official aid. In six months, $13 billion was raised—a world record.[6]

In the first months, much of the reconstruction money reached its intended recipients: NGOs and aid agencies brought emergency food and water, tents and temporary lean-tos; rich countries sent medical teams and supplies. The camps were built as a stopgap, to give people a roof while permanent homes were constructed. There was certainly enough money to get those homes built. But when I was in Sri Lanka six months later, progress had all but stopped; there were almost no permanent homes, and the temporary camps were starting to look less like emergency shelters and more like entrenched shantytowns.

Aid workers complained that the Sri Lankan government was putting up roadblocks at every turn—first declaring the buffer zone, then refusing to provide alternative land to build on, then commissioning an endless series of studies and master plans from outside experts. As the bureaucrats argued, survivors of the tsunami waited in the sweltering inland camps, living off rations, too far from the ocean to begin fishing again. While the delays were often blamed on "red tape" and poor management, there was in fact far more at stake.

Before the Wave: Foiled Plans

The grand plan to remake Sri Lanka predated the tsunami by two years. It began when the civil war ended and the usual players descended on the country to plot Sri Lanka's entry into the world economy—most prominently USAID, the World Bank and its offshoot the Asian Development Bank. A consensus emerged that Sri Lanka's most significant competitive advantage lay in the fact that it was one of last places left uncolonized by go-go globalization, a by-product of its long war. For such a small country, Sri Lanka still had a remarkable amount of surviving wildlife—leopards, monkeys, thousands of wild elephants. Its beaches were strangers to high-rises, and its mountains were dotted with Hindu, Buddhist and Muslim temples and holy sites. Best of all, raved USAID, it was "all contained in a space the size of West Virginia."[7]

Under the plan, Sri Lanka's jungles, which provided such effective cover for guerrilla fighters, would be opened up to adventure ecotourists, who would ride the elephants and swing like Tarzan through the canopies the way they do in Costa Rica. Its religions, accomplices in so much bloodshed, would be retrofitted to nourish the spiritual needs of Western visitors—Buddhist monks could run meditation centers, Hindu women could perform colorful dances at hotels, Ayurvedic medical clinics could soothe aches and pains.

In short, the rest of Asia could keep the sweatshops, call centers and frenetic stock markets; Sri Lanka would be there waiting when the captains of those industries needed a place to rest up. Precisely because of the enormous wealth created in the other outposts of deregulated capitalism, money would be no object when it came to enjoying the perfectly calibrated combination of luxury and wilderness, adventure and attentive service. Sri Lanka's future, the foreign consultants were convinced, rested with chains like Aman Resorts, which has recently opened two stunning properties on the southern coast, with rooms going for $800 a night and plunge pools in every suite.

The U.S. government was so enthusiastic about Sri Lanka's potential as a high-end tourism destination, with all the possibilities for resort chains and tour operators, that USAID launched a program to organize the Sri Lankan tourism industry into a powerful Washington-style lobby group. It takes credit for increasing the budget for tourism promotion "from less than $500,000 a year up to approximately $10 million a year."[8] The U.S. embassy, meanwhile, launched the Competitiveness Program, an outpost mandated to advance U.S. economic interests in the country. The program's director, a graying economist named John Varley, told me that he thought the Sri Lanka Tourist Board was thinking small when it talked about attracting a million tourists a year by the end of the decade. "Personally, I think they could double that." Peter Harrold, an Englishman who directs the World Bank operation in Sri Lanka, told me, "I've always thought of Bali as the perfect comparator."

There is no question that high-end tourism is a bankable growth market. The overall revenues for luxury hotels, where rooms cost an average of $405 a night, went up a rather striking 70 percent between 2001 and 2005—not bad for a period that included the post–September 11 slump, the war in Iraq and spiraling fuel costs. In many ways, the phenomenal growth of the sector is a by-product of the extreme inequality that resulted from the generalized triumph of Chicago School economics. Regardless of the overall state of the economy, there is now a large enough elite made up of new multi-millionaires and billionaires for Wall Street to see the group as "superconsumers," able to carry consumer demand all on their own. Ajay Kapur, the former head of Citigroup Smith Barney's global equity strategy group in New York, encourages his clients to invest in his "Plutonomy basket" of stocks, featuring companies like Bulgari, Porsche, Four Seasons and Sotheby's. "If plutonomy continues, which we think it will, if income inequality is allowed to persist and widen, the plutonomy basket should continue to do very well."[9]

But before Sri Lanka could fulfill its destiny as a playground for the plutonomy set, there were a few areas that needed some drastic improvements—fast. First off, to attract top-notch resorts, the government had to drop the barriers to private land ownership (roughly 80 percent of Sri Lanka's land was owned by the state).[10] It needed more "flexible" labor laws under which investors would staff their resorts. And it needed to modernize its infrastructure—highways, swank airports, better water and electricity systems. However, since Sri Lanka had driven itself deep into debt buying weapons, the government could not pay for all these rapid upgrades on its own. The usual deals were on offer: loans from the World Bank and IMF in exchange for agreements to open the economy to privatization and "public-private partnerships."

All these plans and terms were neatly laid out in *Regaining Sri Lanka*, the country's World Bank-approved shock therapy program finalized in early 2003. Its prime local advocate was a Sri Lankan politician/entrepreneur named Mano Tittawella, a man who bears a striking resemblance to Newt Gingrich, both physically and ideologically.[11]

Like all such shock therapy plans, *Regaining Sri Lanka* demanded many sacrifices in the name of kick-starting rapid economic growth. Millions of people would have to leave traditional villages to free up the beaches for tourists and the land for resorts and highways. What fishing remained would be dominated by large industrial trawlers operating out of deep ports—not wooden boats that launch from the beaches.[12] And of course, as has been the case in similar circumstances from Buenos Aires to Baghdad, there would be mass layoffs at state companies, and the prices of services would have to go up.

The problem for the plan's advocates was that many Sri Lankans simply didn't believe that the sacrifices would pay off. This was 2003, and the starry-eyed faith in globalization had long since been extinguished, especially after the horrors of the Asian economic crisis. The legacy of war also proved to be an obstacle. Tens of thousands of Sri Lankans had lost their lives in the conflict in the name of "nation," "homeland" and "territory." Now, when peace had finally arrived, the poorest among them were being asked to give up the little plots of land and property they had—a vegetable garden, a simple house, a boat—so that a Marriott or a Hilton could build a golf course (and villagers could pursue careers as street hawkers in Colombo). It seemed like a lousy deal, and Sri Lankans responded accordingly.

Regaining Sri Lanka was rejected first through a wave of militant strikes and street protests, then, decisively, at the polls. In April 2004, Sri Lankans defied all the foreign experts and their local partners and voted in a coalition of center-leftists and self-identified Marxists who vowed to scrap the entire *Regaining Sri Lanka* plan.[13] At the time, many of the key privatization schemes had not yet gone through, including water and electricity, and the highway projects were being challenged in court. For those dreaming of building a plutonomy playground, it was a major setback: 2004 was supposed to have been Year One of the new investor-friendly, privatized Sri Lanka; now all bets were off.

Eight months after those fateful elections, the tsunami hit. Among those mourning the demise of *Regaining Sri Lanka*, the significance of the event was understood immediately. The newly elected government would need billions from foreign creditors to reconstruct the homes, roads, schools and railways destroyed in the storm—and those creditors knew well that when faced with a devastating crisis, even the most committed economic national-ists suddenly become flexible. As for the militant farmers and fishing people who had blocked roadways and staged mass rallies to derail their previous at-tempts to clear the land for development, well, Sri Lanka's villagers were otherwise occupied at the moment.

After the Wave: A Second Chance

In Colombo, the national government moved instantly to prove to the wealthy countries who control the aid dollars that it was ready to renounce its past. President Chandrika Kumaratunga, elected on an overtly antipriva-tization platform, claimed that the tsunami had been, for her, a kind of reli-gious epiphany, helping her to see the free-market light. She traveled to the storm-ravaged coast and, standing amid the rubble, announced, "We are a country blessed with so many natural resources, and we have not made use of them fully. . . . So nature itself must have thought 'enough is enough' and whacked us from all sides and taught us a lesson to be together."[14] It was a novel interpretation—the tsunami as divine punishment for failing to sell off Sri Lanka's beaches and forests.

The penance began immediately. Just four days after the wave hit, her government pushed a bill through that paved the way for water privatization, a plan citizens had been forcefully resisting for years. Of course now, with the country still swamped with sea water and graves not yet dug, few even knew it had happened—much like the timing of Iraq's new oil law. The government also chose this moment of extreme hardship to make life even harder by raising the price of gasoline—a move designed to send lenders an unmistakable message about Colombo's fiscal responsibility. It also began developing legislation to break up the national electricity company, with plans to open it up to the private sector.[15]

Herman Kumara, the head of Sri Lanka's National Fisheries Solidarity Movement, which represents the small boats, referred to the reconstruction as "a second tsunami of corporate globalization." He saw it as a deliberate attempt to exploit his constituents when they were most injured and weakened—as pillage follows war, so this second tsunami rushed in after the first. "People were vehemently opposed to these policies in the past," he told me. "But now they are starving in the camps, and they are just thinking about how to survive the next day—they don't have a place to sleep, they don't have a place to be, they have lost their source of income, they have no idea how they will feed themselves in the future. So it's in that situation that the government pushes ahead with this plan. When people recover, they will find out what had been decided, but by then the damage will already be done."

If the Washington lenders were able to move quickly to exploit the tsunami, it was because they had done something remarkably similar before. The dress rehearsal for posttsunami disaster capitalism took place in a little-examined episode following Hurricane Mitch.

In October 1998, for an entire interminable week, Mitch had parked itself over Central America, lashing the coasts and mountains of Honduras, Guatemala and Nicaragua, swallowing villages whole and killing more than nine thousand people. The already impoverished countries could not dig themselves out without generous foreign aid—and it came, but at a steep price. In the two months after Mitch struck, with the country still knee-deep in rubble, corpses and mud, the Honduran congress passed laws allowing the privatization of airports, seaports and highways and fast-tracked plans to privatize the state telephone company, the national electric company and parts of the water sector. It overturned progressive land-reform laws, making it far easier for foreigners to buy and sell property, and rammed through a radically pro-business mining law (drafted by industry) that lowered environmental standards and made it easier to evict people from homes that stood in the way of new mines.[16]

It was much the same in neighboring countries: in the same two months post-Mitch, Guatemala announced plans to sell off its phone system, and Nicaragua did likewise, along with its electric company and its petroleum sector. According to *The Wall Street Journal*, "The World Bank and International Monetary Fund had thrown their weight behind the [telecom] sale, making it a condition for release of roughly $47 million in aid annually over three years and linking it to about $4.4 billion in foreign-debt relief for Nicaragua."[17] Phone privatization had nothing to do with hurricane reconstruction, of course, except inside the logic of the disaster capitalists at Washington's financial institutions.

Over the next few years, the sales went through, often at prices far below market value. The buyers, for the most part, were former state-owned companies from other countries that had been privatized themselves and were now scouring the globe for new purchases that would increase their share prices. Telmex, Mexico's privatized phone company, snapped up Guatemala's telecom company; the Spanish energy company Unión Fenosa bought up Nicaragua's energy companies; San Francisco International Airport, now a private company, bought all four Honduran airports. And Nicaragua sold off 40 percent of its telephone company for only $33 million, when PricewaterhouseCoopers had estimated the value at $80 million.[18] "Destruction carries with it an opportunity for foreign investment," announced Guatemala's foreign minister on a trip to the World Economic Forum in Davos in 1999.[19]

By the time the tsunami hit, Washington was ready to take the Mitch model to the next level—aiming not just at individual new laws but at direct corporate control over the reconstruction. Any country hit by a disaster on the scale of the 2004 tsunami needs a comprehensive plan for reconstruction, one that will make the wisest use of the influx of foreign aid and ensure that the funds reach their intended recipients. But Sri Lanka's president, under pressure from Washington lenders, decided that the planning could not be entrusted to her government's elected politicians. Instead, just one week after the tsunami leveled the coasts, she created a brand-new body called the Task Force to Rebuild the Nation. This group, and not Sri Lanka's Parliament, would have full power to develop and implement a master plan for a new Sri Lanka. The task force was made up of the country's most powerful business executives from banking and industry. And not just any industry—five of the ten members of the task force had direct holdings in the beach tourism sector, representing some of the largest resorts in the country.[20] There was no one from the fishing or farming sectors on the task force, not a single environmental expert or scientist or even a disaster-reconstruction specialist. The chair was Mano Tittawella, the former privatization czar. "This is an opportunity to build a model nation," he declared.[21]

The creation of the task force represented a new kind of corporate coup d'état, one achieved through the force of a natural disaster. As in so many other countries, in Sri Lanka, Chicago School policies had been blocked by the normal rules of democracy; the 2004 elections proved that. But with the country's citizens pulling together to meet a national emergency, and politicians desperate to unlock aid money, the express wishes of voters could be summarily brushed aside and replaced with direct unelected rule by industry—a first for disaster capitalism.

Somehow, in only ten days, and without leaving the capital, the business leaders on the task force were able to draft a complete national reconstruction blueprint, from housing to highways. It was this plan that called for the buffer zones and that kindly exempted hotels. The task force also redirected the aid money to the superhighways and industrial fishing ports that had met so much resistance before the catastrophe. "We see this economic agenda as a bigger disaster than the tsunami, which is why we had been fighting so hard to prevent it before and why we defeated it in the last elections," Sarath Fernando, a Sri Lankan land-rights activist told me. "But now, just three weeks after the tsunami, they give us the same plan. It's obvious that they had it all ready to go before."*

Washington backed up the task force with the kind of reconstruction aid that was by now familiar from Iraq: megacontracts to its own companies. CH2M Hill, the engineering and construction giant from Colorado, had been awarded $28.5 million to oversee other major contractors in Iraq. Despite its central role in the Baghdad reconstruction debacle, it was given an additional $33 million contract in Sri Lanka (later expanded to $48 million), primarily to work on three deep-water harbors for industrial fishing fleets and to build a new bridge to Arugam Bay, part of the plan to turn the town into a "tourist paradise."[22] Both of these programs—carried out in the name of tsunami relief—were disastrous for the primary victims of the tsunami,

---

* Fernando is head of the Movement for Land and Agricultural Reform (MONLAR), a coalition of Sri Lankan NGOs that began calling for "a people's reconstruction process" shortly after the disaster.

since the trawlers scooped up their fish, and the hotels didn't want them on the beach. As Kumari put it, "It's not just that the 'aid' isn't aiding, it is that it is hurting."

When I asked him why the U.S. government was spending its aid money on projects that ensured the displacement of tsunami survivors, John Varley, director of USAID's Competitiveness Program, explained that "you don't want to restrict the aid so it only goes to tsunami victims. . . . Let it be for the benefit of all Sri Lanka; let it contribute to growth." Varley compared the plan to an elevator in a high-rise building: on the first trip it picks up one group of passengers and takes them to the top, where they create wealth that allows the elevator to go back down and pick more people up. The people waiting at the bottom have to know that the elevator will be back for them too—eventually.

The only direct money that the U.S. government was spending on small-scale fishing people was a $1 million grant to "upgrade" the temporary shelters where they were being warehoused while the beaches were redeveloped.[23] It was a good indication that the tin-and-particle-board shelters were temporary in name only; that they were indeed destined to become permanent shantytowns—the kind that ring most major cities in the global South. There are no great relief drives to help the people who live in those slums, of course, but the tsunami victims were supposed to be different. The world watched them lose their homes and livelihoods on live TV, and the arbitrariness of their fate provoked a visceral, global feeling that what was lost needed and deserved to be replaced—not through trickle-down economics, but directly, with hand-to-hand aid. But the World Bank and USAID understood something that most of us did not: that soon enough, the distinctiveness of the tsunami survivors would fade and they would melt into the billions of faceless poor worldwide, so many of whom already live in tin shacks without water. The proliferation of these shacks has become as much an accepted feature of the global economy as the explosion of $800-a-night hotels.

In one of the most desolate inland camps on the southern coast of Sri Lanka, I met a young mother named Renuka, arrestingly beautiful even in rags, and one of the people waiting for Varley's elevator. Her youngest child, a girl, was six months old, born two days after the tsunami. Renuka had summoned superhuman strength to grab both of her boys and run, nine months pregnant and in water up to her neck, away from the wave. Yet after this extraordinary feat of survival, she and her family were now quietly going hungry on a parched piece of land in the middle of nowhere. A couple of canoes, donated by a well-meaning NGO, made a pitiful sight: three kilometers from the water, and with not even a bicycle for transportation, they were little more than a cruel reminder of a former life. She asked us to carry a message to everyone who was trying to help the tsunami survivors. "If you have something for me," she said, "put it in my hand."

The Wider Wave

Sri Lanka wasn't the only country that got hit by this second tsunami — similar stories of land and law grabs have come out of Thailand, the Maldives, and Indonesia. In India, tsunami survivors in Tamil Nadu were left so impoverished that up to 150 women were driven to sell their kidneys in order to buy food. An aid worker explained to *The Guardian* that the state government "would prefer the coast was used to build hotels, but the result is desperate people." All the tsunami-struck countries imposed "buffer zones" preventing villagers from rebuilding on the coasts, freeing up the land for increased development. (In Aceh, Indonesia, the zones were two kilometers wide, though the government was eventually forced to repeal the edict.)[24]

A year after the tsunami, the respected NGO ActionAid, which monitors foreign aid spending, published the results of an extensive survey of fifty thousand tsunami survivors in five countries. The same patterns repeated everywhere: residents were barred from rebuilding, but hotels were showered with incentives; temporary camps were miserable militarized holding pens, and almost no permanent reconstruction had been done; entire ways of life were being extinguished. It concluded that the setbacks could not be chalked up to the usual villains of poor communication, underfunding or corruption. The problems were structural and deliberate: "Governments have largely failed in their responsibility to provide land for permanent housing," the report concluded. "They have stood by or been complicit as land has been grabbed and coastal communities pushed aside in favour of commercial interests."[25]

When it came to posttsunami opportunism, however, nowhere compared with the Maldives, perhaps the least understood of the affected countries. There, the government wasn't satisfied with merely clearing the poor people from the coasts — it used the tsunami to try to clear its citizens out of the vast majority of the country's livable zones.

The Maldives, a chain of roughly two hundred inhabited islands off the coast of India, is a tourism republic in the same way that certain Central

American countries used to be called banana republics. Its export product is not tropical fruit but tropical leisure, with a staggering 90 percent of the state's revenues coming directly from beach holidays.[26] The leisure that the Maldives sells is a particularly decadent, enticing kind. Nearly one hundred of its islands are "resort islands," patches of lush vegetation surrounded by halos of white sand that are entirely controlled by hotels, cruise lines or wealthy individuals. Some are leased for up to fifty years. The most luxurious of the Maldivian islands cater to an elite clientele (Tom Cruise and Katie Holmes on their honeymoon, as an example) that is drawn not just to the beauty and the diving but to the promise of total seclusion that only private islands can provide.

With architecture "inspired" by traditional fishing villages, the spa-resorts compete over who can pack their thatched huts on stilts with the most exciting array of plutonomy toys and perks—Bose Surround Sound home entertainment, Philippe Starck fixtures in outdoor bathrooms, sheets so fine that they practically dissolve on touch. The islands also outdo one another to erase the boundaries between land and sea—the villas at Coco Palm are built over the lagoon and have rope ladders from the decks into the water beneath, the Four Seasons' sleeping quarters "float" on the ocean, and the Hilton boasts the first underwater restaurant, built on a coral reef. Many suites feature maids' quarters, and on one private island, a twenty-four-hour-a-day "dedicated Maldivian butler—a 'Thakuru' " who takes care of such details as "how you like your martini—shaken or stirred." Villas at these James Bondian resorts go as high as $5,000 a night.[27]

The man who reigns over this pleasure kingdom is Asia's longest-running ruler, President Maumoon Abdul Gayoom, who has held on to power since 1978. During his tenure, the government has jailed opposition leaders and been accused of torturing "dissidents" for such crimes as writing for antigovernment Web sites.[28] With critics kept out of sight on prison islands, Gayoom and his entourage have been free to lavish their attention on the tourism business.

Before the tsunami, the Maldives government had been looking to expand the number of resort islands to meet the growing demand for luxury getaways. It faced the usual obstacle: people. Maldivians are subsistence fishers, many of whom live in traditional villages scattered throughout the island atolls. This way of life created some challenges because the rustic charm of seeing fish skinned on the beach is definitely not the Maldives scene. Well before the tsunami, the Gayoom government had been trying to persuade its citizens to move to a handful of larger, more heavily populated islands that tourists rarely visit. Those islands were supposed to offer better protection from rising waters caused by global warming. But it was difficult even for a repressive regime to uproot tens of thousands of people from their ancestral islands, and the "population consolidation" program was largely unsuccessful.[29]

After the tsunami, Gayoom's government immediately announced that the disaster proved that many islands were "unsafe and unsuitable for habitation" and launched a far more aggressive relocation program than it had previously attempted, declaring that anyone who wanted state assistance with tsunami recovery would need to move to one of five designated "safe islands."[30] The entire populations of several islands have already been evacuated and more are in process, conveniently freeing up more land for tourism.

The Maldives government claims that the Safe Island Program, supported and funded by the World Bank and other agencies, is being driven by public demand to live on "bigger and safer islands." But many islanders say they would have stayed on their home islands if the infrastructure had been fixed. As ActionAid put it, "People are left with no choice but to move as it is a precondition of housing and livelihood rehabilitation."[31]

Attracting further cynicism about the safety rationale was the fact that the government's concerns evaporated when it came to all the hotels built with precarious architecture on low-lying islands. Not only were the resorts subject to no safety evacuations but, in December 2005, one year after the tsunami, the Gayoom government announced that thirty-five new islands were available to be leased to resorts for up to fifty years.[32] Meanwhile, on the so-called safe islands, unemployment was rampant, and violence was breaking out between the newcomers and the original residents.

Militarized Gentrification

In a way, the second tsunami was just a particularly shocking dose of economic shock therapy: because the storm did such an effective job of clearing the beach, a process of displacement and gentrification that would normally unfold over years took place in a matter of days or weeks. What it looked like was hundreds of thousands of poor, brown-skinned people (the fishing people deemed "unproductive" by the World Bank) being moved against their wishes to make room for ultrarich, mostly light-skinned people (the "high-yield" tourists). The two economic poles of globalization, the ones that seem to live in different centuries, not countries, were suddenly put in direct conflict over the same pieces of coastline, one demanding the right to work, the other demanding the right to play. Backed up by the guns of local police and private security, it was militarized gentrification, class war on the beach.

Some of the most direct clashes took place in Thailand, where, within twenty-four hours of the wave, developers sent in armed private security guards to fence in land they had been coveting for resorts. In some cases the guards wouldn't even let survivors search their old properties for the bodies of their children.[33] The Thailand Tsunami Survivors and Supporters group was hastily convened to deal with the land grabs. One of its first statements declared that, for "businessmen-politicians, the tsunami was the answer to their prayers, since it literally wiped these coastal areas clean of the communities which had previously stood in the way of their plans for resorts, hotels, casinos and shrimp farms. To them, all these coastal areas are now open land!"[34]

Open land. In colonial times, it was a quasi-legal doctrine—*terra nullius*. If the land was declared empty or "wasted," it could be seized and its people eliminated without remorse. In the countries where the tsunami hit, the idea of open land is weighted with this ugly historical resonance, evoking stolen wealth and violent attempts to "civilize" the natives. Nijam, a fisherman I met on the beach in Arugam Bay, saw no real difference. "The government thinks our nets and our fish are ugly and messy, that's why they want us off the beach. In order to satisfy foreigners, they are treating their own people as if they are uncivilized." Rubble, it seemed, was the new *terra nullius*.

When I met Nijam, he was with a group of fishing people who had just returned from the sea, their eyes bloodshot from the salt water. When I raised the government's plan to move the small-boat fishers to another beach, several of them waved broad fish-gutting knives and vowed to "gather their people and strength" and fight for their land. At first, they said they had welcomed the restaurants and hotels. "But now," said a fisherman named Abdul, "because we gave them a little of our land, they want it all." Another, Mansoor, pointed overhead to the palm trees giving us shade, strong enough to withstand the force of the tsunami. "It was my great-great-grandparents who planted these trees. Why should we move to another beach?" One of his relatives made a pledge: "We will leave here only when the sea runs dry."

The influx of reconstruction aid from the tsunami was supposed to offer Sri Lankans a chance to build a lasting peace after suffering so much more than their share of loss. In Arugam Bay, and all along the eastern coast, it seemed to be starting another kind of war, one over who would benefit from those funds—Sinhalese, Tamil or Muslim—and, most of all, whether the real benefits would go to foreigners, at the expense of all locals.

I started to get a sinking feeling of déjà vu, as if the wind was changing and this was about to become another "reconstructed" country slipping back into perpetual destruction. I had heard very similar grievances a year earlier in Iraq, about the reconstruction favoring the Kurds and certain select Shia. Several aid workers I met in Colombo had told me how much more they liked working in Sri Lanka over Iraq or Afghanistan—here, NGOs were still seen as neutral, even helpful, and reconstruction wasn't yet a dirty word. But that was changing. In the capital, I had seen posters featuring crude caricatures of Western aid workers stuffing themselves with money while Sri Lankans starved.

The NGOs bore the brunt of the anger at the reconstruction because they were intensely visible, slapping their logos on every available surface along the coast, while the World Bank, USAID and government officials dreaming up Bali plans rarely left their urban offices. It was ironic, since the aid organizers were the only ones offering any kind of help at all—but also inevitable, because what they offered was so inadequate. Part of the problem was that the aid complex had become so large and so cut off from the people it was serving that the lifestyles of its staffers became, in Sri Lanka, a kind of national obsession. Almost everyone I met commented on what one priest called "the NGO wild life": high-end hotels, beachfront villas and the ultimate lightning rod for popular rage, the brand-new white sport utility vehicles. All the aid organizations had them, monstrous things that were far too wide and powerful for the country's narrow dirt roads. All day long they went roaring past the camps, forcing everyone to eat their dust, their logos billowing on flags in the breeze—Oxfam, World Vision, Save the Children—as if they were visitors from a far-off NGO World. In a country as hot as Sri Lanka, these cars, with their tinted windows and blasting air conditioners, were more than modes of transportation; they were rolling microclimates.

Seeing this resentment build, I couldn't help wondering how long before Sri Lanka went the way of Iraq and Afghanistan, where the reconstruction looked so much like robbery that aid workers became targets. It happened shortly after I left: seventeen Sri Lankans working on tsunami relief for the international NGO Action Against Hunger were massacred in their office near the east-coast port city of Trincomelee. It sparked a new wave of vicious fighting, and tsunami reconstruction was stopped in its tracks. Many aid organizations, fearing for the safety of their staff after several more attacks, left the country. Others shifted focus to the south, the government-controlled area, leaving the harder-hit east and Tamil-controlled north without aid. These decisions only deepened the sense that the reconstruction funds were being spent unfairly, especially after a study conducted in late 2006 found that even though the majority of tsunami-hit homes were still in ruins, the one exception was the president's own electoral district in the south, where a miraculous 173 percent of the homes had been rebuilt.[35]

The aid workers still on the ground in the east, near Arugam Bay, were now dealing with a new wave of displaced people—the hundreds of thousands forced to leave their homes because of the violence. United Nations workers "who originally were contracted to rebuild schools destroyed by the tsunami have been redirected to build toilets for people displaced by the fighting," reported *The New York Times*.[36]

In July 2006, the Tamil Tigers announced that the cease-fire was officially over; the reconstruction was off, and the war was back on. Less than a year later, over four thousand people had been killed in posttsunami fighting. Only a fraction of the homes hit by the tsunami had ever been rebuilt along the east coast, but of the new structures, hundreds were already punctured with bullet holes, just-installed windows were shattered by explosives and brand-new roofs had collapsed from shelling.

It's impossible to say how much the decision to use the tsunami as an opportunity for disaster capitalism contributed to the return to civil war. The peace had always been precarious, and there was bad faith on all sides. One thing was certain, though: if peace was to take root in Sri Lanka, it needed to outweigh the benefits of war including the tangible economic benefits flowing from a war economy, in which the army takes care of the families of its soldiers and the Tamil Tigers look after the families of its fighters and suicide bombers.

The enormous outpouring of generosity after the tsunami had held out the rare possibility of a genuine peace dividend—the resources to imagine a more equitable country, to repair shattered communities in ways that would rebuild trust as well as buildings and roads. Instead, Sri Lanka (like Iraq) received what the University of Ottawa political scientist Roland Paris has termed "a peace penalty"—the imposition of a cutthroat, combative economic model that made life harder for a majority of people at the very moment when what they needed most was reconciliation and an easing of tensions.[37] In truth, the brand of peace Sri Lanka was offered was its own kind of war. Continued violence promised land, sovereignty and glory. What did corporate peace offer, besides the certainty of landlessness in the immediate term and John Varley's elusive elevator in the long term?

Everywhere the Chicago School crusade has triumphed, it has created a permanent underclass of between 25 and 60 percent of the population. It is always a form of war. But when that warlike economic model of mass evictions and discarded cultures is imposed in a country that is already ravaged by disaster and scarred by ethnic conflict, the dangers are far greater. There are, as Keynes argued all those years ago, political consequences to this kind of punitive peace—including the outbreak of even bloodier wars.

CHAPTER 20

DISASTER APARTHEID

A WORLD OF GREEN ZONES
AND RED ZONES

> **Shelve the abiding fiction that disasters do not discriminate—that they flatten everything in their path with "democratic" disregard. Plagues zero in on the dispossessed, on those forced to build their lives in the path of danger. AIDS is no different.**
>
> —Hein Marais, South African writer, 2006[1]

> **Katrina was not unforeseeable. It was the result of a political structure that subcontracts its responsibility to private contractors and abdicates its responsibility altogether.**
>
> —Harry Belafonte, American musician and civil rights activist, September 2005[2]

During the second week of September 2005, I was in New Orleans with my husband, Avi, as well as Andrew, with whom I had traveled in Iraq, shooting documentary footage in the still partially flooded city. As the nightly six o'clock curfew descended, we found ourselves driving in circles, unable to find our way. The traffic lights were out, and half the street signs had been blown over or twisted sideways by the storm. Debris and water obstructed passage along many roads, and most of the people trying to navigate the obstacles were, like us, out-of-towners with no idea where they were going.

The accident was a bad one: a T-bone at full speed in the middle of a major intersection. Our car spun out into a traffic light, went through a wrought-iron fence and parked in a porch. The injuries to the people in both cars were thankfully minor, but before I knew it I was being strapped to a stretcher and driven away. Through the haze of concussion, I was aware that wherever the ambulance was going, it wouldn't be good. I had visions of the horrific scene at the makeshift health clinic at the New Orleans airport—there were so few doctors and nurses that elderly evacuees were being left unattended for hours, slumped in their wheelchairs. I thought about Charity Hospital, New Orleans' primary public emergency room, which we had passed earlier in the day. It flooded during the storm, and its staff had struggled without power to keep patients alive. I pleaded with the paramedics to let me out. I remember telling them that I was fine, really, then I must have passed out.

I came to as we arrived at the most modern and calm hospital I have ever been in. Unlike the clinics crowded with evacuees, at the Ochsner Medical Center—offering "healthcare with peace of mind"—doctors, nurses and orderlies far outnumbered the patients. In fact, there seemed to be only a handful of other patients in the immaculate ward. In minutes I was settled into a spacious private room, my cuts and bruises attended to by a small army of medical staff. Three nurses immediately took me in for a neck X-ray; a genteel Southern doctor removed some glass fragments and put in a couple of stitches.

To a veteran of the Canadian public health care system, these were wholly unfamiliar experiences; I usually wait for forty minutes to see my general practitioner. And this was downtown New Orleans—ground zero of the largest public health emergency in recent U.S. history. A polite administrator came into my room and explained that "in America we pay for health care. I am so sorry, dear—it's really terrible. We wish we had your system. Just fill out this form."

Within a couple of hours, I would have been free to go, were it not for the curfew that had locked down the city. "The biggest problem," a private security guard told me in the lobby where we were both biding time, "is all the junkies; they're jonesing and want to get into the pharmacy."

Since the pharmacy was locked tight, a medical intern was kind enough to slip me a few painkillers. I asked him what it had been like at the hospital at the peak of the storm. "I wasn't on duty, thank God," he said. "I live outside the city."

When I asked if he had gone to any of the shelters to help, he seemed taken aback by the question and a little embarrassed. "I hadn't thought of that," he said. I quickly changed the subject to what I hoped was safer ground: the fate of Charity Hospital. It was so underfunded that it was barely functioning before the storm, and people were already speculating that with the water damage it might never reopen. "They'd better reopen it," he said. "We can't treat those people here."

It occurred to me that this affable young doctor, and the spa-like medical care I had just received, were the embodiment of the culture that had made the horrors of Hurricane Katrina possible, the culture that had left New Orleans' poorest residents to drown. As a graduate of a private medical school and then an intern at a private hospital, he had been trained simply not to see New Orleans' uninsured, overwhelmingly African-American residents as potential patients. That was true before the storm, and it continued to be true even when all of New Orleans turned into a giant emergency room: he had sympathy for the evacuees, but that didn't change the fact that he still could not see them as potential patients of his.

When Katrina hit, the sharp divide between the worlds of Ochsner Hospital and Charity Hospital suddenly played out on the world stage. The economically secure drove out of town, checked into hotels and called their insurance companies. The 120,000 people in New Orleans without cars, who depended on the state to organize their evacuation, waited for help that did not arrive, making desperate SOS signs or rafts out of their refrigerator doors. Those images shocked the world because, even if most of us had resigned ourselves to the daily inequalities of who has access to health care and whose schools have decent equipment, there was still a widespread assumption that disasters were supposed to be different. It was taken for granted that the state—at least in a rich country—would come to the aid of the people during a cataclysmic event. The images from New Orleans showed that this general belief—that disasters are a kind of time-out for cutthroat capitalism, when we all pull together and the state switches into higher gear—had already been abandoned, and with no public debate.

There was a brief window of two or three weeks when it seemed that the drowning of New Orleans would provoke a crisis for the economic logic that had greatly exacerbated the human disaster with its relentless attacks on the public sphere. "The storm exposed the consequences of neoliberalism's lies and mystifications, in a single locale and all at once," wrote the political scientist and New Orleans native Adolph Reed Jr.[3] The facts of this exposure are well known—from the levees that were never repaired, to the underfunded public transit system that failed, to the fact that the city's idea of disaster preparedness was passing out DVDs telling people that if a hurricane came, they should get out of town.

Then there was the Federal Emergency Management Agency (FEMA), a laboratory for the Bush administration's vision of government run by corporations. In the summer of 2004, more than a year before Katrina hit, the State of Louisiana put in a request to FEMA for funds to develop an in-depth contingency plan for a powerful hurricane. The request was refused. "Disaster mitigation"—advance government measures to make the effects of disasters less devastating—was one of the programs gutted under Bush. Yet that same summer FEMA awarded a $500,000 contract to a private firm called Innovative Emergency Management. Its task was to come up with a "catastrophic hurricane disaster plan for Southeast Louisiana and the City of New Orleans."[4]

The private company spared no expense. It brought together more than a hundred experts, and when money ran out, it went back to FEMA for more; eventually the bill for the exercise doubled to $1 million. The company came up with scenarios for a mass evacuation covering everything from delivering water to instructing neighboring communities to identify empty lots that could immediately be transformed into trailer parks for evacuees—all the sensible things that didn't happen when a hurricane like the one they were imagining actually hit. That's partly because, eight months after the contractor submitted its report, no action had been taken. "Money was not available to do the follow-up," explained Michael Brown, head of FEMA at the time.[5] The story is typical of the lopsided state that Bush built: a weak, underfunded, ineffective public sector on the one hand, and a parallel richly funded corporate infrastructure on the other. When it comes to paying contractors, the sky is the limit; when it comes to financing the basic functions of the state, the coffers are empty.

Just as the U.S. occupation authority in Iraq turned out to be an empty shell, when Katrina hit, so did the U.S. federal government at home. In fact, it was so thoroughly absent that FEMA could not seem to locate the New Orleans superdome, where twenty-three thousand people were stranded without food or water, despite the fact that the world media had been there for days.

For some free-market ideologues, this spectacle of what the *New York Times* columnist Paul Krugman termed "the can't do government" provoked a crisis of faith. "The collapsed levees of New Orleans will have consequences for neoconservatism just as long and deep as the collapse of the Wall in East Berlin had on Soviet Communism," wrote the repentant true believer Martin Kelly in a much-circulated essay. "Hopefully all of those who urged the ideology on, myself included, will have a long time to consider the error of our ways." Even neocon stalwarts like Jonah Goldberg were begging "big government" to ride to the rescue: "When a city is sinking into the sea and rioting runs rampant, government probably should saddle-up."[6]

No such soul-searching was in evidence at the Heritage Foundation, where the true disciples of Friedmanism can always be found. Katrina was a tragedy, but, as Milton Friedman wrote in his *Wall Street Journal* op-ed, it was "also an opportunity." On September 13, 2005—fourteen days after the levees were breached—the Heritage Foundation hosted a meeting of like-minded ideologues and Republican lawmakers. They came up with a list of "Pro-Free-Market Ideas for Responding to Hurricane Katrina and High Gas Prices"—thirty-two policies in all, each one straight out of the Chicago School playbook, and all of them packaged as "hurricane relief." The first three items were "automatically suspend Davis-Bacon prevailing wage laws in disaster areas," a reference to the law that required federal contractors to pay a living wage; "make the entire affected area a flat-tax free-enterprise zone"; and "make the entire region an economic competitiveness zone (comprehensive tax incentives and waiving of regulations)." Another demand called for giving parents vouchers to use at charter schools.[7] All these measures were announced by President Bush within the week. He was eventually forced to reinstate the labor standards, though they were largely ignored by contractors.

The meeting produced more ideas that gained presidential support. Climate scientists have directly linked the increased intensity of hurricanes to warming ocean temperatures.[8] This connection, however, didn't stop the working group at the Heritage Foundation from calling on Congress to repeal environmental regulations on the Gulf Coast, give permission for new oil refineries in the United States and green-light "drilling in the Arctic National Wildlife Refuge."[9] All these measures would increase greenhouse gas emissions, the major human contributor to climate change, yet they were immediately championed by the president under the guise of responding to the Katrina disaster.

Within weeks, the Gulf Coast became a domestic laboratory for the same kind of government-run-by-contractors that had been pioneered in Iraq. The companies that snatched up the biggest contracts were the familiar Baghdad gang: Halliburton's KBR unit had a $60 million gig to reconstruct military bases along the coast. Blackwater was hired to protect FEMA employees from looters. Parsons, infamous for its sloppy Iraq work, was brought in for a major bridge construction project in Mississippi. Fluor, Shaw, Bechtel, CH2M Hill—all top contractors in Iraq—were hired by the government to provide mobile homes to evacuees just ten days after the levees broke. Their contracts ended up totaling $3.4 billion, no open bidding required.[10]

As many remarked at the time, within days of the storm it was as if Baghdad's Green Zone had lifted off from its perch on the Tigris and landed on the bayou. The parallels were undeniable. To spearhead its Katrina operation, Shaw hired the former head of the U.S. Army's Iraq reconstruction office. Fluor sent its senior project manager from Iraq to the flood zone. "Our rebuilding work in Iraq is slowing down and this has made some people available to respond to our work in Louisiana," a company representative explained. Joe Allbaugh, whose company New Bridge Strategies had promised to bring Wal-Mart and 7-Eleven to Iraq, was the lobbyist in the middle of many of the deals. The similarities were so striking that some of the mercenary soldiers, fresh from Baghdad, were having trouble adjusting. When David Enders, a reporter, asked an armed guard outside a New Orleans hotel if there had been much action, he replied, "Nope. It's pretty Green Zone here."[11]

Other things were pretty Green Zone too. On contracts valued at $8.75 billion, congressional investigators found "significant overcharges, wasteful spending, or mismanagement."[12] (The fact that exactly the same errors as those made in Iraq were instantly repeated in New Orleans should put to rest the claim that Iraq's occupation was merely a string of mishaps and mistakes marked by incompetence and lack of oversight. When the same mistakes are repeated over and over again, it's time to consider the possibility that they are not mistakes at all.)

In New Orleans, as in Iraq, no opportunity for profit was left untapped. Kenyon, a division of the mega funeral conglomerate Service Corporation International (a major Bush campaign donor), was hired to retrieve the dead from homes and streets. The work was extraordinarily slow, and bodies were left in the broiling sun for days. Emergency workers and local volunteer morticians were forbidden to step in to help because handling the bodies impinged on Kenyon's commercial territory. The company charged the state, on average, $12,500 a victim, and it has since been accused of failing to properly label many bodies. For almost a year after the flood, decayed corpses were still being discovered in attics.[13]

Another pretty Green Zone touch: relevant experience often appeared to have nothing to do with how contracts were allocated. AshBritt, the company paid half a billion dollars to remove debris, reportedly didn't own a single

dump truck and farmed out the entire job to contractors.[14] Even more striking was the company that FEMA paid $5.2 million to perform the crucial role
of building a base camp for emergency workers in St. Bernard Parish, a suburb of New Orleans. The camp construction fell behind schedule and was
never completed. When the contractor was investigated, it emerged that the
company, Lighthouse Disaster Relief, was actually a religious group. "About
the closest thing I have done to this is just organize a youth camp with my
church," confessed Lighthouse's director, Pastor Gary Heldreth.[15]

As in Iraq, government once again played the role of a cash machine
equipped for both withdrawals and deposits. Corporations withdrew funds
through massive contracts, then repaid the government not with reliable
work but with campaign contributions and/or loyal foot soldiers for the next
elections. (According to *The New York Times*, "the top 20 service contractors
have spent nearly $300 million since 2000 on lobbying and have donated
$23 million to political campaigns." The Bush administration, in turn, in-
creased the amount spent on contractors by roughly $200 billion between
2000 and 2006.)[16]

Something else was familiar: the contractors' aversion to hiring local people who might have seen the reconstruction of New Orleans not only as a job
but as part of healing and reempowering their communities. Washington
could easily have made it a condition of every Katrina contract that companies hire local people at decent wages to help them put their lives back together. Instead, the residents of the Gulf Coast, like the people of Iraq, were
expected to watch as contractors created an economic boom based on easy
taxpayer money and relaxed regulations.

The result, predictably, was that after all the layers of subcontractors had
taken their cut, there was next to nothing left for the people doing the work.
For instance, the author Mike Davis tracked the way FEMA paid Shaw $175
a square foot to install blue tarps on damaged roofs, even though the tarps
themselves were provided by the government. Once all the subcontractors
took their share, the workers who actually hammered in the tarps were paid
as little as $2 a square foot. "Every level of the contracting food chain, in
other words, is grotesquely overfed except the bottom rung," Davis wrote,
"where the actual work is carried out."[17]

According to one study, "a quarter of the workers rebuilding the city were
immigrants lacking papers, almost all of them Hispanic, making far less
money than legal workers." In Mississippi, a class-action lawsuit forced several
companies to pay hundreds of thousands of dollars in back wages to immigrant

workers. Some were not paid at all. On one Halliburton/KBR job site, undocumented immigrant workers reported being wakened in the middle of the night by their employer (a subsubcontractor), who allegedly told them that immigration agents were on their way. Most workers fled to avoid arrest; after all, they could end up in one of the new immigration prisons that Halliburton/KBR had been contracted to build for the federal government.*[18]

The attacks on the disadvantaged, carried out in the name of reconstruction and relief, did not stop there. In order to offset the tens of billions going to private companies in contracts and tax breaks, in November 2005 the Republican-controlled Congress announced that it needed to cut $40 billion from the federal budget. Among the programs that were slashed were student loans, Medicaid and food stamps.[19] In other words, the poorest citizens in the country subsidized the contractor bonanza twice—first when Katrina relief morphed into unregulated corporate handouts, providing neither decent jobs nor functional public services, and second when the few programs that directly assist the unemployed and working poor nationwide were gutted to pay those bloated bills.

Not so long ago, disasters were periods of social leveling, rare moments when atomized communities put divisions aside and pulled together. Increasingly, however, disasters are the opposite: they provide windows into a cruel and ruthlessly divided future in which money and race buy survival.

Baghdad's Green Zone is the starkest expression of this world order. It has its own electrical grid, its own phone and sewage systems, its own oil supply and its own state-of-the-art hospital with pristine operating theaters—all protected by five-meter-thick walls. It feels, oddly, like a giant fortified Carnival Cruise Ship parked in the middle of a sea of violence and despair, the boiling Red Zone that is Iraq. If you can get on board, there are poolside drinks, bad Hollywood movies and Nautilus machines. If you are not among the chosen, you can get yourself shot just by standing too close to the wall.

Everywhere in Iraq, the wildly divergent value assigned to different categories of people is crudely evident. Westerners and their Iraqi colleagues have checkpoints at the entrance to their streets, blast walls in front of their houses, body armor and private security guards on call at all hours. They

---

* No extensive studies have been conducted on New Orleans labor conditions, but the Advancement Project, a grassroots advocacy group in New Orleans, estimates that 60 percent of the immigrant workers in New Orleans have not been paid for at least part of their work.

travel the country in menacing armored convoys, with mercenaries pointing guns out the windows as they follow their prime directive to "protect the principal." With every move they broadcast the same unapologetic message: we are the chosen; our lives are infinitely more precious. Middle-class Iraqis, meanwhile, cling to the next rung down the ladder: they can afford to buy protection from local militias, and they are able to pay off kidnappers to have a family member released. But the vast majority of Iraqis have no protection at all. They walk the streets wide open to any possible violence, with nothing between them and the next car bomb but a thin layer of fabric. In Iraq, the lucky get Kevlar, the rest get prayer beads.

At first I thought the Green Zone phenomenon was unique to the war in Iraq. Now, after years spent in other disaster zones, I realize that the Green Zone emerges everywhere that the disaster capitalism complex descends, with the same stark partitions between the included and the excluded, the protected and the damned.

It happened in New Orleans. After the flood, an already divided city turned into a battleground between gated green zones and raging red zones—the result not of water damage but of the "free-market solutions" embraced by the president. The Bush administration refused to allow emergency funds to pay public sector salaries, and the City of New Orleans, which lost its tax base, had to fire three thousand workers in the months after Katrina. Among them were sixteen of the city's planning staff—with shades of "de-Baathification," laid off at the precise moment when New Orleans was in desperate need of planners. Instead, millions of public dollars went to outside consultants, many of whom were powerful real estate developers.[20] And of course thousands of teachers were also fired, paving the way for the conversion of dozens of public schools into charter schools, just as Friedman had called for.

Almost two years after the storm, Charity Hospital was still closed. The court system was barely functioning, and the privatized electricity company, Entergy, had failed to get the whole city back online. After threatening to raise rates dramatically, the company managed to extract a controversial $200 million bailout from the federal government. The public transit system was gutted and lost almost half its workers. The vast majority of publicly owned housing projects stood boarded up and empty, with five thousand units slotted for demolition by the federal housing authority.[21] Much as the tourism lobby in Asia had longed to be rid of the beachfront fishing villages, New Orleans' powerful tourism lobby had been eyeing the housing projects, several of them on prime land close to the French Quarter, the city's tourism magnet.

Endesha Juakali helped set up a protest camp outside one of the boarded-up projects, St. Bernard Public Housing, explaining that "they've had an agenda for St. Bernard a long time, but as long as people lived here, they couldn't do it. So they used the disaster as a way of cleansing the neighborhood when the neighborhood is weakest. . . . This is a great location for bigger houses and condos. The only problem is you got all these poor black people sitting on it!"[22]

Amid the schools, the homes, the hospitals, the transit system and the lack of clean water in many parts of town, New Orleans' public sphere was not being rebuilt, it was being erased, with the storm used as the excuse. At an earlier stage of capitalist "creative destruction," large swaths of the United States lost their manufacturing bases and degenerated into rust belts of shuttered factories and neglected neighborhoods. Post-Katrina New Orleans may be providing the first Western-world image of a new kind of wasted urban landscape: the mold belt, destroyed by the deadly combination of weathered public infrastructure and extreme weather.

The American Society of Civil Engineers said in 2007 that the U.S. had fallen so far behind in maintaining its public infrastructure—roads, bridges, schools, dams—that it would take more than a trillion and half dollars over five years to bring it back up to standard. Instead, these types of expenditures are being cut back.[23] At the same time, public infrastructure around the world is facing unprecedented stress, with hurricanes, cyclones, floods and forest fires all increasing in frequency and intensity. It's easy to imagine a future in which growing numbers of cities have their frail and long-neglected infrastructures knocked out by disasters and then are left to rot, their core services never repaired or rehabilitated. The well-off, meanwhile, will withdraw into gated communities, their needs met by privatized providers.

Signs of that future were already in evidence by the time hurricane season rolled around in 2006. In just one year, the disaster-response industry had exploded, with a slew of new corporations entering the market, promising safety and security should the next Big One hit. One of the more ambitious ventures was launched by an airline in West Palm Beach, Florida. Help Jet bills itself as "the first hurricane escape plan that turns a hurricane evacuation into a jet-setter vacation." When a storm is coming, the airline books holidays for its members at five-star golf resorts, spas or Disneyland. With the reservations all made, the evacuees are then whisked out of the hurricane zone on a luxury jet. "No standing in lines, no hassle with crowds, just a first class experience that turns a problem into a vacation. . . . Enjoy the feeling of avoiding the usual hurricane evacuation nightmare."[24]

For the people left behind, there is a different kind of privatized solution. In 2006, the Red Cross signed a new disaster-response partnership with Wal-Mart. "It's all going to be private enterprise before it's over," said Billy Wagner, chief of emergency management for the Florida Keys. "They've got the expertise. They've got the resources." He was speaking at the National Hurricane Conference in Orlando, Florida, a fast-growing annual trade show for the companies selling everything that might come in handy during the next disaster. "Some folks here said, 'Man, this is huge business—this is my new business. I'm not in the landscaping business anymore; I'm going to be a hurricane debris contractor,'" said Dave Blandford, an exhibitor at the conference, showing off his "self-heating meals."[25]

Much of the parallel disaster economy has been built with taxpayers' money, thanks to the boom in privatized war-zone reconstruction. The giant contractors that have served as "the primes" in Iraq and Afghanistan have come under frequent political fire for spending large portions of their income from government contracts on their own corporate overhead—between 20 and 55 percent, according to a 2006 audit of Iraq contractors.[26] Much of those funds have, quite legally, gone into huge investments in corporate infrastructure—Bechtel's battalions of earth-moving equipment, Halliburton's planes and fleets of trucks, and the surveillance architecture built by L-3, CACI and Booz Allen.

Most dramatic has been Blackwater's investment in its paramilitary infrastructure. Founded in 1996, the company has used the steady stream of contracts during the Bush years to build up a private army of twenty thousand mercenary soldiers on call and a massive military base in North Carolina worth between $40 million and $50 million. According to one account, Blackwater's capacity now includes the following: "A burgeoning logistics operation that can deliver 100- or 200-ton self-contained humanitarian relief response packages faster than the Red Cross. A Florida aviation division with 26 different platforms, from helicopter gunships to a massive Boeing 767. The company even has a Zeppelin. The country's largest tactical driving track. . . . A 20-acre man-made lake with shipping containers that have been mocked up with ship rails and portholes, floating on pontoons, used to teach how to board a hostile ship. A K-9 training facility that currently has 80 dog teams deployed around the world. . . . A 1,200-yard-long firing range for sniper training."*[27]

A right-wing journal in the U.S. pronounced Blackwater "al Qaeda for the good guys."[28] It's a striking analogy. Wherever the disaster capitalism complex has landed, it has produced a proliferation of armed groupings outside the state. That is hardly a surprise: when countries are rebuilt by people who don't believe in governments, the states they build are invariably weak, creating a market for alternative security forces, whether Hezbollah, Blackwater, the Mahdi Army or the gang down the street in New Orleans.

The emergence of this parallel privatized infrastructure reaches far beyond policing. When the contractor infrastructure built up during the Bush years is looked at as a whole, what is seen is a fully articulated state-within-a-state that is as muscular and capable as the actual state is frail and feeble. This corporate shadow state has been built almost exclusively with public resources (90 percent of Blackwater's revenues come from state contracts), including the training of its staff (overwhelmingly former civil servants, politicians and soldiers).[29] Yet the vast infrastructure is all privately owned and controlled. The citizens who have funded it have absolutely no claim to this parallel economy or its resources.

The actual state, meanwhile, has lost the ability to perform its core functions without the help of contractors. Its own equipment is out of date, and the best experts have fled to the private sector. When Katrina hit, FEMA had to hire a contractor to award contracts to contractors. Similarly, when it came time to update the Army Manual on the rules for dealing with contractors, the army contracted out the job to one of its major contractors, MPRI—it no longer had the know-how in-house. The CIA is losing so many staffers to the parallel privatized spy sector that it has had to bar contractors from recruiting in the agency dining room. "One recently retired case officer said he had been approached twice while in line for coffee," reported the *Los Angeles Times*. And when the Department of Homeland Security decided it needed to build "virtual fences" on the U.S. borders with Mexico and Canada, Michael P. Jackson, deputy secretary of the department, told contractors,

---

* One of the most worrying aspects of this industry is how unabashedly partisan it is. Blackwater, for instance, is closely aligned with the antiabortion movement and other right-wing causes. It donates almost exclusively to the Republican Party, rather than hedging its bets like most big corporations. Halliburton sends 87 percent of its campaign contributions to Republicans, CH2M Hill 70 percent. Is it beyond the realm of the imagination to conceive of a day when political parties will hire these companies to spy on their rivals during an election campaign—or to engage in covert operations too shady even for the CIA?

"This is an unusual invitation. . . . We're asking you to come back and tell us how to do our business." The department's inspector general explained that Homeland Security "does not have the capacity needed to effectively plan, oversee and execute the [Secure Border Initiative] program."[30]

Under Bush, the state still has all the trappings of a government—the impressive buildings, presidential press briefings, policy battles—but it no more does the actual work of governing than the employees at Nike's Beaverton campus stitch running shoes.

The implications of the decision by the current crop of politicians to systematically outsource their elected responsibilities will reach far beyond a single administration. Once a market has been created, it needs to be protected. The companies at the heart of the disaster capitalism complex increasingly regard both the state and nonprofits as competitors—from the corporate perspective, whenever governments or charities fulfill their traditional roles, they are denying contractors work that could be performed at a profit.

"Neglected Defense: Mobilizing the Private Sector to Support Homeland Security," a 2006 report whose advisory committee included some of the largest corporations in the sector, warned that "the compassionate federal impulse to provide emergency assistance to the victims of disasters affects the market's approach to managing its exposure to risk."[31] Published by the Council on Foreign Relations, the report argued that if people know the government will come to the rescue, they have no incentive to pay for privatized protection. In a similar vein, a year after Katrina, CEOs from thirty of the largest corporations in the United States joined together under the umbrella of the Business Roundtable, which includes in its membership Fluor, Bechtel and Chevron. The group, calling itself Partnership for Disaster Response, complained of "mission creep" by the nonprofit sector in the aftermath of disasters. Apparently charities and NGOs were infringing on their market by donating building supplies rather than having Home Depot supply them for a fee. The mercenary firms, meanwhile, have been loudly claiming that they are better equipped to engage in peacekeeping in Darfur than the UN.[32]

Much of this new aggressiveness flows from the fact that the corporate world knows that the golden era of bottomless federal contracts cannot last much longer. The U.S. government is barreling toward an economic crisis, in no small part thanks to the deficit spending that has bankrolled the construction of the privatized disaster economy. That means that sooner rather than later, the contracts are going to dip significantly. In late 2006, defense analysts began predicting that the Pentagon's acquisitions budget could shrink by as much as 25 percent in the coming decade.[33]

When the disaster bubble bursts, firms such as Bechtel, Fluor and Blackwater will lose much of their primary revenue streams. They will still have all the high-tech gear and equipment bought at taxpayer expense, but they will need to find a new business model, a new way to cover their high costs. The next phase of the disaster capitalism complex is all too clear: with emergencies on the rise, government no longer able to foot the bill, and citizens stranded by their can't-do state, the parallel corporate state will rent back its disaster infrastructure to whoever can afford it, at whatever price the market will bear. For sale will be everything from helicopter rides off rooftops to drinking water to beds in shelters.

Already wealth provides an escape hatch from most disasters—it buys early-warning systems for tsunami-prone regions and stockpiles of Tamiflu for the next outbreak. It buys bottled water, generators, satellite phones and rent-a-cops. During the Israeli attack on Lebanon in 2006, the U.S. government initially tried to charge its citizens for the cost of their own evacuations, though it was eventually forced to back down.[34] If we continue in this direction, the images of people stranded on New Orleans rooftops will not only be a glimpse of America's unresolved past of racial inequality but will also foreshadow a collective future of disaster apartheid in which survival is determined by who can afford to pay for escape.

Looking ahead to coming disasters, ecological and political, we often assume that we are all going to face them together, that what's needed are leaders who recognize the destructive course we are on. But I'm not so sure. Perhaps part of the reason why so many of our elites, both political and corporate, are so sanguine about climate change is that they are confident they will be able to buy their way out of the worst of it. This may also partially explain why so many Bush supporters are Christian end-timers. It's not just that they need to believe there is an escape hatch from the world they are creating. It's that the Rapture is a parable for what they are building down here—a system that invites destruction and disaster, then swoops in with private helicopters and airlifts them and their friends to divine safety.

As contractors rush to develop alternative stable sources of revenue, one avenue is disaster-proofing other corporations. This was Paul Bremer's line of business before he went to Iraq: turning multinationals into security bubbles, able to function smoothly even if the states in which they are functioning are crumbling around them. The early results can be seen in the lobbies of many major office buildings in New York or London—airport-style check-ins complete with photo-ID requirements and X-ray machines—but the industry has far greater ambitions, including privatized global communications networks, emergency health and electricity, and the ability to locate and provide transportation for a global workforce in the midst of a major disaster. Another potential growth area identified by the disaster capitalism complex is municipal government: the contracting-out of police and fire departments to private security companies. "What they do for the military in downtown Falluja, they can do for the police in downtown Reno," a spokesperson for Lockheed Martin said in November 2004.[35]

The industry predicts that these new markets will expand dramatically over the next decade. A frank vision of where these trends are leading is provided by John Robb, a former covert-action mission commander with Delta Force turned successful management consultant. In a widely circulated manifesto for *Fast Company* magazine, he describes the "end result" of the war on terror as "a new, more resilient approach to national security, one built not around the state but around private citizens and companies. . . . Security will become a function of where you live and whom you work for, much as health care is allocated already."[36]

Robb writes, "Wealthy individuals and multinational corporations will be the first to bail out of our collective system, opting instead to hire private military companies, such as Blackwater and Triple Canopy, to protect their homes and facilities and establish a protective perimeter around daily life. Parallel transportation networks—evolving out of the time-share aircraft companies such as Warren Buffett's NetJets—will cater to this group, leapfrogging its members from one secure, well-appointed lily pad to the next." That elite world is already largely in place, but Robb predicts that the middle class will soon follow suit, "forming suburban collectives to share the costs of security." These "'armored suburbs' will deploy and maintain backup generators and communications links" and be patrolled by private militias "that have received corporate training and boast their own state-of-the-art emergency-response systems."

In other words, a world of suburban Green Zones. As for those outside the secured perimeter, "they will have to make do with the remains of the national system. They will gravitate to America's cities, where they will be subject to ubiquitous surveillance and marginal or nonexistent services. For the poor, there will be no other refuge."

The future Robb described sounds very much like the present in New Orleans, where two very different kinds of gated communities emerged from the rubble. On the one hand were the so-called FEMA-villes: desolate, out-of-the-way trailer camps for low-income evacuees, built by Bechtel or Fluor subcontractors, administered by private security companies who patrolled the gravel lots, restricted visitors, kept journalists out and treated survivors like criminals. On the other hand were the gated communities built in the wealthy areas of the city, such as Audubon and the Garden District, bubbles of functionality that seemed to have seceded from the state altogether. Within weeks of the storm, residents there had water and powerful emergency generators. Their sick were treated in private hospitals, and their children went to new charter schools. As usual, they had no need for public transit. In St. Bernard Parish, a New Orleans suburb, DynCorp had taken over much of the policing; other neighborhoods hired security companies directly. Between the two kinds of privatized sovereign states was the New Orleans version of the Red Zone, where the murder rate soared and neighborhoods like the storied Lower Ninth Ward descended into a post-apocalyptic no-man's-land. A hit song by the rapper Juvenile in the summer after Katrina summed up the atmosphere: "We livin' like Haiti without no government"—failed state U.S.A.[37]

Bill Quigley, a local lawyer and activist, observed, "What is happening in New Orleans is just a more concentrated, more graphic version of what is going on all over our country. Every city in our country has some serious similarities to New Orleans. Every city has some abandoned neighborhoods. Every city in our country has abandoned some public education, public housing, public healthcare, and criminal justice. Those who do not support public education, healthcare, and housing will continue to turn all of our country into the Lower Ninth Ward unless we stop them."[38]

The process is already well under way. Another glimpse of a disaster apartheid future can be found in a wealthy Republican suburb outside Atlanta. Its residents decided that they were tired of watching their property taxes subsidize schools and police in the county's low-income African-American neighborhoods. They voted to incorporate as their own city, Sandy Springs, which could spend its taxes on services for its 100,000 citizens and not have the revenues redistributed throughout the larger Fulton County. The only difficulty was that Sandy Springs had no government structures and needed to build them from scratch—everything from tax collection, to zoning, to parks and recreation. In September 2005, the same month that

New Orleans flooded, the residents of Sandy Springs were approached by the construction and consulting giant CH2M Hill with a unique pitch: let us do it for you. For the starting price of $27 million a year, the contractor pledged to build a complete city from the ground up.[39]

A few months later, Sandy Springs became the first "contract city." Only four people worked directly for the new municipality—everyone else was a contractor. Rick Hirsekorn, heading up the project for CH2M Hill, described Sandy Springs as "a clean sheet of paper with no governmental processes in place." He told another journalist that "no one in our industry has done a complete city of this size before."[40]

The Atlanta Journal-Constitution reported that "when Sandy Springs hired corporate workers to run the new city, it was considered a bold experiment." Within a year, however, contract-city mania was tearing through Atlanta's wealthy suburbs, and it had become "standard procedure in north Fulton [County]." Neighboring communities took their cue from Sandy Springs and also voted to become stand-alone cities and contract out their government. One new city, Milton, immediately hired CH2M Hill for the job—after all, it had the experience. Soon, a campaign began for the new corporate cities to join together to form their own county, which would mean that none of their tax dollars would go to the poor neighborhoods nearby. The plan has encountered fierce opposition outside the proposed enclave, where politicians say that without those tax dollars, they will no longer be able to afford their large public hospital and public transit system; that partitioning the county would create a failed state on the one hand and a hyperserviced one on the other. What they were describing sounded a lot like New Orleans and a little like Baghdad.[41]

In these wealthy Atlanta suburbs, the three-decade corporatist crusade to strip-mine the state was complete: it wasn't just every government service that had been outsourced but also the very function of government, which is to govern. It was particularly fitting that the new ground was broken by CH2M Hill. The corporation was a multimillion-dollar contractor in Iraq, paid to perform the core government function of overseeing other contractors. In Sri Lanka after the tsunami, it had not only built ports and bridges but was "responsible for the overall management of the infrastructure program."[42] In post-Katrina New Orleans, it was awarded $500 million to build FEMA-villes and put on standby to be ready to do the same for the next disaster. A master of privatizing the state during extraordinary circumstances, it was now doing the same under ordinary ones. If Iraq was a laboratory of extreme privatization, the testing phase was clearly over.

CHAPTER 21

LOSING THE PEACE INCENTIVE

ISRAEL AS WARNING

> Big border fences belong not to the world of the gulag but to the world of noise barriers along highways, luxury boxes in sports stadiums, no-smoking areas, security zones in airports and "gated communities." . . . They make explicit the privileges of the haves and the envy of the have-nots in a way that is embarrassing for both. That is not the same as saying they do not work.
> —Christopher Caldwell, senior editor, *The Weekly Standard*, November 2006[1]

For decades, the conventional wisdom was that generalized mayhem was a drain on the global economy. Individual shocks and crises could be harnessed as leverage to force open new markets, of course, but after the initial shock had done its work, relative peace and stability were required for sustained economic growth. That was the accepted explanation for why the nineties had been such prosperous years: with the Cold War over, economies were liberated to concentrate on trade and investment, and as countries became more enmeshed and interdependent, they were far less likely to bomb each other.

At the 2007 World Economic Forum in Davos, Switzerland, however, political and corporate leaders were scratching their heads over a state of affairs that seemed to flout this conventional wisdom. It was being called the "Davos Dilemma," which the *Financial Times* columnist Martin Wolf described as "the contrast between the world's favourable economics and troublesome politics." As he put it, the economy had faced "a series of shocks: the stock market crash after 2000; the terrorist outrages of September 11, 2001; wars in Afghanistan and Iraq; friction over US policies; a jump in real oil prices to levels not seen since the 1970s; the cessation of negotiations in the Doha round [of WTO talks]; and the confrontation over Iran's nuclear ambitions"—and yet it found itself in "a golden period of broadly shared growth." Put bluntly, the world was going to hell, there was no stability in sight and the global economy was roaring its approval. Soon after, former U.S. Treasury Secretary Lawrence Summers described the "near complete disconnect" between politics and markets as "something out of Dickens, you talk to international relations experts and it's the worst of all times. Then you talk to potential investors and it's one of the best of all times."[2]

This puzzling trend has also been observed through an economic indicator called "the guns-to-caviar index." The index tracks the sales of fighter jets (guns) and executive jets (caviar). For seventeen years, it consistently found that when fighter jets were selling briskly, sales of luxury executive jets went down and vice versa: when executive jet sales were on the rise, fighter jet sales dipped. Of course, a handful of war profiteers always managed to get rich from selling guns, but they were economically insignificant. It was a truism of the contemporary market that you couldn't have booming economic growth in the midst of violence and instability.

But that truism is no longer true. Since 2003, the year of the Iraq invasion, the index found that spending has been going up on both fighter jets and executive jets rapidly and simultaneously, which means that the world is becoming less peaceful while accumulating significantly more profit.[3] The galloping economic growth in China and India played a part in the increased demand for luxury items, but so did the expansion of the narrow military-industrial complex into the sprawling disaster capitalism complex. Today, global instability does not just benefit a small group of arms dealers; it generates huge profits for the high-tech security sector, for heavy construction, for private health care companies treating wounded soldiers, for the oil and gas sectors—and of course for defense contractors.

The scale of the revenues at stake is certainly enough to fuel an economic boom. Lockheed Martin, whose former vice president chaired the committee loudly agitating for war in Iraq, received $25 billion of U.S. taxpayer dollars in 2005 alone. The Democratic congressman Henry Waxman noted that the sum "exceeded the gross domestic product of 103 countries, including Iceland, Jordan, and Costa Rica . . . [and] was also larger than the combined budgets of the Department of Commerce, the Department of the

Interior, the Small Business Administration, and the entire legislative branch of government." Lockheed itself was an "emerging market." Companies like Lockheed (whose stock price tripled between 2000 and 2005) are a large part of the reason why the U.S. stock markets were saved from a prolonged crash following September 11. While conventional stock prices have underperformed, the Spade Defense Index, "a benchmark for defense, homeland security and aerospace stocks," went up every year from 2001 to 2006 by an average of 15 percent—seven and a half times the Standard & Poor's 500 average increase in that same period.[4]

The Davos Dilemma is being further fueled by the intensely profitable model of privatized reconstruction that was forged in Iraq. Heavy-construction stocks, which include the big engineering firms that land juicy no-bid contracts after wars and natural disasters, went up 250 percent between 2001 and April 2007. Reconstruction is now such big business that every new destruction is greeted with the excitement of hot initial public stock offerings: $30 billion for Iraq reconstruction, $13 billion for tsunami reconstruction, $100 billion for New Orleans and the Gulf Coast, $7.6 billion for Lebanon.[5]

Terrorist attacks, which used to send the stock market spiraling downward, now receive a similarly upbeat market reception. After September 11, 2001, the Dow Jones plummeted 685 points as soon as markets reopened. In sharp contrast, on July 7, 2005, the day four bombs ripped through London's public transport system, killing dozens and injuring hundreds, the U.S. stock market closed higher than it did the day before, with the Nasdaq up 7 points. The following August, on the day British law enforcement agencies arrested twenty-four suspects allegedly planning to blow up jetliners headed to the U.S., the Nasdaq closed 11.4 points higher, largely thanks to soaring homeland security stocks.

Then there are the outrageous fortunes of the oil sector—a $40 billion profit in 2006 for ExxonMobil alone, the largest profit ever recorded, and its colleagues at rival companies like Chevron were not far behind.[6] Like those corporations linked to defense, heavy construction and homeland security, the oil sector's fortunes improve with every war, terrorist attack and Category 5 hurricane. In addition to reaping the short-term benefits of high prices linked to uncertainty in key oil-producing regions, the oil industry has consistently managed to turn disasters to its long-term advantage, whether by ensuring that a large portion of the reconstruction funds in Afghanistan went into the expensive road infrastructure for a new pipeline (while most other major reconstruction projects stalled), by pushing through Iraq's oil law while the country burned, or by piggybacking on Hurricane Katrina to plan the first new refineries in the United States since the seventies. The oil and gas industry is so intimately entwined with the economy of disaster—both as root cause behind many disasters and as a beneficiary from them—that it deserves to be treated as an honorary adjunct of the disaster capitalism complex.

No Conspiracies Required

The recent spate of disasters has translated into such spectacular profits that many people around the world have come to the same conclusion: the rich and powerful must be deliberately causing the catastrophes so that they can exploit them. In July 2006, a national poll of U.S. residents found that more than a third of respondents believed that the government had a hand in the 9/11 attacks or took no action to stop them "because they wanted the United States to go to war in the Middle East." Similar suspicions dog most of the catastrophes of recent years. In Louisiana in the aftermath of Katrina, the shelters were alive with rumors that the levees hadn't broken but had been covertly blown up in order "to destroy the black part of town and keep the white part dry," as the Nation of Islam's leader, Louis Farrakhan, suggested.[7] In Sri Lanka I often heard that the tsunami had been caused by underwater explosions detonated by the United States so that it could send troops into Southeast Asia and take full control over the region's economies.

The truth is at once less sinister and more dangerous. An economic system that requires constant growth, while bucking almost all serious attempts at environmental regulation, generates a steady stream of disasters all on its own, whether military, ecological or financial. The appetite for easy, short-term profits offered by purely speculative investment has turned the stock, currency and real estate markets into crisis-creation machines, as the Asian financial crisis, the Mexican peso crisis and the dot-com collapse all demonstrate. Our common addiction to dirty, nonrenewable energy sources keeps other kinds of emergencies coming: natural disasters (up 430 percent since 1975) and wars waged for control over scarce resources (not just Iraq and Afghanistan but lower-intensity conflicts such as those that rage in Nigeria, Colombia and Sudan), which in turn create terrorist blowback (a 2007 study calculated that the number of terrorist attacks since the start of the Iraq war had increased sevenfold).[8]

Given the boiling temperatures, both climatic and political, future disasters need not be cooked up in dark conspiracies. All indications are that simply by staying the current course, they will keep coming with ever more ferocious intensity. Disaster generation can therefore be left to the market's invisible hand. This is one area in which it actually delivers.

While the disaster capitalism complex does not deliberately scheme to create the cataclysms on which it feeds (though Iraq may be a notable exception), there is plenty of evidence that its component industries work very hard indeed to make sure that current disastrous trends continue unchallenged. Large oil companies have bankrolled the climate-change-denial movement for years; ExxonMobil has spent an estimated $16 million on the crusade over the past decade. While this phenomenon is well known, the interplay between disaster contractors and elite opinion-makers is far less understood. Several influential Washington think tanks—including the National Institute for Public Policy and the Center for Security Policy—are heavily funded by weapons and homeland security contractors, which profit directly from these institutes' ceaseless portrayal of the world as a dark and menacing place, its troubles responsive only to force. The homeland security sector is also becoming increasingly integrated with media corporations, a development with Orwellian implications. In 2004, the digital communications giant LexisNexis paid $775 million for Seisint, a data-mining company that works closely on surveillance with federal and state agencies. That same year, General Electric, which owns NBC, purchased InVision, the major producer of controversial high-tech bomb-detection devices used in airports and other public spaces. InVision received a staggering $15 billion in Homeland Security contracts between 2001 and 2006, more of such contracts than any other company.[9]

The creeping expansion of the disaster capitalism complex into media may prove to be a new kind of corporate synergy, one building on the vertical integration so popular in the nineties. It certainly makes sound business sense. The more panicked our societies become, convinced that there are terrorists lurking in every mosque, the higher the news ratings soar, the more biometric IDs and liquid-explosive-detection devices the complex sells, and the more high-tech fences it builds. If the dream of the open, borderless "small planet" was the ticket to profits in the nineties, the nightmare of the menacing, fortressed Western continents, under siege from jihadists and illegal immigrants, plays the same role in the new millennium. The only prospect that threatens the booming disaster economy on which so much wealth depends—from weapons to oil to engineering to surveillance to

patented drugs—is the possibility of achieving some measure of climatic stability and geopolitical peace.

Israel and the Standing Disaster Apartheid State

As analysts struggle to understand the Davos Dilemma, a new consensus is
emerging. It is not that the market has become immune to instability, at least
not exactly. It is that a steady flow of disasters is now so expected that the ever-
adaptable market has changed to fit this new status quo—instability is the new
stability. In discussions of this post-9/11 economic phenomenon, Israel is often
held up as a sort of Exhibit A. For much of the past decade, Israel has been ex-
periencing its own miniaturized Davos Dilemma: wars and terrorist attacks
have been increasing, but the Tel Aviv Stock Exchange has been rising to
record levels right alongside this violence. As one stock analyst noted on Fox
News after the July 7 London bombings, "In Israel they deal with the threat of
terror daily, and that market is up for the year."[10] Like the global economy in
general, Israel's political situation is, most agree, disastrous, but its economy has
never been stronger, with 2007 growth rates rivaling those of China and India.

What makes Israel interesting as a guns-and-caviar model is not only that
its economy is resilient in the face of major political shocks such as the 2006
war with Lebanon or Hamas's 2007 takeover of Gaza, but also that Israel has
crafted an economy that expands markedly in direct response to escalating
violence. The reasons for Israeli industry's comfort level with disaster are not
mysterious. Years before U.S. and European companies grasped the potential of the global security boom, Israeli technology firms were busily pioneering the homeland security industry, and they continue to dominate the
sector today. The Israeli Export Institute estimates that Israel has 350 corporations dedicated to selling homeland security products, and 30 new ones
entered the market in 2007. From a corporate perspective, this development
has made Israel a model to be emulated in the post-9/11 market. From a social and political perspective, however, Israel should serve as something
else—a stark warning. The fact that Israel continues to enjoy booming prosperity, even as it wages war against its neighbors and escalates the brutality in
the occupied territories, demonstrates just how perilous it is to build an
economy based on the premise of continual war and deepening disasters.

Israel's current ability to combine guns and caviar is the culmination of a
dramatic shift in the nature of its economy over the past fifteen years, one

that has had a profound and little-examined impact on the parallel disintegration of prospects for peace. The last time there was a credible prospect of peace breaking out in the Middle East was the early nineties, a time when a powerful constituency of Israelis believed that continued conflict was no longer an option. Communism had collapsed, the information revolution was beginning, and there was a widespread conviction inside Israel's business community that the bloody occupation of Gaza and the West Bank, compounded by the boycott of Israel by Arab states, was putting Israel's economic future in peril. Seeing the explosion of "emerging markets" around the world, Israeli corporations were tired of being held back by war; they wanted to be part of the high-profit borderless world, not penned in by regional strife. If the Israeli government could negotiate some sort of peace agreement with the Palestinians, Israel's neighbors would have to lift their boycotts, and the country would be perfectly positioned to be the Middle East's free-trade hub.

In 1993, Dan Gillerman, then president of the Federation of Israeli Chambers of Commerce, was a vocal proponent of this position. "Israel could become just another state . . . or, it could become the strategic, logistic and marketing center of the whole region like a Middle Eastern Singapore or Hong Kong where multinational companies base their head offices. . . . We are talking about an utterly different economy. . . . Israel must act and fast to adjust or this once in a lifetime economic opportunity will be missed only for us to say: 'we could have.'"[11]

That same year, Shimon Peres, then foreign minister, explained to a group of Israeli journalists that peace was now inevitable. It was a very particular kind of peace, however. "We are not seeking a peace of flags," Peres said, "we are interested in a peace of markets."[12] A few months later, the Israeli prime minister, Yitzhak Rabin, and the Palestinian Liberation Organization chairman, Yasser Arafat, shook hands on the White House lawn to mark the inauguration of the Oslo Accords. The world cheered, the three men shared the 1994 Nobel Peace Prize—and then it all went horribly wrong.

Oslo may have been the most optimistic period in Israeli-Palestinian relations, but the famous handshake did not mark the sealing of a deal. It was merely an agreement to start a process, with all the most contentious questions left unresolved. Arafat was in a terrible bargaining position, having to negotiate his own return to the occupied territories, and he secured no agreement on the fate of Jerusalem, on Palestinian refugees, on Jewish settlers or even on the right to Palestinian self-determination. The Oslo strategy, the negotiators claimed, was to push ahead with the "peace of markets" based on the idea that the rest would fall into place: by flinging open borders and joining the global-ization juggernaut, both Israelis and Palestinians were supposed to experience such concrete improvements in daily life that a more hospitable context would be created for a "peace of flags" in the negotiations to come. That, at least, was the Oslo promise.

Many factors contributed to the subsequent breakdown. Israelis tend to blame suicide bombings and Rabin's assassination. Palestinians point to Is-rael's frenetic expansion of illegal settlements during the Oslo period as proof that the peace process was founded, in the words of Shlomo Ben-Ami, Israel's foreign minister in the Labor government of Ehud Barak, "on a neo-colonialist basis," designed so that "when there will finally be peace between us and the Palestinians, there will be a situation of dependence, of a struc-tured lack of equality between the two entities."[13] The debates about who derailed the peace process, or whether peace was ever the real goal of the process, are well known and have been exhaustively explored. However, two factors that contributed to Israel's retreat into unilateralism are little under-stood and rarely discussed, both related to the unique ways that the Chicago School free-market crusade played out in Israel. One was the influx of Soviet Jews, which was a direct result of Russia's shock therapy experiment. The other was the flipping of Israel's export economy from one based on tradi-tional goods and high technology to one disproportionately dependent on selling expertise and devices relating to counterterrorism. Both factors were greatly disruptive to the Oslo process: the arrival of Russians reduced Israel's reliance on Palestinian labor and allowed it to seal in the occupied territo-ries, while the rapid expansion of the high-tech security economy created a powerful appetite inside Israel's wealthy and most powerful sectors for aban-doning peace in favor of fighting a continual, and continuously expanding, War on Terror.

By unfortunate historical coincidence, the start of the Oslo period coincided precisely with the most painful phase of the Chicago School experiment in Russia. The handshake on the White House lawn was on September 13, 1993; exactly three weeks later, Yeltsin sent in the tanks to set fire to the par-liament building, paving the way for his most brutal dose of economic shock.

Over the course of the 1990s, roughly 1 million Jews left the former So-viet Union and moved to Israel. Immigrants who came from the former Soviet Union in this period now make up more than 18 percent of Israel's total Jewish population.[14] It's hard to overstate the impact of such a large and rapid population transfer to a country as small as Israel. Proportionally, it would be the equivalent of every person in Angola, Cambodia and Peru packing their bags and moving to the United States all at once. In Europe, it would be equivalent to all of Greece moving to France.

When the first wave of Soviet Jews headed for Israel, many were choosing to live in a Jewish state after a lifetime of religious persecution. Following that initial wave, however, the number of Russian immigrants to Israel increased dramatically and in direct relation to the amount of pain being inflicted on the Russian people by their economic shock doctors. These later waves of Soviet immigrants were not idealistic Zionists (many had quite tenuous claims to being Jewish); they were desperate economic refugees. "It is not where we are going that is most important, but from where we are coming," an emigrant waiting outside the Israeli embassy in Moscow told *The Washington Times* in 1992. A spokesperson for the Soviet Jewry Zionist Forum confessed of the exodus that "they are not drawn to Israel, they feel expelled from the USSR by the political instability and economic deterioration there." By far the largest wave came in the wake of Yeltsin's coup in 1993—just as the peace process was beginning in Israel. After that, an additional 600,000 people moved from former Soviet states to Israel.[15]

This demographic transformation upended the agreement's already precarious dynamic. Before the arrival of the Soviet refugees, Israel could not have severed itself for any length of time from the Palestinian populations in Gaza and the West Bank; its economy could no more survive without Palestinian labor than California could run without Mexicans. Roughly 150,000 Palestinians left their homes in Gaza and the West Bank every day and traveled to Israel to clean streets and build roads, while Palestinian farmers and tradespeople filled trucks with goods and sold them in Israel and in other parts of the territories.[16] Each side depended on the other economically, and Israel took aggressive measures to prevent the Palestinian territories from developing autonomous trade relationships with Arab states.

Then, just as Oslo came into effect, that deeply interdependent relationship was abruptly severed. Unlike Palestinian workers, whose presence in Israel challenged the Zionist project by making demands on the Israeli state for restitution of stolen land and for equal citizenship rights, the hundreds of thousands of Russians who came to Israel at this juncture had the opposite effect. They bolstered Zionist goals by markedly increasing the ratio of Jews to Arabs, while simultaneously providing a new pool of cheap labor. Suddenly, Tel Aviv had the power to launch a new era in Palestinian relations. On March 30, 1993, Israel began its policy of "closure," sealing off the border between Israel and the occupied territories, often for days or weeks at a time, preventing Palestinians from getting to their jobs and selling their goods. Closure began as a temporary measure, ostensibly as an emergency response to the threat of terrorism. It quickly became the new status quo, with territories sealed off not just from Israel but from each other, policed through an ever more elaborate and demeaning system of checkpoints.

Nineteen ninety-three had been held up as the dawn of a new hopeful era; instead, it was the year that the occupied territories were transformed from run-down dormitories housing the underclass of the Israeli state into suffocating prisons. In this same period, between 1993 and 2000, the Israeli settlers living in the occupied territories doubled their numbers.[17] What had been in many places rough-hewn settler outposts were transformed into lush, fortified suburbs with their own restricted-access roads, clearly designed to be an addition to the Israeli state. During the Oslo years, Israel also continued to claim key water reserves in the West Bank, feeding the settlements and diverting scarce water back to Israel.

The new immigrants played a little-examined part here as well. Many residents of the former Soviet Union who arrived in Israel penniless after seeing their life savings disappear in the shock therapy devaluations were easily lured into the occupied territories, where houses and apartments were far cheaper, and special loans and bonuses were on offer. Some of the most ambitious settlements—such as Ariel in the West Bank, which boasts a university, a hotel and a Texas mini golf course—aggressively recruited in the former Soviet Union, sending scouts and launching Russian-language Web sites. Ariel managed to double its population thanks to this approach, and today it stands as a kind of mini-Moscow, with store signs advertising in both Hebrew and Russian. Half its residents are new immigrants from the former Soviet Union. The Israeli group Peace Now estimates that about twenty-five thousand Israeli citizens living in illegal settlements fall into this category, and it also notes that many Russians made the move "without a clear understanding of where they were going."[18]

In Israel, the years after the Oslo Accords delivered on their promise of trading conflict for prosperity in dramatic fashion. In the mid- and late nineties, Israeli companies took the global economy by storm, particularly high-tech firms specializing in telecommunications and Web technology, with Tel Aviv and Haifa becoming Middle Eastern outposts of Silicon Valley. At the peak of the dot-com bubble, 15 percent of Israel's gross domestic product came from high tech and about half its exports. That made Israel's economy "the most tech-dependent in the world," according to *Business-Week*—twice as dependent as the United States.[19]

Once again, the new arrivals played a decisive role in the boom. Among the hundreds of thousands of Soviets who came to Israel in the nineties were more highly trained scientists than Israel's top tech institute had graduated in the eighty years of its existence. These were many of the scientists who had kept up the Soviet side of the Cold War—and as one Israeli economist put it, they became "the rocket fuel for [Israel's] tech industry." Shlomo Ben-Ami describes the years after the White House handshake as "one of the most breathtaking eras of economic growth and opening up of markets in [Israel's] history."[20]

That opening of markets had promised to benefit both sides in the conflict, but with the exception of a corrupt elite around Arafat, Palestinians were conspicuously absent from the post-Oslo boom. The biggest obstacle was closure, a policy that was never once lifted in the fourteen years since it was first imposed in 1993. According to the Harvard Middle East specialist Sara Roy, when the borders were abruptly sealed in 1993, the effects on Palestinian economic life were catastrophic. "Closure has been the single most damaging feature to the economy during the Oslo period and since, the one measure that has imposed the greatest damage on an already compromised economy," she said in an interview.

Workers couldn't work, traders couldn't sell their goods, farmers couldn't reach their fields. In 1993 per capita GNP in the occupied territories plummeted close to 30 percent; by the following year, poverty among Palestinians was up 33 percent. By 1996, says Roy, who has extensively documented the economic impact of closure, "66 per cent of the Palestinian labor force was either unemployed or severely under-employed."[21] Far from a "peace of markets," what Oslo meant for Palestinians was disappearing markets, less work, less freedom—and, crucially, as the settlements expanded, less land. It was this utterly untenable situation that turned the occupied territories into the tinderbox that went up in flames when Ariel Sharon visited the site in Jerusalem called al-Haram al-Sharif by Muslims (by Jews, the Temple Mount) in September 2000, setting off the second intifada.

In Israel and the international press, it is generally argued that the reason the peace process collapsed was that Ehud Barak's offer at Camp David in July

2000 was the best deal the Palestinians were ever going to get, and Arafat turned his back on Israel's generosity, thus proving that he was never genuine in the quest for peace. After that experience, and the eruption of the second intifada, Israelis lost faith in negotiation, elected Ariel Sharon and started building what they call the security barrier, and Palestinians call the Apartheid Wall—the network of concrete walls and steel fences that protrudes from the 1967 green-line border, reaching hungrily into Palestinian territory and pulling huge settlement blocks into the Israeli state, as well as 30 percent of the water sources in some areas.[22]

There is no doubt that Arafat wanted a better deal than the ones produced either at Camp David or Taba in January 2001, but these deals were also not the prizes they have been made out to be. Though consistently presented by Israelis as an offer unparalleled in its generosity, Camp David would have provided almost no redress to Palestinians who had been forced from their homes and land when the Israeli state was created in 1948, and it did not come close to satisfying the minimal rights of Palestinians to self-determination. In 2006, Shlomo Ben-Ami, a lead negotiator for the Israeli government at both Camp David and Taba, broke ranks with the party line and admitted that "Camp David was not the missed opportunity for the Palestinians, and if I were Palestinian I would have rejected Camp David, as well."[23]

There were other factors contributing to Tel Aviv's abandonment of serious negotiations at peace talks post-2001—factors just as powerful as Arafat's alleged intransigence or Sharon's personal drive to create a "greater Israel." One related to the rise of Israel's tech economy. In the early nineties, Israel's economic elites wanted peace for prosperity, but the kind of prosperity they then built during the Oslo years ended up relying far less on peace than they had originally assumed. When Israel's niche in the global economy turned out to be information technologies, it meant that the key to growth was sending software and computer chips to Los Angeles and London, not shipping heavy cargo to Beirut and Damascus. Success in the tech sector did not require Israel to have friendly relationships with its Arab neighbors or to end its occupation of the territories. The rise of the tech economy was only the first phase of Israel's fateful economic transformation, however. The second came after the dot-com economy crashed in 2000, and Israel's leading companies needed to find a new niche in the global market.

With the most tech-dependent economy in the world, Israel was hit harder by the dot-com crash than anywhere else. The country went into immediate free fall, and by June 2001, analysts were predicting that roughly three hundred high-tech Israeli firms would go bankrupt, with tens of thousands of layoffs. The Tel Aviv business newspaper *Globes* declared in a headline that 2002 was the "Worst Year for Israeli Economy Since 1953."[24]

The only reason the recession was not even worse, the newspaper observed, was that the Israeli government quickly intervened with a powerful 10.7 percent increase in military spending, partially financed through cutbacks in social services. The government also encouraged the tech industry to branch out from information and communication technologies and into security and surveillance. In this period, the Israeli Defence Forces played a role similar to a business incubator. Young Israeli soldiers experimented with network systems and surveillance devices while they fulfilled their mandatory military service, then turned their findings into business plans when they returned to civilian life. A slew of new start-ups were launched, specializing in everything from "search and nail" data mining, to surveillance cameras, to terrorist profiling.[25] When the market for these services and devices exploded in the years after September 11, the Israeli state openly embraced a new national economic vision: the growth provided by the dot-com bubble would be replaced with a homeland security boom. It was the perfect marriage of the Likud Party's hawkishness and its radical embrace of Chicago School economics, as embodied by Sharon's finance minister, Benjamin Netanyahu, and Israel's new central bank chief, Stanley Fischer, chief architect of the IMF's shock therapy adventures in Russia and Asia.

By 2003, Israel was already making a stunning recovery, and by 2004 the country had seemed to pull off a miracle: after its calamitous crash, it was performing better than almost any Western economy. Much of this growth was due to Israel's savvy positioning of itself as a kind of shopping mall for homeland security technologies. The timing was perfect. Governments around the world were suddenly desperate for terrorist hunting tools, as well as for human intelligence know-how in the Arab world. Under the leadership of the Likud Party, the Israeli state billed itself as a showroom for the cutting-edge homeland security state, drawing on its decades of experience and expertise fighting Arab and Muslim threats. Israel's pitch to North America and Europe was straightforward: the War on Terror you are just embarking on is one we have been fighting since our birth. Let our high-tech firms and privatized spy companies show you how it's done.

Overnight, Israel became, in the words of *Forbes* magazine, "the go-to country for antiterrorism technologies."[26] Every year since 2002, Israel has played host to at least half a dozen major homeland security conferences for lawmakers, police chiefs, sheriffs and CEOs from around the world, with their size and scope growing annually. As traditional tourism suffered in the face of security fears, this kind of official counterterror tourism emerged to partially fill the gap.

During one such gathering in February 2006, billed as a "behind-the-scenes tour of [Israel's] struggle against terrorism," delegates from the FBI, Microsoft and Singapore's Mass Transit System (among others) traveled to some of Israel's most popular tourism destinations: the Knesset, the Temple Mount, the Wailing Wall. At each location, the visitors examined and admired the fortress-style security systems to see what they could apply at home. In May 2007, Israel hosted the directors of several large U.S. airports, who attended workshops on the types of aggressive passenger profiling and screening used at Ben Gurion International Airport near Tel Aviv. Steven Grossman, head of aviation at the international airport in Oakland, California, explained that he was there because "the Israelis are legendary for their security." Some of the events are macabre and theatrical. At the International Homeland Security Conference 2006, for instance, the Israeli military staged an elaborate "simulation of a mass casualty disaster that started in the City of Ness Ziona and concluded in Asaf Harofeh Hospital," according to the organizers.[27]

These are not policy conferences, but highly lucrative trade shows designed to demonstrate the prowess of Israeli security firms. As a result, Israel's exports in counter terrorism–related products and services increased by 15 percent in 2006 and were projected to grow by 20 percent in 2007, totalling $1.2 billion annually. The country's defense exports in 2006 reached a record $3.4 billion (compared to $1.6 billion in 1992), making Israel the fourth largest arms dealer in the world, larger than the U.K. Israel has more technology stocks listed on the Nasdaq exchange—many of them security related—than any other foreign country, and it has more tech patents registered in the U.S. than China and India combined. Its technology sector, much of it linked to security, now makes up 60 percent of all exports.[28]

Len Rosen, a prominent Israeli investment banker, told *Fortune* magazine, "It's security that matters more than peace." During Oslo, "people were looking for peace to provide growth. Now they're looking for security so violence doesn't curtail growth."[29] He could have gone much further: the business of providing "security"—in Israel and around the world—is directly responsible for much of Israel's meteoric economic growth in recent years. It is not an exaggeration to say that the War on Terror industry saved Israel's faltering economy, much as the disaster capitalism complex helped rescue the global stock markets.

Here is a small sample of the industry's reach:

- A call made to the New York Police Department will be recorded and analyzed on technology created by Nice Systems, an Israeli firm. Nice also monitors communication for the L.A. Police and Time Warner, as well as providing video surveillance cameras to Ronald Reagan National Airport, among dozens of other top clients.[30]
- Images captured in the London tube system are recorded on Verint video surveillance cameras, owned by the Israeli technology giant Comverse. Verint surveillance gear is also used at the U.S. Department of Defense, Washington's Dulles International Airport, on Capitol Hill and the Montreal Métro. The company has surveillance clients in more than fifty countries and also helps corporate giants like Home Depot and Target keep an eye on their workers.[31]
- Employees of the cities of Los Angeles and Columbus, Ohio, carry electronic "smartcard" IDs made by the Israeli company SuperCom, which boasts the former CIA director James Woolsey as the chair of its advisory board. An unnamed European country has gone with Super-Com for a national ID program; another has commissioned a pilot program for "biometric passports," both highly controversial initiatives.[32]
- The firewalls in the computer networks of some of the largest electricity companies in the U.S. were built by the Israeli tech giant Check Point, though the corporations have chosen to keep their names secret. According to the company, "89% of Fortune 500 companies use Check Point security solutions."[33]
- In the run-up to the 2007 Super Bowl, all the workers at the Miami International Airport received training to identify "bad people, not just bad things" using a psychological system called Behavior Pattern Recognition, developed by the Israeli firm New Age Security Solutions. The company's CEO is the former head of security at Israel's Ben Gurion Airport. Other airports that have contracted with New Age in recent years to train workers in passenger profiling include Boston, San Francisco, Glasgow, Athens and London Heathrow, as well as many others. Port workers in the conflict-ridden Niger Delta have received New Age training, as have employees at the Netherlands Ministry of Justice, guards for the Statue of Liberty and agents with the New York Police Department's Counter Terrorism Bureau.[34]

- When the wealthy New Orleans neighborhood of Audubon Place decided it needed its own police force after Hurricane Katrina, it hired the Israel private security firm Instinctive Shooting International.[35]
- Agents with the Royal Canadian Mounted Police, Canada's federal police agency, have received training from International Security Instructors, a Virginia-based company that specializes in training law enforcement and soldiers. Advertising its "hard won Israeli experience," its instructors are "veterans of Israeli special task forces from . . . Israel Defense Force, Israel National Police Counter Terrorism units [and] General Security Services (GSS or 'Shin Beit')." The company's elite list of clients includes the FBI, the U.S. Army, the U.S. Marine Corps, the U.S. Navy SEALs, and London's Metropolitan Police Service.[36]
- In April 2007, special immigration agents with the U.S. Department of Homeland Security, working along the Mexican border, went through an intensive eight-day training course put on by the Golan Group. The Golan Group was founded by ex–Israeli Special Forces officers and boasts more than 3,500 employees in seven countries. "Essentially we put an Israeli security spin on our procedures," Thomas Pearson, the company's head of operations, explained of the training course, which covered everything from hand-to-hand combat to target practice to "getting really proactive with their SUV." The Golan Group, now based in Florida but still marketing its Israeli advantage, also produces X-ray machines, metal detectors and rifles. In addition to many governments and celebrities, its clients include ExxonMobil, Shell, Texaco, Levi's, Sony, Citigroup and Pizza Hut.[37]
- When Buckingham Palace needed a new security system, it selected a design by Magal, one of two Israeli companies that have been most involved in building the Israeli "security barrier."[38]
- When Boeing begins building the planned $2.5 billion "virtual fences" on the U.S. borders with Mexico and Canada—complete with electronic sensors, unmanned aircraft, surveillance cameras and eighteen hundred towers—one of its main partners will be Elbit. Elbit is the other Israeli firm most involved in building Israel's hugely controversial wall, which is "the largest construction project in Israel's history" and has also cost $2.5 billion.[39]

With more and more countries turning themselves into fortresses (walls and high-tech fences are going up on the border between India and Kashmir, Saudi

Arabia and Iraq, Afghanistan and Pakistan), "security barriers" may prove to be the biggest disaster market of all. That's why Elbit and Magal don't mind the relentless negative publicity that Israel's wall attracts around the world—in fact, they consider it free advertising. "People believe we are the only ones who have experience testing this equipment in real life," explained Magal CEO Jacob Even-Ezra.[40] Elbit and Magal have seen their stock prices more than double since September 11, a standard performance for Israeli homeland security stocks. Verint—dubbed "the granddaddy of the video surveillance space"— wasn't profitable at all before September 11, but between 2002 and 2006 its stock price has more than tripled, thanks to the surveillance boom.[41]

The extraordinary performance of Israel's homeland security companies is well known to stock watchers, but it is rarely discussed as a factor in the politics of the region. It should be. It is not a coincidence that the Israeli state's decision to put "counterterrorism" at the center of its export economy has coincided precisely with its abandonment of peace negotiations, as well as a clear strategy to reframe its conflict with the Palestinians not as a battle against a nationalist movement with specific goals for land and rights but rather as part of the global War on Terror—one against illogical, fanatical forces bent only on destruction.

Economics is by no means the primary motivator for the escalation in the region since 2001. There is, of course, no shortage of fuel for violence on all sides. Yet within this context that is so weighted against peace, economics has, at certain points, been a countervailing force, pushing reluctant political leaders into negotiations, as was the case in the early nineties. What the homeland security boom has done is change the direction of that pressure, creating yet another powerful sector invested in continued violence.

As has been the case on previous Chicago School frontiers, Israel's post-9/11 growth spurt has been marked by the rapid stratification of society between rich and poor inside the state. The security buildup has been accompanied by a wave of privatizations and funding cuts to social programs that has virtually annihilated the economic legacy of Labor Zionism and created an epidemic of inequality the likes of which Israelis have never known. In 2007, 24.4 percent of Israelis were living below the poverty line, with 35.2 percent of all children in poverty—compared with 8 percent of children twenty years earlier.[42] Yet even though the benefits of the boom have not been widely shared, they have been so lucrative for a small sector of Israelis, particularly the powerful segment that is seamlessly integrated into both the military and government (with all the familiar corporatist corruption scandals), that a crucial incentive for peace has been obliterated.

The Israeli business sector's shift in political direction has been dramatic. The vision that captivates the Tel Aviv Stock Exchange today is no longer that of Israel as a regional trade hub but rather as a futuristic fortress, able to survive even in a sea of determined enemies. The revised attitude was most pronounced in the summer of 2006, when the Israeli government turned what should have been a prisoner exchange negotiation with Hezbollah into a full-scale war. Israel's largest corporations didn't just support the war, they sponsored it. Bank Leumi, Israel's newly privatized megabank, distributed bumper stickers with the slogans "We Will Be Victorious" and "We Are Strong," while, as the Israeli journalist and novelist Yitzhak Laor wrote at the time, "the current war is the first to become a branding opportunity for one of our largest mobile phone companies, which is using it to run a huge promotional campaign."[43]

Clearly, Israeli industry no longer has reason to fear war. In contrast to 1993, when conflict was seen as a barrier to growth, the Tel Aviv Stock Exchange went up in August 2006, the month of the devastating war with Lebanon. In the final quarter of the year, which had also included the bloody escalation in the West Bank and Gaza following the election of Hamas, Israel's overall economy grew by a staggering 8 percent—more than triple the growth rate of the U.S. economy in the same period. The Palestinian economy, meanwhile, contracted by between 10 and 15 percent in 2006, with poverty rates reaching close to 70 percent.[44]

One month after the UN declared a cease-fire between Israel and Hezbollah, the New York Stock Exchange hosted a special conference on investing in Israel. More than two hundred Israeli firms attended, many of them in the homeland security sector. At that moment in Lebanon, economic activity was at a virtual standstill and roughly 140 factories—manufacturers of everything from prefab homes to medical products to milk—were clearing away the rubble after being hit by Israeli bombs and missiles. Impervious to the impact of the war, the message of the New York gatherings was upbeat: "Israel is open for business—has always been open for business," announced Israel's ambassador to the United Nations, Dan Gillerman, welcoming delegates to the event.[45]

Only a decade earlier, this kind of wartime exuberance would have been unimaginable. It was Gillerman who, as head of the Israeli Federation of Chambers of Commerce, had called for Israel to seize the historic opportunity and become "a Middle Eastern Singapore." Now he was one of the most inflammatory of Israel's pro-war hawks, pushing for an even wider escalation. On CNN, Gillerman said that "while it may be politically incorrect and maybe even untrue to say that all Muslims are terrorists, it happens to be very true that nearly all terrorists are Muslim. So this is not just Israel's war. This is the world's war."[46]

This recipe for endless worldwide war is the same one that the Bush administration offered as a business prospectus to the nascent disaster capitalism complex after September 11. It is not a war that can be won by any country, but winning is not the point. The point is to create "security" inside fortress states bolstered by endless low-level conflict outside their walls. In a way, it is the same goal that the private security companies have in Iraq: secure the perimeter, protect the principal. Baghdad, New Orleans and Sandy Springs provide glimpses of a kind of gated future built and run by the disaster capitalism complex. It is in Israel, however, that this process is most advanced: an entire country has turned itself into a fortified gated community, surrounded by locked-out people living in permanently excluded red zones. This is what a society looks like when it has lost its economic incentive for peace and is heavily invested in fighting and profiting from an endless and unwinnable War on Terror. One part looks like Israel; the other part looks like Gaza.

Israel's case is extreme, but the kind of society it is creating may not be unique. The disaster capitalism complex thrives in conditions of low-intensity grinding conflict. That seems to be the end point in all the disaster zones, from New Orleans to Iraq. In April 2007, U.S. soldiers began implementing a plan to turn several volatile Baghdad neighborhoods into "gated communities," surrounded by checkpoints and concrete walls, where residents would be tracked using biometric technology. "We'll be like the Palestinians," predicted one resident of Adhamiya, watching his neighborhood being sealed in by the barrier.[47] After it becomes clear that Baghdad is never going to be Dubai, and New Orleans won't be Disneyland, Plan B is to settle into another Colombia or Nigeria—never-ending war, fought in large measure by private soldiers and paramilitaries, damped down just enough to get the natural resources out of the ground, helped along by mercenaries guarding the pipelines, platforms and water reserves.

It has become commonplace to compare the militarized ghettos of Gaza and the West Bank, with their concrete walls, electrified fences and checkpoints, to the Bantustan system in South Africa, which kept blacks in ghettos and demanded passes when they left. "Israel's laws and practices in the OPT [occupied Palestinian territories] certainly resemble aspects of apartheid," said John Dugard, the South African lawyer who is the UN's special rapporteur on human rights in the Palestinian territories, in February 2007.[48] The similarities are stark, but there are differences too. South Africa's Bantustans were essentially work camps, a way to keep African laborers under tight surveillance and control so they would work cheaply in the mines. What Israel has constructed is a system designed to do the opposite: to keep workers from working, a network of open holding pens for millions of people who have been categorized as surplus humanity.

Palestinians are not the only people in the world who have been so categorized: millions of Russians also became surplus in their own country, which is why so many fled their homes in the hope of finding a job and a decent life in Israel. Although the original Bantustans have been dismantled in South Africa, the one in four people who live in shacks in fast-expanding slums are also surplus in the new, neoliberal South Africa.[49] This discarding of 25 to 60 percent of the population has been the hallmark of the Chicago School crusade since the "misery villages" began mushrooming throughout the Southern Cone in the seventies. In South Africa, Russia and New Orleans the rich build walls around themselves. Israel has taken this disposal process a step further: it has built walls around the dangerous poor.

SHOCK WEARS OFF

THE RISE OF PEOPLE'S RECONSTRUCTION

I want to say to you, my Indian brothers concentrated here in Bolivia, that the five-hundred-year campaign of resistance has not been in vain. This democratic, cultural fight is part of the fight of our ancestors, it is the continuity of the fight of [the indigenous anticolonial leader] Tupac Katari, it is a continuity of the fight of Che Guevara.
—Evo Morales, after being sworn in as president of Bolivia, January 22, 2006[1]

People know best. They know every corner and every detail of their community best. They also know their weak points.
—Pichit Ratakul, executive director of the Asian Disaster Preparedness Center, October 30, 2006[2]

The people from the barrio built the city twice: during the day we built the houses of the well-off. At night and at weekends, with solidarity, we built our own homes, our barrio.
—Andrés Antillano, resident of Caracas, April 15, 2004[3]

When Milton Friedman died in November 2006, many of the obituaries were imbued with a sense of fear that his death marked the end of an era. In Canada's *National Post*, Terence Corcoran, one of Friedman's most devoted disciples, wondered whether the global movement the economist had launched could carry on. "As the last great lion of free market economics,

Friedman leaves a void. . . . There is no one alive today of equal stature. Will the principles Friedman fought for and articulated survive over the long term without a new generation of solid, charismatic and able intellectual leadership? Hard to say."[4]

Corcoran's grim assessment did not begin to encompass the state of disarray in which the quest for unfettered capitalism found itself that November. Friedman's intellectual heirs in the United States, the neocons who launched the disaster capitalism complex, were at the lowest point in their history. The movement's pinnacle had been the winning of the U.S. Congress by the Republicans in 1994; just nine days before Friedman's death, they lost it again to a Democratic majority. The three key issues that contributed to the Republican defeat in the 2006 midterm elections were political corruption, the mismanagement of the Iraq war and the perception, best articulated by a winning Democratic candidate for the U.S. Senate, Jim Webb, that the country had drifted "toward a class-based system, the likes of which we have not seen since the 19th century."[5] In each case, the core tenets of Chicago School economics—privatization, deregulation and cuts to government services—had laid the foundation for the breakdowns.

In 1976, Orlando Letelier, one of the counterrevolution's first victims, had insisted that the massive wealth inequalities that the Chicago Boys opened up in Chile were "not an economic liability but a temporary political success." For Letelier, it was obvious that the dictatorship's "free market" rules were doing exactly what they were designed to do: they were not creating a perfectly harmonious economy but turning the already wealthy into the superrich and the organized working class into the disposable poor. These patterns of stratification have been repeated everywhere that the Chicago School ideology has triumphed. In China, despite its stunning economic growth, the gap between the incomes of city dwellers and the 800 million rural poor has doubled over the past twenty years. In Argentina, where in 1970 the richest 10 percent of the population earned 12 times as much as the poorest, the rich were by 2002 earning 43 times as much. Chile's "political success" has truly been globalized. In December 2006, a month after Friedman died, a UN study found that "the richest 2 per cent of adults in the world own more than half of global household wealth." The shift has been starkest in the U.S., where CEOs made 43 times what the average worker earned in 1980, when Reagan kicked off the Friedmanite crusade. By 2005, CEOs earned 411 times as much. For those executives, the counterrevolution that began in the basement of the Social Sciences building in the

1950s has indeed been a success, but the cost of that victory has been the widespread loss of faith in the core free-market promise—that increased wealth will be shared. As Webb said during the midterm campaign, "Trickle-down economics didn't happen."[6]

The hoarding of so much wealth by a tiny minority of the world's population was not a peaceful process, as we have seen, nor, often, was it a legal one. Corcoran was right to question the caliber of the movement's leadership, but the problem was not simply that there were no figureheads of Friedman's stature. It was that many of the men who had been on the front lines of the international drive to liberate the markets from all restrictions were at that moment caught up in an astonishing array of scandals and criminal proceedings, dating from the earliest laboratories in Latin America to the most recent one in Iraq. Throughout its thirty-five-year history, the Chicago School agenda has advanced through the intimate cooperation of powerful business figures, crusading ideologues and strong-arm political leaders. By 2006, key players from each camp were either in jail or up on charges.

Augusto Pinochet, the first leader to put Friedman's shock treatment into effect, was under house arrest (though he died before trials could go ahead on either the corruption or murder charges). The day after Friedman died, Uruguayan police came to arrest to Juan María Bordaberry on charges related to the killing of four prominent leftists in 1976. Bordaberry had led Uruguay during its brutal embrace of Chicago School economics, with Friedman's colleagues and students serving as prominent advisers. In Argentina, the courts have stripped the country's former junta leaders of immunity, sending ex-president Jorge Videla and Admiral Emilio Massera to jail for life. Domingo Cavallo, who had headed the central bank during the dictatorship and had gone on to impose the sweeping shock therapy program under democracy, was also indicted on charges of "fraud in public administration." A debt deal that Cavallo engineered with foreign banks in 2001 cost the country tens of billions of dollars, and the judge, who froze $10 million of Cavallo's personal assets, asserted that the administration had acted with "absolute consciousness" of the detrimental outcome.[7]

In Bolivia, former president Gonzalo Sánchez de Lozada, in whose living room the economic "atomic bomb" had been built, was wanted on several charges relating to the gunning down of protesters and his signing of contracts with foreign gas companies that allegedly violated Bolivian laws.[8] In Russia, not only had the Harvard Men been found guilty of fraud but many

of the Russian oligarchs, the well-connected businessmen who made billions from the overnight privatizations that the Harvard team had helped engineer, were either in jail or living in exile. Mikhail Khodorkovsky, former
head of the oil giant Yukos, was serving an eight-year sentence in a Siberian
prison. His colleague and principal shareholder, Leonid Nevzlin, was in exile in Israel, as was fellow oligarch Vladimir Gusinsky, while the infamous
Boris Berezovsky had settled in London, unable to return to Moscow for fear
of arrest on fraud charges; yet all these men deny wrongdoing.[9] Conrad
Black, who, with his newspaper chain, was the most powerful ideological
amplifier of Friedmanism in Canada, was facing charges in the U.S. that he
had defrauded the shareholders of Hollinger International, treating the company, according to prosecutors, like "the bank of Conrad Black." Also in the
United States, Enron's Ken Lay—the poster boy for the ill effects of energy
deregulation—died in July 2006, having been convicted of conspiracy and
fraud. And Grover Norquist, the Friedmanite think-tanker who had made
progressives' hair stand on end by declaring, "I don't want to abolish government. I simply want to reduce it to the size where I can drag it into the bath-
room and drown it in the bathtub," was neck-deep in the influence-peddling
scandal surrounding the Washington lobbyist Jack Abramoff, though no
charges had been laid.[10]

Despite the attempts of everyone from Pinochet to Cavallo to Berezovsky
to Black to portray himself as a victim of baseless political persecution, this
list, by no means complete, represents a radical departure from the neoliberal creation myth. The economic crusade managed to cling to a veneer of
respectability and lawfulness as it progressed. Now that veneer was being very
publicly stripped away to reveal a system of gross wealth inequalities, often
opened up with the aid of grotesque criminality.

Besides legal trouble, there was another cloud on the horizon. The effects
of the shocks that had been so integral to creating the illusion of ideological
consensus were beginning to wear off. Rodolfo Walsh, another early casualty, had regarded the Chicago School ascendancy in Argentina as a setback,
not a lasting defeat. The terror tactics used by the junta had put his country
into a state of shock, but Walsh knew that shock, by its very nature, is a temporary state. Before he was gunned down on the streets of Buenos Aires, Walsh estimated that it would take twenty to thirty years until the effects of the terror
receded and Argentines regained their footing, courage and confidence, ready
once again to fight for economic and social equality. It was in 2001, twenty-
four years later, that Argentina erupted in protest against IMF-prescribed

austerity measures and then proceeded to force out five presidents in only three weeks.

I was living in Buenos Aires in that period, and people kept exclaiming, "The dictatorship just ended!" At the time I didn't understand the meaning behind the jubilation, since the dictatorship had been over for seventeen years. Now I think I do: the state of shock had finally worn off, just as Walsh predicted.

In the years since, that wide-awake shock resistance has spread to many other former shock labs—Chile, Bolivia, China, Lebanon. And as people shed the collective fear that was first instilled with tanks and cattle prods, with sudden flights of capital and brutal cutbacks, many are demanding more democracy and more control over markets. These demands represent the greatest threat of all to Friedman's legacy because they challenge his most central claim: that capitalism and freedom are part of the same indivisible project.

The Bush administration remains so committed to perpetuating this false union that, in 2002, it embedded it in the National Security Strategy of the United States of America. "The great struggles of the twentieth century between liberty and totalitarianism ended with a decisive victory for the forces of freedom—a single sustainable model for national success: freedom, democracy and free enterprise."[11] This assertion, made with the full force of the U.S. military arsenal behind it, was not enough to hold back the tide of citizens using their various freedoms to reject free-market orthodoxy—even in the United States. As a headline in *The Miami Herald* after the 2006 midterm elections put it, "Democrats won big by opposing free-trade agreements." A *New York Times*/CBS poll a few months later found that 64 percent of U.S. citizens believed the government should guarantee health care coverage to all and "showed a striking willingness . . . to make tradeoffs" to achieve that goal, including paying up to $500 a year more in taxes.[12]

On the international stage, the staunchest opponents of neoliberal economics were winning election after election. The Venezuelan president Hugo Chávez, running on a platform of "21st Century Socialism," was re-elected in 2006 for a third term with 63 percent of the vote. Despite attempts by the Bush administration to paint Venezuela as a pseudodemocracy, a poll that same year recorded that 57 percent of Venezuelans were happy with the state of their democracy, an approval rating on the continent second only to Uruguay's, where the left-wing coalition party Frente Amplio had been elected to government and where a series of referendums had blocked major privatizations.[13] In other words, in the two Latin American states where voting had resulted in real challenges to the Washington Consensus, citizens had renewed their faith in the power of democracy to improve their lives. In stark contrast to this enthusiasm, in countries where economic policies remain largely unchanged regardless of the promises made during campaigns, polls consistently track an eroding faith in democracy, reflected in dwindling turnout for elections, deep cynicism toward politicians and a rise in religious fundamentalism.

More clashes between free markets and free people took place in Europe in 2005, when the European Constitution was rejected in two national referendums. In France, the document came to be seen as the codification of the corporatist order. It was the first time citizens had ever been asked for their direct input into whether free-market rules should reign in Europe, and they seized the opportunity to say no. As the Paris-based author and activist Susan George put it, "People really didn't know Europe was all encapsulated, all written down in a single document. . . . Once you start to quote it, and people find out what's actually in this and find out what's going to be constitutionalized and not revisable and not amendable, they get scared to death."[14]

The powerful rejection of what the French call "savage capitalism" takes many different forms, including reactionary and racist ones. In the U.S., rage at the shrinking of the middle class has been easily redirected to calls for border fences, with CNN's Lou Dobbs leading a nightly campaign against the "invasion of illegal aliens" waging "war on the American middle class"—stealing jobs, spreading crime, as well as bringing in "highly contagious diseases."[15] (This kind of scapegoating provoked the largest immigrants' rights protests in U.S. history, with more than a million people participating in a series of marches in 2006—another sign of a new fearlessness among casualties of economic shocks.)

In the Netherlands, the 2005 referendum on the European Constitution was similarly hijacked by anti-immigration parties, turning it into a vote less against a corporate order than against the specter of Polish tradespeople flooding into Western Europe to push down wages. What drove many voters in both the French and Dutch referendums was "fear of the Polish plumber"—or "plumber phobia," in the words of the former European Union commissioner Pascal Lamy.[16]

In Poland, meanwhile, the backlash against the policies that impoverished so many in the nineties has unleashed its own set of disturbing phobias.

When Solidarity betrayed the workers who had built the movement, many Poles turned to new organizations, eventually putting the ultraconservative Law and Justice Party into power. Poland is now ruled by President Lech Kaczyński, a disaffected Solidarity activist who, when he was mayor of Warsaw, made a name for himself by banning a gay-pride-day march and participating in a "normal people pride" event.* Kaczyński and his twin brother, Jaroslaw (now prime minister), won the 2005 elections with a campaign largely based on rhetoric attacking Chicago School policies. Their main opponents were promising to do away with the public pension system and to introduce a 15 percent flat tax—both straight out of the Friedman playbook. The twins pointed out that these policies would steal from the poor and enrich a nexus of big-business and on-the-take politicians. When the Law and Justice Party came to power, however, it switched its aim to easier targets: gays, Jews, feminists, foreigners, Communists. As one Polish newspaper editor put it, "Their project is definitely an indictment of the past 17 years."[17]

In Russia, the Putin era is seen by many as a similar backlash against the shock therapy era. With tens of millions of impoverished citizens still excluded from the fast-growing economy, politicians have no difficulty riling up public sentiment about the events of the early nineties, which are frequently portrayed as a foreign conspiracy to bring the Soviet empire to its knees and put Russia "under external management."[18] Despite the fact that Putin's legal moves against several oligarchs have mostly been symbolic—with a new breed of "state oligarch" rising around the Kremlin—the memory of the chaos of the nineties has made many Russians grateful for the order Putin has restored, even as growing numbers of journalists and other critics die mysteriously, and the secret police enjoy seemingly total impunity.

With socialism still closely associated with the decades of brutality carried out in its name, public anger has few outlets for expression except nationalism and protofascism. Incidents of ethnic-based violence are up roughly 30 percent a year and in 2006 were reported almost daily. The slogan "Russia for Russians" is supported by close to 60 percent of the population.[19] "The authorities are fully aware that their social and economic policy is very flawed with respect to providing acceptable living conditions to the majority of the population," said Yuri Vdovin, an antifascist activist. Yet "all the failures are

---

* This prejudice is not unique to Poland. In March 2007, London's mayor, Ken Livingstone, warned of a dangerous "gale of reaction against lesbian and gay rights blowing across eastern Europe."

allegedly due to the presence of other people with the wrong religion, the wrong skin colour or other ethnic background."[20]

It is a bitter irony that when shock therapy was prescribed in Russia and Eastern Europe, its painful effects were often justified as the only way to prevent a repeat of the conditions in Weimar Germany that led to the rise of Nazism. The casual exclusion of tens of millions of people by free-market ideologues has reproduced frighteningly similar explosive conditions: proud populations that perceive themselves as humiliated by foreign forces, looking to regain their national pride by targeting the most vulnerable in their midst.

In Latin America, the original Chicago School laboratory, the backlash takes a distinctly more hopeful form. It is not directed at the weak or the vulnerable but focuses squarely on the ideology at the root of economic exclusion. And unlike the situation in Russia and Eastern Europe, there is an irrepressible enthusiasm for trying the ideas that were subverted in the past.

Despite the Bush administration's claim that the twentieth century ended with a "decisive victory" for free markets over all forms of socialism, many Latin Americans understand perfectly well that it was authoritarian communism that failed in Eastern Europe and parts of Asia. Democratic socialism, meaning not only socialist parties brought to power through elections but also democratically run workplaces and land holdings, has worked in many regions, from Scandinavia to the thriving and historic cooperative economy in Italy's Emilia-Romagna region. It was a version of this combination of democracy and socialism that Allende was attempting to bring to Chile between 1970 and 1973. Gorbachev had a similar, though less radical, vision to turn the Soviet Union into a "socialist beacon" on the Scandinavian model. South Africa's Freedom Charter, the dream that animated the long liberation struggle, was a version of this same third way: not state communism, but markets existing alongside the nationalization of the banks and mines, with the income used to build comfortable neighborhoods and decent schools—economic as well as political democracy. The workers who founded Solidarity in 1980 pledged to struggle not against socialism but for it, with workers eventually winning the power to run their workplaces and country democratically.

The dirty secret of the neoliberal era is that these ideas were never defeated in a great battle of ideas, nor were they voted down in elections. They were shocked out of the way at key political junctures. When resistance was fierce, they were defeated with overt violence—rolled over by Pinochet's,

Yeltsin's and Deng Xiaoping's tanks. At other times, they were simply betrayed through what John Williamson called "voodoo politics": the Bolivian president Víctor Paz Estenssoro's postelection secret economic team (and mass kidnapping of union leaders); the ANC's backroom bargaining-away of the Freedom Charter in favor of Thabo Mbeki's top-secret economic program; Solidarity's exhausted adherents succumbing to economic shock therapy after the elections in exchange for a bailout. It is precisely because the dream of economic equality is so popular, and so difficult to defeat in a fair fight, that the shock doctrine was embraced in the first place.

Washington has always regarded democratic socialism as a greater threat than totalitarian Communism, which was easy to vilify and made for a handy enemy. In the sixties and seventies, the favored tactic for dealing with the inconvenient popularity of developmentalism and democratic socialism was to try to equate them with Stalinism, deliberately blurring the clear differences between the worldviews. (Conflating all opposition with terrorism plays a similar role today.) A stark example of this strategy comes from the early days of the Chicago crusade, deep inside the declassified Chile documents. Despite the CIA-funded propaganda campaign painting Allende as a Soviet-style dictator, Washington's real concerns about the Allende election victory were relayed by Henry Kissinger in a 1970 memo to Nixon: "The example of a successful elected Marxist government in Chile would surely have an impact on—and even precedent value for—other parts of the world, especially in Italy; the imitative spread of similar phenomena elsewhere would in turn significantly affect the world balance and our own position in it."[21] In other words, Allende needed to be taken out before his democratic third way spread.

The dream he represented was never defeated. It was, as Walsh noted, temporarily silenced, pushed under the surface by fear. Which is why, as Latin America emerges from its decades of shock, the old ideas are bubbling back up—along with the "imitative spread" Kissinger so feared. Ever since the Argentine collapse in 2001, opposition to privatization has become the defining issue of the continent, able to make governments and break them; by late 2006, it was practically creating a domino effect. Luiz Inácio Lula da Silva was reelected as president of Brazil largely because he turned the vote into a referendum on privatization. His opponent, from the party responsible for Brazil's major sell-offs in the nineties, resorted to appearing in public looking like a socialist NASCAR driver, wearing a jacket and baseball hat covered in logos from the public companies that had not yet been sold. Voters weren't persuaded, and Lula got 61 percent of the vote, despite disillusionment with the corruption scandals plaguing his government. Shortly afterward in Nicaragua, Daniel Ortega, former head of the Sandinistas, made the country's frequent blackouts the center of his winning campaign; the sale of the national electricity company to the Spanish firm Unión Fenosa after Hurricane Mitch, he asserted, was the source of the problem. "You, brothers, are suffering the effects of these outages every day!" he bellowed. "Who brought Unión Fenosa to this country? The government of the rich did, those who are in the service of barbarian capitalism."[22]

In November 2006, Ecuador's presidential elections turned into a similar ideological battleground. Rafael Correa, a forty-three-year-old left-wing economist, won the vote against Álvaro Noboa, a banana tycoon and one of the richest men in the country. With Twisted Sister's "We're Not Going to Take It" as his official campaign song, Correa called for the country "to overcome all the fallacies of neo-liberalism." When he won, the new president of Ecuador declared himself "no fan of Milton Friedman."[23] By then, the Bolivian president Evo Morales was already approaching the end of his first year in office. After sending in the army to take back the gas fields from multinational "plunderers," he moved on to nationalize parts of the mining sector. In this same period in Mexico, the results of the fraud-tainted 2006 elections were being contested through the creation of an unprecedented "parallel government" of the people, with votes held in the streets and plaza outside the seat of government in Mexico City. In the Mexican state of Oaxaca, the right-wing government sent in riot police to break a strike by teachers who were demanding an annual pay raise. It provoked a statewide rebellion against the corruption of the corporatist state that raged for months.

Chile and Argentina are both led by politicians who define themselves against their countries' Chicago School experiments, though the extent to which they provide genuine alternatives remains a subject of intense debate. The symbolism, however, represents its own kind of victory. Several of the people in the cabinet of the Argentine president, Néstor Kirchner, including Kirchner himself, were imprisoned during the dictatorship. On March 24, 2006, the thirtieth anniversary of the 1976 military coup, Kirchner addressed demonstrators in the Plaza de Mayo, where the mothers of the disappeared held their weekly vigils. "We are back," he declared, referring to the generation that had been terrorized in the seventies. In the huge assembled crowd, he said, were "the faces of the 30,000 disappeared compañeros returning to this plaza today."[24] Chile's president, Michelle Bachelet, was one of the thousands who were victims of Pinochet's reign of terror. In 1975, she and her mother were imprisoned and tortured in Villa Grimaldi, known for its wooden isolation cubicles, so small that prisoners could only crouch. Her father, a military officer, had refused to go along with the coup and was murdered by Pinochet's men.

In December 2006, a month after Friedman's death, Latin America's leaders gathered for a historic summit in Bolivia, held in the city of Cochabamba, where a popular uprising against water privatization had forced Bechtel out of the country several years earlier. Morales began the proceedings with a vow to close "the open veins of Latin America."[25] It was a reference to Eduardo Galeano's book *Open Veins of Latin America: Five Centuries of the Pillage of a Continent,* a lyrical accounting of the violent plunder that had turned a rich continent into a poor one. The book was first published in 1971, two years before Allende was overthrown for daring to try to close those open veins by nationalizing his country's copper mines. That event ushered in a new era of furious pillage, during which the structures built by the continent's developmentalist movements were sacked, stripped and sold off.

Today Latin Americans are picking up the project that was so brutally interrupted all those years ago. Many of the policies cropping up are familiar: nationalization of key sectors of the economy, land reform, major new investments in education, literacy and health care. These are not revolutionary ideas, but in their unapologetic vision of a government that helps reach for equality, they are certainly a rebuke to Friedman's 1975 assertion to Pinochet that "the major error, in my opinion, was . . . to believe that it is possible to do good with other people's money."

Though clearly drawing on a long militant history, Latin America's contemporary movements are not direct replicas of their predecessors. Of all the differences, the most striking is an acute awareness of the need for protection from the shocks of the past—the coups, the foreign shock therapists, the U.S.-trained torturers, as well as the debt shocks and currency collapses of the eighties and nineties. Latin America's mass movements, which have powered the wave of election victories for left-wing candidates, are learning how to build shock absorbers into their organizing models. They are, for example, less centralized than in the sixties, making it harder to demobilize whole movements by eliminating a few leaders. Despite the overwhelming cult of personality surrounding Chávez, and his moves to centralize power at the state level, the progressive networks in Venezuela are at the same time highly decentralized, with power dispersed at the grass roots and community level, through thousands of neighborhood councils and co-ops. In Bolivia, the indigenous people's movements that put Morales in office function similarly and have made it clear that Morales does not have their unconditional support: the barrios will back him as long as he stays true to his democratic mandate, and not a moment longer. This kind of network approach is what allowed Chávez to survive the 2002 coup attempt: when their revolution was threatened, his supporters poured down from the shantytowns surrounding Caracas to demand his reinstatement, a kind of popular mobilization that did not happen during the coups of the seventies.

Latin America's new leaders are also taking bold measures to block any future U.S.-backed coups that could attempt to undermine their democratic victories. The governments of Venezuela, Costa Rica, Argentina and Uruguay have all announced that they will no longer send students to the School of the Americas (now called the Western Hemisphere Institute for Security Cooperation) — the infamous police and military training center in Fort Benning, Georgia, where so many of the continent's notorious killers learned the latest in "counterterrorism" techniques, then promptly directed them against farmers in El Salvador and auto workers in Argentina.[26] Bolivia looks set to cut its ties with the school, as does Ecuador. Chávez has let it be known that if an extremist right-wing element in Bolivia's Santa Cruz province makes good on its threats against the government of Evo Morales, Venezuelan troops will help defend Bolivia's democracy. Rafael Correa is set to take the most radical step of all. The Ecuadorean port city of Manta currently hosts the largest U.S. military base in South America, which serves as a staging area for the "war on drugs," largely fought in Colombia. Correa's government has announced that when the agreement for the base expires in 2009, it will not be renewed. "Ecuador is a sovereign nation," said the minister of foreign relations, María Fernanda Espinosa. "We do not need any foreign troops in our country."[27] If the U.S. military does not have bases or training programs, its power to inflict shocks will be greatly eroded.

The new leaders in Latin America are also becoming better prepared for the kinds of shocks inflicted by volatile markets. One of the most destabilizing forces of recent decades has been the speed with which capital can pick up and move, or how a sudden drop in commodity prices can devastate an entire agricultural sector. But in much of Latin America these shocks have already happened, leaving behind ghostly industrial suburbs and huge stretches of fallow farmland. The task of the region's new left, therefore, has become a matter of taking the detritus of globalization and putting it back to work. In Brazil, the phenomenon is best seen in the million and a half farmers of the Landless Peoples Movement (MST) who have formed hundreds of cooperatives to reclaim unused land. In Argentina, it is clearest in the movement of "recovered companies," two hundred bankrupt businesses that have been resuscitated by their workers, who have turned them into democratically run cooperatives. For the cooperatives, there is no fear of facing an economic shock of investors leaving, because the investors have already left. In a way, the reclamation experiments are a new kind of post-disaster reconstruction—reconstruction from the slow-motion disaster of neoliberalism. In sharp contrast to the model offered by the disaster capitalism complex in Iraq, Afghanistan and the Gulf Coast, the leaders of Latin America's rebuilding efforts are the people most affected by the devastation. And unsurprisingly, their spontaneous solutions look very much like the real third way that had been so effectively shocked out of the way by the Chicago School campaign around the world—democracy in daily life.

In Venezuela, Chávez has made the co-ops a top political priority, giving them first refusal on government contracts and offering them economic incentives to trade with one another. By 2006, there were roughly 100,000 cooperatives in the country, employing more than 700,000 workers.[28] Many are pieces of state infrastructure—toll booths, highway maintenance, health clinics—handed over to the communities to run. It's a reverse of the logic of government outsourcing—rather than auctioning off pieces of the state to large corporations and losing democratic control, the people who use the resources are given the power to manage them, creating, at least in theory, both jobs and more responsive public services. Chávez's many critics have derided these initiatives as handouts and unfair subsidies, of course. Yet in an era when Halliburton treats the U.S. government as its personal ATM for six years, withdraws upward of $20 billion in Iraq contracts alone, refuses to hire local workers either on the Gulf Coast or in Iraq, then expresses its gratitude to U.S. taxpayers by moving its corporate headquarters to Dubai (with all the attendant tax and legal benefits), Chávez's direct subsidies to regular people look significantly less radical.

Latin America's most significant protection from future shocks (and therefore from the shock doctrine) flows from the continent's emerging independence from Washington's financial institutions, the result of greater integration among regional governments. The Bolivarian Alternative for the Americas (ALBA) is the continent's retort to the Free Trade Area of the Americas, the now buried corporatist dream of a free-trade zone stretching from Alaska to Tierra del Fuego. Though ALBA is still in its early stages, Emir Sader, the Brazil-based sociologist, describes its promise as "a perfect example of genuinely fair trade: each country provides what it is best placed to produce, in return for what it most needs, independent of global market prices."[29] So Bolivia provides gas at stable discounted prices; Venezuela offers heavily subsidized oil to poorer countries and shares expertise in developing reserves; and Cuba sends thousands of doctors to deliver free health care all over the continent, while training students from other countries at its medical schools. This is a very different model from the kind of academic exchange that began at the University of Chicago in the mid-fifties, when Latin American students learned a single rigid ideology and were sent home to impose it with uniformity across the continent. The major benefit is that ALBA is essentially a barter system, in which countries decide for themselves what any given commodity or service is worth, rather than letting traders in New York, Chicago or London set the prices for them. That makes trade far less vulnerable to the kind of sudden price fluctuations that devastated Latin American economies in the recent past. Surrounded by turbulent financial waters, Latin America is creating a zone of relative economic calm and predictability, a feat presumed impossible in the globalization era.

When one country does face a financial shortfall, this increased integration means that it does not need to turn to the IMF or the U.S. Treasury for a bailout. That's fortunate because the 2006 U.S. National Security Strategy makes it clear that for Washington, the shock doctrine is still very much alive: "If crises occur, the IMF's response must reinforce each country's responsibility for its own economic choices," the document states. "A refocused IMF will strengthen market institutions and market discipline over financial decisions." This kind of "market discipline" can only be enforced if governments actually go to Washington for help—as Stanley Fischer explained during the Asian financial crisis, the IMF can help only if it is asked, "but when [a country is] out of money, it hasn't got many places to turn."[30] That is no longer the case. Thanks to high oil prices, Venezuela has emerged as a major lender to other developing countries, allowing them to do an end run around Washington.

The results have been dramatic. Brazil, so long shackled to Washington by its enormous debt, is refusing to enter into a new agreement with the

IMF. Nicaragua is negotiating to quit the fund, Venezuela has withdrawn from both the IMF and the World Bank, and even Argentina, Washington's former "model pupil," has been part of the trend. In his 2007 State of the Union address, President Néstor Kirchner said that the country's foreign creditors had told him, " 'You must have an agreement with the International Fund to be able to pay the debt.' We say to them, 'Sirs, we are sovereign. We want to pay the debt, but no way in hell are we going to make an agreement again with the IMF.' " As a result, the IMF, supremely powerful in the eighties and nineties, is no longer a force on the continent. In 2005, Latin America made up 80 percent of the IMF's total lending portfolio; in 2007, the continent represented just 1 percent—a sea change in only two years. "There is life after the IMF," Kirchner declared, "and it's a good life."[31]

The transformation reaches beyond Latin America. In just three years, the IMF's worldwide lending portfolio had shrunk from $81 billion to $11.8 billion, with almost all of that going to Turkey. The IMF, a pariah in so many countries where it has treated crises as profit-making opportunities, is starting to wither away. The World Bank faces an equally grim future. In April 2007, Ecuador's president, Rafael Correa, revealed that he had suspended all loans from the bank and declared the institution's representative in Ecuador persona non grata—an extraordinary step. Two years earlier, Correa explained, the World Bank had used a $100-million loan to defeat economic legislation that would have redistributed oil revenues to the country's poor. "Ecuador is a sovereign country, and we will not stand for extortion from this international bureaucracy," he said. At the same time, Evo Morales announced that Bolivia would quit the World Bank's arbitration court, the body that allows multinational corporations to sue national governments for measures that cost them profits. "The governments of Latin America, and I think the world, never win the cases. The multinationals always win," Morales said. When Paul Wolfowitz was forced to announce his resignation as president of the World Bank in May 2007, it was clear that the institution needed to take desperate measures to rescue itself from its profound crisis of credibility. In the midst of the Wolfowitz affair, *The Financial Times* reported that when World Bank managers dispensed advice in the developing world, "they were now laughed at."[32] Add the collapse of the World Trade Organization talks in 2006 (prompting declarations that "globalization is dead"), and the futures of the three main institutions that had imposed the Chicago School ideology under the guise of economic inevitability are at risk of extinction.

It stands to reason that the revolt against neoliberalism would be in its most advanced stage in Latin America—as inhabitants of the first shock lab, Latin Americans have had the most time to recover their bearings. Years of street protests have created new political groupings, eventually gaining the strength not just to take state power but to begin to change the power structures of the state. There are signs that other former shock laboratories are on the same path. In South Africa, 2005 and 2006 were the years that the long-neglected slums decisively abandoned their party loyalty to the ANC and began protesting against the broken promises of the Freedom Charter. Foreign journalists commented that this kind of upheaval had not been seen since the townships rose up against apartheid. But the most remarkable mood change is taking place in China. For many years, the raw terror of the Tiananmen Square massacre succeeded in supressing popular anger at the erosion of workers' rights and deepening rural poverty. Not anymore. According to official government sources, in 2005 there were a staggering eighty-seven thousand large protests in China, involving more than 4 million workers and peasants.*[33] China's activist wave has been met with the most extreme state repression since 1989, but it has also resulted in several concrete victories: major new spending in rural areas, better health care, pledges to eliminate education fees. China too is coming out of shock.

Any strategy based on exploiting the window of opportunity opened by a traumatic shock relies heavily on the element of surprise. A state of shock, by definition, is a moment when there is a gap between fast-moving events and the information that exists to explain them. The late French theorist Jean Baudrillard described terrorist events as an "excess of reality"; in this sense, in North America, the September 11 attacks were, at first, pure event, raw reality, unprocessed by story, narrative or anything that could bridge the gap between reality and understanding.[34] Without a story, we are, as many of us were after September 11, intensely vulnerable to those people who are ready to take advantage of the chaos for their own ends. As soon as we have a new narrative that offers a perspective on the shocking events, we become reoriented and the world begins to make sense once again.

---

* "Four million workers!" exclaimed a group of U.S. labor writers. "In the US we celebrated the birth of a new global social movement when 60,000 people showed up for the 'Battle of Seattle' in 1999."

Prison interrogators intent on inducing shock and regression understand this process well. It is the reason the CIA's manuals stress the importance of cutting detainees off from anything that will help them establish a new narrative—their own sensory input, other prisoners, even communication with guards. "Prisoners should be segregated immediately," the 1983 manual states. "Isolation, both physical and psychological, must be maintained from the moment of apprehension."[35] The interrogators know that prisoners talk. They warn each other about what's to come; they pass notes between the bars. Once that happens, the captors lose their edge. They still have the power to inflict bodily pain, but they have lost their most effective psychological tools to manipulate and "break" their prisoners: confusion, disorientation and surprise. Without those elements, there is no shock.

The same is true for wider societies. Once the mechanics of the shock doctrine are deeply and collectively understood, whole communities become harder to take by surprise, more difficult to confuse—shock resistant. The intensely violent brand of disaster capitalism that has dominated since September 11 emerged in part because lesser shocks—debt crises, currency crashes, the threat of being left behind "in history"—were already losing much of their potency, largely because of overuse. Yet today, even the cataclysmic shocks of wars and natural disasters do not always provoke the level of disorientation required to impose unwanted economic shock therapy. There are just too many people in the world who have had direct experience with the shock doctrine: they know how it works, have talked to other prisoners, passed notes between the bars; the crucial element of surprise is missing.

A striking example is the response of millions of Lebanese to attempts by international lenders to impose free-market "reforms" as a condition of reconstruction aid after the Israeli attacks in 2006. By all rights, that scheme should have worked: the country could not have been more desperate for funds. Even before the war, Lebanon had one of the heaviest debts in the world, while the new losses from attacks on roads, bridges and airport runways were estimated at $9 billion. So when delegates from thirty wealthy nations got together in Paris in January 2007 to pledge $7.6 billion in reconstruction loans and grants, they naturally assumed that Lebanon's government would accept whatever strings they attached to the aid. The conditions were the usual ones: phone and electricity privatizations, price increases on fuel, cuts to the public service and an increase to an already controversial tax on consumer purchases. Kamal Hamdan, a Lebanese economist, estimated that, as a result, "household bills [would] increase by 15 percent because of increased taxes and adjusted prices"—a classic peace penalty. As for the reconstruction itself, the jobs would of course go to the giants of disaster capitalism, with no requirement to hire or subcontract locally.[36]

The U.S. secretary of state, Condoleezza Rice, was questioned about whether such sweeping demands constituted foreign interference in Lebanon's affairs. She replied, "Lebanon is a democracy. That said, Lebanon is also undertaking some important economic reforms that are critical to making any of this work." Fouad Siniora, Lebanon's prime minister, backed by the West, easily agreed to the terms, shrugging and saying that "Lebanon did not invent privatization." Further demonstrating his willingness to play ball, he hired the Bush-connected surveillance giant Booz Allen Hamilton to broker Lebanon's telecom privatization.[37]

Many Lebanese citizens, however, were distinctly less cooperative. Despite the fact that a lot of their homes still lay in ruins, thousands participated in a general strike, organized by a coalition of unions and political parties, including the Islamist party Hezbollah. The demonstrators insisted that if receiving reconstruction funds meant raising the cost of living for a war-ravaged people, it hardly deserved to be called aid. So while Siniora was reassuring donors in Paris, strikes and road blockades brought the country to a halt—the first national revolt specifically targeting postwar disaster capitalism. Demonstrators also staged a sit-in, which went on for two months, turning downtown Beirut into a cross between a tent city and a street carnival. Most reporters characterized these events as shows of strength by Hezbollah, but Mohamad Bazzi, the Middle East bureau chief for New York's *Newsday*, said that this interpretation missed their true significance: "The biggest motivator driving many of those camped out in downtown isn't Iran or Syria, or Sunni versus Shiite. It's the economic inequality that has haunted Lebanese Shiites for decades. It's a poor and working-class people's revolt."[38]

The location of the sit-in provided the most eloquent explanation for why Lebanon was proving so shock resistant. The protest was in the part of downtown Beirut that residents refer to as Solidere, after the private development company that built and owns almost everything in its confines. Solidere is the result of Lebanon's last reconstruction effort. In the early nineties, after the fifteen-year civil war, the country was shattered and the state was in debt, with no money to rebuild. The billionaire businessman (and later prime minister) Rafiq Hariri made a proposal: give him the land rights to the entire downtown core and let him and his new real estate company, Solidere, turn it into the "Singapore of the Middle East." Hariri, who was killed in a car bombing in February 2005, bulldozed almost all the standing structures, turning the city into a blank slate. Marinas, luxurious condominiums (some with elevators for limousines) and lavish shopping malls replaced the ancient souks.[39] Almost everything in the business district—buildings, plazas, security forces—is owned by Solidere.

To the outside world, Solidere was the shining symbol of Lebanon's postwar rebirth, but for many Lebanese it had always been a kind of holograph. Outside the ultramodern downtown core, much of Beirut lacked basic infrastructure, from electricity to public transit, and the bullet holes inflicted during the civil war were never repaired on the facades of many buildings. It was in those neglected slums surrounding the gleaming center that Hezbollah built its loyal base, rigging up generators and transmitters, organizing trash removal, providing security—becoming the much vilified "state within a state." When the residents of the run-down suburbs ventured into the Solidere enclave, they were often thrown out by Hariri's private security guards; their presence frightened the tourists.

Raida Hatoum, a social justice activist in Beirut, told me that when Solidere began its reconstruction, "people were so happy the war was over and the streets were being rebuilt. By the time we became aware that the streets had been sold, that they were privately owned, it was too late. We didn't know that the money was a loan and we'd have to pay it back later." That rude awakening of finding out that the least advantaged people had been stuck with the bill for a makeover that benefited only a small elite has made the Lebanese experts in the mechanics of disaster capitalism. It is this experience that helped keep the country oriented and organized after the 2006 war. By choosing to hold their mass sit-in inside the Solidere bubble, with Palestinian refugees camped outside the Virgin megastore and high-end latte joints ("If I ate a sandwich here, I'd be broke for a week," one protester remarked), the demonstrators were sending a clear message. They did not want another reconstruction of Solidere-style bubbles and rotting suburbs— of fortressed green zones and raging red zones—but a reconstruction for the entire country. "How can we still accept this government that steals?" one demonstrator asked. "This government that built this downtown and accumulated this huge debt? Who's going to pay for it? I have to pay for it, and my son is going to pay for it after me."[40]

Lebanon's shock resistance went beyond protest. It was also expressed through a far-reaching parallel reconstruction effort. Within days of the cease-fire, Hezbollah's neighborhood committees had visited many of the homes hit by the air attacks, assessed the damage and were already handing out $12,000 in cash to displaced families to cover a year's worth of rent and furnishings. As the independent journalists Ana Nogueira and Saseen Kawzally observed from Beirut, "That is six times the dollar amount that survivors of Hurricane Katrina received from FEMA." And in what would have been music to the ears of Katrina survivors, the Hezbollah leader, Sheik Hassan Nasrallah, promised the country in a televised address, "You won't need to ask a favor of anyone, queue up anywhere." Hezbollah's version of aid did not filter through the government or foreign NGOs. It did not go to build five-star hotels, as in Kabul, or Olympic swimming pools for police trainers, as in Iraq. Instead, Hezbollah did what Renuka, the Sri Lankan tsunami survivor, told me she wished someone would do for her family: put the help in their hands. Hezbollah also included community members in the reconstruction—it hired local construction crews (working in exchange for the scrap metal they collected), mobilized fifteen hundred engineers and organized teams of volunteers. All that help meant that a week after the bombing stopped, the reconstruction was already well under way.[41]

In the U.S. press, these initiatives were almost universally derided as bribery or clientelism—Hezbollah's attempt to purchase popular support after it had provoked the attack from which the country was reeling (David Frum even suggested that the bills Hezbollah was handing out were counterfeit).[42] There is no question that Hezbollah is engaged in politics as well as charity, and that Iranian funds made Hezbollah's generosity possible. Equally important to its efficiency, however, was Hezbollah's status as a local, indigenous organization, one that rose up from the neighborhoods being rebuilt. Unlike the alien corporate reconstruction agencies imposing their designs from far-off bureaucracies via imported management, private security and translators, Hezbollah could act fast because it knew every back alley and every jury-rigged transmitter, as well as who could be trusted to get the work done. If the residents of Lebanon were grateful for the results, it was also because they knew the alternative. The alternative was Solidere.

We do not always respond to shocks with regression. Sometimes, in the face of crisis, we grow up—fast. This impulse was in powerful evidence in Spain, on March 11, 2004, when ten bombs ripped through commuter trains and rail stations in Madrid, killing nearly two hundred people. President José María Aznar immediately went on television and told Spaniards to blame the Basque separatists and to give him their support for the war in Iraq. "No negotiation is possible or desirable with these assassins who so many times have sown death all around Spain. Only with firmness can we end the attacks," he said.[43]

Spaniards reacted badly to that kind of talk. "We are still hearing the echoes of Franco," said José Antonio Martines Soler, a prominent Madrid newspaper editor who had been persecuted under Francisco Franco's dictatorship. "In every act, in every gesture, in every sentence, Aznar told the people he was right, that he was the owner of the truth and those who disagreed with him were his enemies."[44] In other words, the very same qualities that Americans identified as "strong leadership" in their president after September 11 were, in Spain, regarded as ominous signs of a rising fascism. The country was three days away from national elections, and, remembering a time when fear governed politics, voters defeated Aznar and chose a party that would pull troops out of Iraq. As in Lebanon, it was the collective memory of past shocks that made Spain resistant to the new ones.

All shock therapists are intent on the erasure of memory. Ewen Cameron was convinced that he needed to wipe out the minds of his patients before he could rebuild them. The U.S. occupiers of Iraq felt no need to stop the looting of Iraq's museums and libraries, thinking it might make their jobs easier. But like Cameron's former patient Gail Kastner, with her intricate architecture of papers, books and lists, recollections can be rebuilt, new narratives can be created. Memory, both individual and collective, turns out to be the greatest shock absorber of all.

Despite all the successful attempts to exploit the 2004 tsunami, memory also proved to be an effective tool of resistance in some areas where it struck, particularly in Thailand. Dozens of coastal villages were flattened by the wave, but unlike in Sri Lanka, many Thai settlements were successfully rebuilt within months. The difference did not come from the government. Thailand's politicians were just as eager as those elsewhere to use the storm as an excuse to evict fishing people and hand over land tenure to large resorts. Yet what set Thailand apart was that villagers approached all government promises with intense skepticism and refused to wait patiently in camps for an official reconstruction plan. Instead, within weeks, hundreds of villagers engaged in what they called land "reinvasions." They marched past the armed guards on the payroll of developers, tools in hand, and began marking off the sites where their old houses had been. In some cases, reconstruction began immediately. "I am willing to bet my life on this land, because it is ours," said Ratree Kongwatmai, who lost most of her family in the tsunami.[45]

The most daring reinvasions were performed by Thailand's indigenous fishing peoples called the Moken, or "sea gypsies." After centuries of disenfranchisement, the Moken had no illusions that a benevolent state would give them a decent piece of land in exchange for the coastal properties that had been seized. So, in one dramatic case, the residents of the Ban Tung Wah Village in the Phang Nga province "gathered themselves together and marched right back home, where they encircled their wrecked village with rope, in a symbolic gesture to mark their land ownership," explained a report by a Thai NGO. "With the entire community camping out there, it became difficult for the authorities to chase them away, especially given the intense media attention being focused on tsunami rehabilitation." In the end, the villagers negotiated a deal with the government to give up part of their oceanfront property in exchange for legal security on the rest of their ancestral land. Today, the rebuilt village is a showcase of Moken culture, complete with museum, community center, school and market. "Now, officials from the sub-district come to Ban Tung Wah to learn about 'people-managed tsunami rehabilitation' while researchers and university students turn up there by the bus-full to study 'indigenous people's wisdom.' "[46]

All along the Thai coast where the tsunami hit, this kind of direct-action reconstruction is the norm. The key to their success, community leaders say, is that "people negotiate for their land rights from a position of being in occupation"; some have dubbed the practice "negotiating with your hands."[47] Thailand's survivors have also insisted on a different kind of aid—rather than settling for handouts, they have demanded the tools to carry out their own reconstruction. Dozens of Thai architecture students and professors, for example, volunteered to help community members design their new houses and draw their own rebuilding plans; master boat builders trained villagers to make their own, more sophisticated fishing vessels. The results are communities stronger than they were before the wave. The houses on stilts built by Thai villagers in Ban Tung Wah and Baan Nairai are beautiful and sturdy; they are also cheaper, larger and cooler than the sweltering prefab cubicles on offer there from foreign contractors. A manifesto drafted by a coalition of Thai tsunami survivor communities explains the philosophy: "The rebuilding work should be done by local communities themselves, as much as possible. Keep contractors out, let communities take responsibility for their own housing."[48]

A year after Katrina hit, a remarkable exchange took place in Thailand between the leaders of that country's grassroots reconstruction effort and a small delegation of hurricane survivors from New Orleans. The visitors from the United States toured several rebuilt Thai villages and were taken aback by the speed with which rehabilitation had become a reality. "In New Orleans, we're waiting around on the government to do things for us, but here you all are doing by yourselves," said Endesha Juakali, founder of the "survivors' village" in New Orleans. "When we go back," he pledged, "your model is our new goal."[49]

After the community leaders from New Orleans returned home, there was indeed a wave of direct action in the city. Juakali, whose own neighborhood was still in ruins, organized teams of local contractors and volunteers to gut the flood-damaged interiors in every house on the block; then they moved on to the next one. He said that his trip to the tsunami region gave him "a good perspective on . . . how the people of New Orleans are going to have to put FEMA aside and the city and state government aside and begin to say, 'What can we do right now to start to bring our neighborhoods back in spite of the government, not because of it?'" Another veteran of the Asia trip, Viola Washington, also returned to her New Orleans neighborhood, Gentilly, with an entirely new attitude. She "broke down a map of Gentilly into sections, organized representative committees for each section and appointed leaders who meet to discuss rebuilding needs." She explained that "as we fight the government to get our money we don't want to be doing nothing to try and get ourselves back."[50]

There was still more direct action in New Orleans. In February 2007, groups of residents who had lived in the public housing projects that the Bush administration was planning to demolish began "reinvading" their old homes and taking up residence. Volunteers helped clean out apartments and raised money to buy generators and solar panels. "My home is my castle, and I'm taking it back," announced Gloria Williams, a resident of the housing project C. J. Peete. The reinvasion turned into a block party complete with a New Orleans brass band.[51] There was much to celebrate: at least for now, this one community had escaped the great cultural bulldozer that calls itself reconstruction.

Uniting all these examples of people rebuilding for themselves is a common theme: participants say they are not just repairing buildings but healing themselves. It makes perfect sense. The universal experience of living through a great shock is the feeling of being completely powerless: in the face of awesome forces, parents lose the ability to save their children, spouses are separated, homes—places of protection—become death traps. The best way to recover from helplessness turns out to be helping—having the right to be part of a communal recovery. "Reopening our school says this is a very special community, tied together by more than location but by spirituality, by bloodlines and by a desire to come home," said the assistant principal of Dr. Martin Luther King Jr. Elementary School in the Lower Ninth Ward of New Orleans.[52]

Such people's reconstruction efforts represent the antithesis of the disaster capitalism complex's ethos, with its perpetual quest for clean sheets and blank slates on which to build model states. Like Latin America's farm and factory co-ops, they are inherently improvisational, making do with whoever is left behind and whatever rusty tools have not been swept away, broken or stolen. Unlike the fantasy of the Rapture, the apocalyptic erasure that allows the ethereal escape of true believers, local people's renewal movements begin from the premise that there is no escape from the substantial messes we have created and that there has already been enough erasure—of history, of culture, of memory. These are movements that do not seek to start from scratch but rather from scrap, from the rubble that is all around. As the corporatist crusade continues its violent decline, turning up the shock dial to blast through the mounting resistance it encounters, these projects point a way forward between fundamentalisms. Radical only in their intense practicality, rooted in the communities where they live, these men and women see themselves as mere repair people, taking what's there and fixing it, reinforcing it, making it better and more equal. Most of all, they are building in resilience—for when the next shock hits.

NOTES

N.B.: Quotations and facts that come from interviews with the author are generally not cited in the notes.

Unless otherwise indicated, all translations from Spanish to English were done by Shana Yael Shubs.

All dollar amounts in the book are in U.S. currency.

In some cases where there are sources for multiple facts in a paragraph, one super-script note number appears at the end of the paragraph rather than a number after each individual fact. In the notes section here, the sources are listed in the order in which the facts appear in the paragraph.

If there is a source for a footnote, it is cited in the numbered endnote most closely following the asterisk in the text; such sources are marked FOOTNOTE.

Web addresses for news articles available online are not included because of the transient nature of Web architecture. In cases where a document is available exclusively online, the home page where it appears is cited, not the longer URL for the specific text, once again because links change frequently.

Many original documents cited in the text, as well as Web links and an extensive bibliography and filmography, can be found at www.naomiklein.org.

INTRODUCTION

Blank Is Beautiful: Three Decades of Erasing and Remaking the World

1. Bud Edney, "Appendix A: Thoughts on Rapid Dominance," in Harlan K. Ullman and James P. Wade, *Shock and Awe: Achieving Rapid Dominance* (Washington, DC: NDU Press Book, 1996), 110.
2. John Harwood, "Washington Wire: A Special Weekly Report from The Wall Street Journal's Capital Bureau," *Wall Street Journal*, September 9, 2005.
3. Gary Rivlin, "A Mogul Who Would Rebuild New Orleans," *New York Times*, September 29, 2005.
4. "The Promise of Vouchers," *Wall Street Journal*, December 5, 2005.
5. Ibid.
6. Milton Friedman, *Capitalism and Freedom* (1962, repr. Chicago: University of Chicago Press, 1982), 2.
7. Interview with Joe DeRose, United Teachers of New Orleans, September 18, 2006; Michael Kunzelman, "Post-Katrina, Educators, Students Embrace Charter Schools," Associated Press, April 17, 2007.
8. Steve Ritea, "N.O. Teachers Union Loses Its Force in Storm's Wake," *Times-Picayune* (New Orleans), March 6, 2006.
9. Susan Saulny, "U.S. Gives Charter Schools a Big Push in New Orleans," *New York*

Times, June 13, 2006; Veronique de Rugy and Kathryn G. Newmark, "Hope after Katrina" *Education Next,* October 1, 2006, www.aei.org.

10. "Educational Land Grab," *Rethinking Schools,* Fall 2006.

11. Milton Friedman, *Inflation: Causes and Consequences* (New York: Asia Publishing House, 1963), 1.

12. Friedman, *Capitalism and Freedom,* ix.

13. Milton Friedman and Rose Friedman, *Tyranny of the Status Quo* (San Diego: Harcourt Brace Jovanovich, 1984), 3.

14. Milton Friedman and Rose D. Friedman, *Two Lucky People: Memoirs* (Chicago: University of Chicago Press, 1998), 592.

15. Eduardo Galeano, *Days and Nights of Love and War,* trans. Judith Brister (New York: Monthly Review Press, 1983), 130.

16. Ullman and Wade, *Shock and Awe,* xxviii.

17. Thomas Crampton, "Iraq Official Warns on Fast Economic Shift," *International Herald Tribune* (Paris), October 14, 2003.

18. Alison Rice, *Post-Tsunami Tourism and Reconstruction: A Second Disaster?* (London: Tourism Concern, October 2005), www.tourismconcern.org.uk.

19. Nicholas Powers, "The Ground below Zero," *Indypendent,* August 31, 2006, www.indypendent.org.

20. Neil King Jr. and Yochi J. Dreazen, "Amid Chaos in Iraq, Tiny Security Firm Found Opportunity," *Wall Street Journal,* August 13, 2004.

21. Eric Eckholm, "U.S. Contractor Found Guilty of $3 Million Fraud in Iraq," *New York Times,* March 10, 2006.

22. Davison L. Budhoo, *Enough Is Enough: Dear Mr. Camdessus . . . Open Letter of Resignation to the Managing Director of the International Monetary Fund* (New York: New Horizons Press, 1990), 102.

23. Michael Lewis, "The World's Biggest Going-Out-of-Business Sale," *The New York Times Magazine,* May 31, 1998.

24. Bob Sipchen, "Are Public Schools Worth the Effort?" *Los Angeles Times,* July 3, 2006.

25. Paul Tough, David Frum, William Kristol et al., "A Revolution or Business as Usual?: A Harper's Forum," *Harper's,* March 1995.

26. Rachel Monahan and Elena Herrero Beaumont, "Big Time Security," *Forbes,* August 3, 2006; Gary Stoller, "Homeland Security Generates Multibillion Dollar Business," *USA Today,* September 10, 2006.

27. Evan Ratliff, "Fear, Inc.," *Wired,* December 2005.

28. Veronique de Rugy, American Enterprise Institute, "Facts and Figures about Homeland Security Spending," December 14, 2006, www.aei.org.

29. Bryan Bender, "Economists Say Cost of War Could Top $2 Trillion," *Boston Globe,* January 8, 2006.

30. Thomas L. Friedman, "Big Mac I," *New York Times,* December 8, 1996.

31. Steve Quinn, "Halliburton's 3Q Earnings Hit $611M," Associated Press, October 22, 2006.

32. Steven R. Hurst, "October Deadliest Month Ever in Iraq," Associated Press, November 22, 2006.

33. James Glanz and Floyd Norris, "Report Says Iraq Contractor Is Hiding Data from U.S.," *New York Times,* October 28, 2006.

34. Wency Leung, "Success Through Disaster: B.C.-Made Wood Houses Hold Great Potential for Disaster Relief," *Vancouver Sun,* May 15, 2006.

35. Joseph B. Treaster, "Earnings for Insurers Are Soaring," *New York Times*, October 14, 2006.
36. Central Intelligence Agency, *Kubark Counterintelligence Interrogation*, July 1963, 1, 101. Declassified manual is available in full, www.gwu.edu/~nsarchiv.
37. Ibid, 66.
38. Mao Tse-Tung, "Introducing a Cooperative," *Peking Review* 1, no. 15 (June 10, 1958): 6.
39. Friedman and Friedman, *Two Lucky People*, 594.
40. Ibid.
41. "The Rising Risk of Recession," *Time*, December 19, 1969.
42. George Jones, "Thatcher Praises Friedman, Her Freedom Fighter," *Daily Telegraph* (London), November 17, 2006; Friedman and Friedman, *Two Lucky People*, 388–89.
43. Francis Fukuyama, "The End of History?" *The National Interest*, Summer 1989.
44. Justin Fox, "The Curious Capitalist," *Fortune*, November 16, 2006; House of Representatives, 109th Congr., 2nd Sess., "H. Res. 1089: Honoring the Life of Milton Friedman," December 6, 2006; Jon Ortiz, "State to Honor Friedman," *Sacramento Bee*, January 24, 2007; Thomas Sowell, "Freedom Man," *Wall Street Journal*, November 18, 2006.
45. Stéphane Courtois et al., *The Black Book of Communism: Crimes, Terror, Repression*, trans. Jonathan Murphy and Mark Kramer (Cambridge, MA: Harvard University Press, 1999), 2.

1. The Torture Lab: Ewen Cameron, the CIA and the Maniacal Quest to Erase and Remake the Human Mind

1. Cyril J. C. Kennedy and David Anchel, "Regressive Electric-Shock in Schizophrenics Refractory to Other Shock Therapies," *Psychiatric Quarterly* 22, no. 2 (April 1948): 318.
2. Ugo Cerletti, "Electroshock Therapy," *Journal of Clinical and Experimental Psychopathology and Quarterly Review of Psychiatry and Neurology* 15 (September 1954): 192–93.
3. Judy Foreman, "How CIA Stole Their Minds," *Boston Globe*, October 30, 1998; Stephen Bindman, "Brainwashing Victims to Get $100,000," *Gazette* (Montreal), November 18, 1992.
4. Gordon Thomas, *Journey into Madness* (New York: Bantam Books, 1989), 148.
5. Harvey M. Weinstein, *Psychiatry and the CIA: Victims of Mind Control* (Washington, DC: American Psychiatric Press, 1990), 92, 99.
6. D. Ewen Cameron, "Psychic Driving," *American Journal of Psychiatry* 112, no. 7 (1956): 502–509.
7. D. Ewen Cameron and S. K. Pande, "Treatment of the Chronic Paranoid Schizophrenic Patient," *Canadian Medical Association Journal* 78 (January 15, 1958): 95.
8. Aristotle, "On the Soul, Book III," in *Aristotle I, Great Books of the Western World*, vol. 8, ed. Mortimer J. Adler, trans. W. D. Ross (Chicago: Encyclopaedia Britannica, 1952), 662.
9. Berton Rouché, "As Empty as Eve," *The New Yorker*, September 9, 1974.
10. D. Ewen Cameron, "Production of Differential Amnesia as a Factor in the Treatment of Schizophrenia," *Comprehensive Psychiatry* 1, no. 1 (1960): 32–33.
11. D. Ewen Cameron, J. G. Lohrenz and K. A. Handcock, "The Depatterning Treatment of Schizophrenia," *Comprehensive Psychiatry* 3, no. 2 (1962): 67.
12. Cameron, "Psychic Driving," 503–504.

13. Weinstein, *Psychiatry and the CIA*, 120. FOOTNOTE: Thomas, *Journey into Madness*, 129.

14. "CIA, Memorandum for the Record, Subject: Project ARTICHOKE," January 31, 1975, www.gwu.edu/~nsarchiv.

15. Alfred W. McCoy, "Cruel Science: CIA Torture & Foreign Policy," *New England Journal of Public Policy* 19, no. 2 (Winter 2005): 218.

16. Alfred W. McCoy, *A Question of Torture: CIA Interrogation, from the Cold War to the War on Terror* (New York: Metropolitan Books, 2006), 22, 30.

17. Those who found themselves taking LSD in this period of experimentation included North Korean POWs; a group of patients at a drug treatment center in Lexington, Kentucky; seven thousand American soldiers at Maryland's Edgewood Chemical Arsenal; and inmates of California's Vacaville Prison. Ibid., 27, 29.

18. "[A]n anonymous handwritten note found in the archives identifies Dr. Caryl Haskins and Commander R. J. Williams as CIA representatives at the meeting." David Vienneau, "Ottawa Paid for '50s Brainwashing Experiments, Files Show," *Toronto Star*, April 14, 1986; "Minutes of June 1, 1951, Canada/US/UK Meeting Re: Communist 'Brainwashing' Techniques during the Korean War," meeting at Ritz-Carlton Hotel, Montreal, June 1, 1951, page 5.

19. D. O. Hebb, W. Heron and W. H. Bexton, *Annual Report*, Contract DRB X38, Experimental Studies of Attitude, 1953.

20. *Defense Research Board Report to Treasury Board*, August 3, 1954, declassified, 2.

21. "Distribution of Proceedings of Fourth Symposium, Military Medicine, 1952," declassified.

22. Zuhair Kashmeri, "Data Show CIA Monitored Deprivation Experiments," *Globe and Mail* (Toronto), February 18, 1984.

23. Ibid.

24. Hebb, Heron and Bexton, *Annual Report*, Contract DRB X38, 1–2.

25. Juliet O'Neill, "Brain Washing Tests Assailed by Experts," *Globe and Mail* (Toronto), November 27, 1986.

26. Weinstein, *Psychiatry and the CIA*, 122. Thomas, *Journey into Madness*, 103; John D. Marks, *The Search for the Manchurian Candidate: The CIA and Mind Control* (New York: Times Books, 1979), 133.

27. R. J. Russell, L. G. M. Page and R. L. Jillett, "Intensified Electroconvulsant Therapy," *Lancet* (December 5, 1953): 1178.

28. Cameron, Lohrenz and Handcock, "The Depatterning Treatment of Schizophrenia," 68.

29. Cameron, "Psychic Driving," 504.

30. Thomas, *Journey into Madness*, 180.

31. D. Ewen Cameron et al., "Sensory Deprivation: Effects upon the Functioning Human in Space Systems," *Symposium on Psychophysiological Aspects of Space Flight*, ed. Bernard E. Flaherty (New York: Columbia University Press, 1961), 231; Cameron, "Psychic Driving," 504.

32. Marks, *The Search for the Manchurian Candidate*, 138.

33. Cameron and Pande, "Treatment of the Chronic Paranoid Schizophrenic Patient," 92.

34. D. Ewen Cameron, "Production of Differential Amnesia as a Factor in the Treatment of Schizophrenia," 27.

35. Thomas, *Journey into Madness*, 234.

36. Cameron et al., "Sensory Deprivation," 226, 232.

37. Lawrence Weschler, A *Miracle, a Universe: Settling Accounts with Torturers* (New York: Pantheon Books, 1990), 125.
38. Interview appeared in the Canadian magazine *Weekend*, quoted in Thomas, *Journey into Madness*, 169.
39. Cameron, "Psychic Driving," 508.
40. Cameron was citing another researcher, Norman Rosenzweig, to support his thesis. Cameron et al., "Sensory Deprivation," 229.
41. Weinstein, *Psychiatry and the CIA*, 222.
42. "Project MKUltra, The CIA's Program of Research in Behavioral Modification," *Joint Hearings Before the Select Committee on Intelligence and the Subcommittee on Health and Scientific Research of the Committee on Human Resources*, United States Senate, 95th Congr., 1st Sess., August 3, 1977. Quoted in Weinstein, *Psychiatry and the CIA*, 178.
43. Ibid., 143.
44. James LeMoyne, "Testifying to Torture," *New York Times*, June 5, 1988.
45. Jennifer Harbury, *Truth, Torture and the American Way: The History and Consequences of U.S. Involvement in Torture* (Boston: Beacon Press, 2005), 87.
46. Senate Select Committee on Intelligence, "Transcript of Proceedings before the Select Committee on Intelligence: Honduran Interrogation Manual Hearing," June 16, 1988 (Box 1 CIA Training Manuals, Folder: Interrogation Manual Hearings, National Security Archives). Quoted in McCoy, *A Question of Torture*, 96.
47. Tim Weiner, "Interrogation, C.I.A.-Style," *New York Times*, February 9, 1997; Steven M. Kleinman, "KUBARK Counterintelligence Interrogation Review: Observations of an Interrogator," February 2006 in Intelligence Science Board, *Educing Information* (Washington D.C.: National Defense Intelligence College, December 2006), 96.
48. Central Intelligence Agency, *Kubark Counterintelligence Interrogation*, July 1963, pages 1 and 8. Declassified manual is available in full from the National Security Archives, www.gwu.edu/~nsarchiv. Emphasis added.
49. Ibid., 1, 38.
50. Ibid., 1–2.
51. Ibid., 88.
52. Ibid., 90.
53. Central Intelligence Agency, *Human Resource Exploitation Training Manual–1983*. Declassified manual is available in full from the National Security Archives, www.gwu.edu/~nsarchiv. FOOTNOTE: Ibid.
54. Central Intelligence Agency, *Kubark Counterintelligence Interrogation*, July 1963, 49–50, 76–77.
55. Ibid., 41, 66.
56. McCoy, *A Question of Torture*, 8.
57. McCoy, "Cruel Science," 220.
58. Frantz Fanon, *A Dying Colonialism*, trans. Haakon Chevalier (1965, repr. New York: Grove Press, 1967), 138.
59. Pierre Messmer, French minister of defense from 1960 to 1969, says that the Americans invited the French to train soldiers in the U.S. In response, General Paul Aussaresses, the most notorious and unrepentant of France's torture experts, went to Fort Bragg and instructed U.S. soldiers on "seizure, interrogation, torture" techniques. *Death Squadrons: The French School*, documentary directed by Marie-Monique Robin (Idéale Audience, 2003).

60. McCoy, *A Question of Torture*, 65.

61. Dianna Ortiz, *The Blindfold's Eyes* (New York: Orbis Books, 2002), 32.

62. Harbury, *Truth, Torture and the American Way*.

63. United Nations, *Geneva Convention Relative to the Treatment of Prisoners of War*, Adopted August 12, 1949, www.ohchr.org; *Uniform Code of Military Justice*, Subchapter 10: Punitive Articles, Section 893, Article 93, www.au.af.mil.

64. Central Intelligence Agency, *Kubark Counterintelligence Interrogation*, 2; Central Intelligence Agency, *Human Resource Exploitation Training Manual—1983*.

65. Craig Gilbert, "War Will Be Stealthy," *Milwaukee Journal Sentinel*, September 17, 2001; Garry Wills, *Reagan's America: Innocents at Home* (New York: Doubleday, 1987), 378.

66. Katharine Q. Seelye, "A Nation Challenged," *New York Times*, March 29, 2002; Alberto R. Gonzales, *Memorandum for the President*, January 25, 2002, www.nsbc.msn.com.

67. Jerald Phifer, "Subject: Request for Approval of Counter-Resistance Strategies," *Memorandum for Commander, Joint Task Force 170*, October 11, 2002: 6. Declassified, www.npr.org.

68. U.S. Department of Justice, Office of Legal Counsel, Office of the Assistant Attorney General, *Memorandum for Alberto R. Gonzales, Counsel to the President*, August 1, 2002, www.washingtonpost.com. FOOTNOTE: "Military Commissions Act of 2006," Subchapter VII, Sec. 6, thomas.loc.gov; Alfred W. McCoy, "The U.S. Has a History of Using Torture," History News Network, George Mason University, December 4, 2006, www.hnn.us; "The Imperial Presidency at Work," *New York Times*, January 15, 2006.

69. Kleinman, "KUBARK Counterintelligence Interrogation Review," 95.

70. Dan Eggen, "Padilla Case Raises Questions about Anti-Terror Tactics," *Washington Post*, November 19, 2006.

71. Curt Anderson, "Lawyers Show Images of Padilla in Chains," Associated Press, December 4, 2006; John Grant, "Why Did They Torture Jose Padilla," *Philadelphia Daily News*, December 12, 2006.

72. AAP, "US Handling of Hicks Poor: PM," *Sydney Morning Herald*, February 6, 2007.

73. Shafiq Rasul, Asif Iqbal and Rhuhel Ahmed, *Composite Statement: Detention in Afghanistan and Guantánamo Bay* (New York: Center for Constitutional Rights, July 26, 2004), 95, www.ccr-ny.org.

74. Adam Zagorin and Michael Duffy, "Inside the Interrogation of Detainee 063," *Time*, June 20, 2005.

75. James Yee and Aimee Molloy, *For God and Country: Faith and Patriotism under Fire* (New York: Public Affairs, 2005), 101–102; Tim Golden and Margot Williams, "Hunger Strike Breaks Out at Guantánamo," *New York Times*, April 8, 2007.

76. Craig Whitlock, "In Letter, Radical Cleric Details CIA Abduction, Egyptian Torture," *Washington Post*, November 10, 2006.

77. Ibid.

78. Amnesty International, "Italy, Abu Omar: Italian Authorities Must Cooperate Fully with All Investigations," Public Statement, November 16, 2006, www.amnesty.org.

79. Jumah al-Dossari, "Days of Adverse Hardship in U.S. Detention Camps—Testimony of Guantánamo Detainee Jumah al-Dossari," Amnesty International, December 16, 2005.

80. Mark Landler and Souad Mekhennet, "Freed German Detainee Questions His Country's Role," *New York Times*, November 4, 2006.

81. A. E. Schwartzman and P. E. Termansen, "Intensive Electroconvulsive Therapy: A Follow-Up Study," *Canadian Psychiatric Association Journal* 12, no. 2 (1967): 217.

82. Erik Eckholm, "Winning Hearts of Iraqis with a Sewage Pipeline," *New York Times*, September 5, 2004.

2. The Other Doctor Shock: Milton Friedman and the Search for a Laissez-Faire Laboratory

1. Arnold C. Harberger, "Letter to a Younger Generation," *Journal of Applied Economics* 1, no. 1 (1998): 2.
2. Katherine Anderson and Thomas Skinner, "The Power of Choice: The Life and Times of Milton Friedman," aired on PBS on January 29, 2007.
3. Jonathan Peterson, "Milton Friedman, 1912–2006," *Los Angeles Times*, November 17, 2006.
4. Frank H. Knight, "The Newer Economics and the Control of Economic Activity," *Journal of Political Economy* 40, no. 4 (August 1932): 455.
5. Daniel Bell, "Models and Reality in Economic Discourse," *The Crisis in Economic Theory*, eds. Daniel Bell and Irving Kristol (New York: Basic Books, 1981), 57–58.
6. Milton Friedman and Rose D. Friedman, *Two Lucky People: Memoirs* (Chicago: University of Chicago Press, 1998), 24.
7. Larry Kudlow, "The Hand of Friedman," The Corner web log on the National Review Online, November 16, 2006, www.nationalreview.com.
8. Friedman and Friedman, *Two Lucky People*, 21.
9. Milton Friedman, *Capitalism and Freedom* (1962, repr. Chicago: University of Chicago Press, 1982), 15.
10. Don Patinkin, *Essays on and in the Chicago Tradition* (Durham, NC: Duke University Press, 1981), 4.
11. Friedrich A. Hayek, *The Road to Serfdom* (Chicago: University of Chicago Press, 1944).
12. Interview with Arnold Harberger conducted October 3, 2000, for *Commanding Heights: The Battle for the World Economy* [television series for PBS], executive producers Daniel Yergin and Sue Lena Thompson, series producer William Cran (Boston: Heights Productions, 2002), full interview transcript available at www.pbs.org.
13. John Maynard Keynes, *The End of Laissez-Faire* (London: L & Virginia Woolf, 1926).
14. John Maynard Keynes, "From Keynes to Roosevelt: Our Recovery Plan Assayed," *New York Times*, December 31, 1933.
15. John Kenneth Galbraith, *The Great Crash of 1929* (1954, repr. New York: Avon, 1979), 168.
16. John Maynard Keynes, *The Economic Consequences of the Peace* (1919, repr. Westminster, UK: Labour Research Department, 1920), 251.
17. Friedman and Friedman, *Two Lucky People*, 594.
18. Stephen Kinzer, *All the Shah's Men: An American Coup and the Roots of Middle East Terror* (Hoboken, NJ: John Wiley & Sons, 2003), 153–54; Stephen Kinzer, *Overthrow: America's Century of Regime Change from Hawaii to Iraq* (New York: Times Books, 2006), 4.
19. *El Imparcial*, March 16, 1951, cited in Stephen C. Schlesinger, Stephen Kinzer and John H. Coatsworth, *Bitter Fruit: The Story of the American Coup in Guatemala* (Cambridge, MA: Harvard University Press, 1999), 52.
20. Patterson described Argentine and Brazilian economists as "pink" in an interview with Juan Gabriel Valdés. He spoke of the need to "change the formation of the men" to the U.S. ambassador to Chile, Willard Beaulac. Juan Gabriel Valdés, *Pinochet's*

Economists: The Chicago School in Chile (Cambridge: Cambridge University Press, 1995), 110–13.

21. Ibid., 89.
22. The quotation comes from Joseph Grunwald, a Columbia University economist working at the time at the University of Chile. Valdés, *Pinochet's Economists*, 135.
23. Harberger, "Letter to a Younger Generation," 2.
24. André Gunder Frank, *Economic Genocide in Chile: Monetarist Theory Versus Humanity* (Nottingham, UK: Spokesman Books, 1976), 7–8.
25. Kenneth W. Clements, "Larry Sjaastad, The Last Chicagoan," *Journal of International Money and Finance* 24 (2005): 867–69.
26. Gunder Frank, *Economic Genocide in Chile*, 8.
27. Memorandum to William Carmichael, via Jeffrey Puryear, from James W. Trowbridge, October 24, 1984, page 4, cited in Valdés, *Pinochet's Economists*, 194.
28. Ibid., 206. FOOTNOTE: "The Rising Risk of Recession," *Time*, December 19, 1969.
29. In 1963, de Castro himself was on leave from Santiago to further his studies at the University of Chicago. He became chairman in 1965. Valdés, *Pinochet's Economists*, 140, 165.
30. Ibid., 159. The quotation comes from Ernesto Fontaine, a Chicago grad and a professor at the Catholic University in Santiago.
31. Ibid., 6, 13.
32. Third report to the Catholic University of Chile and the International Cooperation Administration, August 1957, signed by Gregg Lewis, University of Chicago, page 3, cited in Valdés, *Pinochet's Economists*, 132.
33. Interview with Ricardo Lagos conducted January 19, 2002, for *Commanding Heights: The Battle for the World Economy*, www.pbs.org.
34. Friedman and Friedman, *Two Lucky People*, 388.
35. Central Intelligence Agency, *Notes on Meeting with the President on Chile*, September 15, 1970, declassified, www.gwu.edu/~nsarchiv.
36. "The Last Dope from Chile," mimeo signed "Al H.," dated Santiago, September 7, 1970, cited in Valdés, *Pinochet's Economists*, 242–43.
37. Sue Branford and Bernardo Kucinski, *Debt Squads: The U.S., the Banks, and Latin America* (London: Zed Books, 1988), 40, 51–52.
38. Subcommittee on Multinational Corporations, "The International Telephone and Telegraph Company and Chile, 1970–71," *Report to the Committee on Foreign Relations United States Senate by the Subcommittee on Multinational Corporations*, June 21, 1973, 13.
39. Ibid., 15.
40. Francisco Letelier, interview, *Democracy Now!* September 21, 2006.
41. Subcommittee on Multinational Corporations, "The International Telephone and Telegraph Company and Chile, 1970–71," 4, 18.
42. Ibid., 11, 15.
43. Ibid., 17.
44. Archdiocese of São Paulo, *Torture in Brazil: A Shocking Report on the Pervasive Use of Torture by Brazilian Military Governments, 1964–1979*, ed. Joan Dassin, trans. Jaime Wright (Austin: University of Texas Press, 1986), 53.
45. William Blum, *Killing Hope: U.S. Military and CIA Interventions Since WWII* (Monroe, ME: Common Courage Press, 1995), 195; "Times Diary: Liquidating Sukarno," *Times* (London), August 8, 1986.

46. Kathy Kadane, "U.S. Officials' Lists Aided Indonesian Bloodbath in '60s," *Washington Post*, May 21, 1990.

47. Kadane first published the account of the lists, based on taped on-the-record interviews with top U.S. officials posted in Indonesia at the time, in *The Washington Post*. The information about radios and weapons appears in a letter to the editor written by Kadane in *The New York Review of Books*, April 10, 1997, based on the same interviews. Kadane's interview transcripts are now with the National Security Archive in Washington, DC. Kadane, "U.S. Officials' Lists Aided Indonesian Bloodbath in '60s."

48. John Hughes, *Indonesian Upheaval* (New York: David McKay Company, Inc., 1967), 132.

49. The 500,000 figure is the most commonly used, including by *The Washington Post* in 1966. Britain's ambassador to Indonesia estimated the number at 400,000, but he reported that the Swedish ambassador, who had done additional research, deemed it "a very serious under-estimate." Some put the number as high as a million, though the CIA claimed in a 1968 report that 250,000 had been killed, calling it "one of the worst mass murders of the 20th century." "Silent Settlement," *Time*, December 17, 1965; John Pilger, *The New Rulers of the World* (London: Verso, 2002), 34; Kadane, "U.S. Officials' Lists Aided Indonesian Bloodbath in '60s."

50. "Silent Settlement."

51. David Ransom, "Ford Country: Building an Elite for Indonesia," *The Trojan Horse: A Radical Look at Foreign Aid*, ed. Steve Weissman (Palo Alto, CA: Ramparts Press, 1975), 99.

52. FOOTNOTE: Ibid., 100.

53. Robert Lubar, "Indonesia's Potholed Road Back," *Fortune*, June 1, 1968.

54. Goenawan Mohamad, *Celebrating Indonesia: Fifty Years with the Ford Foundation 1953–2003* (Jakarta: Ford Foundation, 2003), 59.

55. In the original text, the author spells the general's name Soeharto; I changed it to the more common spelling Suharto for the sake of consistency. Mohammad Sadli, "Recollections of My Career," *Bulletin of Indonesian Economic Studies* 29, no. 1 (April 1993): 40.

56. The following posts were filled with graduates of the Ford program: minister of finance, minister of trade and commerce, chair of the National Planning Board, vice-chair of the National Planning Board, secretary-general of Marketing and Trade Research, chairman of the Technical Team of Foreign Investment, secretary-general of industry and ambassador to Washington. Ransom, "Ford Country," 110.

57. Richard Nixon, "Asia After Vietnam," *Foreign Affairs* 46, no. 1 (October 1967): 111. FOOTNOTE: Arnold C. Harberger, *Curriculum Vitae*, November 2003, www.econ.ucla.edu.

58. Pilger, *The New Rulers of the World*, 36–37.

59. CIA, "Secret Cable from Headquarters [Blueprint for Fomenting a Coup Climate], September 27, 1970," in Peter Kornbluh, *The Pinochet File: A Declassified Dossier on Atrocity and Accountability* (New York: New Press, 2003), 49–56.

60. Valdés, *Pinochet's Economists*, 251.

61. Ibid., 248–49.

62. Ibid., 250.

63. Select Committee to Study Governmental Operations with Respect to Intelligence Activities, United States Senate, *Covert Action in Chile 1963–1973* (Washington, DC: U.S. Government Printing Office, December 18, 1975), 30.

64. Ibid., 40.

65. Eduardo Silva, *The State and Capital in Chile: Business Elites, Technocrats, and Market Economics* (Boulder, CO: Westview Press, 1996), 74.

66. Orlando Letelier, "The Chicago Boys in Chile: Economic Freedom's Awful Toll," *The Nation*, August 28, 1976.

3. States of Shock: The Bloody Birth of the Counterrevolution

1. Niccolò Machiavelli, *The Prince*, trans. W. K. Marriott (Toronto: Alfred A. Knopf, 1992), 42.

2. Milton Friedman and Rose D. Friedman, *Two Lucky People: Memoirs* (Chicago: University of Chicago Press, 1998), 592.

3. *Batalla de Chile* [three-part documentary film series] compiled by Patricia Guzmán, originally produced 1975–79 (New York: First Run/Icarus Films, 1993).

4. John Dinges and Saul Landau, *Assassination on Embassy Row* (New York: Pantheon Books, 1980), 64.

5. *Report of the Chilean National Commission on Truth and Reconciliation*, vol. 1, trans. Phillip E. Berryman (Notre Dame: University of Notre Dame Press, 1993), 153; Peter Kornbluh, *The Pinochet File: A Declassified Dossier on Atrocity and Accountability* (New York: New Press, 2003), 153–54.

6. Kornbluh, *The Pinochet File*, 155–56.

7. These numbers are contested because the military government was notorious for covering up and denying its crimes. Jonathan Kandell, "Augusto Pinochet, 91, Dictator Who Ruled by Terror in Chile, Dies," *New York Times*, December 11, 2006; *Chile Since Independence*, ed. Leslie Bethell (New York: Cambridge University Press, 1993), 178; Rupert Cornwell, "The General Willing to Kill His People to Win the Battle against Communism," *Independent* (London), December 11, 2006.

8. Juan Gabriel Valdés, *Pinochet's Economists: The Chicago School in Chile* (Cambridge: Cambridge University Press, 1995), 252.

9. Pamela Constable and Arturo Valenzuela, *A Nation of Enemies: Chile Under Pinochet* (New York: W. W. Norton & Company, 1991), 187.

10. Robert Harvey, "Chile's Counter-Revolution: The Fight Goes On," *The Economist*, February 2, 1980.

11. José Piñera, "How the Power of Ideas Can Transform a Country," www.josepinera.com.

12. Constable and Valenzuela, *A Nation of Enemies*, 74–75.

13. Ibid., 69.

14. Valdés, *Pinochet's Economists*, 31.

15. Constable and Valenzuela, *A Nation of Enemies*, 70.

16. Pinochet's only trade barrier was a 10 percent tariff on imports, which does not constitute a trade barrier but a minor import tax. André Gunder Frank, *Economic Genocide in Chile: Monetarist Theory versus Humanity* (Nottingham, UK: Spokesman Books, 1976), 81.

17. These are conservative estimates. Gunder Frank writes that in the first year of junta rule, inflation reached 508 percent and may have been close to 1,000 percent for "basic necessities." In 1972, Allende's last year in office, inflation reached 163 percent. Constable and Valenzuela, *A Nation of Enemies*, 170; Gunder Frank, *Economic Genocide in Chile*, 62.

18. *Que Pasa* (Santiago), January 16, 1975, cited in Gunder Frank, *Economic Genocide in Chile*, 26.

19. *La Tercera* (Santiago), April 9, 1975, cited in Orlando Letelier, "The Chicago Boys in Chile," *The Nation*, August 28, 1976.
20. *El Mercurio* (Santiago), March 23, 1976, cited in ibid.
21. *Que Pasa* (Santiago), April 3, 1975, cited in ibid.
22. Friedman and Friedman, *Two Lucky People*, 399.
23. Ibid., 593–94.
24. Ibid., 592–94.
25. Ibid., 594.
26. Gunder Frank, *Economic Genocide in Chile*, 34.
27. Constable and Valenzuela, *A Nation of Enemies*, 172–73.
28. "In 1980, public spending on health had decreased by 17.6 per cent compared to 1970, and education by 11.3 per cent." Valdés, *Pinochet's Economists*, 23, 26; Constable and Valenzuela, *A Nation of Enemies*, 172–73; Robert Harvey, "Chile's Counter-Revolution," *The Economist*, February 2, 1980.
29. Valdés, *Pinochet's Economists*, 22.
30. Albert O. Hirschman, "The Political Economy of Latin American Development: Seven Exercises in Retrospection," *Latin American Research Review* 12, no. 3 (1987): 15.
31. Public Citizen, "The Uses of Chile: How Politics Trumped Truth in the Neo-Liberal Revision of Chile's Development," discussion paper, September 2006, www.citizen.org.
32. "A Draconian Cure for Chile's Economic Ills?" *BusinessWeek*, January 12, 1976.
33. Peter Dworkin, "Chile's Brave New World of Reaganomics," *Fortune*, November 2, 1981; Valdés, *Pinochet's Economists*, 23; Letelier, "The Chicago Boys in Chile."
34. Hirschman, "The Political Economy of Latin American Development,"15.
35. Junta finance minister Jorge Cauas made the statement. Constable and Valenzuela, *Nation of Enemies*, 173.
36. Ann Crittenden, "Loans from Abroad Flow to Chile's Rightist Junta," *New York Times*, February 20, 1976.
37. "A Draconian Cure for Chile's Economic Ills?" *BusinessWeek*, January 12, 1976.
38. Gunder Frank, *Economic Genocide in Chile*, 58.
39. Ibid., 65–66.
40. Harvey, "Chile's Counter-Revolution"; Letelier, "The Chicago Boys in Chile."
41. Gunder Frank, *Economic Genocide in Chile*, 42.
42. Piñera, "How the Power of Ideas Can Transform a Country."
43. Robert M. Bleiberg, "Why Attack Chile?" *Barron's*, June 22, 1987.
44. Jonathan Kandell, "Chile, Lab Test for a Theorist," *New York Times*, March 21, 1976.
45. Kandell, "Augusto Pinochet, 91, Dictator Who Ruled by Terror in Chile, Dies"; "A Dictator's Double Standard," *Washington Post*, December 12, 2006.
46. Greg Grandin, *Empire's Workshop: Latin America and the Roots of U.S. Imperialism* (New York: Metropolitan Books, 2006), 171.
47. Ibid., 171.
48. Constable and Valenzuela, *A Nation of Enemies*, 197–98.
49. José Piñera, "Wealth through Ownership: Creating Property Rights in Chilean Mining," *Cato Journal* 24, no. 3 (Fall 2004): 296.
50. Interview with Alejandro Foxley conducted March 26, 2001, for *Commanding Heights: The Battle for the World Economy*, www.pbs.org.
51. Constable and Valenzuela, *A Nation of Enemies*, 219.
52. Central Intelligence Agency, "Field Listing—Distribution of family income—Gini index," *World Factbook 2007*, www.cia.gov.

53. Letelier, "The Chicago Boys in Chile."

54. Milton Friedman, "Economic Miracles," *Newsweek*, January 21, 1974.

55. Glen Biglaiser, "The Internationalization of Chicago's Economics in Latin America," *Economic Development and Cultural Change* 50 (2002): 280.

56. Lawrence Weschler, A *Miracle, a Universe: Settling Accounts with Torturers* (New York: Pantheon Books, 1990), 149.

57. The quotation comes from notes taken by Brazil's ambassador to Argentina at the time, João Baptista Pinheiro. Reuters, "Argentine Military Warned Brazil, Chile of '76 Coup," CNN, March 21, 2007.

58. Mario I. Blejer was Argentina's secretary of finance during the dictatorship. He received a PhD in economics at the University of Chicago the year before the coup. Adolfo Diz, PhD, University of Chicago, was president of the central bank during the dictatorship. Fernando De Santibáñes, Chicago PhD, worked in the central bank during the dictatorship. Ricardo López Murphy, MA in Chicago, national director of the Office of Economic Research and Fiscal Analysis in the Treasury Department of the Finance Ministry (1974–1983). Several other Chicago grads held lower-level economic positions in the dictatorship, as consultants and advisers.

59. Michael McCaughan, *True Crimes: Rodolfo Walsh* (London: Latin America Bureau, 2002), 284–90; "The Province of Buenos Aires: Vibrant Growth and Opportunity," *BusinessWeek*, July 14, 1980, special advertising section.

60. Henry Kissinger and César Augusto Guzzetti, Memorandum of Conversation, June 10, 1976, declassified, www.gwu.edu/~nsarchiv.

61. "The Province of Buenos Aires." FOOTNOTE: Ibid.

62. McCaughan, *True Crimes*, 299.

63. Reuters, "Argentine Military Warned Brazil, Chile of '76 Coup."

64. *Report of the Chilean National Commission on Truth and Reconciliation*, vol. 2, trans. Phillip E. Berryman (Notre Dame: University of Notre Dame Press, 1993), 501.

65. Marguerite Feitlowitz, A *Lexicon of Terror: Argentina and the Legacies of Torture* (New York: Oxford University Press, 1998), ix.

66. Ibid., 149, 175.

67. Feitlowitz, A *Lexicon of Terror*, 165.

68. Weschler, A *Miracle, a Universe*, 170.

69. Amnesty International, *Report on an Amnesty International Mission to Argentina 6–15 November 1976* (London: Amnesty International Publications, 1977), 35; Feitlowitz, A *Lexicon of Terror*, 158.

70. Alex Sanchez, Council on Hemispheric Affairs, "Uruguay: Keeping the Military in Check," November 20, 2006, www.coha.org.

71. Gunder Frank, *Economic Genocide in Chile*, 43; *Batalla de Chile*.

72. United States Senate, Select Committee to Study Governmental Operations with Respect to Intelligence Activities, *Covert Action in Chile 1963–1973* (Washington, DC: U.S. Government Printing Office, December 18, 1975), 40.

73. Archdiocese of São Paulo, *Brasil: Nunca Mais/Torture in Brazil: A Shocking Report on the Pervasive Use of Torture by Brazilian Military Governments, 1964–1979*, ed. Joan Dassin, trans. Jaime Wright (Austin: University of Texas Press, 1986), 13–14.

74. Eduardo Galeano, "A Century of Wind," *Memory of Fire*, vol. 3, trans. Cedric Belfrage (London: Quartet Books, 1989), 208.

75. *Report of the Chilean National Commission on Truth and Reconciliation*, vol. 1, 153.

76. Kornbluh, *The Pinochet File*, 162.

77. Weschler, *A Miracle, a Universe*, 145. FOOTNOTE: Jane Mayer, "The Experiment," *The New Yorker*, July 11, 2005.
78. This estimate is based on the fact that Brazil had 8,400 political prisoners in this period, and thousands of them were tortured. Uruguay had 60,000 political prisoners, and according to the Red Cross, torture in the jails was systemic. An estimated 50,000 Chileans faced torture and at least 30,000 Argentines did, which would make the 100,000 figure very conservative. Larry Rohter, "Brazil Rights Group Hopes to Bar Doctors Linked to Torture," *New York Times*, March 11, 1999; Organization of American States, Inter-American Commission on Human Rights, *Report on the Situation of Human Rights in Uruguay*, January 31, 1978, www.cidh.org; Duncan Campbell and Jonathan Franklin, "Last Chance to Clean the Slate of the Pinochet Era," *Guardian* (London), September 1, 2003; Feitlowitz, *A Lexicon of Terror*, ix.
79. McCaughan, *True Crimes*, 290.
80. Ibid., 274.
81. Ibid., 285–89.
82. Ibid., 280–82.
83. Feitlowitz, *A Lexicon of Terror*, 25–26.
84. "Covert Action in Chile 1963–1973," 45.
85. Weschler, *A Miracle, a Universe*, 110; Department of State, "Subject: Secretary's Meeting with Argentine Foreign Minister Guzzetti," Memorandum of Conversation, October 7, 1976, declassified, www.gwu.edu/~nsarchiv.
86. In Attendance—Friday, March 26, 1976, declassified document available from the National Security Archive, www.gwu.edu/~nsarchiv.

4. Cleaning the Slate: Terror Does Its Work

1. Daniel Feierstein and Guillermo Levy, *Hasta que la muerte nos separe: Prácticas sociales genocidas en América Latina* (Buenos Aires: Ediciones al margen, 2004), 76.
2. Marguerite Feitlowitz, *A Lexicon of Terror: Argentina and the Legacies of Torture* (New York: Oxford University Press, 1998), xii.
3. Orlando Letelier, "The Chicago Boys in Chile," *The Nation*, August 28, 1976.
4. Ibid.
5. John Dinges and Saul Landau, *Assassination on Embassy Row* (New York: Pantheon Books, 1980), 207–10.
6. Pamela Constable and Arturo Valenzuela, *A Nation of Enemies: Chile Under Pinochet* (New York: W. W. Norton & Company, 1991), 103–107; Peter Kornbluh, *The Pinochet File: A Declassified Dossier on Atrocity and Accountability* (New York: New Press, 2003), 167.
7. Eduardo Gallardo, "In Posthumous Letter, Lonely Ex-Dictator Justifies 1973 Chile Coup," Associated Press, December 24, 2006.
8. "Dos Veces Desaparecido," *Página 12*, September 21, 2006.
9. Carlos Rozanski was the lead author of the ruling, which was cowritten by judges Norberto Lorenzo and Horacio A. Insaurralde. Federal Oral Court No. 1, Case NE 2251/06, September 2006, www.rodolfowalsh.org.
10. Federal Oral Court No. 1, Case NE 2251/06, September 2006, www.rodolfowalsh.org.
11. Ibid.
12. United Nations Office of the High Commissioner for Human Rights, "Convention on

the Prevention and Punishment of the Crime of Genocide," approved December 9, 1948, www.ohchr.org.

13. Leo Kuper, "Genocide: Its Political Use in the Twentieth Century," in Alexander Laban Hinton, ed., *Genocide: An Anthropological Reader* (Malden, MA: Blackwell, 2002), 56.

14. Beth Van Schaack, "The Crime of Political Genocide: Repairing the Genocide Convention's Blind Spot," *Yale Law Journal* 107, no. 7 (May 1997).

15. "Auto de la Sala de lo Penal de la Audiencia Nacional confirmando la jurisdicción de España para conocer de los crimines de genocidio y terrorismo cometidos durante la dictadura argentina," Madrid, November 4, 1998, www.derechos.org. FOOTNOTE: Van Schaack, "The Crime of Political Genocide."

16. Baltasar Garzón, "Auto de Procesamiento a Militares Argentinos," Madrid, November 2, 1999, www.derechos.org.

17. Michael McCaughan, *True Crimes: Rodolfo Walsh* (London: Latin America Bureau, 2002), 182.

18. Constable and Valenzuela, *A Nation of Enemies*, 16.

19. Guillermo Levy, "Considerations on the Connections between Race, Politics, Economics, and Genocide," *Journal of Genocide Research* 8, no. 2 (June 2006): 142.

20. Juan Gabriel Valdés, *Pinochet's Economists: The Chicago School in Chile* (Cambridge: Cambridge University Press, 1995), 7–8 and 113.

21. Constable and Valenzuela, *A Nation of Enemies*, 16.

22. Ibid., 39; Alfred Rosenberg, *Myth of the Twentieth Century: An Evaluation of the Spiritual-Intellectual Confrontations of Our Age* (1930, repr. Newport Beach, CA: Noontide Press, 1993), 333.

23. André Gunder Frank, *Economic Genocide in Chile: Monetarist Theory Versus Humanity* (Nottingham, UK: Spokesman Books, 1976), 41.

24. Ibid.

25. Amnesty International, *Report on an Amnesty International Mission to Argentina 6–15 November 1976* (London: Amnesty International Publications, 1977), 65.

26. Ibid.

27. Marguerite Feitlowitz, *A Lexicon of Terror: Argentina and the Legacies of Torture* (New York: Oxford University Press, 1998), 159.

28. Diana Taylor, *Disappearing Acts: Spectacles of Gender and Nationalism in Argentina's "Dirty War"* (Durham, NC: Duke University Press, 1997), 105.

29. *Report of the Chilean National Commission on Truth and Reconciliation*, vol. 1, trans. Phillip E. Berryman (South Bend, IN: University of Notre Dame Press, 1993), 140.

30. The editorial appeared in *La Prensa* (Buenos Aires). Cited in Feitlowitz, *A Lexicon of Terror*, 153.

31. Constable and Valenzuela, *A Nation of Enemies*, 153.

32. Archdiocese of São Paulo, *Brasil: Nunca Mais/Torture in Brazil: A Shocking Report on the Pervasive Use of Torture by Brazilian Military Governments, 1964–1979*, ed. Joan Dassin, trans. Jaime Wright (Austin: University of Texas Press, 1986), 106–110.

33. *Report of the Chilean National Commission on Truth and Reconciliation*, vol. 1, 149.

34. Letelier, "The Chicago Boys in Chile."

35. *Nunca Más* (Never again): *The Report of the Argentine National Commission of the Disappeared* (New York: Farrar, Straus and Giroux, 1986), 369.

36. Ibid., 371.

37. Amnesty International, *Report on an Amnesty International Mission to Argentina 6–15 November 1976*, 9.

38. Taylor, *Disappearing Acts*, 111.

39. Archdiocese of São Paulo, *Torture in Brazil*, 64.
40. Karen Robert, "The Falcon Remembered," *NACLA Report on the Americas* 39, no. 3 (November–December 2005): 12.
41. Victoria Basualdo, "Complicidad patronal-militar en la última dictadura argentina," *Engranajes: Boletín de FETIA*, no. 5, special edition, March 2006.
42. Transcript of interviews conducted by Rodrigo Gutiérrez with Pedro Troiani and Carlos Alberto Propato, both former Ford workers and union activists, for a forthcoming documentary film on the Ford Falcon, *Falcon*.
43. "Demandan a la Ford por el secuestro de gremialistas durante la dictadura," *Página 12*, February 24, 2006.
44. Robert, "The Falcon Remembered,"13–15; transcript of Gutiérrez's interviews with Troiani and Propato.
45. "Demandan a la Ford por el secuestro de gremialistas durante la dictadura."
46. Ibid.
47. Larry Rohter, "Ford Motor Is Linked to Argentina's 'Dirty War,'" *New York Times*, November 27, 2002.
48. Ibid.; Sergio Correa, "Los desaparecidos de Mercedes-Benz," *BBC Mundo*, November 5, 2002.
49. Robert, "The Falcon Remembered," 14.
50. McCaughan, *True Crimes*, 290.
51. *Nunca Más: The Report of the Argentine National Commission of the Disappeared*, 22.
52. Quoting Padre Santano. Patricia Marchak, *God's Assassins: State Terrorism in Argentina in the 1970s* (Montreal: McGill-Queen's University Press, 1999), 241.
53. Marchak, *God's Assassins*, 155.
54. Levy, "Considerations on the Connections between Race, Politics, Economics, and Genocide," 142.
55. Marchak, *God's Assassins*, 161.
56. Feitlowitz, *A Lexicon of Terror*, 42.
57. Constable and Valenzuela, *A Nation of Enemies*, 171, 188.
58. Ibid., 147.
59. The editorial appeared in *La Prensa* (Buenos Aires), cited in Feitlowitz, *A Lexicon of Terror*, 153.
60. Constable and Valenzuela, *A Nation of Enemies*, 78. FOOTNOTE: L. M. Shirlaw, "A Cure for Devils," *Medical World* 94 (January 1961): 56, cited in Leonard Roy Frank, ed., *History of Shock Treatment* (San Francisco: Frank, September 1978), 2.
61. McCaughan, *True Crimes*, 295.
62. Feitlowitz, *A Lexicon of Terror*, 77.
63. David Rose, "Guantanamo Briton 'in Handcuff Torture,'" *Observer* (London), January 2, 2005.
64. Milton Friedman and Rose D. Friedman, *Two Lucky People: Memoirs* (Chicago: University of Chicago Press, 1998), 596. FOOTNOTE: David Rose, "Guantanamo Briton 'in Handcuff Torture,'" *Observer* (London), January 2, 2005.
65. Arnold C. Harberger, "Letter to a Younger Generation," *Journal of Applied Economics* 1, no. 1 (1998): 4.
66. Amnesty International, *Report on an Amnesty International Mission to Argentina 6–15 November 1976*, 34–35.
67. Robert Jay Lifton, *The Nazi Doctors: Medical Killing and the Psychology of Genocide* (1986, repr. New York: Basic Books, 2000), 16; François Ponchaud, *Cambodia Year Zero*, trans. Nancy Amphoux (1977, repr. New York: Rinehart and Winston, 1978), 50.

68. United Nations Office of the High Commissioner for Human Rights, "Convention on the Prevention and Punishment of the Crime of Genocide," approved December 9, 1948, www.ohchr.org.

69. HIJOS (a human rights organization of the children of the disappeared) estimate over five hundred children. HIJOS, "Lineamientos," www.hijos.org.ar; the figure of two hundred cases cited in Human Rights Watch, *Annual Report 2001*, www.hrw.org.

70. Silvana Boschi, "Desaparición de menores durante la dictadura militar: Presentan un documento clave," *Clarín* (Buenos Aires), September 14, 1997.

71. Feitlowitz, *A Lexicon of Terror*, 89.

5. "Entirely Unrelated": How an Ideology Was Cleansed of Its Crimes

1. Donald Rumsfeld, *Secretary of Defense Donald H. Rumsfeld Speaking at Tribute to Milton Friedman*, White House, Washington, DC, May 9, 2002, www .defenselink.mil.

2. Lawrence Weschler, A *Miracle, a Universe: Settling Accounts with Torturers* (New York: Pantheon Books, 1990), 147.

3. Anthony Lewis, "For Which We Stand: II," *New York Times*, October 2, 1975.

4. "A Draconian Cure for Chile's Economic Ills?" *BusinessWeek*, January 12, 1976; Milton Friedman and Rose D. Friedman, *Two Lucky People: Memoirs* (Chicago: University of Chicago Press, 1998), 601.

5. Milton Friedman, "Free Markets and the Generals," *Newsweek*, January 25, 1982; Juan Gabriel Valdés, *Pinochet's Economists: The Chicago School in Chile* (Cambridge: Cambridge University Press, 1995), 156.

6. Friedman and Friedman, *Two Lucky People*, 596.

7. Ibid., 398.

8. Interview with Milton Friedman conducted October 1, 2000, for *Commanding Heights: The Battle for the World Economy*, www.pbs.org.

9. The Nobel Prize in Economics is separate from other prizes chosen by the Nobel Committee. The award's full name is the Sveriges Riksbank Prize in Economic Sciences in Memory of Alfred Nobel.

10. Milton Friedman, "Inflation and Unemployment," Nobel Memorial Lecture, December 13, 1976, www.nobelprize.org.

11. Orlando Letelier, "The Chicago Boys in Chile," *The Nation*, August 28, 1976.

12. Neil Sheehan, "Aid by CIA Groups Put in the Millions," *New York Times*, February 19, 1967.

13. Amnesty International, *Report on an Amnesty International Mission to Argentina 6–15 November 1976* (London: Amnesty International Publications, 1977), copyright page; Yves Dezalay and Bryant G. Garth, *The Internationalization of Palace Wars: Lawyers, Economists, and the Contest to Transform Latin American States* (Chicago: University of Chicago Press, 2002), 71.

14. Amnesty International, *Report on an Amnesty International Mission to Argentina 6–15 November 1976*, 48.

15. The Peace Committee had been renamed the Vicariate by the time Ford began funding it. Americas Watch was part of Human Rights Watch, which started, under the name Helsinki Watch, with a $500,000 grant from the Ford Foundation. The $30 million figure comes from an interview with Alfred Ironside in the Office of Communications at the Ford Foundation. According to Ironside, most of the money

was spent in the 1980s. He said that "there was virtually none spent on human rights in Latin America in the fifties" and that "there were a series of grants in the sixties geared toward human rights in the ball park of $700,000."

16. Dezalay and Garth, *The Internationalization of Palace Wars*, 69.

17. David Ransom, "Ford Country: Building an Elite for Indonesia," *The Trojan Horse: A Radical Look at Foreign Aid*, ed. Steve Weissman (Palo Alto, CA: Ramparts Press, 1975), 96.

18. Valdés, *Pinochet's Economists*, 158, 186, 308.

19. Ford Foundation, "History," 2006, www.fordfound.org.

20. Goenawan Mohamad, *Celebrating Indonesia: Fifty Years with the Ford Foundation 1953–2003* (Jakarta: Ford Foundation, 2003), 56.

21. Dezalay and Garth, *The Internationalization of Palace Wars*, 148.

22. Ford Foundation, "History," 2006, www.fordfound.org. FOOTNOTE: Frances Stonor Saunders, *The Cultural Cold War: The CIA and the World of Arts and Letters* (New York: New Press, 2000).

23. Archdiocese of São Paulo, *Torture in Brazil: A Shocking Report on the Pervasive Use of Torture by Brazilian Military Governments, 1964–1979*, ed. Joan Dassin, trans. Jaime Wright (Austin: University of Texas Press, 1986), 50.

24. Simone de Beauvoir and Gisèle Halimi, *Djamila Boupacha*, trans. Peter Green (New York: Macmillan, 1962), 19, 21, 31.

25. Marguerite Feitlowitz, *A Lexicon of Terror: Argentina and the Legacies of Torture* (New York: Oxford University Press, 1998), 113.

26. I have made slight changes in Feitlowitz's translation for clarity. Feitlowitz, *A Lexicon of Terror*, 113–15. Emphasis in original.

6. Saved by a War: Thatcherism and Its Useful Enemies

1. Translated by Peter Sillem. Carl Schmitt, *Politische Theologie: Vier Kapitel zur Lehre von der Souveränität* (1922, repr. Berlin: Duncker & Humblot, 1993), 13.

2. Correspondence in the Hayek Collection, box 101, folder 26, Hoover Institution Archives, Palo Alto, CA. Thatcher's letter is dated February 17. Thanks to Greg Grandin.

3. Peter Dworkin, "Chile's Brave New World of Reaganomics," *Fortune*, November 2, 1981.

4. Milton Friedman and Rose D. Friedman, *Two Lucky People: Memoirs* (Chicago: University of Chicago Press, 1998), 387.

5. Donald Rumsfeld, *Secretary of Defense Donald H. Rumsfeld Speaking at Tribute to Milton Friedman*, White House, Washington, DC, May 9, 2002, www.defenselink.mil.

6. Milton Friedman, "Economic Miracles," *Newsweek*, January 21, 1974.

7. In the transcript of the speech there is an error. Rumsfeld is quoted saying, "They're going to learn the going to learn the wrong lesson." I removed the repetition to avoid confusion. Rumsfeld, *Secretary of Defense Donald H. Rumsfeld Speaking at Tribute to Milton Friedman*.

8. Henry Allen, "Hayek, the Answer Man," *Washington Post*, December 2, 1982.

9. Interview with Milton Friedman conducted October 1, 2000, for *Commanding Heights: The Battle for the World Economy*, www.pbs.org.

10. Arnold C. Harberger, *Curriculum Vitae*, November 2003, www.econ.ucla.edu.

11. Ibid.; Friedman and Friedman, *Two Lucky People*, 607–609.

12. *The Political Economy of Policy Reform*, ed. John Williamson (Washington, DC: Institute for International Economics, 1994), 467.

13. Carmen DeNavas-Walt, Bernadette D. Proctor, Cheryl Hill Lee, U.S. Census Bureau, *Income, Poverty and Health Insurance Coverage in the United States: 2005*, August 2006, www.census.gov; Central Intelligence Agency, *World Factbook 2007*, www.cia.gov.

14. Allan H. Meltzer, "Choosing Freely: The Friedmans' Influence on Economic and Social Policy," in *The Legacy of Milton and Rose Friedman's Free to Choose*, eds. M. Wynne, H. Rosenblum and R. Formaini (Dallas: Federal Reserve Bank of Dallas, 2004), 204, www.dallasfed.org.

15. John Campbell, *Margaret Thatcher: The Iron Lady*, vol. 2 (London: Jonathan Cape, 2003), 174–75; Patrick Cosgrave, *Thatcher: The First Term* (London: Bodley Head, 1985), 158–59.

16. Kevin Jefferys, *Finest & Darkest Hours: The Decisive Events in British Politics from Churchill to Blair* (London: Atlantic Books, 2002), 208.

17. Based on MORI poll results (Gallup had Thatcher at 23 percent). "President Bush: Overall Job Rating," www.pollingreport.com, accessed May 12, 2007; Malcolm Rutherford, "1982: Margaret Thatcher's Year," *Financial Times* (London), December 31, 1982.

18. Samuel P. Huntington, *The Third Wave: Democratization in the Late Twentieth Century* (Norman, OK: University of Oklahoma Press, 1991).

19. Hossein Bashiriyeh, *The State and Revolution in Iran, 1962–1982* (New York: St. Martin's Press, 1984), 170–71.

20. "On the Record," *Time*, February 14, 1983.

21. Campbell, *Margaret Thatcher: The Iron Lady*, vol. 2, 128.

22. Leonard Downie Jr. and Jay Ross, "Britain: South Georgia Taken," *Washington Post*, April 26, 1982; "Jingoism Is Not the Way," *Financial Times* (London), April 5, 1982.

23. Tony Benn, *The End of an Era: Diaries 1980–90*, ed. Ruth Winstone (London: Hutchinson, 1992), 206.

24. Angus Deming, "Britain's Iron Lady," *Newsweek*, May 14, 1979; Jefferys, *Finest & Darkest Hours*, 226.

25. BBC News, "1982: First Briton Dies in Falklands Campaign," *On This Day, 24 April*, news.bbc.co.uk.

26. Rutherford, "1982."

27. Michael Getler, "Dockers' Union Agrees to Settle Strike in Britain," *Washington Post*, July 21, 1984.

28. "TUC at Blackpool (Miners' Strike): Labour Urged to Legislate on NUM Strike Fines," *Guardian* (London), September 4, 1985; Seumas Milne, *The Enemy Within: Thatcher's Secret War against the Miners* (London: Verso, 2004); Seumas Milne, "What Stella Left Out," *Guardian* (London), October 3, 2000.

29. Seumas Milne, "MI5's Secret War," *New Statesman & Society*, November 25, 1994.

30. *Coal War: Thatcher vs. Scargill*, director Liam O'Rinn, episode 8093 of the series *Turning Points of History*, telecast June 16, 2005.

31. Ibid.

32. Warren Brown, "U.S. Rules Out Rehiring Striking Air Controllers," *Washington Post*, August 7, 1981; Steve Twomey, "Reunion Marks 10 Years Outside the Tower," *Washington Post*, August 2, 1991.

33. Milton Friedman, Preface, *Capitalism and Freedom* (1962, repr. Chicago: University of Chicago Press, 1982), ix.

34. J. McLane, "Milton Friedman's Philosophy of Economics and Public Policy," *Conference to Honor Milton Friedman on His Ninetieth Birthday*, November 25, 2002, www.chibus.com.
35. N. Bukharin and E. Preobrazhensky, *The ABC of Communism: A Popular Explanation of the Program of the Communist Party of Russia*, trans. Eden and Cedar Paul (1922, repr. Ann Arbor: University of Michigan Press, 1967), 340–41.
36. *The Political Economy of Policy Reform*, 19.
37. Friedman and Friedman, *Two Lucky People*, 603.

7. The New Doctor Shock: Economic Warfare Replaces Dictatorship

1. "U.S. Operations Mission to Bolivia," *Problems in the Economic Development of Bolivia, La Paz: United States Operation Mission to Bolivia*, 1956, 212.
2. Susan Sontag, *Illness as Metaphor* (New York: Farrar, Straus and Giroux, 1977), 84.
3. "Bolivia Drug Crackdown Brews Trouble," *New York Times*, September 12, 1984; Joel Brinkley, "Drug Crops Are Up in Export Nations, State Dept. Says," *New York Times*, February 15, 1985.
4. Jeffrey D. Sachs, *The End of Poverty: Economic Possibilities for Our Time* (New York: Penguin, 2005), 90–93.
5. John Maynard Keynes, *The Economic Consequences of the Peace* (1919, repr. London: Labour Research Department, 1920), 220–21.
6. Interview with the author, October 2006, New York City.
7. Robert E. Norton, "The American Out to Save Poland," *Fortune*, January 29, 1990.
8. Interview with Jeffrey Sachs conducted June 15, 2000, for *Commanding Heights: The Battle for the World Economy*, www.pbs.org.
9. "A Draconian Cure for Chile's Economic Ills?" *BusinessWeek*, January 12, 1976.
10. Sachs, *The End of Poverty*, 93.
11. Sachs, *Commanding Heights*.
12. Catherine M. Conaghan and James M. Malloy, *Unsettling Statecraft: Democracy and Neoliberalism in the Central Andes* (Pittsburgh, PA: University of Pittsburgh Press, 1994), 127.
13. Sachs, *The End of Poverty*, 95.
14. Susan Velasco Portillo, "Víctor Paz: Decreto es coyuntural, pero puede durar 10 ó 20 años," *La Prensa* (La Paz), August 28, 2005.
15. Ibid.
16. Conaghan and Malloy, *Unsettling Statecraft*, 129.
17. Alberto Zuazo, "Bolivian Labor Unions Dealt Setback," United Press International, October 9, 1985; Juan de Onis, "Economic Anarchy Ends," *Los Angeles Times*, November 6, 1985.
18. The official's comments are based on the recollections of the members of the emergency economic team. Velasco Portillo, "Víctor Paz: Decreto es coyuntural, pero puede durar 10 ó 20 años."
19. Ibid.
20. Harlan K. Ullman and James P. Wade, *Shock and Awe: Achieving Rapid Dominance* (Washington, DC: NDU Press, 1996), xxv.
21. Conaghan and Malloy, *Unsettling Statecraft*, 186.
22. Peter McFarren, "48-hour Strike Hurts Country," Associated Press, September 5, 1985; Mike Reid, "Sitting Out the Bolivian Miracle," *Guardian* (London), May 9, 1987.

23. Robert J. Alexander, *A History of Organized Labor in Bolivia* (Westport, CT: Praeger, 2005), 169.

24. Sam Zuckerman, "Bolivian Bankers See Some Hope After Years of Economic Chaos," *American Banker*, March 13, 1987; Waltraud Queiser Morales, *Bolivia: Land of Struggle* (San Francisco: Westview Press, 1992), 159.

25. Statistics come from the Inter-American Development Bank. Morales, *Bolivia*, 159.

26. Erick Foronda, "Bolivia: Paz Has Trouble Selling 'Economic Miracle,'" *Latinamerica Press* 21, no. 5 (February 16, 1989): 7, cited in Morales, *Bolivia*, 160.

27. Alexander, *A History of Organized Labor in Bolivia*, 169.

28. Interview with Gonzalo Sánchez de Lozada conducted March 20, 2001, for *Commanding Heights: The Battle for the World Economy*, www.pbs.org.

29. Peter McFarren, "Farmers' Siege of Police Points Up Bolivia's Drug-Dealing Problems," Associated Press, January 12, 1986.

30. Peter McFarren, "Bolivia—Bleak but Now Hopeful," Associated Press, May 23, 1989.

31. Conaghan and Malloy write that "there is little doubt that the drug trade (like the international aid that Paz received) helped soften the blows of stabilization. In addition to generating income, the injection of 'coca-dollars' into the banking system is believed to have helped stabilize the currency during the second half of the decade." Conaghan and Malloy, *Unsettling Statecraft*, 198.

32. Tyler Bridges, "Bolivia Turns to Free Enterprise Among Hard Times," *Dallas Morning News*, June 29, 1987; Conaghan and Malloy, *Unsettling Statecraft*, 198.

33. John Sedgwick, "The World of Doctor Debt," *Boston Magazine*, May 1991.

34. "Taming the Beast," *The Economist*, November 15, 1986.

35. Sachs, *Commanding Heights*.

36. Peter Passell, "Dr. Jeffrey Sachs, Shock Therapist," *New York Times*, June 27, 1993.

37. "New Austerity Package Revealed," *Latin American Regional Reports: Andean Group*, December 13, 1985.

38. The banker was quoted anonymously. Zuckerman, "Bolivian Bankers See Some Hope after Years of Economic Chaos."

39. *The Political Economy of Policy Reform*, ed. John Williamson (Washington, DC: Institute for International Economics, 1994), 479.

40. Associated Press, "Bolivia Now Under State of Siege," *New York Times*, September 20, 1985.

41. "Bolivia to Lift State of Siege," United Press International, December 17, 1985; "Bolivia Now Under State of Siege."

42. Conaghan and Malloy, *Unsettling Statecraft*, 149.

43. Reuters, "Bolivia Strike Crumbling," *Globe and Mail* (Toronto), September 21, 1985.

44. Peter McFarren, "Detainees Sent to Internment Camps," Associated Press, August 29, 1986; "Bolivia: Government Frees Detainees, Puts Off Plans for Mines," Inter Press Service, September 16, 1986.

45. Sachs, *The End of Poverty*, 96.

46. Sánchez de Lozada, *Commanding Heights*.

47. Conaghan and Malloy, *Unsettling Statecraft*, 149.

8. Crisis Works: The Packaging of Shock Therapy

1. A. E. Hotchner, *Papa Hemingway* (1966, repr. New York: Carroll & Graf, 1999), 280.

2. Jim Shultz, "Deadly Consequences: The International Monetary Fund and Bolivia's

'Black February,' " (Cochabamba, Bolivia: The Democracy Center, April 2005), 14, www.democracyctr.org.

3. Albert O. Hirschman, "Reflections on the Latin American Experience," in *The Politics of Inflation and Economic Stagnation: Theoretical Approaches and International Case Studies*, ed. Leon N. Lindberg and Charles S. Maier (Washington, DC: Brookings Institution, 1985), 76.

4. Banco Central de la República Argentina, *Memoria Anual 1985*, www.bcra.gov.ar; Lawrence Weschler, *A Miracle, a Universe: Settling Accounts with Torturers* (New York: Pantheon Books, 1990), 152; "Brazil Refinancing Foreign Debt Load," *New York Times*, July 2, 1964; Alan Riding, "Brazil's Leader Urges Negotiations on Debt," *New York Times*, September 22, 1985.

5. Robert Harvey, "Chile's Counter-Revolution," *The Economist*, February 2, 1980; World Bank, *Economic Memorandum: Argentina* (Washington, DC: World Bank, 1985), 17.

6. The adviser was Franklin Willis. Michael Hirsh, "Follow the Money," *Newsweek*, April 4, 2005.

7. Terence O'Hara, "6 U.S. Banks Held Pinochet's Accounts," *Washington Post*, March 16, 2005.

8. United Press International, "Former Cabinet Minister Arrested in Argentina," *Seattle Times*, November 17, 1984.

9. World Bank, *Economic Memorandum: Argentina*, page 17; "Documentación que prueba los ilícitos de Martínez de Hoz," *La Voz del Interior*, October 6, 1984, cited in H. Hernandez, *Justicia y Deuda Externa Argentina* (Santa Fe, Argentina: Editorial Universidad de Santa Fe, 1988), 36.

10. Hernandez, *Justicia y Deuda Externa Argentina*, 37.

11. Ibid.

12. She described it as a "report about how to make investments in the Bahamas, Luxembourg, Panama, Switzerland, and Lichtenstein. There was also a section—quite technical—on the tax situation in these places." Marguerite Feitlowitz, *A Lexicon of Terror: Argentina and the Legacies of Torture* (New York: Oxford University Press, 1998), 57.

13. Norberto Galasso, *De la Banca Baring al FMI* (Buenos Aires: Ediciones Colihue, 2002), 246; Adolfo Pérez Esquivel, "¿Cuándo comenzo el terror del 24 de marzo de 1976?" *La Fogata*, March 24, 2004, www.lafogata.org.

14. U.S. State Department, Memorandum of Conversation, Subject: Secretary's Meeting with Argentine Foreign Minister Guzzetti, October 7, 1976, declassified, www.gwu.edu/~nsarchiv.

15. Sue Branford and Bernardo Kucinski, *The Debt Squads: The US, the Banks, and Latin America* (London: Zed Books, 1988), 95.

16. Matthew L. Wald, "A House, Once Again, Is Just Shelter," *New York Times*, February 6, 1983.

17. Jaime Poniachik, "Cómo empezó la deuda externa," *La Nación* (Buenos Aires), May 6, 2001.

18. Donald V. Coes, *Macroeconomic Crises: Politics and Growth in Brazil, 1964–1990* (Washington, DC: World Bank, 1995), 187; Eghosa E. Osaghae, *Structural Adjustment and Ethnicity in Nigeria* (Uppsala, Sweden: Nordiska Afrikainstitutet, 1995), 24; T. Ademola Oyejide and Mufutau I. Raheem, "Nigeria," in *The Rocky Road to Reform: Adjustment, Income Distribution, and Growth in the Developing World*, ed. Lance Taylor (Cambridge, MA: MIT Press, 1993), 302.

19. International Monetary Fund, *Fund Assistance for Countries Facing Exogenous Shock*, August 8, 2003, page 37, www.imf.org.

20. Banco Central de la República Argentina, *Memoria Anual 1989*, www.bcra.gov.ar.

21. "Interview with Arnold Harberger," *The Region*, Federal Reserve Bank of Minneapolis, March 1999, www.minneapolisfed.org.

22. The former Chicago professor and fellow Stanley Fischer was first deputy managing director of the IMF in 1994, Raghuram Rajan was the IMF's chief economist in 2003, Michael Mussa was director of the department of research at the IMF in 1991 and Danyang Xie was senior economist in the IMF's African department in 2003.

23. International Monetary Fund, "Article I—Purposes," *Articles of Agreement of the International Monetary Fund*, www.imf.org.

24. "Speech by Lord Keynes in Moving to Accept the Final Act at the Closing Plenary Session, Bretton Woods, 22 July, 1944," *Collected Writings of John Maynard Keynes*, vol. 26, ed. Donald Moggridge (London: Macmillan, 1980), 103.

25. John Williamson, "In Search of a Manual for Technopols," in John Williamson, ed., *The Political Economy of Policy Reform* (Washington, DC: Institute for International Economics, 1994), 18.

26. "Appendix: The 'Washington Consensus,'" in *The Political Economy of Policy Reform*, 27.

27. Williamson, *The Political Economy of Policy Reform*, 17.

28. Joseph E. Stiglitz, *Globalization and Its Discontents* (New York: W. W. Norton & Company, 2002), 13.

29. Davison L. Budhoo, *Enough Is Enough: Dear Mr. Camdessus . . . Open Letter of Resignation to the Managing Director of the International Monetary Fund*, foreword by Errol K. McLeod (New York: New Horizons Press, 1990), 102.

30. Dani Rodrik, "The Rush to Free Trade in the Developing World: Why So Late? Why Now? Will It Last?" in *Voting for Reform: Democracy, Political Liberalization and Economic Adjustment*, ed. Stephan Haggard and Steven B. Webb (New York: Oxford University Press, 1994), 82. Emphasis added.

31. Ibid., 81.

32. ". . . [W]hatever the merits of trade reform, the causal link drawn between trade regimes and propensity to macroeconomic crisis was bad economics." Dani Rodrik, "The Limits of Trade Policy Reform in Developing Countries," *Journal of Economic Perspectives* 6, no. 1 (Winter 1992): 95.

33. Herasto Reyes, "Argentina: historia de una crisis," *La Prensa* (Panama City), January 12, 2002.

34. Nathaniel C. Nash, "Turmoil, Then Hope in Argentina," *New York Times*, January 31, 1991.

35. "Interview with Arnold Harberger."

36. José Natanson, *Buenos muchachos: Vida y obra de los economistas del establishment* (Buenos Aires: Libros del Zorzal, 2004).

37. Paul Blustein, *And the Money Kept Rolling In (and Out): Wall Street, the IMF, and the Bankrupting of Argentina* (New York: PublicAffairs, 2005), 21.

38. Ibid., 24; interview with Domingo Cavallo conducted January 30, 2002, for *Commanding Heights: The Battle for the World Economy*, www.pbs.org; César V. Herrera and Marcelo García, "A 10 años de la privatización de YPF—Análisis y consecuencias en la Argentina y en la Cuenca del Golfo San Jorge (versión ampliada)," Centro Regional de Estudios Económicos de la Patagonia Central, January 23, 2003, www.creepace.com.ar; Antonio Camou, "Saber técnico y política en los orígenes del

menemismo," *Perfiles Latinoamericanos* 7, no. 12 (June 1998); Carlos Saúl Menem, speech given during a lunch with Mexican president Ernesto Zedillo, November 26, 1997, zedillo.presidencia.gob.mx. FOOTNOTE: Interview with Alejandro Olmos Gaona, "Las deudas hay que pagarlas, las estafas no," *LaVaca*, January 10, 2006, www.lavaca.org.
39. "Menem's Miracle," *Time International*, July 13, 1992.
40. Cavallo, *Commanding Heights*.

9. Slamming the Door on History: A Crisis in Poland, a Massacre in China

1. Leszek Balcerowicz, "Losing Milton Friedman, A Revolutionary Muse of Liberty," *Daily Star* (Beirut), November 22, 2006.
2. Michael Freedman, "The Radical," *Forbes*, February 13, 2006.
3. Joseph Fewsmith, *China Since Tiananmen: The Politics of Transition* (Cambridge: Cambridge University Press, 2001), 35.
4. The embryo of Solidarity was a semi-independent union called Free Labour Unions of the Coast, formed in 1978. This was the group that organized the strikes that eventually led to the creation of Solidarity.
5. Thomas A. Sancton, "He Dared to Hope," *Time*, January 4, 1982.
6. Ibid.
7. "Solidarity's Programme Adopted by the First National Congress," in Peter Raina, *Poland 1981: Towards Social Renewal* (London: George Allen & Unwin, 1985), 326–80.
8. Sancton, "He Dared to Hope."
9. Egil Aarvik, "The Nobel Peace Prize 1983 Presentation Speech," Oslo, Norway, December 10, 1983, www.nobelprize.org.
10. Lawrence Weschler, "A Grand Experiment," *The New Yorker*, November 13, 1989.
11. Jeffrey D. Sachs, *The End of Poverty: Economic Possibilities for Our Time* (New York: Penguin, 2005), 120; Magdalena Wyganowska, "Transformation of the Polish Agricultural Sector and the Role of the Donor Community," *USAID Mission to Poland*, September 1998, www.usaid.gov.
12. James Risen, "Cowboy of Poland's Economy," *Los Angeles Times*, February 9, 1990.
13. Sachs, *The End of Poverty*, 111.
14. Weschler, "A Grand Experiment."
15. Sachs, *The End of Poverty*, 114.
16. Ibid.; Weschler, "A Grand Experiment."
17. Interview with Jeffrey Sachs conducted June 15, 2000, for *Commanding Heights: The Battle for the World Economy*, www.pbs.org.
18. Przemyslaw Wielgosz, "25 Years of Solidarity," unpublished lecture, August 2005. Courtesy of the author.
19. Sachs, *The End of Poverty*, 117. FOOTNOTE: Randy Boyagoda, "Europe's Original Sin," *The Walrus*, February 2007, www.walrusmagazine.com.
20. Weschler, "A Grand Experiment"; Interview with Gonzalo Sánchez de Lozada conducted March 20, 2001, for *Commanding Heights: The Battle for the World Economy*, www.pbs.org.
21. Weschler, "A Grand Experiment."
22. Balcerowicz, "Losing Milton Friedman."
23. "Walesa: U.S. Has Stake in Poland's Success," United Press International, August 25, 1989.

24. The quotation is from Zofia Kuratowska, "Solidarity's foremost expert on health services and now a leading legislator." Weschler, "A Grand Experiment."

25. John Tagliabue, "Poles Approve Solidarity-Led Cabinet," *New York Times*, September 13, 1989.

26. Weschler, "A Grand Experiment"; "Mazowiecki Taken Ill in Parliament," *Guardian Weekly* (London), September 17, 1989.

27. Anne Applebaum, "Exhausted Polish PM's Cabinet Is Acclaimed," *Independent* (London), September 13, 1989.

28. Weschler, "A Grand Experiment."

29. Ibid.

30. Leszek Balcerowicz, "Poland," in *The Political Economy of Policy Reform*, ed. John Williamson (Washington, DC: Institute for International Economics, 1994), 177.

31. Ibid., 176–77.

32. Ibid., 163.

33. Thomas Carothers, "The End of the Transition Paradigm," *Journal of Democracy* 13, no. 1 (January 2002): 6–7.

34. George J. Church, "The Education of Mikhail Sergeyevich Gorbachev," *Time*, January 4, 1988.

35. Francis Fukuyama, "The End of History?" *The National Interest*, Summer 1989. FOOTNOTE: Francis Fukuyama, *The End of History and the Last Man* (New York: Free Press, 1992).

36. Milton Friedman and Rose D. Friedman, *Two Lucky People: Memoirs* (Chicago: University of Chicago Press, 1998), 603.

37. Fukuyama, "The End of History?"

38. Ibid.

39. Friedman and Friedman, *Two Lucky People*, 520–22.

40. Ibid., 558; Milton Friedman, "If Only the United States Were as Free as Hong Kong," *Wall Street Journal*, July 8, 1997.

41. Maurice Meisner, *The Deng Xiaoping Era: An Inquiry into the Fate of Chinese Socialism, 1978–1994* (New York: Hill and Wang, 1996), 455; "Deng's June 9 Speech: 'We Face a Rebellious Clique' and 'Dregs of Society,'" *New York Times*, June 30, 1989.

42. Friedman had been invited to China in various capacities—as a conference participant, a university lecturer—but in his memoirs he characterized it as a state visit: "I was mostly the guest of governmental entities," Friedman writes. Friedman and Friedman, *Two Lucky People*, 601.

43. Ibid., 517, 537, 609. Emphasis in original.

44. Ibid., 601–602.

45. Wang Hui, *China's New Order: Society, Politics, and Economy in Transition* (Cambridge, MA: Harvard University Press, 2003), 45, 54.

46. Ibid., 54.

47. Ibid., 57.

48. Meisner, *The Deng Xiaoping Era*, 463–65.

49. "China's Harsh Actions Threaten to Set Back 10-Year Reform Drive," *Wall Street Journal*, June 5, 1989.

50. "Deng's June 9 Speech: 'We Face a Rebellious Clique' and 'Dregs of Society.'" FOOTNOTE: Henry Kissinger, "The Caricature of Deng as a Tyrant Is Unfair," *Washington Post*, August 1, 1989.

51. Interview with Orville Schell conducted on December 13, 2005, for PBS's *Frontline* episode "The Tank Man"; full interview transcript available at www.pbs.org.

52. Wang, *China's New Order*, 65–66.

53. Meisner, *The Deng Xiaoping Era*, 482. FOOTNOTE: David Harvey, *A Brief History of Neoliberalism* (Oxford: Oxford University Press, 2005), 135.

54. Mo Ming, "90 Percent of China's Billionaires Are Children of Senior Officials," *China Digital Times*, November 2, 2006, www.chinadigitaltimes.net.

55. Human Rights Watch, "Race to the Bottom: Corporate Complicity in Chinese Internet Censorship," *Human Rights Watch* 18, no. 8(c) (August 2006): 28, 43; Wang, *China's New Order*, 65.

56. Friedman and Friedman, *Two Lucky People*, 516.

57. Jaroslaw Urbanski, "Workers in Poland After 1989," Workers Initiative Poland, paspartoo .w.interia.pl; Weschler, "A Grand Experiment."

58. Mark Kramer, "Polish Workers and the Post-Communist Transition, 1989–93," *Europe-Asia Studies*, June 1995; World Bank, World Development Indicators 2006, www .worldbank.org; Andrew Curry, "The Case against Poland's New President," *New Republic*, November 17, 2005; Wielgosz, "25 Years of Solidarity."

59. Wielgosz, "25 Years of Solidarity."

60. David Ost, *The Defeat of Solidarity: Anger and Politics in Postcommunist Europe* (Ithaca, NY: Cornell University Press, 2005), 62.

61. *Statistical Yearly* (Warsaw: Polish Main Statistical Office, 1997), 139.

62. Kramer, "Polish Workers and the Post-Communist Transition, 1989–93."

10. Democracy Born in Chains: South Africa's Constricted Freedom

1. "South Africa; Tutu Says Poverty, Aids Could Destabilise Nation," AllAfrica.com, November 2001.

2. Martin J. Murray, *The Revolution Deferred* (London: Verso, 1994), 12.

3. "ANC Leader Affirms Support for State Control of Industry," *Times* (London), January 26, 1990.

4. Ismail Vadi, *The Congress of the People and Freedom Charter Campaign*, foreword by Walter Sisulu (New Delhi: Sterling Publishers, 1995), www.sahistory.org.za.

5. Nelson Mandela, *A Long Walk to Freedom: The Autobiography of Nelson Mandela* (New York: Little, Brown and Company, 1994), 150.

6. "The Freedom Charter," adopted at the Congress of the People, Kliptown, on June 26, 1955, www.anc.org.za.

7. William Mervin Gumede, *Thabo Mbeki and the Battle for the Soul of the ANC* (Cape Town: Zebra Press, 2005), 219–20.

8. Mandela, *A Long Walk to Freedom*, 490–91.

9. Simple majority rule was actually delayed until 1999. Until then, executive power was shared among all the political parties that won more than 5 percent of the popular vote. Unpublished interview with Nelson Mandela by the filmmaker Ben Cashdan, 2001; Hein Marais, *South Africa: Limits to Change: The Political Economy of Transition* (Cape Town: University of Cape Town Press, 2001), 91–92.

10. FOOTNOTE: Milton Friedman, "Milton Friedman—Banquet Speech," given at the Nobel Banquet, December 10, 1976, www.nobelprize.org.

11. Bill Keller, "Can Both Wealth and Justice Flourish in a New South Africa?" *New York Times*, May 9, 1994.

12. Mark Horton, "Role of Fiscal Policy in Stabilization and Poverty Alleviation," in

Post-Apartheid South Africa: The First Ten Years, ed. Michael Nowak and Luca Antonio Ricci (Washington DC: International Monetary Fund, 2005), 84.

13. FOOTNOTE: Juan Gabriel Valdés, *Pinochet's Economists: The Chicago School in Chile* (Cambridge: Cambridge University Press, 1995), 31, 33, quoting Pinochet's minister of economy Pablo Baraona's definition of the "new democracy"; Robert Harvey, "Chile's Counter- Revolution: The Fight Goes On," *The Economist*, February 2, 1980 (Harvey was quoting Sergio Fernandez, the minister of the interior); José Piñera, "Wealth Through Ownership: Creating Property Rights in Chilean Mining," *Cato Journal* 24, no. 3 (Fall 2004): 298.

14. James Brew, "South Africa — Habitat: A Good Home Is Still Hard to Own," Inter Press Service, March 11, 1997.

15. David McDonald, "Water: Attack the Problem Not the Data," *Sunday Independent* (London), June 19, 2003.

16. Bill Keller, "Cracks in South Africa's White Monopolies," *New York Times*, June 17, 1993.

17. Gumede cites Businessmap statistics asserting that "around 98 percent of executive directors of JSE-listed companies are white, and they preside over 97 percent of the exchange's total value." Simon Robinson, "The New Rand Lords," *Time*, April 25, 2005; Gumede, *Thabo Mbeki and the Battle for the Soul of the ANC*, 220.

18. Gumede, *Thabo Mbeki and the Battle for the Soul of the ANC*, 112.

19. Moyiga Nduru, "S. Africa: Politician Washed Anti-AIDS Efforts Down the Drain," Inter Press Service, April 11, 2006.

20. "Study: AIDS Slashes SA's Life Expectancy," *Mail & Guardian* (Johannesburg), December 11, 2006.

21. The rand recovered slightly by the end of the day, closing 7 percent lower. Jim Jones, "Foreign Investors Take Fright at Hardline Stance," *Financial Times* (London), February 13, 1990.

22. Steven Mufson, "South Africa 1990," *Foreign Affairs* [Special Edition: *America and the World*], 1990/1991.

23. Thomas L. Friedman, *The Lexus and the Olive Branch* (New York: Random House, 2000), 113.

24. Gumede, *Thabo Mbeki and the Battle for the Soul of the ANC*, 69.

25. Ibid., 85; "South Africa: Issues of Rugby and Race," *The Economist*, August 24, 1996.

26. Nelson Mandela, "Report by the President of the ANC to the 50th National Conference of the African National Congress," December 16, 1997.

27. Gumede, *Thabo Mbeki and the Battle for the Soul of the ANC*, 33–39, 69.

28. Ibid., 79.

29. Marais, *South Africa*, 122. FOOTNOTE: ANC, *Ready to Govern: ANC Policy Guidelines for a Democratic South Africa Adopted at the National Conference*, May 28–31, 1992, www.anc.org.za.

30. Ken Wells, "U.S. Investment in South Africa Quickens," *Wall Street Journal*, October 6, 1994.

31. Gumede, *Thabo Mbeki and the Battle for the Soul of the ANC*, 88.

32. Ibid., 87.

33. Marais, *South Africa*, 162.

34. Ibid., 170.

35. Gumede, *Thabo Mbeki and the Battle for the Soul of the ANC*, 89.

36. Ginger Thompson, "South African Commission Ends Its Work," *New York Times*, March 22, 2003.

37. ANC, "The State and Social Transformation," discussion document, November 1996, www.anc.org.za; Ginger Thompson, "South Africa to Pay $3,900 to Each Family of Apartheid Victims," *New York Times*, April 16, 2003; Mandela unpublished interview with Cashdan, 2001.

38. Gumede, *Thabo Mbeki and the Battle for the Soul of the ANC*, 108.

39. Ibid., 119.

40. South African Communist Party, "The Debt Debate: Confusion Heaped on Confusion" November-December 1998, www.sacp.org.za; Jeff Rudin, "Apartheid Debt: Questions and Answers," Alternative Information and Development Centre, March 16, 1999, www.aidc.org.za. FOOTNOTE: Congress of South Africa Trade Unions, "Submission on the Public Investment Corporation Draft Bill," June 25, 2004, www.cosatu.org.za; Rudin, "Apartheid Debt"; South African Communist Party, "The Debt Debate."

41. "The Freedom Charter."

42. Nomvula Mokonyane, "Budget Speech for 2005/06 Financial Year by MEC for Housing in Gauteng," Speech made in the Guateng Legislature on June 13, 2005, www.info.gov.za.

43. Lucille Davie and Mary Alexander, "Kliptown and the Freedom Charter," June 27, 2005, www.southafrica.info; Blue IQ, *The Plan for a Smart Province—Guateng*.

44. Gumede, *Thabo Mbeki and the Battle for the Soul of the ANC*, 215.

45. Scott Baldauf, "Class Struggle: South Africa's New, and Few, Black Rich," *Christian Science Monitor*, October 31, 2006; "Human Development Report 2006," United Nations Development Programme, www.undp.org.

46. "South Africa: The Statistics," *Le Monde Diplomatique*, September 2006; Michael Wines and Sharon LaFraniere, "Decade of Democracy Fills Gaps in South Africa," *New York Times*, April 26, 2004.

47. Simon Robinson, "The New Rand Lords."

48. Michael Wines, "Shantytown Dwellers in South Africa Protest the Sluggish Pace of Change," *New York Times*, December 25, 2005.

49. Mark Wegerif, Bev Russell and Irma Grundling, *Summary of Key Findings from the National Evictions Survey* (Polokwane, South Africa: Nkuzi Development Association, 2005), 7, www.nkuzi.org.za.

50. Wines, "Shantytown Dwellers in South Africa Protest . . ."

51. Gumede, *Thabo Mbeki and the Battle for the Soul of the ANC*, 72. Internal quotation: Asghar Adelzadeh, "From the RDP to GEAR: The Gradual Embracing of Neo-liberalism in Economic Policy," *Transformation* 31, 1996.

52. Ibid., 70.

53. Stephen F. Cohen, *Failed Crusade: America and the Tragedy of Post-Communist Russia* (New York: W. W. Norton & Company, 2001), 30.

11. Bonfire of a Young Democracy: Russia Chooses "The Pinochet Option"

1. Boris Kagarlitsky, *Square Wheels: How Russian Democracy Got Derailed*, trans. Leslie A. Auerbach et al. (New York: Monthly Review Press, 1994), 191.

2. William Keegan, *The Spectre of Capitalism: The Future of the World Economy After the Fall of Communism* (London: Radius, 1992), 109.

3. George J. Church, "The Education of Mikhail Sergeyevich Gorbachev," *Time*, January 4, 1988; Gidske Anderson, "The Nobel Peace Prize 1990 Presentation Speech," www.nobelprize.org.

4. Marshall Pomer, Introduction, in *The New Russia: Transition Gone Awry*, eds. Lawrence R. Klein and Marshall Pomer (Stanford: Stanford University Press: 2001), 1.

5. Anderson, "The Nobel Peace Prize 1990 Presentation Speech"; Church, "The Education of Mikhail Sergeyevich Gorbachev."

6. Mikhail Gorbachev, Foreword, in Klein and Pomer, eds., *The New Russia*, xiv.

7. The unprecedented joint report called for "radical reform" and insisted that borders should be opened to trade simultaneously with any stabilization plan, the two-for-one special discussed by Dani Rodrik in chapter 8. International Monetary Fund, The World Bank, Organization for Economic Cooperation and Development, European Bank for Reconstruction and Development, *The Economy of the USSR: Summary and Recommendations* (Washington, DC: World Bank, 1990); author's interview with Jeffrey Sachs, October 2006, New York City.

8. "Order, Order," *The Economist*, December 22, 1990.

9. Ibid.; Michael Schrage, "Pinochet's Chile a Pragmatic Model for Soviet Economy," *Washington Post*, August 23, 1991.

10. *Return of the Czar*, an episode of *Frontline* [television series for PBS], producer Sherry Jones, telecast May 9, 2000.

11. Vadim Nikitin, "'91 Foes Linked by Anger and Regret," *Moscow Times*, August 21, 2006.

12. Stephen F. Cohen, "America's Failed Crusade in Russia," *The Nation*, February 28, 1994.

13. Author's interview with Jeffrey Sachs.

14. Peter Passell, "Dr. Jeffrey Sachs, Shock Therapist," *New York Times*, June 27, 1993.

15. Peter Reddaway and Dmitri Glinski, *The Tragedy of Russia's Reforms: Market Bolshevism against Democracy* (Washington, DC: United States Institute for Peace Press, 2001), 291.

16. Jeffrey D. Sachs, *The End of Poverty: Economic Possibilities for Our Time* (New York: Penguin Books, 2005), 137.

17. Reddaway and Glinski, *The Tragedy of Russia's Reforms*, 253.

18. *The Agony of Reform*, an episode of *Commanding Heights: The Battle for the World Economy* [television series for PBS], executive producers Daniel Yergin and Sue Lena Thompson, series producer William Cran (Boston: Heights Productions, 2002); Reddaway and Glinski, *The Tragedy of Russia's Reforms*, 237, 298.

19. Mikhail Leontyev, "Two Economists Will Head Russian Reform; Current Digest of the Soviet Press," *Nezavisimaya Gazeta*, November 9, 1991, digest available on December 11, 1991.

20. Chrystia Freeland, *Sale of the Century: Russia's Wild Ride from Communism to Capitalism* (New York: Crown, 2000), 56.

21. Boris Yeltsin, "Speech to the RSFSR Congress of People's Deputies," October 28, 1991.

22. David McClintick, "How Harvard Lost Russia," *Institutional Investor*, January 1, 2006.

23. Georgi Arbatov, "Origins and Consequences of 'Shock Therapy,'" in Klein and Pomer, eds., *The New Russia*, 171.

24. Vladimir Mau, "Russia," in *The Political Economy of Policy Reform*, ed. John Williamson (Washington, DC: Institute for International Economics, 1994), 435.

25. Ibid., 434–35.

26. Joseph E. Stiglitz, Preface, in Klein and Pomer, eds., *The New Russia*, xxii.

27. Joseph E. Stiglitz, *Globalization and Its Discontents* (New York: W. W. Norton & Company, 2002), 136.

28. Yeltsin, "Speech to the RSFSR Congress of People's Deputies."
29. Stephen F. Cohen, "Can We 'Convert' Russia?" *Washington Post*, March 28, 1993; Helen Womack, "Russians Shell Out as Cashless Society Looms," *Independent* (London), August 27, 1992.
30. *Russian Economic Trends*, 1997, page 46, cited in Thane Gustafson, *Capitalism Russian-Style* (Cambridge: Cambridge University Press, 1999), 171.
31. *The Agony of Reform.*
32. Gwen Ifill, "Clinton Meets Russian on Assistance Proposal," *New York Times*, March 25, 1993.
33. Malcolm Gray, "After Bloody Monday," *Maclean's*, October 18, 1993; Leyla Boulton, "Powers of Persuasion," *Financial Times* (London), November 5, 1993.
34. Serge Schmemann, "The Fight to Lead Russia," *New York Times*, March 13, 1993.
35. Margaret Shapiro and Fred Hiatt, "Troops Move in to Put Down Uprising After Yeltsin Foes Rampage in Moscow," *Washington Post*, October 4, 1993.
36. John Kenneth White and Philip John Davies, *Political Parties and the Collapse of the Old Orders* (Albany: State University of New York Press, 1998), 209.
37. "Testimony Statement by the Honorable Lawrence H. Summers Under Secretary for International Affairs U.S. Treasury Department Before the Committee on Foreign Relations of the U.S. Senate, September 7, 1993."
38. Reddaway and Glinski, *The Tragedy of Russia's Reforms*, 294.
39. Ibid., 299.
40. Celestine Bohlen, "Rancor Grows in Russian Parliament," *New York Times*, March 28, 1993.
41. "The Threat That Was," *The Economist*, April 28, 1993; Shapiro and Hiatt, "Troops Move in to Put Down Uprising After Yeltsin Foes Rampage in Moscow."
42. Serge Schmemann, "Riot in Moscow Amid New Calls for Compromise," *New York Times*, October 3, 1993.
43. Leslie H. Gelb, "How to Help Russia," *New York Times*, March 14, 1993. FOOT-NOTE: Shapiro and Hiatt, "Troops Move in to Put Down Uprising After Yeltsin Foes Rampage in Moscow."
44. Fred Kaplan, "Yeltsin in Command as Hard-Liners Give Up," *Boston Globe*, October 5, 1993.
45. "The authorities declared that in the course of two days, 142 people were killed in Moscow. This was a mockery—the real number of dead had to have been several times greater. No one even tried to determine the precise number who were wounded and beaten. Thousands were arrested." Kagarlitsky, *Square Wheels*, 218.
46. Reddaway and Glinski, *The Tragedy of Russia's Reforms*, 427.
47. Kagarlitsky, *Square Wheels*, 212.
48. John M. Goshko, "Victory Seen for Democracy," *Washington Post*, October 5, 1993; David Nyhan, "Russia Escapes a Return to the Dungeon of Its Past," *Boston Globe*, October 5, 1993; Reddaway and Glinski, *The Tragedy of Russia's Reforms*, 431.
49. *Return of the Czar.*
50. Nikitin, " '91 Foes Linked by Anger and Regret."
51. Cacilie Rohwedder, "Sachs Defends His Capitalist Shock Therapy," *Wall Street Journal Europe*, October 25, 1993.
52. Sachs, *The End of Poverty.*
53. Arthur Spiegelman, "Western Experts Call for Russian Shock Therapy," Reuters, October 6, 1993.
54. Dorinda Elliott and Betsy McKay, "Yeltsin's Free-Market Offensive," *Newsweek*,

October 18, 1993; Adi Ignatius and Claudia Rosett, "Yeltsin Now Faces Divided Nation," *Asian Wall Street Journal*, October 5, 1993.

55. Stanley Fischer, "Russia and the Soviet Union Then and Now," in *The Transition in Eastern Europe*, ed. Olivier Jean Blanchard, Kenneth A. Froot and Jeffrey D. Sachs, *Country Studies*, vol. 1 (Chicago: University of Chicago Press: 1994), 237.

56. Lawrence H. Summers, "Comment," in *The Transition in Eastern Europe, Country Studies*, vol. 1, 253.

57. Jeffrey Tayler, "Russia Is Finished," *Atlantic Monthly*, May 2001; "The World's Billionaires, According to *Forbes* Magazine, Listed by Country," Associated Press, February 27, 2003.

58. E. S. Browning, "Bond Investors Gamble on Russian Stocks," *Wall Street Journal*, March 24, 1995.

59. Legislator Sergei Yushenkov is quoting Oleg Lobov. Carlotta Gall and Thomas De Waal, *Chechnya: Calamity in the Caucasus* (New York: New York University Press, 1998), 161.

60. Vsevolod Vilchek, "Ultimatum on Bended Knees," *Moscow News*, May 2, 1996.

61. Passell, "Dr. Jeffrey Sachs, Shock Therapist."

62. David Hoffman, "Yeltsin's 'Ruthless' Bureaucrat," *Washington Post*, November 22, 1996.

63. Svetlana P. Glinkina et al., "Crime and Corruption," in Klein and Pomer, eds., *The New Russia*, 241; Matt Bivens and Jonas Bernstein, "The Russia You Never Met," *Demokratizatsiya: The Journal of Post-Soviet Democracy* 6, no. 4 (Fall 1998): 630, www.demokratizatsiya.org.

64. Bivens and Bernstein, "The Russia You Never Met," 627–28; Total, *Factbook 1998–2006*, April 2006, page 2, www.total.com; The profit figure is for 2000: Marshall I. Goldman, *The Piratization of Russia: Russian Reform Goes Awry* (New York: Routledge, 2003), 120; "Yukos Offers 12.5 Percent Stake against Debts to State-Owned Former Unit," Associated Press, June 5, 2006; the $2.8 billion figure is based on the fact that in 1997 British Petroleum paid $571 million for a 10 percent stake in Sidanko, and at that rate the 51 percent stake would have been worth more than $2.8 billion: Freeland, *Sale of the Century*, 183; Stanislav Lunev, "Russian Organized Crime Spreads Beyond Russia's Borders," *Prism* 3, no. 8 (May 30, 1997).

65. Bivens and Bernstein, "The Russia You Never Met," 629.

66. Reddaway and Glinski, *The Tragedy of Russia's Reforms*, 254.

67. Freeland, *Sale of the Century*, 299.

68. *Return of the Czar.*

69. Bivens and Bernstein report that "allegations surfaced that Chubais and four of his reform lieutenants—all of them men who had been supported by Chubais's USAID-funded patronage—had accepted $90,000 each in bribes disguised as a book advance from Uneximbank" (one of the main oligarchic firms that was winning lucrative privatization contracts from these men). In a similar controversy, Alfred Kokh, second in charge of privatization for the Yeltsin government, was paid $100,000 by a company linked to one of the main oligarchs to whom he was awarding privatization contracts; fittingly, the money was supposedly for a book he was to write on the efficiency of privatized companies. Ultimately, neither man was prosecuted in connection with the separate book deals. Bivens and Bernstein, "The Russia You Never Met," 636; Vladimir Isachenkov, "Prosecutors Investigate Russia's Ex-Privatization Czar," Associated Press, October 1, 1997.

70. McClintick, "How Harvard Lost Russia."

71. U.S. District Court, District of Massachusetts, "United States of America, Plaintiff, v.

President and Fellows of Harvard College, Andrei Shleifer and Jonathan Hay, Defendants: Civil Action No. 00–11977-DPW," *Memorandum and Order*, June 28, 2004; McClintick, "How Harvard Lost Russia."

72. McClintick, "How Harvard Lost Russia."

73. Dan Josefsson, "The Art of Ruining a Country with a Little Professional Help from Sweden," *ETC* (Stockholm) English edition, 1999.

74. Ernest Beck, "Soros Begins Investing in Eastern Europe," *Wall Street Journal*, June 1, 1994; Andrew Jack, Arkady Ostrovsky and Charles Pretzlik, "Soros to Sell 'The Worst Investment of My Life,'" *Financial Times* (London), March 17, 2004.

75. Brian Whitmore, "Latest Polls Showing Communists Ahead," *Moscow Times*, September 8, 1999.

76. *Return of the Czar.*

77. Helen Womack, "Terror Alert in Moscow as Third Bombing Kills 73," *Independent* (London), September 14, 1999.

78. Aslan Nurbiyev, "Last Bodies Cleared from Rebels' Secret Grozny Cemetery," Agence France-Presse, April 6, 2006.

79. Sabrina Tavernise, "Farms as Business in Russia," *New York Times*, November 6, 2001; Josefsson, "The Art of Ruining a Country with a Little Professional Help from Sweden"; "News Conference by James Wolfensohn, President of the World Bank Re: IMF Spring Meeting," Washington, DC, April 22, 1999, www.imf.org; Branko Milanovic, *Income, Inequality and Poverty during the Transition from Planned to Market Economy* (Washington, DC: World Bank, 1998), 68; Working Center for Economic Reform, Government of the Russian Federation, *Russian Economic Trends* 5, no. 1 (1996): 56–57, cited in Bertram Silverman and Murray Yanowitch, *New Rich, New Poor, New Russia: Winners and Losers on the Russian Road to Capitalism* (Armonk, NY: M.E. Sharpe, 2000), 47.

80. The 715,000 statistic comes from the Russian health and social development minister. "Russia Has More Than 715,000 Homeless Children—Health Minister," RIA Novosti news agency, February 23, 2006; Carel De Rooy, UNICEF, *Children in the Russian Federation*, November 16, 2004, page 5, www.unicef.org.

81. In 1987, Russia's per capita alcohol consumption was 3.9 liters. In 2003 it reached 8.87 liters. World Health Organization Regional Office for Europe, "3050 Pure Alcohol Consumption, Litres Per Capita, 1987, 2003," European Health for All Database (HFA-DB), data.euro.who.int/hfadb; "In Sad Tally, Russia Counts More Than 4 Million Addicts," *Pravda* (Moscow), February 20, 2004; UNAIDS, "Annex 1: Russian Federation," *2006 Global Report on the AIDS Epidemic*, May 2006, page 437, www.unaids.org; Interview with Natalya Katsap, Manager, Media Partnerships, Transatlantic Partners Against AIDS, June 2006.

82. World Health Organization Regional Office for Europe, "1780 SDR, Suicide and Self-Inflicted Injury, All Ages Per 100,000, 1986–1994," European Health for All Database (HFA-DB), data.euro.who.int/hfadb; In 1986, the rate of homicide and intentional injuries per 100,000 people was 7.3; in 1994 it reached its high of 32.9; in 2004 it was down to 25.2. World Health Organization Regional Office for Europe, "1793 SDR, Homicide and Intentional Injury, All Ages Per 100,000, 1986–2004," European Health for All Database.

83. Nikitin, "'91 Foes Linked by Anger and Regret"; Stephen F. Cohen, "The New American Cold War," *The Nation*, July 10, 2006; Central Intelligence Agency, "Russia," *World Factbook 1992* (Washington, DC: CIA, 1992), 287; Central Intelligence Agency, "Russia," *World Factbook 2007*, www.cia.gov.

84. Colin McMahon, "Shortages Leave Russia's East Out in the Cold," *Chicago Tribune*, November 19, 1998.

85. Arbatov, "Origins and Consequences of 'Shock Therapy,'" 177.

86. Richard Pipes, "Russia's Chance," *Commentary* 93, no. 3 (March 1992): 30.

87. Richard E. Ericson, "The Classical Soviet-Type Economy: Nature of the System and Implications for Reform," *Journal of Economic Perspectives* 5, no. 4 (Autumn 1991): 25.

88. Tayler, "Russia Is Finished"; Richard Lourie, "Shock of Calamity," *Los Angeles Times*, March 21, 1999.

89. Josefsson, "The Art of Ruining a Country with a Little Professional Help from Sweden."

90. Tatyana Koshkareva and Rustam Narzikulov, *Nezavisimaya Gazeta* (Moscow), October 31, 1997; Paul Klebnikov and Carrie Shook, "Russia and Central Europe: The New Frontier," *Forbes*, July 28, 1997.

91. Adam Smith, *The Wealth of Nations*, ed. Edwin Cannan (New York: Modern Library, 1937), 532.

92. I am indebted to David Harvey for informing this analysis. David Harvey, *A Brief History of Neoliberalism* (New York: Oxford University Press, 2005).

93. Michael Schuman, "Billionaires in the Making," *Forbes*, July 18, 1994; Harvey, *A Brief History of Neoliberalism*, 103.

94. "YPFB: Selling a National Symbol," *Institutional Investor*, March 1, 1997; Jonathan Friedland, "Money Transfer," *Wall Street Journal*, August 15, 1995.

95. Friedland, "Money Transfer."

96. Paul Blustein, *And the Money Kept Rolling In (and Out): Wall Street, the IMF, and the Bankrupting of Argentina* (New York: PublicAffairs, 2005), 24, 29; Nathaniel C. Nash, "Argentina's President, Praised Abroad, Finds Himself in Trouble at Home," *New York Times*, June 8, 1991; Tod Robberson, "Argentine President's Exit Inspires Mixed Emotions," *Dallas Morning News*, October 18, 1999.

97. Paul Brinkley-Rogers, "Chaos Reigns as President Flees Uprising," *Daily Telegraph* (London), December 22, 2001.

98. Jean Friedman-Rudovsky, "Bolivia Calls Ex-President to Court," *Time*, February 6, 2007.

12: The Capitalist Id: Russia and the New Era of the Boor Market

1. John Maynard Keynes, "From Keynes to Roosevelt: Our Recovery Plan Assayed," *New York Times*, December 31, 1933.

2. Ashley M. Herer, "Oprah, Bono Promote Clothing Line, iPod," Associated Press, October 13, 2006.

3. T. Christian Miller, *Blood Money: Wasted Billions, Lost Lives, and Corporate Greed in Iraq* (New York: Little, Brown and Company, 2006), 123. FOOTNOTE p. 248: John Cassidy, "Always with Us," *The New Yorker*, April 11, 2005.

4. Peter Passell, "Dr. Jeffrey Sachs, Shock Therapist," *New York Times*, June 27, 1993.

5. Jeffrey Sachs, "Life in the Economic Emergency Room," in *The Political Economy of Policy Reform*, ed. John Williamson (Washington, DC: Institute for International Economics, 1994), 516.

6. "Roosevelt Victor by 7,054,520 Votes," *New York Times*, December 25, 1932; Raymond Moley, *After Seven Years* (New York: Harper & Brothers, 1939), 305.

7. Carolyn Eisenberg, *Drawing the Line: The American Decision to Divide Germany, 1944–1949* (New York: Cambridge University Press, 1996).

8. *The Political Economy of Policy Reform*, 44.
9. Sachs, "Life in the Economic Emergency Room," 503–504, 513.
10. John Williamson, *The Political Economy of Policy Reform*, 19, 26.
11. John Williamson and Stephan Haggard, "The Political Conditions for Economic Reform," in *The Political Economy of Policy Reform*, 565.
12. Williamson, *The Political Economy of Policy Reform*, 20.
13. John Toye, *The Political Economy of Policy Reform*, 41.
14. Bruce Little, "Debt Crisis Looms, Study Warns," *Globe and Mail* (Toronto), February 16, 1993; The TV report was on W5 on CTV, hosted by Eric Malling. Linda McQuaig, *Shooting the Hippo: Death by Deficit and Other Canadian Myths* (Toronto: Penguin, 1995), 3.
15. The information in this paragraph is drawn from McQuaig, *Shooting the Hippo*, 18, 42–44, 117.
16. Ibid., 44, 46.
17. "How to Invent a Crisis in Education," *Globe and Mail* (Toronto), September 15, 1995.
18. Information in the next two paragraphs is drawn from Michael Bruno, *Deep Crises and Reform: What Have We Learned?* (Washington, DC: World Bank, 1996), 4, 6, 13, 25. Emphasis in original.
19. Ibid., 6. Emphasis added.
20. The figure for World Bank membership refers to 1995. There are now 185 member countries.
21. Information in the next four paragraphs is drawn from Davison L. Budhoo, *Enough Is Enough: Dear Mr. Camdessus . . . Open Letter of Resignation to the Managing Director of the International Monetary Fund* (New York: New Horizons Press, 1990), 2–27.
22. Most of Budhoo's allegations center on the discrepancies in the calculations for Trinidad and Tobago's Relative Unit Labor Cost, which is an extremely important economic indicator that measures countries' productivity. He writes, "On the basis of calculations made by our divisional statistician last year after the Fund mission returned from the field, the Relative Unit Labour Cost in Trinidad and Tobago increased by 69 percent only, instead of the 145.8 percent as stated in our 1985 reports, and the 142.9 percent as claimed in the 1986 Fund documents. Between 1980–85 the RULC actually rose by a mere 66.1 percent instead of our assertion of 164.7 percent made in the 1986 reports. Over 1983–85 relative unit labour costs moved up by only 14.9 percent, not by the 36.9 percent that was mooted to the world community in 1986. In 1985, instead of rising by the 9 percent that we had stated in the RED and Staff Report, the RULC Index fell by 1.7 percent. And in 1986 relative unit labour costs slid downward spectacularly by 46.5 percent although there is no record of this in the 1987 report or anywhere else in official Fund documentation." Ibid., 17.
23. "Bitter Calypsos in the Caribbean," *Guardian* (London), July 30, 1990; Robert Weissman, "Playing with Numbers: The IMF's Fraud in Trinidad and Tobago," *Multinational Monitor* 11, no. 6 (June 1990).
24. Lawrence Van Gelder, "Mr. Budhoo's Letter of Resignation from the I.M.F. (50 Years Is Enough)," *New York Times*, March 20, 1996.

13. Let It Burn: The Looting of Asia and "The Fall of a Second Berlin Wall"

1. Anita Raghavan, "Wall Street Is Scavenging in Asia-Pacific," *Wall Street Journal*, February 10, 1998.

2. R. William Liddle, "Year One of the Yudhoyono–Kalla Duumvirate," *Bulletin of Indonesian Economic Studies* 41, no. 3 (December 2005): 337.
3. "The Weakest Link," *The Economist*, February 8, 2003.
4. Irma Adelman, "Lessons from Korea," in *The New Russia: Transition Gone Awry*, eds. Lawrence R. Klein and Marshall Pomer (Stanford, CA: Stanford University Press, 2001), 129.
5. David McNally, "Globalization on Trial" *Monthly Review*, September 1998.
6. "Apec Highlights Social Impact of Asian Financial Crisis," Bernama news agency, May 25, 1998.
7. Hur Nam-Il, "Gold Rush . . . Korean Style," *Business Korea*, March 1998; "Selling Pressure Mounts on Korean Won—Report," *Korea Herald* (Seoul), May 12, 1998.
8. "Elderly Suicide Rate on the Increase," *Korea Herald* (Seoul), October 27, 1999; "Economic Woes Driving More to Suicide," *Korea Times* (Seoul), April 23, 1998.
9. The crisis hit in 1994, but the loan did not come through until early 1995.
10. "Milton Friedman Discusses the IMF," CNN *Moneyline with Lou Dobbs*, January 22, 1998; George P. Shultz, William E. Simon and Walter B. Wriston, "Who Needs the IMF," *Wall Street Journal*, February 3, 1998.
11. Milken Institute, "Global Overview," *Global Conference 1998*, Los Angeles, March 12, 1998, www.milkeninstitute.org.
12. Bill Clinton, "Joint Press Conference with Prime Minister Chrétien," November 23, 1997, www.clintonfoundation.org.
13. Milken Institute, "Global Overview."
14. José Piñera, "The 'Third Way' Keeps Countries in the Third World," prepared for the Cato Institute's 16th Annual Monetary Conference cosponsored with *The Economist*, Washington, DC, October 22, 1998; José Piñera, "The Fall of a Second Berlin Wall," October 22, 1998, www.josepinera.com.
15. "U.S. Senate Committee on Foreign Relations Holds Hearing on the Role of the IMF in the Asian Financial Crisis," February 12, 1998; "Text–Greenspan's Speech to New York Economic Club," Reuters News, December 3, 1997.
16. M. Perez and S. Tobarra, "Los países asiáticos tendrán que aceptar cierta flexibilidad que no era necesaria hasta ahora," *El País International Edition* (Madrid), December 8, 1997; "IMF Chief Calls for Abandon of 'Asian Model,'" Agence France-Presse, December 1, 1997.
17. Interview with Mahathir Mohamad conducted July 2, 2001, for *Commanding Heights: The Battle for the World Economy*, www.pbs.org.
18. Interview with Stanley Fischer conducted May 9, 2001, for *Commanding Heights*, www.pbs.org.
19. Stephen Grenville, "The IMF and the Indonesian Crisis," background paper, Independent Evaluation Office of the IMF, May 2004, page 8, www.imf.org.
20. Walden Bello, "The IMF's Hidden Agenda," *The Nation* (Bangkok), January 25, 1998.
21. Fischer, *Commanding Heights*; Joseph Kahn, "I.M.F.'s Hand Often Heavy, a Study Says," *New York Times*, October 21, 2000. FOOTNOTE: Paul Blustein, *The Chastening: Inside the Crisis That Rocked the Global Financial System and Humbled the IMF* (New York: PublicAffairs, 2001), 6–7.
22. The IMF agreement with South Korea explicitly demanded "easing restrictions in the labor market over redundancies (to enable businesses to move from one industry to another)." Cited in Martin Hart-Landsberg and Paul Burkett, "Economic Crisis and

Restructuring in South Korea: Beyond the Free Market-Statist Debate," *Critical Asian Studies* 33, no. 3 (2001): 421; Alkman Granitsas and Dan Biers, "Economies: The Next Step: The IMF Has Stopped Asia's Financial Panic," *Far Eastern Economic Review*, April 23, 1998; Cindy Shiner, "Economic Crisis Clouds Indonesian's Reforms," *Washington Post*, September 10, 1998.

23. Soren Ambrose, "South Korean Union Sues the IMF," *Economic Justice News* 2, no. 4 (January 2000).

24. Nicola Bullard, *Taming the Tigers: The IMF and the Asian Crisis* (London: Focus on the Global South, March 2, 1999), www.focusweb.org; Walden Bello, *A Siamese Tragedy: The Collapse of Democracy in Thailand* (London: Focus on the Global South, September 29, 2006), www.focusweb.org.

25. Jeffrey Sachs, "Power Unto Itself," *Financial Times* (London), December 11, 1997.

26. Michael Lewis "The World's Biggest Going-Out-of-Business Sale," *New York Times Magazine*, May 31, 1998.

27. Ian Chalmers, "Tommy's Toys Trashed," *Inside Indonesia* 56 (October–December 1998).

28. Paul Blustein and Sandra Sugawara, "Rescue Plan for Indonesia in Jeopardy," *Washington Post*, January 7, 1998; Grenville, "The IMF and the Indonesian Crisis," 10.

29. McNally, "Globalization on Trial."

30. "Magic Arts of Jakarta's 'Witch-Doctor,'" *Financial Times* (London), November 3, 1997.

31. Susan Sim, "Jakarta's Technocrats vs. the Technologists," *Straits Times* (Singapore), November 30, 1997; Kahn, "I.M.F.'s Hand Often Heavy, a Study Says."

32. International Monetary Fund, *The IMF's Response to the Asian Crisis*, January 1999, www.imf.org.

33. Paul Blustein, "At the IMF, a Struggle Shrouded in Secrecy," *Washington Post*, March 30, 1998; Martin Feldstein, "Refocusing the IMF," *Foreign Affairs*, March–April 1998; Jeffrey Sachs, "The IMF and the Asian Flu," *American Prospect*, March–April 1998.

34. South Korea went from 2.6 to 7.6 percent, Indonesia from 4 to 12 percent. Similar patterns occurred in the other countries. International Labour Organization, "ILO Governing Body to Examine Response to Asia Crisis," press release, March 16, 1999; Mary Jordan, "Middle Class Plunging Back to Poverty," *Washington Post*, September 6, 1998; McNally, "Globalization on Trial"; Florence Lowe-Lee, "Where Is Korea's Middle Class?" *Korea Insight* 2, no. 11 (November 2000): 1; James D. Wolfensohn, "Opening Address by the President of the World Bank Group," *Summary Proceedings of the Fifty-Third Annual Meeting of the Board of Governors* (Washington, DC: International Monetary Fund, October 6–8, 1998), 31, www.imf.org.

35. "Array of Crimes Linked to the Financial Crisis, Meeting Told," *New Straits Times* (Kuala Lumpur), June 1, 1999; Nussara Sawatsawang, "Prostitution—Alarm Bells Sound Amid Child Sex Rise," *Bangkok Post*, December 24, 1999; Luz Baguioro, "Child Labour Rampant in the Philippines," *Straits Times* (Singapore), February 12, 2000; "Asian Financial Crisis Rapidly Creating Human Crisis: World Bank," Agence France-Presse, September 29, 1998.

36. Laura Myers, "Albright Offers Thais Used F-16s, Presses Banking Reforms," Associated Press, March 4, 1999.

37. Independent Evaluation Office of the IMF, *The IMF and Recent Capital Account Crises: Indonesia, Korea, Brazil* (Washington, DC: International Monetary Fund,

September 12, 2003): 42–43, www.imf.org; Grenville, "The IMF and the Indonesian Crisis," 8.

38. Craig Mellow, "Treacherous Times," *Institutional Investor International Edition*, May 1999.

39. Raghavan, "Wall Street Is Scavenging in Asia-Pacific."

40. Rory McCarthy, "Merrill Lynch Buys Yamaichi Branches, Now Japan's Biggest Foreign Broker," Agence France-Presse, February 12, 1998; "Phatra Thanakit Announces Partnership with Merrill Lynch," Merrill Lynch press release, June 4, 1998; United Nations Conference on Trade and Development, *World Investment Report 1998: Trends and Determinants* (New York: United Nations, 1998): 337; James Xiaoning Zhan and Terutomo Ozawa, *Business Restructuring in Asia: Cross-Border M&As in the Crisis Period* (Copenhagen: Copenhagen Business School Press, 2001), 100; "Advisory Board for Salomon," *Financial Times* (London), May 18, 1999; "Korea Ssangyong Sells Info Unit Shares to Carlyle," Reuters News, January 2, 2001; "JP Morgan—Carlyle Consortium to Become Largest Shareholder of KorAm," *Korea Times* (Seoul), September 9, 2000.

41. Nicholas D. Kristof, "Worsening Financial Flu in Asia Lowers Immunity to U.S. Business," *New York Times*, February 1, 1998.

42. Lewis, "The World's Biggest Going-Out-of-Business Sale"; Mark L. Clifford, "Invasion of the Bargain Snatchers," *BusinessWeek*, March 2, 1998.

43. United Nations Conference on Trade and Development, *World Investment Report 1998*, 336; Zhan and Ozawa, *Business Restructuring in Asia*, 99; "Chronology-GM Takeover Talks with Daewoo Motor Creditors," Reuters, April 30, 2002.

44. Zhan and Ozawa, *Business Restructuring in Asia*, 96–102; Clifford, "Invasion of the Bargain Snatchers."

45. Alexandra Harney, "GM Close to Taking 67% Stake in Daewoo for $400M," *Financial Times* (London), September 20, 2001; Stephanie Strom, "Korea to Sell Control of Banks to U.S. Investors," *New York Times*, January 1, 1999.

46. Charlene Barshefsky, "Trade Issues with Asian Countries," Testimony before the Subcommittee on Trade of the House Committee on Ways and Means, February 24, 1998.

47. "International Water—Ayala Consortium Wins Manila Water Privatization Contract," Business Wire, January 23, 1997; "Bechtel Wins Contract to Build Oil Refinery in Indonesia," Asia Pulse news agency, September 22, 1999; "Mergers of S. Korean Handset Makers with Foreign Cos on the Rise," Asia Pulse news agency, November 1, 2004; United Nations Conference on Trade and Development, *World Investment Report 1998*, 337; Zhan and Ozawa, *Business Restructuring in Asia*, 96–99.

48. Zhan and Ozawa, *Business Restructuring in Asia*, 96–102; Robert Wade and Frank Veneroso, "The Asian Crisis: The High Debt Model Versus the Wall Street-Treasury-IMF Complex," *New Left Review* 228 (March-April 1998).

49. "Milton Friedman Discusses the IMF," *CNN Moneyline with Lou Dobbs*, January 22, 1998.

50. In 1995, the suicide rate was 11.8 per 100,000 people; in 2005 it was 26.1 per 100,000, an increase of 121 percent. *World Factbook 1997* (Washington, DC: Central Intelligence Agency, 1997); *World Factbook 2007*, www.cia.gov; "S. Korea Has Top Suicide Rate among OECD Countries: Report," Asia Pulse news agency, September 18, 2006; "S. Korean Police Confirm Actress Suicide," Agence France-Presse, February 12, 2007.

51. United Nations Human Settlements Program, *2005 Annual Report* (Nairobi: UN-

HABITAT, 2006), 5–6, www.unchs.org; Rainer Maria Rilke, *Duino Elegies and the Sonnets to Orpheus*, trans. A. Poulin Jr. (Boston: Houghton Mifflin, 1977), 51.

52. "Indonesia Admits to Rapes during Riots," *Washington Post*, December 22, 1998.
53. "The Weakest Link"; Thomas L. Friedman, *The Lexus and the Olive Tree* (New York: Farrar, Straus and, Giroux, 1999), 452–53.
54. "The Critics of Capitalism," *Financial Times* (London), November 27, 1999.
55. Fischer, *Commanding Heights*; Blustein, *The Chastening*, 6–7.

14. Shock Therapy in the U.S.A.: The Homeland Security Bubble

1. Tom Baldwin, "Revenge of the Battered Generals," *Times* (London), April 18, 2006.
2. Reuters, "Britain's Ranking on Surveillance Worries Privacy Advocate," *New York Times*, November 3, 2006.
3. Daniel Gross, "The Homeland Security Bubble," Slate.com, June 1, 2005.
4. Robert Burns, "Defense Chief Shuns Involvement in Weapons and Merger Decisions to Avoid Conflict of Interest," Associated Press, August 23, 2001.
5. John Burgess, "Tuning in to a Trophy Technology," *Washington Post*, March 24, 1992; "TIS Worldwide Announces the Appointment of the Honorable Donald Rumsfeld to its Board of Advisors," PR Newswire, April 25, 2000; Geoffrey Lean and Jonathan Owen, "Donald Rumsfeld Makes $5M Killing on Bird Flu Drug," *Independent* (London), March 12, 2006.
6. George W. Bush, "Bush Delivers Remarks with Rumsfeld, Gates," CQ Transcripts Wire, November 8, 2006.
7. Joseph L. Galloway, "After Losing War Game, Rumsfeld Packed Up His Military and Went to War," Knight-Ridder, April 26, 2006.
8. Jeffrey H. Birnbaum, "Mr. CEO Goes to Washington," *Fortune*, March 19, 2001.
9. Donald H. Rumsfeld, "Secretary Rumsfeld's Remarks to the Johns Hopkins, Paul H. Nitze School of Advanced International Studies," December 5, 2005, www.defenselink.mil; Tom Peters, *The Circle of Innovation* (New York: Alfred A. Knopf, 1997), 16.
10. Information on the next 2 pages is drawn from Donald H. Rumsfeld, "DoD Acquisition and Logistics Excellence Week Kickoff—Bureaucracy to Battlefield," speech made at the Pentagon, September 10, 2001, www.defenselink.mil.
11. Carolyn Skorneck, "Senate Committee Approves New Base Closings, Cuts $1.3 Billion from Missile Defense," Associated Press, September 7, 2001; Rumsfeld, "DoD Acquisition and Logistics Excellence Week Kickoff."
12. Bill Hemmer and Jamie McIntyre, "Defense Secretary Declares War on the Pentagon's Bureaucracy," *CNN Evening News*, September 10, 2001.
13. Donald Rumsfeld, "Tribute to Milton Friedman," Washington, DC, May 9, 2002, www.defenselink.mil; Milton Friedman and Rose D. Friedman, *Two Lucky People: Memoirs* (Chicago: University of Chicago Press, 1998), 345.
14. Friedman and Friedman, *Two Lucky People*, 391.
15. William Gruber, "Rumsfeld Reflects on Politics, Business," *Chicago Tribune*, October 20, 1993; Stephen J. Hedges, "Winter Comes for a Beltway Lion," *Chicago Tribune*, November 12, 2006.
16. Greg Schneider, "Rumsfeld Shunning Weapons Decisions," *Washington Post*, August 24, 2001; Andrew Cockburn, *Rumsfeld: His Rise, Fall, and Catastrophic Legacy* (New York: Scribner, 2007), 89–90; Randeep Ramesh, "The Two Faces of Rumsfeld,"

Guardian (London), May 9, 2003; Richard Behar, "Rummy's North Korea Connection," *Fortune*, May 12, 2003.

17. Joe Palca, "Salk Polio Vaccine Conquered Terrifying Disease," *National Public Radio: Morning Edition*, April 12, 2005; David M. Oshinsky, *Polio: An American Story* (Oxford: Oxford University Press, 2005), 210–11. FOOTNOTE: Carly Weeks, "Tamiflu Linked to 10 Deaths," Gazette (Montreal), November 30, 2006; Dorsey Griffith, "Psychiatric Warning Put on Flu Drug," *Sacramento Bee*, November 14, 2006.

18. Knowledge Ecology International, "KEI Request for Investigation into Anticompetitive Aspects of Gilead Voluntary Licenses for Patents on Tenofivir and Emtricitabine," February 12, 2007, www.keionline.org.

19. John Stanton, "Big Stakes in Tamiflu Debate," *Roll Call*, December 15, 2005.

20. Information in the next two paragraphs is drawn from T. Christian Miller, *Blood Money: Wasted Billions, Lost Lives and Corporate Greed in Iraq* (New York: Little, Brown and Company, 2006), 77–79.

21. Joan Didion, "Cheney: The Fatal Touch," *The New York Review of Books*, October 5, 2006.

22. Dan Briody, *Halliburton Agenda: The Politics of Oil and Money* (New Jersey: John Wiley & Sons, 2004), 198–99; David H. Hackworth, "Balkans Good for Texas-Based Business," *Sun-Sentinel* (Fort Lauderdale), August 16, 2001.

23. Antonia Juhasz, *Bush Agenda: Invading the World, One Economy at a Time* (New York: Regan Books, 2006), 120.

24. Jonathan D. Salant, "Cheney: I'll Forfeit Options," Associated Press, September 1, 2000.

25. "Lynne Cheney Resigns from Lockheed Martin Board," Dow Jones News Service, January 5, 2001.

26. Tim Weiner, "Lockheed and the Future of Warfare," *New York Times*, November 28, 2004. FOOTNOTE: Jeff McDonald, "City Looks at County's Outsourcing as Blueprint," *San Diego Union-Tribune*, July 23, 2006.

27. Sam Howe Verhovek, "Clinton Reining in Role for Business in Welfare Effort," *New York Times*, May 11, 1997; Barbara Vobejda, "Privatization of Social Programs Curbed," *Washington Post*, May 10, 1997.

28. Michelle Breyer and Mike Ward, "Running Prisons for a Profit," *Austin American-Statesman*, September 4, 1994; Judith Greene, "Bailing Out Private Jails," *The American Prospect*, September 10, 2001; Madeline Baro, "Tape Shows Inmates Bit by Dogs, Kicked, Stunned," Associated Press, August 19, 1997.

29. Matt Moffett, "Pension Reform Pied Piper Loves Private Accounts," *Wall Street Journal*, March 3, 2005.

30. "Governor George W. Bush Delivers Remarks on Government Reform," *FDCH Political Transcripts*, Philadelphia, June 9, 2000.

31. Jon Elliston, "Disaster in the Making," *Tucson Weekly*, September 23, 2004.

32. Joe M. Allbaugh, "Current FEMA Instructions & Manuals Numerical Index," Testimony of Federal Emergency Management Agency Director Joe M. Allbaugh before the Veterans Affairs, Housing and Urban Development and Independent Agencies Subcommittee of the Senate Appropriations Committee, May 16, 2001.

33. John F. Harris and Dana Milbank, "For Bush, New Emergencies Ushered in a New Agenda," *Washington Post*, September 22, 2001; United States General Accounting Office, *Aviation Security: Long-Standing Problems Impair Airport Screeners' Performance*, June 2000, page 25, www.gao.gov.

34. National Commission on Terrorist Attacks upon the United States, *The 9/11*

Commission Report: Final Report of the National Commission on Terrorist Attacks Upon the United States, 2004, page 85, www.gpoaccess.gov.

35. Anita Manning, "Company Hopes to Restart Production of Anthrax Vaccine," *USA Today*, November 5, 2001.

36. J. McLane, "Conference to Honor Milton Friedman on His Ninetieth Birthday," *Chicago Business*, November 25, 2002, www.chibus.com.

37. Joan Ryan, "Home of the Brave," *San Francisco Chronicle*, October 23, 2001; George W. Bush, "President Honors Public Servants," Washington, DC, October 15, 2001.

38. George W. Bush, "President Discusses War on Terrorism," Atlanta, Georgia, November 8, 2001.

39. Harris and Milbank, "For Bush, New Emergencies Ushered in a New Agenda."

40. Andrew Bacevich, "Why Read Clausewitz When Shock and Awe Can Make a Clean Sweep of Things?" *London Review of Books*, June 8, 2006. FOOTNOTE: Scott Shane and Ron Nixon, "In Washington, Contractors Take on Biggest Role Ever," *New York Times*, February 4, 2007.

41. Evan Ratliff, "Fear, Inc.," *Wired*, December 2005.

42. Shane and Nixon, "In Washington, Contractors Take on Biggest Role Ever."

43. Matt Richtel, "Tech Investors Cull Start-ups for Pentagon," *Washington Post*, May 7, 2007; Defense Venture Catalyst Initiative, "An Overview of the Defense Venture Catalyst Initiative," devenci.dtic.mil.

44. Ratliff, "Fear, Inc."

45. Jason Vest, "Inheriting a Shambles at Defense" *Texas Observer* (Austin), December 1, 2006; Ratliff, "Fear, Inc."; Paladin Capital Group, "Lt. General (Ret) USAF Kenneth A. Minihan," Paladin Team, December 2, 2003, www.paladincapgroup.com.

46. Office of Homeland Security, *National Strategy for Homeland Security*, July 2002, page 1, www.whitehouse.gov; Ron Suskind, *The One Percent Doctrine: Deep Inside America's Pursuit of Its Enemies Since 9/11* (New York: Simon & Schuster, 2006); "Terror Fight Spawns Startups," *Red Herring*, December 5, 2005.

47. United States House of Representatives, Committee on Government Reform—Minority Staff, Special Investigations Division, *Dollars, Not Sense: Government Contracting Under the Bush Administration*, Prepared for Rep. Henry A. Waxman, June 2006, page 5, www.democrats.reform.house.gov; Tim Shorrock, "The Corporate Takeover of U.S. Intelligence," *Salon*, June 1, 2007, www.salon.com; Rachel Monahan and Elena Herrero Beaumont, "Big Time Security," *Forbes*, August 3, 2006; Central Intelligence Agency, *World Fact Book 2007*, www.cia.gov; "US Government Spending in States Up 6 Pct in FY'03," Reuters, October 7, 2004; Frank Rich, "The Road from K Street to Yusufiya," *New York Times*, June 25, 2006.

48. Monahan and Herrero Beaumont, "Big Time Security"; Ratliff, "Fear, Inc."

49. The figure comes from Roger Cressey, a former Bush counterterrorism official now President of Good Harbor Consulting. Rob Evans and Alexi Mostrous, "Britain's Surveillance Future," *Guardian* (London), November 2, 2006; Mark Johnson, "Video, Sound Advances Aimed at War on Terror," Associated Press, August 2, 2006; Ellen McCarthy, "8 Firms Vie for Pieces of Air Force Contract," *Washington Post*, September 14, 2004.

50. Brian Bergstein, "Attacks Spawned a Tech-Security Market That Remains Young Yet Rich," Associated Press, September 4, 2006.

51. Mure Dickie, "Yahoo Backed on Helping China Trace Writer," *Financial Times* (London), November 10, 2005; Leslie Cauley, "NSA Has Massive Database of Americans' Phone Calls," *USA Today*, May 11, 2006; "Boeing Team Awarded SBInet

Contract by Department of Homeland Security," press release, September 21, 2006, www.boeing.com.

52. Robert O'Harrow Jr., *No Place to Hide* (New York: Free Press, 2005).

53. "Terror Fight Spawns Startups."

54. Justine Rood, "FBI Terror Watch List 'Out of Control'," *The Blotter blog on ABC News*, June 13, 2007, www.abcnews.com; Ed Pilkington, "Millions Assigned Terror Risk Score on Trips to the US," *Guardian* (London), December 2, 2006.

55. Rick Anderson, "Flog Is My Co-Pilot," *Seattle Weekly*, November 29, 2006; Jane Mayer, "The C.I.A.'s Travel Agent," *The New Yorker*, October 30, 2006; Brian Knowlton, "Report Rejects European Denial of CIA Prisons," *New York Times*, November 29, 2006; Mayer, "The C.I.A.'s Travel Agent"; Stephen Grey, *Ghost Plane: The True Story of the CIA Torture Program* (New York: St. Martin's Press, 2006), 80; Pat Milton, "ACLU File: Suit Against Boeing Subsidiary, Saying It Enabled Secret Overseas Torture," Associated Press, May 31, 2007.

56. Andrew Buncombe, "New Maximum-Security Jail to Open at Guantanamo Bay," *Independent* (London), July 30, 2006; Pratap Chatterjee, "Intelligence in Iraq: L-3 Supplies Spy Support," *CorpWatch*, August 9, 2006, www.corpwatch.com.

57. Michelle Faul, "Guantanamo Prisoners for Sale," Associated Press, May 31, 2005; John Simpson, "No Surprises in the War on Terror," *BBC News*, February 13, 2006; John Mintz, "Detainees Say They Were Charity Workers," *Washington Post*, May 26, 2002.

58. The prisoner in question was Adel Fattough Ali Algazzar. Dave Gilson, "Why Am I in Cuba?" *Mother Jones*, September–October 2006; Simpson, "No Surprises in the War on Terror"; Andrew O. Selsky, "AP: Some Gitmo Detainees Freed Elsewhere," *USA Today*, December 15, 2006.

59. Gary Stoller, "Homeland Security Generates Multibillion Dollar Business," *USA Today*, September 10, 2006.

60. Sarah Anderson, John Cavanagh, Chuck Collins and Eric Benjamin, "Executive Excess 2006: Defense and Oil Executives Cash in on Conflict," August 30, 2006, page 1, www.faireconomy.org.

61. Ratliff, "Fear, Inc."

62. O'Harrow, *No Place to Hide*, 9.

15. A Corporatist State: Removing the Revolving Door, Putting in an Archway

1. Jim Krane, "Former President Bush Battles Arab Critics of His Son," Associated Press, November 21, 2006.

2. Scott Shane and Ron Nixon, "In Washington, Contractors Take on Biggest Role Ever," *New York Times*, February 4, 2007.

3. Jane Mayer, "Contract Sport," *The New Yorker*, February 16, 2004.

4. "HR 5122: John Warner National Defense Authorization Act for Fiscal Year 2007 (Enrolled as Agreed to or Passed by Both House and Senate)," thomas.loc.gov.

5. "Remarks of Sen. Patrick Leahy on National Defense Authorization Act for Fiscal Year 2007, Conference Report, Congressional Record," States News Service, September 29, 2006.

6. Gilead Sciences, "Stock Information: Historical Price Lookup," www.gilead.com.

7. Interview with Stephen Kinzer, *Democracy Now!* April 21, 2006, www.democracy now.org.

8. The phrase "interrelated and mutually reinforcing" comes from the historian James

A. Bill. Stephen Kinzer, *Overthrow: America's Century of Regime Change from Hawaii to Iraq* (New York: Times Books, 2006), 122.

9. Robert Burns, "Defense Chief Shuns Involvement in Weapons and Merger Decisions to Avoid Conflict of Interest," Associated Press, August 23, 2001; Matt Kelley, "Defense Secretary Sold Up to $91 Million in Assets to Comply with Ethics Rules, Complains about Disclosure Form," Associated Press, June 18, 2002; Pauline Jelinek, "Rumsfeld Asks for Deadline Extension," Associated Press, July 17, 2001.

10. John Stanton, "Big Stakes in Tamiflu Debate," *Roll Call*, December 15, 2005.

11. Rumsfeld's 2005 disclosure report shows that he holds "shares worth up to $95.9m, from which he got an income of up to $13m, owned land worth up to $17m, and made $1m from renting it out." Geoffrey Lean and Jonathan Owen, "Donald Rumsfeld Makes $5m Killing on Bird Flu Drug," *Independent* (London), March 12, 2006; Kelley, "Defense Secretary Sold up to $91 Million in Assets . . ."

12. Burns, "Defense Chief Shuns Involvement . . ."

13. Stanton, "Big Stakes in Tamiflu Debate."

14. Nelson D. Schwartz, "Rumsfeld's Growing Stake in Tamiflu," *Fortune*, October 31, 2005.

15. Gilead Sciences, "Stock Information: Historical Price Lookup," www.gilead.com.

16. Cassell Bryan-Low, "Cheney Cashed in Halliburton Options Worth $35 Million," *Wall Street Journal*, September 20, 2000.

17. Ken Herman, "Cheneys Earn $8.8 Million to Bushes' $735,000," Austin *American-Statesman*, April 15, 2006; Halliburton, Investor Relations, "Historical Price Lookup," www.halliburton.com.

18. Sarah Karush, "Once Privileged in Iraq, Russian Oil Companies Hope to Compete on Equal Footing After Saddam," Associated Press, March 14, 2003; Saeed Shah, "Oil Giants Scramble for Iraqi Riches," *Independent* (London), March 14, 2003.

19. "Waiting for the Green Light," *Petroleum Economist*, October 1, 2006.

20. Lean and Owen, "Donald Rumsfeld Makes $5m Killing on Bird Flu Drug."

21. Jonathan Weisman, "Embattled Rep. Ney Won't Seek Reelection," *Washington Post*, August 8, 2006; Sonya Geis and Charles R. Babcock, "Former GOP Lawmaker Gets 8 Years," *Washington Post*, March 4, 2006; Judy Bachrach, "Washington Babylon," *Vanity Fair*, August 1, 2006.

22. Eric Lipton, "Former Antiterror Officials Find Industry Pays Better," *New York Times*, June 18, 2006.

23. Ellen Nakashima, "Ashcroft Finds Private-Sector Niche," *Washington Post*, August 12, 2006; Lipton, "Former Antiterror Officials Find Industry Pays Better"; Good Harbor Consulting, LLC., www.goodharbor.net; Paladin Capital Group, "R. James Woolsey—VP," Paladin Team, www.paladincapgroup.com; Booz Allen Hamilton, "R James Woolsey," www.boozallen.com; Douglas Jehl, "Insiders' New Firm Consults on Iraq," *New York Times*, September 30, 2003; "Former FEMA Head to Start Consulting Business on Emergency Planning," Associated Press, November 24, 2005.

24. "Former FEMA Head Discussed Wardrobe during Katrina Crisis," Associated Press, November 3, 2005.

25. Seymour M. Hersh, "The Spoils of the Gulf War," *New Yorker*, September 6, 1993.

26. Michael Isikoff and Mark Hosenball, "A Legal Counterattack," *Newsweek*, April 16, 2003; John Council, "Baker Botts' 'Love Shack' for Clients," *Texas Lawyer*, March 6, 2006; Erin E. Arvedlund, "Russian Oil Politics in a Texas Court," *New York Times*, February 15, 2005; Robert Bryce, "It's a Baker Botts World," *The Nation*, October 11, 2004.

27. Peter Smith and James Politi, "Record Pay-Outs from Carlyle and KKR," *Financial Times* (London), October 20, 2004.

28. "Cutting James Baker's Ties," *New York Times*, December 12, 2003.

29. The information in the next two paragraphs is drawn from Naomi Klein, "James Baker's Double Life: A Special Investigation," *The Nation*, posted online October 12, 2004, www.thenation.com.

30. David Leigh, "Carlyle Pulls Out of Iraq Debt Recovery Consortium," *Guardian* (London), October 15, 2004; United Nations Compensation Commission, "Payment of Compensation," press releases, 2005–2006, www.unog.ch; Klein, "James Baker's Double Life"; World Bank, "Data Sheet for Iraq," October 23, 2006, www.worldbank.org.

31. Eric Schmitt, "New Group Will Lobby for Change in Iraqi Rule," *New York Times*, November 15, 2002; George P. Shultz, "Act Now," *Washington Post*, September 6, 2002; Harry Esteve, "Ex-Secretary Stumps for Gubernatorial Hopeful," *Oregonian* (Portland), February 12, 2002; David R. Baker, "Bechtel Pulling Out after 3 Rough Years of Rebuilding Work," *San Francisco Chronicle*, November 1, 2006.

32. Tim Weiner, "Lockheed and the Future of Warfare," *New York Times*, November 28, 2004; Schmitt, "New Group Will Lobby for Change in Iraqi Rule"; John Laughland, "The Prague Racket," *Guardian* (London), November 22, 2002; John B. Judis, "Minister without Portfolio," *The American Prospect*, May 2003; Lockheed Martin, Investor Relations, "Stock Price Details," www.lockheedmartin.com.

33. Bob Woodward, *State of Denial* (New York: Simon & Schuster, 2006), 406–407.

34. James Dao, "Making a Return to the Political Stage," *New York Times*, November 28, 2002; Leslie H. Gelb, "Kissinger Means Business," *New York Times*, April 20, 1986; Jeff Gerth, "Ethics Disclosure Filed with Panel," *New York Times*, March 9, 1989.

35. James Harding, "Kissinger Second Take," *Financial Times* (London), December 14, 2002.

36. Seymour M. Hersh, "Lunch with the Chairman," *The New Yorker*, March 17, 2003.

37. Ibid.; Thomas Donnelly and Richard Perle, "Gas Stations in the Sky," *Wall Street Journal*, August 14, 2003. FOOTNOTE: R. Jeffrey Smith, "Tanker Inquiry Finds Rumsfeld's Attention Was Elsewhere," *Washington Post*, June 20, 2006; Tony Capaccio, "Boeing Proposes Bonds for 767 Lease Deal," *Seattle Times*, March 4, 2003.

38. Hersh, "Lunch with the Chairman"; Tom Hamburger and Dennis Berman, "U.S. Adviser Perle Resigns as Head of Defense Board," *Wall Street Journal*, March 28, 2003.

39. Interview with Richard Perle, *CNN: Late Edition with Wolf Blitzer*, March 9, 2003.

40. Judis, "Minister without Portfolio"; David S. Hilzenrath, "Richard N. Perle's Many Business Ventures Followed His Years as a Defense Official," *Washington Post*, May 24, 2004; Hersh, "Lunch with the Chairman"; T. Christian Miller, *Blood Money: Wasted Billions, Lost Lives and Corporate Greed in Iraq* (New York: Little, Brown and Company, 2006), 73.

16. Erasing Iraq: In Search of a "Model" for the Middle East

1. Andrew M. Wyllie, "Convulsion Therapy of the Psychoses," *Journal of Mental Science* 86 (March 1940): 248.

2. Richard Cohen, "The Lingo of Vietnam," *Washington Post*, November 21, 2006.

3. "Deputy Secretary Wolfowitz Interview with Sam Tannenhaus, Vanity Fair," News Transcript, May 9, 2003, www.defenselink.mil.

4. FOOTNOTE: *2007 Index of Economic Freedom* (Washington, DC: Heritage Foundation and *The Wall Street Journal*, 2007), 326, www.heritage.org.

5. Thomas L. Friedman, "The Long Bomb," *New York Times*, March 2, 2003; Joshua Muravchik, "Democracy's Quiet Victory," *New York Times*, August 19, 2002; Robert Dreyfuss, "Just the Beginning," *American Prospect*, April 1, 2003. FOOTNOTE: John Norris, *Collision Course: NATO, Russia, and Kosovo* (Westport, CT: Praeger, 2005), xxii–xxiii.

6. George W. Bush, "President Discusses Education, Entrepreneurship & Home Ownership at Indiana Black Expo," Indianapolis, Indiana, July 14, 2005.

7. Edwin Chen and Maura Reynolds, "Bush Seeks U.S.-Mideast Trade Zone to Bring Peace, Prosperity to Region," *Los Angeles Times*, May 10, 2003.

8. Harlan Ullman, " 'Shock and Awe' Misunderstood," *USA Today*, April 8, 2003.

9. Peter Johnson, "Media's War Footing Looks Solid," *USA Today*, February 17, 2003.

10. Thomas L. Friedman, "What Were They Thinking?" *New York Times*, October 7, 2005.

11. United States Department of State, "Memoranda of Conversation," June 10, 1976, declassified, www.gwu.edu/~nsarchiv.

12. George W. Bush, speech made at 2005 Inauguration, January 20, 2005.

13. Norman Friedman, *Desert Victory: The War for Kuwait* (Annapolis, MD: Naval Institute Press, 1991), 185; Michael R. Gordon and Bernard E. Trainor, *Cobra II: The Inside Story of the Invasion and Occupation of Iraq* (New York: Pantheon Books, 2006), 551.

14. Anthony Shadid, *Night Draws Near: Iraq's People in the Shadow of America's War* (New York: Henry Holt, 2005), galley, 95. Quoted with the author's permission.

15. Harlan K. Ullman and James P. Wade, *Shock and Awe: Achieving Rapid Dominance* (Washington, DC: NDU Press Book, 1996), 55; Ron Suskind, *The One Percent Doctrine: Deep Inside America's Pursuit of Its Enemies Since 9/11* (New York: Simon & Schuster, 2006), 123, 214.

16. Ullman and Wade, *Shock and Awe*, xxv, 17, 23, 29.

17. Maher Arar, " 'I Am Not a Terrorist—I Am Not a Member of Al-Qaida,' " *Vancouver Sun*, November 5, 2003.

18. "Iraq Faces Massive U.S. Missile Barrage," *CBS News*, January 24, 2003.

19. "U.S. Tests Massive Bomb," *CNN: Wolf Blitzer Reports*, March 11, 2003.

20. Ibid.

21. Rajiv Chandrasekaran and Peter Baker, "Allies Struggle for Supply Lines," *Washington Post*, March 30, 2003; Jon Lee Anderson, *The Fall of Baghdad* (New York: Penguin Press, 2004), 199; Gordon and Trainor, *Cobra II*, 465. FOOTNOTE: Charles Duelfer, *Comprehensive Report of the Special Advisor to the DCI on Iraq's WMD*, vol. 1, September 30, 2004, 11, www.cia.gov.

22. Shadid, *Night Draws Near*, 71.

23. Suzanne Goldenberg, "War in the Gulf: In an Instant We Were Plunged into Endless Night," *Guardian* (London), April 4, 2003.

24. "Restoring a Treasured Past," *Los Angeles Times*, April 17, 2003.

25. Charles J. Hanley, "Looters Ransack Iraq's National Library," Associated Press, April 15, 2003.

26. Michael D. Lemonick, "Lost to the Ages," *Time*, April 28, 2003; Louise Witt, "The End of Civilization," *Salon*, April 17, 2003, www.salon.com.

27. Thomas E. Ricks and Anthony Shadid, "A Tale of Two Baghdads," *Washington Post*, June 2, 2003.

28. Frank Rich, "And Now: 'Operation Iraqi Looting,'" *New York Times*, April 27, 2003.

29. Donald H. Rumsfeld, "DoD News Briefing—Secretary Rumsfeld and Gen. Myers," April 11, 2003, www.defenselink.mil; Simon Robinson, "Grounding Planes the Wrong Way," *Time*, July 14, 2003.

30. Rajiv Chandrasekaran, *Imperial Life in the Emerald City: Inside Iraq's Green Zone* (New York: Alfred A. Knopf, 2006), 119–20.

31. Ibid., 165–66.

32. World Bank, *World Development Report 1990* (Oxford: World Bank, 1990), 178–79; New Mexico Coalition for Literacy, New Mexico Literacy Profile, 2005–2006 Programs, www.nmcl.org. FOOTNOTE: Chandrasekaran, *Imperial Life in the Emerald City*, 5.

33. Shafiq Rasul, Asif Iqbal and Rhuhel Ahmed, *Composite Statement: Detention in Afghanistan and Guantanamo Bay* (New York: Center for Constitutional Rights, July 26, 2004), 96, 99, www.ccr-ny.org.

34. Ibid., 9, 10, 21, 26, 72.

35. John F. Burns, "Looking Beyond His Critics, Bremer Sees Reason for Both Hope and Caution," *New York Times*, June 29, 2004; Steve Kirby, "Bremer Says Iraq Open for Business," Agence France-Presse, May 25, 2003.

36. Thomas B. Edsall and Juliet Eilperin, "Lobbyists Set Sights on Money-Making Opportunities in Iraq," *Washington Post*, October 2, 2003.

17. Ideological Blowback: A Very Capitalist Disaster

1. According to Jeffrey Goldberg, Rice made the comment at a dinner in a Georgetown restaurant. He writes, "The remark stunned the other guests. [Brent] Scowcroft, as he later told friends, was flummoxed by Rice's 'evangelical tone.'" Jeffrey Goldberg, "Breaking Ranks," *The New Yorker*, October 31, 2005.

2. Fareed Zakaria, "What Bush Got Right," *Newsweek*, March 14, 2005.

3. Phillip Kurata, "Eastern Europeans Urge Iraq to Adopt Rapid Market Reforms," Washington File, Bureau of International Information Programs, U.S. Department of State, September 26, 2003, usinfo.state.gov; "Iraq Poll Finds Poverty Main Worry, Sadr Popular," Reuters, May 20, 2004.

4. Joseph Stiglitz, "Shock without the Therapy," *Business Day* (Johannesburg), February 20, 2004; Jim Krane, "U.S. Aims to Keep Iraq Military Control," Associated Press, March 13, 2004.

5. Interview with Richard Perle, CNN: *Anderson Cooper 360 Degrees*, November 6, 2006; Interview with David Frum, CNN: *Late Edition with Wolf Blitzer*, November 19, 2006.

6. L. Paul Bremer III, *My Year in Iraq: The Struggle to Build a Future of Hope* (New York: Simon & Schuster, 2006), 21.

7. Interview with Paul Bremer, PBS: *The Charlie Rose Show*, January 11, 2006.

8. Noelle Knox, "Companies Rush to Account for Staff," *USA Today*, September 13, 2001; Harlan S. Byrne, "Disaster Relief: Insurance Brokers AON, Marsh Look to Recover, Even Benefit Post-September 11," *Barron's*, November 19, 2001.

9. General Garner's plan for Iraq was straightforward enough: fix the infrastructure, hold quick and dirty elections, leave the shock therapy to the International Monetary Fund and concentrate on securing U.S. military bases on the model of the Philippines. "I think we should look right now at Iraq as our coaling station in the Middle East," he

told the BBC. Interview with General Jay Garner, conducted by Greg Palast, "Iraq for Sale," BBC TV, March 19, 2004, www.gregpalast.com; Thomas Crampton, "Iraq Official Warns on Fast Economic Shift," *International Herald Tribune* (Paris), October 14, 2003; Rajiv Chandrasekaran, "Attacks Force Retreat from Wide-Ranging Plans for Iraq," *Washington Post*, December 28, 2003.

10. "Let's All Go to the Yard Sale," *The Economist*, September 27, 2003.

11. Coalition Provisional Authority, *Order Number 37 Tax Strategy for 2003*, September 19, 2003, www.iraqcoalition.org; Coalition Provisional Authority, *Order Number 39 Foreign Investment*, December 20, 2003, www.iraqcoalition.org; Dana Milbank and Walter Pincus, "U.S. Administrator Imposes Flat Tax System on Iraq," *Washington Post*, November 2, 2003; Rajiv Chandrasekaran, "U.S. Funds for Iraq Are Largely Unspent," *Washington Post*, July 4, 2004. FOOTNOTE: Mark Gregory, "Baghdad's 'Missing Billions,'" *BBC News*, November 9, 2006; David Pallister, "How the US Sent $12bn in Cash to Iraq. And Watched It Vanish," *Guardian* (London), February 8, 2007.

12. Central Bank of Iraq and the Coalition Provisional Authority, "Saddam-Free Dinar Becomes Iraq's Official Currency," January 15, 2004, www.cpa-iraq.org; "Half of Iraqis Lack Drinking Water—Minister," Agence France-Presse, November 4, 2003; Charles Clover and Peter Spiegel, "Petrol Queues Block Baghdad as Black Market Drains Off," *Financial Times* (London), December 9, 2003.

13. Donald H. Rumsfeld, "Prepared Statement for the Senate Appropriations Committee," Washington, DC, September 24, 2003, www.defenselink.mil; Borzou Daragahi, "Iraq's Ailing Banking Industry Is Slowly Reviving," *New York Times*, December 30, 2004; Laura MacInnis, "Citigroup, U.S. to Propose Backing Iraqi Imports," Reuters, February 17, 2004; Justin Blum, "Big Oil Companies Train Iraqi Workers Free," *Washington Post*, November 6, 2004.

14. Congressional Budget Office, *Paying for Iraq's Reconstruction: An Update*, December 2006, page 15, www.cbo.gov; Chandrasekaran, "U.S. Funds for Iraq Are Largely Unspent."

15. George W. Bush, "President Bush Addresses United Nations General Assembly," New York City, September 23, 2003; George W. Bush, "President Addresses the Nation," September 7, 2003.

16. James Glanz, "Violence in Iraq Curbs Work of 2 Big Contractors," *New York Times*, April 22, 2004.

17. Rajiv Chandrasekaran, "Best-Connected Were Sent to Rebuild Iraq," *Washington Post*, September 17, 2006; Holly Yeager, "Halliburton's Iraq Army Contract to End," *Financial Times* (London), July 13, 2006.

18. Office of Inspector General, USAID, *Audit of USAID/Iraq's Economic Reform Program*, Audit Report Number E-266–04–004-P, September 20, 2004, pages 5–6, www.usaid.gov; USAID, "Award/Contract," RAN-C-00–03–00043–00, www.usaid.gov; Mark Brunswick, "Opening of Schools to Test Iraqis' Confidence," *Star Tribune* (Minneapolis), September 17, 2006. FOOTNOTE: James Rupert, "Schools a Bright Spot in Iraq," *Seattle Times*, June 30, 2004.

19. Ron Wyden, "Dorgan, Wyden, Waxman, Dingell Call to End Outsourcing of Oversight for Iraq Reconstruction," press release, May 5, 2004, wyden.senate.gov; "Carolinas Companies Find Profits in Iraq," Associated Press, May 2, 2004; James Mayfield, "Understanding Islam and Terrorism—9/11," August 6, 2002, was at www.texashoustonmission.org, accessed January 7, 2005; Sis Mayfield, "Letters from President Mayfield," February 27, 2004, was at www.texashoustonmission.org, accessed January 7, 2005.

20. Rajiv Chandrasekaran, "Defense Skirts State in Reviving Iraqi Industry," *Washington Post*, May 14, 2007.

21. This account of Gaidar's comments comes from Mark Masarskii, an adviser on entrepreneurship to the Moscow government. Jim Krane, "Iraq's Fast Track to Capitalism Scares Baghdad's Businessmen," The Associated Press, December 3, 2003; Lynn D. Nelson and Irina Y. Kuzes, "Privatization and the New Business Class," in *Russia in Transition: Politics, Privatization, and Inequality*, ed. David Lane (London: Longman, 1995), 129. FOOTNOTE: Kevin Begos, "Good Intentions Meet Harsh Reality," *Winston-Salem Journal*, December 19, 2004.

22. Dahr Jamail and Ali al-Fadhily, "U.S. Resorting to 'Collective Punishment,'" Inter Press Service, September 18, 2006.

23. Gilbert Burnham et al., "Mortality after the 2003 Invasion of Iraq: A Cross-Sectional Cluster Sample Survey," *Lancet* 368 (October 12, 2006): 1421–28.

24. Ralph Peters, "Last Gasps in Iraq," *USA Today*, November 2, 2006.

25. Oxford Research International, *National Survey of Iraq*, February 2004, page 20, news.bbc.co.uk; Donald MacIntyre, "Sistani Most Popular Iraqi Leader, US Pollsters Find," *Independent* (London), August 31, 2004.

26. Bremer, *My Year in Iraq*, 71.

27. "The Lost Year in Iraq," PBS *Frontline*, October 17, 2006.

28. Patrick Graham, "Beyond Fallujah: A Year with the Iraqi Resistance," *Harper's*, June 1, 2004.

29. Rajiv Chandrasekaran, *Imperial Life in the Emerald City: Inside Iraq's Green Zone* (New York: Alfred A. Knopf, 2006), 118.

30. Alan Wolfe, "Why Conservatives Can't Govern," *Washington Monthly*, July/August 2006.

31. Ariana Eunjung Cha, "In Iraq, the Job Opportunity of a Lifetime," *Washington Post*, May 23, 2004.

32. Chandrasekaran, *Imperial Life in the Emerald City*, 214–18; T. Christian Miller, "U.S. Priorities Set Back Its Healthcare Goals in Iraq," *Los Angeles Times*, October 30, 2005.

33. Jim Krane, "Iraqi Businessmen Now Face Competition," Associated Press, December 3, 2003.

34. Chandrasekaran, *Imperial Life in the Emerald City*, 288.

35. "National Defense Authorization Act for Fiscal Year 2007," *Congressional Record— Senate*, June 14, 2006, page S5855.

36. Griff Witte, "Despite Billions Spent, Rebuilding Incomplete," *Washington Post*, November 12, 2006; Dan Murphy, "Quick School Fixes Won Few Iraqi Hearts," *Christian Science Monitor*, June 28, 2004.

37. Griff Witte, "Contractors Rarely Held Responsible for Misdeeds in Iraq," *Washington Post*, November 4, 2006; T. Christian Miller, "Contractor's Plans Lie Among Ruins of Iraq," *Los Angeles Times*, April 29, 2006; James Glanz, "Inspectors Find Rebuilt Projects Crumbling in Iraq," *New York Times*, April 29, 2007; James Glanz, "Billions in Oil Missing in Iraq, U.S. Study Says," *New York Times*, May 12, 2007.

38. E-mail interview with Kristine Belisle, deputy assistant inspector general for Congressional and Public Affairs, special inspector general for Iraq reconstruction, December 15, 2006.

39. Griff Witte, "Invoices Detail Fairfax Firm's Billing for Iraq Work," *Washington Post*, May 11, 2005; Charles R. Babcock, "Contractor Bilked U.S. on Iraq Work, Federal Jury Rules," *Washington Post*, March 10, 2006; Erik Eckholm, "Lawsuit Accuses a Contractor of Defrauding U.S. Over Work in Iraq," *New York Times*, October 9, 2004.

40. Renae Merle, "Verdict against Iraq Contractor Overturned," *Washington Post*, August 19, 2006; Erik Eckholm, "On Technical Grounds, Judge Sets Aside Verdict of Billing Fraud in Iraq Rebuilding," *New York Times*, August 19, 2006.

41. Dahr Jamail and Ali al-Fadhily, "Bechtel Departure Removes More Illusions," Inter Press Service, November 9, 2006; Witte, "Despite Billions Spent, Rebuilding Incomplete."

42. Anthony Shadid, *Night Draws Near: Iraq's People in the Shadow of America's War* (New York: Henry Holt, 2005), 173, 175.

18. Full Circle: From Blank Slate to Scorched Earth

1. Bertolt Brecht, "The Solution," *Poems, 1913–1956*, ed. John Willett and Ralph Manheim (1976, repr. New York: Methuen, 1979), 440.

2. Sylvia Pfeifer, "Where Majors Fear to Tread," *Sunday Telegraph* (London), January 7, 2007.

3. L. Paul Bremer III, "New Risks in International Business," *Viewpoint*, November 2, 2001, was at www.mmc.com, accessed May 26, 2003.

4. Maxine McKew, "Confessions of an American Hawk," *The Diplomat*, October–November 2005.

5. L. Paul Bremer III, *My Year in Iraq: The Struggle to Build a Future of Hope* (New York: Simon & Schuster, 2006), 93.

6. Interview with Paul Bremer conducted June 26, 2006, and August 18, 2006, for "The Lost Year in Iraq," PBS *Frontline*, October 17, 2006.

7. William Booth and Rajiv Chandrasekaran, "Occupation Forces Halting Elections Throughout Iraq," *Washington Post*, June 28, 2003; Michael R. Gordon and Bernard E. Trainor, *Cobra II: The Inside Story of the Invasion and the Occupation of Iraq* (New York: Pantheon Books, 2006), 490; William Booth, "In Najaf, New Mayor Is Outsider Viewed with Suspicion," *Washington Post*, May 14, 2003.

8. Ariana Eunjung Cha, "Hope and Confusion Mark Iraq's Democracy Lessons," *Washington Post*, November 24, 2003; Booth and Chandrasekaran, "Occupation Forces Halting Elections Throughout Iraq."

9. Christopher Foote, William Block, Keith Crane, and Simon Gray, *Economic Policy and Prospects in Iraq*, Public Policy Discussion Papers, no. 04–1 (Boston: Federal Reserve Bank of Boston, May 4, 2004), 37, www.bosfed.org.

10. Salim Lone, "Iraq: This Election Is a Sham," *International Herald Tribune* (Paris), January 28, 2005.

11. "Al-Sistani's Representatives Threaten Demonstrations, Clashes in Iraq," *BBC Monitoring International Reports*, report by Lebanese Hezbollah TV Al-Manar, January 16, 2004; Nadia Abou El-Magd, "U.S. Commander Urges Saddam Holdouts to Surrender," Associated Press, January 16, 2004.

12. Michael Moss, "Iraq's Legal System Staggers Beneath the Weight of War," *New York Times*, December 17, 2006.

13. Gordon and Trainor, *Cobra II*, 4, 555; Julian Borger, "Knives Come Out for Rumsfeld as the Generals Fight Back," *Guardian* (London), March 31, 2003.

14. Jeremy Scahill, *Blackwater: The Rise of the World's Most Powerful Mercenary Army* (New York: Nation Books, 2007), 199.

15. Peter Maass, "The Way of the Commandos," *New York Times*, May 1, 2005; "Jim Steele Bio," Premiere Speakers Bureau, www.premierespeakers.com; Michael Hirsh and John Barry, "'The Salvador Option,'" *Newsweek*, January 8, 2005.

16. "Email from Cpt. William Ponce," PBS *Frontline: The Torture Question*, August 2003, www.pbs.org; Josh White, "Soldiers' 'Wish Lists' of Detainee Tactics Cited," *Washington Post*, April 19, 2005.

17. Brigadier General Janis Karpinski, commander in charge of Abu Ghraib, says Miller said this to her. Scott Wilson and Sewell Chan, "As Insurgency Grew, So Did Prison Abuse," *Washington Post*, May 10, 2004.

18. One month later, Sanchez sent another memo clarifying and somewhat tempering the earlier memo but creating much confusion in the field about which procedures applied. Ricardo S. Sanchez, *Memorandum, Subject: CJTF-7 Interrogation and Counter-Resistance Policy*, September 14, 2003, www.aclu.org.

19. The information in the next three paragraphs is drawn from Human Rights Watch, *No Blood, No Foul: Soldiers' Accounts of Detainee Abuse in Iraq*, July 2006, pages 6–14, www.hrw.org.

20. Ibid., 26, 28.

21. Richard P. Formica, "Article 15–6 Investigation of CJSOTF–AP and 5th SF Group Detention Operations," finalized on November 8, 2004, declassified, www.aclu.org.

22. *USMC Alleged Detainee Abuse Cases Since 11 Sep 01*, unclassified, July 8, 2004, www.aclu.org.

23. "Web Magazine Raises Doubts Over a Symbol of Abu Ghraib," *New York Times*, March 14, 2006; Interview with Haj Ali, "Few Bad Men?" *PBS Now*, April 29, 2005.

24. "Haj Ali's Story," *PBS Now* Web site, www.pbs.org; Chris Kraul, "War Funding Feud Has Iraqis Uneasy," *Los Angeles Times*, April 28, 2007.

25. Human Rights Watch, *Leadership Failure: Firsthand Accounts of Torture of Iraqi Detainees by the U.S. Army's 82nd Airborne Division*, September 2005, pages 9, 12, www.hrw.org.

26. Human Rights Watch, *The New Iraq? Torture and Ill-Treatment of Detainees in Iraqi Custody*, January 2005, pages 2, 4, www.hrw.org; Bradley Graham, "Army Warns Iraqi Forces on Abuse of Detainees," *Washington Post*, May 20, 2005; Moss, "Iraq's Legal System Staggers Beneath the Weight of War."

27. Maass, "The Way of the Commandos."

28. Interview with Allan Nairn, *Democracy Now!* January 10, 2005, www.democracynow .org; Solomon Moore, "Killings Linked to Shiite Squads in Iraqi Police Force," *Los Angeles Times*, November 29, 2005.

29. Moss, "Iraq's Legal System Staggers Beneath the Weight of War"; Thanassis Cambanis, "Confessions Rivet Iraqis," *Boston Globe*, March 18, 2005; Maass, "The Way of the Commandos."

30. Ibid; John F. Burns, "Torture Alleged at Ministry Site Outside Baghdad," *New York Times*, November 16, 2005; Moore, "Killings Linked to Shiite Squads in Iraqi Police Force."

31. Anne Collins, *In the Sleep Room: The Story of the CIA Brainwashing Experiments in Canada* (Toronto: Lester and Orpen Dennys, 1988), 174.

32. Maxine McKew, "Confessions of an American Hawk," *The Diplomat*, October–November 2005.

33. Charles Krauthammer, "In Baker's Blunder, a Chance for Bush," *Washington Post*, December 15, 2006; Frederick W. Kagan, *Choosing Victory: A Plan for Success in Iraq*, Phase I Report, January 4, 2007, page 34, www.aei.org.

34. Dahr Jamail and Ali Al-Fadhily, "Iraq: Schools Crumbling Along with Iraqi Society," Inter Press Service, December 18, 2006; Charles Crain, "Professor Says Approximately 300 Academics Have Been Assassinated," *USA Today*, January 17,

2005; Michael E. O'Hanlon and Jason H. Campbell, Brookings Institution, *Iraq Index: Tracking Variables of Reconstruction & Security in Post-Saddam Iraq*, February 22, 2007, page 35, www.brookings.edu; Ron Redmond, "Iraq Displacement," press briefing, Geneva, November 3, 2006, www.unhcr.org; "Iraq's Refugees Must Be Saved from Disaster," *Financial Times* (London), April 19, 2007.

35. "Nearly 20,000 People Kidnapped in Iraq This Year: Survey," Agence France-Presse, April 19, 2006; Human Rights Watch, *The New Iraq?* 32, 54, www.hrw.org.

36. HSBC was originally supposed to open branches across Iraq. Instead it bought a 79 percent stake in Iraq's Dar es-Salaam bank. John M. Broder and James Risen, "Contractor Deaths in Iraq Soar to Record," *New York Times*, May 19, 2007; Paul Richter, "New Iraq Not Tempting to Corporations," *Los Angeles Times*, July 1, 2004; Yochi J. Dreazen, "An Iraqi's Western Dream," *Wall Street Journal*, March 14, 2005; "Syria and Iraq: Unbanked and Unstable," *Euromoney*, September 2006; Ariana Eunjung Cha and Jackie Spinner, "U.S. Companies Put Little Capital into Iraq," *Washington Post*, May 15, 2004.

37. Andy Mosher and Griff Witte, "Much Undone in Rebuilding Iraq, Audit Says," *Washington Post*, August 2, 2006; Julian Borger, "Brutal Killing of Americans in Iraq Raises Questions over Security Firms," *Guardian* (London), April 2, 2004; Office of the Special Inspector General for Iraq Reconstruction, *Review of Administrative Task Orders for Iraq Reconstruction Contracts*, October 23, 2006, page 11, www.sigir.mil.

38. Griff Witte, "Despite Billions Spent, Rebuilding Incomplete," *Washington Post*, November 12, 2006.

39. Aqeel Hussein and Colin Freeman, "US to Reopen Iraq's Factories in $10m U-turn," *Sunday Telegraph* (London), January 29, 2007.

40. Josh White and Griff Witte, "To Stem Iraqi Violence, U.S. Looks to Factories," *Washington Post*, December 12, 2006.

41. James A. Baker III, Lee H. Hamilton, Lawrence S. Eagleburger, et al., *Iraq Study Group Report*, December 2006, page 57, www.usip.org.

42. Pfeifer, "Where Majors Fear to Tread."

43. "Iraq's Refugee Crisis Is Nearing Catastrophe," *Financial Times* (London), February 8, 2007; Joshua Gallu, "Will Iraq's Oil Blessing Become a Curse?" *Der Spiegel*, December 22, 2006; Danny Fortson, Andrew Murray-Watson and Tim Webb, "Future of Iraq: The Spoils of War," *Independent* (London), January 7, 2007.

44. Iraqi Labor Union Leadership, "Iraqi Trade Union Statement on the Oil Law," December 10–14, 2006, www.carbonweb.org.

45. Edward Wong, "Iraqi Cabinet Approves Draft of Oil Law," *New York Times*, February 26, 2007.

46. Steven L. Schooner, "Contractor Atrocities at Abu Ghraib: Compromised Accountability in a Streamlined Outsourced Government," *Stanford Law & Policy Review* 16, no. 2 (2005): 552.

47. Jeremy Scahill, *Blackwater: The Rise of the World's Most Powerful Mercenary Army* (New York: Nation Books, 2007), 123.

48. Jim Krane, "A Private Army Grows Around the U.S. Mission in Iraq and Around the World," Associated Press, October 30, 2003; Jeremy Scahill, "Mercenary Jackpot," *The Nation*, August 28, 2006; Jeremy Scahill, "Exile on K Street," *The Nation*, February 20, 2006; Mark Hemingway, "Warriors for Hire," *Weekly Standard*, December 18, 2006.

49. Griff Witte, "Contractors Were Poorly Monitored, GAO Says," *Washington Post*, April 30, 2005.

50. T. Christian Miller, *Blood Money: Wasted Billions, Lost Lives, and Corporate Greed*

in Iraq (New York: Little, Brown and Company, 2006), 87. FOOTNOTE: George R. Fay, *AR 15–6 Investigation of the Abu Ghraib Detention Facility and 205th Military Intelligence Brigade*, pages 19, 50, 52, www4.army.mil.

51. Renae Merle, "Army Tries Private Pitch for Recruits," *Washington Post*, September 6, 2006.
52. Andrew Taylor, "Defense Contractor CEOs See Pay Double Since 9/11 Attacks," Associated Press, August 29, 2006; Steve Vogel and Renae Merle, "Privatized Walter Reed Workforce Gets Scrutiny," *Washington Post*, March 10, 2007; Donna Borak, "Walter Reed Deal Hindered by Disputes," Associated Press, March 19, 2007.
53. According to Thomas Ricks, "When the U.S. troop level was about 150,000, and the allied troop contributions totaled 25,000, there were about 60,000 additional civilian contractors supporting the effort." That means there were 175,000 coalition soldiers to 60,000 contractors, a ratio of 1 contractor to every 2.9 soldiers. Nelson D. Schwartz, "The Pentagon's Private Army," *Fortune*, March 17, 2003; Thomas E. Ricks, *Fiasco: The American Military Adventure in Iraq* (New York: Penguin, 2006), 37; Renae Merle, "Census Counts 100,000 Contractors in Iraq," *Washington Post*, December 5, 2006.
54. Ian Bruce, "Soldier of Fortune Deaths Go Missing in Iraq," *Herald* (Glasgow), January 13, 2007; Brian Brady, "Mercenaries to Fill Iraq Troop Gap," *Scotland on Sunday* (Edinburgh), February 25, 2007; Michelle Roberts, "Iraq War Exacts Toll on Contractors," Associated Press, February 24, 2007.
55. United Nations Department of Public Information, "Background Note: 31 December 2006," United Nations Peacekeeping Operations, www.un.org; James Glanz and Floyd Norris, "Report Says Iraq Contractor Is Hiding Data from U.S.," *New York Times*, October 28, 2006; Brady, "Mercenaries to Fill Iraq Troop Gap."
56. FOOTNOTE: James Boxell, "Man of Arms Explores New Areas of Combat," *Financial Times* (London), March 11, 2007.
57. Special Inspector General for Iraq Reconstruction, *Iraq Reconstruction: Lessons in Contracting and Procurement*, July 2006, pages 98–99, www.sigir.mil; George W. Bush, State of the Union Address, Washington, DC, January 23, 2007.
58. Guy Dinmore, "US Prepares List of Unstable Nations," *Financial Times* (London), March 29, 2005.

19. Blanking the Beach: "The Second Tsunami"

1. Seth Mydans, "Builders Swoop in, Angering Thai Survivors," *International Herald Tribune* (Paris), March 10, 2005.
2. ActionAid International et al., *Tsunami Response: A Human Rights Assessment*, January 2006, page 13, www.actionaidusa.org.
3. *Sri Lanka: A Travel Survival Kit* (Victoria, Australia: Lonely Planet, 2005), 267.
4. John Lancaster, "After Tsunami, Sri Lankans Fear Paving of Paradise," *Washington Post*, June 5, 2005.
5. National Physical Planning Department, *Arugam Bay Resource Development Plan: Reconstruction Towards Prosperity*, Final Report, pages 4, 5, 7, 18, 33, April 25, 2005; Lancaster, "After Tsunami, Sri Lankans Fear Paving of Paradise."
6. "South Asians Mark Tsunami Anniversary," United Press International, June 26, 2005.
7. USAID/Sri Lanka, "USAID Elicits 'Real Reform' of Tourism," January 2006, www.usaid.gov.

8. Ibid.
9. E-mail interview with Karen Preston, public relations manager, Leading Hotels of the World, August 16, 2006; Ajay Kapur, Niall Macleod, and Narendra Singh, "Plutonomy: Buying Luxury, Explaining Global Imbalances," Citigroup: Industry Note, Equity Strategy, October 16, 2005, pages 27, 30.
10. United Nations Environment Programme, "Sri Lanka Environment Profile," National Environment Outlook, www.unep.net.
11. Tittawella was director general of the Public Enterprises Reform Commission of Sri Lanka from 1997 to 2001, during which time he oversaw the privatization of Sri Lanka Telecom (August 1997) and Sri Lankan Air Lines (March 1998). After the 2004 elections, he was named chairman and CEO of the government-run Strategic Enterprises Management Agency, which continued the project of privatization under the updated language of "public-private partnerships." Public Enterprises Reform Commission of Sri Lanka, "Past Divestitures," 2005, www.perc.gov.lk; "SEMA to Rejuvenate Key State Enterprises," June 15, 2004, www.priu.gov.lk.
12. Movement for National Land and Agricultural Reform, Sri Lanka, *A Proposal for a People's Planning Commission for Recovery After Tsunami*, www.monlar.org.
13. "Privatizations in Sri Lanka Likely to Slow Because of Election Results," Associated Press, April 5, 2004.
14. "Sri Lanka Begins Tsunami Rebuilding Amid Fresh Peace Moves," Agence France-Presse, January 19, 2005.
15. Movement for National Land and Agricultural Reform, Sri Lanka, *A Proposal for a People's Planning Commission for Recovery After Tsunami*, www.monlar.org; "Sri Lanka Raises Fuel Prices Amid Worsening Economic Crisis," Agence France-Presse, June 5, 2005; "Panic Buying Grips Sri Lanka Amid Oil Strike Fears," Agence France-Presse, March 28, 2005.
16. James Wilson and Richard Lapper, "Honduras May Speed Sell-Offs After Storm," *Financial Times* (London), November 11, 1998; Organization of American States, "Honduras," *1999 National Trade Estimate Report on Foreign Trade Barriers*, page 165, www.sice.oas.org; Sandra Cuffe, Rights Action, *A Backwards, Upside-Down Kind of Development: Global Actors, Mining and Community-Based Resistance in Honduras and Guatemala*, February 2005, www.rightsaction.org.
17. Mexico's Telmex Unveils Guatemala Telecom Alliance," Reuters, October 29, 1998; Consultative Group for the Reconstruction and Transformation of Central America, Inter-American Development Bank, "Nicaragua," *Central America After Hurricane Mitch: The Challenge of Turning a Disaster into an Opportunity*, May 2000, www.iadb.org; Pamela Druckerman, "No Sale: Do You Want to Buy a Phone Company?" *Wall Street Journal*, July 14, 1999.
18. "Mexico's Telmex Unveils Guatemala Telecom Alliance"; "Spain's Fenosa Buys Nicaragua Energy Distributors," Reuters, September 12, 2000; "San Francisco Group Wins Honduras Airport Deal," Reuters, March 9, 2000; "CEO–Govt. to Sell Remaining Enitel Stake This Year," *Business News Americas*, February 14, 2003.
19. Quotation from Eduardo Stein Barillas. "Central America After Hurricane Mitch," World Economic Forum Annual Meeting, Davos, Switzerland, January 30, 1999.
20. Alison Rice, Tsunami Concern, *Post-Tsunami Tourism and Reconstruction: A Second Disaster?* October 2005, page 11, www.tourismconcern.org.uk.
21. TAFREN, "An Agenda for Sri Lanka's Post-Tsunami Recovery," *Progress & News*, July 2005, page 2.

22. USAID Sri Lanka, "Fishermen and Tradesmen to Benefit from U.S. Funded $33 Million Contract for Post-Tsunami Infrastructure Projects," press release, September 8, 2005, www.usaid.gov; United States Government Accountability Office, *USAID Signature Tsunami Reconstruction Efforts in Indonesia and Sri Lanka Exceed Initial Cost and Schedule Estimates, and Face Further Risks,* Report to Congressional Committee, GAO-07–357, February 2007; National Physical Planning Department, *Arugam Bay Resource Development Plan: Reconstruction Towards Prosperity,* Final Report, April 25, 2005, page 18.

23. United States Embassy, "U.S. Provides $1 Million to Maintain Tsunami Shelter Communities," May 18, 2006, www.usaid.gov.

24. Randeep Ramesh, "Indian Tsunami Victims Sold Their Kidneys to Survive," *Guardian* (London), January 18, 2007; ActionAid International et al., *Tsunami Response,* 17; www.actionaidusa.org; Nick Meo, "Thousands of Indonesians Still in Tents," *Globe and Mail* (Toronto), December 27, 2005.

25. ActionAid International et al., *Tsunami Response,* 9.

26. Central Intelligence Agency, "Maldives," *The World Factbook 2007,* www.cia.gov.

27. Coco Palm Dhuni Kolhu, www.cocopalm.com; Four Seasons Resort, Maldives at Landaa Giraavaru, www.fourseasons.com; Hilton Maldives Resort and Spa, Rangali Island, www.hilton.com; "Dhoni Mighili Island," Private Islands Online, www.private islandsonline.com.

28. Roland Buerck, "Maldives Opposition Plan Protest," *BBC News,* April 20, 2007; Asian Human Rights Commission, "Extrajudicial Killings, Disappearances, Torture and Other Forms of Gross Human Rights Violations Still Engulf Asia's Nations," December 8, 2006, www.ahrchk.net; Amnesty International, "Republic of Maldives: Repression of Peaceful Political Opposition," July 30, 2003, www.amnesty.org.

29. Ashok Sharma, "Maldives to Develop 'Safe' Islands for Tsunami-Hit People," Associated Press, January 19, 2005.

30. Ministry of Planning and National Development, Republic of Maldives, *National Recovery and Reconstruction Plan,* Second Printing, March 2005, page 29, www.tsunam imaldives.mv.

31. Ibid.; ActionAid International et al., *Tsunami Response,* 18.

32. The leases are for twenty-five years, but the fine print of the bids allows them to be extended to fifty under certain ownership structures. Ministry of Tourism and Civil Aviation, *Bidding Documents: For Lease of New Islands to Develop as Tourist Resorts* (Malé: Republic of Maldives, July 16, 2006), 4, www.maldivestourism.gov.

33. Penchan Charoensuthipan, "Survivors Fighting for Land Rights," *Bangkok Post,* December 14, 2005; Mydans, "Builders Swoop in, Angering Thai Survivors."

34. Asian Coalition for Housing Rights, "The Tsunami in Thailand: January–March 2005," www.achr.net.

35. Shimali Senanayake and Somini Sengupta, "Monitors Say Troops Killed Aid Workers in Sri Lanka," *New York Times,* August 31, 2006; Amantha Perera, "Tsunami Recovery Skewed by Sectarian Strife," Inter Press Service, January 3, 2007.

36. Shimali Senanayake, "An Ethnic War Slows Tsunami Recovery in Sri Lanka," *New York Times,* October 19, 2006.

37. Roland Paris, *At War's End: Building Peace After Civil Conflict* (Cambridge: Cambridge University Press, 2004), 200.

20. Disaster Apartheid: A World of Green Zones and Red Zones

1. Hein Marais, "A Plague of Inequality," *Mail & Guardian* (Johannesburg), May 19, 2006.
2. "Names and Faces," *Washington Post*, September 19, 2005.
3. Adolph Reed Jr., "Undone by Neoliberalism," *The Nation*, September 18, 2006.
4. Jon Elliston, "Disaster in the Making," *Tucson Weekly*, September 23, 2004; Innovative Emergency Management, "IEM Team to Develop Catastrophic Hurricane Disaster Plan for New Orleans & Southeast Louisiana," press release, June 3, 2004, www.ieminc.com.
5. Ron Fournier and Ted Bridis, "Hurricane Simulation Predicted 61,290 Dead," Associated Press, September 9, 2005.
6. Paul Krugman, "A Can't Do Government," *New York Times*, September 2, 2005; Martin Kelly, "Neoconservatism's Berlin Wall," The G–Gnome Rides Out blog, September 1, 2005, www.theggnomeridesout.blogspot.com; Jonah Goldberg, "The Feds," the Corner blog on the National Review Online, August 31, 2005, www.nationalreview.com.
7. Milton Friedman, "The Promise of Vouchers," *Wall Street Journal*, December 5, 2005; John R. Wilke and Brody Mullins, "After Katrina, Republicans Back a Sea of Conservative Ideas," *Wall Street Journal*, September 15, 2005; Paul S. Teller, deputy director, House Republican Study Committee, "Pro-Free-Market Ideas for Responding to Hurricane Katrina and High Gas Prices," e-mail sent on September 13, 2005.
8. Intergovernmental Panel on Climate Change, *Climate Change 2007: The Physical Science Basis*, Summary for Policymakers, February 2007, page 16, www.ipcc.ch.
9. Teller, "Pro-Free-Market Ideas for Responding to Hurricane Katrina and High Gas Prices."
10. Eric Lipton and Ron Nixon, "Many Contracts for Storm Work Raise Questions," *New York Times*, September 26, 2005; Anita Kumar, "Speedy Relief Effort Opens Door to Fraud," *St. Petersburg Times*, September 18, 2005; Jeremy Scahill, "In the Black(water)," *The Nation*, June 5, 2006; Spencer S. Hsu, "$400 Million FEMA Contracts Now Total $3.4 Billion," *Washington Post*, August 9, 2006.
11. Shaw Group, "Shaw Announces Charles M. Hess to Head Shaw's FEMA Hurricane Recovery Program," press release, September 21, 2005, www.shawgrp.com; "Fluor's Slowed Iraq Work Frees It for Gulf Coast," Reuters, September 9, 2005; Thomas B. Edsall, "Former FEMA Chief Is at Work on Gulf Coast," *Washington Post*, September 8, 2005; David Enders, "Surviving New Orleans," *Mother Jones*, September 7, 2005, www.motherjones.com.
12. United States House of Representatives, Committee on Government Reform— Minority Staff, Special Investigations Division, *Waste, Fraud and Abuse in Hurricane Katrina Contracts*, August 2006, page i, www.oversight.house.gov.
13. Rita J. King, CorpWatch, *Big, Easy Money: Disaster Profiteering on the American Gulf Coast*, August 2006, www.corpwatch.org; Dan Barry, "A City's Future, and a Dead Man's Past," *New York Times*, August 27, 2006.
14. Patrick Danner, "AshBritt Cleans Up in Wake of Storms," *Miami Herald*, December 5, 2005.
15. "Private Companies Rebuild Gulf," *PBS NewsHour with Jim Lehrer*, October 4, 2005.
16. Scott Shane and Ron Nixon, "In Washington, Contractors Take on Biggest Role Ever," *New York Times*, February 4, 2007.
17. Mike Davis, "Who Is Killing New Orleans?" *The Nation*, April 10, 2006.

18. Leslie Eaton, "Immigrants Hired After Storm Sue New Orleans Hotel Executive," *New York Times*, August 17, 2006; King, CorpWatch, *Big, Easy Money*; Gary Stoller, "Homeland Security Generates Multibillion Dollar Business," *USA Today*, September 11, 2006. FOOTNOTE: Judith Browne-Dianis, Jennifer Lai, Marielena Hincapie et al., *And Injustice for All: Workers' Lives in the Reconstruction of New Orleans*, Advancement Project, July 6, 2006, page 29, www.advancementproject.org.

19. Rick Klein, "Senate Votes to Extend Patriot Act for 6 Months," *Boston Globe*, December 22, 2005.

20. Jeff Duncan, "The Unkindest Cut," *Times-Picayune* (New Orleans), March 28, 2006; Paul Nussbaum, "City at a Crossroads," *Philadelphia Inquirer*, August 29, 2006.

21. Ed Anderson, "Federal Money for Entergy Approved," *Times-Picayune* (New Orleans), December 5, 2006; Frank Donze, "146 N.O. Transit Layoffs Planned," *Times-Picayune* (New Orleans), August 25, 2006; Bill Quigley, "Robin Hood in Reverse: The Looting of the Gulf Coast," justiceforneworleans.org, November 14, 2006.

22. Asian Coalition for Housing Rights, "Mr. Endesha Juakali," www.achr.net.

23. Bob Herbert, "Our Crumbling Foundation," *New York Times*, April 5, 2007.

24. Help Jet, www.helpjet.us.

25. Seth Borenstein, "Private Industry Responding to Hurricanes," Associated Press, April 15, 2006.

26. James Glanz, "Idle Contractors Add Millions to Iraq Rebuilding," *New York Times*, October 25, 2006.

27. Mark Hemingway, "Warriors for Hire," *Weekly Standard*, December 18, 2006. FOOTNOTE: Jeremy Scahill, "Blackwater Down," *The Nation*, October 10, 2005; Center for Responsive Politics, "Oil & Gas: Top Contributors to Federal Candidates and Parties," Election Cycle 2004, www.opensecrets.org; Center for Responsive Politics, "Construction: Top Contributors to Federal Candidates and Parties," Election Cycle 2004, www.opensecrets.org.

28. Josh Manchester, "Al Qaeda for the Good Guys: The Road to Anti-Qaeda," *TCSDaily*, December 19, 2006, www.tcsdaily.com.

29. Bill Sizemore and Joanne Kimberlin, "Profitable Patriotism," *The Virginian-Pilot* (Norfolk), July 24, 2006.

30. King, CorpWatch, *Big, Easy Money*; Leslie Wayne, "America's For-Profit Secret Army," *New York Times*, October 13, 2002; Greg Miller, "Spy Agencies Outsourcing to Fill Key Jobs," *Los Angeles Times*, September 17, 2006; Shane and Nixon, "In Washington, Contractors Take on Biggest Role Ever."

31. The corporations on the advisory committee include Lockheed Martin, Boeing and Booz Allen. Stephen E. Flynn and Daniel B. Prieto, Council on Foreign Relations, *Neglected Defense: Mobilizing the Private Sector to Support Homeland Security*, CSR No. 13, March 2006, page 26, www.cfr.org.

32. Mindy Fetterman, "Strategizing on Disaster Relief," *USA Today*, October 12, 2006; Frank Langfitt, "Private Military Firm Pitches Its Services in Darfur," *National Public Radio: All Things Considered*, May 26, 2006.

33. Peter Pae, "Defense Companies Bracing for Slowdown," *Los Angeles Times*, October 2, 2006.

34. Johanna Neuman and Peter Spiegel, "Pay-as-You-Go Evacuation Roils Capitol Hill," *Los Angeles Times*, July 19, 2006.

35. Tim Weiner, "Lockheed and the Future of Warfare," *New York Times*, November 28, 2004.

36. Information in the next two paragraphs is drawn from John Robb, "Security: Power to the People," *Fast Company*, March 2006.

37. Juvenile, "Got Ya Hustle On," on the album *Reality Check*, Atlanta/WEA label, 2006.

38. Bill Quigley, "Ten Months After Katrina: Gutting New Orleans," CommonDreams.org, June 29, 2006, www.commondreams.org.

39. Doug Nurse, "New City Bets Millions on Privatization," *Atlanta Journal-Constitution*, November 12, 2005.

40. Annie Gentile, "Fewer Cities Increase Outsourced Services," *American City & County*, September 1, 2006; Nurse, "New City Bets Millions on Privatization."

41. Doug Nurse, "City Hall Inc. a Growing Business in North Fulton," *Atlanta Journal-Constitution*, September 6, 2006; Doug Gross, "Proposal to Split Georgia County Drawing Cries of Racism," *Seattle Times*, January 24, 2007.

42. United Nations Office for the Coordination of Humanitarian Affairs, "Humanitarian Situation Report—Sri Lanka," September 2–8, 2005, www.reliefweb.int.

21. Losing the Peace Incentive: Israel as Warning

1. Christopher Caldwell, "The Walls That Work Too Well," *Financial Times* (London), November 18, 2006.

2. Martin Wolf, "A Divided World of Economic Success and Political Turmoil," *Financial Times* (London), January 31, 2007; "Ex–Treasury Chief Summers Warns on Market Risks," Reuters, March 20, 2007.

3. Richard Aboulafia, Teal Group, "Guns-to-Caviar Index," 2007.

4. United States House of Representatives, Committee on Government Reform—Minority Staff, Special Investigations Division, *Dollars, Not Sense: Government Contracting Under the Bush Administration*, Prepared for Rep. Henry A. Waxman, June 2006, page 6, www.oversight.house.gov; Tim Weiner, "Lockheed and the Future of Warfare," *New York Times*, November 28, 2004; Matthew Swibel, "Defensive Play," *Forbes*, June 5, 2006.

5. Dow Jones U.S. Heavy Construction Index closed at $143.34 on September 10, 2001, and closed at 507.43 on June 4, 2007. DJ_2357, "Historical Quotes," money.cnn.com; James Glanz, "Iraq Reconstruction Running Low on Funds," *International Herald Tribune* (Paris), October 31, 2005; Ellen Nakashima, "A Wave of Memories," *Washington Post*, December 26, 2005; Ann M. Simmons, Richard Fausset and Stephen Braun, "Katrina Aid Far from Flowing," *Los Angeles Times*, August 27, 2006; Helene Cooper, "Aid Conference Raises $7.6 Billion for Lebanese Government," *New York Times*, January 26, 2007.

6. Shawn McCarthy, "Exxon's 'Outlandish' Earnings Spark Furor," *Globe and Mail* (Toronto), February 2, 2007.

7. Jonathan Curiel, "The Conspiracy to Rewrite 9/11," *San Francisco Chronicle*, September 3, 2006; Jim Wooten, "Public Figures' Rants Widen Racial Chasm," *Atlanta Journal-Constitution*, January 22, 2006.

8. EM–DAT, The OFDA/CRED International Disaster Database, "2006 Disasters in Numbers," www.em-dat.net; Peter Bergen and Paul Cruickshank, "The Iraq Effect: War Has Increased Terrorism Sevenfold Worldwide," *Mother Jones*, March–April 2007.

9. McCarthy, "Exxon's 'Outlandish' Earnings Spark Furor"; William Hartung and Michelle Ciarrocca, "The Military-Industrial-Think Tank Complex," *Multinational Monitor*, January–February 2003; Robert O'Harrow Jr., "LexisNexis to Buy Seisint for

$775 Million," *Washington Post*, July 15, 2004; Rachel Monahan and Elena Herrero Beaumont, "Big Time Security," *Forbes*, August 3, 2006.

10. "Recap of Saturday, July 9, 2005," *Fox News: The Cost of Freedom*, www.foxnews.com.

11. Dan Gillerman, "The Economic Opportunities of Peace," press statement, Chambers of Commerce, September 6, 1993, cited in Guy Ben-Porat, "A New Middle East?: Globalization, Peace and the 'Double Movement,'" *International Relations* 19, no. 1 (2005): 50.

12. Efraim Davidi, "Globalization and Economy in the Middle East—A Peace of Markets or a Peace of Flags?" *Palestine-Israel Journal* 7, nos. 1 and 2 (2000): 33.

13. Shlomo Ben-Ami, *A Place for All* (Tel Aviv: Hakibbutz Hameuchad, 1998), 113, cited in Davidi, "Globalization and Economy in the Middle East," 38.

14. Americans for Peace Now, "The Russians," *Settlements in Focus* 1, no. 16 (December 23, 2005), www.peacenow.org.

15. Gerald Nadler, "Exodus or Renaissance?" *Washington Times*, January 19, 1992; Peter Ford, "Welcome and Woes Await Soviet Jews in Israel," *Christian Science Monitor*, July 25, 1991; Lisa Talesnick, "Unrest Will Spur Russian Jews to Israel, Official Says," Associated Press, October 5, 1993; "Israel's Alienated Russian Voters Cry Betrayal," Agence France-Presse, May 8, 2006.

16. Greg Myre, "Israel Economy Hums Despite Annual Tumult," *International Herald Tribune* (Paris), December 31, 2006; "Israel Reopens Gaza Strip," United Press International, March 22, 1992.

17. Peter Hirschberg, "Barak Settlement Policy Remains Virtually the Same as Netanyahu's," *Jerusalem Report*, December 4, 2000.

18. Americans for Peace Now, "The Russians."

19. David Simons, "Cold Calculation of Terror," *Forbes*, May 28, 2002; Zeev Klein, "January–May Trade Deficit Shoots up 16% to $3.59 Billion," *Globes* (Tel Aviv), June 12, 2001; Neal Sandler, "As if the Intifada Weren't Enough," *BusinessWeek*, June 18, 2001.

20. "Rocket fuel" quote is from Shlomo Maital, a professor at Israel's Technion Institute of Management. Nelson D. Schwartz, "Prosperity without Peace," *Fortune*, June 13, 2005; Shlomo Ben-Ami, *Scars of War, Wounds of Peace: The Israeli-Arab Tragedy* (Oxford: Oxford University Press, 2006), 230.

21. United Nations Special Coordinator in the Occupied Territories, *Quarterly Report on Economic and Social Conditions in the West Bank and Gaza Strip*, April 1, 1997; Ben-Ami, *Scars of War, Wounds of Peace*, 231; Sara Roy, "Why Peace Failed: An Oslo Autopsy," *Current History* 101, no. 651 (January 2002): 13.

22. Chris McGreal, "Deadly Thirst," *Guardian* (London), January 13, 2004.

23. "Norman Finkelstein & Former Israeli Foreign Minister Shlomo Ben-Ami Debate," *Democracy Now!* February 14, 2006, www.democracynow.org.

24. According to the Israeli business newspaper *Globes*, between 2001 to 2003 Israel was looking at "a cumulative 8.5 per cent drop in per capita growth," a stunning decline. Zeev Klein, "2002 Worst Year for Israeli Economy Since 1953," *Globes* (Tel Aviv), December 31, 2002; Sandler, "As if the Intifada Weren't Enough."

25. Aron Heller and James Bagnall, "After the Intifada: Why Israel's Tech Titans Are Challenging Canadian Entrepreneurs as a Global Force," *Ottawa Citizen*, April 28, 2005; Schwartz, "Prosperity without Peace."

26. Susan Karlin, "Get Smart," *Forbes*, December 12, 2005.

27. Ran Dagoni, "O'seas Cos, Gov'ts to Inspect Israeli Anti-Terror Methods," *Globes* (Tel Aviv), January 22, 2006; Ben Winograd, "U.S. Airport Directors Study Tough Israeli Security Measures Ahead of Summer Travel," Associated Press, May 8, 2007; State of

Israel, Ministry of Public Security, "International Homeland Security Conference, 2006," March 19, 2006, www.mops.gov.il.

28. Heller and Bagnall, "After the Intifada"; Yaakov Katz, "Defense Officials Aim High at Paris Show," *Jerusalem Post*, June 10, 2007; Hadas Manor, "Israel in Fourth Place among Defense Exporters," *Globes* (Tel Aviv), June 10, 2007; Steve Rodan and Jose Rosenfeld "Discount Dealers," *Jerusalem Post*, September 2, 1994; Gary Dorsch, "The Incredible Israeli Shekel, as Israel's Economy Continues to Boom," The Market Oracle, May 8, 2007, www.marketoracle.co.uk.

29. Schwartz, "Prosperity without Peace."

30. Ibid.; Nice Systems, "Nice Digital Video Surveillance Solution Selected by Ronald Reagan Washington National Airport," press release, January 29, 2007, www.nice.com; Nice Systems, "Time Warner (Charlotte)," Success Stories, www.nice.com.

31. James Bagnall, "A World of Risk: Israel's Tech Sector Offers Lessons on Doing Business in the New Age of Terror," *Ottawa Citizen*, August 31, 2006; Electa Draper, "Durango Office Keeps Watch in War on Terror," *Denver Post*, August 14, 2005.

32. SuperCom, "SuperCom Signs $50m National Multi Id Agreement with a European Country," press release, September 19, 2006; SuperCom, "City of Los Angeles to Deploy Supercom's IRMS Mobile Credentialing and Handheld Verification System," press release, November 29, 2006; SuperCom, "SuperCom Signs $1.5m ePassport Pilot Agreement with European Country," press release, August 14, 2006, www.supercomgroup.com.

33. Check Point, "Facts at a Glance," www.checkpoint.com.

34. David Machlis, "US Gets Israeli Security for Super Bowl," *Jerusalem Post*, February 4, 2007; New Age Security Solutions, "Partial Client List," www.nasscorp.com.

35. Kevin Johnson, "Mansions Spared on Uptown's High Ground," *USA Today*, September 12, 2005.

36. International Security Instructors, "About" and "Clients," www.isiusa.us.

37. "Golan Group Launches Rigorous VIP Protection Classes," press release, April 2007; Golan Group, "Clients," www.golangroup.com.

38. Schwartz, "Prosperity without Peace"; Neil Sandler, "Israeli Security Barrier Provides High-Tech Niche," *Engineering News-Record*, May 31, 2004.

39. David Hubler, "SBInet Trawls for Small-Business Partners," *Federal Computer Week*, October 2, 2006; Sandler, "Israeli Security Barrier Provides High-Tech Niche."

40. Schwartz, "Prosperity without Peace."

41. Elbit Systems Ltd. and Magal Security Systems Ltd, "Historical Prices," Yahoo! Finance, finance.yahoo.com; Barbara Wall, "Fear Factor," *International Herald Tribune* (Paris), January 28, 2006; Electa Draper, "Verint Systems Emerges as Leader in Video Surveillance Market."

42. Thomas L. Friedman, "Outsource the Cabinet?" *New York Times*, February 28, 2007; Ruth Eglash, "Report Paints Gloomy Picture of Life for Israeli Children," *Jerusalem Post*, December 28, 2006.

43. Karen Katzman, "Some Stories You May Not Have Heard," report to the Jewish Federation of Greater Washington, www.shalomdc.org; Yitzhak Laor, "You Are Terrorists, We Are Virtuous," *London Review of Books*, August 17, 2006.

44. Tel Aviv Stock Exchange Ltd., TASE *Main Indicators*, August 31, 2006, www.tase.co.il; Friedman, "Outsource the Cabinet?"; Reuters, "GDP Growth Figure Slashed," *Los Angeles Times*, March 1, 2007; Greg Myre, "Amid Political Upheaval, Israeli Economy Stays Healthy," *New York Times*, December 31, 2006; World Bank Group, *West Bank and Gaza Update*, September 2006, www.worldbank.org.

45. Susan Lerner, "Israeli Companies Shine in Big Apple," *Jerusalem Post*, September 17, 2006; Osama Habib, "Labor Minister Says War Led to Huge Jump in Number of Unemployed," *Daily Star* (Beirut), October 21, 2006.

46. Interview with Dan Gillerman, *CNN: Lou Dobbs Tonight*, July 14, 2006.

47. Karin Brulliard, "'Gated Communities' for the War-Ravaged," *Washington Post*, April 23, 2007; Dean Yates, "Baghdad Wall Sparks Confusion, Divisions in Iraq," Reuters, April 23, 2007.

48. Rory McCarthy, "Occupied Gaza like Apartheid South Africa, Says UN Report," *Guardian* (London), February 23, 2007.

49. Michael Wines, "Shantytown Dwellers in South Africa Protest the Sluggish Pace of Change," *New York Times*, December 25, 2005.

Conclusion: Shock Wears Off: The Rise of People's Reconstruction

1. Juan Forero, "Bolivia Indians Hail the Swearing In of One of Their Own as President," *New York Times*, January 23, 2006.

2. Tom Kerr, Asian Coalition for Housing Rights, "People's Leadership in Disaster Recovery: Rights, Resilience and Empowerment," Phuket disaster seminar, October 30–November 3, 2006, Phuket City, www.achr.net.

3. Antillano belongs to the Land Committee of La Vega, Caracas. *Hablemos del Poder/Talking of Power*, documentary directed by Nina López, produced by Global Women's Strike, 2005, www.globalwomenstrike.net.

4. Terence Corcoran, "Free Markets Lose Their Last Lion," *National Post* (Toronto), November 17, 2006.

5. Jim Webb, "Class Struggle," *Wall Street Journal*, November 15, 2006.

6. Geoffrey York, "Beijing to Target Rural Poverty," *Globe and Mail* (Toronto), March 6, 2006; Larry Rohter, "A Widening Gap Erodes Argentina's Egalitarian Image," *New York Times*, December 25, 2006; World Institute for Development Economics Research, "Pioneering Study Shows Richest Two Percent Own Half World Wealth," press release, December 5, 2006, www.wider.unu.edu; Sarah Anderson et al., *Executive Excess 2006: Defense and Oil Executives Cash in on Conflict*, August 30, 2006, page 1, www.faireconomy.org; Webb, "Class Struggle."

7. Raul Garces, "Former Uruguayan Dictator Arrested," Associated Press, November 17, 2006; "Argentine Judge Paves Way for New Trial of Ex-Dictator Videla," Agence France-Presse, September 5, 2006; "Former Argentine Leader Indicted for 2001 Bond Swap," MercoPress, September 29, 2006, www.mercopress.com.

8. "Former Latin American Leaders Facing Legal Troubles," *Miami Herald*, January 18, 2007.

9. Andrew Osborn, "The A–Z of Oligarchs," *Independent* (London), May 26, 2006.

10. Paul Waldie, "Hollinger: Publisher or 'Bank of Conrad Black'?" *Globe and Mail* (Toronto), February 7, 2007; "Political Activist Grover Norquist," *National Public Radio Morning Edition*, May 25, 2001; Jonathan Weisman, "Powerful GOP Activist Sees His Influence Slip over Abramoff Dealings," *Washington Post*, July 9, 2006.

11. George W. Bush, *The National Security Strategy of the United States*, September 2002, www.whitehouse.gov.

12. Jane Bussey, "Democrats Won Big by Opposing Free-Trade Agreements," *Miami Herald*, November 20, 2006; Robin Toner and Janet Elder, "Most Support U.S. Guarantee of Health Care," *New York Times*, March 2, 2007.

13. Corporación Latinobarómetro, *Latinobarómetro Report 2006*, www.latinobaro metro.org.

14. Susan George and Erik Wesselius, "Why French and Dutch Citizens Are Saying NO," Transnational Institute, May 21, 2005, www.tni.org.

15. Lou Dobbs, CNN: *Lou Dobbs Tonight*, April 14, 2005.

16. Martin Arnold, "Polish Plumber Symbolic of all French Fear about Constitution," *Financial Times* (London), May 28, 2005.

17. Andrew Curry, "The Case Against Poland's New President," *New Republic*, November 17, 2005; Fred Halliday, "Warsaw's Populist Twins," *openDemocracy*, September 1, 2006, www.opendemocracy.net; Ian Traynor, "After Communism: Ambitious, Eccentric — Polish Twins Prescribe a Dose of Harsh Reality," *Guardian* (London), September 1, 2006. FOOTNOTE: Ken Livingstone, "Facing Phobias," *Guardian* (London), March 2, 2007.

18. Perry Anderson, "Russia's Managed Democracy," *London Review of Books*, January 25, 2007.

19. Vladimir Radyuhin, "Racial Tension on the Rise in Russia," *The Hindu*, September 16, 2006; Amnesty International, *Russian Federation: Violent Racism Out of Control*, May 4, 2006, www.amnesty.org.

20. Helen Womack, "No Hiding Place for Scared Foreigners in Racist Russia," *Sydney Morning Herald*, May 6, 2006.

21. Henry A. Kissinger, *Memorandum to the President, Subject: NSC Meeting, November 6 — Chile*, November 5, 1970, declassified, www.gwu.edu/~nsarchiv.

22. Jack Chang, "Fear of Privatization Gives Brazilian President a Lead in Runoff," Knight Ridder, October 26, 2006; Hector Tobar, "Nicaragua Sees Red Over Blackouts," *Los Angeles Times*, October 30, 2006.

23. Nikolas Kozloff, "The Rise of Rafael Correa," *CounterPunch*, November 26, 2007; Simon Romero, "Leftist Candidate in Ecuador Is Ahead in Vote, Exit Polls Show," *New York Times*, November 27, 2006.

24. "Argentine President Marks Third Year in Office with Campaign-Style Rally," BBC Monitoring International Reports, May 26, 2006.

25. Dan Keane, "South American Leaders Dream of Integration, Continental Parliament," Associated Press, December 9, 2006.

26. Duncan Campbell, "Argentina and Uruguay Shun US Military Academy," *Guardian* (London), April 6, 2006; "Costa Rica Quits US Training at Ex-School of the Americas," Agence France-Press, May 19, 2007.

27. Roger Burbach, "Ecuador's Government Cautiously Takes Its First Steps," *NACLA News*, February 19, 2007, www.nacla.org.

28. Chris Kraul, "Big Cooperative Push in Venezuela," *Los Angeles Times*, August 21, 2006.

29. Emir Sader, "Latin American Dossier: Free Trade in Reciprocity," *Le Monde Diplomatique*, February 2006.

30. George W. Bush, *The National Security Strategy of the United States of America*, March 2006, page 30, www.whitehouse.gov; interview with Stanley Fischer conducted May 9, 2001, for *Commanding Heights: The Battle for the World Economy*, www.pbs.org.

31. Jorge Rueda, "Chavez Says Venezuela Will Pull out of the IMF, World Bank," Associated Press, May 1, 2007; Fiona Ortiz, "Argentina's Kirchner Says No New IMF Program," Reuters, March 1, 2007; Christopher Swann, Bloomberg News, "Hugo Chávez Exploits Oil Wealth to Push IMF Aside," *International Herald Tribune* (Paris), March 1, 2007.

32. Ibid.; "Ecuador Expels World Bank Representative," Agence France-Press, April 27, 2007; Reuters, "Latin Leftists Mull Quitting World Bank Arbitrator," *Washington Post*, April 29, 2007; Eoin Callan and Krishna Guha, "Scandal Threatens World Bank's Role," *Financial Times* (London), April 23, 2007.

33. Michael Wines, "Shantytown Dwellers in South Africa Protest the Sluggish Pace of Change," *New York Times*, December 25, 2005; Brendan Smith et al., "China's Emerging Labor Movement," Commondreams.org, October 5, 2006, www.commondreams.org. FOOTNOTE: Ibid.

34. Jean Baudrillard, *Power Inferno* (Paris: Galilée, 2002), 83.

35. Central Intelligence Agency, Human Resource Exploitation Training Manual—1983, www.gwu.edu/~nsarchiv.

36. Andrew England, "Siniora Flies to Paris as Lebanon Protests Called Off," *Financial Times* (London), January 23, 2007; Kim Ghattas, "Pressure Builds for Lebanon Reform," BBC News, January 22, 2007; Lysandra Ohrstrom, "Reconstruction Chief Says He's Stepping Down," *Daily Star* (Beirut), August 24, 2006.

37. Helene Cooper, "Aid Conference Raises $7.6 Billion for Lebanese Government," *New York Times*, January 26, 2007; Osama Habib, "Siniora Unveils Reform Plan Aimed at Impressing Paris III Donors," *Daily Star* (Beirut), January 3, 2007; Osama Habib, "Plans for Telecom Sale Move Ahead," *Daily Star* (Beirut), September 30, 2006.

38. Mohamad Bazzi, "People's Revolt in Lebanon," *The Nation*, January 8, 2007; Trish Schuh, "On the Edge of Civil War: The Cedar Revolution Goes South," *CounterPunch*, January 23, 2007, www.counterpunch.org.

39. Mary Hennock, "Lebanon's Economic Champion," *BBC News*, February 14, 2005; Randy Gragg, "Beirut," *Metropolis*, November 1995, pages 21, 26; "A Bombed-Out Beirut Is Being Born Again—Fitfully," *Architectural Record* 188, no. 4 (April 2000).

40. Bazzi, "People's Revolt in Lebanon."

41. Ana Nogueira and Saseen Kawzally, "Lebanon Rebuilds (Again)," *Indypendent*, August 31, 2006, www.indypendent.org; Kambiz Foroohar, "Hezbollah, with $100 Bills, Struggles to Repair Lebanon Damage," Bloomberg News, September 28, 2006; Omayma Abdel-Latif, "Rising From the Ashes," *Al-Ahram Weekly*, August 31, 2006.

42. David Frum, "Counterfeit News," *National Post* (Toronto), August 26, 2006.

43. "Spain's Aznar Rules Out Talks with Basque Group ETA," Associated Press, March 11, 2004.

44. Elaine Sciolino, "In Spain's Vote, a Shock from Democracy (and the Past)," *New York Times*, March 21, 2004.

45. Santisuda Ekachai, "This Land Is Our Land," *Bangkok Post*, March 2, 2005.

46. Tom Kerr, Asian Coalition for Housing Rights, "New Orleans Visits Asian Tsunami Areas—September 9–17, 2006," www.achr.net.

47. Ibid.

48. Kerr, "People's Leadership in Disaster Recovery: Rights, Resilience and Empowerment."

49. Kerr, "New Orleans Visits Asian Tsunami Areas."

50. Richard A. Webster, "N.O. Survivors Learn Lessons from Tsunami Rebuilders," *New Orleans Business*, November 13, 2006.

51. Residents of Public Housing, "Public Housing Residents Take Back Their Homes," press release, February 11, 2007, www.peoplesorganizing.org.

52. Quote from Joseph Recasner. Steve Ritea, "The Dream Team," *Times-Picayune* (New Orleans), August 1, 2006.

ACKNOWLEDGMENTS

I think there may be some literary rule against dedicating two books to the same person. I need to break that rule for this book. This project would simply not have been physically, intellectually or emotionally possible without my husband, Avi Lewis. He is my collaborator in all things: editor, travel partner (to Sri Lanka, South Africa, New Orleans), life enhancer. We did this together.

The task would also have defeated me without the extraordinary work of my research assistant, Debra Levy. Debra gave her life over to this book for three years, pausing only to have a child. Her dazzling research skills have left their mark on every page. She unearthed new and exciting information, managed and organized unwieldy sources, conducted several interviews, then fact-checked the entire manuscript. I am so unspeakably grateful to have been joined at every stage by such a dedicated and talented colleague. Debra extends her love and appreciation to Kyle Yamada and Ari Yamada-Levy, as do I.

Two editors, working in an unusually collaborative and rewarding editorial relationship, shaped this manuscript in ways too profound to describe: Frances Coady for Metropolitan Books and Louise Dennys at Knopf Canada. Frances and Louise, who are also my close friends and mentors, pushed me to take the thesis into entirely new areas and granted me the months of necessary time to follow through on their rigorous challenges. Louise has been my faithful editor and fierce defender since No Logo, and I remain in awe of her ability to tone me down and toughen me up simultaneously. When I handed in the revised and much expanded draft, Frances restructured and refined it with stunning commitment at every stage. The fact that the publishing world still has space for intellectual titans like these two women gives me hope for the future of books.

The manuscript was further sharpened thanks to incisive feedback from Helen Conford at Penguin UK, who worked closely with us from the earliest days. Alison Reid's boundless passion for this project as well as her attentiveness to polishing the text make the title "copy editor" wholly inadequate. I am in her debt.

My brilliant agent, Amanda Urban, believed in this book when it was supposed to be only about Iraq, and her faith and loyalty grew through each missed deadline and every revised and expanded outline. She also happens to have the sharpest, coolest team going: Margaret Halton, Kate Jones, Elizabeth Iveson, Daisy Meyrick, Karolina Sutton and Liz Farrell. Surrounded by the women of ICM Books, one feels ready for anything. We are all grateful for the groundwork laid by Nicole Winstanley and Bruce Westwood.

Jackie Joiner is the office manager for Klein Lewis Productions. For two years she acted as human shield, keeping the world at bay so I could focus. Then, when the draft was complete, Jackie set us all in motion like a magnificent orchestra conductor. To say more about Jackie's daily feats of creative administration would invite envy, so I will leave it there.

The ICM team found perfect publishing homes for this book around the world, thereby giving me the luxury to put together an international team of researchers and fact-checkers, without whom Debra and I could never have completed a project of this scope. Each researcher took on crucial pieces of the puzzle, drawing on his or her own specialized skills and areas of expertise.

My dear friend Andréa Schmidt, with whom I travelled in Iraq, was a constant intellectual companion, not just supplying me with fat binders of hyperorganized readings on the grimmest of subjects but educating me and pushing me to go further and deeper into the horror. The sections on torture in particular are very much the product of our never-ending conversation. She also read drafts of the manuscript and gave me some of the most important feedback.

Aaron Maté was my primary researcher in 2003–05, when my journalism focused almost exclusively on Iraq's economic transformation. It was a blessing to work with Aaron, a great intellect and terrific journalist. Aaron's imprint is unmistakable in the chapters on Iraq, as well as on Israel/Palestine.

Fernando Rouaux and Shana Yael Shubs, both up-and-coming Latin American studies scholars, uncovered a largely unexplored cache of economic writings on the interrelationship between crisis and neoliberal reforms. It was this material that revealed to me the centrality of the shock doctrine at the highest reaches of the international financial institutions. Fernando conducted several background interviews for me in Buenos Aires, and Shana translated dozens of documents and articles from Spanish to English. They also rigorously fact-checked the chapters of the book on Argentina.

The wonderful Amanda Alexander was my primary researcher on the South Africa chapter, fact-finding, fact-checking and transcribing interview tapes, along with the enormously helpful Audrey Sasson. Amanda also conducted key research on China's shock therapy period. Several other researchers joined the team at various points: Bruno Anili, Emily Lodish (particularly on Russia), Hannah Holleman (the Asian financial crisis), Wes Enzinna (including last-minute interviews in Bolivia), Emma Ruby-Sachs, Grace Wu and Nepomuceno Malaluan.

Debra Levy, a librarian herself, wishes to thank her personal back-office: the patient and resourceful staffs of the University of Oregon libraries, Corvallis-Benton County Public Library and the Eugene Public Library.

My reporting in the field also relied on many researchers, translators, fixers and friends—too many to mention, but here is a start. In Iraq: Salam Onibi, Linda Albermani and Khalid al-Ansary, one of the best journalists in Baghdad, as well as my friend and fellow traveler Andrew Stern. In South Africa: Patrick Bond, Heinrich Bohmke, Richard Pithouse, Raj Patel and, as always, the brilliant and unstoppable Ashwin Desai. Special thanks to Ben Cashdan and his crew for sharing their interviews with Nelson Mandela and Archbishop Desmond Tutu, and for much else. In New Orleans: Jordan Flaherty, Jacquie Soohen and Buddy and Annie Spell. In Sri Lanka: Kumari and Dileepa Witharana were my and Avi's spiritual and intellectual guides, not to mention translators. Sarath Fernando, Kath Noble and the rest of the team at MONLAR were our home base and the reason we made the trip in the first place. When I returned to Canada, Stuart Laidlaw transcribed hours of interviews, and Loganathan Sellathurai and Anusha Kathiravelu transcribed and translated from Tamil and Sinhala.

Boris Kagarlitsky helped with the Russia chapter. Przemyslaw Wielgosz, Marcin Starnawski and Tadeusz Kowalik all spent time educating me about Poland's transition. Marcela Oliviera linked me up with participants in Bolivia anti–shock therapy movements. Tom Kerr at the Asian Coalition for Housing Rights was our bridge to tsunami reconstruction in Thailand.

The genesis of this book was a year spent living in Argentina, where a group of newfound friends taught me about the bloody roots of the Chicago School project, often by sharing their own wrenching stories and family histories. Those patient teachers are, among others, Marta Dillon, Claudia Acuña, Sergio Ciancaglini, Nora Strejilevich, Silvia Delfino, Ezequiel Adamovsky, Sebastian Hacher, Cecilia Sainz, Julian A. Massaldi-Fuchs, Esteban Magnani, Susana Guichal and Tomás Bril Mascarenhas. They changed the way I saw the world. The analysis of torture that appears in this book was shaped by dozens of interviews conducted with people who experienced prison abuse themselves, and also by those who have dedicated their lives to counseling survivors. I want in particular to thank Federico Allodi and Miralinda Friere, both founders of the Canadian Centre for the Victims of Torture, as well as Shokoufeh Sakhi, Carmen Sillato and Juan Miranda.

Some of the people closest to me are writers specializing in themes touched on in this book, and several of them read drafts of the manuscript and spent hours talking through ideas. Kyo Maclear was always slipping me books and forwarding articles, and her feedback on the first draft informed my understanding of the layering of colonialism; Seumas Milne, who turned *The Guardian's* op-ed page into a truly global debating forum, was my tutor on the Thatcher years and my political counsel on much else; Michael Hardt sent me back to the drawing board and put up with my emergent Keynesianism; Betsy Reed, my editor at *The Nation*, helped me frame the thesis and edited my first article on disaster capitalism, as well as dozens of columns; the fearless Jeremy Scahill read early chapters and swapped panic and research about the state of war (and life) privatization; Katharine Viner was the light at the end of the tunnel and is making *The Guardian* the launch pad for this book. Most of all, these dear friends, who also happen to be colleagues, kept me company and inspired me during years of lonely writing.

I am not an economist, but my brother, Seth Klein, director of the indispensable British Columbia Canadian Centre for Policy Alternatives, is my secret weapon. He put up with calls at odd hours requesting impromptu tutorials in monetarist theory and carefully edited the first draft, pushing me and protecting me as best he could. Ricardo Grinspun, a brilliant economist specializing in Latin America at York University (cited in the text), was kind enough to read the manuscript and provide important specialized feedback. So did Stephen McBride, director of the Centre for Global Political Economy at Simon Fraser University. I am honored that both took time out of their overloaded schedules to accept another student, and neither should be held responsible for any errors on my part.

My parents, Bonnie and Michael Klein, gave me terrific feedback on drafts and took excellent care of me when I moved to their neck of the woods for the writing. Both have passionately protected the idea of a public sphere outside the market for their entire lives, Michael in health care and Bonnie in the arts. My hero of a mother-in-law, Michele Landsberg, read the manuscript and cheered me on, as only she can. The insistence of my father-in-law, Stephen Lewis, on placing the AIDS pandemic firmly within the context of free-market fundamentalism emboldened me to write this book.

Many other stellar publishers and their teams have thrown their support behind this project, including Brad Martin at Random House of Canada, John Sterling at Henry Holt and Sara Bershtel at Metropolitan in New York, Stefan McGrath and the creative and intelligent team at Penguin UK, Peter Sillem at S. Fischer Verlag, Carlo Brioschi at Rizzoli, Erik Visser at De Geus, Claudia Casanova at Paidós, Jan-Erik Petterson at Ordfront, Ingeri Engelstad at Oktober, Roman Kozyrev at Dobraya Kniga, Marie-Catherine Vacher at Actes Sud and Lise Bergevin and everyone at Leméac.

All of us owe a huge debt to the unflappable Adrienne Phillips, acting managing editor at Knopf Canada. Not only did she keep this unwieldy team on track but, along with Margaret Halton and Jackie Joiner, she made it possible for the book to come out in seven languages simultaneously, something of a publishing miracle. I am also enormously grateful to Lisa Fyfe for her powerful jacket design, to Doris Cowan for her careful proofreading and to Beate Schwirtlich for her expert typesetting. Barney Gilmore is, once again, the master indexer. Mark A. Fowler is the very best kind of libel lawyer and was a pleasure to argue with. I also thank Sharon Klein, Tara Kennedy, Maggie Richards, Preena Gadher and Rosie Glaisher, as well as all the translators who will bring this text to readers around the world.

In addition to the researchers who worked directly on this project, many activists and writers helped me along the way. The incredible team members at Focus on the Global South in Bangkok were the first to identify "reconstruction" as the new frontier of neocolonialism, an extension of their longtime work on the exploitation of crises. I am particularly grateful to the acuity of Shalmali Guttal and Walden Bello. For their outstanding investigations exposing disaster capitalism in New Orleans, I am indebted to Chris Kromm and the team at the Institute for Southern Studies as well as to the writings and activism of the human rights lawyer Bill Quigley. Soren Ambrose, formerly of Fifty Years Is Enough, was a tremendous resource on the international financial institutions. My research on contemporary prisoner abuse was greatly aided by Michael Ratner and the courageous team at the Center for Constitutional Rights, as well as John Sifton and Human Rights Watch, the reports of Amnesty International and Jameel Jaffer at the American Civil Liberties Union.

Many of the declassified documents cited in the text were unearthed by the extraordinary people at the National Security Archive. Another important resource has been the interviews from PBS's 2002 documentary trilogy *Commanding Heights: The Battle for the World Economy*. Most of the quotations that appear in the text did not make it into the films, but the producers made the rare decision to put their raw interview transcripts online. I am also grateful to Amy Goodman and the entire team at *Democracy Now!* Their groundbreaking interviews are not only an addictive source of daily news (www.democracynow.org), but a precious ongoing research tool.

Hundreds of other investigative journalists and authors whose work I draw on are acknowledged in the text and the endnotes. An extensive bibliography can be accessed through www.naomiklein.org, with direct links to many original documents. A few books were of such tremendous and repeated help that endnotes and bibliographies don't suffice to indicate their importance: Stephen F. Cohen's *Failed Crusade*, Alfred McCoy's *A Question of Torture*, Anthony Shadid's *Night Draws Near*, Rajiv Chandrasekaran's *Imperial Life in the Emerald City*, Marguerite Feitlowitz's *A Lexicon of Terror*, Michael McCaughan's *True Crimes: Rodolfo Walsh*, Lawrence Weschler's *A Miracle, a Universe*, Greg Grandin's *Empire's Workshop*, T. Christian Miller's *Blood Money*, Antonia Juhasz's *Bush Agenda*, Juan Gabriel Valdés's *Pinochet's Economists*, Peter Reddaway and Dmitri Glinski's *The Tragedy of Russia's Reforms*, William Mervin Gumede's *Thabo Mbeki and the Battle for the Soul of the ANC*, Joseph E. Stiglitz's *Globalization and Its Discontents*, Judith Butler's *Precarious Life*, John Perkins's *Confessions of an Economic Hitman*, Peter Kornbluh's *The Pinochet File* and John Pilger's *The New Rulers of the World*, among many of his other works. I am also in debt to many documentary filmmakers whose footage helped me to understand events that I was not able to witness firsthand. Patricio Guzmán's definitive trilogy *The Battle of Chile* demands particular mention.

Several theorists and chroniclers of neoliberalism have shaped my thinking well beyond what citations can reflect: David Harvey (particularly *A Brief History of Neoliberalism*), and pretty much everything ever written by John Berger, Mike Davis and Arundhati Roy. When I read and reread the work of Eduardo Galeano I feel as if everything has been said. I hope that he will forgive my attempts here to put a few asterisks in the margin, just to emphasize the point.

I also want to honor five exquisitely diverse models of the engaged, enraged intellectual, each one a personal hero of mine, who passed away while I was writing this book. The loss of Susan Sontag, John Kenneth Galbraith, Molly Ivins, Jane Jacobs and Kurt Vonnegut will, for me as for so many others, be difficult to bear.

The following people all lent a hand: Misha Klein, Nancy Friedland, Anthony Arnove, John Montesano, Esther Kaplan, John Cusack, Kashaelle Gagnon, Stefan Christoff, Kamil Mahdi, Pratap Chatterjee, Sara Angel, Manuel Rozenthal, John Jordan, Justin Podur, Jonah Gindin, Ewa Jasiewicz, Maude Barlow, Justin Alexander, Jeremy Pikser, Ric Young, Arthur Manuel, Joe Nigrini, David Wall, John Greyson, David Meslin, Carly Stasko, Brendan Martin, Bill Fletcher, David Martinez, Joseph Huff-Hannon, Ofelia Whiteley, Barr Gilmore and my patient colleagues at the *New York Times* Syndicate, Gloria Anderson and Mike Oricchio.

Roger Hodge sent me to Iraq for *Harper's*, on assignment for the piece that turned into this book, and Sharon Oddie Brown and Andreas Schroeder set me up in their perfect writer's cabin when I returned. I am, as always, grateful to Katrina vanden Heuvel, Peter Rothberg and Hamilton Fish for making The Nation feel like home.

It may take a village to raise a child, but looking at this long list, I realize that it took a global conspiracy to make this book. I'm so fortunate to have been supported by this amazing web of humanity.

INDEX

ABOUT THE AUTHOR

Naomi Klein is the award-winning author of the bestselling books *No Logo* and *Fences and Windows* and cocreator of the documentary film *The Take*. Her books have been translated into twenty-eight languages and received awards. Her column for *The Guardian* and *The Nation* is syndicated around the world.